BLUE GUIDE   LITERARY BRITAIN

W9-AOI-084

Ian Ousby was educated at Cambridge and Harvard and has taught at universities in both England and America. His publications include *Bloodhounds of Heaven: The Detective in English Fiction from Godwin to Doyle,* and (with L. Bradley) *The Correspondence of John Ruskin and Charles Eliot Norton.* He is currently working on a new edition of *Blue Guide England.*

Frontispiece by Richard Doyle to Laurence Oliphant, Piccadilly *(1870). Courtesy of Cambridge University Library*

BLUE GUIDE

LITERARY
BRITAIN
AND IRELAND.

Ian Ousby

A & C Black Limited
London

W W Norton & Company Inc
New York

First published 1985 by
A & C Black (Publishers) Limited
35 Bedford Row, London WC1R 4JH

© A & C Black (Publishers) Limited 1985

Published in the United States of America by
W W Norton & Company Inc
500 Fifth Avenue, New York, NY 10110

Printed in Great Britain

ISBN 0-7136-2735-2

ISBN 0-393-30077-3   (U.S.A.)

British Library Cataloguing in Publication Data

Ousby, Ian
    Literary Britain: and Ireland. — (Blue guide)
    1. Literary landmarks — Great Britain —
    Dictionaries
    I. Title   II. Series
    941′.003′21   PR109

    ISBN 0-7136-2735-2

CONTENTS

Maps

INTRODUCTION

In academic circles at least, a formalistic approach to literature still holds sway, as it has done for some forty years or so. Practitioners of the various branches of higher literary criticism continue in their effort to restrict texts to the pages on which they are printed, chastely oblivious to the circumstances of writers' lives, the conditions under which they worked and published, the places where their books were written and the places with which they deal—actual, imagined or some delicate combination of the two. Yet to authors themselves and to general readers such factors have often seemed more than merely incidental. Above all, they are moved by what D.H. Lawrence in the first chapter of *Studies in Classic American Literature* called 'The Spirit of Place' and, indeed, may cherish the literary associations of a particular locale over its strictly historical significance. 'Don't talk to me of the Duke of Monmouth,' commanded Tennyson on a visit to Lyme Regis, his imagination stimulated less by seventeenth-century politics than by Jane Austen's *Persuasion*. 'Show me the exact spot where Louisa Musgrove fell "and was taken up lifeless".'

Such reverence is not peculiar to Tennyson or his age. By the seventeenth century, antiquaries were already snatching hopefully at fragments of folklore to connect Warwickshire's highways and byways with Shakespeare's youth, Ben Jonson was celebrating Sir Philip Sidney's more certain connection with Penshurst in Kent, and (according to John Aubrey) Milton's birthplace on Bread Street was becoming an attraction for the curious during the writer's lifetime. And today Lyme itself, aided since Tennyson's time by its position on the southern edge of Hardy's 'Wessex' and more recently by the popularity of John Fowles' *The French Lieutenant's Woman*, continues to be a minor shrine for the literary pilgrim. Nor is there any lack of major shrines, especially prominent on the itineraries of those foreign visitors whose notions of England have been partly formed by its literature: Poets' Corner in Westminster Abbey, Haworth Parsonage in West Yorkshire, not to mention the various sights, varnished and unvarnished, that Stratford-upon-Avon can boast. In more general terms, the tourist industries of Dorset and Cumbria owe more than a little to the fame of Hardy and the Lake Poets respectively.

Admittedly, this approach to literature and to travel has its limitations, disappointments and dangers. Had he read his *Persuasion* carefully Tennyson's guide at Lyme would have been able to satisfy the poet's request, but even the most precisely realised scene in a book can prove elusive on the map. The places that can be found may sometimes disappoint, like the scenes of childhood, by being smaller than we envisaged them: both Hardy's 'Egdon Heath' and Blackmore's Doone Valley, for example, are larger in imagination than in actuality. Writers, too, are notorious for their tendency to frustrate the literal-minded researcher by moving real places across the country in obedience to imaginative requirements, by conflating several into one composite fictional entity, or simply by inventing a single place to epitomise the character of a whole terrain. On being asked to point out the building in Canterbury he had used as model for Dr Strong's Academy in *David Copperfield* Dickens gave a reply that speaks for his profession: 'there were several that would do.'

Even those firmer landmarks constituted by writers' birthplaces, homes and graves are subject to their own particular hazards. The Rev. Francis Gastrell, eighteenth-century owner of New Place in Stratford, was driven to destroy a mulberry tree that Shakespeare had supposedly planted because so many people wanted to see it. We do things differently today and modern vandalism is more likely to take the form of excessive commercialisation than outright destruction. Too often the visitor finds his fond imaginings brought unpleasantly down to earth by advertisements for Shakespeare teas or Brontë ice creams—products that contribute little to his appreciation of literature, topography or, for that matter, food. Places that do not lend themselves to such intense exploitation are still not immune from the natural processes of change. The example of Joyce's Dublin is especially poignant, for surely no other writer of this century has empowered an urban landscape with such rich delight and exactitude. But Joyce's re-creation of his native city in *Ulysses* took place at a necessary remove, in Trieste and Zurich and Paris: it was an act of reminiscence, both intensely personal and profoundly scholarly, not of immediate observation. In conversation with Frank Morley, Joyce recommended the same distance to his readers: 'if you wished to enjoy *Ulysses*, you should not make enjoyment more difficult by going to look at a changed Dublin.'

Yet the topographical approach to literature can still bring both innocent pleasure and real enlightenment. To stand in the quiet Chelsea house where Carlyle so frequently interrupted work to complain about the noise of his neighbours' chickens, to compare the modest homeliness of Hardy's birthplace with the frigid respectability of the house he built for himself in later years; these acts bring us closer to the impalpable atmosphere which spilled naturally over from writers' lives into their books. Lawrence's Midlands, Arnold Bennett's Five Towns, and even those parts of London where change has not completely banished the occasional whiff of Dickens or Dr Johnson: all these have their particular story still to tell. However insensibly, they deepen our acquaintance with literature. The relations between topography and text can eventually become reciprocal: knowledge of place enhances our appreciation of literature, just as knowledge of literature sharpens our enjoyment of place. We make the discovery Henry James made in *English Hours*: 'Reading over Thackeray to help me further to Winchelsea, I became conscious, of a sudden, that Winchelsea—which I already in a manner knew—was helping me further to Thackeray.'

The present volume is designed to aid such discovery by giving an account of the associations between writers and the British places they knew and wrote about. Given the sheer size of this subject, much remains to be said about the criteria by which this book has been compiled and the methods by which it has been organised. Its scope embraces Scotland, Wales and Ireland as well as England, a wide and rich terrain but one that excludes consideration of those foreign travels which have played so crucial a part in the lives of British writers from Chaucer to Joyce. For obvious reasons the authors treated have been limited to dead ones, while the term 'author' itself has been taken to mean a writer of imaginative literature—a definition that omits essayists, political economists, theologians, philosophers, monarchs with a penchant for diaries or pamphlets, and all the other various folk who sometimes find shelter under that large umbrella which the universities call 'English Literature.' The distinction, of course, is by no means as neat as it may at first appear and an indulgent policy has been adopted towards, for example, those Grub Street writers of the eighteenth century who made a movable feast of their talents. By the same token, room has been found for writers like Pepys and Ruskin who, without being imaginative in the commonly accepted sense of the term, yet managed to establish a strong connection with place in their work and so to leave their imprint on our landscape.

Although such guidelines provide both breadth and variety, they are not meant to guarantee anything like completeness. Many lesser figures have been omitted, often regretfully, as have minor events in the lives and works of all the writers dealt with—especially the most productive ones and those whose circumstances, whether affluent or indigent, made them relentlessly peripatetic. A similar form of discretion has been applied to the inclusion of places. The location of a writer's birth and death is always indicated, when these facts are known, but otherwise there has seemed little point in giving more than passing mention, if that, to places so despoiled that they have lost their original character. However pleasant it may be to read nostalgic evocations of bygone places over the winter fireside, it is usually unrewarding to gaze at the modern roundabout or office block or shopping centre under which they have disappeared. Even here, of course, exceptions have to be made since certain places, though sites rather than sights, are of such resonant importance it would be foolish to ignore their memory. Shakespeare's Globe Theatre is the most obvious example.

Above all, this is a guidebook. It is organised not as a gazetteer of placenames but as an aid for the traveller seeking to further his interest in writers with whom he is already tolerably familiar. The first section assigns major writers individual entries, which are subdivided region by region. Inside each region the account is presented according to the tried and tested *Blue Guide* method of convenient itineraries or outings. The second section limits itself to shorter entries for lesser figures—that is to say, for writers of lesser reputation or achievement, those who make less conspicuous or precise use of place in their work, and those whose lives are too obscure to make topographical identification easy. Because these entries are relatively brief a region-by-region division is not needed and the account is loosely organised according to the chronology of the subject's life.

Headnotes are added to both types of entry providing a selected list of the subject's main works and their dates—the dates given for plays referring to publication rather than first performance, since this is sometimes an uncertain matter in the case of early dramatists. In the entries themselves generous use is made of quotations to remind the reader how a particular writer viewed a particular place or used it in his work. The sources of quotations are indicated by chapter numbers for novels, act and scene numbers for plays and line or stanza numbers for poems of any length.

Details of opening arrangements for public buildings are given at the end of short entries and at the end of routes in the long entries. It is necessary, however, to repeat the common guidebook warning that, while every effort has been made to ensure this information is correct at the time of writing, opening hours frequently change from year to year and travellers would be wise to confirm them in advance.

It can normally be assumed that cathedrals and parish churches are open during all reasonable daylight hours. (Nowadays more and more churches are kept locked when services are not being held, but there is usually a notice outside explaining arrangements for getting the key.) Oxford and Cambridge colleges are not now as hospitable to the tourist as they used to be, though the present restrictions are not of a sort that lend themselves to ready summary in the endnotes to separate entries. In general, the visitor to Oxford will fare better in the afternoon than the morning, and Cambridge should be avoided during the examination period (mid April to early June), when some of the more heavily trafficked colleges are closed to the general public.

ACKNOWLEDGEMENTS

Although my errors are all my own it is still pleasant to thank the people who have helped me towards accuracy. Particularly because of the great help I have received from the staff of various organisations connected with tourism or literature, the full list is too long to catalogue but I should mention the following, who generously went out of their way to answer my queries: Timothy Aldous, Norwich Amenities Leisure Section; Heather Armitage, Oxford Information Centre; Janet Barnes, Ruskin Gallery, Sheffield; Claire Benson, National Gardens Scheme; Mary Boudren, Bord Fáilte (Irish Tourist Board); Robin Bowers, Dorset College of Agriculture; A. Brew, Town Clerk, Peel; Margaret Bridgman and Alistair W. Hankey, British Tourist Authority; M. Christine Brookes, Rydal Mount; John Bunch, Cumbria Tourist Board; D.J. Burkett, General Cemetery Company, Kensal Green; Alison Connell, Ayrshire Valleys Tourist Board; Liz Foulkes, South East England Tourist Board; Canon D. Ingram Hill, Canterbury Cathedral; T.J. Hogarth, Leisure Services Department, Rochester upon Medway; Gillian Jacobs, West Dorset Tourist Information; David Jones, Chelmsford and Essex Museum; Ron Jones, Merseyside County Council Tourism; Dr T. McCormick, Dove Cottage; David Mander, Hackney Archives Department; Pauline F. Millward, Historical Collections, Calderdale Museums Service; C.W. Nicholls, National Coal Board, Coleorton; Dr G.W. Nicholls, Samuel Johnson Birthplace Museum; Robert Nicholson, Joyce Tower; Pam Petersen, Norwich Tourist Information; Diana Rumens, Southern Tourist Board; Robert Sabourin, Hauteville House; Commander Charles Shears, Chapter House, St Paul's Cathedral; Dr Richard S. Smith, William Morris Society; V. Tyrrell, Stoke-on-Trent Library Services.

At Cambridge University Library the staff of the Map Room and Photography Department have been unfailingly helpful; Janice Fairholm has continually made my work in the West Room easier and more pleasant. Robert Mathews and Mary Turner kindly supplied points of specific information while, particularly in the early stages of the project, Annette Kelley gave generous encouragement. Tom Neville has throughout been the most patient and knowledgeable of editors.

A NOTE ON FURTHER READING

The interest in writers and places described in my introduction has bred a large attendant literature. The earliest example I have seen is J. Storer's *Cowper, Illustrated by a Series of Views, in, or near, the Park Of Weston-Underwood, Bucks*, published in 1803. A hundred years afterwards the bookshelf had lengthened to include a host of volumes of the 'homes and haunts,' 'inns and taverns,' 'in the footsteps' variety, some of them dealing with figures more cherished by the Victorians than by later readers and many showing greater familiarity with the books they discuss than their modern counterparts do. These modern counterparts range from slender volumes garnished with appetising photographs through personal evocations of literary rambles to scholarly gazetteers and specialist studies. The most restricted in scope are usually the best. Outstanding among recent book-length studies are Richard Ellmann's *Ulysses on the Liffey* (1972) and Denys Kay-Robinson's *Hardy's Wessex Reappraised* (1972) and, among recent pamphlets, Geoffrey Fletcher's *Pocket Guide to Dickens' London* (1976) and Graham Nicholls' *Literary Lichfield* (1981). Of more ambitious works, George Williams' *Guide to Literary London* (1973) is particularly useful. The list could easily be extended but it may be more valuable instead to point out that some of the best studies come from writers who are themselves considered in this volume. Edward Thomas' *A Literary Pilgrim in England* is still immensely readable and Henry James' *English Hours*, without attempting any of the humbler duties of the guidebook, shows its author to be the very model of the traveller sensitive to literary associations.

SYMBOLS AND ABBREVIATIONS

As in other *Blue Guides* asterisks and double asterisks draw attention to places of special interest, whether individual buildings or more general areas, but in this volume the criteria are necessarily different. To qualify, a place has to be interesting in its own right and also important to the writer under discussion. Thus Hatfield House, which receives a well deserved asterisk in *Blue Guide England*, does not get one when it is mentioned in the entry for Dickens since his connection with the house was only slight. By the same token Carlyle's House, double asterisked in the entry for Carlyle, gets no distinction when it crops up in connection with Tennyson and Ruskin, mere visitors there. It is hardly necessary to add that, though the system of asterisks may have an appearance of objectivity, it is inevitably the vehicle for personal opinion. The reader will quickly detect (without necessarily sharing) my belief that writers' birthplaces, if they are merely that, do not always hold a strictly literary interest and that, when opened to the public, writers' houses too often lose the interest they once held and take on a sterile, lifeless atmosphere.

In quotations from verse an oblique stroke marks a break between lines.

Abbreviations for points of the compass, days of the week and months of the year will be either familiar or self-explanatory, but some others may require explanation:

aetat.=age

b.=born

BH=Bank Holiday

Bk=Book

C=century

c.=(circa) approximately

Ch.=Chapter

d.=died

DoE=The Department of the Environment, which since the creation of the English Heritage now administers only royal palaces in England. Public properties in Wales continue to be the responsibility of the DoE/Welsh Office and in Scotland of the DoE/Scottish Development Department (SDD).

English Heritage=The popular name for the Historic Buildings and Monuments Commission, which in 1984 assumed responsibility for all English properties formerly administered by the Department of the Environment, except royal palaces.

GLC=Greater London Council

l.=left

ms(s).= manuscript(s)

n.d.=not dated

NGS=The National Gardens Scheme, an independent charitable trust which supervises the opening of private gardens to the public. Since opening days vary greatly from year to year, details are not given in my text and readers are referred to the annual listing available from bookshops or directly from NGS at 57 Lower Belgrave Street, London SW1W 0LR.

No(s).=Number(s)

NT=The National Trust

NTS=The National Trust for Scotland

q.v. (qq.v.)=(*quod vide*) see entry (entries) for this name (these names)

r.=right

Rte = Route

s.v.=(*sub voce*) see entry under this word

Vol.=Volume

PART ONE

CHARLES DICKENS

b. Portsmouth, Hampshire, 1812; d. Gad's Hill, Kent, 1870. *The Pickwick Papers* (1836–37); *Oliver Twist* (1837); *Nicholas Nickleby* (1838–39); *The Old Curiosity Shop* (1840–41); *Barnaby Rudge* (1841); *A Christmas Carol* (1843); *Martin Chuzzlewit* (1843–44); *Dombey and Son* (1846–48); *David Copperfield* (1849–50); *Bleak House* (1852–53); *Hard Times* (1854); *Little Dorrit* (1855–57); *A Tale of Two Cities* (1859): *The Uncommercial Traveller* (1860); *Great Expectations* (1860–61); *Our Mutual Friend* (1864-65); *The Mystery of Edwin Drood* (unfinished; 1870).

In the Preface to *The Uncommercial Traveller* Dickens gave this description of himself:

> I am both a town traveller and a country traveller and am always on the road. Figuratively speaking, I travel for the great house of Human Interest Brothers, and have rather a large connection in the fancy goods way. Literally speaking, I am always wandering here and there from my rooms in Covent Garden, London—now about the city streets, now about the country by-roads—seeing many little things, and some great things, which, because they interest me, I think may interest others.

It makes a fitting introduction to a man whose life was restlessly mobile. He began his career as a touring election reporter and ended it, to large extent, as a travelling reader from his own published works. His private life was characterised by a love of moving house, an eager interest in new coastal resorts where he might holiday and a willingness to take his amateur theatrical productions anywhere that might welcome them. The result was an unusually detailed knowledge of England's various regions—though not of Scotland, Wales or Ireland—which had a vivid impact on his writings. Kent (Rte 11) and Eastern England (Rte 16) stand out in particular.

It is also fitting that the passage from *The Uncommercial Traveller* should identify Dickens first as a 'town traveller' and cite London as the centre from which his wanderings begin. For London was the hub round which both his professional and personal life revolved, the 'magic lantern' (to use his own striking phrase) whose varied sights continually informed his fiction. Yet a word of caution is necessary about the changes that have overtaken the city whose former topography he knew so intimately. Of the twenty-two addresses he inhabited in London only one, in Doughty Street (Rte 1), survives intact; the two grandest, No. 1 Devonshire Terrace near the York Gate of Regent's Park and Tavistock House in Tavistock Square, have vanished beneath later development. Major thoroughfares he frequented, like the Strand and Holborn, have changed almost beyond recognition while poorer sections and much of London's dockland would now seem to him a foreign country. Dickens himself would not necessarily have lamented such transformations. For his first London residence in Camden Town (Rte 8) he seems to have felt a marked antipathy, while his friend and biographer John Forster remarked that 'any special regard for houses he had lived in was not a thing noticeable in him.' For ancient buildings, particularly public ones, he felt no intrinsic respect, taking satisfaction in the burning of the old Houses of Parliament in 1834. The jerry-built slums which were Victorian England's most distinctive contribution to the urban landscape inspired real horror. The Dickensian pilgrim of today need not greatly regret these changes either, for, by using a selective eye, he will find probably more surviving and well preserved buildings—not only in London but throughout the country—than can be connected with the name of any other English writer.

London

1   Holborn to the City

This route, the longest but also the richest of the London itineraries in this section, encompasses Dickens' only remaining London residence, as well as legal London and Fleet Street, two of the areas he knew best and which have undergone least change. It ends in the financial district of the City.

From Russell Square Underground Station (Piccadilly Line) we walk east along Guilford Street. To the left lie Coram Fields, site of the Foundling Hospital (now at No. 40 Brunswick Square) established by Captain Thomas Coram in 1739. Only its gateway survives but readers of *Little Dorrit* will remember that the aptly nicknamed Tattycoram, rebellious servant to Pet Meagles, was brought up here.

A right turn leads to Doughty Street and *Dickens House (formerly No. 48), a handsome terraced house of three storeys, attic and basement which Dickens rented between 1837 and 1839, following his marriage to Catherine Hogarth, for £80 a year. During his residence he finished *Pickwick Papers* and wrote *Oliver Twist* and *Nicholas Nickleby*, as well as suffering the shock of his sister-in-law Mary's sudden death. Dickens House is now owned and administered by the Dickens Fellowship. Its large and varied collection includes: an extensive Dickensian library; holograph letters; portraits; parts of the mss. of *Pickwick Papers* and *Nicholas Nickleby* (Suzannet Gift of 1971); relics from William Shaw's Academy at Bowes (Rte 17); the desk Dickens used at Ellis and Blackmore's (see Gray's Inn below); and the supposed original of the Wooden Midshipman that advertised Solomon Gills' shop to the world and is fancifully described in Chapter 4 of *Dombey and Son*. The basement houses a replica of the Dingley Dell kitchen from *Pickwick Papers*.

We continue down John Street, the southern extension of Doughty Street, to the junction with Theobald's Road, where a left turn leads to the Gray's Inn Road, which is followed south. On the right is Gray's Inn, one of the four Inns of Court and to Dickens ('Chambers' in *The Uncommercial Traveller*) a 'stronghold of Melancholy' and 'one of the most depressing institutions in brick and mortar, known to the children of men.' Mr Pickwick's long-suffering solicitor, Mr Perker, had chambers at an unspecified location here, while in South Square (then Holborn Court), beyond the Hall and to the left, Dickens worked at the excellently preserved No. 1 as a clerk for the firm of Ellis and Blackmore at the age of 15, in 1827 and 1828. At the top of a 'crazy old staircase' in No. 2 (rebuilt) next door Tommy Traddles lived after his marriage to Sophy and was visited by David Copperfield in Chapter 59 of the novel.

Beyond Gray's Inn, on the left of Gray's Inn Road, Brooke's Court, a right on Leather Lane and a left on Greville Street give access to Bleeding Heart Yard (r.). In *Little Dorrit* the Yard is the home of the Plornishes, the site of Doyce and Clennam's factory, and the property of the apparently philanthropic Mr Casby, a place

> with some relish of ancient greatness about it. Two or three mighty stacks of chimneys, and a few large dark rooms which had escaped being walled and subdivided out of recognition of their old proportions, gave the Yard a character. It was inhabited by poor people, who set up their rest among its faded glories, as Arabs of the desert pitch their tents among the fallen stones of the Pyramids; but there was a family sentimental feeling prevalent in the Yard, that it had a character. (Ch. 12)

Today most of even that tenuous character has gone, though a few reminders still remain.

Gray's Inn Road ends with Holborn, at a point opposite the distinctive half-timbered frontage of *Staple Inn. Despite restoration, war-time bombing and the loss of its former status as an Inn of Chancery, Staple Inn retains some of the rural peace that led Mr Snagsby of *Bleak House*, a man much in need of solace, to seek refuge here and caused Dickens himself to describe it in these terms in *The Mystery of Edwin Drood*:

> It is one of those nooks, the turning into which out of the clashing street, imparts to the relieved pedestrian the sensation of having put cotton in his ears, and velvet soles on his boots. It is one of those nooks where a few smoky sparrows twitter in smoky trees, as though they called to one another, 'Let us play at country,' and where a few feet of garden mould and a few yards of gravel enable them to do that refreshing violence to their tiny understandings. (Ch. 11)

Mr Grewgious, the kindly solicitor in *Edwin Drood*, had chambers in the second court at the building on the left with the inscription 'PJT' over its door. Dickens humorously interprets the initials to mean 'Perhaps John Thomas,' 'Perhaps Joe Tyler' or 'Pretty Jolly Too' (Ch. 11), though in fact they commemorate President James Taylor of the Society of Antients of Staple Inn.

Beyond Staple Inn to the east we come to Furnival Street, which leads to the tiny Took's Court (r.). This appears under the transparent disguise of 'Cook's Court' in *Bleak House*—'a shady place' (Ch. 10) where Mr Snagsby conducts his business as a law stationer under the watchful eye of his wife. By turning right on to Cursitor Street at the end of Took's Court we join Chancery Lane opposite the gatehouse entrance to *Lincoln's Inn, perhaps the most impressive and best preserved of the Inns of Court, as well as the one most pervaded by Dickensian associations. The 15C Old Hall facing the entrance was until 1873 occupied by the Court of Chancery and is hence the scene of the memorable opening to *Bleak House*. Behind it are the spacious and handsome Lincoln's Inn Fields. In Chapter 23 of *David Copperfield* Betsey Trotwood took lodgings at 'a kind of private hotel' here, mainly because of its convenient exit in the roof, 'my aunt being firmly persuaded that every house in London was going to be burnt down every night.' *No. 58, a handsome 18C house in the style of Inigo Jones with 19C alterations, on the west side of the Fields, was the home of Dickens' friend John Forster between

1834 and 1856. Dickens made use of it as the residence of Mr Tulkinghorn, the sinister and close-mouthed lawyer in *Bleak House*, where it is first described in Chapter 10.

The Old Curiosity Shop on Portsmouth Street, reached from the SW corner of Lincoln's Inn Fields, owes its name to the commercial opportunism of a late-Victorian proprietor rather than to any genuine connection with the novel.

Chancery Lane continues south to Fleet Street. To the right of the junction stood Temple Bar (called a 'leaden-headed old obstruction' in Chapter 1 of *Bleak House*), marking the formal boundary between Westminster and the City proper until increased traffic made its removal necessary in 1878. The Strand to the west is explored in Rte 3. The present route continues east along Fleet Street towards Ludgate Circus.

The first notable site, immediately south of the present Temple Bar Memorial, is No. 1 Fleet Street, Child's Bank (now assimilated into Williams and Glyn's Bank). Though the present building dates from 1878 Child's itself is one of London's oldest banking institutions and served as the model for 'Tellson's Bank' in *A Tale of Two Cities*:

> an old-fashioned place, even in the year one thousand seven hundred and eighty ... very small, very dark, very ugly, very incommodious ... After bursting open a door of idiotic obstinacy with a weak rattle in its throat, you fell into Tellson's down two steps, and came to your senses in a miserable little shop, with two little counters, where the oldest of men made your cheque shake as if the wind rustled it, while they examined the signature by the dingiest of windows, which were always under a shower-bath of mud from Fleet Street, and which were made the dingier by their own iron bars proper, and the heavy shadow of Temple Bar. (Bk 2, Ch. 1)

Tellson's entrance was guarded by Jerry Cruncher and its interior operations supervised by Jarvis Lorry. Shortly beyond and also on the south side of the street Middle Temple Lane gives access to the charming *Fountain Court (r.), a place of 'slow vegetation' where, according to *Martin Chuzzlewit*, Ruth Pinch was in the habit of meeting her brother Tom (Ch. 45) and where she later took to meeting her lover John Westlock (Ch. 53).

On the north side of Fleet Street, after the junction with Chancery Lane, stands the gatehouse entrance to Clifford's Inn Passage, though the site of the former Inn itself is now occupied by a block of flats. Here Tip, brother to Little Dorrit, worked for an attorney and 'languished ... for six months and at the expiration of that term, sauntered back one evening with his hands in his pockets, and incidentally observed to his sister that he was not going back again' (Ch. 7). In Book 1, Chapter 8 of *Our Mutual Friend* the rather more enterprising 'John Rokesmith,' as John Harmon calls himself for most of the novel, uses Clifford's Inn as the scene of the interview that leads to his becoming Mr Boffin's secretary. Immediately beyond we find St Dunstan in the West, a handsome church of 1831 by John Shaw. On their way from Lincoln's Inn Fields to Doctors' Commons David Copperfield and his aunt Betsey Trotwood stopped to watch the jacks of the 17C clock strike noon.

Johnson's Court, leading from the N side of the street, once housed the offices of Chapman and Hall, publishers of the *Monthly Magazine*, to whom in 1833 the young Dickens delivered 'stealthily one evening at twilight, with fear and trembling' his first literary attempt—a sketch called 'A Dinner at Poplar Walk' but reprinted in *Sketches by Boz* (1836) as 'Mr Minns and His Cousin.' *Pickwick Papers* began a more famous and enduring association between Dickens and the publishing firm. In Wine Office Court but entered from No. 145 Fleet Street is the Cheshire Cheese, a restaurant famous as a literary gathering place since the 18C but now perhaps over-celebrated. It was, inevitably, familiar to Dickens and he may have had it in mind as the scene of Sydney Carton and Charles Darnay's meal in Book 2, Chapter 4 of *A Tale of Two Cities*, just after the former has aided the latter's acquittal from a charge of High Treason at the Old Bailey.

Off Whitefriars Street, on the S side of Fleet Street almost opposite Wine Office Court, we find the picturesquely named Hanging Sword Alley, where Jerry Cruncher of *A Tale of Two Cities* has his lodgings and from which he makes his nocturnal forays as body-snatcher.

From Ludgate Circus we ascend Ludgate Hill. Immediately to the left stood La Belle Sauvage Inn, headquarters of Tony Weller in

Ludgate Hill, by Gustav Doré. From Blanchard Jerrold, London: A Pilgrimage *(1872). Courtesy of Cambridge University Library*

Pickwick Papers. Behind Seacoal Lane on the same of the Hill stood the Fleet Prison, where Mr Pickwick's confinement for debt began in Chapter 50 of the novel. At the end of Old Bailey, again to the left, the Central Criminal Court covers the site occupied until 1902 by Newgate Prison. Fagin spent a memorable night in the jail (Chapter 52 of *Oliver Twist*) while awaiting public execution in Newgate Street beyond; Pip visited it with Wemmick as his guide in Chapter 32 of *Great Expectations*, before returning to Mr Jaggers' offices in Little Britain (reached by a right turn on Newgate Street and a left up King Edward Street). The destruction of the 18C prison by the Gordon Rioters is described in *Barnaby Rudge*, Chapters 58ff.

At the top of Ludgate Hill we reach St Paul's Churchyard where, in Chapter 23 of *David Copperfield*, Betsey Trotwood met the mysterious man who David later discovered was her estranged husband. On Dean's Court to the south stands the handsome Old Deanery. It is the one surviving remnant of Doctors' Commons, where Dickens came to work as a legal reporter in 1829 and Mr Jingle obtained the marriage license he never got the chance to use (Chapter 10 of *Pickwick Papers*).

We follow Cannon Street, the eastern continuation of St Paul's Churchyard, make an oblique left up Queen Victoria Street and change to Cornhill at Bank Underground Station and the Bank of England. Near the top of Cornhill the little St Michael's Alley (r.) leads to the George and Vulture, which retains the atmosphere of the days when it served as a recurring location in *Pickwick Papers* and as Mr Pickwick's London lodging after circumstances made it advisable for him to leave Mrs Bardell's house. Of the several scenes taking place here perhaps the most notable is in Chapter 40, when Messrs Namby and Smouch arrive to take Mr Pickwick to prison for non-payment of damages in Mrs Bardell's suit against him. The next alley off Cornhill, St Peter's, brings us to the churchyard garden Bradley Headstone chose as the scene for his anguished and impassioned proposal of marriage to Lizzie Hexam in Book 2, Chapter 15 of *Our Mutual Friend*.

Route 2 below offers a convenient extension of this route.

Dickens House, Doughty Street. Open Mon to Sat 10–5; closed Sun, BH and public holidays. Fee.

2 Southwark

Southwark or—to use the proper title by which Dickens habitually refers to it—the Borough is being progressively overtaken by the modern development to which most of London's South Bank is now subject. Yet it retains both specific and atmospheric reminders of its appearances in the pages of his fiction, especially *Little Dorrit*, and of that unhappy period during his childhood when his father was imprisoned for debt and he himself forced to work in the blacking factory.

The route indicated may be treated either as an extension of Rte 1 above, by following Gracechurch Street from the top of Cornhill to the river, or separately, by starting from Bank Underground Station

(Central and Northern Lines) and taking King William Street to the river. In either case the Thames is crossed by London Bridge, a modern structure that prepares the visitor for some of the transformations the Borough itself has undergone in recent years.

Beyond the railway bridge on the left side of Borough High Street stood the inns from which the London–Dover coaching route originated. *Pickwick Papers*, while lamenting the decline of such inns elsewhere, was able to celebrate their survival in Southwark:

> In the Borough, especially, there still remain some half dozen old inns, which have preserved their external features unchanged, and which have escaped alike the rage for public improvement, and the encroachments of private speculation. Great, rambling, queer, old places they are, with galleries, and passages, and staircases, wide enough and antiquated enough to furnish materials for a hundred ghost stories ... (Ch. 10)

Today the King's Head, Tabard and Queen's Head have vanished, and so has the White Hart where Mr Jingle brings Rachel Wardle and Mr Pickwick first meets Sam Weller in Chapter 10. But one wing of the *George remains, with a half-timbered gallery and interior (rebuilt in 1676 after fire destroyed an earlier building on the same spot), enjoying a double character as inn and National Trust property. Although the George receives only a passing mention in Dickens' work (Ch. 22 of *Little Dorrit*) it is of considerable interest as the type of those similar establishments, in the Borough and other districts of London, that appear so often in the pages of his novels.

Further down the High Street, on the left and marked by a plaque, is the site of the Marshalsea debtors' prison from 1811 until its closure in 1842: 'an oblong pile of barrack building, partitioned into squalid houses standing back to back, so that there were no back rooms; environed by a narrow paved yard, hemmed in by high walls duly spiked at top' (*Little Dorrit*, Ch. 6). John Dickens was brought here by his improvidence in 1824 and the effect of the episode on his young son is best reflected, perhaps, in *Little Dorrit*, where the prison is a central location and Mr Dorrit, to some extent modelled on John Dickens, is an inmate long enough to acquire the title 'Father of the Marshalsea.' Beyond the site of the prison stands the 18C church of St George the Martyr, where Little Dorrit is christened and married to Arthur Clennam; there is a modern window commemorating her at the east end.

Lant Street leads right from Borough High Street shortly afterwards, surrounded by a network of sidestreets with suitably Dickensian names but greatly changed since the 19C. While his father was in the Marshalsea and he himself working in the blacking factory the young Dickens had lodgings in a house whose site is now occupied by the Charles Dickens Primary School of 1877. In *Pickwick Papers* he gave this understandably sombre account of the street's atmosphere:

> There is a repose about Lant Street ... which sheds a gentle melancholy upon the soul. There are always a good many houses to let in the street: it is a bye-street too, and its dulness is soothing. A house in Lant Street would not come within the denomination of a first-rate residence, in the strict acceptation of the term; but it is a most desirable spot nevertheless. If a man wished to abstract himself from the world—to remove himself from within the reach of temptation—to place himself beyond the possibility of inducement to look out of the window—he should by all means go to Lant Street. (Ch. 32)

The medical student Bob Sawyer occupies a back attic on the street, living on hostile terms with his landlady; the disastrous evening when he entertains Mr Pickwick to dinner is described in Chapter 32.

Sam Weller, Mr Perker, Mr Wardle and Mr Pickwick in the yard of the White Hart, by 'Phiz.' From Pickwick Papers. *Courtesy of Cambridge University Library*

3   The Strand and Covent Garden

The Strand and its environs are much changed since Dickens' day but a few isolated features of interest survive.

We begin at Aldwych Underground Station (Piccadilly Line). In St Mary-le-Strand, a fine Gibbs church of 1714 in the middle of the Strand opposite, Dickens' parents were married in 1809. On Maiden Lane in Covent Garden, reached by walking east along the Strand and turning right up Southampton Street, Rules Restaurant lovingly maintains the atmosphere it possessed when Dickens patronised it. Charing Cross Station covers the site of No. 30 Hungerford Stairs, where Dickens underwent his childhood ordeal in the blacking factory: 'a crazy, tumble-down old house, abutting, of course, the river, and literally overrun with rats.' On the steps of St Martin's in the-Fields, visible to the right and reached via Duncannon Street, David Copperfield met Peggotty during the latter's search for his daughter Little Em'ly (Ch. 40).

4   Westminster

The starting point is Westminster Underground Station (District and Circle Line).

In Poets' Corner (fee) of Westminster Abbey a slab marks Dickens' grave. He had earlier expressed wishes to be buried, variously, in Kensal Green Cemetery (Rte 7) as well as at Shorne and Rochester Cathedral (Rte 11).

By walking south along Millbank and taking a right turn on to Dean Stanley Street we come to Smith Square, where Jenny Wren, the crippled dolls' dressmaker of *Our Mutual Friend*, lodged. Dickens uncharitably called its 18C church of St John the Evangelist, now restored as a lecture and concert hall after war-time bomb damage, 'very hideous ... with four towers at the four corners, generally resembling some petrified monster, frightful and gigantic, on its back with its legs in the air' (Book 2, Ch. 1).

5   Chelsea

More rural and more clearly separated from the central parts of London in the 19C than it is today, Chelsea was a favourite destination on Dickens' frequent, energetic walks.

Starting at South Kensington Underground Station (District, Circle and Piccadilly Lines), we go south via Onslow Place and Sydney Place, take a right into Fulham Road and then a left into Sydney Street. St Luke's Church, an early 19C Gothic building halfway down on the left, was the scene of Dickens' marriage to Catherine Hogarth in 1836.

By continuing down Sydney Street, turning right on to the King's Road and then left on Oakley Street, we reach the river where it is spanned by the Albert Bridge. A right along Cheyne Walk and another right up Cheyne Row bring us to Carlyle's House on the right, home of the writer and his wife Jane from 1834 until the end of their lives. As friend and admirer of Carlyle, Dickens was inevitably a visitor here. The house may also stand as a type of the quiet, modestly elegant Chelsea houses he knew well in other contexts. See under Carlyle for a full description.

Carlyle's House (NT). Open Apr to end Oct, Wed to Sun & BH Mon 11–5. Closed Good Fri. Fee.

6   Richmond

With its rural atmosphere, river scenery and dignified houses Richmond, like Chelsea, held obvious attractions for a man of Dickens' tastes. Although only two specific places of interest to Dickensians are included in the itinerary below, the visitor will find the area also worth casual exploration.

The walking tour begins at Richmond Station (British Rail and District Underground Line) and leads south via the Quadrant, George Street, Hill Street and Richmond Hill. On the right Star and Garter House, a 20C building for disabled soldiers and sailors, replaces the old Star and Garter Inn. It was a favourite haunt of Dickens for celebrations, most notably the publication of *David Copperfield* in 1850 when his dinner guests included Tennyson and Thackeray (qq.v.). We continue south via Star and Garter Hill to Petersham Road and Elm Lodge (then Elm Cottage) which Dickens rented for a holiday in 1839.

7   Kensal Green

Kensal Green Cemetery, opposite Kensal Green Station (British Rail and Bakerloo Underground Line) contains the grave of Dickens' beloved sister-in-law Mary Hogarth, who died in 1837 while he was living on Doughty Street (Rte 1). After a visit to the spot he wrote that 'the grass around it was as green and the flowers as bright, as if nothing of the earth in which they grew could ever wither or fade.' He originally intended to be buried beside her, but in the event only other members of the Hogarth family were laid in the plot. It is No. 977 in Square 33, on North Avenue near the main entrance.

Kensal Green Cemetery. Open Mon to Sat 9–5.30 (or dusk, if earlier), Sun 2–5.30 (or dusk); Good Fri 2–5.30, Christmas Day 10–2. Closes at 1 on BH.

8   Camden Town

The district is connected with Dickens' childhood and with the onset of the financial difficulties that led to his father's imprisonment. Its character when Dickens first knew it is well evoked in the portrait of Staggs's Gardens in Chapter 6 of *Dombey and Son*:

> It was a little row of houses, with little squalid patches of ground before them, fenced off with old doors, barrel staves, scraps of tarpaulin, and dead bushes; with bottomless tin kettles and exhausted iron fenders, thrust into the gaps. Here the Staggs's Gardeners trained scarlet beans, kept fowls and rabbits, erected rotten summer houses (one was an old boat), dried clothes, and smoked pipes.

Its subsequent destruction by the opening of the Euston–Birmingham railway line is described in Chapter 16:

There was no such place as Staggs's Gardens. It had vanished from the earth. Where the old rotten summer houses once had stood, palaces now reared their heads, and granite columns of gigantic girth opened up a new vista to the railway world beyond. The miserable waste ground, where the refuse-matter had been heaped of yore, was swallowed up and gone; and in its frowsty stead were tiers of warehouses, crammed with rich goods and costly merchandise. The old by-streets now swarmed with passengers and vehicles of every kind: the new streets that had stopped disheartened in the mud and waggon-ruts, formed towns within themselves, originating wholesome comforts and conveniences belonging to themselves, and never tried nor thought of until they sprung into existence.

We begin at Camden Town Underground Station (Northern Line) and take Bayham Street to the south. The Dickens family lived at No. 16 in 1823–24, when John Dickens' work for the Navy Office first brought them from Chatham. The house itself no longer stands, its site being covered by a hospital, but surviving terraced houses nearby give an idea of what it was like.

Bayham Street issues into Crowndale Road, where a right and then a left turn lead into Hampstead Road. At No. 247 of this otherwise unremarkable thoroughfare, on the right by the junction with Granby Terrace, stood the Wellington House Academy which Dickens began attending in June 1824 after his family's fortunes had improved enough to release him from work in the blacking factory.

9   Hampstead

Although it has been thoroughly assimilated into London's urban complex since the 19C, Hampstead, particularly its old Village and adjacent Heath, still possesses some of the quiet rural character that frequently drew Dickens here.

A walking tour begins at Hampstead Underground Station (Northern Line) and leads north on Heath Street to Whitestone Pond, stranded in the centre of a large road junction. To the east lies Hampstead Heath, which Dickens loved to walk over on his way to and from central London and which Bill Sikes crossed in Chapter 48 of *Oliver Twist* as he fled the scene of Nancy's murder. The Hampstead Ponds, about whose sources Mr Pickwick engaged in learned speculation (Ch. 1), are to the south east and may be reached via East Heath Road. The large castellated building immediately beyond Whitestone Pond is Jack Straw's Castle; it replaces an older inn of the same name familiar to Dickens.

By heading north on North End Way we come to the Bull and Bush, behind which stands Wylde's (formerly Collins's Farm), a part-Elizabethan cottage where Dickens came from Doughty Street in May 1837 to recuperate from the shock of Mary Hogarth's sudden death. 'I have been so unnerved and hurt that I have been compelled for once to give up all idea of my monthly work, and to try a fortnight's rest and quiet,' he wrote to a friend. A footpath leads across the heath (a route undoubtedly known to Dickens) to Spaniards Road. To the left, where the old toll house still straddles the road, is the *Spaniards Inn (formerly the Spaniards Tea Gardens), a finely preserved but often crowded pub. Mrs Bardell chose its garden in Chapter 46 of

Pickwick Papers for the ill-fated celebratory party which was interrupted by the arrival of Mr Jackson to take her to the Fleet Prison
for non-payment of Dodson and Fogg's fees.

10 Limehouse

Only one place of interest survives in the Thames dockland area that
Dickens knew well and several times used in his fiction, most notably
in his last complete novel, *Our Mutual Friend*.

From Shadwell Underground Station (Metropolitan Line, East
London section; closed Sundays) we cut south to The Highway, once
the Ratcliff Highway and a notorious haunt of thieves, following it
and its extension, Narrow Street, to the east (l.). The Grapes Inn at
No. 76, overlooking both the river and Limehouse Basin, is commonly
identified with Miss Abbey Potterson's 'Six Jolly Fellowship Porters':

> a tavern of dropsical appearance, . . . long settled down into a state of
> hale infirmity . . . Externally, it was a narrow lopsided wooden jumble of
> corpulent windows heaped one upon another as you might heap as many
> toppling oranges, with a crazy wooden verandah impending over the
> water; indeed the whole house, inclusive of the complaining flag-staff on
> the roof, impended over the water, but seemed to have got into the
> condition of a faint-hearted diver who has paused so long on the brink
> that he will never go in at all. (*Our Mutual Friend*, Bk 1, Ch. 6)

Inside, the Grapes now boasts a Dickens Bar.

South-Eastern England

11 London to Broadstairs via Rochester and Canterbury

'I have many happy recollections connected with Kent and am
scarcely less interested in it than if I had been a Kentish man bred
and born, and had resided in the county all my life,' Dickens once
wrote. The present route incorporates places familiar to him
throughout his life but especially associated with his childhood and
later years, as well as retracing in part or whole some of the most
famous journeys described in his fiction: the first expedition of Mr
Pickwick and his friends, David Copperfield's flight from Murdstone
and Grinby's to the refuge of Betsey Trotwood's home, and Pip's
various travels between the humble scenes of his childhood and the
delusive glamour of London in *Great Expectations*.

A2 leaves London by the Old Kent Road, New Cross and Blackheath
(7 miles), where it becomes a motorised bypass, the Rochester Way.
A more rewarding way to continue is by A207, Shooter's Hill Road,
the old Watling Street and traditional Dover road. On the incline of
Shooter's Hill, in Book 1, Chapter 2 of *A Tale of Two Cities*, Jarvis

Lorry and his fellow passengers were forced to get out and walk because 'the harness, and the mud, and the mail, were all so heavy, that the horses had three times already come to a stop, besides once drawing the coach across the road, with the mutinous intent of taking it back to Blackheath,' allowing the banker to be overtaken by Jerry Cruncher with the momentous news that Dr Manette, long-time prisoner in the Bastille, had been 'recalled to life.'

At Dartford (16 miles) the route diverges left on the A226 through Gravesend (23 miles), a Thames port that Dickens knew but hardly refers to in his writing, to Chalk (26 miles). In 1836 Dickens spent his honeymoon in the village, now on the fringe of London's urban sprawl, though attempts to identify the cottage where he and his wife Kate stayed have led to considerable confusion and the building apparently no longer stands. The old forge, today a private house, at the corner of the road to Singlewell and Cobham is regarded as the model for Joe Gargery's in *Great Expectations*. The church and churchyard, reached by a lane leading left from the main road, were a frequent stopping place for Dickens on his walks through the area.

A mile beyond Chalk a detour leads south from A226 through Shorne, a village in whose churchyard Dickens once expressed a desire to be buried, across the A2 to Cobham (3 miles), a favourite haunt throughout his life. Its chief point of interest is the **Leather Bottle Inn, an ancient building splendidly preserved and maintained despite fire damage in the 1880s, and now boasting a large, varied collection of Dickens relics on the walls of its bar. It was here that the lovesick and apparently suicidal Mr Tupman took refuge and was discovered by his fellow Pickwickians in 'a long, low-roofed room, furnished with a large number of high-backed leather-cushioned chairs of fantastic shapes and embellished with a great variety of old portraits and roughly coloured prints of some antiquity,' enjoying 'a roast fowl, bacon, ale, and et ceteras . . . looking as unlike a man who has taken his leave of the world, as possible' (Ch. 10). In the churchyard opposite, Mr Pickwick encountered little difficulty persuading his friend to rejoin the Club and its peregrinations. On his way back to the Leather Bottle he found the mysterious stone whose apparently ancient inscription was deciphered by his rival and enemy Mr Blotton as reading: '+BILL STUMPS HIS MARK.' Dickensians have placed a facsimile at the corner of the inn. At the east end of the village Cobham Park, landscaped by Repton, formed one of Dickens' common routes in his rambles from Gad's Hill. The park and its mansion, Cobham Hall, had earlier been affectionately evoked in the description of the Pickwickians' search for the missing Mr Tupman:

> The ivy and the moss crept in thick clusters over the old trees, and the soft green turf overspread the ground like a silken mat. They emerged upon an open park, with an ancient hall, displaying the quaint and picturesque architecture of Elizabeth's time. Long vistas of stately oaks and elm trees appeared on every side: large herds of deer were cropping the fresh grass; and occasionally a startled hare scoured along the ground, with the speed of the shadows thrown by the light clouds which swept across a sunny landscape like a passing breath of summer. (Ch. 10)

At Higham (28 miles) a second detour leads from the main road north-east towards the Isle of Grain, via B2000 to Cooling (5 miles). The bleak countryside of this area, which may also be viewed from

Cliffe at N end of B2000, dominates the opening chapters of *Great Expectations*: 'the marsh country, down by the river, within, as the river wound, twenty miles of the sea' (Ch. 1). In Cooling *churchyard lies a row of seven small 18C gravestones commemorating the children of the Comport family, a melancholy spectacle that inspired Pip's contemplation of his dead siblings (though Dickens alters the number):

> To five little stone lozenges, each about a foot and a half long, . . . sacred to the memory of five little brothers of mine—who gave up trying to get a living exceedingly early in that universal struggle—I am indebted for a belief I religiously entertained that they had all been born on their backs with their hands in their trousers pockets, and had never taken them out in this state of existence. (Ch. 1)

On the hill leaving Higham and opposite the Sir John Falstaff Inn stands Gad's Hill Place, the 'little Kentish freehold' Dickens bought in 1857 and used as his main residence until his death there in 1870, the years of separation from his wife, public reading tours, *A Tale of Two Cities*, *The Uncommercial Traveller*, *Great Expectations*, *Our Mutual Friend* and the unfinished *Mystery of Edwin Drood*. A letter announcing his new purchase reveals the special significance that this 'grave red brick house' held for him:

> It has always a curious interest for me, because when I was a small boy down in these parts I thought it the most beautiful house (I suppose because of its famous old cedar-trees) ever seen. And my poor father used to bring me to look at it, and used to say that if I ever grew up to be a clever man perhaps I might own the house, or another such house. In remembrance of which, . . . it has never been to me like any other house.

Another letter shows him keenly, if fancifully, appreciative of the place's connection with Shakespeare (q.v.) and *Henry IV, Part One*: 'The robbery was committed before the door, on the man with the treasure, and Falstaff ran away from the identical spot of ground now covered by the room in which I write.' Such nostalgic considerations did not prevent him altering and modernising the late 18C property (which he apparently thought dated from the Queen Anne period) with customary energy: 'I have added . . . and stuck bits upon in all manner of ways, so that it is as pleasantly irregular and as violently opposed to all architectural ideas, as the most hopeful man could possibly desire.' A tunnel connecting the main grounds with their extension, which Dickens called 'The Wilderness,' leads under the main road. The house is now a school.

**Rochester (31 miles) is, after London, the English city most intimately connected with Dickens. Its combination of historic associations, quiet provinciality and periodic bustle caused by its crucial position on the coaching route and by the nearby military dockyards gave it a special appeal for him. He uses the city in three of his novels: under its own name as the first halting place in the travels of Mr Pickwick and his companions; anonymously as the provincial centre nearest the countryside of Pip's childhood in *Great Expectations*; and as 'Cloisterham,' the 'drowsy city' where most of *The Mystery of Edwin Drood* takes place.

The bridge over the Medway by which travellers now approach the town is a later and altogether less picturesque construction than the stone bridge from which Mr Pickwick admired prospects of the city and the river before being interrupted by the 'dismal man' (Ch. 5). A convenient walking tour begins nearby at the north end of the

High Street. On the right stands the Royal Victoria and Bull Hotel (formerly the Bull Hotel), a building of red brick and grey stone well known to Dickens but now extensively and not always happily modernised. The Pickwickians and Mr Jingle stay here in Chapter 2 of the novel, Mr Pickwick's own room being pointed out as either No. 11 or No. 17. In its assembly room Mr Jingle and Mr Tupman attended the ball that led, by a series of typically Pickwickian accidents, to Mr Winkle almost fighting a duel with Dr Slammer at Fort Pitt Fields in neighbouring Chatham. In *Great Expectations* the Bull reappears as the 'Blue Boar,' where Pip's apprenticeship to Joe is celebrated by the Gargerys, Uncle Pumblechook and Mr Wopsle, whose vigorous recitation of Collins' 'Ode to the Passions' provokes complaint from other guests: 'The Commercials underneath sent up their compliments and it wasn't the Tumbler's Arms' (Ch. 13). The coffee room, now a bar to the left of the main entrance, is the scene of Pip's hostile encounter with Bentley Drummle in Chapter 43. Opposite the Bull is the 17C Guildhall, now a local museum, in whose courtroom Pip was formally bound apprentice. Dickens' description of the room as 'a queer place . . . with higher pews in it than a church' (Ch. 13), though in keeping with the mood of the incident, makes no mention of its magnificent plaster ceiling. The Corn Exchange on the left is notable for being 'oddly garnished with a queer old clock, as if Time carried on business there.' *Chertsey's Gate, an arched gatehouse spanning the pavement at the junction of High Street and Boley Hill, is now popularly known as 'Jasper's Gate' since its upper apartment became the residence of the sinister choirmaster in *Edwin Drood*. Beyond it is the half-timbered building occupied by the verger Mr Topes in the same novel and used as a temporary lodging by that mysterious visitor to 'Cloisterham,' Dick Datchery.

A right turn up Boley Hill leads immediately to the imposing five-storey Norman keep of Rochester Castle, which called forth enthusiastic reactions from the members of Mr Pickwick's party. To the poetic Mr Snodgrass it was a 'magnificent ruin,' and to the scholarly Mr Pickwick 'a study for an antiquarian,' while to the telegrammatic Mr Jingle it conjured up visions of 'frowning walls—tottering arches—dark nooks—crumbling staircases' (Ch. 2). The *Cathedral opposite, dating from 12C–14C but with its present tower and spire rebuilt in 1904, is the central location around which much of the plot of *Edwin Drood* revolves. Dickens wished to be buried here, though in the event Westminster Abbey (Rte 4) enjoyed that honour; a memorial to him can be found in the south transept. Minor Canon Row, south of the Cathedral, is the home of Mr Crisparkle in *Edwin Drood*.

On the continuation of the High Street, still retaining some of the quiet provincial atmosphere Dickens relished, is (left) Watts' Charity, founded in 1579 at the bequest of Richard Watts for the accommodation of 'Six Poor Travellers' and the inspiration for 'Seven Poor Travellers,' Dickens' Christmas story for 1854. Eastgate House beyond, a brick Elizabethan building, now houses a substantial museum. Its contents include reconstructed tableaux of famous scenes from the novels, but the most conspicuous and interesting item is the *Swiss chalet given to Dickens by the actor Charles Fechter and originally erected in the grounds of Gad's Hill as an alternative study to his ground-floor room in the house itself. He wrote his last pages, Chapter 23 of the unfinished *Edwin Drood*, in it on the day before his death in June 1870, Eastgate House may have served as the model for 'Westgate House,' the school for young ladies where Mr Pickwick has his embarrassing adventure in Chapter 16, though the novel represents the incident as occurring in Bury St Edmunds (Rte 16). It is certainly the 'Nuns' House' of *Edwin Drood*, where Miss Twinkleton runs the academy at which Rosa Bud is a pupil. The gabled Tudor building nearly opposite is associated with Mr Pumblechook's premises 'of a peppery and farinaceous character' (Ch. 8) in *Great Expectations* and, more somberly, with the residence of Mr Sapsea, the pompous Mayor of 'Cloisterham' in *Edwin Drood*.

Crow Lane leads right from the High Street to Restoration House (l.), a Tudor mansion so called because of its connection with Charles II. To Dickens it provided the suggestion for Miss Havisham's house in *Great Expectations* though he took its fictional name, 'Satis House,' from another building (on Bakers Walk). From Vines Lane to the right the pedestrian may enter The Vines, formerly a monks' vineyard and in Chapter 14 of *Edwin Drood* the scene of Edwin's ominous encounter with the Princess Puffer. Its tree-shaded walk may also have provided hints for the setting of Jasper's equally sinister interview with Rosa Bud in Chapter 19, though for the sake of plausibility the scene is transferred to the garden of the 'Nuns' House.' A return route may easily be traced through The Vines, down Boley Hill and back to the High Street.

Chatham, separated from Rochester only by an indistinct boundary in the nineteenth century and now officially amalgamated into the same borough, has undergone greater change than its sister town since Dickens' childhood residence there (1817–23). The advent of modern technology has rendered the Royal Naval Dockyard, in particular, virtually unrecognisable from his various descriptions, the most extended of which is the essay 'Chatham Dockyard' in *The Uncommercial Traveller*. The house at No. 11 (then No. 2) Ordnance Terrace, opposite the railway station, first occupied by the Dickens family after their arrival survives and is marked by a plaque; but even by the time of 'Dullborough Town' in *The Uncommercial Traveller* Dickens had cause to lament the alteration that time and the coming of the railway had made to its previously rural setting. The more modest house in The Brook, to which the family was forced to move in 1821, does not survive.

From Chatham via A2 to Canterbury (58 miles), a city with which Dickens was thoroughly familiar but whose surviving landmarks associate it chiefly with *David Copperfield*. In St Dunstan's Street near Westgate the traveller can find The House of Agnes (now a hotel), popularly identified with Mr Wickfield's residence where David met his future second wife Agnes and the ingratiating Uriah Heep:

> a very old house bulging out over the road; a house with long low lattice windows bulging out still farther, and beams with carved heads on the ends bulging out too, so that I fancied the whole house was leaning forward, trying to see who was passing on the narrow pavement below. (Ch. 15)

The Sun Inn (formerly the Little Inn) at the corner of Sun Street and Guildhall Street, between the High Street and the Cathedral, apparently provided accommodation for the Micawbers on their trip to Canterbury, when they entertained David to a 'beautiful little dinner' in Chapter 17. It is no longer an inn but its Dickensian association is remembered by an inscription. Attempts to identify the school run by Dr Strong which David attends with King's School in the Cathedral precincts are not convincing.

From Canterbury via A28 to Margate (74 miles) and A255 to Broadstairs (78 miles), a seaside resort fashionable in the 19C and still popular today. Dickens, who found it 'the healthiest and freshest of places,' spent his holidays here nearly every summer between 1837 and 1850, returning again from May to November 1851 and for a final one-week stay in 1859. Substantial parts of *Pickwick Papers*, *Nicholas Nickleby*, *The Old Curiosity Shop*, *Barnaby Rudge*, *David Copperfield* and *Bleak House* were written or planned during these visits. Though unnamed, Broadstairs is the subject of an affectionately ironic portrait, 'Our English Watering-Place' (1851; later included in *Reprinted Pieces*). Dickens had already given a shorter but equally vivid account of the place and his activities there in a letter of 1843:

> This is a little fishing-place; intensely quiet; built on a cliff, whereon—in the centre of a tiny semi-circular bay—our house stands; the sea rolling and dashing under the windows. Seven miles out are the Goodwin Sands . . . whence floating lights perpetually wink after dark, as if they were carrying on intrigues with the servants. Also there is a big lighthouse called the North Foreland on a hill beyond the village, a severe parsonic light, which reproves the young and giddy floaters, and stares grimly out upon the sea. Under the cliff are rare good sands, where all the children assemble every morning and throw up impossible fortifications, which the sea throws down again at high water. Old gentlemen and ancient ladies flirt after their own manner in two reading-rooms and on a great many scattered seats in the open air. Other old gentlemen look all day through telescopes and never see anything. In a bay window in a one-pair sits, from nine o'clock to one, a gentleman with rather long hair and no neckcloth, who writes and grins as if he thought he were very funny indeed. His name is Boz. At one he disappears, and presently emerges from a bathing machine, and may be seen—a kind of salmon-coloured porpoise—splashing about in the ocean. After that he may be seen in another bay window on the ground floor, eating a strong lunch; after that, walking a dozen miles or so, or lying on his back in the sand reading a book. Nobody bothers him unless they know he is disposed to be talked to; and I am told he is very comfortable indeed.

Although recent development and the inevitable increase of summer tourism have altered the town's character, much of the atmosphere Dickens enjoyed and some of the buildings most intimately connected with him remain.

A convenient walking tour begins on the High Street, which slopes towards the bay, where a plaque over the present Woolworths marks the site of No. 12, Dickens' lodging during his first visit. At the bottom of the hill stands the Royal Albion Hotel, now incorporating the house he occupied on an early visit; he was a guest at the hotel itself (then simply the Albion Hotel) during his farewell visit of 1859. A brief walk down Victoria Parade and a right turn lead immediately to Dickens House. In the 1840s and 1850s it was the home of Mary Pearson Strong from whom, it is said, Dickens borrowed several of the characteristics attributed to Betsey Trotwood in *David Copperfield*, including an aversion to donkeys. The house is identified with the 'very neat little cottage with cheerful bow-windows; in front of it, a small gravelled court or garden full of flowers, carefully tended, and smelling deliciously' (Ch. 13) where Miss Trotwood lives, though the novel locates it near Dover. It now contains items associated with Dickens, prints and photographs of Broadstairs during the period he knew it, and a reconstruction of Miss Trotwood's parlour based on 'Phiz's' illustration of her encounter with the Murdstones (Ch. 14). The northern end of Victoria Parade leads to Harbour Street, a footpath spanned by Archway House (formerly Lawn House), where Dickens wrote part of *Barnaby Rudge* in 1841. On top of the cliff beyond stands *Bleak House (formerly Fort House), Dickens' lodging in 1850 and again in 1851. It derives its present name from the fact he planned part of the novel there and not from any resemblance to Jarndyce's home, which is placed near St Albans. Though its external appearance was greatly altered by an extension of 1901 that doubled the size of the house, the rooms Dickens occupied are well preserved and contain a fine exhibition of Dickensiana. Of particular interest are: the lectern used for his public readings; the 'airy nest' of a study overlooking the sea, where *David Copperfield* was written; and the writing chair from Gad's Hill immortalised in Luke Fildes' mourning picture, 'The Empty Chair—10 June 1870.'

A week-long Dickens festival is held in June each year.

An extension of the route leads from Broadstairs south to Dover (A256; 20 miles), which Dickens barely knew when he chose to place Miss Trotwood's house in its vicinity and which he found 'not quite to my taste' when he stayed there for the summer of 1852. Folkestone (A20; 28 miles) proved more congenial in the summer of 1855, when he was writing the opening instalments of *Little Dorrit*, and still has much of the atmosphere that appealed to him. His lodging at Copperfield House (then simply No. 3), Albion Villas still stands and is marked by a plaque but has suffered a change of more than name. Folkestone also enjoys the distinction of being the first town where Dickens gave a public reading, from *A Christmas Carol* at the end of his 1855 visit, in an unidentifiable 'carpenter's shop, which looks far more alarming as a place to hear in than the Town Hall at Birmingham.'

Cobham Hall. Open Good Fri to Easter Mon 2–6; 29 July to 2 Sept, Wed, Thurs, Sun, also BH Mon 2–6. Fee.

Guildhall, Rochester. Open daily 10–12.30, 2–5.30. Fee.

Rochester Castle (English Heritage). Open 15 March to 15 Oct, Mon to Sat 9.30–6.30, Sun 2–6.30 (Apr to Sept, Sun 9.30–6.30); 16 Oct to 14 March, Mon to Sat 9.30–4, Sun 2–4. Closed Christmas Eve, Christmas Day, Boxing Day and New Year's Day. Fee.

Watts' Charity, Rochester. Open 1 March to 31 Oct, Tues to Sat 2–5.

Eastgate House (Charles Dickens Centre), Rochester. Open daily 10–12.30, 2–5.30; closed over Christmas. Fee.

Dickens House, Broadstairs. Open 7 Apr to 28 Oct, daily 2.30–5.30. Fee.

Bleak House (Dickens and Maritime Museum), Broadstairs. Open March to Nov, daily 10–6 (until 9 in July to Sept). Fee.

12   Brighton and Portsmouth

Brighton may be reached from London via A23 and M23 (53 miles). An alternative route (72 miles or 104 miles) leads across country from

Broadstairs or Folkestone at the end of the previous itinerary, via Rye, Hastings, Bexhill and Lewes.

It was inevitable that Brighton, with its proximity to London and its popularity as a seaside resort well established since the Regency, should have attracted Dickens. He spent several holidays here between the 1830s and 1850s, and included it in his public reading tours, reporting to a friend that it was 'a gay place for a week or so.' The Regency atmosphere, which still lingers today, contributed to his understanding of a period he delighted to satirise in his novels. Turveydrop, the Model of Deportment in *Bleak House*, was accustomed to visit Brighton 'at fashionable times' and it was outside the Royal Pavilion that he received the supreme honour of being noticed by the Prince Regent, who graciously enquired: 'Who is he? Who the Devil is he? Why don't I know him? Why hasn't he thirty thousand a year?' (Ch. 14).

The surviving reminders of Dickens' visits are situated along the seafront and can best be seen by a walk beginning at the west end of King's Road. He lodged at No. 148, near the Norfolk Hotel, in 1847 and at the Bedford Hotel beyond in 1848 and again in 1849. These were the years of *Dombey and Son* and the Bedford finds its way into the book as the chosen residence of Mr Dombey during his trips to see his son Paul. He entertained Major Bagstock, who had followed him from London to scrape an acquaintance, to dinner in the hotel and had his breakfast interrupted by Walter Gay and the well-intentioned but maladroit Captain Cuttle (Ch. 10). The Old Ship Hotel, between West and Palace Piers, was the scene of earlier visits in 1837 and 1841, when Dickens was working on *Oliver Twist* and *Barnaby Rudge* respectively. By following the continuation of King's Road as Marine Parade and King's Cliff Parade we reach Chichester House, at the nearest end of Chichester Terrace. According to the novelist Harrison Ainsworth (q.v.), whom Dickens saw in Brighton, this imposing building is the original of Dr Blimber's Academy, 'a mighty fine house, fronting the sea' (Ch. 11), where Paul Dombey attended school and made friends with Mr Toots, that amiable victim of the hothouse method of education.

From Brighton west via Chichester (A27) to Portsmouth (A27, A3; 104 miles), the town of Dickens' birth and early childhood (1812– 14) but greatly changed since that time.

His birthplace, an unremarkable but respectable house, survives as No. 393 Commercial Road, Landport, south of the Continental Ferry Port; in Dickens' day it was No. 1 Mile End Terrace. It is now a museum with a collection including the couch from Gad's Hill on which he died and is well furnished in the 19C style. A second Portsmouth house to which the family moved when he was six months old was destroyed by war-time bombing. Dickens revisited Portsmouth in 1838 in search of local colour for the hero's theatrical adventures with Mr Vincent Crummles and his company in *Nicholas Nickleby* (Chs 22–25, 29 and 30) and again in later life with George Dolby, the manager of his reading tours, when he found himself unable to identify the house of his birth.

We may cross from Portsmouth Harbour Station by ferry to Ryde, on the Isle of Wight. At the pretty village of Bonchurch near Ventnor on the south coast of the island (12 miles from Ryde) is Winterbourne, now a residential hotel but in 1849 'a most delightful and beautiful house' which Dickens rented for the summer. The Swinburne (q.v.)

family were among his neighbours and he admired their son, a 'golden-haired lad' of twelve. His initial enthusiasm for the area quickly faded and he was soon complaining to his friend John Forster about the climate:

> Of all the places I have ever been in, I have never been in one so difficult to exist in, pleasantly. Naples is hot and dirty, New York feverish, Washington bilious, Genoa exciting, Paris rainy—but Bonchurch, smashing. I'm quite convinced that I should die here, in a year. It's not hot, it's not close, I don't know what it is, but the prostration of it is *awful.*

Charles Dickens Birthplace Museum, Portsmouth. Open daily 10.30–5.30. Closed Christmas Day & Boxing Day. Fee.

South-Western England

13 Salisbury, Bath, Exeter and Clovelly

Dickens' knowledge of South-Western England, derived mainly from an 1835 excursion as an election reporter and subsequent fleeting visits for holidays, amateur theatricals and public readings, is probably sparser than his knowledge of any other English region of comparable size. Its fictional appearances are inevitably less frequent and less topographically precise than his use of more familiar areas like Kent and Eastern England. The following places, too dispersed to fall conveniently into a single itinerary, are worth noting.

Salisbury is a recurrent location in *Martin Chuzzlewit.* In Chapter 5 Tom Pinch visits the city under the impression that it is 'a very desperate sort of place' and takes 'a stroll about the streets with a vague and not unpleasant idea that they teemed with all kinds of mystery and bedevilment.' He ends the day safely enough playing the organ in the Cathedral. Various attempts, none of them notably persuasive, have been made to identify the nearby Wiltshire village where the Pecksniffs live and Tom Pinch usually plays the organ. Perhaps the best candidate is Winterslow, 8 miles NE and reached via A30. Some ten years after the novel's publication T.H. Wyatt restored the exterior of the church but left the interior relatively unscathed.

Bath. In Chapter 35 of *Pickwick Papers* the hero selects the fashionable spa as a holiday refuge from the anxieties caused by Mrs Bardell's impending lawsuit for breach of promise. His journey westward allows Dickens to comment jocularly on his theft of Pickwick's name from Moses Pickwick, owner of the London–Bath coaching service and proprietor of a Bath hotel, but once the city is reached it is described only in the most general terms and emphasis falls on social satire at the expense of Cyrus Bantam, Esquire and the footmen's 'swarry.' The only precise and memorable location is the Royal Crescent, scene in Chapter 36 of the 'extraordinary calamity' that prompted Mr Winkle to flee to Bristol. A visit of 1840 brought Dickens to the home of his friend Walter Savage Landor at No. 35 St James Square, behind the Royal Crescent and now marked by a plaque. It was here, to Landor's great pride, that Dickens first conceived the character of Little Nell in *The Old Curiosity Shop*.

Exeter. At Alphington 1½ miles to the south, once a village but now almost absorbed into the city, is Mile End Cottage, standing opposite the Post Office. A tablet bears witness to the fact that Dickens rented it as a home for his parents in 1839, an unsuccessful experiment ending in 1843 with their return to London.

Clovelly (12 miles west of Bideford via A39). In late 1860 Dickens visited this village on the north Devon coast, then just made famous by Charles Kingsley (q.v.) in *Westward Ho!* and still popular with tourists for its steep pedestrian street leading down to a fine bay. It appears as 'Steepways' in 'A Message from the Sea,' his Christmas story for that year written in collaboration with his companion on the trip, Wilkie Collins (q.v.):

> There was no road in it, there was no wheeled vehicle in it, there was not a level yard in it. From the sea-beach to the cliff-top two irregular rows of white houses, placed opposite to one another, and twisting here and there, and there and here, rose, like the sides of a long succession of stages of crooked ladders, and you climbed up the village or climbed down the village by the staves between, some six feet wide or so, and made of sharp irregular stones ... No two houses in the village were alike, in chimney, size, shape, door, window, gable, roof-tree, anything. The sides of the ladders were musical with water, running clear and bright. The staves were musical with the clattering feet of the pack-horses and pack-donkeys, and the voices of the fishermen's wives and their many children. The pier was musical with the wash of the sea, the creaking of capstans and windlasses, and the airy fluttering of little vanes and sails. The rough, bleached sea-boulders of the shore, were brown with drying nets. The red-brown cliffs, richly wooded to their extremest verge, had their softened and beautiful forms reflected in the bluest water ... (Ch. 1)

Central England

14 London to Grantham via Rockingham

We leave London via A1 to Hatfield (21 miles), where the old town lies to the east of the road. In Chapter 48 of *Oliver Twist* Bill Sikes came to this 'quiet village' after fleeing London and the scene of Nancy's murder by a route that had taken him through Islington, Highgate, Hampstead Heath (Rte 9) and Hendon, and later continued to St Albans. The picturesque 17C Eight Bells at the corner of Fore Street and Park Street is commonly identified with 'the small public house' where his refreshment was spoiled by the pedlar's attempt to use his blood-stained hat in a sales demonstration for a patent stain remover. The fire that briefly distracts him from the agonies of guilt was undoubtedly suggested by one in 1835 at the Jacobean mansion of Hatfield House nearby, which destroyed the west wing and killed the aged Marchioness of Salisbury. Dickens interrupted work on the opening chapters of *Pickwick Papers* to report the disaster.

A1 continues north, bypassing Welwyn Garden City. Knebworth

House (27 miles) may be reached via B656. This originally Tudor mansion rebuilt in a highly fanciful style at the beginning of the nineteenth century was the residence of Edward Bulwer-Lytton (s.v. Lytton), popular novelist as well as Dickens' friend and co-patron of the Guild of Literature and Art, designed to help less fortunate writers. Dickens' fundraising on behalf of the Guild brought him to Knebworth in November 1850 for performances in the banqueting hall of Jonson's *Every Man in His Humour* (q.v.), which allowed him to distinguish himself in the role of Captain Bobadil, and the farce *Animal Magnetism*. During a visit in 1861 he accepted Lytton's suggestion that the original, unhappy ending of *Great Expectations* be changed to the happier version eventually printed. He returned again in 1865 for a banquet celebrating the opening of three Gothic cottages (now standing near the Stevenage road) intended for recipients of the Guild's charity. The failure of the scheme led to their conversion into almshouses.

A1 north via Sandy (50 miles) and Norman Cross (80 miles) to the junction with A605 (84 miles). A left turn leads on a route via Oundle (97 miles), where we transfer to A427, and Corby (107 miles), where we take A6116 and then B6003 to **Rockingham Castle (110 miles)** on the hill overlooking the stone-built high street of the village.

Of all English country houses Rockingham is the one where Dickens felt most at home and which left the greatest imprint on his writing. He first met its owner, the Hon. Richard Watson, and his wife Lavinia at Lausanne in 1846 and a quickly developing friendship (reflected in the Dedication of *David Copperfield*) led to a visit in November 1849. A letter to his friend John Forster describes the part Norman, part Tudor castle and his reception there in terms of mock awe:

> Picture to yourself . . . a large old castle, approached by an ancient keep, portcullis, &c, &c, filled with company, waited on by six-and-twenty servants; the slops (and wine-glasses) continually being emptied; and my clothes (with myself in them) always being carried off to all sorts of places.

The house party acted scenes from Sheridan's *School for Scandal* and the episode of the gentleman in small clothes from Chapter 41 of *Nicholas Nickleby*. Dickens returned for more elaborate productions in the Castle in the New Year of 1851 and visited Rockingham again, after Richard Watson's death, in 1855 during a public reading tour.

Rockingham appears unmistakably in *Bleak House* as 'Chesney Wold.' country seat of Sir Leicester and Lady Dedlock, though it is transplanted from Northamptonshire to Lincolnshire and given a name suitable to that county. The main features that the novel uses are: the Yew Walk, which becomes the 'Ghost's Walk' whose history the housekeeper Mrs Rouncewell relates in Chapter 7; the 'shady, ancient, solemn little church' (Ch. 18) in the park, where Esther first sees Lady Dedlock; the turret where the lawyer Tulkinghorn lodges during his visits to the house; and the Sondes Arms in Rockingham's main street, which becomes the 'Dedlock Arms.' Relics of Dickens' visits and his friendship with the Watsons are now on display in the Long Gallery.

From Rockingham the route returns to the A1 by retracing A427 between Corby and Oundle to Weldon (114 miles) and heading north on A43 to Stamford (127 miles). On the lefthand side of the High Street at Grantham (148 miles) stands the George Hotel, an 18C coaching inn where Dickens and his illustrator Hablôt Browne ('Phiz')

'Chesney Wold,' by 'Phiz.' From Bleak House. *Courtesy of Cambridge University Library*

stayed in January 1838 on their way to research Yorkshire schools for *Nicholas Nickleby*. His enthusiastic reports of the George are echoed in the novel, where it is called 'one of the best inns in England' (Ch. 5), though Nicholas, making an altogether less pleasant journey north with Wackford Squeers and his new pupils, does not have the good fortune to stay there.

For a continuation of this journey see Rte 17.

Hatfield House. House and west gardens open end of March to beginning of Oct, Tues to Sat 12–5, Sun 2–5.30. Closed Good Fri but open BH Mon 11–5. Park open daily 10.30–8. Fee.

Knebworth House. Open 1 Apr to 21 May, Sun & BH Mon 11.30–4.30; 1 June to 15 Sept, Tues to Sun & BH Mon 11.30–4.30; 15 Sept to 30 Sept, Sun 11.30–4.30. Fee.

Rockingham Castle. Open Easter Sun to 30 Sept, Thurs, Sun & BH Mon & Tues 2–6; also Tues in Aug 2–6. Fee.

15 London to Shrewsbury via Leamington, Stratford and Tewkesbury

Leaving London by M1 we diverge left at 20½ miles on the A5 and travel via Dunstable (27 miles) and Stony Stratford (45½ miles) to Towcester (53½ miles). Among its several surviving old inns is the Pomfret Arms (Saracen's Head in Dickens' day), which Mr Pickwick found in Chapter 51 to fulfill Sam Weller's promise of 'everything clean and comfortable,' though his stay was disrupted by the stormy encounter between those two sworn political enemies, Mr Pott of the *Eatanswill Gazette* and Mr Slurk of the *Eatanswill Independent*.

From Towcester the A5 continues to Weedon Bec (61½ miles) and the A45 turning for Daventry (65½ miles), where A425 leads via Southam (75½ miles) to Royal Leamington Spa (82½ miles). Dickens included Leamington on itineraries for his public readings in later life but his most important visit took place in October 1838, the year when Queen Victoria bestowed the prefix 'Royal' on the town and the period when the popularity of its medicinal waters was well on the way to being established. Its fashionable semi-Regency atmosphere, still appreciable today, made Leamington a natural setting for Major Bagstock to introduce Mr Dombey to the grotesquely faded Mrs Skewton and her daughter Edith, destined to become the second Mrs Dombey, in Chapter 21 of the novel. Among the places where their acquaintance was renewed is the Royal Pump Room (rebuilt in 1925), near Victoria Bridge which spans the River Leam.

Nearby Warwick Castle (85 miles; W on A425) is the object in Chapter 27 of a visit by Mr Dombey's party. Dickens' description of the castle's exterior, 18C interiors and collection of paintings is generalised in the extreme ('They made the tour of the pictures, the walls, crow's nest, and so forth') but he makes good use of the occasion to ridicule Mrs Skewton's slavish adulation of the past: 'Those darling byegone times . . . with their delicious fortresses, and their dear old dungeons, and their delightful places of torture, and their romantic vengeances, and their picturesque assaults and sieges, and everything that makes life truly charming!'

From Warwick the traveller may take a detour 5 miles north to Kenilworth Castle, founded in 12C, enlarged in the Renaissance, allowed to decay after the Civil War and restored since it became national property in 1937. Mr Dombey's party admired its 'haunted ruins' (Ch. 27).

From Warwick the main route leads south on A46 to Stratford-upon-Avon (93 miles). Dickens, who later donated proceeds from amateur theatrical tours to the curatorship of the Birthplace in Henley Street, visited the major sights of Stratford (described under the entry for Shakespeare) during the same tour that took him and Hablôt Browne to Leamington. The visit is mainly memorable for providing Mrs Nickleby with one of the flightiest of those reminiscences that habitually enliven her conversation:

> 'After we had seen Shakespeare's tomb and birthplace, we went back to the inn there, where we slept that night, and I recollect that all night long I dreamt of nothing but a black gentleman, at full length, in plaster-of-Paris, with a lay-down collar tied with two tassels, leaning against a post and thinking; and when I woke in the morning and described him to Mr

Nickleby, he said it was Shakespeare just as he had been when he was alive, which was very curious indeed.' (Ch. 27)

A46 leads south from Stratford via Broadway (107 miles) and Toddington (111½-miles), where A438 branches right to the abbey town of Tewkesbury (122 miles). Of chief interest to the Dickensian is the Royal Hop Pole (formerly the Hop Pole) on Church Street near the Abbey, with a fine 14C fireplace as well as a Pickwick Bar and a Sam Weller Bar. Over dinner at the Hop Pole, on his way to Birmingham and his unsuccessful interview with Mr Winkle senior, Mr Pickwick found that the combination of bottled ale, madeira and port on top of milk punch earlier in the day helped make him more tolerant of Bob Sawyer's high-spirited antics during the journey.

The route continues north from Tewkesbury on A38 to Worcester (137 miles), A449 to Kidderminster (152 miles), A442 to Bridgnorth (166 miles) and then successively on A442 and A4169 to Shifnal (178 miles). The half-timbered houses of this town are sometimes associated with those glimpsed by Little Nell during the last stages of her journey with her grandfather and the schoolmaster from the industrial Midlands, in Chapter 46 of *The Old Curiosity Shop*:

They passed a large church; and in the streets were a number of old houses, built of a kind of earth or plaster, crossed and re-crossed in a great many directions with black beams which gave them a remarkable and very ancient look. The doors, too, were arched and low, some with oaken portals and quaint benches, where the former inhabitants had sat on summer evenings. The windows were latticed in little diamond panes, that seemed to wink and blink upon the passengers as if they were dim of sight.

The small village of Tong to the east (180 miles) can be more certainly identified, on Dickens' own authority, as Nell's destination and final resting-place. The •church of St Bartholomew, notable for its fine array of ornate tombs, monuments and effigies, bears a plaque outside the south door in memory of Dickens' most famous heroine.

We return to Shifnal and head west on A464, using M64 to bypass Oakengates and Wellington, and take A5 to Shrewsbury (198 miles). During their 1838 tour Dickens and Browne stayed at the Lion, a fine building with a part half-timbered and part 18C frontage, on Wyle Cop. Shrewsbury itself, which boasts perhaps the finest examples of Shropshire black-and-white architecture, has a rival claim to Shifnal as the original of the half-timbered town described in the quotation above.

Warwick Castle. Open 1 March to end Oct, daily 10–5.30; 1 Nov to end Feb daily 10–4.30. Fee.

Kenilworth Castle (English Heritage). Open 15 March to 15 Oct, Mon to Sat 9.30–6.30, Sun 2–6.30 (Apr to Sept, Sun 9.30–6.30); 16 Oct to 14 March, Mon to Sat 9.30–4, Sun –4. Closed Christmas Eve, Christmas Day, Boxing Day & New Year's Day. Fee.

Eastern England

16 London to Yarmouth via Ipswich and Bury St Edmunds

After London and Kent, Eastern England is probably the region that Dickens knew and loved best and the one that finds its way most persistently into his writing. He first visited it as a young reporter covering Suffolk elections in 1834 and 1835, acquiring a familiarity with the county's inns and an affection for its rural scenery that left their obvious mark on *Pickwick Papers*. A trip in early 1849 extended his knowledge to Norfolk and provided locales for *David Copperfield*. In the 1850s and 1860s he included the region's main towns in his public reading tours.

We leave London by A11 which originates as the Whitechapel Road in the East End, and at Leytonstone (8½ miles) transfer to A12, the main road for the rest of this route.

At Redbridge (11 miles) a detour leads left on A123 to Chigwell (4 miles), hyperbolically praised by Dickens as 'the greatest place in the world' and, despite the encroachments of London's outer suburbs, still preserving its village centre. Its chief attraction is the ****King's Head**, which appears in *Barnaby Rudge* as the 'Maypole Inn,' that massive symbol of traditional England presided over by the equally traditional landlord, John Willett. The appearance and atmosphere of the King's Head today still answer to Dickens' opening description of the 'Maypole':

> an old building, with more gable ends than a lazy man would care to count on a sunny day; huge zig-zag chimneys, out of which it seemed as though smoke could not choose but come in more than naturally fantastic shapes, imparted to it in its tortuous progress . . . Its windows were old diamond-pane lattices, its floors were sunken and uneven, its ceilings blackened by the hand of time, and heavy with massive beams. (Ch. 1)

The Chester Room is named in memory of the encounter that took place there between Mr Chester and Reuben Haredale in Chapter 29.

A12 continues to Chelmsford (35 miles), a town that singularly failed to impress Dickens when he made it his first stop during his East Anglian travels of 1834. The Black Boy Inn where he stayed and where Mr Jingle and Job Trotter join Tony Weller's coach in Chapter 20 of *Pickwick Papers* was demolished in the author's lifetime.

The route then bypasses Colchester (57 miles) and reaches Ipswich (75 miles), another of Dickens' stops on both his reporting tour (1835) and his reading tours (1859–61). During his first visit he lodged at the ***Great White Horse**, which is reached from the market place, Cornhill, by following Tavern Street to the corner of Northgate Street. This is how Mr Pickwick, Sam Weller and their accidental travelling companion Mr Magnus approach the inn in Chapter 22 of 'Pickwick Papers,' where it appears under its own name and in a highly unfavourable light. The stone effigy of a horse over the portico is ridiculed as 'a rampacious animal with flowing mane and tail, distantly resembling an insane cart-horse.' The gloomy and confusing interior ('Never were such labyrinths of uncarpeted passages, such clusters of mouldy ill-lighted rooms, such huge numbers of small dens for eating and sleeping in') provides an appropriate setting for Mr Pickwick's embarrassing intrusion into the bedroom properly belonging to the lady in the yellow curl papers. Modernised but retaining its historic character, with remnants of half-timbering visible in the roofed-over courtyard, the present Great White Horse hardly deserves such strictures.

A detour leads NW from Ipswich along A45 via Stowmarket (12 miles) and Suffolk countryside of the sort that, according to the urban Sam Weller, 'beats the chimley pots' (Ch. 16) to Bury St Edmunds (26 miles). Despite its inevitable growth since the 19C Bury is still the 'bright little town' Dickens praised at the expense of London in *The Uncommercial Traveller*. He knew it from a visit in the 1830s as well as return trips in 1859 and 1861, when he gave public readings at the 18C Athenaeum on Angel Hill by the entrance to the Abbey ruins. Also on Angel Hill is the *Angel Hotel, an imposing Georgian building, where he slept on his later visits. It was in the courtyard of the Angel that Sam Weller, using the pump to help himself recover from the previous evening's 'conviviality,' met Job Trotter for the first time and was innocently beguiled into entangling Mr Pickwick in his unfortunate adventure at a local school for young ladies (Ch. 16). The scene of that episode, 'Westgate House,' ('a large, old, red-brick house, just outside the town') is sometimes identified as Southgate House on Southgate Street, reached from St Mary's Square, though Eastgate House in Rochester (Rte 11) has rival claims.

From Ipswich the main A12 route continues to Lowestoft (118 miles) and the region Dickens toured in 1849.

A detour from A12 3 miles north of Lowestoft leads left to Blundeston, which by an easy process of transliteration suggested 'Blunderstone,' the village where David Copperfield is born and spends his early years. Attempts have been made to associate the 'Rookery' of his childhood with both the Rectory and Blundeston Hall but these should not be trusted, since Dickens himself implied in a letter that it was not so much the topography of the village as 'the sound of its name' of which he made use. The round Norman tower of Blundeston church has been restored as a memorial to him. At Somerleyton Hall 2 miles beyond he was the guest of Sir Morton Peto, the railway magnate who in 1844 had vastly extended his 17C manor house.

A12 leads north to Great Yarmouth (128 miles) which Dickens reported on the basis of his 1849 visit to be 'the strangest place in the world,' apparently because of the flatness of the surrounding countryside. Its subsequent growth into the most popular resort on the Norfolk coast has robbed it of the atmosphere he found and made David Copperfield share in the opening chapters of the novel. However, the visitor should not neglect the Denes, near the monument to Nelson, where the Peggotty family had their eccentric dwelling: 'a black barge, or some other kind of superannuated boat, ... high and dry on the ground, with an iron funnel sticking out of it for a chimney and smoking very cosily' (Ch. 3)

Somerleyton Hall. Open Easter Sun to end Sept, Thurs, Sun & BH Mon (also Tues & Wed in July & Aug) 2–5.30. Gardens open all other days except Sat 2-5.30. Fee.

Northern England

17   London to Carrock Fell via Barnard Castle and Bowes

Dickens' most important connection with Northern England dates from the trip he made with his illustrator, Hablôt Browne, in 1838 to the notorious Yorkshire private schools as part of his research for *Nicholas Nickleby*.

This route may be treated as a continuation of Rte 14 or taken by itself, travelling directly up A1 via Grantham (112 miles) and Doncaster (163 miles).

At 188 miles A64 offers a detour NE to York (14 miles). 'The Five Sisters,' lancet lights of 13C glass in the north transept of York Minster, inspire the fanciful story told to Nicholas by the 'grey-headed gentleman' in Chapter 6 of the novel.

The main route continues north on A1 to Scotch Corner (239 miles), where A66 leads NW. At Greta Bridge (248 miles), near the junction of the Greta and the Tees, Dickens proved unresponsive to scenery that impressed Sir Walter Scott (q.v.), Turner and Cotman, finding it merely 'a bare place . . . in the midst of a dreary moor.' His friendly reception at the George and New Inn (now a private house) mollified him and may have encouraged the tributes to local good-heartedness and hospitality which offset his otherwise rather bleak picture of the region in *Nicholas Nickleby*.

To the NW is the attractive market town of Barnard Castle (252 miles). The King's Head, where Dickens and Browne lodged, is recommended to Nicholas by Newman Noggs for its good ale (Ch. 7). Almost opposite the hotel stood a clockmaker's shop belonging to a Master Humphrey, which gave Dickens the title for the ill-fated miscellany in which he attempted to revive Mr Pickwick and Sam Weller but managed to rescue by using as a framework for *The Old Curiosity Shop* and *Barnaby Rudge*.

From Barnard Castle A688 leads SW to Bowes (257 miles). The *low stone building, now converted into apartments, at the end of the village's only street was undoubtedly Dickens' main model for the cruel and horrifying 'Dotheboys Hall,' though he also drew hints from several other schools in the Bowes area: 'a long, cold-looking house, with a few straggling outbuildings behind and a barn and a stable adjoining' (Ch. 9). At the time of Dickens' visit it housed an academy run by William Shaw (a one-eyed man, like his fictional counterpart Squeers), who had already achieved minor notoriety in 1823 when he was twice tried for cruelty to his pupils. Relics from the academy are exhibited at Dickens House in London (Rte 1). The church contains a memorial window to Shaw, donated in 1896, while he and his family lie in the churchyard. Its most interesting feature is the gravestone commemorating George Ashton Taylor, a pupil of Shaw's who died 'suddenly' at the age of 19 in 1822. Dickens read the inscription and later remarked: 'I think his ghost put Smike into my head, on the spot.'

A66 continues W via Brough (270 miles) and Penrith (291 miles) to a right turn, later dwindling into a track, at 301 miles, leading to Mungrisdale, Mosedale and Carrock Fell (308 miles; 2174ft). The fell was the main object of an abortive tour of Cumbria made by Dickens and Wilkie Collins (q.v.) in September 1857. Guided by a local publican who later confessed he had not tackled Carrock for twenty years they managed to reach the top, but their descent was beset by a series of accidents in which Dickens broke his compass and Collins sprained his ankle. Chapter 1 of *The Lazy Tour of Two Idle Apprentices*, jointly written by the two novelists and serialised in 1857, gives a comic account of their expedition.

THOMAS HARDY

b. Higher Bockhampton, Dorset, 1840; d. Dorchester, Dorset, 1928. *Desperate Remedies* (1871); *Under the Greenwood Tree* (1872); *A Pair of Blue Eyes* (1873); *Far from the Madding Crowd* (1874); *The Hand of Ethelberta* (1876); *The Return of the Native* (1878); *The Trumpet-Major* (1880); *A Laodicean* (1881); *Two on a Tower* (1882); *The Mayor of Casterbridge* (1886); *The Woodlanders* (1887); *Wessex Tales* (1888); *A Group of Noble Dames* (1891); *Tess of the d'Urbervilles* (1891); *Life's Little Ironies* (1894); *Jude the Obscure* (1896); *The Well-Beloved* (1897); *Wessex Poems* (1898); *Poems of the Past and Present* (1902); *The Dynasts* (1903–08); *Time's Laughingstocks* (1909); *A Changed Man and Other Tales* (1913); *Satires of Circumstance* (1914); *Moments of Vision* (1917); *Late Lyrics and Earlier* (1922); *The Famous Tragedy of the Queen of Cornwall* (1923); *Human Shows* (1925); *Winter Words* (1928); *The Life of Thomas Hardy 1840–1891†* (1928); *The Life of Thomas Hardy 1892–1928†* (1930); *An Indiscretion in the Life of an Heiress* (1934); *Our Exploits at West Poley* (1952).

† written by Hardy but published under the name of his second wife, Florence Emily. Republished in one volume as *Life of Thomas Hardy 1840–1928*.

Thomas Hardy, by William Strang (1919). Courtesy of National Portrait Gallery

Hardy needs little by way of general introduction, if only because his 'Wessex,' home for most of his long life and setting for the bulk of his writing, stands at or very near the top of any literary pilgrim's itinerary. This is quite natural, for in its combination of literary interest with architectural and natural beauty 'Wessex' is probably unrivalled among the sights described in this volume. Even the detailed tours suggested under South-Western England (Rtes 5–14) and Central England.(Rte 15) do not exhaust its richness. They are supplemented by reminders of Hardy's connection with London (Rtes 1–4) and Cambridge (Rte 16).

London

Hardy's acquaintance with the city was both larger and more significant than the common image of him would admit. We fall into serious misunderstanding if we suppose him a massively rooted provincial, a reclusive countryman whose knowledge of the world was limited to his native Dorset. In fact, he knew London well. From 1862 until 1867, crucial years when he was in his twenties, he worked as assistant to the London architect Arthur Blomfield. He returned in 1874–76 and 1878–81, the early years of his marriage, clearly wondering if London were not the necessary place for a writer to pursue his career, just as he had earlier supposed the same thing to hold true for an architect. When he did settle permanently in Dorset in the 1880s he was, like Clym Yeobright, no longer simply a native but a returned native: his love of home was now mixed with the detachment that comes from experience of other, different places. He still journeyed up to London for the fashionable season each year until extreme old age, taking innocent pride in the *entrée* he enjoyed to aristocratic dinner tables and in the ease with which he could slip again into the role of a 'London man.'

1   Adelphi

From Charing Cross Station (British Rail, and Northern, Bakerloo and Jubilee Underground Lines) we walk east along the Strand and make a right turn towards the river on Adam Street. This quickly brings us to Adelphi Terrace, a building of 1938 replacing the original 18C one by the Adam brothers. In 1863 Hardy's employer, the church architect Arthur Blomfield, moved his office to No. 8 and Hardy wrote enthusiastically to his sister Mary that it was 'a capital place. It is on the first floor and on a terrace that overlooks the river. We can see from our window right across the Thames, and on a clear day every bridge is visible' (*Life*, Aetat. 21–27). He later recalled with some affection: 'I sat there drawing, . . . occasionally varying the experience by idling on the balcony. I saw from there the Embankment and Charing Cross Bridge built . . . The rooms contained at that date fine Adam mantelpieces in white marble, on which we used to sketch caricatures in pencil' (*Life*, Aetat. 21–27). The mention of 'idling' is perhaps misleading for, apart from his conscientious application to architecture, Hardy's years with Blomfield were a period of great intellectual growth. He wrote poetry that was not to the taste of magazine editors and turned to fiction instead, producing *The Poor Man and the Lady*. The novel was never published, and Hardy later destroyed the manuscript, but the opinion of George Meredith (q.v.) was favourable enough to encourage him. By the time he returned home to Dorset in 1867, exhausted and in poor health, he was already wavering between literature and architecture as careers.

2   Westminster Abbey

Hardy's tablet in Poets' Corner (fee) marks the site of perhaps the most grotesquely inappropriate funeral suffered by an English writer. He had felt no love for the Abbey authorities, satirising the Dean for his exclusion of Byron (q.v.) in his poem 'A Refusal,' and had wished to lie by his family in Stinsford churchyard (Rte 9). But before consulting the relatives his literary co-executor Sydney Cockerell zealously went ahead with arrangements for a grand public funeral in the Abbey, and the resulting conflict had to be resolved by an expedient that sounds like a grim joke from Hardy's own writing. His heart, removed by the local doctor, was reserved for Stinsford while the rest of him was buried at Westminster, with leading literary men of the day acting as pallbearers: Barrie, Galsworthy, Housman, Kipling and Shaw (qq.v.).

3   Paddington and Maida Vale

Hardy lodged in Paddington while working for Arthur Blomfield in 1862–67 and returned to the area in 1874 for his marriage to Emma Gifford at St Peter's on Elgin Avenue, SW of Maida Vale Underground Station (Bakerloo Line). When he came to write his disguised autobiography at the end of his life he was still proud enough of Emma's genteel connections to note that the service was performed by 'her uncle Dr E. Hamilton Gifford, Canon of Worcester, and afterwards Archdeacon of London' (*Life*, Aetat. 33–36). More sentimentally, she remembered that the wedding took place on 'a perfect September day . . . not of brilliant sunshine, but wearing a soft sunny luminousness; just as it should be' (*Life*, Aetat. 29–30). The couple spent their honeymoon on the Continent and then lived briefly in Surbiton and Yeovil before setting up their first real home together at Sturminster Newton (Rte 7).

4   Tooting

We begin this visit to Hardy's south London home in 1878–81 at
Tooting Bec Underground Station (Northern Line).

Near Tooting Bec Common, reached via Tooting Bec Road to the
south, he saw the unhappily loitering couple who appear in his poem
'Beyond the Last Lamp.' Our main route takes us north up Trinity
Road to Arundel Terrace, a block of Victorian villas on the right-hand
side near the junction with Brodrick Road and the outskirts of
Wandsworth Common. A plaque at No. 1 (now No. 172 Trinity Road)
marks the dreary house where Hardy and his first wife Emma lived
after their 'idyll' at Sturminster Newton (Rte 7) and before their move
to Wimborne (Rte 9). Hardy later wrote that he 'by degrees fell into
line as a London man again' (*Life*, Aetat. 37–39) but in his diary also
spoke of a 'horror at lying down in close proximity to "a monster
whose body had four million heads and eight million eyes"' (*Life*,
Aetat. 39–40). Shortly after his arrival *The Return of the Native*,
written in Sturminster Newton, was published. At Arundel Terrace
he wrote *The Trumpet-Major* and *A Laodicean*, the latter inevitably
damaged by the internal haemorrhage that kept him bed-ridden for
the last five months of his stay.

South-Western England

Hardy did not use the term 'Wessex' until Chapter 50 of his fourth
novel, *Far from the Madding Crowd*, where 'Greenhill Fair' (really
Woodbury Fair outside Bere Regis) is described in an unpromisingly
obscure phrase as 'the Nijni Novgorod of South Wessex.' Once
introduced, it opened up suggestive possibilities for a writer who was
both methodical and deeply attached to the principle of the classical
unities. He later explained in a preface to the book:

> The series of novels I projected being mainly of the kind called local, they
> seemed to require a territorial definition of some sort to lend unity to their
> scene. Finding that the area of a single county did not afford a canvas
> large enough for this purpose, and that there were objections to an
> invented name, I disinterred the old one.

This may take retrospective credit for a more systematic intent than
he really possessed when he stood on the threshold of his career as
a major novelist, but the fact remains that his development into this
status—and his subsequent blossoming into a major poet—required
the creation, elaboration, extension and, finally, the commanding
possession of a fictional territory. He needed a solid, defined stage
for his invented dramas. The mood of Hardy's art may shift from the
comic to the tragic (indeed, we can already see this happening in
Far from the Madding Crowd), and the preoccupations embodied in
his central characters may change with the years, but his people act
out their differing fates against a landscape which remains constant
and familiar.

Hardy began the creation of 'Wessex' with a mild inaccuracy,

Map of 'Wessex' from the Wessex edition of Hardy's work (1912-31).
Courtesy of Cambridge University Library

Map of the
WESSEX
of the
Novels and Poems

Scale of Miles

Septentrio

Oriens

Occidens

Meridies

Lumsdon Christminster

R. Thames

NORTH
The Brown House Alfredston
Cresscombe
Marygreen
WESSEX
MID
Marlbury
Downs
Gaymead
Kennetbridge
Castle
Royal
Aldbrickham

WESSEX
The Great
Plain
Inkpen Beacon
Stoke Barehills
Weydon
Priors
Icenway
House
Quartershot
Stonehenge
UPPER
our Head
Melchester
WESSEX
Wintoncester
Kennel Hall
Deansleigh
Park
Shaston Wingreen
Marlott The Chase
The Slopes
Trantridge Cross Chaseborough
Shotcastle Kingsbere Nuttlebury Nulls
Lornton
Inn
The Great
Bramshurst
Forest
Southampton
Portsmouth

Shottsford Forum
Warborne
Kingsbere
Weatherbury
Welland
Budmouth
Heath
Havenpool
Nether Mynton
Casterbridge
Corvsgate
Sandbourne
Knollsea
The
Island
Solentsea

Castle
stshp

The Channel

Emery Walker sc

borrowing its name from the ancient Saxon kingdom whose centre lay east of the region he had in mind. In all else, however, he kept as near the facts as possible. Indeed, he possessed the rarest sort of artistic tact: an instinctive knowledge that imagination is sometimes superfluous and mere literal accuracy is eloquent enough. His home county of Dorset becomes 'South Wessex,' Hampshire 'Upper Wessex,' Wiltshire 'Mid-Wessex' and Somerset 'Outer Wessex.' The north-east boundary of 'North Wessex' reaches into Central England's Berkshire and Oxfordshire, the urbanised landscape of *Jude the Obscure*. Beyond Devon, called 'Lower Wessex' but virtually ignored in his writing, 'Off Wessex' extends westward to an unspecified point somewhere near the north Cornish coast, countryside charged with the memory of his first wife.

Of course, this territory does not completely enclose the action of the novels: characters travel to London, even to France, the United States and South America. Yet the world beyond 'Wessex' is shadowy, insubstantial, only vaguely seen. Hardy may regard Cainy Ball's innocent, wondering misconceptions about Bath with amusement (*Far from the Madding Crowd*, Ch. 33), yet his own acute sense of place deserts him when he turns his gaze to the larger scene. Sergeant Troy is given an improbable career as 'Professor of Gymnastics, Sword Exercise, Fencing, and Pugilism' in the United States (*Madding Crowd*, Ch. 50), while the account of Swithin St Cleeve's journey in *Two on a Tower* (Ch. 40) suggests that Hardy believed Boston and Cambridge, Massachusetts were a considerable distance apart. In *Tess of the d'Urbervilles* (Ch. 41) he writes of Angel Clare falling ill from fever in the 'clay lands' near Curbita, a Brazilian city in fact situated on a high plateau.

The blurriness at the outer edge of Hardy's vision serves to emphasise how sharply in focus is his depiction of 'Wessex.' Here landscape and buildings are seen with a vivid precision that constantly invokes the real geography of South-Western England. Hardy commonly keeps the existing names of natural landmarks like rivers and hills, while his towns, villages and hamlets wear only the thinnest of disguises. Who could fail to detect the name of Dorchester in 'Casterbridge,' for example, or Weymouth in 'Budmouth' or Cerne Abbas in 'Abbot's Cernel'? Elsewhere an older name is revived, making Shaftesbury into 'Shaston.' Thrifty in his art as well as in his life, Hardy sometimes finds that the discarded name of a real place comes in handy for a character. Jude Fawley's surname is derived from the village that had become 'Marygreen,' while we can find Troy (*Far from the Madding Crowd*), Chickerell (*The Hand of Ethelberta*), Melbury and Winterbourne (*The Woodlanders*) among the small print of the Ordnance Survey map.

As the popularity of his work attracted visitors to South-Western England, Hardy sometimes found it necessary to insist on the imaginary character of a particular place, like the 'Little Hintock' of *The Woodlanders*, or to admit that his imagination had enlarged Puddletown Heath or the Vale of Blackmore beyond their actual scope. But on the whole he showed little of the writer's customary annoyance at seekers after 'real-life originals' and was proud to accept the identification of 'Wessex' with his native region. The General Preface of 1912 to the Wessex Edition spoke of his scenery as having been 'done from the real' and provided a key to some of its major landmarks. By this time he had already smiled on the publication of several guides to 'Wessex,' the first by B.C.A. Windle in 1901, and was actively helping Hermann Lea in his exhaustive study of 1913. The Wessex Edition itself reproduced photographs of real places identified by their fictional names.

This may sound disturbingly like the insistent desire for actuality in art which led the Victorians to introduce running streams and live rabbits into their productions of *As You Like It*. Such a taste certainly helped the reception of the 'Wessex' novels, and it appealed to one aspect of Hardy's complex temperament. He had the antiquarian's respect for facts and the countryman's zest for odd ones. His architect's training had developed a mathematically precise eye for distances and spatial relations, and left him with the sort of technical vocabulary he could never resist: his pen readily notes architraves and ogee curves, or ponders distinctions between the various stages of Gothic. In the larger view, he possessed at least some of the instincts necessary to the social realist and could speak, in his General Preface, of the 'humble supplementary quality' his novels had in their relation to social history:

> At the dates represented in the various narrations things were like that in Wessex: the inhabitants lived in certain ways, engaged in certain occupations, kept alive certain customs, just as they are shown doing in these pages.

In our own age, uneasily conscious of the destruction of rural England and its traditional ways of life, he has come to be treasured above all as the historian—indeed, the elegist—of a vanished culture.

Yet he himself was quick to add that this aspect of his achievement was 'quite unintentional and unforeseen.' He was not Emile Zola nor even George Eliot (q.v.), though he conscientiously read both these authors. If 'Wessex' is 'partly real' it is also, he firmly reminded us, 'partly dream.' The dream-like quality comes not from sentimental regret at the death of rural England nor from occasional rebellions against the facts of geography. It comes, rather, from his own highly distinctive vision: an imaginative grasp, shaping and coherent, which underlies even his most dogged moments of literal-mindedness. When we finish one of his novels we are left with the impression of a detailed map, but also with a more elemental image of man's position in the order of things, an image admirably summed up by Lionel Johnson in one of the earliest criticisms of Hardy:

> A rolling down country, crossed by a Roman road: here a gray standing stone, of what sacrificial, ritual origins I can but guess; there a grassy burrow, with its great bones, its red brown jars, its rude gold ornaments, still safe in the earth: a broad sky burning with stars: and a solitary man.

This, of course, is not to deny the real benefits—let alone the many incidental pleasures—to be taken from visits to the landscape he had in mind for his fiction. We should be guided by Hardy's own evident belief that the way to universals lies through the most careful attention to particulars.

For the sake of convenience, the tours suggested below begin with Dorchester, the cultural though not the literal centre of 'Wessex,' and then proceed to a series of journeys radiating outward from the town.

5   Dorchester

**Dorchester, the single most important town in Hardy's life and work, was changing greatly in his time and has continued to change since then. The atmosphere conjured up so expressively in *The Mayor of Casterbridge* belonged to the years before his birth:

> Casterbridge was the complement of the rural life around; not its urban opposite. Bees and butterflies in the cornfields at the top of the town, who desired to get to the meads at the bottom, took no circuitous course, but flew straight down High Street without any apparent consciousness that they were traversing strange latitudes. And in autumn airy spheres of thistledown floated into the same street, lodged upon the shop fronts, blew into drains, and innumerable tawny and yellow leaves skimmed along the pavement, and stole through people's doorways into their passages with a hesitating scratch on the floor, like the skirts of timid visitors. (Ch. 9)

The railway came in 1847 when he was still a young boy, forging a link with London and bringing with it telegraphs and daily newspapers. By the time Hardy was working here as an apprentice architect (1856–61) and living with his parents at Higher Bockhampton (Rte 9) he was, he realised, a commuter between two radically different ways of life, observer of 'rustic and borough doings in a juxtaposition peculiarly close' (*Life*, Aetat. 16–21). Later he sometimes had reason to lament the destruction of local landmarks like the old Three Mariners Inn.

'Looking up the High Street of Casterbridge.' From the Wessex edition of The Mayor of Casterbridge. *Cambridge University Library*

Even though the visitor should be ready for exhaust fumes rather than butterflies or thistledown in the streets, he will also find Dorchester a remarkable survival. It has suffered much less from modernisation than most county towns; its main buildings and its quiet corners would be familiar to Hardy and his characters.

The town is best explored by a series of walking tours starting from the centre formed by the junction of Cornhill, High West Street and High East Street. The distinctive landmark at this spot is St Peter's with the statue of William Barnes (q.v.), Hardy's friend and fellow poet, outside. The local architect John Hicks was finishing a major restoration of the church when Hardy joined his office in 1856, and Hardy himself may have worked on alterations to the east window and the north vestry. At any rate, there is an architectural plan signed by him on a pillar in the south aisle. Hardy, who developed a snobbishly selective approach to his ancestors, liked to believe that he was descended from the Elizabethan Thomas Hardy, founder of Dorchester's grammar school, commemorated by a chapel and a separate tablet. The 8 o'clock curfew which the bells of St Peter's used to sound is mentioned in *The Mayor of Casterbridge* (Ch. 4).

The •Dorset County Museum next door has a collection rich in Roman antiquities, agricultural equipment and musical instruments used by the old church 'quires'—all subjects of great interest to Hardy. Also on display is a reconstruction of his study at Max Gate, and an arch with a mask as its keystone, formerly part of Colliton House. So grotesque an object was bound to catch Hardy's attention:

> Originally the mask had exhibited a comic leer, as could still be discerned; but generations of Casterbridge boys had thrown stones at the mask, aiming at its open mouth; and the blows thereon had chipped off the lips and jaws as if they had been eaten away by disease. (*Mayor*, Ch. 21)

We start our first walking tour by descending High East Street. Immediately on our left is the Town Hall and Corn Exchange, built in 1847 and so presumably the setting Hardy had in mind for two important scenes: Henchard's confrontation with the furmity-woman who had witnessed the wife-sale (*Mayor*, Ch. 28) and Bathsheba Everdene's first triumphant appearance among the local farmers (*Far from the Madding Crowd*, Ch. 12). Next we come to the •King's Arms Hotel, conspicuous for its handsome portico with a bow window above. Looking in through this window Mrs Henchard saw her husband presiding as Mayor over the public dinner (Ch. 5). Henchard's bankruptcy hearing was held in another front room (Ch. 31).

Opposite the hotel stands All Saints' Church, a 19C building no longer used for worship. After Sunday service the choir filed across to the Three Mariners Inn and met a drunken Michael Henchard demanding that they play the 'cursing psalm' (Ch. 33). The Elizabethan inn has gone and the site is occupied by the British Legion Club. As we approach the bottom of High East Street we find, again on our left, the White Hart. In this now sadly altered building Sergeant Troy met Pennyways before going on to make his disastrous appearance at Boldwood's Christmas party (*Madding Crowd*, Ch. 52).

At the bottom of the hill is Swan Bridge, modern replacement of a much older structure. Hardy mentions it as one of two bridges which attracted 'all the failures of the town; those who had failed in business, in love, in sobriety, in crime' (*Mayor*, Ch. 32). To reach the second,

Grey's Bridge, and so to retrace the steps of Michael Henchard when his fortunes had sunk to their lowest, we continue straight ahead along the London road with the flat expanse of Durnover Moor stretching on either side. From Grey's Bridge a footpath leads left along the riverside to Ten Hatches, the sluice gates and weir where Henchard contemplates suicide but is stopped by the appearance of his own effigy in the water (Ch. 41).

Returning to the bridge we cross the road and take King's Road to the turning on the right for Mill Street, the disreputable 'Mixen Lane':

> It was the hiding-place of those who were in distress, and in debt, and trouble of every kind. Farm-labourers and other peasants, who combined a little poaching with their farming, and a little brawling and bibbing with their poaching, found themselves sooner or later in Mixen Lane. Rural mechanics too idle to mechanise, rural servants too rebellious to serve, drifted or were forced into Mixen Lane. (*Mayor*, Ch. 36)

The neighbourhood had already risen when Hardy wrote the novel and it has changed beyond recognition since then. In the years of her widowhood Florence Emily, Hardy's second wife, took an active part in its improvement.

At the top of King's Road we come to Fordington Cross, centre of the area Hardy calls 'Durnover' and mentions in *The Mayor of Casterbridge* as the site of the corn merchants' granaries. It is most important as a reminder of Hardy's youthful friendship with the Moule family. Rev. Henry Moule was Vicar of Fordington and his church, St George's, is reached by turning right at the Cross, following Fordington Hill, and then branching right on Fordington High Street. In the churchyard lies Moule's son Horace (properly Horatio), friend of Hardy, the first person to encourage his literary ambitions and, by his suicide in 1873, a partial model for the ill-fated Boldwood in *Far from the Madding Crowd* and Jude Fawley. Hardy's poem 'Before My Friend Arrived' describes his visit to the newly dug grave the night before Moule's body was returned from Cambridge (Rte 16). After St George's we descend Fordington High Street to Swan Bridge and return to the centre of town.

We start a second excursion from Cornhill by taking the narrow lane between St Peter's and the Town Hall, scene of the collision between Henchard and Farfrae's wagons (*Mayor*, Ch. 27). The same chapter recalls that North Square beyond once boasted stocks and a stone post to which oxen were tied for baiting by dogs, in the belief it would make their meat tender.

From North Square we descend Friary Hill, cross the river and take the path to our left. Henchard came here after reading the letter from his dead wife, for the neighbourhood suited his mood by embodying 'the mournful phases of Casterbridge life' (*Mayor*, Ch. 19). On the opposite bank of the river rises the unpicturesque shape of the Prison, a modern building that preserves the 'classic archway of ashlar' noted by Gertrude Lodge in the short story, 'The Withered Arm'. Boldwood knocked at the gate to give himself up after shooting Troy (*Madding Crowd*, Ch. 54). In the first half of the nineteenth century executions were still held outside the prison, and these spectacles played a part in the development of Hardy's sometimes morbid sensibility. The hanging of the murderess Martha Brown, which he witnessed in 1856, may have helped suggest the final scene of *Tess of the d'Urbervilles*. His *Life* recounts a grotesque memory of 1858:

One summer morning at Bockhampton, just before he sat down to breakfast, he remembered that a man was to be hanged at eight o'clock at Dorchester. He took up the big brass telescope that had been handed on in the family, and hastened to a hill on the heath a quarter of a mile away from the house, whence he looked towards the town. The sun behind his back shone straight on the white stone façade of the gaol, the gallows upon it, and the form of the murderer in white fustian, the executioner and officials in dark clothing and the crowd below being invisible at this distance of nearly three miles. At the moment of his placing the glass to his eye the white figure dropped downwards, and the faint note of the town clock struck eight.

The whole thing had been so sudden that the glass nearly fell from Hardy's hands. He seemed alone on the heath with the hanged man, and crept homeward wishing he had not been so curious. (Aetat. 16–21)

We cross the river at the next bridge and, as the road bends to the right, find Hangman's Cottage. The public hangman still lived in this picturesque building when Hardy was a boy, and Gertrude Lodge pays him a memorable visit in 'The Withered Arm.' Almost opposite is the entrance to North Walk, one of several distinctive tree-lined avenues that mark the line of Dorchester's old Roman walls. We follow the Walk to the right and then bear left on Colliton Walk, which runs alongside The Grove. Henchard walked here with Farfrae, persuading him not to emigrate but to stay in 'Casterbridge' instead (Ch. 9).

Close to the Top o' Town junction near the end of Colliton Walk is Eric Kennington's statue of Hardy, unveiled in 1931 by Sir James Barrie (q.v.). We turn left into High West Street and, just before reaching Shire Hall, take another left into Glyde Path Road. Behind

'The Hangman's Cottage at Casterbridge.' From the Wessex edition of Wessex Tales. *Courtesy of Cambridge University Library*

the row of houses on its left-hand side stood No. 7 Shire Hall Place, Hardy's home in 1883–85, when he was writing *The Mayor of Casterbridge* and waiting for Max Gate to be completed. Further along we find Colliton House, now part of the offices of Dorset County Council. The 18C building was probably the model for 'High Place Hall,' home of Lucetta Templeman:

> The Hall, with its grey façade and parapet, was the only residence of its sort so near the centre of town . . . The house was entirely of stone, and formed an example of dignity without great size. It was not altogether aristocratic, still less consequential, yet the old-fashioned stranger instinctively said, 'Blood built it, and wealth enjoys it,' however vague his opinions of these accessories might be. (*Mayor*, Ch. 21)

In the process of turning Colliton House into 'High Place Hall' Hardy moved it to Cornhill so that it could enjoy a panoramic view of Dorchester's market. As the start of our third tour we should examine Cornhill more closely, since it is a recurrent location for the public scenes in his novels: 'The *carrefour* was like the regulation Open Place in spectacular dramas, where the incidents that occur always happen to bear on the lives of the adjoining residents' (*Mayor*, Ch. 24). Mother Cuxsom and the rural chorus gather round the town pump, which still survives, to gossip about Mrs Henchard's death (*Mayor*, Ch. 18) and in *Far from the Madding Crowd* Gabriel Oak plays flute to console himself after failing to get a job at the hiring fair (Ch. 6). On the right is the impressive frontage of the Antelope Hotel where Henchard waits in vain to give Lucetta back her letters (*Mayor*, Ch. 18).

Cornhill leads to South Street ('Corn Street') where, beyond the entrance to Tudor Arcade on the left, we find the fine 18C house 'faced with dull red-and-grey old brick' (Ch. 9) that Hardy used as Michael Henchard's home. It is now a branch of Barclays Bank. Further on, Napper's Mite was once almshouses and the Hardye Arcade, a modern shopping precinct, occupies the site of Hardye's Grammar School, whose pupils included Sergeant Troy. The scene opposite is more interesting. Next to each other and marked by plaques are the house of William Barnes and the offices of the architect John Hicks, where Hardy worked in 1856–61 and again after his return from London in 1867. His *Life* (Aetat. 16–21) remembers that he would sometimes slip out of the office to get Barnes' advice on a point of Greek grammar.

From the large road junction at the bottom of South Street we may take Great Western Road and its continuation as Damers Road right to the former Union Workhouse, now Damers Hospital. Fanny Robin came here to die in Chapter 40 of *Far from the Madding Crowd* and Hardy used the occasion for a laconic comment: 'A neighbouring earl once said that he would give up a year's rental to have at his own door the view enjoyed by the inmates from theirs—and very probably the inmates would have given up the view for his year's rental.'

Returning to the South Street junction we continue south on Weymouth Avenue. After passing near the railway station on our left we come to ˙Maumbury Rings, the Roman amphitheatre which Hardy usually calls 'The Ring.' As a child he was brought by his father to see effigies of the Pope and Cardinal Wiseman burnt during the No-Popery Riots, and in *The Mayor of Casterbridge* (Ch. 11) he made 'The Ring' setting for Henchard's reunion with his wife. The scene includes a fine evocation of the place's gloomy history.

°Max Gate, the final point of interest in a tour of Dorchester, lies about a mile from the centre and is best reached by car, following the Wareham road (A352) south-east, past a modern pub named after *The Trumpet-Major*, to the turning on the left for Syward Road. The house occupies the corner site. Hardy designed it himself, had it built by his brother Henry, moved to it in 1885 and stayed for the rest of his life. *Tess of the d'Urbervilles* and *Jude the Obscure* were written here during the years of crisis in his marriage to Emma. Many of the poems he wrote after abandoning fiction in the 1890s are rooted in domestic incidents at Max Gate. After Emma's death in 1912 he brought his second wife, Florence Emily, to the house. The 1920s, when he had become the Grand Old Man of English Letters, saw a procession of distinguished visitors: T.E. Lawrence (q.v.), then living nearby at Clouds Hill, was the most welcome and Virginia Woolf (q.v.), daughter of Hardy's old friend Leslie Stephen, the most ironically perceptive. His manner of receiving guests was described by Siegfried Sassoon in the poem 'At Max Gate':

> Old Mr Hardy, upright in his chair,
> Courteous to visiting acquaintance chatted
> With unaloof alertness while he patted
> The sheep dog whose society he preferred.
> He wore an air of never having heard
> That there was much that needed putting right.
> Hardy, the Wessex wizard, wasn't there,
> Good care was taken to keep him out of sight.

For all this wealth of personal history, the house is neither attractive nor expressive. One can appreciate Hardy's choice of the site, with its fine views over the surrounding countryside; it allowed him, incidentally, to walk by a path that cuts off the curve of A352 to William Barnes' rectory. But the building itself, bleakly angular, is a disappointing creation by a man who elsewhere shows himself so sensitive to architectural nuance. It would have been more appropriate for a successful town councillor or businessman than for the novelist who described his birthplace at Higher Bockhampton or Bathsheba's farmhouse or the old buildings of Dorchester so lovingly. Its gloomy atmosphere is intensified by the heavy screen of trees, mostly planted by Hardy himself, a forcible reminder of his carefully guarded privacy in later life.

Dorset County Museum. Open Mon to Fri 10–5, Sat 10–1, 2–5. Closed Christmas Day, Boxing Day & Good Fri. Fee.

6   Dorchester to Sherborne via Cerne Abbas and Cross-in-Hand

The route takes us north from Dorchester through countryside mainly associated with *The Woodlanders* and *Tess of the d'Urbervilles*. It begins at the Top o' Town, where we follow A37 (the Yeovil road) and branch right after 1½ miles on A352 towards Sherborne.

At 7 miles we reach Cerne Abbas ('Abbot's Cernel'), a village so satisfyingly picturesque that it acts as a powerful magnet for summer visitors. South of The Folly, the street by which we approach the main village from A352, is the medieval Tithe Barn that once belonged to the Abbey. Together with the one at Abbotsbury (Rte 12), it is claimed as model for the shearing barn enthusiastically celebrated by Hardy in *Far from the Madding Crowd*:

> One could say about this barn, what could hardly be said of either the church or the castle, akin to it in age and style, that the purpose which had dictated its original erection was the same with that to which it was still applied. Unlike and superior to either of those two typical remnants of mediaevalism, the old barn embodied practices which had suffered no mutilation at the hands of time. Here at least the spirit of the ancient builders was one with the spirit of the modern beholder. Standing before this abraded pile, the eye regarded its present usage, the mind dwelt upon its past history, with a satisfied sense of functional continuity throughout—a feeling almost of gratitude, and quite of pride, at the permanence of the idea which had heaped it up . . . The defence and salvation of the body by daily bread is still a study, a religion, and a desire. (Ch. 22)

The charming Abbey Street leads north past the church to a beautiful 15C gatehouse, only surviving fragment of the Abbey where Hardy's poem 'The Lost Pyx' begins.

As we leave the village on A352 we have on the right a fine view of the Cerne Giant (NT), the massive chalk figure carved on the hillside. Our route is now following the coaching road travelled by Mrs Dollery's van in the opening chapter of *The Woodlanders*, though it no longer has quite the forsaken atmosphere Hardy pondered:

> The physiognomy of a deserted highway expresses solitude to a degree that is not reached by mere dales or downs, and bespeaks a tomb-like stillness more emphatic than that of glades and pools. The contrast of what is with what might be, probably accounts for this. To step, for instance, . . . from the edge of the plantation into the adjoining thoroughfare, and pause amid its emptiness for a moment, was to exchange by the act of a single stride the simple absence of human companionship for an incubus of the forlorn.

With Minterne Magna (9 miles) we reach 'Great Hintock,' one of the few certainly identifiable locations in a novel whose elusive topography will shortly be considered.

A mile north of the village we turn left on the unclassified road that leads across the high uplands of Batcombe Down towards Holywell and Evershot. On our right we soon find 'Cross-in-Hand (11½ miles), a short stone pillar of uncertain date surmounted by an almost indecipherable design. 'The Lost Pyx' describes one legend explaining this mysterious landmark. In *Tess*, when the heroine passes it on her journey to Angel Clare's parents, Hardy suggests that it 'marks the site of a miracle, or murder, or both' (Ch. 44). In the following chapter, when she has a dramatic encounter with Alec d'Urberville here on her return journey, Hardy adds:

> Some authorities stated that a devotional cross had once formed the complete erection thereon, of which the present relic was but the stump; others that the stone as it stood was entire, and that it had been fixed there to mark a boundary or place of meeting. Anyhow, whatever the origin of the relic, there was and is something sinister, or solemn, according to mood, in the scene amid which it stands; something tending to impress the most phlegmatic passer-by. (Ch. 45)

The scene is certainly striking, for from this bleak height spreads one of the widest views in Dorset. To the west, on our left, rises Bubb Down and to the east High Stoy. The Blackmore (or Blackmoor) Vale—home of Tess' childhood (Rte 7)—stretches north and east of High Stoy.

Somewhere in the nearer reaches of this expanse is the setting of *The Woodlanders*, a countryside of 'extensive woodlands, interspersed with apple-orchards' (Ch. 1). In creating 'Little Hintock,' home of the Melbury family and the book's main location, Hardy abandoned his normally precise use of the map and took a certain delight in the confusion he caused his more earnest readers:

> I once spent several hours on a bicycle with a friend in a serious attempt to discover the real spot; but the search ended in failure; though tourists assure me positively that they have found it without trouble, and that it answers in every particular to the description given in this volume. At all events, . . . the commanding heights called 'High-Stoy' and 'Bubb-Down Hill' overlook the landscape in which it is supposed to be hid. (Preface of 1912)

From Cross-in-Hand we return to A352 and continue north. The junction with A3030 (20 miles) marks the site of the Sherborne turnpike where Gabriel Oak and Jan Coggan overtake Bathsheba on her secret journey to Bath (*Madding Crowd*, Ch. 32).

At 22 miles A352 brings us to Sherborne, Hardy's 'Sherton Abbas' and still one of the pleasantest towns in Dorset. Its chief sight is the magnificent Abbey, where Grace Melbury and Giles Winterbourne sit among the tombs (*Woodlanders*, Ch. 38). The tombs again caught Hardy's attention in the poem 'In Sherborne Abbey.' East of the river at the edge of the town lie the ruins of the Old Castle and the 16C Sherborne Castle. Already of interest to the literary-minded visitor for their connection with Sir Walter Ralegh (q.v.), the buildings were used by Hardy as the setting for 'Anna Lady Baxby' in *A Group of Noble Dames*. Grace Melbury inspects the Old Castle in Chapter 23 of *The Woodlanders*.

Sherborne Old Castle (English Heritage). Open 15 March to 15 Oct, Mon to Sat 9.30–6.30, Sun 2–6.30 (Apr to Sept, Sun 9.30–6.30); 16 Oct to 14 March, Mon to Sat 9.30–4, Sun 2–4. Closed Christmas Eve, Christmas Day, Boxing Day & New Year's Day. Fee.

Sherborne Castle. Open Easter Sat to end Sept, Thurs, Sat, Sun, BH Mon 2–6. Fee.

7   Dorchester to Cranborne via Sturminster Newton, Marnhull, Shaftesbury and Wardour Castle

This journey takes us through scenes from *Tess of the d'Urbervilles* and *Jude the Obscure*, as well as Hardy's life in the years following his marriage to Emma.

We start by heading east from Dorchester on the Puddletown road (A35) and branching left on B3143 just beyond Grey's Bridge over the Frome. B3143 leads north through Piddlehinton, White Lackington and Piddletrenthide (about 7 miles) to an unclassified road on the right for Plush (8½ miles). The village lies in the middle of the area where several locations have been proposed for 'Flintcomb-Ash,' the 'starve-acre place' where Tess goes to work in Chapter 43 and where she experiences her greatest suffering. None of the suggestions is entirely convincing and together they serve to remind us that Hardy was in the habit of hiding or muddling the identity of unpleasant places in his novels.

From Plush we continue NE to Mappowder (11½ miles). Some 2 miles east of the village rises Bulbarrow, second highest point in Dorset and one of the hills celebrated in the poem 'Wessex Heights.' It also marks one boundary of the Vale of Blackmore or Blackmoor (see also Rte 6), familiar to readers of *Tess*:

> This fertile and sheltered tract of country, in which the fields are never brown and the springs never dry, is bounded on the south by the bold chalk ridge that embraces the prominences of Hambledon Hill, Bulbarrow, Nettlecombe-Tout, Dogbury, High Stoy, and Bubb Down. The traveller from the coast, who, after plodding northward for a score of miles over calcareous downs and corn-lands, suddenly reaches the verge of one of these escarpments, is surprised and delighted to behold, extended like a map beneath him, a country differing absolutely from that which he has passed through. Behind him the hills are open, the sun blazes down upon fields so large as to give an unenclosed character to the landscape, the lanes are white, the hedges low and plashed, the atmosphere colourless. Here, in the valley, the world seems to be constructed upon a smaller and more delicate scale; the fields are mere paddocks, so reduced that from this height their hedgerows appear a network of dark green threads overspreading the paler green of the grass. The atmosphere beneath is languorous, and is so tinged with azure that what artists call the middle distance partakes also of that hue, while the horizon beyond is of the deepest ultramarine. Arable lands are few and limited; with but slight exceptions the prospect is a broad rich mass of grass and trees, mantling minor hills and dales within the major. (Ch. 2)

We enter this country on unclassified roads leading via Hazelbury Bryan ('Nuttlebury' in *Tess*) to the junction with A357 and, immediately north, Sturminster Newton (18 miles).

This quiet market town, the 'Stourcastle' of *Tess*, was Hardy's home from 1876, when he and Emma left furnished lodgings in Yeovil, until they went to London in 1878 (Rte 4). *The Return of the Native* was written at Riverside Villa, their house overlooking the Stour west of the town. Hardy later described the excitement of setting up what was in effect their first married home, hastily furnishing it 'by going to Bristol and buying £100 worth of mid-Victorian furniture in two hours' (*Life*, Aetat. 36–37). He came to treasure the 'Sturminster idyll' as the happiest phase of a marriage that later settled into quiet, entrenched unhappiness:

> Yes; such it was;
> Just those two seasons unsought,
> Sweeping like summertide wind on our ways;
> Moving, as straws,
> Hearts quick as ours in those days;
> Going like wind, too, and rated as nought
> Save as the prelude to plays
> Soon to come—larger, life-fraught:
> Yes; such it was.
>
> ('A Two-Years' Idyll,' first stanza)

'The To-Be-Forgotten' was written after a return visit in 1899. In *Moments of Vision* three poems—'Overlooking the River Stour', 'The

Musical Box' and 'On Sturminster Foot-Bridge'—combine memories of scenes near his house with retrospective fears that he paid too little attention to Emma.

On B3092 to the north is Marnhull (21 miles), a sprawling village and the 'Marlott' of *Tess*. None of the inevitable attempts to identify the Durbeyfields' cottage is persuasive, though the Crown Inn by the church presumably suggested Hardy's 'Pure Drop Inn.' B3092 continues to the junction with A30 (24 miles), which leads east to *Shaftesbury (28 miles). This stone-built town, marvellously situated on a hill enjoying superb views of the surrounding country, appears under its old local name as 'Shaston' in *Jude the Obscure*, where Hardy quite rightly calls it 'one of the queerest and quaintest spots in England' (Part 4, Ch. 1). His account, however, omits mention of Gold Hill, perhaps Shaftesbury's queerest and quaintest spot. 'Old-Grove Place,' the home of Sue and her schoolmaster-husband Phillotson, is the Ox House on Bimport, off the north end of the High Street. We may follow Jude's example and take Abbey Walk from Bimport to Park Walk, with its fine view of the country to the south. The Grosvenor Arms in the Market Place is presumably the 'Duke's Arms,' where Jude missed his coach at the end of his visit.

From Shaftesbury we can make a detour (20 miles in all) to Wardour Castle by following A30 NE towards Salisbury and then branching left at 6 miles for Tisbury. The Castle, built in 1769–76 by James Paine, has lost the collection of pictures admired by Jude and Sue (*Jude the Obscure*, Part 3, Ch. 2) as well as some of its decorated ceilings and panelling. It is now a school. The medieval ruins of Wardour Old Castle, which did not attract the severely classical Sue Bridehead, are ¾ mile SE.

To the SE of Shaftesbury is Cranborne Chase, still preserving its character as 'a country of ragged woodland, which, though intruded on by the plough at places, remained largely intact from prehistoric times, and still abounded with yews of gigantic growth and oaks tufted with mistletoe' (*Two on a Tower*, Ch. 39). Tess Durbeyfield is raped here by Alec (Ch. 11). We cross the Chase by taking the scenic B3081 to the junction with B3078 (42 miles), where a left turn brings us to Cranborne (43 miles). Because unpleasant, the 'Trantridge' of *Tess of the d'Urbervilles* cannot be identified but Cranborne is certainly 'Chaseborough'—though in Hardy's description, 'decayed market-town' (Ch. 10), the adjective is no longer appropriate. The Fleur-de-Lys is obviously the 'Flower-de-Luce' mentioned by Alec when he offers to rescue Tess from the revelling of the 'Trantridge' labourers.

Wardour Castle. Open 20 July to 5 Sept, Mon, Wed, Fri, Sat 2.30–6. Fee.

Wardour Old Castle (English Heritage). Open 15 March to 15 Oct, Mon to Sat 9.30–6.30, Sun 2–6.30; 16th Oct to 14 March, Mon to Sat 9.30–4, Sun –4. Closed Christmas Eve, Christmas Day, Boxing Day & New Year's Day. Fee.

8   Salisbury and Stonehenge

This can easily be treated as an extension of Rte 7 by making the 17-mile journey from Cranborne to Salisbury on B3078 east and A338 north or by taking A30 12 miles NE after visiting Wardour Castle.

Salisbury ('Melchester') is richly connected with several of Hardy's works, especially *Jude the Obscure*. If we took Sue Bridehead's advice in that novel we would begin a walking tour at the railway station, which she believes has replaced the Cathedral and other historic buildings as the 'centre of town life' (Part 3, Ch. 1). Instead, we start by the north end of the High Street at St Thomas of Canterbury, the 'grey Perpendicular church with a low-pitched roof' (Part 3, Ch. 7) where Sue is given away by Jude at her marriage to Phillotson. We then make the short walk south on the High Street to enter the *Cathedral Close by its North Gate.

Hardy paid tribute to these stately and impressive surroundings in a diary note made in 1897:

> Went into the Close late at night. The moon was visible through both the north and south clerestory windows to me standing on the turf on the north side . . . Walked to the west front, and watched the moonlight creep round upon the statuary of the façade—stroking tentatively and then more and more firmly the prophets, the martyrs, the bishops, the kings, and the queens . . . Upon the whole the Close of Salisbury under the full summer moon on a windless night, is as beautiful a scene as any I know in England—or for the matter of that elsewhere. (*Life*, Aetat. 57–58)

His impressions on this occasion appear again in the poem 'A Cathedral Façade at Midnight,' while the Close is several times described in his fiction. In *Two on a Tower*, for example, Louis Glanville finds it 'damp and venerable, . . . level as a bowling-green, and beloved of rooks' (Ch. 39) when he comes to visit the Bishop of Melchester at his Palace (on the south side of the Cathedral and now the Cathedral School). The most important visitor, though, is Jude Fawley, attracted by the prospect of 'a quiet and soothing place, almost entirely ecclesiastical in its tone; a spot where worldly learning and intellectual smartness had no establishment; where the altruistic feeling that he did possess would perhaps be more highly estimated than a brilliancy which he did not' (Part 3, Ch. 1). Less wisely, he is also drawn by the presence of Sue Bridehead at the training college, attended in real life by Hardy's sisters, housed in the medieval Old Deanery and King's House on the west side of the Close.

Jude works as a mason on the restoration of the Cathedral, Hardy presumably having in mind the alterations begun by Gilbert Scott in 1859. These went some way towards modifying the damage done to the interior by Wyatt in the 18C. Wyatt's inappropriately neat reorganisation of the monuments survives, however, and is given a sideglance by Hardy in *The Hand of Ethelberta* when the heroine inspects 'the sallow monuments which lined the grizzled pile' while Christopher Julian plays the organ (Ch. 39). Hardy's poem 'The Impercipient' finely records the feelings of an agnostic during a service, estranged by his doubts from the 'bright believing band' of worshippers.

Tess Durbeyfield and Angel Clare also come to Salisbury, but only to pass quickly through the city in their flight from the law: 'It was about midnight when they went along the deserted streets, lighted fitfully by the few lamps, keeping off the pavement that it might not echo their footsteps. The graceful pile of cathedral architecture rose dimly on their left hand, but it was lost upon them now' (Ch. 58). The end of their journey is *Stonehenge, which we may reach by following A345 north and A303 west (10 miles). Hardy indulges his love of nocturnal scenes and gives a wonderfully atmospheric yet precise description of their arrival at the stone circle:

> The wind, playing upon the edifice, produced a booming tune, like the note of some gigantic one-stringed harp. No other sound came from it, and lifting his hand and advancing a step or two, Clare felt the vertical surface of the structure. It seemed to be of solid stone, without joint or moulding. Carrying his fingers onward he found that what he had come in contact with was a colossal rectangular pillar; by stretching out his left hand he could feel a similar one adjoining. At an indefinite height overhead something made the black sky blacker, which had the semblance of a vast architrave uniting the pillars horizontally. They carefully entered beneath and between; the surfaces echoed their soft rustle; but they seemed to be still out of doors. The place was roofless. Tess drew her breath fearfully, and Angel, perplexed, said—
> 'What can it be?'
> Feeling sideways they encountered another tower-like pillar, square and uncompromising as the first; beyond it another and another. The place was all doors and pillars, some connected above by continuous architraves.
> 'A very Temple of the Winds,' he said.
> The next pillar was isolated; others composing a trilithon; others were prostrate, their flanks forming a causeway wide enough for a carriage; and it was soon obvious that they made up a forest of monoliths grouped upon the grassy expanse of the plain. The couple advanced further into this pavilion of the night till they stood in its midst.
> 'It is Stonehenge!' said Clare. (Ch. 58)

Modern visitors may no longer wander in between the pillars and they will find some of the fallen stones restored to their original position; but the Altar stone where Tess is sleeping next morning when the police arrive can still be seen.

Stonehenge (English Heritage). Open 15 March to 15 Oct, Mon to Sat 9.30–6.30, Sun 2–6.30 (Apr to Sept, Sun 9.30–6.30); 16 Oct to 14 March, Mon to Sat 9.30–4, Sun 2–4. Closed Christmas Eve, Christmas Day, Boxing Day & New Year's Day. Fee.

9   Dorchester to Wimborne Minster via Stinsford, Puddletown, Bere Regis and Milton Abbas

We go east from Dorchester on A35 and, half a mile after crossing the River Frome, bear right on an unclassified road for Stinsford (2 miles), the hamlet which gives its name to the dispersed parish including Lower Bockhampton and Higher Bockhampton. Stinsford parish was the scene of Hardy's childhood and much of his youth, and it remained at the very centre of his affections throughout his life. As 'Mellstock' it appears in his writings from the early *Under the Greenwood Tree* to his last poems.

Our first destination is the little *church and churchyard where Hardy's heart lies buried near the graves of his relatives. The inclusion of an engraving showing the entrance to the churchyard as frontispiece to his first volume of poems showed its importance to him, not just as a repository of family history but as the place for solemn (or ironic) meditation. It was his Stoke Poges, he once told a friend. Of the several poems set here, perhaps the most poignant are 'Voices from Things Growing in a Churchyard.' 'The Dead Quire' and 'Friends Beyond.'

The interior of the church has changed since the days Hardy first knew it, having lost its traditional barrel roof, tall pews and the west gallery where as a youth he continued the tradition of his father and grandfather by playing in the 'quire'. His sketch of the gallery, marking the places occupied by the various musicians, is on display and there is a plaque commemorating his family's forty-year service. The poem 'A Church Romance' describes how his mother first saw his father when

> She turned in the high pew, until her sight
> Swept the west gallery, and caught its row
> Of music-men with viol, book and bow
> Against the sinking sad tower-window light.

> (first stanza)

Among the monuments we should note the one in the south chancel to the 18C Lady Susan Strangways and her actor-husband, a marriage that appealed to Hardy's interest in social disparities and provided the subject for 'The Noble Lady's Tale,' and the tablet to Benjamin Bowring, mentioned in 'Voices from Things Growing in a Churchyard.'

From the church we retrace our route north and then turn right on the road for Bockhampton Cross. On our right is the entrance to Kingston Maurward House and the Old Manor House, now the Dorset College of Agriculture. In Hardy's time the House was occupied by Julia Augusta Martin, who took a strong interest in his education and encouraged the precocious development of his talents. It is clearly the chief model for 'Knapwater House,' home of Mrs Aldclyffe in his first published novel, *Desperate Remedies*.

. From Bockhampton Cross a left turn brings us to Higher Bockhampton and at 3½ miles the lane leading to **Hardy's Birthplace. The Birthplace cannot be reached by car and so we park on the right by the head of the lane. From here we can walk directly to the house but a better route takes us through Thorncombe Wood (NT), marking the western edge of the old Puddletown Heath, one of a loosely connected series that stretched SE from Higher Bockhampton towards Bournemouth. Development, modern farming techniques and the activities of the National Forestry Commission have restricted its scope, but even in Hardy's time it was smaller and considerably less dramatic than the 'Egdon Heath' familiar to readers of *The Return of the Native* and the closing chapters of *The Mayor of Casterbridge*. About 1 mile east of the car park and reached by footpath lie Rainbarrows, the mound Hardy called 'Rainbarrow,' where Eustacia Vye stands at the opening of *The Return of the Native*.

From whatever direction it is approached the Birthplace is a satisfyingly picturesque building, lovingly described as Tranter

Dewy's home in *Under the Greenwood Tree*:

> It was a long low cottage with a hipped roof of thatch, having dormer windows breaking up into the eaves, a chimney standing in the middle of the ridge and another at each end. The window-shutters were not yet closed, and the fire-and candle-light within radiated forth upon the thick bushes of box and laurestinus growing in clumps outside, and upon the bare boughs of several codlin-trees hanging about in various distorted shapes, the result of earlier training as espaliers combined with careless climbing into their boughs in later years. The walls of the dwelling were for the most part covered with creepers, though these were rather beaten back from the doorway—a feature which was worn and scratched by much passing in and out, giving it by day the appearance of an old keyhole. (Ch. 2)

The cottage is little altered since it was built at the turn of the 19C. Hardy lived here with his parents until he went to London in 1862 and on his return, dispirited and unhealthy, in 1867. During the years that followed he wrote *Under the Greenwood Tree* and *Far from the Madding Crowd*, the novels that stick most closely to the countryside of his childhood and the first of his books to mine a rich vein of local traditions, anecdotes and humour. *Far from the Madding Crowd* was composed 'sometimes indoors, sometimes out—when he would occasionally find himself without a scrap of paper at the very moment he felt volumes. In such circumstances, he would use large dead leaves, white chips left by the wood-cutters, or pieces of stone or slate that came to hand. He used to say that when he carried a pocket-book his mind was barren as the Sahara' (*Life*, Aetat. 33–36).

Leaving the Birthplace, we turn right at the head of the lane and follow the hill to the A35, which we take eastward. On the left we pass Yellowham Wood, 'Yalbury Wood' and the home of Keeper Day in *Under the Greenwood Tree*, before reaching Puddletown (5½ miles). Victorian improvements swept away many of the buildings Hardy knew from childhood visits to his mother's relatives and described in his portrait of 'Weatherbury' in *Far from the Madding Crowd*. Yet Puddletown is still an agreeable place and its *church is of special interest, for among its lovely furnishings it retains the 17C west gallery formerly used by the 'quire'. Though the tower does have gargoyles the visitor will look in vain for the particularly fearsome one that destroyed Fanny Robin's grave (Ch. 46).

Hardy himself admitted the liberty he had taken with the location of Bathsheba's home, 'Weatherbury Upper Farm,' which the novel places on the outskirts of Puddletown. Its original, the 16C–17C Waterston Manor lies 1½ miles NW of the village via B3142. Though it has risen from the status of rented farm to which it had sunk in Hardy's day, and though it suffered severe damage from fire later in the 19C, the Manor has kept much of the character which called forth one of his most openly loving architectural descriptions:

> Fluted pilasters, worked from the solid stone, decorated its front, and above the roof the chimneys were panelled or columnar, some coped gables with finials and like features still retaining traces of their Gothic extraction. Soft brown mosses, like faded velveteen, formed cushions upon the stone tiling, and tufts of the houseleek or sengreen sprouted from the eaves of the low surrounding buildings ... The main staircase was of hard oak, the balusters, heavy as bed-posts, being turned and moulded in the quaint fashion of their century, the handrail as stout as a parapet-top, and the stairs themselves continually twisting round like a person trying to look over his shoulder. Going up, the floors above were found to have a very irregular surface, rising to ridges, sinking into

valleys; and being just then uncarpeted, the face of the boards was seen to be eaten into innumerable vermiculations. Every window replied by a clang to the opening and shutting of every door, a tremble followed every bustling movement, and a creak accompanied a walker about the house, like a spirit, wherever he went. (Ch. 9)

Returning to A35 we continue eastward to another country house that Hardy knew well: Athelhampton Manor (9½ miles). The largely Tudor building appears as 'Athelhall' in *A Group of Noble Dames.*

Further east on A35 is Bere Regis (13½ miles), Hardy's 'Kingsbere.' The ˙interior of its church is exactly what the reader of *Tess of the d'Urbervilles* (Ch. 52) would expect, with canopied tombs and 'beautifully traceried windows of many lights' commemorating the Turberville family. East of the village rises Woodbury Hill, site of 'Greenhill Fair' at which Sergeant Troy makes an unwelcome reappearance in Bathsheba's life (*Madding Crowd*, Ch. 50).

From Bere Regis an unclassified road leads NW via Milborne St Andrew (16½ miles) and across A354 to Milton Abbas (20 miles). The Earl of Dorchester built this model village in the 1780s when he cleared the original market town from beside his new mansion, Milton Abbey. It lies near the Abbey church, 1 mile west of the present village, and is now a school. Hardy clearly had it in mind as the original of 'Middleton Abbey,' Felice Charmond's house in *The Woodlanders*, influenced no doubt as much by the building's autocratic history as by its architecture. Unclassified roads continue north from Milton Abbas via Winterbourne Strickland to Turnworth (24½ miles). As assistant to Crickmay, John Hicks' successor, Hardy worked on Turnworth church in 1869. The delicately embellished capitals and corbels he contributed remind us how sensitive a church architect he could be.

We retrace our route south from Turnworth and turn east at Winterbourne Strickland for A354, which quickly brings us to Blandford Forum (31 miles), a handsome town mentioned as 'Shottsford Forum' but never really described in the 'Wessex' novels. B3082 now leads SE to Wimborne Minster (40 miles). Hardy and Emma lived here in 1881–83 before moving to Dorchester, and found in its old-world charm (now a little diminished) an echo of their 'idyll' at Sturminster Newton (Rte 7). But the chief point of interest for the visitor is the Abbey, whose rich, cluttered interior is evoked in the poem 'Copying Architecture in an Old Minster.'

5 miles west of Wimborne, on A31 heading back towards Bere Regis, we pass the entrance to Charborough Park, whose Gothic tower (rebuilt 1840) gave Hardy some hints for the one at 'Welland House,' the ingeniously composite setting for *Two on a Tower.* On the coast 8 miles SE of Wimborne is Bournemouth, whose atmosphere is neatly captured by the description of 'Sandbourne' in *Tess of the d'Urbervilles*: 'a fairy palace suddenly created by the stroke of a wand, and allowed to get a little dusty' (Ch. 55).

Kingston Maurward House (Dorset College of Agriculture). Visitors by prior appointment.

Hardy's Birthplace, Higher Bockhampton (NT). Interior by prior appointment with the tenant. Exterior can be seen from the end of the garden Apr to end Oct, daily except Tues morning (including Good Fri) 11–6 or dusk if earlier. Fee for interior.

Athelhampton Manor. Open 18 Apr to 14 Oct, Wed, Thurs, Sun 2–6; also Good

Fri & BH, plus Tues & Fri in Aug. Fee.

Milton Abbey. House open Easter and summer holidays, 10–7.30 or dusk. Fee. Abbey church open at all reasonable times.

10 Dorchester to Lulworth Cove via West Stafford, Woodsford and Wool

This route heads eastward from Dorchester through scenes mainly associated with *Tess of the d'Urbervilles*. We begin by taking A352 towards Wool and at 2 miles branch left on the unclassified road which leads to the Frome, and, beyond, Stinsford parish (Rte 9). Before this, however, we turn right for the village of West Stafford (4 miles), beginning a journey along the southern bank of the river and through the 'Valley of the Great Dairies.' Most readers will remember the passage where Tess Durbeyfield first sees this 'valley in which milk and butter grew to rankness, and were produced more profusely, if less delicately, than at her home—the verdant plain so well watered by the river Var or Froom':

> It was intrinsically different from the Vale of Little Dairies, Blackmoor Vale [Rtes 6 and 7] ... The world was drawn to a larger pattern here. The enclosures numbered fifty acres instead of ten, the farmsteads were more extended, the groups of cattle formed tribes hereabout; there only families. These myriads of cows stretching under her eyes from the far east to the far west outnumbered any she had ever seen at one glance before. The green lea was speckled as thickly with them as a canvas by Van Alsoot or Sallaert with burghers. The ripe hues of the red and dun kine absorbed the evening sunlight, which the white-coated animals returned to the eye in rays almost dazzling, even at the distant elevation on which she stood.
>
> The bird's-eye perspective before her was not so luxuriantly beautiful, perhaps, as that other one which she knew so well; yet it was more cheering. It lacked the intensely blue atmosphere of the rival vale, and its heavy soils and scents; the new air was clear, bracing, ethereal. The river itself, which nourished the grass and cows of those renowned dairies, flowed not like the streams in Blackmoor. Those were slow, silent, often turbid; flowing over beds of mud into which the incautious wader might sink and vanish unawares. The Froom waters were clear as the pure River of Life shown to the Evangelist, rapid as the shadow of a cloud, with pebbly shallows that prattled to the sky all day long. There the water-flower was the lily; the crowfoot here. (Ch. 16)

As a general description it still holds true, and it is with pervasive atmosphere rather than specific places that the visitor to this countryside should be content. Unlike most buildings in Hardy's work, 'Talbothays,' the dairy farm where Tess meets Angel Clare, does not seem to have a real-life model. He took its name from the farm bought by his father in West Stafford. The farmhouse Hardy designed and his brother Henry built in 1913 still stands; Hardy's sisters Mary and Kate lived here. It has been suggested that Lower Lewell Farm, on the Woodsford Road just after the turning for Crossways, may occupy the spot where Hardy envisaged the fictional 'Talbothays.'

Woodsford Castle, standing on the left as we enter the village of Woodsford (6½ miles), can be more certainly identified with Hardy's work. The melodramatic poem 'A Sound in the Night' narrates the legend of an 18C murder in this pleasant patchwork of virtually every architectural period from the medieval onwards. The footpath nearby leads to the river at a point within sight of Sturt's Weir, the 'Shadwater Weir' where Eustacia Vye and Damon Wildeve drown in *The Return of the Native* (Bk 5, Ch. 9).

From Woodsford our route continues south-east via Moreton to Wool (13 miles), the 'Wellbridge' where Angel Clare takes Tess after their wedding (Ch. 34). The Manor where they spend their disastrous honeymoon is north of the town just beyond the Elizabethan stone bridge mentioned by Hardy. It is now a hotel, but still displays the Turberville portraits which so impress Clare. Half a mile east of Wool on the road to East Stoke we find the scanty ruins of Bindon Abbey, rather less romantic than they are made to appear in the famous sleep-walking scene (Ch. 37), though the coffin of Abbot Maners in which Clare lays Tess survives. Near the Abbey ruins stands the mill whose workings Clare planned to investigate.

We complete our journey by taking B3070 south from Wool to Lulworth Cove (17 miles), a fine circular bay of chalk cliffs. It is the subject of the poem 'At Lulworth Cove a Century Back' and, as 'Lulwind Cove,' it is a recurrent location in the novels. Owen and Cytherea Graye come here by paddle-steamer excursion from Weymouth in *Desperate Remedies* (Ch. 2), while in *Far from the Madding Crowd* (Ch. 47) Sergeant Troy takes the swim that leads to his presumed death by drowning. The atmosphere that Hardy found has been greatly changed by the Cove's popularity with summer visitors as well as by the neighbouring military camp and firing range.

11 Dorchester to Sutton Poyntz via Maiden Castle, Weymouth and Isle of Portland

2 miles SW of Dorchester and reached by an unclassified road leading right from A354 stands one of Dorset's finest antiquities, *Maiden Castle. This earthen hill fort, covering some 116 acres, was first occupied in about 2000 BC and fell to the Roman general Vespasian in AD 43. The outermost of its ramparts—there are as many as eight at one point—offers a splendid walk with views over the surrounding countryside. It was inevitable that Hardy, with his strong sense of prehistory, should have used it in his writing. As 'Mai Dun' the fort appears in 'Tryst at an Ancient Earthworks,' more an evocation of place than a short story, as well as in *The Mayor of Casterbridge*, where Henchard proposes its 'pleasant upland' as the scene for his unsuccessful public entertainment (Ch. 16) and uses it to spy on Farfrae's courtship of Elizabeth-Jane (Ch. 43).

Returning to A354 we continue south to the large and popular seaside resort of Weymouth (8½ miles). As 'Budmouth' it is frequently mentioned but rarely described in Hardy's work. The most specific glimpses are given by his novel of the Napoleonic Wars, *The Trumpet-Major*, which conjures up the town's atmosphere when it became a centre of military activity and was graced by the presence of George III. The colourful statue of the King at the south end of the Esplanade stands as a monument to this period of Weymouth's history, while the Esplanade itself has preserved much of its Georgian elegance. The Gloucester Hotel is an enlarged version of Gloucester Lodge where, as *The Trumpet-Major* notes, the King stayed.

A354 leads south to the Isle of Portland, not an island proper but a limestone peninsula 'like a great crouching animal tethered to the mainland' (*Trumpet-Major*, Ch. 12). Hardy chose its bleak and rocky expanse, in striking contrast to the scenery that typifies the rest of Dorset, as the setting for *The Well-Beloved* and renamed it 'The Isle of Slingers.' A354 approaches Portland via Chesil Bank, 'a long thin neck of pebbles "cast up by the rages of the sea" and unparalleled in its kind in Europe' (*Well-Beloved*, Ch. 1) and reaches Fortuneswell (13½ miles), Hardy's 'Street of Wells.' The 'roomy cottage or homestead' belonging to the Caro family, where Jocelyn Pierston woos successive generations of Avices, lies 1½ miles further south on the road leaving Easton for Pennsylvania Castle and is now a 'bygones' museum.

From Portland we retrace our route back to Weymouth and take A353 NE along the coast. It passes through Overcombe (which gave its name but apparently no more to the chief setting of *The Trumpet-Major*) and Preston (24 miles), where an unclassified road leads left to Sutton Poyntz (24½ miles). This large and much extended village was Hardy's model for 'Overcombe,' though the visitor will look in vain for Loveday's mill. North of the village a footpath heads half a mile NE to the downs and the chalk figure of George III on horseback, another reminder of the area's close connections with the Napoleonic period.

Portland Museum (Avice Caro's Cottage). Open in summer Mon to Sat 10–5.30, Sun 11–5, in winter Tues to Sat 10–5. Fee.

12 Dorchester to Bridport via Martinstown, Blackdown Hill and Abbotsbury

From Dorchester's Top o' Town we take A35 west towards Bridport but turn left after 1 mile on the unclassified road to Martinstown (3 miles). The poem 'Last Look Round St Martin's Fair' recalls the time when its horse market attracted people from as far away as the New Forest. At the west end of the village an unclassified road leads SW over Blackdown Hill where, at a point commanding particularly fine views, we find a monument of 1844 to Admiral Hardy, whom the writer liked to claim as an ancestor. A left turn at the crossroads beyond the monument takes us to Portesham (7 miles), from which B3157 continues west to Abbotsbury (8½ miles). With its ruined Benedictine Abbey, swannery and sub-tropical gardens the village has established itself as one of Dorset's tourist showcases. In Hardy's work it is variously called 'Abbot's Beach' and 'Abbotsea,' and its Abbey barn, like the one at Cerne Abbas (Rte 6), is claimed as the original of the shearing barn in *Far from the Madding Crowd*.

B3157 westwards offers a fine scenic route paralleling the coast and Chesil Bank (Rte 11) to Bridport (14½ miles). Its enviable site near the sea—the harbour is at West Bay a mile south—means that Bridport has expanded considerably since the 19C but its old centre by the Town Hall preserves much of the charm Hardy conjured up in his picture of 'Port Bredy,' setting for his short story 'The Fellow Townsmen.'

13 Dorchester to Windwhistle Hill via Beaminster and Winyard's Gap

The route proceeds NW from Dorchester through some of Dorset's finest downland, as well as scenes associated with *Far from the Madding Crowd* and *Tess of the d'Urbervilles*, ending over the border in Somerset.

From the Top o' Town junction in Dorchester we take A37 (the Yeovil road), branching left after 4½ miles on A356 for Crewkerne. Maiden Newton (8 miles) is Hardy's 'Chalk-Newton' but greatly changed from the days when it was mentioned in 'The Grave by the Handpost' and Tess Durbeyfield stopped for breakfast on her way to 'Flintcomb-Ash' (Ch. 42).

At about 9 miles we turn left on an unclassified road for Toller Porcorum (10 miles) and follow sideroads that sometimes dwindle to narrow lanes through Lower Kingcombe and Higher Kingcombe to Hooke (12½ miles). The rich chalk •downland through which we pass is the scene for the opening chapters of *Far from the Madding Crowd*, when Gabriel Oak proposes in vain to Bathsheba and loses his flock of sheep in the chalk pit. The precise location of 'Norcombe Hill' cannot be identified, for Hardy obviously created it from the general characteristics of the area.

From Hooke we take unclassified roads to the junction with B3163 (14½ miles), where a left turn brings us to the pleasant little town of Beaminster (16½ miles). As 'Emminster,' a name echoing the local pronunciation, it is the home of the Clare family and the goal of Tess' abortive journey from 'Flintcomb-Ash' (Ch. 44). The vicarage and the church (with a fine tower) where she lingers can still be seen.

We leave Beaminster by retracing our route along B3163 but stay on this road after the turning for Hooke and cross Toller Down to join A356 (20½ miles), which is followed towards Crewkerne. The road climbs steeply to •Winyard's Gap (23½ miles), where the old stone pub on the left is the 'cosy house' mentioned in Stanza 4 of the poem 'A Trampwoman's Tragedy.' The view from this height and from the adjoining woods (NT) is admired by the speakers in the dialogue poem 'At Wynyard's Gap.'

A356 descends to the market town of Crewkerne (27½ miles), mentioned by its own name in the same poem, from which A30 leads west along the ridge of Windwhistle Hill. At 31½ miles we reach on our right another haunt of Hardy's trampwoman, the Windwhistle Inn. Hardy's note to the poem recalls a visit to the pub before it was modernised:

The highness and dryness of Windwhistle Inn was impressed upon the writer . . . when, after climbing on a hot afternoon to the beautiful spot near which it stands and entering the inn for tea he was informed by the landlady that none could be had, unless he would fetch water from a valley half a mile off, the house containing not a drop, owing to its situation. However, a tantalizing row of full barrels behind her back testified to a wetness of a certain sort, which was not at that time desired.

14 Launceston to Lanhydrock House via Beeny Cliff, Boscastle and Tintagel

Why go to Saint-Juliot? What's Juliot to me?
>   Some strange necromancy
>   But charmed me to fancy
That much of my life claims the spot as its key.

('Dream or No,' first stanza)

For Hardy the landscape of northern Cornwall was identified with his courtship of Emma Gifford, his first wife. It was 'Lyonesse,' a territory of special magic and special pain. He first met Emma here in 1870 during the course of his work for Crickmay, successor to the Dorchester architect John Hicks. The first excited feelings for Emma and Cornwall made their way into his third novel, *A Pair of Blue Eyes*. In 1913, the year after her death, he returned to the scenes of their romance, making a 'penitential pilgrimage' that swelled the flood of over fifty poems about her, including the magnificent 'Poems of 1912–1913.'

We begin our tour near the Devon border at the pleasant little town of Launceston (on A30), where the railway deposited Hardy on his 1870 visit. 'St Launce's Revisited,' written on his return years later, noted the ruins of the Norman 'castle and keep uprearing / Gray' (lines 3–4) on the hill. In the Market Place and also mentioned in the poem is the White Hart Hotel, distinguished by the archway from the Augustinian priory, where he had hired horse and trap to take him the remaining distance to the tiny hamlet of St Juliot.

We make that journey by driving west and north towards Boscastle via A30, A395, B3262 and A39. Just beyond Marshgate at 14½ miles we take the unclassified road on the left for Tresparrett, and in the valley of the River Valency, the *church of St Juliot (16 miles). The former Rectory lies about ½ a mile beyond, off the road leading north from the valley. Like 'Endelstow Rectory' in *A Pair of Blue Eyes* it is situated in 'a little dell' (Ch. 2).

Emma Gifford, sister-in-law to the Rector of St Juliot, immediately struck Hardy as '*living*': 'Though her features were not regular her complexion at this date was perfect in hue, her figure and movement graceful, and her corn-coloured hair abundant in its coils' (*Life*, Aetat. 29–30). The 'Recollections' Hardy quoted in his autobiography record the rather less romantic impression he made on her: 'I thought him much older than he was. He had a beard, and a rather shabby greatcoat, and had quite a business appearance. Afterwards he seemed younger, and by daylight especially so' (Aetat. 29–30). She was surprised to learn that the blue paper sticking out of his pocket was not an architectural plan but the manuscript of a poem he had been drafting during his journey. Hardy later imagined her feelings as she awaited his arrival in the poem 'A Man Was Drawing Near To Me.'

The main reason for Hardy's visit was to supervise restoration of the church, then 'in its original condition of picturesque neglect' (*Life*, Aetat. 29–30). The nave and tower were rebuilt and the furnishings renewed, though Hardy later 'much regretted the obliteration in this manner of the church's history, and, too, that he should be instrumental in such obliteration, the building as he had first set eyes on it having been so associated with what was romantic in his life' (*Life*, Aetat. 29–30). The fate of the chancel screen reminds us why he became, in larger ways, disillusioned with what passed for church restoration in the 19C:

> Hardy had made a careful drawing of it, with its decayed tracery, posts, and gilding, marking thereon where sundry patchings and scarfings were to be applied. Reaching the building one day he found a new and highly varnished travesty of the old screen standing in its place. 'Well, Mr Hardy,' replied the builder in answer to his astonished inquiries, 'I said to myself, I won't stand on a pound or two while I'm about it, and I'll give 'em a new screen instead of that patched-up old thing.' (*Life*, Aetat. 29–30)

The church displays drawings he made on the site as well as two tablets, the first commemorating his role in the alterations and the second, erected by Hardy in 1913, recording that Emma laid the foundation stone of the new aisle and tower (see the poems 'The Marble Tablet' and 'The Monument-Maker').

From St Juliot we head north to B3263, which is followed westward. After 1 mile, as we are nearing Boscastle, we find on our right a

'Harbour of Castle Boterel.' From the Wessex edition of A Pair of Blue Eyes. *Courtesy of Cambridge University Library*

footpath leading to the richly dramatic coastline where Hardy often walked with Emma and where he later imagined her in poems like 'The Phantom Horsewoman.' Pentargan Bay ($\frac{1}{2}$ mile) is the scene of his meditations in 'After a Journey,' and after another $\frac{1}{4}$ mile we reach the splendid *Beeny Cliff, which gave its name to Hardy's most vibrant recollection of Emma. In a notebook entry of 1872 he had described the scene:

> green towards the land, blue-black towards the sea. Every ledge has a little, starved, green grass upon it; all vertical parts bare. Seaward, a dark-grey ocean beneath a pale green sky, upon which lie branches of red cloud. A lather of foam around the base of each rock. The sea is full of motion internally, but still as a whole. Quiet and silent in the distance, noisy and restless close at hand.

As 'The Cliff Without a Name' it is the scene of Henry Knight's memorable ordeal in *A Pair of Blue Eyes* (Chs 21–22).

Boscastle (21 miles), its charming little *harbour flanked by steep cliffs at the mouth of the Valency, is the setting of 'At Castle Boterel.'

By B3263 3 miles south-west is Tintagel and the ruined castle on the promontory of Tintagel Head. Hardy and Emma came here in 1870 and 'owing to their lingering too long among the ruins, they found themselves locked in, only narrowly escaping being imprisoned there for the night by much signalling with their handkerchiefs to cottagers in the valley.' He added: 'The lingering might have been considered prophetic, seeing that, after it had been smouldering in his mind for between forty and fifty years, he constructed *The Famous Tragedy of the Queen of Cornwall* from the legends connected with that romantic spot' (*Life*, Aetat. 29–30).

From Tintagel we follow B3263 and B3266 SE to Camelford ('Camelton'), where the continuation of B3266 and A389 take us south to Bodmin (41 miles). In the valley of the Fowey off B3268 2$\frac{1}{2}$ miles SE is Lanhydrock House. This 17C mansion, largely rebuilt after a fire in 1881 but remaining one of the grandest in Cornwall, suggested features of 'Endelstow House,' home of the Luxellians in *A Pair of Blue Eyes*. Among other minor liberties with geography the novel transplants it to the immediate neighbourhood of St Juliot.

Launceston Castle (English Heritage). Open 15 March to 15 Oct, Mon to Sat 9.30–6.30, Sun 2–6.30 (Apr to Sept, Sun 9.30–6.30); 16 Oct to 14 March, Mon to Sat 9.30–4, Sun 2–4. Closed Christmas Eve, Christmas Day, Boxing Day and New Year's Day. Fee.

Tintagel Castle (English Heritage). Open 15 March to 15 Oct, Mon to Sat 9.30–6.30, Sun 2–6.30 (Apr to Sept, Sun 9.30–6.30); 16 Oct to 14 March, Mon to Sat 9.30–4, Sun 2–4. Closed Christmas Eve, Christmas Day, Boxing Day and New Year's Day. Fee.

Lanhydrock House (NT). Open Apr to end Oct, daily 11–6; Nov to March, garden only, in daylight. Fee.

Central England

15   Reading to Oxford via Fawley

The route takes us through scenes mainly associated with *Jude the Obscure*, a novel set on the northern fringes of 'Wessex' and away from the older rural world described in the earlier fiction.

We begin at Reading ('Aldbrickham'), suitably unromantic surroundings for later episodes in the hero's depressing career. The main identifiable building is the George Hotel on King Street east of the Market Place, where Jude takes Arabella for their night of reunion (Part 3, Ch. 8) and, by one of the unhappy accidents that dog his fortunes, brings Sue Bridehead when she leaves her husband (Part 4, Ch. 5).

From Reading we take A4 SW via Newbury (16 miles), called 'Kennetbridge' in the novel after its position on the River Kennet, to Hungerford (24 miles). At Hungerford we turn north on A338 and cross the Berkshire Downs.

Off A338 at 31 miles is Fawley, birthplace of Hardy's grandmother, Mary Head Hardy, and under the ironic name of 'Marygreen' setting for the opening scenes of *Jude the Obscure*. There have been changes to its village green since the novel was written but the result is no more attractive:

> Many of the thatched and dormered dwelling-houses had been pulled down of late years, and many trees felled on the green. Above all, the original church, hump-backed, wood-turreted, and quaintly hipped, had been taken down, and either cracked up into heaps of road-metal in the lane, or utilised as pig-sty walls, garden seats, guard-stones to fences, and rockeries in the flower-beds of the neighbourhood. In place of it a tall new building of modern Gothic design, unfamiliar to English eyes, had been erected on a new piece of ground by a certain obliterator of historic records who had run down from London and back in a day. (Part 1, Ch. 1)

The offending architect of St Mary (1866) was G.E. Street.

At the top of the hill 2 miles after we return to A338 the road is joined by the old Ridgeway. To the left stood the Red ('Brown') House from which the young Jude admired the distant, tantalising prospect of Oxford ('Christminster') in Part 1, Chapter 3. We reach Oxford (52 miles) by continuing through Wantage ('Alfredston') and joining A420.

Hardy's portrait of the city as 'Christminster' departs from his normally detailed use of place, perhaps because this seemed inappropriate to the hero's abstract and idealised view of the city, perhaps because he wished to take some of the local sting out of his bitter satire—a wise precaution in a man who would later ride down the High in triumph as an honorary Doctor of Letters. Our first glimpse of 'Christminster' is atmospheric rather than precise, one of the nocturnal scenes beloved by Hardy:

> It was a windy, whispering, moonless night. To guide himself he opened under a lamp a map he had brought. The breeze ruffled and fluttered it,

but he could see enough to decide on the direction he should take to reach the heart of the place.

After many turnings he came up to the first ancient mediaeval pile that he had encountered. It was a college, as he could see by the gateway. He entered it, walked round, and penetrated to dark corners which no lamplight reached. Close to this college was another; and a little further on another; and then he began to be encircled as it were with the breath and sentiment of the venerable city. When he passed objects out of harmony with its general expression he allowed his eyes to slip over them as if he did not see them.

A bell began clanging, and he listened till a hundred-and-one strokes had sounded. He must have made a mistake, he thought: it was meant for a hundred.

When the gates were shut, and he could no longer get into the quadrangles, he rambled under the walls and doorways, feeling with his fingers the contours of their mouldings and carving. The minutes passed, fewer and fewer people were visible, and still he serpentined among the shadows, for had he not imagined these scenes for ten bygone years, and what mattered a night's rest for once? High against the black sky the flash of a lamp would show crocketed pinnacles and indented battlements. Down obscure alleys, apparently never trodden now by the foot of man, and whose very existence seemed to be forgotten, there would jut into the path porticoes, oriels, doorways of enriched and florid middle-age design, their extinct air being accentuated by the rottenness of the stones. It seemed impossible that modern thought could house itself in such decrepit and superseded chambers. (Part 2, Ch. 1)

Just as we can identify the curfew bell in this passage as 'Great Tom' in Christ Church's Tom Tower, so we can work out a table of correspondence for the 'Christminster' landmarks Hardy mentions elsewhere. 'Beersheba' is the Jericho area off Walton Street in NW Oxford, and 'St Silas' (Part 2, Ch. 3) is the Victorian church of St Barnabas, by Hardy's ex-employer Arthur Blomfield, near the end of Cardigan Street and the canal. 'Crozier College' is Oriel, 'Cardinal College' is Christ Church, and 'Rubric College' may be Brasenose. Yet this is still a short and sketchy list by comparison with the richly saturated portrait of, say, Dorchester in *The Mayor of Casterbridge*.

A few landmarks, however, require special notice. The Lamb and Flag, off St Giles by St John's College, is an enlarged and more respectable version of the 'obscure and low-ceiled tavern up a court' where Jude gets drunk and recites the Nicene Creed (Part 2, Ch. 7). In the pavement of Broad Street opposite Balliol College is the spot where Cranmer, Ridley and Latimer met their martyrdom, Jude's ill-omened choice of meeting-place for his first appointment with Sue Bridehead (Part 2, Ch. 4). Further east on Broad Street is Wren's Sheldonian Theatre. On 'Remembrance Day' (Commemoration Day) Jude brings his family to this 'circular theatre with that well-known lantern above it, which stood in his mind as the sad symbol of his abandoned hopes' and makes his speech to the crowd assembled outside, confessing failure in his academic ambitions and admitting: 'It takes two or three generations to do what I tried to do in one' (Part 6, Ch. 1).

Sheldonian Theatre. Open 15 Feb to 15 Nov, Mon to Sat 10–1 & 2–5; 16 Nov to 14 Feb, Mon to Sat 10–1 & 2–4. Fee.

Eastern England

16 Cambridge

Hardy's acquaintance with Cambridge produced no equivalent to his portrayal of Oxford as 'Christminster' in *Jude the Obscure* (Rte 15), but it has its own poignancy.

To him Cambridge was important for its connection with the unhappy career of his friend and mentor Horace Moule, son of the Vicar of Fordington (Rte 5). After an abortive period as an undergraduate at Oxford, Moule entered Queen's College in 1854 but did not receive his B.A. until 1867, a delay hinting at the bouts of depression and alcoholism that clouded his academic promise. In 1870 he was back again at Queen's and during the summer treated Hardy, visiting Cambridge for the first time, to a tour of the sights which commonly attract the stranger. Hardy's diary records of 21 June:

> Next morning went with H.M. to King's Chapel early. M. opened the great West doors to show the interior vista: we got upon the roof where we could see Ely Cathedral gleaming in the distant sunlight. A never-to-be-forgotten morning. H.M.M. saw me off for London. His last smile. (*Life*, Aetat. 30–33)

In September Moule committed suicide in his college rooms. Hardy's marginalia to his copy of *In Memoriam* show that he associated him with Arthur Henry Hallam, another Cambridge graduate who died young and left a poet to mourn him.

He returned twice in 1913, the year he received an honorary Litt. D. from the University. On both occasions he visited Magdalene College, which elected him to an Honorary Fellowship.

The Fitzwilliam Museum has the famous portrait by Augustus John presenting him in his capacity as the grand old man of English Letters.

Fitzwilliam Museum. Upper galleries (paintings) open Tues to Sat & BH Mon 2–5, Sun 2.15–5. Closed Christmas Eve to New Year's Day & Good Fri.

JAMES JOYCE

b. Dublin, 1882; d. Zurich, Switzerland, 1941. *Chamber Music* (1907); *Dubliners* (1914); *A Portrait of the Artist as a Young Man* (1916); *Exiles: A Play in Three Acts* (1918); *Ulysses* (1922); *Pomes Penyeach* (1927); *Finnegans Wake* (1939); *Stephen Hero: Part of the First Draft of A Portrait of the Artist as a Young Man* (edited by T. Spencer; 1944).

Dublin and Vicinity

On the face of it, Joyce's life and work regard each other across a gaping paradox. He left his native Dublin in 1904, when he was twenty-two, and returned only for the briefest of visits. The rest of his life, the years when he produced his major work, passed in an odyssey whose main stopping points were summarised in the byline at the end of *Ulysses*: Trieste, Zurich, Paris. And yet, like everything else Joyce wrote, that novel has nothing to say about these cities and everything to say about Dublin. The man who so deliberately transformed himself from an Irishman into a European, the writer whose style developed from the merely cosmopolitan to the riotously polyglot, never needed to stray beyond the boundaries of Dublin in his choice of subject. From Trieste and Zurich and Paris he sought in *Ulysses* to recreate Dublin as it had been on 16 June 1904. Where the Renaissance sonneteer used to boast that his poem would outlive the ephemeral beauty of the woman it praised, it was Joyce's hope that if Dublin were destroyed it could be reconstructed from the pages of his novel.

Joyce himself always insisted that he had no imagination: his muse was Thom's city directory of Dublin. Besides, his voluntary exile on the Continent was never intended to break with the past. 'We are what we are,' he told his brother Stanislaus in explanation of *A Portrait of the Artist as a Young Man*. 'Our maturity is an extension of our childhood.' In *Portrait* itself the voyages of maturity are prophesied when the young Stephen Dedalus writes in the flyleaf of his exercise book at Clongowes:

Stephen Dedalus
Class of Elements
Clongowes Wood College
Sallins
County Kildare
Ireland
Europe
The World
The Universe
(Ch. 1)

The adult Joyce came to doubt this simple diagram of concentric rings and to concede that classification of the elements was a trickier business than the child had foreseen, but he never swerved in his belief that the way towards the universal significance aimed at and achieved in *Ulysses* and *Finnegans Wake* could begin only with minute inspection of his own point of origin.

So Joyce's Dublin is uniquely challenging to the literary tourist. The city is there in the book and the book there in the city to a degree that is without parallel in modern literature. For this reason *Ulysses* requires special treatment and is made the separate subject of Rtes 1–4 below. They begin in the SE, where the novel itself starts, and explore the city by taking the course of Paddy Dignam's funeral procession as an organising framework. In this description the eighteen untitled episodes of Joyce's novel are identified by the Homeric names which he privately used and scholars have subsequently adopted. They are, in order: 'Telemachus,' 'Proteus,' 'Nestor,' 'Calypso,' 'Lotos Eaters,' 'Hades,' 'Aeolus,' 'Lestrygonians,' 'Scylla and Charybdis,' 'Wandering Rocks,' 'Sirens,' 'Cyclops,' 'Nausicaa,' 'Oxen of the Sun,' 'Circe,' 'Eumaeus,' 'Ithaca,' 'Penelope.'

The attentive reader of *Ulysses* will quickly note that the locations of several episodes are missing from the suggested itineraries, and this is because Dublin, already changing as Joyce wrote, has continued to change with alarming rapidity. It was inevitable, of course, that the trams, horse-drawn traffic and other street furniture should have vanished and taken much of the atmosphere of *Ulysses* with them. It was inevitable, too, that Night-town ('Circe') and Barney Kiernan's on Little Britain Street ('Cyclops') should go with the passage of the years, that the interiors of Joyce's bars and hotels should change beyond recognition, and that the Holles Street Hospital should transform itself to benefit its patients but disappoint readers of 'Oxen of the Sun.' However, the demolition of Nelson's Pillar would have been vandalism even if Joyce had not memorialised it in 'Aeolus' and 'Hades.' The most recent loss is No. 7 Eccles Street, home of Leopold Bloom. In moments of depression the modern visitor may feel that Dubliners are bent on testing Joyce's claim for *Ulysses*, though as yet they have shown little inclination to reconstruct the city from his pages. There is all the more reason, then, to cherish those public buildings that do survive—the National Library, Trinity College, the Four Courts, Prospect Cemetery—and to marvel at the good fortune that has kept the Martello Tower in Sandycove not only intact but honourably preserved for its connection with Joyce.

Rtes 5–11 chronicle the scenes of Joyce's early life, and of *Dubliners* and *A Portrait of the Artist*, beginning again in the SE and working round the compass to the NE. Here the record of survival is perhaps more impressive and nine addresses where Joyce lived are mentioned, though even this list cannot claim to be complete. In their variety these houses are striking witness to the ups and downs, but mainly downs, in the fortunes of the writer's father, John Joyce. Together, they remind us how early in life Joyce became a traveller, how little of Ithaca he could savour even as a child. The restless, enforced movement of his childhood and youth was training for his adult travels, and it helps explain why, when he turned to his native city in *Ulysses*, he saw it through the eyes of Stephen Dedalus and Leopold Bloom, two dispossessed wanderers who each set out on 16 June 1904 without a doorkey.

1   'Ulysses' in South-East Dublin: Sandycove and Sandymount

We begin at Sandycove Point on the coast some 8 miles SE of central Dublin and just outside the city boundary. The *James Joyce Museum is an excellent starting point for the enthusiast, its interest lying not so much in the collection of relics and books as in the building that houses them, one of the Martello Towers built along the coast to answer the threat of Napoleonic invasion. It was opened to the public in 1962 by Sylvia Beach, Joyce's friend and patron as well as the first publisher of *Ulysses*.

In biographical terms, the squat fortress-like tower has only a slender connection with Joyce, being among the most transitory of his many Dublin addresses. It was rented in August 1904 (for £8 a year) by Oliver St John Gogarty, poet, medical student and, according to Stanislaus Joyce, a man 'full of bustling energy, wit, and profanity.' At that time he was in violent reaction against the provinciality of Dublin life and liked to regard the tower as an *omphalos*, not just because of its shape but because, like the navel-stone at Delphi, it would become the centre and symbol of an enlightened culture. Joyce, who had left his father's house in Cabra (Rte 10) earlier that year, arrived on 9 September. Though he sympathised with his friend's criticism of Dublin and Ireland, he soon found Gogarty's charm wearing thin, and his temper was frayed even more by the presence of another guest, the Anglo-Irishman Samuel Chenevix Trench. These tensions reached breaking point on 15 September, when Trench woke screaming from a nightmare about a black panther and began firing shots from his revolver. Gogarty disarmed him and, when Trench started screaming again, fired into the wall above Joyce's bed. Joyce wisely took this as a cue to leave, making a dramatic exit from the tower in the middle of the night and in the pouring rain.

With any other writer the matter would probably have ended there and we would have no reason to remember the episode or its setting. But Joyce felt aggrieved, and he knew well that through art the artist can revenge himself for the petty humiliations of ordinary life. He made the Martello Tower scene for the opening of *Ulysses*, the 'Telemachus' episode. With his bawdy profanities and his dream of Hellenising Ireland, Buck Mulligan is identifiably Gogarty and Trench has become the 'ponderous Saxon' Haines. Yet the fiction subtly alters the facts from which it sprang, for it is Stephen Dedalus who pays the rent, however reluctantly, and Buck Mulligan is not host but 'usurper,' the embodiment of the dispossessing tyrannies suffered by the Irish artist in his native country.

Such is the transforming power of art that the modern visitor comes to Sandycove to view the tower in the light of *Ulysses* rather than life, to remember Dedalus and Mulligan rather than Joyce and Gogarty. The roofdeck on top is where Mulligan paused in his shaving to rebuke Stephen for his treatment of his dying mother and to expatiate on the Homeric associations of the sea below: 'The snotgreen sea. The scrotumtightening sea.' Nearby is the Forty-Foot Hole where Stephen, no lover of water, watches with distaste as the athletic Mulligan takes his morning dip.

Stephen's day continues with a journey south to Dalkey, where (like his creator) he works as a schoolteacher, but little survives in that suburb to reward the reader of 'Nestor' and so our route goes NW from Sandycove along the shoreline towards Dublin. At 3 miles we pass through Blackrock, whose connection with Joyce (not echoed in *Ulysses*) is described in Rte 5.

Sandymount Strand (reached by diverging right from Merrion Road at 4½ miles) is a recurrent location in *Ulysses*, as befits a book that has begun by taking its cue from Homer and announcing the sea as one of its major images. Since Joyce's day, however, the appearance of the Strand has been changed by enlargement of the harbour. We stop at 6 miles by the junction of Beach Road and Leahy's Terrace. In 'Proteus' the sight of the midwives emerging from the Terrace prompts Stephen to agonised meditation on the relations of substance to spirit and on his own humiliating entrapment in the chain of heredity. Later in the book ('Nausicaa') Bloom comes to the same spot, or one very close by, to engage in his own rather different sort of meditation on the flesh: tumescent delight at the spectacle of Gertie MacDowell on the beach. On Leahy's Terrace lies Mary, Star of the Sea, parish church of both Gertie and Paddy Dignam; the dedication gives the keynote to much of the symbolism of the 'Nausicaa' episode. Dignam lived at No. 9 Newbridge Avenue, on the other side of Tritonville Road beyond the church, and his funeral cortège in 'Hades' starts from here. Rtes 2 and 3 below follow its course through Dublin.

James Joyce Tower and Museum, Sandycove. Open 1 May to 10 Sept, Mon to Sat 10–1, 2–5 & Sun 2.30–6. Fee.

2 'Ulysses' in South-East and South Dublin: Sandymount to O'Connell Bridge

Of all the many journeys through the city in *Ulysses* certainly the most extensive and perhaps the most detailed is Paddy Bloom's funeral procession in 'Hades,' from Sandymount in the SE to Prospect Cemetery in the north. It passes by or near most of the central locations in the novel and so offers an ideal thread for Joyce's readers to follow in their own tours through the city. The route suggested here covers the first half of the procession, with diversions to the other major sights of south Dublin. Rte 3 deals with Dublin north of the Liffey in similar fashion.

We begin where Rte 1 ended, in Sandymount at the junction of Newbridge Avenue and Tritonville Road. Leopold Bloom joins his fellow mourners—Martin Cunningham, Mr Power and Stephen Dedalus' father, Simon—in the carriage outside Paddy Dignam's house. They proceed up Tritonville Road (then still a 'cobbled causeway') and its continuation as Irishtown Road. Stephen Dedalus is also in the neighbourhood (see 'Proteus' in Rte 1) and a brief glimpse of him from the carriage window prompts Mr Bloom to reflections about fathers and sons and to memories of his own dead son, Rudy.

The party turns left, crosses the River Dodder and continues down Ringsend Road. They are held up at the bridge over the Grand Canal within sight and smell of the gas works: 'Whooping cough they say it cures,' thinks Bloom with a characteristic dip into his seemingly inexhaustible store of folk wisdom. Ahead lies the dull expanse of Pearse Street (then Great Brunswick Street) where Bloom notes the 'bleak' 18C church of St Mark on the right. The odd-shaped monument to the Dublin surgeon Sir Philip Crampton has gone.

We may vary this route by turning left from Pearse Street into Westland Row at the corner by the railway station. In 'Lotos Eaters' Bloom collects the letter from Martha Clifford here and enters the 19C church of St Andrew (All Hallows) to watch Mass in progress. At the junction with Lincoln Place at the southern end of Westland Row he buys his cake of lemon soap. By walking down Lincoln Place and crossing Leinster Street we quickly come to Kildare Street and Sir Thomas Deane's *National Library. At the end of 'Lestrygonians' Bloom dashes into the building, eager to avoid an encounter with his wife's lover, Blazes Boylan. The stone goddesses guarding the entrance, which he notes even in his hurry, have now gone but we may still visit the Reading Room inside where in the next chapter, 'Scylla and Charybdis,' Stephen Dedalus puts forward his theory of *Hamlet*.

By taking Molesworth Street opposite the Library entrance and turning right on Dawson Street we come to Duke Street, on our left. 'Here we are. Must eat,' thinks Bloom in 'Lestrygonians.' In the 'Burton' restaurant, really Bailey's, he is repelled by the sight of meat-eating customers and retreats to Davy Byrne's nearby, where he enjoys a modest cheese sandwich and glass of Burgundy. Both restaurants still flourish but Bloom would scarcely recognise their interiors. (He would, however, recognise the door displayed in the Bailey restaurant, for it was taken from No. 7 Eccles Street when it was demolished.)

From the west end of Duke Street a right turn up Grafton Street brings us to College Green where, on his way to lunch in 'Lestrygonians,' Bloom had paused briefly to contemplate the 'surly front' of Trinity College. The university grounds are also passed, in grander fashion, by the Viceroy's procession in 'Wandering Rocks.' As Westmoreland Street leads north to the Liffey and the O'Connell Bridge we pass a statue of the Irish poet Thomas Moore (1779–1852). 'Meeting of the waters,' thinks Bloom in 'Lestrygonians,' in allusion to one of Moore's lyrics and to the fact his effigy stands over a public lavatory.

National Library, Kildare Street. Open Mon to Thurs 10–9 (10–5 from mid July to mid Aug), Fri 10–5, Sat 10–1. Closed Sun and BH.

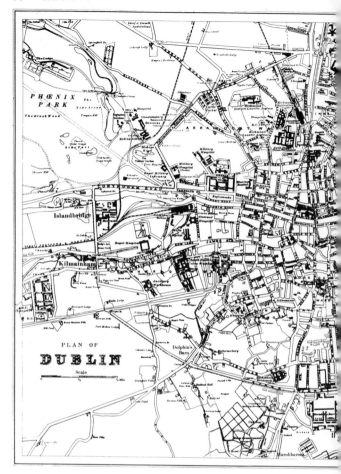

Plan of Dublin. From G. W. Bacon, Commercial and Library Atlas of the British Isles *(1902). Courtesy of Cambridge University Library*

3   'Ulysses' in North Dublin: O'Connell Bridge to Prospect Cemetery

We begin on the northern side of the O'Connell Bridge, our finishing point for the previous route. In 'Hades' the funeral cortège goes directly up O'Connell Street but we should take the time to walk west along Bachelor's Walk and Ormond Quay by the bank of the Liffey. Our goals are the Ormond Hotel, where Miss Douce and Miss Kennedy presided over the musical 'Sirens' episode, and the battered but still magnificent 18C façade of the Four Courts. From its porch Ritchie Goulding watches the Viceroy's procession pass in 'Wandering Rocks.'

Back at O'Connell Bridge we can contemplate O'Connell Street and an object lesson in the changes that have overtaken Dublin since Joyce's day. In 1904 (when it was still Sackville Street) it had already lost its residential character and become a commercial thoroughfare, but some shreds of 18C elegance remained. These have since been swept away, partly by the violence of 1916 and 1922. Gone, too, is its most distinctive landmark, Nelson's Pillar, 'the statue of the onehandled adulterer' which recurs throughout 'Aeolus' and is noted more respectfully by Bloom in 'Hades.' Of the street's remaining monuments, 'Hades' pauses to mention the 'hugecloaked Liberator's form,' the statue of Daniel O'Connell by the bridge, and further north, the statue of Sir John Gray, 19C Protestant Irish patriot and owner of the *Freeman's Journal.*

At the north end of O'Connell Street is the Rotunda—an 18C Hospital and Assembly Rooms, the latter now serving as cinema—where the sight of a child's hearse turns Bloom's mind to thoughts of his own dead son. These thoughts follow him as Paddy Dignam's funeral procession makes its way up Parnell Square, then not dedicated to the nationalist hero and still known as Rutland Square. The carriage leaves the square by its NE corner and follows Frederick Street North to Upper Dorset Street. It then crosses to take Blessington Street and Berkeley Street to the North Circular Road. Bloom is pleased to note that the route takes them past Eccles Street ('My house down there') but we should resist the temptation to explore it and reserve this neighbourhood for a separate tour (Rte 4).

At the North Circular Road the funeral party is delayed by a herd of cattle, a hazard the modern visitor need not fear, before making its way up Phibsborough Road over the Royal Canal to Prospect (or Glasnevin) Cemetery. Rather than using the Prospect Square entrance near the Botanic Gardens, they turn left on Finglas Road. This takes them past Bengal Terrace on the right, which Mr Power remembers as the scene of Samuel Childs' alleged murder of his brother in 1899. They enter the cemetery near the mortuary chapel and the 'lofty cone' of the Round Tower commemorating Daniel O'Connell, whose remains were reburied in the crypt beneath.

4   'Ulysses' in North and North-East Dublin: Eccles Street to Mountjoy Square

We begin on Eccles Street, between Phibsborough Road and Upper Dorset Street, passed in the course of Rte 3. And we begin with a disappointment, for No. 7, Leopold Bloom's home in *Ulysses* and perhaps the most notable address in Dublin's literary history, was finally demolished in 1982 to make way for a new extension of the Mater Misericordiae Hospital. Joyce visited the modest terraced house on a return visit to Ireland in 1909, when it was the home of his friend J.F. Byrne, and used it in *Ulysses* after consultation of Thom's city directory had reassured him it had been vacant in 1904, when the action of *Ulysses* takes place. We can take some consolation from the older buildings of the Hospital where, as Bloom is reminded in 'Hades,' Mrs Riordan died and he himself was treated for a bee sting.

From the south-eastern end of Eccles Street we cross Upper Dorset Street, where Bloom bought his breakfast kidney in 'Calypso,' to Great St George's Church, with its spire recalling St Martin's-in-the-Fields in London. The sound of its bells remind Bloom of the dead Paddy Dignam in the morning ('Calypso'), while at the end of the day Molly Bloom lies awake in bed listening to the striking of the hours ('Penelope').

Beyond the church we follow Temple Street and take a left on Gardiner's Place to enter Mountjoy Square, once but no longer a centre of fashionable life. It is a focal point in the walk taken by the sociable Father Conmee in 'Wandering Rocks.' The Square is also the starting point of Rte 11, which deals with Joyce's childhood and education in this part of Dublin.

5   South-East Dublin: Blackrock

Blackrock lies just outside the city boundary on the coast between Sandycove and Sandymount (Rte 1). When they left Bray in 1892 the Joyce family came to live on Carysfoot Avenue, which runs NW from Main Street; their home at No. 23 no longer has the stone lions which went with its name, Leoville. In *Portrait of the Artist* (Ch. 2) Joyce remembers his granduncle Charles taking him for running practice under the eye of Mike Flynn in Blackrock Park (reached from the northern end of Main Street via Rock Hill). He remembers, too, that the family's hasty departure the next year for NE Dublin (Rte 11) was the first time he caught a glimpse of the money troubles that now beset John Joyce: 'He understood little or nothing of it at first but he became slowly aware that his father had enemies and that some fight was going to take place' (Ch. 2).

6   South Dublin: Rathgar and Rathmines

This tour covers the two earliest of Joyce's childhood homes. We begin on Harold's Cross Road south of Mount Jerome Cemetery. To the left is Brighton Square, where Joyce was born at No. 41 on 2 February 1882. He grew up to be superstitious in his reverence for numbers and dates, and arranged to see the first copies of both *Ulysses* and *Finnegans Wake* on his birthday.

He embarked on the perpetual journeying of which his life would consist at the age of two when his family moved about a mile north to Rathmines. We may follow them by taking Harold's Cross Road north to Leinster Road, which is followed to the right; a second right on Rathmines Road brings us to Castlewood Avenue. The Joyces' house at No. 23 (at the corner of Cambridge Road) is probably the handsomest of their many homes and a reminder of their relative prosperity during the writer's infancy. They left here in 1887 for Bray (Rte 12).

7   South Dublin: University College

On Earlsfort Terrace south of St Stephen's Green we find the granite block of University College, greatly changed in appearance from the original building of 1865 and in function, for it now houses only the faculties of Medicine and Architecture. Joyce attended the College in 1898–1902, too late to profit from the presence of Gerard Manley Hopkins (q.v.) but in time to be taught by Thomas, brother of Matthew Arnold (q.v.). The brief glimpse of Stephen Dedalus at university in *A Portrait of the Artist* (Ch. 5) reflects his creator's attitude of deliberately maintained aloofness and genuine boredom.

8   South Dublin: Usher's Island

Usher's Island is a quay on the south bank of the Liffey between the Queen Maeve Bridge and the Rory O'More Bridge. It can be reached from the north bank via Arran Quay, near the Four Courts (visited in Rte 3). No. 15, now occupied by a seed merchant, is the 'dark gaunt house' where the Misses Morkan live in 'The Dead,' the last and perhaps the most powerful story in *Dubliners*.

9   North Dublin: Church Street

Church Street runs north from the Liffey by the Father Matthew Bridge and the Four Courts (Rte 3). Beyond the fine St Michan's Church and the entrance to May Lane on the left lies the Capuchin Church of St Mary of the Angels, the Church Street chapel where Stephen Dedalus comes burdened with adolescent guilt to make his confession at the end of Chapter 3 in *A Portrait of the Artist*. Kneeling in the nave afterwards, he feels his prayers ascend 'from his purified heart like perfume streaming upwards from a heart of white rose.'

10   North-West Dublin: Cabra

Joyce left Dublin for Paris in December 1902, but the following April he received a dramatic telegram: 'MOTHER DYING COME HOME FATHER.' By that time home was No. 7 St Peter's Terrace, one of a row of 19C houses now assimilated into St Peter's Road, which leads north from Cabra Road opposite St Peter's Church. John Joyce had bought the modest terraced house at the sacrifice of half his pension and his son returned to find the family more than usually plagued by money problems. The months until May Joyce's death in August were fraught with tension, much of it provoked by Joyce's refusal of his mother's plea that he make his confession and take communion. His intransigence is remembered in *Ulysses*, where Stephen Dedalus views it with a combination of defiant pride and underlying guilt. Joyce finally left St Peter's Terrace in 1904—his immediate excuse being that he could no longer practice music after his father had pawned the piano—for a succession of lodgings of which the most famous is the Martello Tower in Sandycove (Rte 1).

11   North-East Dublin: Mountjoy Square to North Bull Island via Fairview

This route explores several of the neighbourhoods which Joyce knew after his family's return to the city in 1893, neighbourhoods whose character strongly influenced *Dubliners* and *A Portrait of the Artist as a Young Man*. Its starting point is also the end of Rte 4.

It is certainly fitting to begin in Mountjoy Square. In Chapter 2 of *A Portrait of the Artist* the young and newly arrived Stephen Dedalus at first confines himself to 'circling timidly' round it before he plucks up courage to explore the 'new and complex sensation' of the city beyond. And a chance encounter here between Joyce's father and Father John Conmee led to the young Joyce being enrolled at the Jesuit school on Great Denmark Street beyond Gardiner's Place to the south of the Square. Joyce studied at the 18C Belvedere House from 1893 to 1898. Chapter 4 of *A Portrait of the Artist* is memorable for the interview at which the Director of Belvedere suggests that Stephen consider joining the Society of Jesus, a suggestion both he and his creator set their faces against.

We retrace our steps to Mountjoy Square and continue north on Fitzgibbon Street, where the Joyce family lived in 1893–94 in a house that has since been demolished, to Richmond Place. On his last visit to Dublin, in August 1912, Joyce stayed at Nos 17 and 21. By turning right and crossing the street we reach the entrance to •North Richmond Street. Before entering Belvedere Joyce had briefly been a pupil at the Christian Brothers school here, the only time when his schooling was not in Jesuit hands. No. 17 became the Joyce's family home from 1895 to 1898, when they were already sinking from former prosperity. To judge from his writing, North Richmond Street was to him the most important of his many childhood homes. In *A Portrait of the Artist* he ignores several of the upheavals he suffered in real life and prolongs the Dedalus family's stay in the area. North Richmond is also the 'blind' street that makes so powerful a location for 'Araby' in *Dubliners*.

From Richmond Place we now take Summerhill Parade and Ballybough Road north to the Royal Canal and the River Tolka. Beyond the bridge Richmond Road leads left and becomes Millbourne Avenue after it enters Drumcondra. The Joyces lived at the semi-detached No. 2 in their brief interlude between Fitzgibbon Street and North Richmond Street. It now seems one of the dreariest of their Dublin addresses and was then hardly a respectable neighbourhood, but Stanislaus Joyce reported: 'I liked it because it was almost in the country at the foot of a low hill, and just near it were fields with a weir into the Tolka and woods where my school-friends and I could trespass at pleasure.'

Returning to the bridge we then follow Fairview Strand NE. A left on Philipsburgh Avenue and another left on Melrose Avenue bring us to Inverness Road. The Joyces lived at No. 8 in 1900–01, when the street was called Royal Terrace. Their house backs on to a convent and, when he leaves for the university one morning, Stephen Dedalus hears 'a mad nun screeching in the nuns' madhouse beyond the wall' (*Portrait*, Ch. 5). Further NE along Fairview Strand is Windsor Avenue, on the left, where No. 29 was yet another of the Joyces' homes (1898–1900).

For the last part of this tour we take a walk of some 2½ miles to the scene of a crucial episode in *A Portrait of the Artist*. Fairview Strand is followed as it skirts Fairview Park, built on land reclaimed from the sea; Stephen Dedalus is familiar with 'the sloblands of Fairview' (Ch. 5). Clontarf Road then leads along the shoreline to Bull Bridge. After his interview with the Director of Belvedere College Stephen arrives here on 'a day of dappled seaborne clouds' (Ch. 4) and is depressed to meet 'a squad of christian brothers' crossing the bridge. On North Bull Island beyond he completes his liberation from Ireland and the Roman Catholicism in which he has been brought up. The clouds remind him of the world that lies beyond the country of his birth and hint at a future of travel:

> The Europe they had come from lay out there beyond the Irish Sea, Europe of strange tongues and valleyed and woodbegirt and citadelled and of entrenched and marshalled races. He heard a confused music with him as of memories and names which he was almost conscious of but could not capture even for an instant . . .

The sight of a girl on the strand, like 'a strange and beautiful seabird,' brings about a Joycean epiphany: a moment of luminous realisation that has all the intensity of religious experience but is directed towards the material, secular, even mundane, world.

Wicklow and Kildare
12 Bray

John Joyce moved his family to Bray from Dublin (Rte 6) in 1887, when Joyce was five, and remained until 1892. Bray (on the coast 13 miles south of Dublin via N11) was already a popular and fashionable resort and the Joyce's home at No. 1 Martello Terrace, by the Promenade, reflects their prosperity during this period. The opening chapter of *A Portrait of the Artist* remembers the writer's childhood playmate Eileen Vance, who lived at No. 4 (not No. 7 as Joyce states), and gives a notable account of the explosive Christmas dinner at Bray in 1891. Behind the argument between Joyce's father and his first teacher, Dante Conway, lay the shadow of Parnell's recent death, an event which John Joyce came to identify with the beginning of his own decline in fortune.

13 Clongowes Wood College

The Jesuit school stands in wooded countryside near the Liffey some 38 miles west of Joyce's childhood home at Bray (Rte 12) and 2 miles north of Clane (off L25 between Naas and Kilcock). Its buildings incorporate part of a medieval castle. Joyce's father sent him here in 1888—he gave his age as 'half past six' and acquired this as his school nickname—and withdrew him in 1891. The first chapter of *A Portrait of the Artist* is based on vivid recollections of his years with the Jesuits at Clongowes ('a smell of air and rain and turf and corduroy'). The 'square ditch' in front of the castle is the one into which Wells pushes the young Stephen Dedalus.

County Cork
14 Cork

The Joyces came from Cork, on the south coast of Ireland and now the second city of the Republic. In 1867–70 the writer's father, John Joyce, studied medicine at University College (then Queen's College); he was popular with his fellow students but failed his exams. Beset by money troubles, he returned to Córk in February 1894 to dispose of the remaining property he had inherited, and took his twelve-year old son with him. Chapter 2 of *A Portrait of the Artist* describes how Simon Dedalus takes Stephen on a tour of the College's neo-Tudor buildings (in the SW of the city) and how Stephen 'listened without sympathy to his father's evocation of Cork and of scenes of his youth, a tale broken by sighs or draughts from his pocketflask whenever the image of some dead friend appeared in it or whenever the evoker remembered suddenly the purpose of his actual visit.'

THE LAKE POETS: WORDSWORTH, COLERIDGE AND SOUTHEY

William Wordsworth: b. Cockermouth, Cumbria, 1770; d. Rydal, Cumbria, 1850. *Lyrical Ballads* (with Coleridge; 1798; second edition with Preface, 1800); *Poems in Two Volumes* (1807); *The Excursion, Being a Portion of The Recluse* (1814); *The White Doe of Rylstone: or the Fate of the Nortons* (1815); *Peter Bell: a Tale in Verse* (1819); *Ecclesiastical Sketches* (1822); *Memorials of a Tour on the Continent 1820* (1822); *A Description of the Scenery of the Lakes in the North of England* (1822); *Yarrow Revisited, and Other Poems* (1835); *The Prelude, or Growth of a Poet's Mind* (1850).

Samuel Taylor Coleridge: b. Ottery St Mary, Devon, 1772; d. London, 1834. *The Fall of Robespierre: An Historic Drama* (with Southey; 1794); *Poems on Various Subjects* (1796); *Fears in Solitude, Written in 1798 During the Alarm of an Invasion* (1798); *Lyrical Ballads* (with Wordsworth; 1798); *The Friend* (1809–10); *Christabel; Kubla Khan; A Vision; The Pains of Sleep* (1816); *Lay Sermons* (1816–17); *Biographia Literaria: or Biographical Sketches of My Literary Life and Opinions* (1817); *On the Constitution of the Church and State According to the Idea of Each* (1830).

Robert Southey: b. Bristol, Avon, 1774; d. Keswick, Cumbria, 1843. *The Fall of Robespierre: An Historic Drama* (with Coleridge; 1794); *Joan of Arc: An Epic Poem* (1796); *Letters Written During a Short Residence in Spain and Portugal* (1797); *Thalaba the Destroyer* (1801); *Madoc: A Poem in Two Parts* (1805); *The Life of Nelson* (1813); *Wat Tyler: A Dramatic Poem* (1817); *Journal of a Tour in Scotland in 1819* (1929); *The Life of Wesley, and the Rise and Progress of Methodism* (1820); *A Vision of Judgment* (1821).

Related works: Dorothy Wordsworth, *Journals* (edited by Ernest de Selincourt; 1941); Thomas De Quincey, *Recollections of the Lake Poets* (1835–40).

It is, of course, hazardous to follow the lead of contemporaries and group Wordsworth, Coleridge and Southey together as 'The Lake Poets,' for on not very close inspection they turn out to be distinguished as much by their differences as their agreements. As so often proves the case with members of what critics call a school, they crossed each other's paths at a fertile, receptive point in youth—Coleridge and Southey to share their impractical dream of 'Pantisocracy,' Wordsworth and Coleridge to collaborate on the *Lyrical Ballads*—and then pursued increasingly divergent ways. Those ways led not merely to a relaxation of their early friendship punctuated by the occasional quarrel but also to very different literary careers. Wordsworth became a poet whose lonely greatness is in no way illuminated by associating him with a school and then declined into conventionality without encouragement from his fellow poets. Coleridge wrote fitfully and sometimes waywardly, never managing to leave a paper record that gives posterity more than fragmented glimpses into his strength of intellect. Southey developed into one of literature's conscientious journeymen and England's many undistinguished Poet Laureates.

Yet, if we persist in regarding them as a school, it is completely understandable that the school should bear a geographical label and one, moreover, which identifies them with the Lake District. For all its oversimplification, the term 'Lake Poets' pays inevitable tribute to the way these writers—but particularly Wordsworth—changed the relation of literature to landscape and, indeed, changed our perception of what the word 'landscape' itself may imply. Early poets had located moral values in the world of pastoral or taken pleasure in the picturesque arrangement of natural effects, but it was left to Wordsworth to find in untouched nature a source of experiences at once liberating and edifying. Among the many and often complex ramifications of this discovery was the simple result that he put his native region on the educated man's map of England. At a time when the Industrial Revolution was making people turn to nature with new, larger and more urgent demands, his poetry about the Lakes and the example of his own life there suggested a tangible, specific destination for the tourist temporarily indulging his discontent with civilisation. Wordsworth's success in this respect was too great for his own complete comfort, for the very popularity of the Lake District was beginning to threaten its original character even in his lifetime, turning the former celebrant of the remote and overlooked into an embattled conservationist.

London

1   Inns of Court, Fleet Street and The Strand

We begin on Holborn at Chancery Lane Underground Station (Central Line). On the left-hand side of Gray's Inn Road to the north lie the pleasant courts and gardens of Gray's Inn, which Southey entered in 1797, though his stay there was only brief. In 1793 Wordsworth lodged with his brother Richard in Staple Inn, the attractive half-timbered building (much rebuilt and no longer an Inn of Court) on the south side of Holborn. This was the poet's second visit of any consequence to the capital, made immediately after his return from France; it undoubtedly contributed to the impressions of the city recorded in Book 7 of *The Prelude*.

Walking west along Holborn, we turn left on Southampton Buildings—where Coleridge lodged with William Hazlitt as a neighbour in the spring of 1811—and follow it to Chancery Lane. It was here that a younger Coleridge on vacation from Cambridge met a recruiting officer and enlisted in the Light Dragoons. He had seen the name, 'Comberbacke,' which he adopted for this brief, disastrous adventure, on a doorway in Lincoln's Inn opposite. Wordsworth himself stayed in Lincoln's Inn from February to August 1795 with his friend Basil Montagu, who had chambers at No. 7 New Square.

Chancery Lane leads south to Fleet Street opposite Middle Temple Lane and the Temple, richly associated with Wordsworth and Coleridge's friend, Charles Lamb. If we walk left along Fleet Street we are following the route trod by Wordsworth early one Sunday morning of April 1808 'in a very thoughtful and melancholy state of mind' about Coleridge, from whom he had just parted. His letter to Sir George Beaumont describing the walk, like his sonnet 'Composed Upon Westminster Bridge' (see Rte 2), is a reminder that it was not only the natural environment which could operate on him as a soothing, consoling force:

> I had passed through Temple Bar and by St Dunstan's, noticing nothing, and entirely preoccupied with my own thoughts, when, looking up, I saw before me the avenue of Fleet Street, silent, empty, and pure white, with a sprinkling of new-fallen snow, not a cart or carriage to obstruct the

view, no noise, only a few soundless and dusky foot-passengers here and there. You remember the elegant line of the curve of Ludgate Hill in which this avenue would terminate, and beyond, towering above it, was the huge and majestic form of St Paul's, solemnised by a thin veil of falling snow. I cannot say how much I was affected at this unthought-of sight in such a place, and what a blessing I felt there is in habits of exalted imagination. My sorrow was controlled, and my uneasiness of mind—not quieted and relieved altogether—seemed at once to receive the gift of an anchor of security.

A left turn from Ludgate Hill on Old Bailey and then a right on Newgate Street bring us to the site of Christ's Hospital, which lay north of the ruined Christ Church. Coleridge's schooldays here (1782–91) are remembered by his younger contemporary, Charles Lamb, in 'Christ's Hospital Five-and-Thirty Years Ago' and imaginatively conjured up by Wordsworth in *The Prelude*:

> I speak to thee, my Friend! to thee,
> Who, yet a liveried schoolboy, in the depths
> Of the huge city, on the leaded roof
> Of that wide edifice, thy school and home,
> Wert used to lie and gaze upon the clouds
> Moving in heaven; or, of that pleasure tired,
> To shut thine eyes, and by internal light
> See trees, and meadows, and thy native stream,
> Far distant, thus beheld from year to year
> Of a long exile.

(Bk 6, lines 265–274)

By retracing our steps down Ludgate Hill and along Fleet Street, and then continuing into the Strand, we may visit a final location

Christ's Hospital, by Thomas Shepherd. From James Elmes,
London and its Environs in the Nineteenth Century *(1829).*
Courtesy of Cambridge University Library

associated with Coleridge. Just before Charing Cross Station Buckingham Arcade leads left to Buckingham Street, where Coleridge lodged at the handsome No. 21 for the winter of 1799–1800. He had left his family behind in Keswick (see Rte 12A) and was making an attempt, doomed to failure, at establishing himself as a regular journalist for the *Morning Post*.

2   Westminster

The obvious starting-point is Westminster Underground Station (District and Circle Lines). The present bridge, built in 1862, replaces the 18C stone structure whose view is celebrated in Wordsworth's sonnet 'Composed Upon Westminster Bridge September 3, 1802.' The occasion that provoked the poem seems actually to have been the last day of July 1802, when Wordsworth and his sister left London on the way to France and a visit to Annette Vallon, who was bringing up his illegitimate child. Dorothy's journal for that day offers a close analogue to her brother's poem:

> We mounted the Dover Coach at Charing Cross. It was a beautiful morning. The City, St Paul's, with the River and a multitude of little Boats, made a most beautiful sight as we crossed Westminster Bridge. The houses were not overhung by their cloud of smoke and they were spread out endlessly, yet the sun shone so brightly with such a pure light that there was even something like the purity of one of nature's own grand spectacles.

In Poets' Corner (fee) of Westminster Abbey we find memorials to all three poets, though none is buried here. The epitaph on Southey is by Wordsworth. Southey attended Westminster School in Little Dean's Yard to the south of the Abbey from 1788 to 1792. He was expelled for protesting against flogging.

3   Highgate and Hampstead

We walk north from Archway Underground Station (Northern Line) up Highgate Hill and Highgate High Street before turning left on South Grove. Coleridge's tomb was removed from the chapel crypt of Highgate School and brought to the early 19C church of St Michael's here in 1961. It now stands in the aisle; near his memorial on the north wall of the nave is one to James and Ann Gillman. Coleridge lived with Dr Gillman and his wife from April 1816 to 1823 at No. 14, the fine early 18C Moreton House. He arrived as a patient desperately seeking help for his drug addiction:

> You will never *hear* any thing but truth from me—Prior Habits render it out of my power to *tell* a falsehood, but unless watched carefully, I dare not promise that I should not with regard to this detested Poison be capable of acting a Lie.—No sixty hours *have yet passed* without my having taken Laudunum—tho' for the last week comparatively trifling doses. I have full belief, that your *anxiety* will need not to be extended beyond the first week; and for the first week I shall not, I *must not be*

permitted to leave your House, unless I should walk out with you.—Delicately or indelicately, this *must* be done, and both the Servant and the young Man must receive absolute commands from you on no account to fetch anything for me.

The doctor's care reduced but never eliminated the problem. Coleridge's presence in the house brought a steady flow of visitors, some of them distinguished, attracted by the prospect of hearing the age's most compelling talker. Leading right from the end of South Grove is The Grove, a handsome late 17C–early 18C terraced street where, in 1823, the Gillmans moved with Coleridge to No. 3. He lived here until his death.

By following Highgate West Hill to the south and turning right on Merton Lane we come to a footpath that leads across Highgate Ponds and continues south of Kenwood House to Hampstead Heath. On this path or a neighbouring one Keats (q.v.) encountered Coleridge and a mutual acquaintance in April 1819:

after enquiring by a look whether it would be agreeable—I walked with him at his alderman-after-dinner pace for near two miles I suppose. In those two miles he broached a thousand things—let me see if I can give you a list—Nightingales, Poetry—on Poetical sensation— Metaphysics —Different genera and species of Dreams—Nightmare—a dream accompanied by a sense of touch—single and double touch—A dream related—First and second consciousness—the difference explained between will and Volition—so my [many] metaphysicians from a want of smoking the second consciousness—Monsters—the Kraken— Mermaids —Southey believes in them—southeys belief too much diluted—a Ghost story—Good morning—I heard his voice as he came towards me—I heard it as he moved away—I heard it all the interval—if it may be called so.

Coleridge later remembered that before he left Keats asked: 'Let me carry away the memory, Coleridge, of having pressed your hand!' It was their only meeting.

A pleasant end to the walk can be made by continuing across the Heath to its western edge, where Heath Street leads south to Hampstead Underground Station (Northern Line).

South-Eastern England
4   Boldre

In 1839 Southey married his second wife, Caroline Bowles, in the church at Boldre, a little Hampshire village 3 miles north of Lymington on the south coast. The vicar of Boldre had earlier been William Gilpin (1724–1804), author of picturesque travel books whose tour of the Wye Valley is mentioned in Rte 8 below. Gilpin is buried in the churchyard and remembered by a monument in the church.

South-Western England

5   Bath to Crewkerne via Bristol, Nether Stowey and Ottery St Mary

In its way South-Western England is almost as rich in associations with all three poets as the Lake District that gave them the label by which they became popularly known. Coleridge and Southey were born and married here, as well as sharing their youthful enthusiasm for 'Pantisocracy.' More important, it was in South-Western England that Coleridge and Wordsworth forged the close bond that led to their literary collaboration on *Lyrical Ballads*.

Bath is not a city we readily associate with the Lake Poets, though all of them came here on one occasion or another. The most important surviving location, now marked with a plaque, is No. 108 Walcot Street near the river, where Southey lived from the age of two to six under the care of his aunt, the fashionable and unpleasant Miss Tyler.

A4 leads NW from Bath to Bristol (12 miles). A walking tour of the city, linking the dispersed places frequented by the three writers, begins in the SE. At the magnificent church of St Mary Redcliffe Coleridge and Southey were married in October and November 1795 respectively to Sara and Edith Fricker, contemptuously described by Byron (q.v.) as 'milliners of Bath' but really daughters of a failed manufacturer of sugar pans who lived on Redcliffe Hill to the south. Southey's marriage lasted until Edith's death in 1837 but Coleridge's ran a much less happy course. He eventually separated from Sara after his return from Malta in 1806.

St Mary Redcliffe's close connection with Chatterton (q.v.) made it an appropriate venue for these ceremonies, since both Coleridge and Southey played a crucial role in the growth of the romantic legend surrounding the 'marvellous Boy.' Southey took a kindly interest in Chatterton's surviving relatives and edited his poems with Joseph Cottle (1803), while Coleridge wrote a lengthy 'Monody on the Death of Chatterton,' revising and adding to it while in Bristol.

From the church we follow Redcliffe Way west over the Floating Harbour and across Queen Square. On King Street, to the right shortly afterwards, stands the old Free Library, which Coleridge used while making erratic preparations for his Bristol lectures. It is now an Employment Centre. At the end of Redcliffe Way we skirt St Augustine's Reach and head left to Bristol Cathedral. The monument to Bishop Butler (d. 1752) in the north transept has an inscription by Southey, while a bust of the poet may be found in the north choir aisle.

College Street leads from the west side of College Green opposite the Cathedral. Now changed beyond all recognition, it was the site of Coleridge and Southey's lodgings in 1795, when they were making plans to found a 'Pantisocratic' community on the banks of the Susquehanna in America. By following College Street's continuation as Frog Lane and turning left on Park Street, we come to Great Park Street (left) and the *Georgian House. The elegant building was the home of John Pretor Pinney, a wealthy West Indies merchant, and the probable scene of Wordsworth and Coleridge's first meeting in autumn 1795. The generosity of John Pinney the younger allowed Wordsworth and his sister Dorothy to live at Racedown Lodge, which we visit later in the course of this tour.

Rte 8 charts a picturesque journey north from Bristol up the valley of the Wye. The present route leaves the city to the SW following the general direction of the M5 for part of the way but shunning the motorway in favour of roads that keep closer to the character of the countryside which Wordsworth and Coleridge knew.

After following A330 signs for Weston-super-Mare we turn right on B3128 and its continuation, B3130, for Clevedon (24 miles), a coastal town vastly grown from the small fishing village where Coleridge stayed. He brought his wife Sara here for his honeymoon in 1795 and tradition, as well as a plaque, identifies No. 55 Old Church Road near the station as 'our Cot o'ergrown/ With white-flower'd Jasmin, and the broad-leav'd Myrtle,' of which he wrote fondly in 'The Eolian Harp' (lines 3–4).

We leave Clevedon by B3133 and branch left at 28½ miles on a sideroad to Wrington (32 miles). All three poets paid visits to the Evangelical Hannah More at Barley Wood, described under the entry devoted to her. It was on a visit here in 1814 that Joseph Cottle, Bristol bookseller and longtime friend of the Lake Poets, first realised the extent of Coleridge's opium addiction when he observed 'his hands shaking to an alarming degree, so that he could not take a glass of wine without spilling it, though one hand supported the other!'

From Wrington we join A38 and head SW, skirting the pleasant and sometimes dramatic landscape of the Mendip Hills. Coleridge came here on walking tours with Southey in 1794 and with the Wordsworths in 1798. At 54 miles we reach Bridgwater. Coleridge preached in its Unitarian Chapel on Dampiet Street (south of and parallel to Fore Street after we cross Town Bridge) in 1797 and again the following year.

From Bridgwater A39 leads west towards the Quantock Hills and the village of •Nether Stowey (62 miles), scene of probably the most important passages in Coleridge's friendship with Wordsworth and Dorothy. Thomas Poole, a prosperous local tanner and farmer of radical sympathies, found a cottage for him here in the winter of 1796. Disillusioned by his recent attempts to launch *The Watchman*, a journal of literature and politics, Coleridge welcomed the prospect of rural retirement: 'I am not *fit* for *public* life; yet the light shall shine to a far distance from my cottage window.' Wordsworth and his sister came to visit in the spring and decided to settle at Alfoxden (described below). In the year that followed their daily intimacy sparked a new creative energy in both poets; its most tangible result was the *Lyrical Ballads*, published in Bristol by Cottle. As recorded by Dorothy in her *Alfoxden Journal*, one of her beautifully precise and unassuming accounts of the landscape and people around her, their time in the Quantocks has an idyllic quality. But it was not without its melodramatic and comic side. The Wordsworths' northern accents, Coleridge's sometimes eccentric manner and a visit by John Thelwall, the prominent radical, combined to generate local suspicion in this nervously anti-Jacobin period. A Dr Daniel Lysons of Bath solemnly reported servants' gossip to the Home Secretary:

I am since informed that the Master of the house has no wife with him, but only a woman who passes for his Sister. The man has Camp Stools which he and his visitors take with them when they go about the country upon their nocturnal or diurnal excursions and have also a Portfolio in which they enter their observations which they have been heard to say were almost finished.

Here is Coleridge's account of the upshot, which has no doubt gained in the memory and the telling, from *Biographia Literaria*:

The dark guesses of some zealous quidnunc met with so congenial a soil in the grave alarm of a titled Dogberry of our neighbourhood that a spy was actually sent down from the government *pour surveillance* of myself and friend. There must have been not only abundance, but variety of these 'honorable men' at the disposal of ministers; for this proved a very honest fellow. After three weeks' truly Indian perseverance in tracking us (for we were commonly together), during all which time seldom were we out of doors but he contrived to be within hearing (and all the while utterly unsuspected; how, indeed, could such a suspicion enter our fancies?), he not only rejected Sir Dogberry's request that he would try yet a little longer, but declared to him his belief that both my friend and myself were as good subjects, for aught he could discover to the contrary, as any in His Majesty's dominions. He had repeatedly hid himself, he said, for hours together, behind a bank at the sea-side (our favorite seat), and overheard our conversation. At first he fancied that we were aware of our danger; for he often heard me talk of one *Spy Nozy* [ie. Spinoza], which he was inclined to interpret of himself, and of a remarkable feature belonging to him; but he was speedily convinced that it was the name of a man who had made a book and lived long ago. (Vol. 1, Ch. 10)

Nether Stowey's church (right of A39) has on its south wall a tablet to Thomas Poole remembering his friendship with Wordsworth, Coleridge and Southey. On the north side of the tower arch is a Latin epitaph to Richard Camplin (d. 1752) translated by Coleridge in the lines beginning 'Depart in joy from this world's noise and strife.' Poole's house, a solid 18C building marred by the addition of a shopfront, stands on Castle Street (left of A39). Constrained by a lame foot to rest in the garden while the Wordsworths took their visitor, Charles Lamb, for a walk in the countryside, Coleridge wrote the lovely 'This Lime-Tree Bower My Prison':

Well, they are gone, and here I must remain,
This lime-tree bower my prison! I have lost
Beauties and feelings, such as would have been
Most sweet to my remembrance even when age
Had dimm'd mine eyes to blindness! They, meanwhile,
Friends, whom I never more may meet again,
On springy heath, along the hill-top edge,
Wander in gladness, and wind down, perchance,
To that still roaring dell, of which I told . . .

Globe House next door was formerly the Globe Inn, where the government agent pumped the landlord for incriminating information against the poets. Coleridge Cottage on Lime Street, enlarged, altered and still bearing obvious marks of its later career as an inn, is now owned by the National Trust. At the time of writing only the parlour is shown.

Alfoxden (or Alfoxton) Park, then the Wordsworth's home and now a hotel, lies to the left of A39 near Holford (64 miles). Dorothy described its situation vividly in a letter written soon after their arrival:

Here we are in a large mansion, in a large park, with seventy head of deer around us . . . In front is a little court, with grass plot, gravel walk, and shrubs; the moss roses were in full beauty a month ago. The front of the house is to the south, but it is screened from the sun by a high hill which rises immediately from it. This hill is beautiful, scattered irregularly and abundantly with trees, and topped with fern, which spreads a considerable way down it. The deer dwell here, and sheep, so that we have a living prospect. From the end of the house we have a view of the sea, over a woody meadow-country; and exactly opposite the window where I now sit is an immense wood, whose round top from this point has exactly the appearance of a mighty dome. In some parts of this wood there is an under grove of hollies which are now very beautiful. In a glen at the bottom of the wood is the waterfall of which I spoke, a quarter of a mile from the house . . . Wherever we turn we have woods, smooth downs and valleys with small brooks running down them through green meadows, hardly ever intersected with hedgerows, but scattered over with trees. The hills that cradle these valleys are either covered with fern and bilberries or oak woods which are cut for charcoal . . . The Tor of Glastonbury is before our eyes during more than half of our walk to Stowey; and in the park wherever we go, keeping about fifteen yards above the house, it makes a part of our prospect.

Wordsworth's little poem entitled 'To My Sister' records his enthusiastic reaction to their surroundings.

At Williton (72 miles) A39 continues NW along the coast to Porlock, home of the anonymous person whose business interrupted the writing of 'Kubla Khan' and so doomed the poem to incompleteness, like so many of Coleridge's other projects. The Exmoor farm where the famous incident occurred has not been satisfactorily identified and so, instead of pursuing this direction, we turn left on A358, which takes us via Taunton (87 miles) to the junction with A303 (96 miles), which is followed SW. After bypassing Honiton (111 miles), where the road has become A30, we branch left on B3177 to Ottery St Mary (117 miles), the rather unattractive town of Coleridge's birth.

His childhood home does not survive but the fine church where he was baptised and his father was rector still stands. By the Otter south of the town and reached mainly by footpaths we find the cave called Pixie's Parlour, a favourite haunt of Coleridge's. The carving of his name on the wall has long since vanished but the poem, 'Song of the Pixies,' commemorates the occasion when he brought a party of young ladies here in 1793.

The next, and necessarily circuitous, stage of our itinerary begins by leaving Ottery St Mary to the east on B3174 and then changing to A3052 for Lyme Regis (135 miles). We climb north from this charming coastal town on A3070 to the junction with A35 (138 miles), where we follow the hilly B3165 for Crewkerne.

Just beyond Birdsmoor Gate (147½ miles) we find Racedown Lodge. Somewhat to his father's annoyance John Pinney the younger of Bristol lent this Georgian house, now a farmhouse, rent-free to Wordsworth and his sister from September 1795 to July 1797, when they left for Alfoxden. It was an important time for the poet, not least because it gave him his first chance to live with Dorothy since childhood. As Book 11 of *The Prelude* bears witness, her company helped rescue him from the nervous anguish that followed his experiences in France and confirmed his dedication to poetry. The results can be seen in works like 'The Ruined Cottage' and 'The Borderers,' written at Racedown.

At 151 miles we reach Crewkerne, the pleasant market town that was the Wordsworths' centre for shopping and post while at Racedown. From here A30 leads east towards Salisbury Plain, scene of another Wordsworth poem belonging to this period, 'Guilt and Sorrow.'

Georgian House, Bristol. Open Mon to Sat 10–1, 2–5.

Coleridge Cottage, Nether Stowey (NT). Open Apr to end Sept, daily except Fri & Sat 2–5; Oct to March by written appointment with the caretaker. Fee.

Central England

6   Oxford

Southey's expulsion from Westminster School (see Rte 2) stopped him being admitted to Christ Church but he was able to enter Balliol College in 1792. His Oxford years were creative ones, as the early publication date of *Joan of Arc* testifies, though he himself later claimed that the University taught him only rowing and swimming. Coleridge, brought by a mutual friend, first met him in his Balliol rooms in July 1794. Southey quickly pronounced Coleridge to be 'of most uncommon merit—of the strongest genius, the clearest judgment, the best heart,' while Coleridge later wrote in *Biographia Literaria* of 'the strong and sudden, yet I trust not fleeting influence, which my moral being underwent on my acquaintance with him at Oxford' (Vol. 1, Ch. 3). The two young poets together formulated their ideal scheme, 'Pantisocracy,' which took them to Bristol (see Rte 5) though never to America when they left University.

7   Coleorton

Coleorton lies 3 miles NE of Ashby-de-la-Zouch, which is on A50 between Leicester and Burton-upon-Trent. The Hall now belongs to the National Coal Board.

It was built in 1804–08 by George Dance the younger for Sir George Beaumont, amateur landscape painter, patron of the arts, admirer of Wordsworth's poetry and, according to Sir Walter Scott (q.v.), 'by far the most sensible and pleasing man I ever knew.' Wordsworth came here for the winter of 1806–07 with his wife, sister Dorothy and sister-in-law Sara Hutchinson to stay at Hall Farm on the estate. He took an active role in the planting of forest trees; his letter of 17 October 1805 to Sir George makes a striking application of Romantic principles to landscape gardening, insisting on the need 'of having our houses belong to the country, which will of course lead us back to the simplicity of Nature.'

A visit from Coleridge, recently back from Malta, was by no means a happy occasion, since the Wordsworths were troubled by the changes in their friend's life: his separation from his wife, attraction to Sara Hutchinson and increasing dependence on brandy and opium. When Wordsworth read him the first version of *The Prelude*, still known just as the 'poem to Coleridge,' he responded with 'To William Wordsworth,' a poem expressing his own sense of failure and anguished need of love:

> Thy hopes of me, dear Friend! by me unfelt!
> Were troublous to me, almost as a voice,
> Familiar once, and more than musical,—
> To one cast forth, whose hope had seem'd to die
> A wanderer with a worn-out heart
> Mid strangers pining with untended wounds.
>
> (first version, lines 68–73)

Whilst at Coleorton Wordsworth made a sightseeing visit to 'the ivied ruins of forlorn GRACE DIEU,' originally an Augustinian nunnery and later the family home of the Beaumonts. His poem, 'For a Seat in the Groves at Coleorton,' remembers that Francis Beaumont (q.v.), the playwright, was born at Grace Dieu. It can be seen to the right of A512 3 miles east of Coleorton Hall. Returning to the area many years later in 1841 Wordsworth and his wife went to view the building of Mount St Bernard, the first monastery to be founded in England since the Reformation, in Charnwood Forest. He found the spectacle of the Trappist community disquieting: 'The whole appearance had in my eyes something of the nature of a dream, and it has often haunted me since.' Mount St Bernard is reached by continuing east on A512 2 miles beyond Grace Dieu, then turning right on Charley Road and taking a second right on Oaks Road, an additional 3 miles. Its fine church by Pugin (1839) is particularly notable.

Coleorton Hall. Visitors by prior arrangement with the Head of Secretariat.

Mount St Bernard. The abbey welcomes visitors.

8   The Wye Valley

Their connections with Bristol (see Rte 5) assured the Lake Poets' familiarity with the lovely Wye Valley, which winds north from the River Severn on the border between Gloucester and Gwent. A convenient itinerary begins at Chepstow.

In 1795 Coleridge, Southey, the Fricker sisters and Joseph Cottle started their tour of the area by a visit to Chepstow Castle, separated from the town by a ravine and magnificently sited near the river. A quarrel disturbed their dinner at a local inn, for Coleridge had annoyed Southey by his failure to arrive for a publicly announced lecture in Bristol—a failure that all too often marred his career on the podium. To the right of A466 just north of the town is Piercefield Park, where Chepstow racecourse stands in wooded countryside and where Coleridge and Southey reconciled their differences as they walked.

At 5 miles we come to **Tintern Abbey, a grand Cistercian ruin on a patch of level ground by the river and surrounded by some of the finest scenery this journey has to offer. Coleridge and his party had difficulty finding Tintern and arrived late at night but, as Cottle later wrote, this had its picturesque advantages:

At the instant the huge doors unfolded, the horned moon appeared between the opening clouds, and shining through the grand window in the distance. It was a delectable moment; not a little augmented by the unexpected green sward that covered the whole of the floor, and the long-forgotten tombs beneath; whilst the gigantic ivies, in their rivalry, almost concealed the projecting and dark turrets and eminences, reflecting back the lustre of the torch below.

Of Wordsworth's visits the most important resulted in 'Lines Composed a Few Miles Above Tintern Abbey, on Revisiting the Banks of the Wye During a Tour. July 13, 1798':

No poem of mine was composed under circumstances more pleasant for me to remember than this. I began it upon leaving Tintern, after crossing the Wye, and concluded it just as I was entering Bristol in the evening, after a ramble of four or five days, with my sister. Not a line of it was altered, and not any part of it written down till I reached Bristol.

William Gilpin's *Observations on the River Wye ... Made in the Summer of the Year 1770*, a guidebook that Wordsworth in all probability took with him, records aspects of the scene not mentioned by the poet:

Among other things in this scene of desolation, the poverty and wretchedness of the inhabitants were remarkable. They occupy little huts, raised among the ruins of the monastery; and seem to have no employment, but begging; as if a place, once devoted to indolence, could never again become the seat of industry ... The country about *Tintern-abbey* hath been described as a solitary, tranquil scene; but its immediate environs only are meant. Within half a mile of it are carried on great iron-works; which introduce noise and bustle into these regions of tranquillity.

By following A466 north and then changing successively to A40, B4229 and B4228, we reach another magnificent ruin on the banks

Tintern Abbey, by Sir Richard Hoare. From William Coxe, An Historical Tour in Monmouthshire *(1801). Courtesy of Cambridge University Library*

of the river, *Goodrich Castle (23 miles). His encounter with a young girl here in 1793 gave Wordsworth the idea for 'We Are Seven,' one of his contributions to *Lyrical Ballads.*

A possible extension to this journey leads NW from Ross-on-Wye (26 miles), picking up A49 for Hereford (39 miles), where we continue NW on A438 and A480 to Brinsop (45 miles). At Brinsop Court, a mansion still showing its 14C origin, about a mile to the north, Wordsworth several times visited his brother-in-law, Thomas Hutchinson. In the village itself the church of St George has a modern Nativity window in memory of the Wordsworths.

Chepstow Castle (DoE/ Welsh Office). Open 15 March to 15 Oct, daily 9.30–6.30; 16 Oct to 14 March, Mon to Sat 9.30–4, Sun 2–4. Closed Christmas Eve, Christmas Day, Boxing Day & New Year's Day. Fee.

Tintern Abbey (DoE/ Welsh Office). Open 15 March to 15 Oct, Mon to Sat 9.30–6.30, Sun 2–6.30; 16 Oct to 14 March, Mon to Sat 9.30–4, Sun 2–4. Closed Christmas Day, Boxing Day, New Year's Day & 2 May. Fee.

Goodrich Castle (English Heritage). Open 15 March to 15 Oct, Mon to Sat 9.30–6.30, Sun 2–6.30; 16 Oct to 14 March, Mon to Sat 9.30–4, Sun 2–4. Closed Christmas Eve, Christmas Day, Boxing Day & New Year's Day. Fee.

Wales

9   Llangollen to Devil's Bridge via Snowdon

Though he toured Wales three times (in 1791, 1793 and 1824), Wordsworth never carried out his idea of writing a guide to Snowdon and, in his *Description of the Scenery of the Lakes in the North of England*, awarded Cumbria a 'decided superiority' over Wales because of its 'concentration of interest.' The itinerary that follows links the major but dispersed places with which the poet was familiar.

We begin at Llangollen. In 1824 Wordsworth followed in the footsteps of Southey and other literary men of the age by paying a visit to Plas Newydd, an elaborate half-timbered house south of A5. Since 1799 it had been the home of Lady Eleanor Butler and the Hon. Sarah Ponsonby, the eccentric 'Ladies of Llangollen' who lived a secluded life devoted to 'friendship, celibacy, and the knitting of blue stockings.' His sonnet commemorating the occasion was not an entirely happy performance, for it described Plas Newydd as a 'low-roofed Cot' and drew attention to the ladies' age.

From Llangollen we can make a 28-mile detour up A525 to the pleasant Vale of Clwyd beyond Ruthin. Wordsworth stayed here with a friend from Cambridge, Robert Jones, and his sisters on his two earlier visits to Wales. 'Who would not be happy enjoying the company of three young ladies in the Vale of Clwyd without a rival?' Dorothy asked reasonably. Wordsworth dedicated his *Descriptive Sketches Taken During a Pedestrian Tour Among the Alps* (1793) to Jones and apologised in the preface for not paying similar tribute in verse to his friend's native land.

The main route heads NW from Llangollen along A5, changing at Capel Curig (36 miles) to A4086. At the junction with A498 (40miles) we have reached the foothills of Snowdon. Modern tourists usually make the ascent on the Snowdon Mountain Railway from Llanberis (6 miles NW via A4086); Wordsworth climbed the mountain at night from Beddgelert on A498 (47 miles). We cannot be sure whether he did it in 1791 or 1793 but the exact date matters less than the magnificent description that resulted in Book 14 of *The Prelude*:

> as I looked up,
> The Moon hung naked in a firmament
> Of azure without cloud, and at my feet
> Rested a silent sea of hoary mist.
> A hundred hills their dusky backs upheaved
> All over this still ocean; and beyond,
> Far, far beyond, the solid vapours stretched,
> In headlands, tongues, and promontory shapes,
> Into the main Atlantic, that appeared
> To dwindle, and give up his majesty,
> Usurped upon far as the sight could reach.
>
> (lines 39–49)

Returning to Beddgelert in 1824 he was distressed to find it 'much altered for the worse; new and formal houses have supplanted the old rugged and tufted cottages; and a smart hotel has taken the place of the lowly public house in which I took refreshment.'

The last stage of our itinerary involves a lengthy trip south. We follow successively: A498 and A4085 to Penrhyndeudraeth (55 miles); A487 to Maentwrog (59 miles); A470 to Dolgellau (77 miles); and finally, A470 and A487 to Aberystwyth (111 miles). On A4120 east of Aberystwyth we reach Devil's Bridge (123 miles), where the Rheidol and Mynach join to fall dramatically through a rocky cleft. Wordsworth remembered his visit to the spot in 1824 with a sonnet:

> There I seem to stand,
> As in life's morn; permitted to behold,
> From the dread chasm, woods climbing above woods,
> In pomp that fades not; everlasting snows;
> And skies that ne'er relinquish their repose;
> Such power possess the family of floods
> Over the minds of Poets, young or old!

Plas Newydd, Llangollen. Open Easter to end Sept, Mon to Sat 10–7, Sun 10–5. Fee.

Eastern England

10 Cambridge

A walking tour best begins by retracing the last stage of Wordsworth's route when he entered the city by coach as an excited freshman, described as the opening to Book 3 of *The Prelude*. We cross Magdalene Bridge and follow Bridge Street south. Beyond the Round Church, ahead and on our left, stood the Hoop Inn where he dined on his first evening. By turning right on St John's Street we quickly come to *St John's College, scene of his undergraduate career (1787–90).

His rooms were on the present F staircase, on the south side of First Court, and the memory of their disadvantages as well as advantages remained with him when he wrote *The Prelude*:

> The Evangelist St John my Patron was:
> Three Gothic courts are his, and in the first
> Was my abiding-place, a nook obscure;
> Right underneath, the College kitchens made
> A humming sound, less tuneable than bees,
> But hardly less industrious; with shrill notes
> Of sharp command and scolding intermixed.
> Near me hung Trinity's loquacious clock,
> Who never let the quarters, night or day,
> Slip by him unproclaimed, and told the hours
> Twice over with a male and female voice.
> Her pealing organ was my neighbour too;
> And from the pillow, looking forth by light
> Of moon or favouring stars, I could behold
> The antechapel where the statue stood
> Of Newton with his prism and silent face,
> The marble index of a mind for ever
> Voyaging through strange seas of Thought, alone.
>
> (Bk 3, lines 46–63)

A window bearing a commemorative inscription has been moved from his rooms to the Library in Second Court. The Hall, to the right of the screens passage between First and Second Courts, has a portrait by Pickersgill which Wordsworth praised in a sonnet: 'how true/ To life thou art, and, in thy truth, how dear!'

It was inevitable that the Backs and College grounds beyond, not then distinguished by the Bridge of Sighs and New Court (1824), should have held a special attraction for him:

> All winter long, whenever free to choose,
> Did I by night frequent the College groves
> And tributary walks; the last, and oft
> The only one, who had been lingering there
> Through hours of silence, till the porter's bell,
> A punctual follower on the stroke of nine,
> Rang with its blunt unceremonious voice,
> Inexorable summons! Lofty elms,
> Inviting shades of opportune recess,
> Bestowed composure on a neighbourhood
> Unpeaceful in itself.
>
> (*The Prelude*, Bk 6, lines 66–76)

The subtitle of 'Remembrance of Collins,' one of the few poems attributable to Wordsworth's undergraduate years, associates it with the Thames near Richmond but the description of the peaceful, consoling river may also owe something to his walks by the Cam:

> O glide, fair stream! for ever so,
> Thy quiet soul on all bestowing,
> Till all our minds for ever flow
> As thy deep waters now are flowing.
>
> (lines 5–8)

Yet the picture of Cambridge offered in *The Prelude* is that of a place he found ultimately uncongenial. The bewildered excitement of a northern youth in the bustle of a university city gives way to disillusionment with the Fellows of his college, a sense of his own incompatibility with the academic life and a steady realisation that his future lay in very different environments. The academic record supports his conclusion, for by the end of his undergraduate career he did not even attempt his papers in mathematics.

In the ante-chapel at Trinity, St John's neighbour, we can see the fine •statue of Newton by Roubiliac which moved Wordsworth to such magnificent poetry. Wordsworth's younger brother, Christopher, who fulfilled the family hopes his own undergraduate career had disappointed, was Master of the College from 1820 to 1841.

Wordsworth's 'Ode on the Installation of His Royal Highness Prince Albert as Chancellor of the University of Cambridge, July, 1847' was performed in Gibbs' Senate House at the southern end of Trinity Street. It is ironic that Wordsworth's only public poem in his capacity as Poet Laureate should have contributed to an occasion he disapproved of, for Albert's progressive views about university studies were not to his own increasingly conservative taste; and it is not surprising that the poem should have proved the weakest of his later performances. King's College Chapel beyond is the subject of three sonnets (Part 2, Nos 43–45) in *Ecclesiastical Sketches*; the last reaches the unremarkable conclusion that 'They dreamt not of a perishable home/ Who thus could build.'

On Sidney Street, east of Market Hill and the modern Red Lion Yard, stands Christ's College, where the undergraduate Wordsworth paid a reverential visit to Milton's old rooms (q.v.), then occupied by his friend from Hawkshead school, Edward Birkett. The occasion was memorable not so much for the act of literary piety but because, as Wordsworth confesses in *The Prelude* (Bk 3, lines 239–321), he became uncharacteristically drunk.

By heading north on Sidney Street and turning right into Jesus Lane we reach Jesus College, where Coleridge studied from 1791 to 1794. In *Biographia Literaria* (Vol. 1, Ch. 10) he paid passing tribute to 'the friendly cloysters and the happy grove of quiet,' while in *The Prelude* Wordsworth, conscious of the irony that he had so narrowly missed meeting his future friend during their undergraduate days, exclaimed:

> I have thought
> Of thee, thy learning, gorgeous eloquence,
> And all the strength and plumage of thy youth,
> Thy subtle speculations, toils abstruse
> Among the schoolmen, and Platonic forms
> Of wild ideal pageantry, shaped out
> From things well-matched or ill, and words for things,
> The self-created sustenance of a mind
> Debarred from Nature's living images,
> Compelled to be a life unto herself,
> And unrelentingly possessed by thirst
> Of greatness, love, and beauty.
>
> (Bk 6, lines 294–305)

In fact, Coleridge's discovery of his unsuitability to the academic life was as melodramatic and turbulent as Wordsworth's had been modest and inconspicuous. He plunged into debt, apparently meditated suicide, confessed darkly that he had 'fled to Debauchery,' supported an undergraduate charged by the Proctor with radical agitation and interrupted his time at Jesus for his brief, extraordinary career in the Light Dragoons. By the time he left Cambridge Coleridge was firmly committed to the scheme for 'Pantisocracy' that took him to Bristol (Rte 5).

Library, St John's College. Visitors by special application to the Librarian.

Northern England

11 North Yorkshire

This route zigzags west and east from A1, taking the traveller to places recalling various aspects of Wordsworth's life and poetry, as well as to some of England's finest abbeys and natural scenery.

We begin just below Wetherby and the North Yorkshire border at the junction of A1 with A659. The latter road and its continuation as A660 and A65 are followed west along the bank of the River Wharfe to Ilkley (20 miles). After crossing the river we head NW through the magnificent Wharfedale via Beamsley and the junction with A59 to Bolton Abbey (28 miles). After visiting this Augustinian foundation in the autumn of 1807 Wordsworth used its legends in *The White Doe of Rylstone*, his most ambitious attempt at a historical ballad in the manner of Sir Walter Scott (q.v.), and 'The Force of Prayer.'

From Bolton we return on A59 via Harrogate to A1 (50 miles) and head north before branching right (NE) via A168 to Thirsk (68 miles). The next stage of the journey, from here to Brompton, was travelled twice by Wordsworth and his sister: they walked it in July 1802 and returned by coach in October with the poet's bride, Mary Hutchinson. After they breakfasted at The Three Tuns in Thirsk's market place Dorothy noted in her journal: 'We were well treated but when the Landlady understood that we were going to *walk* off and leave our luggage behind she threw out some saucy words in our hearing.'

A170 climbs east from Thirsk up the Hambleton Hills, where we turn left on a sideroad for Scawton and •Rievaulx Abbey (78 miles). Seen on the eve of his wedding day, the view from this stretch of country prompted Wordsworth to a sonnet whose language (like that of so many of his poems) resembles Dorothy's journal entry:

> far far off us, in the western sky, we saw Shapes of Castles, Ruins among groves, a great, spreading wood, rocks, and single trees, a minster with its tower unusually distinct, minarets in another quarter, and a round Grecian Temple also—the colours of the sky of a bright grey and the forms of a sober grey, with a dome.

On her July visit to the Abbey Dorothy found that

> thrushes were singing, cattle feeding among green grown hillocks among the Ruins. These hillocks were scattered over with *grovelets* of wild roses and other shrubs, and covered with wild flowers ... We walked upon Mr Duncombe's terrace and looked down upon the Abbey. It stands in a larger valley among a Brotherhood of valleys of different lengths and breadths all woody, and running up into the hills in all directions.

From Rievaulx B1257 leads south to Helmsley (81 miles), where the Wordsworths visited the ruined 12C Castle.

We now follow A170 east to the little village of Brompton (103 miles), where Mary Hutchinson lived with her uncle. She married Wordsworth on 4 October 1802, Dorothy being too overcome with emotion to attend the ceremony:

> At a little after 8 o'clock I saw them go down the avenue towards the Church. William had parted from me upstairs. I gave him the wedding ring—with how deep a blessing! I took it from my forefinger where I had worn it the whole of the night before—he slipped it again onto my finger

and blessed me fervently. When they were absent my dear little Sara [Hutchinson] prepared the breakfast. I kept myself as quiet as I could, but when I saw the two men running up the walk, coming to tell us it was over, I could stand it no longer and threw myself on the bed where I lay in stillness, neither hearing nor saying anything, till Sara came upstairs to me and said 'They are coming.' This forced me from the bed where I lay and I moved I knew not how straight forward, faster than my strength could carry me till I met my beloved William and fell upon his bosom.

A copy of Wordsworth's marriage certificate can be seen in the church.

From Brompton we return on A170 to Thirsk, where we head north on A168 to Northallerton (145 miles) and A167 for Sockburn (155 miles), charmingly sited in a loop of the Tees. We approach the little village by turning right on B1264 shortly after Great Smeaton, then branching left on a sideroad and footpath which leads across the river. Wordsworth and Coleridge came here to stay with Mary Hutchinson's brother, Thomas, in 1799. Coleridge's poem, 'Love,' dates from this period and it has been suggested that its fourth stanza was inspired by the recumbent effigy of a medieval knight in Sockburn's ruined church.

> She leant against the armèd man,
> The statue of the armèd knight;
> She stood and listened to my lay,
>   Amid the lingering light.

A167 continues to the junction with B1263, which is followed across A1 to the fine town of Richmond (169 miles). On Hipswell Moor to its SW is Hartleap Well (173½ miles), subject of an historical poem by Wordsworth. At Halfpenny House (175 miles) A6108 leads from the edge of the moor to Leyburn (178 miles) and the entrance to the grandeurs of Wensleydale. To the north of Hawes (195 miles) at its western end we find *Hardrow Force, a magnificent waterfall that excited Wordsworth's sensitivity to wild natural spectacles. He marvelled to a friend: 'I cannot express to you the enchanted effect produced by this Arabian scene of colour as the wind blew aside the great waterfall behind which we stood.'

Wordsworth himself recommended the route we have been following through Wensleydale as one of the most picturesque approaches to his beloved Lake District.

Rievaulx Abbey (English Heritage). Open 15 March to 15 Oct, Mon to Sat 9.30–6.30, Sun 2–6.30 (Apr to Sept, Sun 9.30–6.30); 16 Oct to 14 March, Mon to Sat 9.30–4, Sun 2–4. Closed Christmas Eve, Christmas Day, Boxing Day & New Year's Day. Fee.

Rievaulx Terrace (NT). Open Apr to Oct, daily 10.30–6. Closed Good Fri. Fee.

Helmsley Castle (English Heritage). Open 15 March to 15 October, Mon to Sat 9.30–6.30, Sun 2–6.30 (Apr to Sept, Sun 9.30–6.30); 16 Oct to 14 March, Mon to Sat 9.30–4, Sun 2–4. Closed Christmas Eve, Christmas Day, Boxing Day & New Year's Day. Fee.

The Lake District

At the beginning of *A Description of the Scenery of the Lakes in the North of England*, still an excellent handbook for the traveller, Wordsworth describes the main contours of the region by asking the reader to imagine himself suspended in the air between and slightly above the summits of Great Gable and Scafell. From this vantage point the valleys and lakes below appear like so many spokes radiating from the hub of a wheel. Beginning in the SE and moving clockwise, he notes: Langdale and Windermere; Coniston, 'a broken spoke sticking in the rim'; the valley of the River Duddon; Eskdale; Wastdale; Ennerdale; Buttermere, Crummock Water and Lorton Vale; and Borrowdale and Derwent Water. These last run due north and,

Wordsworth on Helvellyn, by Benjamin Haydon (1842). Courtesy of National Portrait Gallery

as Wordsworth admits, the north-eastern sector that follows does not conform neatly to his image. But from the top of Helvellyn to the east a fragment of another wheel is represented by: Thirlmere and St John's Vale; Ullswater; Haweswater (though it is not actually visible from Helvellyn); and finally, the vale of Grasmere, Rydal and Windermere to the south.

It is an instructive exercise for those who like to find underlying pattern in a landscape which, despite its grand vistas and small compass (Wordsworth's wheel is only about 30 miles in diameter), has a complex formation and can easily bewilder the earth-bound tourist. Yet it is more than that, for the very authority with which Wordsworth views his subject from a bird's-eye perspective reminds us how intimately he knew the Lakes. Beneath his imagined spectator's feet lie not just the scenes where major chapters in his life took place, but also the sources of continual stimulus to his poetic imagination. Coleridge and Southey lived in the Lake District too, but Wordsworth possessed and repossessed it in imagination with a force that no previous English poet (and probably no subsequent one) brought to the experience of natural landscape.

In the face of this achievement the customary routes, directions and helpful paraphernalia of the guidebook, however minute an inspection of their subject they may recommend, develop special limitations. Wordsworth said of his poem, 'An Evening Walk': 'The plan of it has not been confined to a particular walk or an individual place; a proof (of which I was unconscious at the time) of my unwillingness to submit the poetic spirit to the chains of fact and circumstance.' We may detect in this something more than the familiar warning that writers take liberties with geography and that the better they know a place the more liberties they are likely to take. It reminds us that only in his later and usually weaker poetry does Wordsworth confine himself entirely to a date and an exact spot, setting down particular impressions of a particular scene on a particular visit. At its finest his poetry, even when the title includes a specific placename, is a palimpsest where the objects being viewed are overlaid by recollections of other experiences, other occasions and other places. So the four itineraries into which Wordsworth's Lake District is divided below are mere skeletons, catalogues of specifically identifiable items from a landscape whose largest, most abiding features and small, most fugitive details permeated his sensibility.

12a Cockermouth to Keswick

We begin with Cockermouth, a small town at the confluence of the Derwent and the Cocker, and a reminder that though much of Wordsworth's life was spent in the central and southern Lake District his origins were in the north, near the Border country. He was born here in 1770, one of the five children of Ann and John Wordsworth, man of business to Sir James Lowther (later first Earl of Lonsdale); his sister Dorothy was born the following year. Their family 'home, a substantial building of 1745 rented from Sir James, stands near the west end of the main street. Now a property of the National Trust, it retains its original panelling, staircase and fireplaces. The River Derwent nearby is remembered by Wordsworth in the opening book of *The Prelude*:

> Was it for this
> That one, the fairest of all rivers, loved
> To blend his murmurs with my nurse's song,
> And, from his alder shades and rocky falls,
> And from his fords and shallows, sent a voice
> That flowed along my dream? For this, didst thou,
> O Derwent! winding among the grassy holms
> Where I was looking on, a babe in arms,
> Make ceaseless music that composed my thoughts
> To more than infant softness, giving me
> Amid the fretful dwellings of mankind
> A foretaste, a dim earnest, of the calm
> That Nature breathes among the hills and groves.
>
> (lines 269–281)

John Wordsworth (d. 1783) is buried in the local churchyard. Returning near the spot in 1833, Wordsworth compared it in a sonnet with his own children's graves (see Grasmere, Rte 12C) and the fact of his own mortality:

> A point of life between my Parent's dust,
> And yours, my buried Little-ones! am I,
> And to those graves looking habitually
> In kindred quiet I repose my trust.

The ruined 13C–15C Cockermouth Castle, built by the Percy family, is remembered in *The Prelude* as 'a shattered monument/ Of feudal sway' (Bk 1, lines 284–285) and made the speaker of another sonnet from his 1833 visit, 'Address From the Spirit of Cockermouth Castle':

> thus did I, thy Tutor,
> Make my young thoughts acquainted with the grave;
> While thou wert chasing the winged butterfly
> Through my green courts; or climbing, a bold suitor,
> Up to the flowers whose golden progeny
> Still round my shattered brow in beauty wave.

From Cockermouth we may detour SW to the coast at Whitehaven (12 miles). As a boy Wordsworth visited his uncle, Richard, here; he returned in 1833 on his way to the Isle of Man (see Rte 13). We follow A595 an additional 6 miles south to Egremont, where the ruined castle with its fine 12C gatehouse is the subject of Wordsworth's historical ballad, 'The Horn of Egremont Castle' (1807). The return to Cockermouth can be made directly by A5086 (14 miles).

The main journey heads SE to Keswick. It can be made on A66 (12 miles), past Bassenthwaite Lake, but this route is less attractive than B5292 and B5289, which take us further south through some of the grandest scenery in the district, going down to Lorton Vale, skirting Crummock Water and Buttermere, and entering Keswick at 22 miles from Borrowdale and the eastern shore of Derwent Water.

In 1800 Coleridge and his family became tenants of Greta Hall, at the west end of Keswick and now part of Keswick School. Its situation greatly pleased him: 'I question if there be a room in England which commands a view of mountains, and lakes, and woods and vales, superior to that in which I am now sitting.' So, too, did the opportunity for regular contact with the Wordsworths at Grasmere (Rte 12C). His stay was notable for two of his finest poems, 'Christabel' and

'Dejection: An Ode.' When it ended in 1803 his real intimacy with Wordsworth and his marriage ended too, for he returned from Malta to a quarrel with his friend and a permanent separation from Sara.

Southey, who had shared the house during the last months of Coleridge's stay, assumed full tenancy after his departure—along with responsibility for Coleridge's family. Mrs Coleridge lived here until her daughter's marriage in 1829. Southey remained until his death in 1843, conscientiously pursuing his career as man of letters and accepting the Poet Laureateship after Sir Walter Scott (q.v.) declined it in 1813. He was visited by Shelley (q.v.), Harriet Westbrook and her sister, Eliza, in the winter of 1811–12; details of the younger poet's stay in the area are given under the appropriate entry. In the main, Southey's life was quiet and bookish. Wordsworth, who 'would rather give up books than men,' lamented 'how completely dead Southey is become to all but *books*,' while Thomas De Quincey disparagingly compared his elegantly appointed library at Greta Hall with the small shelf of thumbed and battered volumes favoured by the older poet. Southey's *Vision of Judgment*, a poem usually remembered only because of the satiric reply it provoked from Byron (q.v.), opens with a description of the view he enjoyed from his study:

'Twas at that sober hour when the light of day is receding,
And from surrounding things the hues wherewith day has adorned them
Fade, like the hopes of youth, till the beauty of earth is departed:
Pensive, though not in thought, I stood at the window, beholding
Mountain and lake and vale; the valley disrobed of its verdure;
Derwent retaining yet from eve a glassy reflection
Where his expanded breast, then still and smooth as a mirror,
Under the woods reposed: the hills that, calm and majestic,
Lifted their heads in the silent sky, from far Glaramar,
Bleacrag, and Maidenmawr, to Grizedal and westermost Withop.
Dark and distinct they rose. The clouds had gather'd above them
High in the middle air, huge, purple, pillowy masses,
While in the west beyond was the last pale tint of twilight.

Southey was buried in the churchyard at Crossthwaite, west of Greta Hall. Wordsworth attended the funeral even though he had not been invited. He had always been a friendly acquaintance rather than a close friend of Southey, and relations had been strained by his sympathy with Southey's daughter in her disputes with the writer's second wife, Caroline, whom he had married in 1839. Southey is commemorated in the church by a marble effigy showing him asleep with a book in his hand; the accompanying poem is by Wordsworth.

Wordsworth House, Cockermouth (NT). Open Apr to end Oct, daily except Thurs and Good Fri 11–5, Sun 2–5. Fee.

12b Penrith to Ullswater via Lowther

This itinerary can easily be linked with the previous route by following A66 17 miles east from Keswick, a journey that takes us past Saddleback.

Penrith itself is closely entwined with Wordsworth's life. His mother, Ann Cookson, and his wife, Mary Hutchinson, were both born here; his sister, Dorothy, returned to live in Penrith as a teenager. Yet these associations have left no visible mark and the most significant feature is Penrith Beacon, NE of the town. As a child of about five, on a visit to his mother's relatives, Wordsworth went riding on the Beacon and came across the site of a disused gibbet; he returned to the place years later with his future wife. Both episodes are recalled in Book 12 of *The Prelude* as examples of those

> spots of time,
> That with distinct pre-eminence retain
> A renovating virtue, whence, depressed
> By false opinion and contentious thought,
> Or aught of heavier or more deadly weight,
> In trivial occupations, and the round
> Of ordinary intercourse, our minds
> Are nourished and invisibly repaired.

(lines 208–215)

From Penrith we follow A6 1 mile south to Eaumont Bridge, where we turn right on B5320. At Moorside (2 miles) a sideroad leads to Askham and Lowther Castle (5 miles). The Castle (1806–11), by Sir Robert Smirke, was demolished in 1957 and its ruins now stand in a park for European wild life. A sonnet of 1833 gloomily prophesied the building's destruction but not the European wild life:

> Fall if ye must, ye Towers and Pinnacles,
> With what ye symbolise; authentic Story
> Will say, Ye disappeared with England's Glory!

Wordsworth came here several times to visit the second Earl of Lonsdale, heir to John Wordsworth's employer, who was instrumental in obtaining for him the much-derided but very useful post as Distributor of Stamps. *The Excursion*, his lengthy philosophical poem, is dedicated to the Earl.

We then return to B5320 and continue SW, passing Sockbridge, birthplace of Wordsworth's father, before reaching Pooley Bridge (11 miles) and the head of **Ullswater. A592 is then followed along the NW shore of the lake. At 16½ miles we find the junction with A5091 to Dockray and a convenient parking place from which to explore *Gowbarrow Park (NT). It contains Lyulph's Tower, a shooting lodge built by the Duke of Norfolk in 1780, and Aira Force, the impressive waterfall that is the scene of Wordsworth's 'mournful tale,', 'The Somnambulist,' and one of his better late poems, 'Airey-Force Valley.' Dorothy Wordsworth's journal for April 1802 has a significant entry:

> When we were in the woods beyond Gowbarrow park we saw a few daffodils close to the water side. We fancied that the lake had floated the seeds ashore and that the little colony had so sprung up. But as we went along there were more and yet more and at last under the boughs of the trees, we saw that there was a long belt of them along the shore, about the breadth of a country turnpike road. I never saw daffodils so beautiful they grew among the mossy stones about and about them, some rested their heads upon these stones as on a pillow for weariness and the rest tossed and reeled and danced and seemed as if they verily laughed with the wind that blew upon them over the lake, they looked so gay ever glancing ever changing. This wind blew directly over the lake to them. There was here and there a little knot and a few stragglers a few yards higher up but they were so few as not to disturb the simplicity and unity and life of that one busy highway.

The very language of her description identifies this occasion as the genesis of her brother's most anthologised poem, written some two years later.

A592 continues to the southern end of Ullswater. The opening book of *The Prelude* describes an early, crucial glimpse of nature's 'unknown modes of being' which took place on this stretch of the lake in a stolen boat:

> like one who rows,
> Proud of his skill, to reach a chosen point
> With an unswerving line, I fixed my view
> Upon the summit of a craggy ridge,
> The horizon's utmost boundary, for above
> Was nothing but the stars and the grey sky.
> She was an elfin pinnace; lustily
> I dipped my oars into the silent lake,
> And, as I rose upon the stroke, my boat
> Went heaving through the water like a swan;
> When, from behind that craggy steep till then
> The horizon's bound, a huge peak, black and huge,
> As if with voluntary power instinct
> Upreared its head. I struck and struck again,
> And growing still in stature the grim shape
> Towered up between me and the stars, and still,
> For so it seemed, with purpose of its own
> And measured motion like a living thing,
> Strode after me. With trembling oars I turned,
> And through the silent water stole my way
> Back to the covert of the willow-tree;
> There in her mooring-place I left my bark,—
> And through the meadows homeward went, in grave
> And serious mood . . .

(lines 367–390)

The furtive expedition began and ended on the southern shore near Patterdale; the 'craggy ridge' on which he fixed his sight is presumably Stybarrow Crag by A592, and the minatory peak, 'black and huge,' Black Crag by Glencoynedale to the west.

Lowther Castle and Wildlife Country Park. Open Easter to October, daily 10–5. Fee.

12c Grasmere to Esthwaite Water via Rydal and Hawkshead

We can reach the starting-point of this tour from the end of Rte 12A by taking A591 12 miles south from Keswick past Thirlmere and Helvellyn (scene of Wordsworth's 'Fidelity') or from the end of Rte 12B by following A592 south from Patterdale through the Kirkstone Pass, diverging right through the Stock Ghyll valley and heading north on A591 at Ambleside, a journey of 11 miles.

Grasmere is ideally situated at the very centre of Wordsworth's Lake District. The opening lines of 'The Recluse'—the ambitious poem he long meditated but left only in fragments—record his first, vivid impressions when he came here as a child from over Langdale Pass to the west:

Once to the verge of yon steep barrier came
A roving School-boy; what the Adventurer's age
Hath now escaped his memory—but the hour,
One of a golden summer holiday,
He well remembers, though the year be gone.
Alone and devious from afar he came;
And, with a sudden influx overpowered
At sight of this seclusion, he forgot
His haste, for hasty had his footsteps been
As boyish his pursuits; and sighing said
'What happy fortune were it here to live.'

He enjoyed this happy fortune from 1799 to 1813, living in a succession of houses in the village, and when he left it was only to move a few miles south.

Rydal Water and Grasmere from Rydal Park, by George Pickering. From Thomas Rose, Westmorland, Cumberland, Durham and Northumberland, Illustrated *(1832). Courtesy of Cambridge University Library*

We begin a walking tour north of the village at Allan Bank, the Wordsworths' home in 1808–11. It was ironic that he should have come to live here, since its construction in 1805 for a Liverpool lawyer had roused him to anger:

Woe to poor Grasmere for ever and ever! A wretched Creature, wretched in name and nature, of the name of *Crump*, goaded on by his still more wretched Wife . . . this same wretch has at last begun to put his long impending threats in execution; and when you next enter the sweet paradise of Grasmere you will see staring you in the face, upon that beautiful ridge that elbows out into the vale (behind the church and towering far above its steeple), a temple of abomination in which are to be enshrined Mr and Mrs Crump. Seriously, this is a great vexation to us as this House will stare you in the face from every part of the Vale, and entirely destroy its character of simplicity and seclusion.

Nor were the events immediately after the poet became Mr Crump's tenant entirely propitious, though his family enjoyed 'the comfort of each having a room of our own' and he was given permission to plant forest trees, some of which remain, in the park. Coleridge's visit in the winter of 1808–09, when he was struggling with his essays for *The Friend*, made his depressed and debilitated condition all too apparent; Wordsworth's comments to the garrulous Basil Montagu reached Coleridge's ears and began a quarrel between the poets, eventually patched up but never completely forgotten.

From Allan Bank we go south to the church of St Oswald. Wordsworth and his family lived at the Old Vicarage, their last home in Grasmere itself, in 1811–13, when Wordsworth tried his hand at teaching in the school, now a shop, at the north entrance to the churchyard. The churchyard contains the graves of Wordsworth himself, his sister Dorothy (d. 1855), his wife Mary (d. 1859), her sister Sara (d. 1835) and Catherine and Thomas (both d. 1812), Wordsworth's son and daughter who died in early childhood, as well as the grave of Coleridge's eldest son, Hartley (d. 1849), who spent most of his life in the region. Inside the church (where Wordsworth's children were baptised and Thomas De Quincey was married) there is a memorial to the poet by Thomas Woolner.

From the church we may follow in Wordsworth's footsteps and make the delightful 3-mile *circuit of Grasmere's lake. The island in its centre was one of his favourite spots and Coleridge has left this description of a picnic party there in 1800:

> Our kettle swung over the fire hanging from the branch of a fir-tree, and I lay and saw the woods, and the mountains, and lake all trembling, and as it were *idealized* through the subtle smoke which rose up from the clear red embers of the fir-apples, which we had collected; afterwards we made a glorious Bonfire on the margin, by some elder-bushes, whose twigs heaved and sobbed in the uprushing column of smoke—and the Image of the Bonfire, and of us that danced round it—ruddy laughing faces in the twilight—the Image of this in a Lake smooth as that Sea to whose waves the Son of God had said, *'Peace.'*

Beyond Loughrigg Terrace we cross the Rothay by a footbridge and re-enter the village from the south at Town End.

Here we find *Dove Cottage, where Wordsworth lived from 1799 to 1808, perhaps his most famous and certainly his most interesting home. The barn opposite has been converted into a Grasmere and Wordsworth Museum of relics and mss.

When Wordsworth and his sister first became tenants of the Cottage, once the Dove and Branch Inn, they took special pleasure in their view of the lake (now spoiled by later building) and what Dorothy called their 'domestic slip of mountain' behind. Inside, one of the ground-floor rooms was used as Dorothy's bedroom and the other as kitchen, with a wash-house at the back; upstairs were the living room and William's bedroom, with only two small extra rooms. The result, as Dorothy confessed, was a house 'crammed edge-full'—particularly after Wordsworth's marriage to Mary Hutchinson in 1802 and the birth of his children. When in 1807 he at last plucked up courage to visit the poet he then revered above all men, Thomas

De Quincey was struck by the extreme simplicity of the Wordsworths' way of life:

> Miss Wordsworth I found making breakfast in the little sitting-room. No urn was there; no glittering breakfast service; a kettle boiled upon the fire, and everything was in harmony with those unpretending arrangements. I, the son of a merchant, and naturally, therefore, in the midst of luxurious (though not ostentatious) display from my childhood, had never seen so humble a *ménage*; and, contrasting the dignity of the man with this honourable poverty, and his courageous avowal of it, his utter absence of all effort to disguise the simple truth of the case, I felt my admiration increase to the uttermost by all I saw.

De Quincey assumed the tenancy of Dove Cottage when the Wordsworths moved to Allan Bank in 1808, but managed to give offence in several ways. He demolished the little 'moss-hut' or summer house they had built in their back orchard; a newer one was later erected on the site. In 1817 he married his mistress, Margaret Sympson, objectionable to the Wordsworths not because she was already pregnant at the time of her wedding but because she was a farmer's daughter. Worst of all, he began in 1835 the series of essays now usually collected as *Recollections of the Lake Poets*, which Wordsworth refused to read, warning Crabb Robinson that 'no friend of mine will ever tell me a word of their contents.' For his part De Quincey had concluded by this time that Wordsworth was a 'mixed creature, made up of special infirmity and special strength.' Despite their subject's disapproval and De Quincey's tendency toward witty malice, the essays still make excellent introductory reading.

A591 winds SE from Town End, following the eastern shore of Grasmere lake and the northern shore of Rydal Water, to Rydal Mount (2 miles), Wordsworth's home from 1813 until his death in 1850. It is now owned by the Wordsworth Trust. Dora's Field overlooking Rydal Water nearby, bought by the poet in 1826 and named after his daughter, is now NT.

Wordsworth's years at Rydal Mount were perhaps the most serene but certainly not the most creative period of his life. His income, previously small and often unreliable, was made more secure when he became Distributor of Stamps in 1813; his reputation was acknowledged by his appointment as Poet Laureate after Southey's death in 1843. In old age he had himself become one of the tourist attractions of the area which his poetry had done so much to put on the map. Keats (q.v.) called when Wordsworth was away from home in 1818, left a note on the mantelpiece by Dorothy's portrait, and reported sourly in a letter: 'Lord Wordsworth, instead of being in retirement, has himself and his house full in the thick of fashionable visitors quite convenient to be pointed at all the summer long.' Later visitors included Matthew Arnold and the twelve-year-old Swinburne (qq.v.). Harriet Martineau, who came to live at Ambleside in 1846 and herself published a guide to the Lakes in 1855, estimated that about five hundred people called each year at Rydal Mount. Her *Autobiography* gives an interesting, though clearly hostile, description of the poet's 'usual manner with strangers.' He took them 'the round of his garden and terraces, relating to persons whose very names he had not attended to, particulars about his writing and other affairs, which each stranger flattered himself was a confidential communication to himself' and concluded the interview by wishing them 'improved health and much enjoyment of the lake scenery.'

A591 continues south to Ambleside (3½ miles) and ••Windermere. Wordsworth's boyhood pleasure in skating on the lake is superby evoked in Book 1 of *The Prelude*:

>   All shod with steel,
> We hissed along the polished ice in games
> Confederate, imitative of the chase
> And woodland pleasures,—the resounding horn,
> The loud pack chiming, and the hunted hare.
>   . . . and oftentimes,
> When we had given our bodies to the wind,
> And all the shadowy banks on either side
> Came sweeping through the darkness, spinning still
> The rapid line of motion, then at once
> Have I, reclining back upon my heels,
> Stopped short; yet the solitary cliffs
> Wheeled by me—even as if the earth had rolled
> With visible motion her diurnal round!
> Behind me did they stretch in solemn train,
> Feebler and feebler, and I stood and watched
> Till all was tranquil as a dreamless sleep.
>   (lines 433–437; 442–453)

The proposal to build the railway line which now runs from the village of Windermere on the east shore of the lake to Kendal roused Wordsworth in 1844 to magnificent protest against the despoliation of natural scenery: 'Is then no nook of English ground secure/ From rash assault?' His public letters, despite their evidently thoughtful concern for conservation, leave one less easy about some of his grounds for objection: 'the imperfectly educated classes are not likely to draw much good from rare visits to the lakes performed in this way.'

The present route, however, takes us SW from Ambleside and west of the lake on A593 and B5286 to Hawkshead (8 miles), scene of Wordsworth's schooling. Despite the influx of summer visitors, the centre of the little town remains charmingly picturesque, though

Windermere, by William Gilpin. From Observations, Relative Chiefly to Picturesque Beauty, Made in the Year 1772, On Several Parts of England *(1786). Courtesy of Cambridge University Library*

Wordsworth looked on its Town Hall of 1790 with the disfavour that men feel for changes to the scenery of their childhood:

> A rude mass
> Of native rock, left midway in the square
> Of our small market village, was the goal
> Or centre of these sports; and when, returned
> After long absence, thither I repaired,
> Gone was the old grey stone, and in its place
> A smart Assembly-room usurped the ground
> That had been ours.
>
> (*The Prelude*, Bk 2, lines 33–40)

From 1779 to 1787 he attended Archbishop Sandys' Grammar School, whose building is now a museum. It preserves Wordsworth's desk with his name carved on it and the housekeeping ledger kept by Ann Tyson, with whom he lodged.

The exact location of this lodging has been the subject of disagreement and confusion. It seems most likely, however, that Wordsworth first stayed with the Tyson family at the house marked with a plaque on Vicarage Lane before moving with them, in about 1783, to the hamlet of Colthouse half a mile east. Green End Cottage here answers to the description of his surroundings, as remembered from a return visit made while on summer vacation from Cambridge:

> The rooms, the court, the garden were not left
> Long unsaluted, nor the sunny seat
> Round the stone table under the dark pine,
> Friendly to studious or to festive hours;
> Nor that unruly child of mountain birth,
> The froward brook, who, soon as he was boxed
> Within our garden, found himself at once,
> As if by trick insidious and unkind,
> Stripped of his voice and left to dimple down
> (Without an effort and without a will)
> A channel paved by man's officious care.
>
> (*The Prelude*, Bk 4, lines 46–56)

Esthwaite Water lies south of Colthouse on B5285. From its shore the nine-year-old Wordsworth watched a drowned body being recovered:

> At last, the dead man, 'mid that beauteous scene
> Of trees and hills and water, bolt upright,
> Rose, with his ghastly face, a spectre shape
> Of terror; yet no soul-debasing fear,
> Young as I was, a child not nine years old,
> Possessed me, for my inner eye had seen
> Such sights before, among the shining streams
> Of faery land, the forest of romance.
> Their spirit hallowed the sad spectacle
> With decoration of ideal grace;
> A dignity, a smoothness, like the words
> Of Grecian art, and purest poesy.
>
> (*The Prelude*, Bk 5, lines 448–459)

Dove Cottage and Museum, Grasmere. Open March & Oct, Mon to Sat 11–4.30, Sun 11–5.30; April to Sept, Mon to Sat 9.30–5.30, Sun 11–5.30. Fee.

Rydal Mount. Open March to Oct, daily 10–5.30; Nov to mid Jan, 10–12.30 & 2–4. Fee.

Hawkshead Grammar School. Open Easter to Oct, Mon, Tues, Thurs–Sat 10–5, Sun 12.30–5.

12d Coniston to Cartmel and Furness Abbey

Our starting point, Coniston, is reached from Hawkshead on Rte 12C by taking B5285 west for 3 miles. We then follow a route which takes us SW towards the coast. Its first stage, an area more readily associated with Ruskin (q.v.) but well known to Wordsworth, follows A593 between the Old Man and Coniston Water to Torver (2½ miles), then goes south on A5084 and, at Lowick (8 miles), A5092. At Greenodd (10 miles) we turn north and east on A590 before branching right on B5278 for Cark (18 miles).

From here we reach Cartmel (20 miles), with its splendid 12C Priory Church and 14C Gatehouse. Its churchyard has the grave of Wordsworth's Hawkshead schoolmaster, William Taylor (d. 1786). *The Prelude* describes the poet's visit in 1794:

> That very morning had I turned aside
> To seek the ground where, 'mid a throng of graves,
> An honoured teacher of my youth was laid,
> And on the stone were graven by his desire
> Lines from the churchyard elegy of Gray.
> This faithful guide, speaking from his death-bed,
> Added no farewell to his parting counsel,
> But said to me, 'My head will soon lie low';
> And when I saw the turf that covered him,
> After the lapse of full eight years, those words
> With sound of voice and countenance of the Man,
> Came back upon me, so that some few tears
> Fell from me in my own despite.
>   (Bk 10, lines 532–544)

The lines from Gray (q.v.) are, in fact, slightly misquoted on the tombstone.

We now retrace our steps to Greenodd (30 miles) and take A590 SW. Beyond Dalton-in-Furness at 38 miles a lane descends left to the 'Vale of Deadly Nightshade' and the ruins of *Furness Abbey:

> a mouldering pile with fractured arch,
> Belfry, and images, and living trees,
> A holy scene!

The Prelude, from which these lines come, goes on superbly to describe the exhilaration of a boyhood ride here:

> With whip and spur we through the chantry flew
> In uncouth race, and left the cross-legged knight,
> And the stone-abbot, and that single wren
> Which one day sang so sweetly in the nave
> Of the old church, that—though from recent showers
> The earth was comfortless, and touched by faint
> Internal breezes, sobbings of the place
> And respirations, from the roofless walls
> The shuddering ivy dripped large drops—yet still
> So sweetly 'mid the gloom the invisible bird
> Sang to herself, that there I could have made
> My dwelling-place, and lived for ever there
> To hear such music.
>   (Bk 2, lines 116–128)

The cross-legged knights, for there are in fact two effigies of knights in armour (c. 1250), can be found in the Infirmary Chapel, together with an ecclesiastical figure, apparently a deacon but presumably Wordsworth's 'stone-abbot.'

Wordsworth's second letter of protest against the Kendal–Windermere Railway noted with satisfaction that plans to cut another line through the ruins of the Abbey had been thwarted and the proposed route changed. Yet it did pass close enough for him to find navvies resting from their work among the ruins when he came here the following summer. The second of two sonnets deriving from this visit expressed pleasure at their reverential manner: 'All seem to feel the spirit of the place.'

Cartmel Priory Gatehouse (NT shop and exhibition centre). Open spring BH to Christmas, daily except Mon 10.30–5; Apr to Spring BH, key available from the Manager, The Priory Hotel, Cartmel.

Furness Abbey (English Heritage). Open 15 March to 15 Oct, Mon to Sat 9.30–6.30, Sun 2–6.30; 16 Oct to 14 March, Mon to Sat 9.30–4, Sun 2–4. Closed Christmas Eve, Christmas Day, Boxing Day & New Year's Day. Fee.

13   The Isle of Man

Although he had viewed it many times in the distance from the Cumbrian coast, Wordsworth did not actually visit the Isle of Man until 1833. He made the crossing to Douglas from Whitehaven (Rte 12A), whereas modern visitors come from Liverpool. The trip produced several sonnets, distinguished (like so many of his later poems) more by their topographical explicitness than any other quality.

The first landmark to catch his attention was the Tower of Refuge in Douglas Bay, built only the previous year at the instigation of Sir William Hillary, founder of the Royal National Lifeboat Institution. Its function is compared favourably with the proud or aggressive intent of medieval fortresses:

> but yon Tower, whose smiles adorn
> This perilous bay, stands clear of all offence;
> Blest work it is of love and innocence,
> A Tower of refuge built for the else forlorn.
> Spare it, ye waves, and lift the mariner,
> Struggling for life, into its saving arms!
> Spare, too, the human helpers! Do they stir
> 'Mid your fierce shock like men afraid to die?
> No; their dread service nerves the heart it warms,
> And they are led by noble HILLARY.

At Ballasalla (8 miles SW of Douglas via A5) lie the modest ruins of Rushden Abbey, an offshoot of Furness Abbey (Rte 12C), now surrounded by a tea garden and other inappropriate entertainments. Wordsworth sought 'repose/ Where ancient trees this convent-pile enclose,/ In ruin beautiful' here. A4 leads north to join A1 at St John's (15 miles) near Tynwald Hill, an ancient mound duly commemorated in another sonnet.

Scotland

Wordsworth visited Scotland four times: with Dorothy and, for part of the way, Coleridge in 1803; with his wife and Sara Hutchinson in 1814; with his daughter Dora in 1831; and with his son John and Crabb Robinson in 1833, though this last excursion—which began with the Isle of Man (see Rte 13)—involved only a brief glimpse of the Inner Hebrides. Apart from allowing him to pay tribute to the memory of Robert Burns (q.v.), these tours brought him into contact with James Hogg (q.v.), the Ettrick Shepherd, and forged a sympathetic friendship with Sir Walter Scott (q.v.). They also inspired a considerable number of poems, of which the best ('The Solitary Reaper' or 'Stepping Westward,' for example) are often the least precisely located and were written in retrospect; in Scotland as elsewhere, the occasional poems he jotted down on the spot too often read like entries from a versified guidebook.

Southey's *Journal of a Tour in Scotland in 1819*, lent a special interest because his companion was Thomas Telford, the engineer and road-builder, was not published until 1929 and is still not as well known as it deserves.

14 Dumfries to Roslin via The Yarrow, Jedburgh, Melrose and Neidpath

The starting-point can easily be reached from the Lake District (Rtes 12A–12D) via Carlisle.

At Dumfries Wordsworth and his sister visited Burns' House in Burns Street, finding his widow away from home but being shown round by the servant, and his grave in St Michael's churchyard nearby, not yet moved to the large mausoleum where modern visitors see it. Of the three poems arising from the occasion, 'At the Grave of Burns 1803' affirms the importance of his predecessor's example to Wordsworth:

> I mourned with thousands, but as one
> More deeply grieved, for He was gone
> Whose light I hailed when first it shone,
>   And showed my youth
> How Verse may build a princely throne
>   On humble truth.
>   (stanza 6)

A701 leads NE, briefly joining A74 before Moffat (20 miles), where we take A708. After St Mary's Loch (36 miles) we enter the lovely *valley of the Yarrow, an area of particular fascination to Wordsworth. He passed close to it with Dorothy in 1803 but, as she recorded, 'came to the conclusion of reserving the pleasure for some future time.' 'Yarrow Unvisited' is perhaps the most simply charming poem inspired by this tour:

> If Care with freezing years should come,
> And wandering seems but folly,—
> Should we be loth to stir from home,

And yet be melancholy;
Should life be dull, and spirits low,
'Twill soothe us in our sorrow,
That earth hath something yet to show,
The bonny holms of Yarrow!

When he did finally come here in 1814 it was only fitting that his guide should be James Hogg (q.v.), a poet whose name is intimately associated with the adjoining valley of the Ettrick. 'Extempore Effusion Upon the Death of James Hogg' later recalled this occasion:

When last along its banks I wandered,
Through groves that had begun to shed
Their golden leaves upon the pathways,
My steps the Border-minstrel led.
(stanza 2)

'Yarrow Visited' begins by expressing mock-disappointment ('And is this—Yarrow?—This the Stream . . .?') but ends with a fine adaptation of the conclusion to his earlier poem:

The vapours linger round the Heights,
They melt, and soon must vanish;
One hour is theirs, nor more is mine—
Sad thought, which I would banish,
But that I know, where'er I go,
Thy genuine image, Yarrow!
Will dwell with me—to heighten joy,
And cheer my mind in sorrow.

In 1831 he walked with Sir Walter Scott (q.v.) among the ruins of Newark Castle, seen across the valley from A708 at 45 miles. 'Yarrow Revisited' is overshadowed by the memory of this last meeting with his friend, an obviously exhausted and dying man.

From Selkirk (48 miles) at the head of the valley we follow A7 south to Hawick (60 miles), where we turn NE again on A698 and B6358 for *Jedburgh (70 miles). On their visit in 1803 Dorothy found the town 'exceedingly beautiful on its low eminence, surmounted by the conventual tower, which is arched over, at the summit, by light stone-work resembling a coronet.' The Abbey impressed them less on close inspection, but both she and her brother were properly conscious of Jedburgh's connection with James Thomson (q.v.). Their lodging at No. 5 Abbey Close, 'one of a line of houses bordering on the churchyard' (as Dorothy described it) and now marked with a plaque, is of some interest. They were intrigued by the contrast between their vivacious elderly landlady and her silent invalid husband:

The joyous Woman is the Mate
Of him in that forlorn estate!
He breathes a subterranean damp;
But bright as Vesper shines her lamp:
He is as mute as Jedborough Tower:
She jocund as it was of yore,
With all its bravery on; in times
When, all alive with merry chimes,
Upon a sun-bright morn of May,
It roused the Vale to holiday.
('The Matron of Jedborough and Her Husband,' lines 25–34)

When he came to see them here Walter Scott 'stayed late, and repeated some of his poem,' the recently finished *Lay of the Last*

Minstrel. Wordsworth was troubled by its resemblance to Coleridge's 'Christabel,' not yet published but known to Scott, though he never doubted that the plagiarism (if it deserved the term) was unconscious.

A68 and then A6091 lead NW to Melrose Abbey (83 miles). Dorothy was disappointed by its situation, which she compared unfavourably with the surroundings of Rievaulx Abbey (see Rte 11), but the visit was made more interesting by having Scott as a guide: 'He was here on his own ground, for he is familiar with all that is known of the authentic history of Melrose and the popular tales connected with it. He pointed out many pieces of beautiful sculpture in obscure corners which would have escaped our notice.' The details of the stone carving are, in fact, Melrose's chief distinction.

It was inevitable that Wordsworth should also have been a guest at Abbotsford, west on A6091 at 86 miles. Scott's home is described in detail under the appropriate entry.

By following A72 west from Abbotsford and passing through Peebles we reach at 105 miles the 13C–15C Neidpath Castle, overlooking the Tweed. In 1803 Wordsworth wrote a sonnet discreetly identified as 'Composed at ——— Castle' denouncing the fourth Duke of Queensberry for stripping the estate of trees:

> Degenerate Douglas! oh, the unworthy Lord!
> Whom mere despite of heart could so far please,
> And love of havoc, (for with such disease
> Fame taxes him,) that he could send forth word
> To level with the dust a noble horde,
> A brotherhood of venerable Trees,
> Leaving an ancient dome, and towers like these,
> Beggared and outraged!

Wordsworth's anger foreshadows the passionate interest in conservation shown in later life by his protests against the construction of the Kendal–Windermere Railway (see Rte 12C). The notorious gambler 'Old Q' seems fully to have deserved Wordsworth's aspersions on his character. He is said to have chopped down the trees to provide a dowry for Maria Fagniani, whom he believed to be his daughter, though George Selwyn also claimed the honour of her paternity.

Roslin Chapel (121 miles), the final goal of the present journey, is reached by returning to Peebles, heading north towards Edinburgh on A703 and A701, and branching right on B7003. Its 'sumptuous roof,/ Pillars, and arches' inspired Wordsworth to a sonnet during his 1831 tour.

Burns House, Dumfries. Open Apr to June, & Sept, Mon & Wed to Sat 10–1 & 2–5, Sun 2–5; July & Aug, daily 10–5; Oct to March, Mon & Wed to Sat 2–5. Fee.

Newark Castle. Apply to Buccleuch Estates, Bowhill.

Jedburgh Abbey (DoE/SDD). Open 15 March to 15 Oct, Mon to Sat 9.30–6.30, Sun 2–6.30; 16 Oct to 14 March, Mon to Sat 9.30–4, Sun 2–4. Closed Christmas Day, Boxing Day, New Year's Day & 2 Jan. Fee.

Melrose Abbey (DoE/SDD). Open Apr to Sept, Mon to Sat 9.30–7, Sun 2–7; Oct to March, Mon to Sat 9.30–4, Sun 2–4. Closed Tues & alternate Wed in winter, Christmas Day, Boxing Day, New Year's Day and 2 Jan. Fee.

Abbotsford. Open 19 March to 31 Oct, Mon to Sat 10–5, Sun 2–5. Fee.

Neidpath Castle. Open 19 Apr to mid Oct, Mon to Sat 10–2, 2–6, Sun 1–6. Fee.

Roslin (or **Rosslyn**) **Chapel**. Open Apr to end Oct, Mon to Sat 10–5. Fee.

15   Dumbarton to Loch Lomond and The Trossachs

This route, which takes us through scenery made famous in the lifetime of the Lake Poets by Sir Walter Scott (q.v.) and still among the most popular beauty spots in Scotland, begins at Dumbarton.

The Castle is dramatically perched on a cleft rock by the banks of the Clyde and is entered from the seaward side. Though she enjoyed the prospects it offered, Dorothy Wordsworth was not impressed by the Castle itself, still garrisoned when she visited it in 1803: 'The Castle and fortification add little effect to the general view of the rock, especially since the building of a modern house, which is white-washed and consequently jars, wherever it is seen, with the natural character of the place.' The offending modern building is the Governor's House. Southey added to her strictures:

> As we approached Dunbarton [sic], the prominent objects were some glass-houses pouring out volumes of smoke; and the remarkable rock upon which the Castle stands. The prints which I have seen convey a very exaggerated notion of this rock; it is picturesque and singular, but has nothing of sublimity, and little magnitude, if those words may be coupled together. The elevation is not great; there are two summits, and between the two the Ordnance, with just such a feeling of propriety as they have shown in erecting a manufactory upon the rock at Edinburgh, have built a barrack-house.

From the town we take A82 north up the valley of the Leven and past the monument to Smollett (q.v.). At 4 miles we reach the junction with A811, close to the southern end of Loch Lomond. Southey found the view from the south to be the most impressive, recommending Cameron (1 mile further north) in particular as a vantage point. Dorothy Wordsworth exclaimed:

> What I had heard of Loch Lomond, or any other place in Great Britain, had given me no idea of anything like what was beheld; it was an outlandish scene—we might have believed ourselves in North America. The islands were of every possible variety of shape and surface—hilly and level, large and small, bare, rocky, pastoral, or covered with wood.

The route she took with Wordsworth and Coleridge in 1803 continued north on the present A82 up the western shore of the Loch to Inveruglas, where they crossed by ferry to Inversnaid, and continued due east for The Trossachs. For all its obviously picturesque attractions, the route had disadvantages even for so hardy a trio of pedestrians. The journey between Luss and Tarbet proved 'a solitude to the eye' and the ferryman surly. On the eastern shore of the Loch they found themselves hungry, nearly benighted and exposed to the curiosity that lost strangers commonly provoke: 'all drew near him, staring at William as nobody could have stared but out of sheer rudeness, except in such a lonely place.' When they found a boatman to take them the length of Loch Katrine, Coleridge insisted on walking along the shore to keep out the cold.

We take a tamer, rather circuitous route and one largely accessible by car; it also includes landmarks seen by Wordsworth and Dorothy on their return through the region in 1803. A811 and A81 are followed to Aberfoyle (22 miles), where B829 leads NW, with Loch Chon and

Ben Lomond beyond to our left, to a country road (32 miles) linking Lomond and Katrine. By turning left we reach Inversnaid on the shore of Lomond (36 miles), where Wordsworth saw the Highland girl, the ferryman's daughter, to whom he addressed his poem. A footpath leads 1 mile north to Rob Roy's Cave, rock crevices which Wordsworth's party inspected. We then return along the road past the junction with B829 to Stronachlachar and the shore of Loch Katrine (41 miles). Wordsworth's poem, 'Roy Roy's Grave,' was based on the belief that the hero was buried near Glengyle to our left on the opposite side of the water. It should be added in his defence that Balquidder (see below), chosen by tradition for the distinction, has only tradition to support its claim.

After returning to Aberfoyle (52 miles) we take A821 to The *Trossachs (59 miles), the gorge connecting the eastern tip of Katrine with Loch Achray. Southey compared the pass to Borrowdale (see Rte 12A), while conceding that it was 'upon a larger scale and better wooded.' He was told the name was 'equivalent to the Wilds—a suspicious translation, however, because one part of this country can hardly be called wilder than another.' Dorothy Wordsworth believed it meant 'many hills.' In fact, it is properly translated as 'the bristly country.' A Wordsworth sonnet of 1831 bids the spectator nourish thoughts of life's brevity

> 'mid Nature's old felicities,
> Rocks, rivers, and smooth lakes more clear than glass
> Untouched, unbreathed upon.

An earlier, altogether more important poem was also suggested by his experiences in The Trossachs. Walking back this way with Dorothy near the end of his 1803 tour, he had a memorable encounter:

> The sun had been set for some time, when, being within a quarter of a mile of the ferryman's hut, our path having led us close to the shore of the calm lake, we met two neatly dressed women, without hats, who had probably been taking their Sunday evening's walk. One of them said to us in a friendly, soft tone of voice, 'What! you are stepping westward?' I cannot describe how affecting this simple expression was in that remote place, with the western sky in front, yet glowing with the departed sun.

The result, of course, was 'Stepping Westward.'

After exploring The Trossachs we continue east on A821, then north on A84, branching left on a sideroad for Balquidder (79 miles) and the head of Loch Voil. Somewhere in the vicinity of the road that leads south from the village and becomes a footpath to Glenfinglas and Loch Katrine, the Wordsworths found 'the fields were quietly—might I be allowed to say pensively?—enlivened by small companies of reapers.' The sight, together with a passage from Thomas Wilkinson's description of the Highlands, gave Wordsworth the idea for 'The Solitary Reaper.'

A possible 40-mile extension to this route continues north and east on A84, A85, A82 and A85 again to Dalmally. From the old road to Inverary SW of the town we get a superb view of Loch Awe and Kilchurn Castle, built by the Breadalbane family, addressed by Wordsworth in a poem from his 1803 tour. Dorothy found it

> a most impressive scene, a ruined castle on an island almost in the middle of the last compartment of the lake, backed by a mountain cove, down which came a roaring stream. The castle occupied every foot of the island that was visible to us, appearing to rise out of the water; mists rested upon the mountain side, with spots of sunshine between; there was a

mild desolation in the low grounds, a solemn grandeur in the mountains, and the castle was wild, yet stately, not dismantled of its turrets, nor the walls broken down, though completely in ruin.

Dumbarton Castle (DoE/SDD). Open 15 March to 15 Oct, Mon to Sat 9.30–6.30, Sun 2–6.30; 16 Oct to 14 March, Mon to Sat 9.30–4, Sun 2–4. Closed Christmas Day, Boxing Day, New Year's Day & 2 Jan. Fee.

16 Oban to The Inner Hebrides

This route can easily be linked with its predecessor by making the 20-mile journey along A85 from Dalmally to Oban on the west coast.

In Oban itself the sight of an eagle imprisoned in Dunollie Castle (now ruined) had provoked an angry sonnet from Wordsworth in 1831. Returning in 1833 he added two further poems on the same subject, noting in the second that even when freed the bird had chosen to remain in the castle's dungeon:

> Poor Bird, even so,
> Doth man of brother man a creature make
> That clings to slavery for its own sad sake.

The Inner Hebridean islands visited by the poet in 1833 and duly commemorated in rather undistinguished sonnets are best visited on the day-long steamer roundtrip from Oban via Staffa and Iona. At Staffa, the rocky outcrop famous for Fingal's Cave, he was at first merely conscious of the disadvantages of travelling with a party of tourists:

> We saw, but surely, in the motley crowd,
> Not One of us has felt the far-famed sight;
> How *could* we feel it? each the other's blight,
> Hurried and hurrying, volatile and loud.

In the second of his four poems about the island, he was able to detect when the crowd had gone a divine architecture that surpassed 'mechanic laws':

> The pillared vestibule,
> Expanding yet precise, the roof embowed,
> Might seem designed to humble man, when proud
> Of his best workmanship by plan or tool.

Iona, inevitably made the subject of several sonnets, called forth

> a thoughtful sigh
> Heaved over ruin with stability
> In urgent contrast.

Ireland

17 Edgeworthstown

Wordsworth's five-week tour of Ireland in 1829, otherwise unremark-able and virtually unique among his tours in not giving rise to topographical verse, took him to one location worth noting. In Edgeworthstown, at the junction of N4 and N55 8 miles SE of the county town of Longford, he visited the novelist Maria Edgeworth (q.v.) and her family; her home is described under the appropriate entry. She was impressed by his 'long thin gaunt looking face—much wrinkled and weather-beaten' but added:

> I enjoyed the snatches of Mr Wordsworth's conversation & I think I had quite as much as was good for me or for *him* in my opinion—He is sensible—but has an abundance, a superfluity of words—and he talks too much like a book & like one of his own books—neither prose nor poetry—He seems as if he had been too much accustomed to be listened to and that he had learned to listen to himself—You know the French expression—'Il s'écoute'—Not that he is absolutely presuming or conceited or *vain* in manner—It is rather a soft slow proud-humility tone—very prosing—as if he were always speaking *ex cathedra* for the instruction of the rising generation and never forgetting that he is MR WORDSWORTH—the author and one of the poets of the lakes.

WILLIAM SHAKESPEARE

b. Stratford-upon-Avon, Warwickshire, 1564; d. Stratford-upon-Avon, 1616.
Henry VI, Part One (1623); *Henry VI, Part Two* (1594); *Henry VI, Part Three*
(1623); *Richard III* (1597); *Titus Andronicus* (1594); *The Comedy of Errors* (1623);
The Taming of the Shrew (1594); *Venus and Adonis* (1593); *The Rape of Lucrece*
(1594); *The Two Gentlemen of Verona* (1623); *Love's Labour's Lost* (1598);
Romeo and Juliet (1597); *Richard II* (1597); *A Midsummer Night's Dream* (1600);
King John (1623); *The Merchant of Venice* (1600); *Henry IV, Part One* (1598);
Henry IV, Part Two (1600); *The Merry Wives of Windsor* (1602); *Much Ado
About Nothing* (1600); *Henry V* (1600); *Julius Caesar* (1623); *As You Like It*
(1623); *Twelfth Night* (1623); *Hamlet* (1603); *Troilus and Cressida* (1609); *All's
Well That Ends Well* (1623); *Othello* (1622); *Measure For Measure* (1623);
Macbeth (1623); *King Lear* (1608); *Timon of Athens* (1609); *Sonnets* (1609);
Antony and Cleopatra (1623); *Coriolanus* (1623); *Pericles* (1609); *Cymbeline*
(1623); *The Winter's Tale* (1623); *The Tempest* (1623); *Henry VIII* (1623).

'Reader, looke/ Not on his Picture, but his Booke,' advised Ben Jonson
(q.v.) in a poem at the beginning of the First Folio of Shakespeare's
works (1623). It was sensible advice, particularly given Martin
Droeshout's accompanying engraving of a moon-faced, lopsided
Bard, and generations of readers and playgoers have been content
to follow it. Yet a certain interest in the man himself was also natural,
beginning with the gossipy anecdotes told by 17C antiquaries and
continuing in the larger though not always less fanciful biographies
of the present day; its history is entertainingly described in Samuel
S. Schoenbaum's *Shakespeare's Lives* (1970). The topographical
enthusiasts came on the scene slightly later, too late to rescue or
even sometimes to record those richly ephemeral quarters of London
where he had lived and worked. At Stratford they were rather luckier:
the town today remains what it has been since the later years of the
18C, England's national literary shrine, an object of pilgrimage where
the documented facts of stone, timber and plaster have been thickly
overlaid with apocryphal legends of poaching misadventures and
drinking exploits.

Only a handful of the allusions to place in Shakespeare's work
reward attention. The same freedom that could endow Bohemia with
a seacoast in *The Winter's Tale* makes his English references, even
to the geography of London in the history plays, generalised and
perfunctory. The spare suggestiveness of the Elizabethan stage,
where the shifting of a bench could change the scene from Rome to
Egypt or from Eastcheap to Shrewsbury, had no room for the patient
topographical fidelity of later realism.

London

Of the date and circumstances of Shakespeare's first arrival in London
we know nothing. They belong in all probability to the 'lost years'
(1585–92) which legend has obligingly filled with stories of a fugitive
from a Stratford magistrate's persecution (or a star-struck admirer of
a touring company of actors or a country schoolmaster) starting his
life in the capital by holding customers' horses at the theatre entrance.
Nor, apart from the occasional reference to his residence in a
particular parish in a particular year, do we know much about where

and how he lived. What we do know is that he was a member of the Lord Chamberlain's Men by 1594 and that he went on to a successful London career as actor, manager and dramatist until his retirement to Stratford in 1611—a working life recorded in account books, the Stationer's Register and the diaries of a few contemporary playgoers. Its scene was largely the City, its eastern and northern fringes and, particularly, its neighbour over the river, Southwark.

1   The City to Southwark

We begin at Liverpool Street Station (British Rail and Central, Circle and Metropolitan Underground Lines).

North of the present station stood the first purpose-built Elizabethan theatres, successors to the galleried inn yards where companies had performed in London and elsewhere. A plaque at Nos 86–88 Curtain Road marks the site of James Burbage's Theatre, built in 1576. Shakespeare was an associate of Burbage and his more famous son Richard, and a member of the Lord Chamberlain's Men when they performed at the nearby Curtain between 1597 and 1599.

Our walking tour leads south on Bishopsgate, following the migratory pattern of the Elizabethan theatres themselves.

Wormwood Street and its continuation as London Wall, to the right of Bishopsgate, offer a lengthy optional detour to the Barbican. In this unappealing modern complex stands the church of St Giles without Cripplegate, whose medieval tower and nave have miraculously survived the onslaught of fire, restoration and bombing. Edward, illegitimate son of Shakespeare's actor brother Edmund, was buried here in 1607. Opposite the Barbican Wood Street leads south from London Wall to Love Lane (left). At the lane's junction with Aldermanbury a garden occupying the site of St Mary Aldermanbury contains a memorial to John Heminge and Henry Condell, actors and co-editors of the First Folio, and to Shakespeare himself, who was living on nearby Silver Street (now gone) in 1604.

The main route continues down Bishopsgate, bringing us to Great St Helen's (left) and the fine medieval church of *St Helen's. Shakespeare lived within its parish in 1597 and so may have attended its services. Bishopsgate becomes Gracechurch Street shortly before its convergence with King William Street. At this busy junction stood the Boar's Head Tavern, the scene in *Henry IV* of Falstaff's carousing with Prince Hal.

By crossing London Bridge we reach Southwark (properly called the Borough), home of Elizabethan London's main theatres after the removal of James Burbage's Theatre from the north bank of the river. Those fragile, fire-prone structures have of course long since vanished and, indeed, successive waves of decay and redevelopment, still in confused progress today, have swept away most of the Borough's historic buildings. Yet its richly associative street names and, in certain fugitive corners, some of its former atmosphere still remain

*Southwark Cathedral, at the south end of the bridge, may fairl claim to have been the actors' church of the Renaissance. By 159 Shakespeare himself was apparently living as well as working withi its parish of St Saviour's. He is commemorated by a modern window

Wenceslaus Hollar's 'Long View of London' (1647). Courtesy of Guildhall Library.

S. of Waterhouse

S. Andre in Holborne

Baynards castle

Paules wharfe

Queene hythe

the Eel Ships

Winchester house

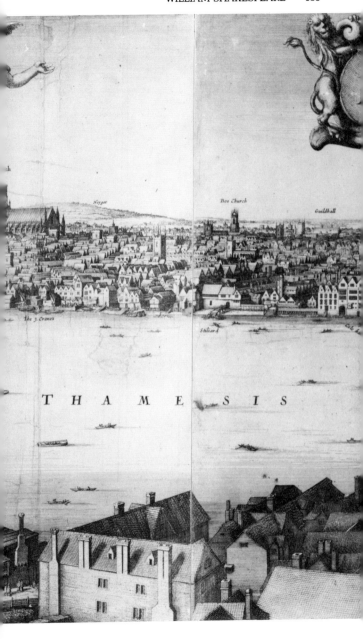

Newgate

Boo Church

Guildhall

the 3 Cranes

Stiliard

T H A M E   S I S

LONDON

Guildhall　4. Alhallows y great　S. Laurence Poultney　the Royal Exchange　S. Michaels　S. Pet

Old fewel hewse　The Old Swan　Fyshmongers hall

FLUVIU

Southwarke

1.S. Magnes   2. Gray Church   S. Dunston in the East

Lyon kay   Billings gate

THE BRIDGE.

The Tower.

Tower Wharfe

Olafe

De Celeberrima & Florentissima
TRINOBANTIADOS AVGVSTÆ CIVITATE

Prostant AMSTELODAMI apud
Cornelium Danckers in via vitulina sub insignt
Gratitudines An°. 1647.

(1954) and recumbent effigy (1911). His brother Edmund, the only other theatrically inclined member of the Shakespeare family, was buried here in 1607.

Wencelaus Hollar's 'Long View' of London (1647), our main and most reliable source for the location of the Renaissance theatres, surveys its subject by looking west from the Cathedral tower towards Blackfriars Bridge. We tour the area by a winding route through picturesque urban decay that begins at the west end of the Cathedral close and continues via Cathedral Street, Clink Street and Bankside. Just after Bankside has passed under Southwark Bridge we reach Rose Alley (left) whose name recalls the Rose Theatre. It was built by Philip Henslowe in 1587 and here a company including Edward Alleyn performed, among other plays, the early tragedy *Titus Andronicus*. On Bear Gardens, again to the left of Bankside, stood the later Hope Theatre. Its site is now occupied by the excellent Bear Gardens Museum which houses a vivid and detailed exhibition of the Renaissance theatres.

At the bottom of Bear Garden we take Park Street to the left. A plaque on the wall of Courage's brewery proclaims the supposed site of the most famous theatre of them all, the Globe, but in fact the building stood further to the east. The plan to reconstruct the Globe near the original spot, by the river on Greenmore Wharf, is still in abeyance at the time of writing.

Shakespeare was a shareholder with Richard Burbage in the erection of the building (1598) from the dismantled timbers of the old Theatre. Its company was originally called the Lord Chamberlain's Men but, in tribute to its pre-eminence, earned the title of the King's Men on the accession of James I. Its apron stage, surrounded by covered galleries for the more fortunate spectators, witnessed the production of at least fifteen plays from the Shakespeare canon. In *The Tempest* Prospero punningly includes 'the great globe itself' (Act 4, Scene 1, line 153) among the transitory things of this world and the reference proved prophetic, for the theatre burnt down during the first performance of *Henry VIII* in 1613. The fire was apparently started by the 'chambers' discharged in Act 1, Scene 4. A second Globe was built in 1614 and demolished in 1644.

Park Street and a right turn on Stoney Street bring us into Borough High Street, at a point slightly south of London Bridge and Southwark Cathedral. On the opposite side of the street stood the famous coaching inns, among them the White Hart, used in *Henry VI, Part Two* by the rebel Jack Cade, who rebukes his followers: 'Hath my sword therefore broke through London gates, that you should leave me at the White Hart in Southwark?' (Act 4, Scene 8). It has not survived but a 17C wing of its companion, the George (NT), remains. During the summer Shakespeare's plays are performed in its yard.

Bear Gardens Museum, Southwark. Open Mon to Fri by appointment, Sat & Sun 10.30–5.30. Fee.

2   The Inns of Court

The Inns of Court, best reached for these purposes from Chancery Lane Underground Station (Central Line), preserve the only London buildings where Shakespeare's plays were performed within their author's lifetime.

Gray's Inn stands north of High Holborn at the junction with Gray's Inn Road. In its Hall *The Comedy of Errors*, usually regarded as Shakespeare's earliest comedy, was performed on 28 December 1594 by the Lord Chamberlain's Men as part of the Christmas revels. The Inn's records, *Gesta Grayorum*, describe how the festivities became so spirited that the ambassador from the Inner Temple withdrew and

> it was thought good not to offer any thing of Account, saving Dancing and Revelling with Gentlewomen; and after such Sports, a Comedy of Errors (like to *Plautus* his *Menechmus*) was played by the Players. So that Night was begun, and continued to the end, in nothing but Confusion and Errors; whereupon, it was ever afterwards called, *The Night of Errors*.

The Hall needed rebuilding after bomb damage during the Second World War but preserves its glass and part of its fine wooden screen intact.

From Gray's Inn we walk south of High Holborn on Chancery Lane to Fleet Street, where the entrance to the Middle Temple lies on the opposite side of the road. According to the diary of John Manningham, a law student, *Twelfth Night* was performed by a company that may have included Shakespeare on 2 February (Candlemas) 1602 in the magnificent 16C •Hall. Feste's description of 'bay windows transparent as barricadoes, and ... clerestories towards the south-north ... as lustrous as ebony' (Act 4, Scene 2, lines 40–41) is sometimes taken as a reference to the building's oriel windows. Like the Hall at Gray's Inn it suffered from wartime bombing but has now been restored.

Gray's Inn Hall. Visitors by prior arrangement with the Under Treasurer.

Middle Temple Hall. Visitors by prior arrangement.

3   Westminster Abbey

Shakespeare is commemorated in Poets' Corner (fee) of the Abbey with a monument by William Kent and a sculpture by Peter Scheemakers (1741). Part of its cost was raised by a benefit performance of *Julius Caesar* in 1739. For Scheemakers' sculpture, see also Wilton House (Rte 5) and Stratford (Rte 6).

4   Windsor Castle

Windsor Castle is reached via M4, 12 miles west of London. It is linked with *The Merry Wives of Windsor* by an unproved tradition that Falstaff owed his revival to Queen Elizabeth's request and by more certain connections with the Garter Feast on St George's Day 1597. Though the comedy may have been performed at Whitehall or Greenwich rather than Windsor it nevertheless refers to the late 15C ·Stalls of St George's Chapel in some detail. In her role as Fairy Queen Mistress Quickly instructs her attendant fairies to prepare their heraldic decorations for the forthcoming Garter ceremonies:

> The several chairs of order look you scour
> With juice of balm and every precious flower;
> Each fair instalment, coat and sev'ral crest,
> With loyal blazon, evermore be blest.
> (Act 5, Scene 5, lines 62–65)

Windsor Castle (DoE). Precincts open mid March to 30 Apr & 1 Sept to late Oct, daily 10–5.15; May to end Aug, daily 10–7.15; late Oct to mid March, daily 10–4.15. State Apartments and St George's Chapel open Mon to Sat from 10.30, Sun from 1.30. Fee for State Apartments and Chapel.

South-Western England
5   Wilton House

At this fine Renaissance mansion (3 miles west of Salisbury) *As You Like It* was performed by the King's Men, Shakespeare himself presumably among them, on 2 December 1603. The occasion was no doubt arranged by Mary Herbert, Countess of Pembroke, sister to Sir Philip Sidney (q.v.) and a distinguished patroness of the arts, while the audience included James I, who had brought his court to Wilton to escape the plague in London.

The north entrance hall has a statue of Shakespeare by Peter Scheemakers (1743), a revised and refined version of his contribution to the monument in Poets' Corner of Westminster Abbey (Rte 3).

Wilton House. Open mid Apr to mid Oct, Tues to Sat & BH Mon 11–6, Sun 1–6. Fee.

Central England
6   London to Stratford-upon-Avon via Oxford

The main lines of this route were in all likelihood followed by Shakespeare on journeys between the capital and his hometown. It has become the most heavily trafficked tourist route in England.

A40 leads NW from London to Oxford (57 miles) where, according to tradition, Shakespeare lodged at the Crown (then the Taverne), a gabled building on Cornmarket near Carfax. Its guest chamber, the Painted Room, is administered by the Oxford Preservation Trust.

Sir William Davenant (1606–68), son of the Crown's landlady and a dramatist himself, took satisfaction in claiming to be Shakespeare's illegitimate son—a claim accepted by contemporaries in search of romantic embellishment to Shakespeare's life but rejected by scholarship. 17C antiquaries reported that Shakespeare admitted to being Davenant's godfather, and so attended his christening at St Martin's Church opposite the Crown.

From Oxford A34 leads NW to Stratford-upon-Avon (97 miles), scene of Shakespeare's birth, early years, retirement and death.

The poet's father John, native of the nearby village of Snitterfield, had moved to this 'proper little mercate town' (as Camden described it) by the early 1550s to pursue his trade as glover—though rival traditions also make him a wool merchant or butcher. The facts of his domestic life and standing in the community are better established. He achieved local eminence with his appointment as Alderman in 1565 and High Bailiff in 1567, the second post making him a Justice of the Peace, but apparently suffered the economic difficulties common among Midlands tradesmen later in the century. In 1557 he had married Mary Arden, daughter of a prosperous yeoman from Wilmcote.

William was the third of their eight children, and the eldest son. The date of his baptism, 26 April 1564, has given Englishmen a

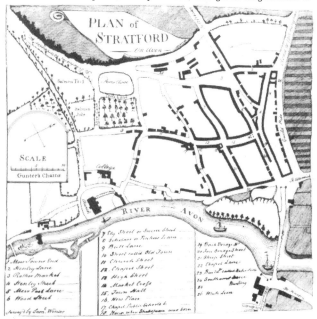

Map of Stratford, by Samual Winter (1759). Courtesy of Shakespeare Birthplace Trust

*The earliest known engraving of Shakespeare's Birthplace, by
B. Cole from a drawing by Richard Greene. From* Gentleman's
Magazine *(1769). Courtesy of Cambridge University Library*

patriotic excuse for celebrating his birthday as 23 April, St George's
Day, an occasion still marked by festivities in the town. Virtually
nothing can be said of his childhood or youth in Stratford beyond the
safe assumption that he attended the local grammar school and the
fact that he married Anne Hathaway of adjoining Shottery in 1582.
Yet even here the record is confused by the almost simultaneous
issue of a license for him to marry an Anne Whateley of Temple
Grafton. Scholarship remains unable to determine whether this
document embodies romantic intrigue or clerical error. Three children
were born of Shakespeare's marriage: Susanna in 1583, and the twins
Judith and Hamnet in 1585. Neither the date nor the occasion of
Shakespeare's departure from Stratford is known, though it evidently
took place during the 'lost years' 1585–92 and is attributed by a
stubborn local legend to his poaching misadventures at Charlecote
Park. He apparently kept close ties with the town, strengthened by
the acquisition of property through inheritance and purchase, and
returned to it in 1611 for the last years of his life. His son Hamnet
had died in infancy but both daughters outlived him and continued
the family association with Stratford. Susanna married Dr John Hall
and Judith married Thomas Quiney, a vintner. Shakespeare's last
direct descendant was Elizabeth Hall, who married Thomas Nash
but left Stratford after his death to become Lady Barnard. She died
in 1670.

After Shakespeare's death in 1616 Stratford's history became
intertwined with the growth of a local literary legend and the creation
of a national literary shrine. The first pilgrimage to the town was
probably made by his old colleagues, the King's Men, during a
provincial tour in 1622. They may well have achieved their presumed
goal of seeing Shakespeare's newly erected monument in the parish
church but their reception reminds us of the Puritan disapproval with
which the town regarded plays and players: they were paid six
shillings not to stage a performance in Stratford. Later in the 17C
antiquaries lent a willing and often gullible ear to Stratford's gossip
about its distinguished son and with the 18C a recognisably modern
tourist industry came to birth. The Rev. Francis Gastrell, owner of

Shakespeare's last home and a man obviously insensible to literary piety, was so annoyed by visitors wanting to see a mulberry tree the poet had planted in his garden that he chopped it down in 1756 and thus provoked a minor local riot. A neighbour, Thomas Sharp, bought the wood and made a small fortune out of carved mulberry knick-knacks, which proved as popular and mysteriously self-multiplying as relics of the true cross. Stratford's pre-eminence on the literary map of England was confirmed by the actor David Garrick's descent on the town for the Jubilee of 1769. The three-day festival celebrated Shakespeare's memory in every conceivable way, except performing his work. It also set an uncomfortable precedent for future literary festivals in being dogged by bad weather and in leaving some participants disillusioned by its evident commercialism. Sam Foote, comic actor and admittedly no friend of Garrick, claimed: 'I was charged nine guineas for six hours' sleep and two shillings for asking a country bumpkin what time it was.' In the 19C Stratford's rise was furthered by the public purchase of the Henley Street Birthplace, a tercentenary festival in 1864 and Charles Edward Flower's successful campaign for a theatre devoted to Shakespeare's plays.

The town's popularity with visitors today shows no signs of decline. Five of its major attractions—the Birthplace, New Place Estate and Hall's Croft in Stratford itself, Anne Hathaway's Cottage at Shottery and Mary Arden's Cottage at Wilmcote—are owned and administered by the Shakespeare Birthplace Trust. A walking tour logically begins on Henley Street at *Shakespeare's Birthplace. The half-timbered structure resting on stone foundations dates from the late 15C or early 16C and originally formed two separate dwellings. John Shakespeare was living in the western (or left-hand) wing by 1552 and apparently using it as his business premises. He bought the other half in 1556; at some later point in the century the two houses were connected and a rear wing added. William inherited the property on his father's death in 1601, though it continued to be inhabited by his mother and sister, Joan Hart. On the latter's death in 1646 it passed to Susanna Hall and then to her daughter Elizabeth. In 1670 it returned to the possession of the Hart family, where it remained until 1806, when it was acquired by the Courts.

During these vicissitudes of ownership the eastern or right-hand wing became an inn known as the Maidenhead and later as the Swan and Maidenhead, while the other part was at one time used as a butcher's shop. But by the 18C the building was already attracting interest as the birthplace and childhood home of England's national poet. Visitors to the 1769 Jubilee were given the chance to sit in a chair that he had supposedly used and shown round the house by custodians who simplified matters by announcing that their name was Shakespeare. Washington Irving's *The Sketch Book of Geoffrey Crayon, Gent*, (1820) gives an entertaining account of the house's character during the years (1793–1820) when the remarkable Mrs Hornby acted as cicerone. Outside, it struck him as 'a small mean-looking edifice of wood and plaster, a true nestling place of genius, which seems to delight in hatching its offspring in bye corners.' Inside he encountered Mrs Hornby's claim to be a lineal descendant of Shakespeare ('she put into my hands a play of her own composition, which set all belief in her consanguinity at defiance'), the famous chair, the inevitable bits of mulberry tree and a wealth of other fictitious relics:

There was the shattered stock of the very matchlock with which Shakespeare shot the deer, on his poaching exploit. There, too, was his tobacco-box; which proves that he was a rival smoker of Sir Walter Raleigh; the sword also with which he played Hamlet; and the identical lanthorn with which Friar Laurence discovered Romeo and Juliet at the tomb!

Nathaniel Hawthorne, a later visitor, was shown a more modest array of exhibits but still, as he admitted in *Our Old Home* (1863), was 'conscious of not the slightest emotion . . ., nor any quickening of the imagination.' He managed, however, to rescue a useful piece of advice for his fellow-countrymen from the disappointing occasion: 'nobody need fear to hold out half-a-crown to any person with whom he has occasion to speak a word in England.'

In 1847 the house had been bought by the Shakespeare Birthplace Committee as the result of a public campaign in which Dickens (q.v.) among other famous contemporaries took part. After restoration, it was reopened as a museum in 1863. Barry, the architect in charge, used an early drawing as a guide and carried out the work as authentically as possible but substantial changes were still judged necessary: adjoining houses with which the Birthplace had formed a continuous row were demolished to minimise the danger of fire; the three vanished gables were reconstructed; and the frontage of the eastern half, brick-clad during its days as an inn, was largely replaced. Henry James (q.v.), a visitor later in the century, left no record of his impressions in *English Hours* (1905) but his short story 'The Birthplace' tells a pleasantly whimsical tale of a custodian who quells moral scruples and learns to take pleasure in conveying the Shakespeare legend to his customers.

Today the western wing of the house is furnished in the manner of Shakespeare's time. The room that tradition has designated his birthroom is on the first floor; its window panes are incised with the signatures of Sir Walter Scott (q.v.) and Carlyle (q.v.) among other famous literary pilgrims. The eastern wing is a museum of books, pictures and objects connected with the writer and his age. The pleasant garden at the back is planted with flowers and trees referred to in the plays.

To the west of the Birthplace stands the Shakespeare Centre of 1964 with its large Shakespeare library. Our tour proceeds to the east, where Henley Street soon gives access to the gridiron of streets which still form the centre of the town as they did in Shakespeare's day. On the corner of Bridge Street and High Street Judith Shakespeare's House, where the poet's daughter lived with her husband, is now the Tourist Information Centre. We follow High Street to the right, passing several fine half-timbered buildings of which the most striking is probably Harvard House (discussed under the entry for 'Marie Corelli'). At the corner of Sheep Street is the Town Hall whose opening in 1769 was the nominal occasion for the Garrick Jubilee. The bust of Shakespeare on its north front, presented to Stratford by the actor, is a copy by John Cheere of Scheemakers' statue at Wilton House (see Rte 5), itself an improved version of the Westminster Abbey monument (see Rte 3). The building formerly housed a portrait of Shakespeare by Benjamin Wilson and Gainsborough's famous portrait of Garrick leaning elegantly against a bust of the poet, but these were destroyed by fire in 1946.

High Street continues as Chapel Street where, on the left, we find

New Place Museum (or Nash's House), home of Shakespeare's granddaughter Elizabeth during her first marriage. Its present contents include an exhibition of the Garrick Jubilee and a table inlaid with wood from the celebrated mulberry tree.

More important, New Place Museum gives access to the site of New Place, at the corner of Chapel Street and Chapel Lane. Originally built for Sir Hugh Clopton near the end of the 15C, the house was still the largest in Stratford when Shakespeare bought it in 1597. He lived there from his retirement until his death (1611–16), when it passed to his elder daughter Susanna and her husband Dr Hall. It was renovated in 1702, when it had returned into the possession of the Cloptons, but suffered a more dramatic fate after it became the property of the infamous Rev. Gastrell in 1753. That gentleman's destruction of the mulberry tree and its accidental encouragement to the Shakespeare relic industry have already been described. By 1759 he had again fallen into conflict with his Stratford neighbours, this time over taxes, a dispute he resolved by the simple expedient of demolishing the house and quitting the town. Today only fragments of foundation are visible and part of the site has been planted as an Elizabethan Knot Garden. The original gardens of New Place, charmingly maintained and inevitably with a mulberry tree claiming descent from the original stock, are entered from Chapel Lane.

We continue south, where the change from Chapel Street to Church Street is marked by the fine Guild Chapel on the left. Beyond stands the Guildhall of 1416–18. Originally built by the Holy Cross Guild it later housed the Grammar School which, it is to be presumed, Shakespeare attended. A left turn at the end of Church Street leads down Old Town and past Hall's Croft, home of Shakespeare's daughter and son-in-law before their move to New Place. It contains a collection of Renaissance furniture.

We then reach the *Collegiate Church of Holy Trinity. Pleasantly situated near the Avon, the 13C–15C building is of considerable interest in its own right but is today visited for its many and intimate connections with the Shakespeare family.

Its exterior is virtually unaltered since the Renaissance except for the replacement of the original spire, short and wooden, by the present one of 1765. A tour of the interior (fee) begins at the west end of the north aisle, where the visitor finds the font in which Shakespeare, as well as his brothers, sisters and children, were christened. A case displays the entries of his baptism and burial in the church register.

His grave lies on the north side of the late 15C chancel. The famous plea of its doggerel inscription (recut) is addressed to the local sexton, who might otherwise be tempted to move the tomb and make room for others, rather than to those later eccentric believers that his grave might contain important secrets:

> GOOD FREND FOR JESUS SAKE FOREBEARE,
> TO DIGG THE DUST ENCLOASED HEARE.
> BLESTE BE YE MEN YT SPARES THES STONES,
> AND CURST BE HE YT MOVES MY BONES.

On the wall above is a monument by Gheerart Janssen (or Gerald Johnson) erected sometime between 1616 and 1623, when it was mentioned by Leonard Digges in his commendatory verse for the First Folio. Shakespeare's bust is flanked by a marble column either side, with a cornice and entablature above and an epitaph beneath.

Sir Walter Scott (q.v.) viewing the Shakespeare monument in the chancel of Holy Trinity. The painting is attributed to Sir Walter Allen. Courtesy of Shakespeare Birthplace Trust

Its English verse is noteworthy for both its early recognition of Shakespeare's importance and its misleading implication that he is actually buried within the monument:

STAY PASSENGER, WHY GOEST THOU BY SO FAST?
READ IF THOU CANST, WHOM ENVIOUS DEATH HATH PLAST,
WITH IN THIS MONUMENT SHAKESPEARE: WITH WHOME,
QUICK NATURE DIDE: WHOSE NAME DOTH DECK YS TOMBE,
FAR MORE THEN COST: SIEH [sic] ALL, YT HE HATH WRITT,
LEAVES LIVING ART, BUT PAGE, TO SERVE HIS WITT.

It has inevitably required and suffered restoration over the centuries. By 1746 the soft stone had become badly eaten away and the actor-manager John Ward staged a local benefit performance of *Othello* to pay for repairs. In 1793 the Shakespearean scholar and editor Edmund Malone persuaded the vicar to have the bust painted white, an act which caused a visitor of 1810 to protest in angry verse:

Stranger to whom this monument is shown,
Invoke the poet's curse upon Malone
Whose meddling zeal his barbarous taste betrays
And smears his tombstone as he marr'd his plays.

It was restored to its present colouring in the 19C. In none of these various states has Janssen's indifferent and inexpressive portrayal of the poet attracted admiration. Washington Irving was being both charitable and fanciful when he found Shakespeare's appearance 'pleasant and serene, with a finely arched forehead; and I thought I could read in it clear indications of that cheerful, social disposition, by which he was as much characterised among his contemporaries as by the vastness of his genius.' Dickens' reaction was more typical when he remarked ironically: 'I have here the counterfeit presentment of a face suggestive above all things of a strong vitality, freshness of spirit, and liveliness of disposition.'

Adjacent memorials in the chancel include those to Shakespeare's wife Anne, who outlived him to die in 1623, his daughter Susanna (remembered as 'witty beyond her sexe') who died in 1649, her husband John Hall (d. 1635), and Thomas Nash (d. 1647), first husband of their daughter Elizabeth. Shakespeare's friend and fellow townsman John Combe (d. 1614) is commemorated in another work by Janssen. The graves of other members of Shakespeare's family are unmarked. The window depicting the Seven Ages of Man from *As You Like It* was donated by American admirers in 1885.

Southern Lane offers a convenient return route from Holy Trinity with the river on our right. On the left we pass The Other Place, the smaller and less formal of the two Stratford theatres maintained by the Royal Shakespeare Company. Its parent building of 1932, the Royal Shakespeare Theatre, lies beyond to the right, on a site where Garrick erected his Rotunda for the 1769 Jubilee and where the Memorial Theatre of 1877–79, destroyed by fire in 1926, previously stood. The only Victorian building to escape the fire now houses a library for Shakespeare students on its ground floor and a Picture Gallery and Museum upstairs. It boasts a remarkable collection of objects and paintings illustrating the stage history of Shakespeare's work but is most notable for the 'Flower Portrait' of Shakespeare, which may be either model for or copy of the Droeshout engraving in the First Folio. Beyond the Theatre, where Southern Lane becomes Waterside and leads to the Clopton Bridge, are the Bancroft Gardens and Lord Ronald Gower's statue of Shakespeare surrounded by characters from the plays.

Apart from their intrinsic charm, the neighbouring countryside and villages around Stratford are rich in Shakespearean associations, whether real or fondly imagined.

Shottery (1 mile NW) can be reached by bus from Bridge Street, by a footpath from Evesham Place or by car via the A422 Shottery Road. Its attraction, of course, is Anne Hathaway's Cottage. The term 'cottage' is something of a misnomer for the timber-framed farmhouse that was the family home of Shakespeare's wife. The Hathaway bedstead, dairy and baking oven in the kitchen are all to be noted.

2½ miles NW of Shottery, off A422, we come to Wilmcote and Mary Arden's Cottage, a handsome 16C farmhouse furnished in the style of the period. Its claim to be the birthplace of Shakespeare's mother is based on the slender authority of John Jordan, self-taught and self-styled Shakespeare expert of the 18C. By continuing 2 miles NW we reach Aston Cantlow, in whose church Mary Arden married John Shakespeare.

At *Charlecote Park (4 miles east of Stratford via B4086) is the restored Renaissance mansion of Sir Thomas Lucy, site of the most persistent and tantalising legend connected with Shakespeare's youth. It was related in its most familiar form by Rowe, 18C editor of the plays:

> He had, by a Misfortune common enough to young Fellows, fallen into ill Company; and amongst them, some that made a frequent practice of Deer-Stealing, engag'd him with them more then once in robbing a Park that belong'd to Sir *Thomas Lucy* of *Cherlecot*, near *Stratford*. For this he was prosecuted by that Gentleman, as he thought, somewhat too severely; and in order to revenge that ill Usage, he made a Ballad upon him. And . . . it is said to have been so very bitter, that it redoubled the Prosecution against him to that degree, that he was oblig'd to leave his Business and Family in *Warwickshire*, for some time, and shelter himself in *London*.

Sir Walter Scott (q.v.) makes use of the story in Chapter 17 of *Kenilworth* (1821). Tradition also supplies several versions of the offending ballad, none of them calculated to advance Shakespeare's reputation as a poet, and points to Justice Shallow in *The Merry Wives of Windsor* as Shakespeare's revenge on his persecutor. Such entertaining possibilities are somewhat dampened by the reminder that Sir William Lucy, ancestor of Sir Thomas, is respectfully treated in *Henry VI, Part One* and that Charlecote did not have a park proper in Shakespeare's time, merely a 'warren' that may or may not have contained roe deer. The sensible tourist abandons speculation and joins Henry James in appreciating grounds 'whose venerable verdure seems a survival from an earlier England and whose innumerable acres, stretching away, in the early evening, to vaguely seen Tudor walls, lie there like the backward years receding to the age of Elizabeth' ('In Warwickshire' in *English Hours*).

The Painted Room, Crown Inn, Oxford. Open Mon to Fri 9.30–1 & 2–5, Sat 9.30–1. Visitors should apply to the office labelled 'Counting House' on the second floor of Greene's Tutorial College, No. 3 Cornmarket and, from 16 July to 15 Aug, to No. 45 Pembroke Street.

Shakespeare Birthplace Properties. Shakespeare's Birthplace and Anne Hathaway's Cottage: open Apr to Sept, Mon to Sat 9–6, Sun 10–6; Oct, Mon to Sat 9–5, Sun 10–5; Nov to March, Mon to Sat 9–4.30, Sun 1.30–4.30. Hall's Croft, Mary Arden's House and New Place: open Apr to Sept, Mon to Sat 9–6, Sun 2–6; Oct, Mon to Sat 9–5, Sun 2–5; Nov to March, Mon to Sat 9–4, closed Sun. Separate admission fees or inclusive ticket for all five properties.

King Edward VI Grammar School, Stratford-upon-Avon. Usually open during Easter and summer holidays.

Royal Shakespeare Company Gallery, Stratford-upon-Avon. Open Mon to Sat 9–6, Sun 12–5. Fee.

Charlecote Park (NT). Open Apr & Oct, Sat, Sun, BH Mon & Tues in week following Easter 11–5; May to end Sept, Tues, Wed, Fri, Sat, Sun & BH Mon 11–6. Fee.

PART TWO

Joseph Addison

b. Milston, Wiltshire, 1672; d. London, 1719. *The Campaign* (1704); contributions to *The Tatler* (1709–11); contributions to *The Spectator* (1711–12); *Cato* (1713).

In the cathedral city of Lichfield, Staffordshire, 16 miles north of Birmingham, a pleasant atmosphere remains to evoke the period of Addison's childhood. The Deanery where he was brought up in a serene and loving family has been replaced by a slightly later building, though a monument to his father (d. 1703) may be found in the Cathedral nearby at the west end of the south aisle. The old Grammar School on St John Street, able to boast Dr Johnson (q.v.) among its subsequent pupils, has gone except for its Headmaster's House, now Council offices.

The scenes of Addison's later education are better preserved. The fine 16C–18C buildings formerly used by Charterhouse, on Charterhouse Square near the Central Meat Market in the City of London, survive and have been well restored. Addison's schoolboy friendship with Richard Steele (q.v.), eventually to issue in their collaboration on *The Tatler* and *The Spectator*, was continued when Addison went to Oxford: first to The Queen's College in 1687 and then to Magdalen, where he later became a Fellow. His love of the river scenery enjoyed by Magdalen is recalled in the naming of Addison's Walk and in this account of his spokesman, Philander, in *Dialogues upon the Usefulness of Ancient Medals*:

> Philander used every morning to take a walk in the neighbouring wood, that stood on the borders of the Thames. It was cut through by abundance of beautiful allies, which terminating on the water, looked like so many painted views in a perspective. The banks of the river and the thickness of the shades drew into them all the birds of the country, that at sun-rising filled the wood with such a variety of notes as made the prettiest confusion imaginable. (Dialogue 3)

He was twice chief secretary to the Lord Lieutenant of Ireland under Whig governments (1709–11 and 1715–16). His connection with Dublin is remembered in similar manner to his years at Oxford, by the name of the riverside walk in the 18C part of the Botanic Gardens at Glasnevin, north of the city.

For evidence of Addison's successful career as essayist, poet and Whig politician we look not in London but to the late 17C house he was able to buy as a country seat in 1711: Bilton Hall, SW of Rugby in Warwickshire. At first sight the decision to spend part of each year so removed from the scene of his normal duties and in an area with which he had no family connection may seem surprising; in fact, it expressed not an early Romantic interest in nature but that adherence to Augustan values which characterised his habits of life as much as the easy elegance of his prose.

In 1716 he married Charlotte, Countess of Warwick, at St Edmund King and Martyr, a Wren church on Lombard Street in the City of London. The couple lived at Holland House, which she had inherited from her first husband, though there is little reason to believe the common rumour that Addison felt ill at ease in these grand surroundings and preferred to take refuge in the coffee houses and taverns of his bachelor days. Holland House, begun by Sir Thomas Cope in the early 17C, stood between Holland Park Avenue and Kensington High Street; only the park and east wing (now restored) survived war-time bombs, their appearance altered by the addition of the modern King George VI Memorial Hostel.

Addison was buried in Westminster Abbey, a building which had prompted these characteristic reflections in No. 26 of his *Spectator* essays:

> When I look upon the tombs of the great, every emotion of envy dies in me; when I read the epitaphs of the beautiful every inordinate desire goes out; when I meet with the grief of parents upon a tomb-stone, my heart melts with compassion; when I see the tomb of the parents themselves, I consider the vanity of grieving for those whom we must quickly follow.

His statue in Poets' Corner (fee) was erected at the beginning of the 19C.

Headmaster's House (Council Offices), Lichfield. Visitors by appointment.

Botanic Gardens, Dublin. Open in summer Mon to Sat 9–6, Sun 11–6; in winter Mon to Sat 10–4.30, Sun 11–4.30.

Charterhouse, City of London. Visitors by written appointment only.

William Harrison Ainsworth

b. Manchester, 1805; d. Reigate, Surrey, 1882. *Rookwood* (1834); *Crichton* (1837); *Jack Sheppard* (1839); *The Tower of London* (1840); *Guy Fawkes, or The Gunpowder Treason* (1841); *Old Saint Paul's: A Tale of the Plague and the Fire* (1841); *Windsor Castle* (1843); *The Lancashire Witches* (1849); *The Flitch of Bacon: or The Custom of Dunmow* (1854); *Mervyn Clitheroe* (1857); *Ovingdean Grange: A Tale of the South Downs* (1860); *Aureol: or The Elixir of Life* (1865).

A plaque now marks Ainsworth's birthplace in Manchester at No. 57 King Street, north of the Town Hall and then a quiet residential area. He was educated at Manchester Grammar School when it was housed in a late 18C building near the Cathedral and the medieval Chetham's Hospital. The semi-autobiographical *Mervyn Clitheroe*, dedicated to his contemporaries at the school, gives a detailed picture of his boyhood there (Bk I, Ch. 2). In 1881, after a long and extremely popular career writing novels that combined Gothic melodrama with historical fiction in the manner of Sir Walter Scott (q.v.), he returned to Manchester for a dinner given in his honour by the Mayor. It was held in Alfred Waterhouse's Town Hall, completed only a few years before.

On that occasion Ainsworth proudly accepted the title of 'The Lancashire Novelist.' His best claim to it is his detailed use of the area around *Pendle Forest in *The Lancashire Witches*, set in the 16C and 17C. A brief tour of its countryside may begin at Whalley, in the valley of the Ribble by the junction of A59 and A671 24 miles north of Manchester. The novel depicts Whalley Abbey, now ruined, in the last days before its dissolution ('Introduction,' Ch. 3). We take A59 north with Pendle Hill, the opening scene of the book, rising on our right. At 6 miles we turn right for the pleasant little village of

Ainsworth presiding at the Dunmow Flitch ceremony. From Illustrated London News *(1855). Courtesy of Cambridge University Library*

Downham, whose manor house Ainsworth made the home of Nicholas Assheton, and cross the hill following the turning for Barley and Newchurch in Pendle. Ainsworth stayed in Newchurch while planning *The Lancashire Witches* and portrayed it as 'Goldshaw.' A proposal at the beginning of this century to erect a memorial window to him in the church was not successful.

Though in Derbyshire rather than Lancashire, the town of Chesterfield (20 miles south of Sheffield on A61) played an important, if accidental, part in the genesis of *Rookwood*. Ainsworth later described how he 'happened, one evening, to enter the spacious cemetery attached to the church with the queer, twisted steeple, which ... seems to menace the ggod town of Chesterfield with destruction. Here an incident occurred, on the opening of a vault, which supplied me with a hint for the commencement of my romance.' He remained tantalisingly silent about the incident but its fictional result certainly got his career as a novelist off to a rousingly melodramatic start.

The Flitch of Bacon brought him to the Essex village of Little Dunmow (just south of A120 between Bishop's Stortford and Braintree), which boasted the ancient custom of awarding a flitch of bacon to the married couple who could prove they had lived together happily for the previous year and a day. His novel makes detailed use of *St Mary, the surviving part of Dunmow Priory, correctly remarking that it is 'the mere fragment of a vast and stately pile, which in its time had formed part of a range of monastic buildings' (Bk I, Ch. 7). Its Fitzwalter tombs and Flitch Chair are noted. The popularity of Ainsworth's novel helped revive a custom that had been falling into disuse and in 1855 he presided at the Flitch ceremony in the Town Hall of Great Dunmow nearby.

From 1853 until 1867 he lived on the Sussex coast in Brighton. A plaque marks his home at No. 5 Arundel Terrace, on the seafront immediately east of Lewes Crescent and Sussex Square in Kemp Town. *Ovingdean Grange* is set in Ovingdean 3 miles east of Kemp Town via Marine Parade and Greenways. It notes that the Grange (or Hall) near the church 'has entirely lost its original and distinctive character' but rightly concedes that it is still 'a fair-proportioned, cheerful-looking domicile' (Bk 1, Ch. 2). Its appearance today, as when Ainsworth wrote his novel, is 18C. *Ovingdean Grange* also takes notice of Lewes, 8 miles NE of Brighton via A27, an 'old picturesque town . . ., with its quaint, climbing houses and its towering castle' (Bk 4, Ch. 1). Southover Grange, an Elizabethan house reached by following Keere Street south from Lewes' High Street, appears as the 'Mock-Beggars Hall,' where the usurer Zachary Trangmar lends money to impoverished Royalists (Bk 4, Ch. 2).

The preface to *Rookwood* acknowledges that its main locale was closely modelled on Cuckfield Place, 16 miles north of Brighton via A23 and A272. The novel enthuses over the Elizabethan house:

> Rookwood Place was a fine, old, irregular pile, of considerable size, presenting a rich, picturesque outline, with its innumerable gable ends, its fantastical coigns, and tall nest of twisted chimneys. There was no uniformity of style about the building, yet the general effect was pleasing and beautiful. Its very irregularity constituted a charm. Nothing except convenience had been consulted in its construction: additions had from time to time been made to it, but everything dropped into its proper place, and, without apparent effort or design, grew into an ornament, and heightened the beauty of the whole. It was, in short, one of those glorious manorial houses that sometimes unexpectedly greet us in our wanderings, and gladden us like the discovery of a hidden treasure. (Bk 1, Ch. 4)

This effect (which we may suspect owes something to Ainsworth's pen as well as to the builder's trowel) was diminished by alterations in 1848, but the brick *gatehouse retains all its original charm.

Ainsworth was buried in London at Kensal Green Cemetery, opposite Kensal Green Station (Bakerloo Underground Line and British Rail) in Harrow Road. His grave is No. 3443 in Square 154, north of West Centre Avenue and west of the church. The cemetery makes an appropriate resting place, not just because several other Victorian novelists lie there but because Ainsworth had lived in the

Harrow Road nearby at Kensal Lodge and then Kensal Manor (1835–53), both gone but both in their day festive gathering places for his fellow writers.

Whalley Abbey (English Heritage). Exterior only, open at all reasonable times.

Southover Grange, Lewes. Gardens open Mon to Sat 8–dusk, Sun & BH 9–dusk.

Cuckfield Place, Cuckfield. Gardens open under NGS. Fee.

Kensal Green Cemetery. Open Mon to Sat 9–5.30 (or dusk, if earlier), Sun 2–5.30 (or dusk); Good Fri 2–5.30, Christmas Day 10–2. Closes at 1 on BH.

Matthew Arnold

b. Laleham, Surrey, 1822; d. Liverpool, Merseyside, 1888. *The Strayed Reveller and Other Poems* (1849); *Empedocles on Etna and Other Poems* (1852); *Poems: A New Edition* (1853); *On Translating Homer: Three Lectures Given at Oxford* (1861); *Essays in Criticism: First Series* (1865); *Culture and Anarchy: An Essay in Political and Social Criticism* (1869); *Friendship's Garland* (1871); *Literature and Dogma: An Essay Towards a Better Apprehension of the Bible* (1873); *God and the Bible: A Review of Objections to Literature and Dogma* (1875); *Discourses in America* (1885); *Essays in Criticism: Second Series* (1888).

The places most intimately connected with Matthew Arnold are found west of London near the course of the Thames. He was born at Laleham, 2 miles south of A30 and Staines via B376. The school which his famous father, Dr Thomas Arnold, kept and he himself later attended (1831–32) no longer stands, but the church of All Saints where Arnold was buried does survive. It is near the junction of B376 (Shepperton Road) and B377 (The Broadway). In his last years Arnold had been living at Cobham, 7 miles SE of Laleham, at the junction of A3 and A245, though his home near the River Mole has gone. Before that he had lived to the north, at Harrow on the Hill. Byron House, his home from 1868 to 1873, is found on Byron Hill Road near the school to which he sent his sons.

Oxford was the most important city in Arnold's life, memorably extolled in the preface to the first series of his *Essays in Criticism*:

> Beautiful city! so venerable, so lovely, so unravaged by the fierce intellectual life of our century, so serene!
>
> There are our young barbarians, all at play! And yet, steeped in sentiment as she lies, spreading her gardens to the moonlight, and whispering from her towers the last enchantments of the Middle Age, who will deny that Oxford, by her ineffable charm, keeps ever calling us nearer to the true goal of all of us, to the ideal, to perfection,—to beauty, in a word, which is only truth seen from another side?—nearer, perhaps, than all the science of Tübingen. Adorable dreamer, whose heart has been so romantic! who hast given thyself so prodigally, given thyself to sides and to heroes not mine, only never to the Philistines! home of lost causes, and forsaken beliefs, and unpopular names, and impossible loyalties!

He was classical scholar at Balliol College from 1841 to 1844, years when the intellectual life of the university was dominated by disputes between his father, Regius Professor of Modern History, and members of the Oxford Movement. Though he won the Newdigate Prize with a poem about Cromwell, Arnold's undergraduate career was marked more by social gaiety than devotion to study; his second-class degree has given consolation and encouragement to poets ever since. In 1845–47 he held a fellowship at Oriel College and in 1857 he was first elected Professor of Poetry.

Two major poems, 'The Scholar-Gipsy' (1853) and 'Thyrsis' (1866), look back to his friendship with Arthur Hugh Clough (q.v.) and the youthful times when he 'shook off all the bonds and formalities of the place, and enjoyed the spring of life and that unforgotten Oxfordshire and Berkshire country.' 'The Scholar-Gipsy,' in particular, 'was meant to fix the remembrance of those delightful wanderings of ours in the Cumner [sic] Hills.' Most of the countryside Arnold wrote about has vanished beneath Oxford's suburban sprawl but the visitor prepared for such change may explore the region by following A420 west from the city centre to Botley and changing at the A34 junction (1½ miles) to the Cumnor Road, which soon crosses what remains of Cumnor Hill. In Arnold's time it was still a suitable spot in which to imagine his lonely scholar gipsy:

> And thou hast climbed the hill
> And gained the white brow of the Cumner range;
> Turned once to watch, while thick the snowflakes fall,
> The line of festal light in Christ-Church hall—
> Then sought thy straw in some sequestered grange.
>
> (lines 126–130)

Bablock Hythe, by the Thames 1½ miles west of Cumnor, was another imagined haunt of Arnold's hero:

> Thee at the ferry Oxford riders blithe,
> Returning home on summer-nights, have met
> Crossing the stripling Thames at Bab-lock-hithe,
> Trailing in the cool stream thy fingers wet,
> As the punt's rope chops round.
>
> (lines 72–75)

Though Oxford and the Thames engrossed Arnold's affection and, indeed, much of his poetic imagination, they were not of course the only centres of his life. From 1828 until his death in 1842 Thomas Arnold was headmaster of the public school at Rugby (on A428 4 miles west of M1 junction 18 and 12 miles east of Coventry). Arnold himself attended the school and served briefly as a master in 1845. The chapel which he made the subject of a famous poem was replaced by Butterfield's building of 1872. Arnold's London home from 1858 to 1868 was in Belgravia at No. 2 Chester Square, now marked by a GLC plaque. It is reached via Eccleston Street from Victoria Station (British Rail; Victoria, District and Circle Lines) and Buckingham Palace Road.

Two locations in Northern England should not be forgotten. The first is Haworth in West Yorkshire, the village described in detail under the entry for the Brontës, where Arnold's poem, 'Haworth Churchyard,' is also considered. The second is in the Lake District, where Thomas Arnold bought Fox How as a holiday home in 1834. From Ambleside at the head of Windermere we follow A591 north until we reach the southern end of Rydal (1½ miles), where a left turn on the Clappersgate road brings us to the foot of Loughrigg Fell and the house after another half mile. Arnold's holidays here brought him into contact with the elderly Wordsworth (s.v. Lake Poets, Rte 12C), then living at Rydal Mount nearby. Both the Arnolds, father and son, are commemorated in Rydal church.

W.H. Auden

b. York, 1907; d. Vienna, Austria, 1973. *Poems* (privately printed; 1928); *The Orators: An English Study* (1932); *The Dance of Death* (1933); *The Dog Beneath the Skin* (with Christopher Isherwood; 1935); *The Ascent of F6* (with Christopher Isherwood; 1936); *Letters from Iceland* (with Louis MacNeice [q.v.]; 1937); *Selected Poems* (1938); *On the Frontier* (with Christopher Isherwood; 1938); *Journey to a War* (with Christopher Isherwood; 1939); *Another Time* (1940); *The Double Man* (1941); *For the Time Being* (1945); *Collected Poetry* (1945); *The Age of Anxiety: A Baroque Eclogue* (1948); *Collected Shorter Poems 1930–1944* (1950); *The Enchafèd Flood: Or the Romantic Iconography of the Sea* (1951); *The Shield of Achilles* (1955); *Homage to Clio* (1960); *The Dyer's Hand and Other Essays* (1963); *About the House* (1965); *Collected Shorter Poems 1927–1957* (1966); *Collected Longer Poems* (1968); *Secondary Worlds* (1968); *City Without Walls* (1969).

Born in York and brought up in Birmingham, Auden was educated at Gresham's School in Holt, 10 miles SW of Cromer on the Norfolk coast. The countryside that made the deepest impression on him as he grew up was that of the Pennines, particularly the fells and moors around Alston in Cumbria (10 miles SE of Brampton via A689). His interest in geology and belief that 'rock creates the only truly human landscape' persisted throughout his life and received fine expression in the poem, 'In Praise of Limestone.'

Auden entered Christ Church, Oxford in 1925, soon changing from Natural Sciences to English (in which his tutor was Nevill Coghill). With his precocious talent for poetry and his wide if unsystematic knowledge, he quickly became an undergraduate celebrity. The poets he gathered round him—Cecil Day-Lewis, Louis MacNeice (qq.v.) and Stephen Spender—were known as 'The Gang'; their abandonment of Oxford aestheticism in favour of harsh, experimental modernity and a growing commitment to left-wing politics set the tone for a generation. Auden's reputation was only a little dented when he was awarded a Third in his exams.

After Oxford he worked as a schoolmaster before embarking on the European and American travels that took him away from England until old age. When he did return it was to Oxford, first as Professor of Poetry (1956–60) and then, in 1972, to live in a cottage in the grounds of Christ Church.

He was buried at Kirchstetten, the Austrian village where he had spent his summers. In 1974 Sir John Betjeman (q.v.), a friend from Auden's undergraduate days, unveiled a memorial stone in Poets' Corner (fee) of Westminster Abbey.

Jane Austen

b. Steventon, Hampshire, 1775; d. Winchester, Hampshire, 1817. *Sense and Sensibility* (1811); *Pride and Prejudice* (1813); *Mansfield Park* (1814); *Emma* (1815); *Northanger Abbey* (1818); *Persuasion* (1818).

An account of Jane Austen can most appropriately begin in South-Western England at **Bath. At a time when the reputation for fashionable gaiety had passed to newer resorts like Brighton and left Bath to enjoy a solidly respectable character Jane Austen made several visits to the city in her youth, lived there after her father's retirement between 1801 and 1806 and made use of it in her novels, especially *Northanger Abbey* and *Persuasion*. Its fictional appearances typify her handling of locales: precise reference to real places abounds (hardly a street or public building in Bath passes without mention of some sort) but the emphasis falls less on physical detail than social atmosphere.

No. 4 Sydney Place, the modest terraced house that was the Austens' main home during their residence in Bath, lies to the east of the city's centre opposite the Holburne Art Museum and is best reached via Pulteney Bridge over the Avon. The other places of interest may be embraced in a single walking tour. We begin in the Paragon, where at No. 1 halfway down Jane Austen lodged during her earlier visits, and walk south to the junction with George Street, which is then followed to the right. Opposite Edgar's Buildings (where Isabella Thorpe in *Northanger Abbey* stayed) the fashionable Milsom Street leads left, bringing us after its pedestrian extension to the Grand Pump Room, built 1792–96 in the classical style. Apart from the Roman Baths it contains the famous gathering place where (to choose but one example from the pages of Jane Austen's fiction) the newly arrived Catherine Morland and Mrs Allen 'paraded up and down for an hour, looking at everybody and speaking to no one' in Chapter 3 of *Northanger Abbey*. From the Grand Pump Room the colonnaded Bath Street leads to Hot Bath Street, which is followed to the left. A right turn at its end takes us past the Elizabethan Hetling House and along James Street West. A left on to Seymour Street brings us to the handsome terrace of Green Park Buildings where, at No. 27, Jane Austen lived in 1804. By returning up Seymour Street, following its continuation as Charles Street and branching right on Chapel Row, we reach the south side of Queen Square, where Jane Austen lodged during an early visit. Leaving the square by its NE corner we take Gay Street (where in 1805 the Austens lived at No. 25) to The Circus. From its right-hand exit we quickly reach the Assembly (or Upper) Rooms, restored to their 18C elegance after the fire of 1942. The ballroom inside was the scene of Catherine Morland's first, disappointing encounter with Bath society in Chapter 2 of *Northanger Abbey* as well as of a later encounter (Ch. 8) with the Thorpes and Henry Tilney. In the Octagon Room, used for concerts, there is a finely handled meeting between Anne Elliot and Captain Wentworth in Chapter 20 of *Persuasion*. The lefthand exit from The Circus leads to Brock Street and the Royal Crescent, Wood's masterpiece of 1769 and a fitting conclusion to the tour.

A visit from Bath to the charming south coastal resort of Lyme Regis, Dorset in 1804 had memorable consequences for her fiction. She gives a fond account of Lyme (which then lacked the royal suffix) and its surrounding area in Chapter 11 of *Persuasion*, her last completed novel. In Chapter 12 her characters venture on to the Cobb, the stone jetty that juts into Lyme Bay, and Louisa Musgrove suffers her famous accident when jumping the steps known as Granny's Teeth from the upper to the lower Cobb. Captain Harville's house, to which she is taken, is popularly identified with Bay Cottage on Marine Parade nearby. The site of Jane Austen's own lodgings, opposite the cottage, has recently been converted into a garden in her memory.

Despite their influence on her fiction the years in South-Western

England were not in themselves productive or entirely happy, being overshadowed by the death of her father in 1805. It was with obvious relief that she returned to South-Eastern England, the territory of her childhood. She had been born at Steventon, a village west of the A30 between Basingstoke and Andover, though the rectory where she grew up was demolished in 1826. She had attended Mrs Latournelle's school in Reading, which occupied the rooms over the gateway of the ruined Abbey in Forbury Road.

On leaving Bath Jane Austen, her sister Cassandra and their widowed mother lived first at a vanished location in Southampton before moving in 1809 to the village of Chawton, 1 mile south of Alton, Hampshire and now mercifully bypassed by A31 to Winchester. In the modest red brick house inevitably renamed *Jane Austen's House she lived until 1817, reworking her early writing into the finely textured novels of her maturity. Much has been made of her limited social environment and cramped domestic circumstances but she herself expressed satisfaction with the place in a doggerel sent to her brother shortly after her arrival:

> Our Chawton Home, how much we find
>   Already in it to our mind;
> And how convinced, that when complete
>   It will all other houses beat
> That ever have been made or mended,
>   With rooms concise or rooms distended.

The 'Chawton Home' is now a museum where visitors may see a fine collection of memorabilia, her bedroom and the livingroom where she wrote, with its creaking door to warn her to hide manuscripts from intruding visitors. The graves of her mother and Cassandra Austen lie in the SE corner of the churchyard of St Nicholas nearby.

Jane Austen was several times a visitor to Great Bookham, Surrey (NE of Chawton and 2 miles SW of Leatherhead) where her cousin Cassandra was wife of the rector Samuel Cooke, who is commemorated in the parish church. Attempts have been made to identify the village with the 'Highbury' of *Emma*. Excursions from Great Bookham to nearby *Box Hill (partly NT), to the east of A24 between Leatherhead and Dorking, had a more certain impact on the novel. In Chapter 43 this fine stretch of down and woodland with its striking views is the object of the expedition organised by Mrs Elton, an occasion marred from the start by 'a languor, a want of spirits, a want of union, which could not be got over.' In the course of the day Frank Churchill flirts with Emma to spite Jane Fairfax while Emma herself is rude to the garrulous Miss Bates, suffers a rebuke from Mr Knightley and makes the journey home in tears.

In Kent Jane Austen stayed at Godmersham Park (by A28 between Canterbury and Ashford), home of her brother Edward, who took the name of his adoptive father, Knight. There is a memorial to him and his wife in the parish church. From the church a lane leads to a public footpath through the park, offering views of the fine 18C house. Her knowledge of it may well have helped the depiction of 'Mansfield Park' in the novel of that title and even of 'Pemberley' in *Pride and Prejudice* (but see note below).

In 1817, already ill with Addison's disease, Jane Austen moved south from Chawton to Winchester. The lodgings where she died later the same year are at No. 8 College Street, a picturesque small house south of the Cathedral Close and adjoining Winchester College.

Her grave is opposite the Wykeham Chantry in the north aisle of the Cathedral nave; above it are a later brass wall plaque and a window in her memory.

A Note on 'Pemberley.' The identity and location of Mr Darcy's estate, which Elizabeth Bennet sees in Chapter 43 of *Pride and Prejudice*, have caused perplexity among Janeites. The visit takes place in the course of Elizabeth's tour through Derbyshire, whose 'celebrated beauties' have been listed in the previous chapter: Matlock, Dovedale and Chatsworth (4 miles NE of Bakewell). The last reference has been taken to rule out the Duke of Devonshire's mansion, but it may well be a deliberate red herring. Chatsworth certainly has the necessary scale and grandeur, though it must be admitted that the description of 'Pemberley,' while effectively making Jane Austen's point about Mr Darcy's taste and good sense, is lacking in salient detail:

> It was a large, handsome, stone building, standing well on rising ground, and backed by a ridge of high woody hills;—and in front, a stream of some natural importance was swelled into greater, but without any artificial appearance. Its banks were neither formal, nor falsely adorned.

Grand Pump Room and Roman Baths, Bath. Open April to Oct daily 9–6; Nov to March, Mon to Sat 9–5, Sun 11–5. Fee.

Assembly Rooms (now Museum of Costume), Bath. Open April to Oct, Mon to Sat 9.30–6, Sun 10–6; Nov to March, Mon to Sat 10–5, Sun 11–5. Fee.

Jane Austen's House, Chawton. Open April to Oct daily 11–4.30; Nov to March, Wed to Sun 11–4.30. Fee.

Chatsworth House. Open end of March to Oct daily, house 11.30–4.30, grounds 11.30–5. Fee.

William Barnes

b. Rush-hay, Dorset, 1801; d. Winterbourne Came, Dorset, 1886. *The Elements of English Grammar, With a Set of Questions and Exercises* (1842); *Poems of Rural Life in the Dorset Dialect, With a Dissertation and Glossary* (1844); *Poems, partly of Rural Life (in National English)* (1846); *A Philological Grammar, Grounded Upon English* (1854); *Views of Labour and Gold* (1859); *Hwomely Rhymes: A Second Collection of Poems in the Dorset Dialect* (1859); *Tiw: Or, A View of the Roots and Stems of the English as a Teutonic Tongue* (1861); *Poems of Rural Life in the Dorset Dialect: Third Collection* (1862); *A Grammar and Glossary of the Dorset Dialect, With the History, Outspreadings and Bearings of South-Western English* (1864); *A Guide to Dorchester* (1864); *Poems of Rural Life in Common English* (1868); *An Outline of English Speech-Craft* (1878).

As his friend Thomas Hardy (q.v.) noted, Barnes was 'emphatically Dorset.' His poetry reproduced its dialect, praised its countryside, recorded its customs and relished its humour. His philological writings, urging the virtues of national purity in language, gave Dorset speech a place of honour for its preservation of Anglo-Saxon forms and preferred it to the polyglot 'Englandish' of standard speech.

He spent his early years at Rush-hay, a 'farmling' 1½ miles W of Sturminster Newton in the Blackmore (or Blackmoor) Vale, a region evoked in the poems 'Rustic Childhood' and 'Our Early Landscape.' Nostalgia for another aspect of the place is expressed in 'Blackmwore Maidens.' The church at Sturminster Newton, where he was baptised, was drastically restored in 1825–27 but has a lectern in his memory. Another church, at Lydlinch 3 miles west on A357, is subject of the lovely 'Lydlinch Bells.'

Only twice did Barnes live outside his native county. From 1823 to 1835 he worked as a schoolmaster in Mere, just over the Wiltshire border on A303. The Tudor Chantry House near the church was his home and school. In 1847 he spent the first of his three terms at St John's College, Cambridge, graduating as a 'ten-year man' in 1850.

Otherwise, his life centred on the county town of Dorchester, where he is today commemorated by a statue outside the church of St Peter. The site is well chosen, as Hardy's obituary of Barnes reminds us:

> Until within the last year or two there were few figures more familiar to the eye in the county town of Dorset on a market day than an aged clergyman, quaintly attired in caped cloak, knee-breeches, and buckled shoes, with a leather satchel slung over his shoulders, and a stout staff in his hand. He seemed usually to prefer the middle of the street to the pavement, and to be thinking of matters which had nothing to do with the scene before him. He plodded along with a broad, firm tread, notwithstanding the slight stoop occasioned by his years. Every Saturday morning he might have been seen thus trudging up the narrow South Street, his shoes coated with mud or dust according to the state of the roads between his rural home and Dorchester, and a little grey dog at his heels, till he reached the four cross ways in the centre of the town. Halting here, opposite the public clock, he would pull his old-fashioned watch from its deep fob, and set it with great precision to London time. This, the invariable first act of his market visit, having been completed to his satisfaction, he turned round and methodically proceeded about his other business.

A plaque marks his house in South Street, next door to the architect's office where the young Hardy worked as assistant.

In 1862 Barnes was appointed Rector of Winterbourne Came. Old Came Rectory, the charming thatched house where he spent his last years, lies off A352 1½ miles SE of Dorchester, a little beyond Hardy's home at Max Gate. An unclassified road leads right from A352 to the church of Winterbourne Came where Barnes was buried. His funeral is finely remembered in Hardy's 'The Last Signal.'

Sir James Barrie

b. Kirriemuir, Tayside Region, 1860; d. London, 1937. *Caught Napping* (1883); *Better Dead* (1888); *Auld Licht Idylls* (1888); *When A Man's Single: A Tale of Literary Life* (1888); *An Edinburgh Eleven: Pencil Portraits From College Life* (1889); *A Window in Thrums* (1889); *My Lady Nicotine* (1890); *The Little Minister* (1891); *Walker, London* (1907); *Sentimental Tommy: The Story of His Boyhood* (1896); *Margaret Ogilvy* (1896); *Tommy and Grizel* (1900); *Quality Street* (1913); *The Admirable Crichton* (1914); *The Little White Bird, or Adventures in Kensington Gardens* (1902); *Peter Pan, or The Boy Who Wouldn't Grow Up* (1928); *Peter Pan in Kensington Gardens* (1906); *What Every Woman Knows* (1928); *Peter and Wendy* (1911); *Dear Brutus* (1928); *Mary Rose: The Island That Wants To Be Visited* (1928); *The Boy David* (1938); *When Wendy Grew Up: An Afterthought* (1957).

Though he is now remembered only as the creator of Peter Pan, Barrie first achieved notice with his sentimental and cynical tales about his hometown of Kirriemuir (16 miles north of Dundee via A929 and A928). 'Thrums,' to give the little manufacturing town its fictional name, appears in *Auld Licht Idylls*, *When A Man's Single*, *A Window in Thrums*, the two novels about Tommy, and Barrie's memoir of his mother, *Margaret Ogilvy*. In Kirriemuir today his birthplace at No. 9 Brechin Road houses a small museum. Visitors may see the wash house at the back where he tried out his first childish attempts at playwriting. In 1872, after two years' absence from Kirriemuir, the Barrie family returned to live in a larger and more comfortable house, Strathview. Barrie married Mary Ansell here in 1894. He was buried near his parents and relatives in the cemetery near the top of the town.

In Glasgow Barrie attended the Academy off Great Western Road near the bridge over the Kelvin. In Edinburgh, 'about the most romantic city on the earth,' he was a student at the University from 1878 to 1882. He was awarded the honorary degree of LL.D. in 1909 and became Chancellor in 1930. His *Edinburgh Eleven* offered a series of light-hearted sketches of famous teachers and former students, including Robert Louis Stevenson (q.v.).

Of Barrie's many return visits to his native Scotland perhaps the most important was in the summer of 1912, when he rented Ahmuinnsuid Castle, a 19C building in the Scottish baronial style, on the west coast of North Harris in the Outer Hebrides. The surrounding landscape influenced *Mary Rose*, in its day one of his most popular plays.

His working life was spent in London. In 1895 he and his wife came to live at No. 133 Gloucester Road in South Kensington, moving in 1901 to Leinster Corner, a Regency house at the corner of Bayswater Road and Leinster Terrace. Kensington Gardens opposite enjoyed a special place in his affections and played an important role in his life. It was here, while walking his dog, that Barrie used to meet the three sons of the charming Sylvia Jocelyn Davies and began to invent stories about Peter Pan. The friendship was strengthened and the fantasy further elaborated during summers in the countryside near Farnham in Surrey, but Barrie paid tribute to the importance of Kensington Gardens by commissioning and paying for the statue of Peter Pan (by Sir George Frampton) that now stands on the western edge of Long Water.

After his divorce in 1909 he moved to No. 3 in the fashionable Adelphi Terrace (since rebuilt), between the Strand and Victoria Embankment Gardens, where he remained until his death.

Barrie Museum, Kirriemuir (NTS). Open 1 May to 30 Sept, Mon to Sat 10–12.30 & 2–6, Sun 2–6. Fee.

Francis Beaumont and John Fletcher

Francis Beaumont: b. Grace Dieu, Leicestershire, 1584; d. London, 1616.

John Fletcher: b. Rye, East Sussex, 1579; d. London, 1625.

Collaborative plays: *The Knight of the Burning Pestle* (1613); *Philaster* (1620); *The Maid's Tragedy* (1619).

The ruins of the family seat where Beaumont was born, Grace Dieu, an Augustinian priory of 1240 with additions after the Beaumonts acquired it in 1539, can be seen in a field by A512 4 miles east of

Ashby-de-la-Zouch. Wordsworth remembered the playwright's connection with the spot when he came here during his visit to Coleorton Hall nearby (s.v. Lake Poets, Rte 7). Beaumont attended Pembroke College (then Broadgates), Oxford and was buried in Poets' Corner (fee) of Westminster Abbey. In fact, his grave near Chaucer and Spenser (qq.v.) is one of the earliest signs that the Abbey reserved a special place for literary men.

Fletcher's birthplace in Rye, between Hastings and Dungeness on the Sussex coast, is popularly identified as the Ancient Rectory in Lion Street; it now bears a plaque. He studied at Corpus Christi College, Cambridge and his residence there is commemorated by the same plaque in *Old Court that mentions Christopher Marlowe (q.v.). Like so many Renaissance dramatists Beaumont and Fletcher lived in Southwark and Fletcher, who died of the plague, was buried in Southwark Cathedral (then St Saviour's), immediately south of London Bridge and at the head of Borough High Street—supposedly in the same grave as his fellow playwright Philip Massinger (q.v.).

William Beckford

b. London? 1760; d. Bath, Avon, 1844. *Vathek, An Arabian Tale* (English translation, probably by Samuel Henley; 1786); *Recollections of an Excursion to the Monasteries of Alcobaća and Batalha* (1835).

When Beckford returned to England in 1796 after a youth and early manhood spent largely on the Continent, he devoted himself to realising in stone the same strain of exotic fantasy already expressed in his novel, *Vathek*. On his estate near Fonthill Bishop, 14 miles west of Salisbury on B3089, Fonthill Abbey grew from the type of Gothick folly by no means uncommon in the age, replaced Beckford's original mansion and became, by its completion in 1812, a monolithic tribute to private obsession: an irregular cruciform dominated by a 225ft octagonal tower, the whole surrounded by rugged landscape in the Romantic manner. Here Beckford lived in an isolation that fed local rumours of his scandalous behaviour, occasionally entertaining distinguished visitors—Turner in 1799, Nelson and Lady Hamilton for an elaborate three-day visit in 1800, and later the poet Samuel Rogers, who appreciated his host's civilised wit, whatever he may have thought of his home.

So eccentric and extravagant an undertaking could not escape problems. The workmen, employed by the hundred and sometimes labouring round the clock, were unalterably fixed in their habit of trimming stone to Palladian smoothness rather than Gothic roughness. The combination of Beckford's eager haste with the love of delay for which his architect, James Wyatt, was notorious created special hazards. The original tower, jerry-built from wood and stucco, fell down in 1797 shortly after its erection while its successor, a timber frame clad in stone, collapsed in 1825. *The Gardener's Magazine* reported:

> Only one man . . . saw it fall. He is said to have described its manner of falling as very beautiful; it first sank perpendicularly and slowly, and then burst and spread over the roofs of the adjoining wings on every side, but rather more on the south-west than others. The cloud of dust which arose

was enormous, and such as completely to darken the air for a considerable distance around for several minutes. Such was the concussion in the interior of the building, that one man was forced along a passage, as if he had been in an air-gun, to the distance of 30ft, among dust so thick as to be felt. Another, on the outside, was in the like manner carried to some distance. Fortunately, no one was seriously injured.

The rest of Fonthill Abbey soon followed the tower into oblivion and today only a fragment of the north wing survives. It stands west of Fonthill Lake on private land in Fonthill Abbey Wood, Fonthill Gifford, 2 miles south of B3089.

By the time of these disasters Beckford's extravagance had already forced him to sell the building. Its collection of curios and paintings was auctioned in 1823. Somewhat surprisingly, he had chosen to live in Bath, where he indulged a minor version of the same itch to build and expand that had created Fonthill. He first bought No. 20 Lansdown Crescent, north of the Royal Crescent, but soon added Nos 18 and 19 and No. 1 Lansdown Place West, which faced No. 20 across a mews entrance. A connecting bridge was built by H.E. Goodridge, the Bath architect who also remodelled the interiors. On Lansdown Hill behind the Crescent, a hill which Beckford lovingly landscaped, Goodridge also constructed a restrained tower in the classical manner. Now usually known as *Beckford's Tower, it houses

Fonthill Abbey from the north west, by John Martin. From John Rutter, Delineations of Fonthill and its Abbey *(1823). Courtesy of Cambridge University Library*

a small collection of memorabilia and has a fine view from the top. When Lansdown Hill was consecrated in 1848 Beckford's tomb was moved from its original resting place in the Abbey to a spot near the foot of his Tower.

Beckford's Tower, Bath. Open 1 April to 28 Oct, Sat, Sun & BH Mon 2–5. Fee.

Sir Max Beerbohm

b. London, 1872; d. Rapallo, Italy, 1956. *The Works of Max Beerbohm* (1896); *The Happy Hypocrite: A Fairy Tale For Tired Men* (1897); *More* (1899); *Yet Again* (1909); *Zuleika Dobson: or An Oxford Love Story* (1911); *A Christmas Garland, Woven by Beerbohm* (1912); *Seven Men* (1919); *And Even Now* (1920).

The writer and caricaturist was born in London at No. 57 Palace Gardens Terrace, which leads south from Notting Hill Gate towards Kensington High Street. He was sent to school at Charterhouse, which had moved in 1872 from its old site in the City to its present buildings in Godalming, by A3100 4 miles SW of Guildford, Surrey. His temperament was not suited to public-school life and he later remarked: 'My delight in having been at Charterhouse was far greater than my delight in being there.' He found a much more congenial environment when he entered Merton College, Oxford in 1890 and took rooms in its medieval Mob Quad. His undergraduate years coincided with the zenith in popularity of the Aesthetic Movement, represented locally by Walter Pater (q.v.) at Brasenose and in London by the circle surrounding Oscar Wilde (q.v.), whom Beerbohm soon met. He did little work at Merton, preferring to draw caricatures of the dons than to write essays for them, and left in 1894 without taking his exams. In *Zuleika Dobson*, a characteristic blend of fantasy and irony, he paid elegant tribute to the university; Merton has returned the compliment by devoting a room leading off its magnificent Library to Beerbohm memorabilia.

After leaving Oxford Beerbohm led a relentlessly social life in London and developed a wide circle of acquaintance among writers. His visits to the elderly Swinburne (q.v.) in Putney were captured in a memorable essay. On his marriage in 1910 he moved to Italy, where he spent the rest of his life except for a return to England during World War Two. His ashes were buried in the crypt of St Paul's Cathedral.

Beerbohm Room, Old Library, Merton College, Oxford. Open Mon to Sat 2–4. Closed Easter and Christmas. Fee.

Crypt, St Paul's Cathedral. Open Mon to Fri 10–3.15 (4.15 in summer), Sat 11–3.15 (4.15 in summer). Entrance may be restricted during special services. Fee.

Hilaire Belloc

b. St Cloud, France, 1870; d. Guildford, Surrey, 1953. *Verses and Sonnets* (1896); *The Bad Child's Book of Beasts* (1896); *A Moral Alphabet* (1899); *Danton* (1899); *Paris* (1900); *Robespierre* (1901); *The Path to Rome* (1902); *The Old Road* (1904); *Emmanuel Burden* (1904); *The Historic Thames* (1907); *Mr Clutterbuck's Election* (1908); *Cautionary Tales For Children: Designed For the Admonition of Children Between the Ages of Eight and Fourteen Years* (1908); *Marie Antoinette* (1909); *Pongo and the Bull* (1910); *The French Revolution* (1911); *British Battles* (1911–13); *The Servile State* (1912); *The Four Men* (1912); *The Jews* (1922); *Sonnets and Verses* (1923); *A History of England* (1925–31); *Oliver Cromwell* (1927); *James the Second* (1928); *Belinda: A Tale of Affection in Youth and Age* (1928); *The Chanty of the Nona* (1928); *How the Reformation Happened* (1928); *Joan of Arc* (1929); *Richelieu* (1929); *New Cautionary Tales* (1930); *Wolsey* (1930); *The Praise of Wine: An Heroic Poem* (1930); *Cranmer* (1931); *Napoleon* (1932); *Charles the First, King of England* (1933); *Return to the Baltic* (1938); *The Last Rally: A Study of Charles II* (1939).

Belloc was educated at the school attached to St Philip Neri, the Roman Catholic Oratory founded by Cardinal Newman in Birmingham. The Oratory itself remains on the Hagley Road in the SW suburb of Edgbaston, though the school has since moved to Goring-on-Thames.

The years between school and university were lively but unsettled. Belloc worked his way across America to California in pursuit of Elodie Hogan, whom he later married, and returned to France, the country he had left when his French father died in 1872, to serve briefly in its navy and for a year in its army. Such experiences made him a notable figure among undergraduates when he entered Balliol College, Oxford in 1893. His rooms were on the ground floor of Staircase 3, almost opposite the main Porter's Lodge. On the surface his undergraduate career was distinguished: his eloquence won him the Presidency of the Oxford Union, and he achieved a First in his examinations. Yet he did not gain the Fellowship at All Souls which he coveted and remained in Oxford after graduation only as a private coach and lecturer for the University Extension. He dwelt with obsessive bitterness on this academic rebuff in later life when financial problems forced him to write pot-boiling historical biographies.

By 1900 Belloc, now married to Elodie, had moved to London. They lived by the river in Chelsea at No. 104 Cheyne Walk, marked with a GLC plaque. In the early years of his literary success he was a close friend and constant companion of G.K. Chesterton (q.v.); the two writers were a familiar pair in the pubs and restaurants of Fleet Street.

Part of Belloc's childhood had been spent in Sussex and in 1906 he moved to Shipley (off B2224 6 miles SW of Horsham). King's Land, a house dating back to the 15C, remained his home for the rest of his life and the surrounding countryside was often celebrated in the aggressively open-necked, beery verses that were his special metier:

> On Sussex hills where I was bred,
> When lanes in autumn rains are red,
> When Arun tumbles in his bed,
>   And busy great gusts go by;
> When branch is bare in Burton Glen
> And Bury Hill is a-whitening, then,
> I drink strong ale with gentlemen;

Which nobody can deny, deny,
    Deny, deny, deny, deny,
Which nobody can deny!
            ('The First Drinking Song' in *The Four Men*)

The reality of his life at Shipley was rather less than vigorously cheerful. Elodie died in 1914 and Belloc afterwards permanently wore mourning clothes, sealed up her room and never passed its door without crossing himself. The pathetic, even grotesque, quality of his old age was intensified after he suffered a disabling stroke in 1942. The 19C smock mill which formed part of Belloc's estate at King's Land has been restored to working order and contains a small museum devoted to him. He was buried with his wife and son in the Roman Catholic churchyard at West Grinstead, by A24 3 miles SE of Shipley.

Belloc Mill, Shipley. Open May to Oct, first weekend in each month and Easter & Aug BH 2.30–5.30. Fee.

Arnold Bennett

b. Hanley, Staffordshire, 1867; d. London, 1931. *A Man from the North* (1898); *The Grand Babylon Hotel: A Fantasia on Modern Themes* (1902); *Anna of the Five Towns* (1902); *The Gates of Wrath: A Melodrama* (1903); *Leonora* (1903); *A Great Man: A Frolic* (1904); *Teresa of Watling Street* (1904); *Tales of the Five Towns* (1905); *The Loot of Cities* (1905); *Sacred and Profane Love* (1905); *Hugo* (1906); *Whom God Hath Joined* (1906); *The Sinews of War* (1906); *The Grim Smile of the Five Towns* (1907); *The City of Pleasure* (1907); *The Statue* (1908); *Buried Alive* (1908); *The Old Wives' Tale* (1908); *The Glimpse: An Adventure of the Soul* (1909); *Helen with the High Hand: An Idyllic Diversion* (1910); *Clayhanger* (1910); *The Card: A Story of Adventure in the Five Towns* (1911); *Hilda Lessways* (1911); *The Matador of the Five Towns, and Other Stories* (1912); *The Regent: A Five Towns Story of Adventure in London* (1913); *The Price of Love* (1914); *These Twain* (1915); *The Lion's Share* (1916); *The Pretty Lady* (1918); *The Roll-Call* (1918); *Mr Prohack* (1922); *Lilian* (1922); *Riceyman Steps* (1923); *Elsie and the Child* (1924); *Lord Raingo* (1926); *The Strange Vanguard: A Fantasia* (1928); *The Woman Who Stole Everything, and Other Stories* (1927); *Accident* (1929); *Imperial Palace* (1930); *The Night Visitor, and Other Stories* (1931).

Bennett was born in The Potteries, the cluster of industrial towns absorbed since 1910 into the single borough of Stoke-upon-Trent (between Manchester and Birmingham on A34, and east of M6). Though he left when he was 22, returning only for visits to relatives, the region became the setting for many of his novels and stories, including books that rank among his finest achievements: *Anna of the Five Towns*, *The Old Wives' Tale* and the *Clayhanger* trilogy. The six pottery towns are reduced (by the omission of Fenton) to the 'Five Towns,' a label that has stuck despite its inaccuracy, Stoke being renamed 'Knype,' Hanley 'Hanbridge,' Burslem 'Bursley', Tunstall 'Turnhill' and Longton 'Longshaw'. This might seem reminiscent of the way his older contemporary Hardy (q.v.) created 'Wessex' out of Dorset and its bordering counties, but in fact Bennett's work looks forward in spirit to Lawrence and Joyce (qq.v.), younger contemporaries whom he generously praised. Like them, Bennett wrote not as a loyal native but as a determined exile—a man who, when he had made his escape, could look back on the world of his youth and find there an interest, even a sort of poetry, to which he had earlier been oblivious.

In the unlovely landscape of The Potteries Bennett detected a 'grim and original beauty.' The first chapter of *Anna of the Five Towns* elaborates the point and gives the reader a panoramic view of the area:

> Five contiguous towns—Turnhill, Bursley, Hanbridge, Knype and Longshaw—united by a single winding thoroughfare some eight miles in length, have inundated the valley like a succession of great lakes. Of these five Bursley is the mother, but Hanbridge is the largest. They are mean and forbidding of aspect—sombre, hard-featured, uncouth; and the vaporous poison of their ovens and chimneys has soiled and shrivelled the surrounding country till there is no village lane within a league but what offers a gaunt and ludicrous travesty of rural charms. Nothing could be more prosaic than the huddled red-brown streets; nothing more seemingly remote from romance. Yet be it said that romance is even here—the romance which, for those who have an eye to perceive it, ever dwells amid the seats of industrial manufacture, softening the coarseness, transfiguring the squalor, of these mighty alchemic operations. Look down into the valley . . ., embrace the whole smoke-girt amphitheatre in a glance, and it may be that you will suddenly comprehend the secret and superb significance of the vast Doing which goes forward below.

In the years since these words were written The Potteries first sank into economic decline and then, recently, emerged into a phase of urban redevelopment. Spoil heaps have been grassed and planted over; the distinctive smoke stacks and bottle kilns have all but disappeared; and, thanks to the Clean Air Act and the introduction of electric firing, the smoke has dispersed. As a result, surviving local scenes connected with Bennett or redolent of his work are relatively few, and the chief ones may be comprised within a single tour of about 3 miles.

It begins in the northern part of Hanley on Hope Street, where the site of the novelist's birthplace at the junction with Hanover Street is marked by a plaque. The neighbourhood was and remains undistinguished: trained as a master potter, Bennett's father was then working unsuccessfully as a draper and pawnbroker. By following Hope Street north toward Burslem we come to Waterloo Road and No. 205, the house Bennett's father built for himself in 1879 after he had finally qualified as a solicitor. Standing on the right just beyond the turning for Rushton Road, the solid red-brick building expresses the social change achieved by the family during the writer's childhood. They had risen from shabby, struggling respectability to middle-class affluence, and it is no surprise that Bennett the novelist should be master of the everyday details which distinguish the two ways of life.

To the north lies the *centre of Burslem, one of the few areas to retain much of the character it had in Bennett's day. It still displays that mixture of coarseness and sophistication, grimness and exuberance which is the hallmark of the Victorian provincial town. From Waterloo Road we turn left on Queen Street and find on our right the Wedgwood Institute, now housing the Public Library and an annexe to the College of Further Education but in the 19C home of the Endowed School which Bennett attended (1877–80). The building's exterior is a remarkable tribute to Burslem's pride in its ceramics. At the end of Queen Street we enter St John's Square, where Bennett's grandparents ran a shop. It is the 'St Luke's Square' of *The Old Wives' Tale* and other novels. A right on Market Place takes us past the Old Town Hall, and by continuing straight ahead we come to Moorland Road, which leads after about a mile to Burslem Cemetery. An obelisk marks the place where the writer's ashes are buried in the family grave.

Arnold Bennett's dining room at Cadogan Square. From 'The London House of Mr Arnold Bennett,' Vogue (September 1924). Courtesy of Vogue

Bennett left The Potteries for London in 1887, soon abandoning his uncongenial work in a solicitor's office for journalism and literature. In 1900, his career as a novelist already launched, he moved to the country—a curious decision for a man so thoroughly urban in his sympathies. Also curious was his choice of Trinity Hall Farm in Hockliffe (on A5 in Bedfordshire at the junction with A4012 for Leighton Buzzard) for, though the house itself is handsome, the village has nothing to recommend it except its position on the ancient

Watling Street. This historic connection prompted Bennett to write the unsuccessful *Teresa of Watling Street*. From 1902 until 1912 he lived in France, returning with a French wife and a yacht, the latter proving an irresistible target to the younger generation of writers who regarded his conspicuously affluent lifestyle as vulgar. His choice of an English home cannot be faulted on the same grounds. Comarques in the village of Thorpe-le-Soken (12 miles east of Colchester, near the Essex coast) is a delightful Queen Anne building.

Bennett's later years were spent in London. After separating from his wife Marguerite he moved in 1922 to No. 75 Cadogan Square (south of Pont Street in Chelsea). Modestly calling it 'a rather fine thing in houses,' he brought all his enthusiasm for plumbing and his taste for opulence to its interior furnishing. In 1930, shortly before his death from typhoid, he moved to a flat in the modern Chiltern Court at the junction of Baker Street and Marylebone Road. His old friend H.G. Wells (q.v.) was a neighbour.

Sir John Betjeman

b. London, 1906; d. Trebetherick, Cornwall, 1984. *Mount Zion* (1932); *Ghastly Good Taste* (1933); *Cornwall* (Shell Guide; 1934); *Devon* (Shell Guide; 1936); *Continual Dew* (1937); *An Oxford University Chest* (1938); *Old Lights for New Chancels* (1940); *Vintage London* (1942); *English Cities and Small Towns* (1943); *Slick, But Not Streamlined* (1947); *Murray's Buckinghamshire Architectural Guide* (with John Piper; 1948); *Murray's Berkshire Architectural Guide* (with John Piper; 1949); *Shropshire* (Shell Guide, with John Piper; 1951); *First and Last Loves* (1952); *A Few Late Chrysanthemums* (1954); *Poems in the Porch* (1954); *Collected Poems* (1958); *Collins Guide to English Parish Churches* (1958); *Summoned by Bells* (1960); *English Churches* (with B. Clarke; 1964); *The City of London Churches* (1965); *High and Low* (1966); *Victorian and Edwardian London from Old Photographs* (1969); *Victorian and Edwardian Oxford from Old Photographs* (with David Vaisey; 1971); *London's Historic Railway Stations* (1972); *Victorian and Edwardian Brighton from Old Photographs* (1972); *West Country Churches* (1973); *A Nip in the Air* (1974); *Archie and the Strict Baptists* (1977); *Church Poems* (1981); *Uncollected Poems* (1982).

'I cannot say how shock'd I am to see/ The *variations* in our scenery,' complains the speaker in 'The Town Clerk's Views' (lines 11–12) and he, of course, is the very antithesis of Betjeman himself, that vigorous opponent of civic uniformity. Probably no other contemporary writer has shown so highly developed and so catholic a sense of place; if we cannot speak of 'Betjeman Country' this is because so few aspects of the English scene escaped his attention, whether as poet, guidebook writer, defender of the architectural heritage or, in his last years, television personality. Rural parish churches, seaside piers, railway stations, Edwardian suburbs, even motorways all caught the eye of a man whose enthusiasm was backed by scholarly knowledge and whose distaste for the modern was tempered by humour and sympathy.

He was born and brought up in north London's Highgate, an area that did much to shape his taste in townscapes. Chapter 1 of his autobiographical poem *Summoned by Bells* remembers his childhood home on West Hill, which leads SW from the top of Highgate High Street. A lifelong love of Victoriana was encouraged by nearby Highgate Cemetery, south of West Hill and entered from Swains

Lane. Family worship is remembered in the poem 'St Saviour's, Aberdeen Park, Highbury, London N.' The Victorian church lies off Highbury Grove, SE of Highgate.

In central London the Euston Road is an appropriate spot for recalling Betjeman's role as champion of our Victorian heritage. He defended St Pancras Station (British Rail, and Piccadilly, Victoria, Northern, Metropolitan and Circle Lines) against criticism and threat but failed to save Euston Station and its classical entrance arch, to the west, from ill-conceived modernisation in 1963–68. By continuing along Euston Road and its extension as Marylebone Road we come to Baker Street Underground Station, where the Metropolitan Line leads NW through the suburbs celebrated as 'Metro-Land' in a successful 1973 TV programme.

Betjeman's support for the restoration fund at St Mary-le-Strand is a reminder that his love of buildings by no means stopped with the 19C. James Gibbs' lovely 18C church stands in the middle of the Strand by the junction with Aldwych.

In Wiltshire the poet attended Marlborough College. Chapter 7 of *Summoned by Bells* describes his unhappiness at school, where his contemporary Louis MacNeice (q.v.) remembered him as looking like 'a will-o'-the-wisp with Latin blood in it' and being 'a mine of useless information and a triumphant misfit.' From Marlborough he went to the more congenial Magdalen College, Oxford, though he was on bad terms with his tutor, C.S. Lewis, and left without a degree in 1928 after failing his qualifying exam in Divinity—an odd result for someone whose later work bears such frequent witness to his devout Anglicanism. Before his departure from Oxford Betjeman came into contact with the group of young poets led by W.H. Auden (q.v.), but his customary friends were the latter-day Aesthetes flamboyantly led by Harold Acton.

His connection with Cornwall, subject of his first guidebook, began in childhood; it is described in Chapters 4 and 8 of *Summoned by Bells*. In adult life he took a summer home on the north coast at Trebetherick (off B3314 13 miles NW of Bodmin). He was buried just south of the village at the little Norman church of St Enodoc, dug out from encroaching sands in 1863 and now stranded in the middle of a golf course. It is the setting for two poems, 'Sunday Afternoon Service in St Enodoc Church, Cornwall' and 'By the Ninth Green, St Enodoc.'

Highgate Cemetery. Tours leave from Swains Lane daily on the hour, Apr to Sept 10–4, Oct to March 10–3.

R.D. Blackmore

b. Longworth, Oxfordshire, 1825; d. London, 1900. *The Fate of Franklin* (1860); *Clara Vaughan* (1864); *Cradock Nowell: A Tale of the New Forest* (1866); *Lorna Doone: A Romance of Exmoor* (1869); *The Maid of Sker* (1872); *Alice Lorraine: A Tale of the South Downs* (1875); *Cripps the Carrier: A Woodland Tale* (1876); *Erema: or My Father's Sin* (1877); *Mary Anerley: A Yorkshire Tale* (1880); *Christowell: A Dartmoor Tale* (1882); *The Remarkable History of Sir Thomas Upmore Bart MP, Formerly Known As 'Tommy Upmore'* (1884); *Springhaven: A Tale of the Great War* (1887); *Kit and Kitty: A Story of West Middlesex* (1890); *Perlycross: A Tale of the Western Hills* (1894); *Fringilla: A Tale in Verse* (1895); *Dariel: A Romance of Surrey* (1897).

Most of Blackmore's adult life was passed in Teddington, then a separate and rural village but now completely absorbed into the suburbs of SW London, where he divided his days between writing and market-gardening. Gomer House, which he bought in 1860, has gone and his long residence there is remembered only by a cluster of street names between Teddington's High Street and Station Road. Yet Blackmore's real loyalty was always to South-Western England and in old age he could still insist: 'In everything, except the accident of birth, I am Devonian; my ancestry were all Devonians; my sympathies and feelings are all Devonian.' He lived in Devon from the age of six to eighteen and permanently identified himself with the county in the popular mind by his most successful novel, *Lorna Doone*. His 'Romance of Exmoor' endowed it with a romantic, literary charm that helped attract visitors whose interest in the north Devon coast had already been stimulated by Charles Kingsley (q.v.) in *Westward Ho!*.

The scenes of Blackmore's childhood and *Lorna Doone* may be encompassed in a tour of some 62 miles beginning in the area round Tiverton, at the junction of A396 and A373 in east Devon. In 1826 his widowed father became curate of Culmstock, 10 miles east of the town via A373 and B3391, and after his remarriage in 1831 was joined by his son. Blackmore created 'Perlycross,' setting for one of his minor novels, from memories of the village and the Blackdown Hills which rise to its NE. By the river in Tiverton itself we find the picturesque old building of Blundell's School (NT), founded in 1604. Drawing on his own schooldays here, Blackmore made Blundell's famous in the opening pages of *Lorna Doone*. In Chapter 2 John Ridd fights Robin Snell on the 'Ironing Box,' a little triangle of turf reserved by the boys for such contests.

We strike NW from Tiverton on B3221, changing to A361 after 14 miles and again to B3226 2 miles beyond South Molton. After another 3 miles, when we have just crossed the River Bray, a sideroad leads left to the village of Charles, where the young Blackmore stayed at the Rectory with his uncle, 'an ancient parson of the North Devon type.' His visits are remembered by a tablet in the church, a building radically changed in the late 19C. Returning to B3226 we continue a further 8 miles north to Blackmoor Gate, which marks the western boundary of what is now the Exmoor National Park. At this point A399 leads NW to Combe Martin (4 miles), one of several parishes where Blackmore's grandfather held the living. The village owes its present popularity with tourists more to its natural setting than its untidy sprawl of buildings, though the church is distinguished by a fine spire.

From Blackmoor Gate our main route enters Exmoor via A39. Just beyond the boundary with Somerset at County Gate a sideroad (12 miles) leads right to Oare. Blackmore knew the village well in his boyhood since it was another of his grandfather's livings, and in *Lorna Doone* made it the home of John Ridd. The little church is the scene of Lorna's murder by Carver Doone on her wedding day (Ch. 74). Its interior was changed in the mid 19C when the chancel was extended.

Malmshead, half a mile west of Oare, gives access to the countryside of the Doones, the savage clan whom Blackmore developed from 17C legends into the main dramatic interest of his story. By 1887 curiosity had brought enough visitors here for Baedeker's *Handbook for Travellers in Great Britain* to offer a warning: 'Readers of *Lorna Doone* will be disappointed if they expect to find a close resemblance between the descriptions of the book and the actual facts of nature.' The novelist, who had been shown this passage before it appeared, conceded its justice in a private letter to the guidebook's editor, James Muirhead: 'If I had dreamed that it would ever be more than a book of the moment, the descriptions of scenery—which I know as well as I know my garden—would have been kept nearer to their fact. I romanced therein not to mislead any other, but solely for the uses of my story.' With this caution in mind we walk south from Malmshead on a track that quickly becomes a footpath following the course of Badgworthy Water. After a mile we pass a memorial erected by Blackmore's admirers in 1969, the centenary of the book's publication. The stream leading to the right has been identified with the 'slide of water' up which John Ridd struggles in Chapter 7. A further ½ mile brings us to the opening of the Doone Valley (right), as it is now known, a pleasant stretch of countryside and worth the walk but altogether milder than the scene described by Blackmore: 'a deep green valley, carved from out the mountains in a perfect oval, with a fence of sheer rock standing round it, eighty feet or a hundred high; from whose brink black wooded hills swept up to the sky-line' (Ch. 4).

Blackmore's minor novels, eclipsed to his great annoyance by the success of *Lorna Doone*, often make similar use of places with which he had been familiar since boyhood. *The Maid of Sker* has as its setting the Elizabethan Sker House on the south Welsh coast NW of Porthcawl, near the home of his mother's family. Oxford is the centre of another area he knew well. He was born in the pleasant village of Longworth, 12 miles SW of the city and north of A420, where his father was curate-in-charge. The Old Rectory, part 16C and part Georgian, still stands. Though his mother's death took him away from Longworth when he was four months old he returned to stay with relatives at Elsfield, 5 miles north of Oxford on a sideroad leading from A40. *Cripps the Carrier* is partly set in Beckley, 2 miles NE of Elsfield beyond B4027. The rest of the novel takes place in Oxford and includes a brief description of the May morning service held on the tower of Magdalen College (Vol. 2, Ch. 14). Blackmore was an undergraduate at Exeter College (1843–47).

His poem *The Fate of Franklin* was written to help the erection of the statue in memory of the Arctic explorer (d. 1847) which now stands in the market place of Spilsby, at the junction of A16 and A1115 in Lincolnshire.

William Blake

b. London, 1757; d. London, 1827. *Poetical Sketches* (1783); *Songs of Innocence* (1789); *The Book of Thel* (1789); *The Marriage of Heaven and Hell* (1790); *Visions of the Daughters of Albion* (1793); *America: A Prophecy* (1793); *Songs of Experience* (1794); *Europe: A Prophecy* (1794); *The First Book of Urizen* (1794); *The Song of Los* (1795); *The Book of Los* (1795); *The Book of Ahania* (1795); *The Ghost of Abel* (1822).

London, evoked so powerfully in one of the best known *Songs of Experience*, now offers only scattered and fragmentary reminders of

Blake's near-lifetime residence. He was baptised in Wren's St James's Church, rebuilt after bomb damage, on Jermyn Street south of Piccadilly. In Soho to the north a plaque by the junction of Broadwick (then Broad) Street and Marshall Street marks the site of his birthplace. Blake returned to the neighbourhood later in life, living on Poland Street (1785–91) and holding an 1810 exhibition of his engravings on Carnaby Street. His apprenticeship (1771–81), when he was already displaying all the characteristics of the eccentric prodigy, was served under the engraver James Basire in Great Queen Street, which continues Long Acre to the junction with Kingsway. His marriage in 1782 to Catherine Boucher, a solid and tolerant companion, took place south of the river in St Mary's, Battersea, reached by a right turn on Battersea Church Road after crossing Battersea Bridge. His last years were spent in the charming little Fountain Court, entered via Middle Temple Lane from the Strand near its junction with Fleet Street. When he visited Blake here the diarist Crabb Robinson found him

> at work engraving in a small bedroom, light, and looking out on a mean yard. Everything in the room squalid and indicating poverty, except himself. And there was a natural gentility about him, and an insensibility to the seeming poverty, which quite removed the impression. Besides, his linen was clean, his hand white, and his air quite unembarrassed when he begged me to sit down as if he were in a palace.

He is buried in the Nonconformist cemetery at Bunhill Fields, bounded by City Road and Bunhill Row in Finsbury. There is a memorial in the crypt of St Paul's Cathedral, whose 'high dome' witnessed the charity service in 'Holy Thursday,' one of his *Songs of Innocence*. A bust by Epstein remembers him in Poets' Corner (fee) of Westminster Abbey, a building whose monuments he sketched as part of his training in Gothic when an apprentice.

The one, brief period of Blake's life outside London was eventful. From 1800 to 1803 he accepted the invitation of William Hayley, mediocre poet but a good patron, to live in Felpham, now a suburb of Bognor Regis on the Sussex coast. His home here has since been re-named Blake's House. The stay came to an end when Blake turned a soldier out of his garden and provoked a charge of sedition. In 1804 he was tried and acquitted at nearby Chichester, in Grey Friars' Church in Priory Park; the medieval building is now the Guildhall Museum.

Bunhill Fields. Open Mon to Fri 7.30–4, Sat & Sun 9.30–4.

Crypt, St Paul's Cathedral. Open Mon to Fri 10–3.15 (4.15 in summer), Sat 11–3.15 (4.15 in summer). Entrance may be restricted during special services. Fee.

Guildhall Museum, Chichester. Open June to Sept, Tues to Sat 1–5.

George Borrow

b. Dumpling Green, Norfolk, 1813; d. Oulton Broad, Suffolk, 1881. *The Zincali: or An Account of the Gypsies in Spain* (1841); *The Bible in Spain: or The Journeys, Adventures and Imprisonments of an Englishman in an Attempt to Circulate the Scriptures in the Peninsula* (1843); *Lavengro, the Scholar, the*

Gypsy, the Priest (1851); *The Romany Rye: A Sequel to Lavengro* (1857); *Wild Wales: Its People, Language and Scenery* (1862).

Borrow's life was itinerant, in childhood because of his father's different military postings and in adulthood because of the temperament that led him to seek 'roving adventure, becoming tinker, gypsy, postillion, ostler; associating with various kinds of people, chiefly of the lower classes' (Ch. 1 of the Appendix to *Romany Rye*). His real homeland, if the term retains any meaning in his case, was Eastern England. Despite his statement at the beginning of *Lavengro*, he seems to have been born not in East Dereham (16 miles west of Norwich via A47) but in Dumpling Green, a little village 1½ miles SE on B1135 where his mother's family lived. East Dereham, however, was certainly the home of his early years and he returned to it several times in the course of his childhood. *Lavengro* remembers it with special affection: 'I love to think on thee, pretty, quiet D——, thou pattern of an English county town, with thy clean but narrow streets branching out from thy modest market-place, with thine old-fashioned houses, with here and there a roof of venerable thatch' (Ch. 3). The town might now cause Borrow to modify this glowing praise a little but remains proud of its connection with William Cowper (q.v.), whom he revered as 'England's sweetest and most pious bard' (Ch. 3).

In 1810 the Borrows moved west to the camp for French prisoners from the Napoleonic Wars at Norman Cross, now marked by a dreary roundabout on the A1 south of Peterborough. Chapter 4 of *Lavengro* gives a fascinating account of the barracks and Chapter 5 describes his first encounter with gipsies in the nearby countryside. In 1813 the family came to Edinburgh, where they were quartered in the Castle. Borrow followed in the footsteps of Sir Walter Scott (q.v.) and became a pupil at the Royal High School, whose old building still stands on Regent Road by Calton Hill:

> High School!—called so, I scarcely know why; neither lofty in structure of tawny stone, with many windows fenced with iron netting—with thy long hall below, and thy five chambers above, for the reception of the five classes, into which the eight hundred urchins, who styled thee instructress, were divided. (*Lavengro*, Ch. 4)

Borrow's boyhood travels were completed by a brief spell in Ireland, a country that stimulated three of his greatest interests: horses, foreign languages and old buildings. At Templemore (11 miles south of Roscrea on N62 in Tipperary) he was struck by the profusion of ruined castles in the 'wild and thinly inhabited country.' Templemore itself has one, built by the Knights Templar, in its Priory Park and Chapter 11 of *Lavengro* describes an adventurous walk to, apparently, the ruins of Loughmoe Castle (15C–17C), left of N62 4 miles south.

By 1816 the Borrows had returned to Eastern England and settled permanently in Norwich. *Lavengro* praises it as a 'fine old city, perhaps the most curious specimen at present extant of the genuine old English town,' a claim that could still be advanced today, and offers this panoramic description of its antiquities:

> Yes, there it spreads from north to south, with its venerable houses, its numerous gardens, its thrice twelve churches, its mighty mound, which, if tradition speaks true, was raised by human hands to serve as the grave heap of an old heathen king, who sits deep within it, with his sword in his hand and his gold and silver treasures about him. There is an old grey castle on top of that mighty mound; and yonder, rising three hundred feet

above the soil, from among those noble forest trees, behold that old Norman master-work, that cloud-encircled cathedral spire around which a garrulous army of rooks and choughs continually wheel their flight. Now, who can wonder that the children of that fine old city are proud of her, and offer up prayers for her prosperity? (Ch. 14)

Borrow attended the Grammar School in the Cathedral Close during the years when 'Old Crome,' the Norwich painter, was a drawing instructor. The family home stands on Willow Lane, reached by following Giles Street west from the Market Place. At the Tombland Easter Fair, then held on open ground south of the Castle, he again met the gipsy whom he called 'Jasper Petulengro' (Ch. 16) and went with him to visit the gipsy encampment on Mousehold Heath, NE of the city centre and reached via Magdalen Street and Sprowston Road (Ch. 17).

Borrow left Norwich in 1824, first to work as a hack writer in London and then to embark on the nomadic adventures in England and abroad which his books celebrate in romantic fashion. His habit of exaggeration, reticence about exact locations and waywardness with dates all make it difficult to deduce an itinerary from his writings, but two places described in *Romany Rye* stand out. In 1825 Borrow came to the pleasant county town of Stafford (by M6 25 miles NW of Birmingham) and worked as head ostler at the Swan Inn on Greengate Street—'a place of infinite life and bustle' (Chs 23–29). He left the Swan when he discovered that 'there was little poetry in keeping an account of the corn, hay and straw which came in, and was given out, and I was fond of poetry.' Later the same year he arrived at Horncastle in Lincolnshire (21 miles east of Lincoln on A158) for the August horse fair (Ch. 37) and correctly decided that the town 'offered no object worthy of attention but its church.' Chapter 43 of *Romany Rye* has an amusing account of a tour of the building with a guide who is more interested in horses than architecture but remembers to point out the scythe blades traditionally said to have been used against Cromwell's army at the Battle of Winceby.

After his marriage in 1840 Borrow gravitated again to Eastern England and his wife's home at Oulton Broad near the Suffolk coast 2 miles west of Lowestoft. The house where he wrote most of his books and lived intermittently until death has gone, though his presence in the area is remembered in the church at Oulton, 1 mile north. In 1853–55 he took lodgings in the seaside resort of Great Yarmouth (8 miles north of Lowestoft via A12). *Romany Rye* was finished at No. 169 King Street.

Of his later travels the most important is his sixteen-week visit to Wales in the autumn of 1854, partly a tour with his wife and stepdaughter Henrietta and partly a series of solitary walking expeditions. Its best record is his own *Wild Wales*. The book is still an excellent traveller's companion, being unusual among Borrow's British books for its precise itinerary and unusual among books about Wales for its passionate—though at times uncritical and unscholarly—interest in Welsh language, literature and history.

A few highlights from Borrow's journey may be selected. He began his tour of north Wales at Wrexham (10 miles SW of Chester via A483), 'a Welsh town, but its appearance is not Welsh' (Ch. 5). He praised the fine exterior of the church of St Giles, the main interest of the town for visitors, but was unimpressed by its interior. Llangollen (9 miles SW of Wrexham via A483 and A5) served as a base for various expeditions. He seems to have been disappointed by Plas Newydd (south of A5), for his account in Chapter 10 is sketchy, but on his return to the area he records local memories of the eccentric 'Ladies of Llangollen' in Chapter 13. Chapter 13 describes Valle Crucis Abbey (1½ miles NW on A542) and Chapter 54 describes Chirk Castle (8 miles SE of Llangollen via A5 and sideroad). Borrow found the latter building 'a mansion ancient and beautiful and abounding with all kinds of agreeable and romantic associations.' His interest in the Welsh poet Huw Morris later took him west of the Castle to the Ceiriog Valley and the little village of Glyn Ceiriog (5 miles from Chirk via B4500). Elsewhere in north Wales Borrow climbed Snowdon (46 miles west of Llangollen via A5 and A4086) with Henrietta. Chapter 29 records how he recited a Welsh poem on the summit to the 'grinning scorn' of other English tourists and the mild confusion of a Welshman, who mistook him for a Breton.

Borrow's account of south Wales provides at least one memorable moment when he arrives at the town of Neath (on A465 8 miles NE of Swansea):

> I had surmounted a hill, and had nearly descended that side of it which looked towards the east, having on my left, that is to the north, a wooded height, when an extraordinary scene presented itself to my eyes. Somewhat to the south rose immense stacks of chimneys surrounded by grimy diabolical-looking buildings, in the neighbourhood of which were huge heaps of cinders and black rubbish. From the chimneys, notwithstanding it was Sunday, smoke was proceeding in volumes, choking the atmosphere all around. From this pandemonium, at the distance of about a quarter of a mile to the south-west, upon a green meadow, stood, looking darkly grey, a ruin of vast size with window holes, towers, spires and arches. Between it and the accursed pandemonium, lay a horrid filthy place, part of which was swamp and part pool: the pool black as soot, and the swamp of a disgusting leaden colour. Across this place of filth stretched a tramway leading from the abominable mansions to the ruin. So strange a scene I had never beheld in nature. (Ch. 102)

With the rise of industry at Neath in the 18C the Abbey had been used as a forge. Traces of this fate are still apparent today.

Though he died at his Suffolk home Borrow was buried in London. He lies next to his wife Mary (d. 1869) among the lavish and respectable monuments of the Brompton Cemetery, north of the Fulham Road. This inappropriate resting place is explained by the fact that in 1860 they had come to live nearby at No. 22 Hereford Square, west of Gloucester Road; Borrow remained at the address, now marked with a GLC plaque, after his wife's death until returning to Suffolk in 1874.

Edinburgh Castle (DoE/SDD). Open May to Oct, Mon to Sat 9.30–6, Sun 11–6; Nov to Apr, Mon to Sat 9.30–5, Sun 12.30–4.30. Closed Christmas Day, Boxing Day and first 3 days of Jan. Fee.

Plas Newydd, Llangollen. Open Easter to end Sept, Mon to Sat 10–7, Sun 10–5. Fee.

Valle Crucis Abbey, near Llangollen (DoE/Welsh Office). Open 15 March to 15 Oct, Mon to Sat 9.30–6.30, Sun 2–6.30 (Apr to Sept, Sun 9.30–6.30); 16 Oct to 14 March, Mon to Sat 9.30–4, Sun 2–4. Closed Christmas Eve, Christmas Day, Boxing Day and 1 Jan. Fee.

Chirk Castle (NT). Open 22 Apr to 30 May, Oct to 4 Nov, Wed & Sun 2–5; 31 May to 30 Sept, Tues, Wed, Thurs & Sun 12–5; all BH Mons 12–5. Closed Good Fri. Fee.

Neath Abbey (DoE/Welsh Office). Open 15 March to 15 Oct, Mon to Sat 9.30–6.30, Sun 2–6.30; 16 Oct to 14 March, Mon to Sat 9.30–4, Sun 2–4. Closed Christmas Eve, Christmas Day, Boxing Day and 1 Jan. Fee.

Anne, Charlotte and Emily Brontë

Anne Brontë: b. Thornton, West Yorkshire, 1820; d. Scarborough, North Yorkshire, 1849. *Agnes Grey* (1847); *The Tenant of Wildfell Hall* (1848).

Charlotte Brontë: b. Thornton, 1816; d. Haworth, West Yorkshire, 1855. *Jane Eyre* (1847); *Shirley* (1849); *Villette* (1853); *The Professor* (1857).

Emily Brontë: b. Thornton, 1818; d. Haworth, 1848. *Wuthering Heights* (1847).

Jointly published: *Poems* (1846). Related reading: Elizabeth Gaskell (q.v.), *The Life of Charlotte Brontë* (1857).

Few literary legends have proved as enduringly popular as the Brontë legend, familiar in its general outline or at least its atmosphere even to those who have not read the novels. And few have been as precisely localised. When Elizabeth Gaskell, the first and still the best biographer of Charlotte Brontë, announced that she had visited all the places connected with her subject's life except 'two small private governessships' she was pointing the way to future pilgrims. Certain landmarks were given authority when Ellen Nussey, Charlotte's friend since their schooldays, advised the illustrator Edmund Morison Wimperis about the real locations of fictional places for the 1872–73 edition of the Brontës' work. Today, the 'Brontë Country' looms large on the tourist map of England, making up for its smallness by the intensity of its cultivation.

Its natural centre is Haworth in West Yorkshire, encircled to the east by the larger industrial centres of Huddersfield, Halifax, Leeds, Bradford and Keighley and to the west by Haworth and Keighley Moors. When the Brontë family arrived in 1820 it was a small worsted weaving town of 4600 people; by 1840 the population had risen to slightly over 6000. Its high, remote situation, seen on the approach from Keighley, was well described by Mrs Gaskell. The town comes into view

> on the side of a pretty steep hill, with a background of dun and purple moors, rising and sweeping away yet higher than the church, which is built at the summit of the long narrow street. All round the horizon there is this same line of sinuous wave-like hills; the scoops into which they fall only revealing other hills beyond, of similar colour and shape, crowned with wild, bleak moors.

We climb Main Street, still paved as it was in the novelists' day with the local millstone grit. On the left at the top we find the Black Bull Inn, favourite haunt of Branwell Brontë (1817–48), whose alcoholism thwarted his artistic career but left behind a colourful legend to serve as tributary to the story of his sisters. Beyond lies the first of Haworth's two major points of interest: the Church of St Michael and All Angels, of which Patrick Branwell Brontë (1777–1861), long-lived father of the family, was incumbent. In fact, the building is greatly changed since his time, restoration of 1879–81 having swept away all but the original tower. Inside, a plaque marks the site of the family vault where all the Brontës except Anne were buried. Matthew Arnold (q.v.) wrote his poem of tribute, 'Haworth Churchyard,' in the belief that the sisters were buried outdoors, and told Mrs Gaskell when she corrected him: 'It really seems to me to put the finishing touch to the strange cross-grained character of the fortunes of that ill-fated family that they should even be placed after death in the wrong, uncongenial spot.'

A lane leads left from Main Street to the Brontë Parsonage Museum, the home to which Patrick Brontë brought his wife, Maria, and their six children. Mrs Brontë soon died, in 1821, and was followed in 1825 by the two eldest daughters, Maria (b. 1813) and Elizabeth (b. 1815). The remaining children—Anne, Charlotte, Emily and Branwell—were brought up by an aunt, Elizabeth Branwell, for whom they never developed great fondness, and the housekeeper Tabitha ('Tabby') Ackroyd, source of those local tales which stimulated their imagination and found their way into later writing. Despite being sent away to school and to work as governesses, the sisters always returned to the Parsonage and wrote all their novels here. Charlotte remained even after her late, surprising marriage in 1854 to her father's curate, Arthur Bell Nicholls, a match vigorously opposed by the old Mr Brontë.

Built in 1782, the heavy stone Parsonage was extended in the 1860s. The Brontë Society, founded in 1893 and for some time limited to a room above the Yorkshire Bank in the Main Street, acquired the building in 1927 and made it a museum that has since become second only to Shakespeare's Birthplace in its popularity. The Parsonage has been refurbished in the style of the early nineteenth century and the simple manner preferred by the Brontës, though both its appearance and atmosphere have suffered from the large crowds of visitors it regularly attracts. Of special note is the Bonnell room with its collection of tiny notebooks filled with the daydreams, fantasies and sagas which played so important a role in the Brontës' childhood. The visitor will also be struck by the small bedroom to which Emily—that hard, strange, indomitable spirit—refused to be confined

Haworth Church and Parsonage, by Edmund Morison Whimperis. From 1872-73 edition of the Brontës' works. Courtesy of Cambridge University Library

The Brontë Waterfall, by Edmund Morison Whimperis. From 1872-73 edition of the Brontës' works. Courtesy of Cambridge University Library

until only a few hours before her early death. The sisters' otherwise enclosed and restricted life had little connection with the town of Haworth itself but much to do with the *moors that lie to the west. Charlotte wrote:

> My sister Emily ... loved the moors ... They were far more to her than a mere spectacle; they were what she lived in & by, as much as the wild

> birds, their tenants, or the heather, their produce ... She found in the
> bleak solitude many and dear delights; and not the least and best loved
> was—liberty.

A favourite walk leads west from the Parsonage Museum along the
course of Sladen Beck, tributary of the River Worth, to the Bridge
and Waterfall that now bear the Brontës' name (2 miles). Charlotte
came here with her husband in November 1854: 'I had often wished
to see it in its winter power—so we walked on. It was fine indeed; a
perfect torrent racing over the rocks, white and beautiful! It began
to rain while we were watching it, and we returned home under a
streaming sky.' Her resulting cold precipitated the illness from which
she died the following March.

Hardy walkers, who will need one of the local maps available from
the Museum, will also wish to venture further across the moors to
see several buildings associated with the novels. The location, though
not the exact appearance, of the ruined Top Withens (or High or Far
Withens) suggested Heathcliff's residence in *Wuthering Heights*.
'Wuthering,' the narrator Lockwood explains, is

> a significant provincial adjective, descriptive of the atmospheric tumult
> to which its station is exposed in stormy weather. Pure, bracing weather
> they must have had up there at all times, indeed: one may guess the
> power of the north wind, blowing over the edge, by the excessive slant
> of a few stunted firs at the end of the house; and by a range of gaunt
> thorns stretching their limbs one way, as if craving alms of the sun.
> Happily, the architect had foresight to build it strong; the narrow windows
> are deeply set in the wall, and the corners defended with large jutting
> stones. (Ch. 1)

Ponden Hall may have suggested 'Thrushcross Grange,' the
altogether more civilised home of the Lintons in the same novel.
Wycoller Hall is traditionally identified with 'Ferndean Manor,' where
Rochester lives in *Jane Eyre* after the fire has destroyed 'Thornfield
Hall'; it is hard to detect any resemblance from the present ruins.

A series of trips may be taken from Haworth to other parts of the
North and north Midlands connected with the Brontës, though these
are too dispersed to be organised into a single tour. The nearest place
to visit is Thornton, on B6145 4 miles west of Bradford and now
absorbed into the suburbs of that city, where Patrick Brontë brought
his wife in the early years of their marriage. A plaque on the modest
house in Market Street, off High Street, marks the birthplace of his
famous children.

In the area round Halifax, 8 miles south of Thornton via B6145 and
A629, we can find several points of interest. The weaving village of
Luddenden (off A646 3½ miles west of Halifax) is connected with
Branwell, who was appointed railway clerk at Luddenden Foot in
1841, though he was dismissed the following year when inspection
of the accounts revealed that some £11 were missing. The Lord
Nelson Inn at Luddenden was the scene of what he called the 'cold
yet malignant debauchery' of his heavy drinking. Emily's post as
governess in a girls' boarding school at Law Hill (1837) brought her
near to Shibden Hall, 1½ miles east of Halifax on Shibden Hall Road
and in Shibden Dale. The fine timber-framed house may have
contributed to the description of 'Thrushcross Grange' in *Wuthering
Heights*. Nearby High Sunderland, which may have suggested the
fancifully carved frontage of Heathcliff's home, has been demolished.
Charlotte several times visited her friend Ellen Nussey at Birstall, on

A643 10 miles east of Halifax, and made its surrounding area the location of *Shirley*. The Elizabethan Oakwell Hall, ¾ of a mile NW of the town and near M62, appears as the heroine's home, 'Fieldhead':

> If Fieldhead had few other merits as a building, it might at least be termed picturesque: its irregular architecture, and the grey and mossy colouring communicated by time, gave it a just claim to this epithet. The old latticed windows, the stone porch, the walls, the roof, the chimney-stacks, were rich in crayon touches and sepia lights and shades. (Ch. 11)

Further afield from Haworth by far the most important site is Cowan Bridge, reached by travelling 8 miles NE of Keighley to join A65 at Skipton and continuing another 30 miles NE. Charlotte and Emily entered the Rev. William Carus Wilson's Clergy Daughters' School in 1824 but were taken away in 1825 after their older sisters Elizabeth and Maria had died of typhus contracted at the institution. Charlotte reacted against the harsh Evangelical regime of the school with passionate resentment. In *Jane Eyre* it became 'Lowood' and Rev. Wilson was transformed into Mr Brocklehurst, while Maria's death suggested the death of Helen Burns. These episodes stirred a controversy that was again inflamed by Mrs Gaskell's charges against Cowan Bridge in her biography. The school's surviving building stands just north of the Leck and is marked by a tablet. *Jane Eyre* also gives a vivid and only lightly fictionalised account of the Sunday journey to hear Rev. Wilson preach in his church at Tunstall, 2 miles SW of Cowan Bridge on A683:

> Sundays were dreary days in that winter season. We had to walk two miles to Brocklebridge Church, where our patron officiated. We set out cold, we arrived at church colder: during the morning service we became almost paralysed. It was too far to return to dinner, and an allowance of cold meat and bread, in the same penurious proportion observed in our ordinary meals, was served round between the services.
>
> At the close of the afternoon service we returned by an exposed and hilly road, where the bitter wind, blowing over a range of snowy summits to the north, almost flayed the skin from our faces. (Ch. 7)

In 1833, after the Brontës' connection with the school had been severed, it was moved to Casterton (3 miles NE of Cowan Bridge on A683), where the Old Hall was Rev. Wilson's home.

Also to the north of the Haworth–Keighley area is •Norton Conyers. This mainly 17C country house stands 4 miles north of Ripon and is reached by following A61 before branching left towards Wath. Charlotte paid a visit, probably in 1839 when she was working as a governess in the area, saw its third-storey attics and heard how a madwoman had been confined there in the 18C. The connection with *Jane Eyre* is obvious.

In May 1849, shortly after Emily's death, Charlotte and Ellen Nussey took Anne to Scarborough on Yorkshire's east coast. She died only three days after their arrival at the resort and was buried in the churchyard of St Mary's on Castle Road above the harbour.

An earlier connection with Hathersage, on A625 in the High Peaks between Manchester and Sheffield, had important results for Charlotte's fiction. She came here to visit Ellen Nussey at the home of her friend's brother, Henry, who had once proposed to her. The 15C Eyre brasses in the church, striking enough in their own right, must surely have suggested the surname of her most famous heroine. Hathersage is also identified with the 'Morton' of *Jane Eyre*, where Jane meets St John Rivers (Ch. 28ff.). This section of the novel certainly draws on Charlotte's impressions of Peak District scenery. In Manchester itself, Charlotte was several times a guest at the Plymouth Grove home of Mrs Gaskell, described more fully under the entry for that novelist.

Emily never visited London and Anne stayed in the city only briefly. After the great success of *Jane Eyre*, however, Charlotte made an extended visit whose best-remembered episode was an unsuccessful evening at the Kensington home of Thackeray, dealt with under the entry devoted to him. Thackeray's daughter described the occasion:

> The room looked very dark, the lamp began to smoke a little, the conversation grew dimmer and more dim, the ladies sat round still expectant, my father was much too perturbed by the gloom and the silence to be able to cope with it at all. Mrs Brookfield, who was in the doorway by the study, near the corner in which Miss Brontë was sitting, leant forward with a little commonplace, since brilliance was not to be the order of the evening. 'Do you like London, Miss Brontë?' she said; another silence, a pause, then Miss Brontë answers, 'Yes and No,' very gravely.

All three sisters are commemorated in Poets' Corner (fee) of Westminster Abbey.

Brontë Parsonage Museum, Haworth. Open Apr to Sept, Mon to Sat 11–5.30, Sun 2–5.30; Oct to March, Mon to Sat 11–4.30, Sun 2–4.30. Closed last 3 weeks of Dec. Fee.

Shibden Hall, Halifax (West Yorkshire Folk Museum). Open Apr to Sept, Mon to Sat 10–6, Sun 2–5; Oct, Nov & March, Mon to Sat 10–5, Sun 2–5; Feb, Sun only 2–5; closed Dec & Jan.

Oakwell Hall, Birstall. Open Apr to Oct, Tues to Sat 10–6, Sun 1–5; Nov to March, Tues to Sat 10–5, Sun 1–5.

Norton Conyers, near Ripon. Open June, July, & Aug, Sun & BH Mon 2–5.30; also 24 July to 4 Aug daily 2–5.30. Fee.

Rupert Brooke

b. Rugby, Warwickshire, 1887; d. Aegean Sea, 1915. *Poems* (1911); *1914 and Other Poems* (1915); *The Old Vicarage, Grantchester* (1916); *John Webster and the Elizabethan Drama* (1916).

Brooke was born in Rugby at No. 5 Hillmorton Road, near the public school where his father taught. He himself entered the school as a pupil in 1901.

In Cambridge the legend of Rupert Brooke still has potency even for tourists indifferent to poetry. It typifies youth in all its carefree innocence and energy, and is made the more poignant by his early death during the First World War. In the city itself the chief point of interest is King's College, where Brooke started his undergraduate career in 1906. His rooms were on A Staircase and then E Staircase in the Fellows' Building opposite the main entrance. His name is recorded on the War Memorial in the sidechapel nearest the altar of the Chapel. Yet the spot most intimately connected with Brooke is Grantchester (2½ miles SW), where he lived while studying for the King's fellowship he was awarded in 1912. Though often crowded in summer, the village retains much of the charm Brooke praised in his most famous poem. It can be reached by following the Trumpington Road and turning right in Trumpington, but the most pleasant approach is the walk from Grantchester Street (beyond the junction of Newnham Road and Fen Causeway) through the meadows that skirt the river. Brooke lodged at The Orchard from June 1909 to December 1910, when he moved to the Old Vicarage nearby. He is remembered on the War Memorial in the little church of St Andrew and St Mary.

Rupert Brooke in the garden of the Old Vicarage, Grantchester.
Courtesy of King's College, Cambridge

Sir Thomas Browne

b. London, 1605; d. Norwich, Norfolk, 1682. *Religio Medici* (1642); *Pseudodoxia Epidemica: or Enquiries into Very Many Received Tenents and Commonly Presumed Truths Which Examined Prove But Vulgar and Common Errors* (1646); *Hydriotaphia, Urne-Buriall: or A Discourse of the Sepulchrall Urnes Lately Found in Norfolk; Together With the Garden of Cyrus: or the Quincunciall Lozenge, or Network Plantations of the Ancients, Artificially, Naturally, Mystically Considered* (1658).

Browne's education began in Hampshire at Winchester College. It was continued in Oxford at Broadgates Hall, refounded under its present name of Pembroke College during his undergraduate career (1623–26).

After studying medicine on the Continent he established his practice at Norwich in 1636. It remained his home until death; indeed, there is no evidence to suggest that he again left Eastern England. This fixity did not restrict the scope of his writings, in which he combined the roles of scientist, antiquary and moralist, or the fame they brought him. In 1671 he was knighted by Charles II at Blackfriars Hall, once the nave of a Dominican church but used as a civic meeting place since the Reformation; it stands on St George Street between St Andrew Street and Blackfriars Bridge. In October the same year he was visited by John Evelyn (q.v.), diarist and like Browne a Fellow of the Royal Society, who found his house near St Peter Mancroft in the Market Place 'a Paradise & Cabinet of rarities, & that of the best collection, especially Medails, books, Plants, natural things.' Browne took his guest on a tour of 'all the remarkable places of this ancient Citty' and Evelyn was 'much astonish'd' to see 'buildings of flint, so exquisitely headed & Squared.' Browne was buried in the noble church of St Peter Mancroft, which has a memorial in the chancel and a statue of him outside.

Winchester College. Open Apr to Sept, Mon to Sat 10–6, Sun 2–6 (guided tours start Mon to Sat 11, 2 & 3.15, Sun 2 & 3.15); Oct to March, Mon to Sat 10–4, Sun 2–4. Fee.

St Andrew's and **Blackfriars' Halls**, Norwich. Open Mon to Sat 9–5, except when in use for public functions.

Robert and Elizabeth Barrett Browning

Robert Browning: b. London, 1812; d. Venice, Italy, 1889. *Pauline: A Fragment of a Confession* (1833); *Paracelsus* (1835); *Strafford: An Historical Tragedy* (1837); *Sordello* (1840); *Pippa Passes* (1841); *A Blot in the 'Scutcheon: A Tragedy in Five Acts* (1843); *Dramatic Romances and Lyrics* (1845); *Men and Women* (1855); *Dramatis Personae* (1864); *The Ring and the Book* (1868–69); *Balaustion's Adventure* (1871); *Prince Hohenstiel-Schwangau, Saviour of Society* (1871); *Fifine at the Fair* (1872); *Red Cotton Night-Cap Country; or Turf and Towers* (1873); *Aristophanes' Apology* (1875); *The Inn Album* (1875); *Pacchiarotto and How He Worked in Distemper; with Other Poems* (1876); *Dramatic Idylls* (First Series, 1879; Second Series, 1880); *Parleyings with Certain People of Importance in Their Day* (1887).

Elizabeth Browning: b. Kelloe, County Durham, 1806; d. Florence, Italy, 1861. *Sonnets from the Portuguese* (1850); *Casa Guidi Windows: A Poem* (1851); *Aurora Leigh* (1857); *Poems Before Congress* (1860).

To his friend and contemporary Henry James (q.v.), Browning was, 'with all his Italianisms and cosmopolitanisms, . . . a magnificent example of the best and least dilenttantish English spirit.' Yet his life, and that of Elizabeth Barrett Browning, belonged only intermittently to England. Their best memorials are in Florence at Casa Guidi, where they lived from 1848 until her death in 1861, and at Elizabeth's elaborate tomb in the Protestant cemetery. England can offer nothing so magnificent by way of rivalry. Camberwell, the scene of Browning's early years, has changed too drastically from the pleasantly leafy south London suburb that Browning knew to repay a visit. The country houses where the young Elizabeth Barrett lived before her father's decline in fortune have vanished or been altered.

Her connection with the south Devon coastal resort of Torquay is better remembered. A plaque at the Regina Hotel (then Bath House) on Beacon Terrace records her convalescent stay in 1838–41.

In London, Marylebone has a rich little cluster of places associated mainly with the crucial years when the two poets met and married. A convenient tour begins at Baker Street Underground Station (Bakerloo, Circle, Metropolitan and Jubilee Lines). We take the Marylebone Road westward and turn left on to Gloucester Place. A GLC plaque at No. 99 (then No. 74) marks the house where Elizabeth and her family first lived in London (1835–38). It was not a congenial environment for a semi-invalid and a letter recording her first impressions describes the city as a 'dungeon' and 'wrapped up like a mummy, in a yellow mist, so closely that I have had scarcely a glimpse of its countenance since we came.' From Gloucester Place we follow Dorset Street to the left. In the summer of 1855 Robert and Elizabeth took lodgings at No. 13, now rebuilt, while he prepared *Men and Women* for publication and she fell under the influence of Daniel Dunglas Home, the fashionable medium. Tennyson (q.v.) came on a memorable evening in September to read *Maud* aloud to the assembled company and be covertly sketched by Rossetti (q.v.) as he did so; Robert responded by reading 'Fra Lippo Lippi.' At the end of Dorset Street we follow Manchester Street, turn left on Blandford Street and cross Marylebone High Street to New Cavendish Street.

This quickly brings us to Wimpole Street and the most famous English address in the Brownings' lives. No. 50, to the left, has been rebuilt but the solidly respectable Georgian façades of the surviving houses in the street preserve the atmosphere Elizabeth found when she came to live here in 1838. Robert paid his first visit in May 1845 and found her leading an enclosed existence in a third-floor bedroom, surrounded by busts and engraved portraits of writers, including himself. The story of their courtship is well known, with Robert coaxing her out of invalidism and Elizabeth gaining the strength to oppose her selfish, tyrannical father. The couple were secretly married in September 1846 at the early 19C church of St Marylebone. To reach it we follow Wimpole Street and its continuation north to the Marylebone Road, where it lies almost immediately to our left, opposite the York Gate to Regent's Park. In a letter written shortly after the ceremony Elizabeth described how her thoughts turned to the other brides who had stood in St Marylebone: 'Not one of them all perhaps, not one perhaps, since that building was a church, has had reasons strong as mine, for an absolute trust and devotion towards the man she married—not one!' She went back only briefly to Wimpole Street before leaving for Italy with her husband.

We may extend this tour by returning to Marylebone Station and taking the Bakerloo Line to Warwick Avenue Underground Station. By following Warwick Avenue south, turning right on Blomfield Road and then crossing the canal we reach Little Venice, the picturesque waterside area where Browning lived from the time of Elizabeth's death in 1861 until 1887. No. 19 Warwick Crescent, the narrow white-stuccoed house he filled with furniture from Casa Guidi, was demolished soon after he moved away but its approximate site is marked by a modern bas-relief. Here he wrote *The Ring and the Book*, blossomed from a widower's seclusion into the active social life at which Henry James marvelled, and submitted to relentless lionisation by the Browning Society.

From Little Venice Browning went to live in Kensington at No. 29 De Vere Gardens, south of Kensington High Street almost opposite the Palace Gate to Kensington Gardens. Henry James was a neighbour.

It was James, too, whose essay in *English Hours* offered appropriate reflections on Browning's burial in Westminster Abbey, taking pleasure in the thought that so modern a writer should rest with the classics in 'the great temple of fame of the English race.' Browning is commemorated by a stone next to Tennyson's in Poets' Corner (fee).

Browning was not conspicuous for his travels inside the British Isles but a visit to Wales in the summer of 1886 was notable. He stayed at Llangollen, Clwyd to be near his friend Lady Martin, formerly Helen Faucit the actress. The church at Llantysilio, off A5 2 miles NW of Llangollen and near Valle Crucis Abbey, has a plaque put up by Lady Martin to commemorate his worship there.

'Mr Robert Browning, Taking Tea with the Browning Society,' by Max Beerbohm (q.v.). Courtesy of Ashmolean Museum

John Bunyan

b. Elstow, Bedfordshire, 1628; d. London, 1688. *Grace Abounding to the Chief of Sinners* (1666); *The Pilgrim's Progress* (1678–84); *The Life and Death of Mr Badman* (1680); *The Holy War* (1682).

Bunyan's life was rooted in Bedford and its surrounding area, that fertile breeding ground of 17C Puritanism.

The site of the humble cottage where he was born, now marked with a stone, is in rough country near the village of Elstow, on A6 1 mile south of the county town. It is best approached by quitting Bedford.in the direction of Harrowden, then branching south on the old country lane that almost immediately crosses a railway line; a footpath leading through fields to the birthplace is indicated by a signpost. In Elstow itself the heavily restored Norman church of St Mary and St Helen, where Bunyan's parents were buried, preserves the octagonal Perpendicular font in which he was baptised and the pulpit from which some of the sermons that first stirred his religious conscience were delivered. Windows of 1880 at the east end of the north and south aisles depict scenes from *The Pilgrim's Progress* and *The Holy War*. The church is also notable for its detached tower whose bells Bunyan as a young man took 'much delight in ringing, but my Conscience beginning to be tender, I thought that such a practice was but vain, and therefore forced myself to leave it' (*Grace Abounding*, Section 33). As his qualms grew stronger he developed the fear that first the bells and then the tower itself might fall on him. *Grace Abounding* also records a rebuke to Sunday amusements, which took place on the village green:

> As I was in the midst of a game at Cat, and having struck it one blow from the hole; just as I was about to strike it the second time, a voice did suddenly dart from Heaven into my Soul, which said, *Wilt thou leave thy sins, and go to Heaven? or have thy sins, and go to Hell?* At this I was put to an exceeding maze; wherefore, leaving my Cat upon the ground, I looked up to Heaven, and was as if I had with the eyes of my understanding, seen the Lord Jesus looking down upon me, as being very hotly displeased with me, and as if he did severely threaten me with some grievous punishment for these, and other my ungodly practices. (Section 22)

On one side of the green stands the •Moot Hall of c. 1500, a fine half-timbered building with an overhanging upper storey. It is now a Museum whose collection illustrates Bunyan's life and times.

Houghton House, off A418 6 miles south of Bedford and near Ampthill, a now ruined but still elegant Jacobean mansion built by Inigo Jones for Mary, Countess of Pembroke and sister to Sir Philip Sidney (q.v.), is sometimes claimed as the original of 'House Beautiful' in the first part of *The Pilgrim's Progress*. Bunyan was arrested in 1660 near Harlington, 6 miles further south, on a charge of preaching without a licence. Harlington Manor House, home of the magistrate who issued the warrant, stands at the main crossing.

Bunyan's preaching took him to several other villages near Bedford. At Stevington, off A428 5 miles NW of Bedford, the village cross is sometimes identified with the one by which Christian shed his burden near the beginning of *The Pilgrim's Progress*, while its mill has been restored in Bunyan's memory.

In Bedford itself Bunyan carried on his family trade as tinker, preached and was imprisoned from his arrest in 1660 until the Declaration of Indulgence in 1672 and again for a shorter period of six months, probably in 1677. Despite a stubborn tradition that places him in the town gaol on the old bridge over the Ouse (now demolished), the scene of his ordeals and 'den' where he wrote *Grace Abounding* and the first part of *The Pilgrim's Progress* was in fact the County Gaol, which stood at the junction of Silver Street and the High Street. He is commemorated today by Boehm's statue of 1874 on St Peter's Green at the northern end of the High Street. On Mill Street to the east of the High Street the Bunyan Meeting of 1850 replaces the earlier building where he preached. The ten panels of its doors, made by Frederick Thrupp in 1876, are decorated with scenes from *The Pilgrim's Progress*. The adjoining Bunyan Museum contains relics.

Bunyan died while visiting London and was buried at Bunhill Fields in Finsbury, a Nonconformist cemetery where Defoe, Blake (qq.v.) and the hymn writer Isaac Watts also lie. South of Old Street Underground Station (Northern Line; closed Sundays), it is bounded by Bunhill Row to the west and City Road to the east. According to Southey (s.v. Lake Poets), Bunyan's gravestone originally bore the inscription: 'The "Pilgrim's Progress" now is finished,/ And Death has laid him on his earthly bed.' It was replaced by a more elaborate monument with a recumbent statue of 1861 by E.C. Papworth, itself in turn restored in 1950 after war-time damage.

A stained glass window (1911) in the north transept of Westminster Abbey depicts episodes from *The Pilgrim's Progress*.

Moot Hall, Elstow. Open Tues to Sat 10–1 & 2–5, Sun 2–5.30 (dusk in winter). Fee.

Houghton House, Ampthill (English Heritage). Open at all reasonable times.

Bunyan Museum, Bedford. Open Apr to Sept, Tues to Sat 2–4. Fee.

Bunhill Fields. Open Mon to Fri 7.30–4, Sat & Sun 9.30–4.

Fanny Burney (Madame D'Arblay)

b. King's Lynn, Norfolk, 1752; d. London, 1840. *Evelina* (1778); *Cecilia* (1782); *Camilla* (1796).

The charming town of King's Lynn, near the Wash, preserves both specific buildings connected with Fanny Burney and much of the atmosphere in which she spent her early years. There is, in fact, some doubt as to her exact birthplace: it may have been No. 84 High Street (now rebuilt) or, as one would prefer to believe, the older but still surviving St Augustine's on Chapel Street, near the Tuesday Market. She was certainly baptised at St Nicholas, north of Chapel Street, a chapel of ease north a visit for its own sake. Her father, Dr Charles Burney, was organist at another fine church, St Margaret's by the Saturday Market. Although the family moved to London in 1760 she returned to King's Lynn throughout her childhood to stay with Mrs Stephen Allen, who became Dr Burney's second wife in 1766. Her lifelong habit of keeping a diary and her early attempts at writing, soon to issue in *Evelina*, date from these years.

The success of *Evelina*, never fully to be repeated, had many fortunate consequences for the novelist and at least one unfortunate one: the invitation from George III's queen to become Second Keeper of the Robes. Her diary records the lonely and frustrating years (1786–91) she spent in this capacity, first at Windsor Castle (west of London via M4 or A4) and then at Kew Palace (in Kew Gardens, SW London). One of the few highlights of this period, vigorously described in her diary, was the trial of Warren Hastings in Westminster Hall.

Her release from these irksome duties initiated an especially happy period of her life, centring on the Surrey town of Mickleham off A24 between Leatherhead and Dorking. She was already familiar with the area from visits to her sister, Susan, and to the Lockes of Norbury Park, a house half a mile west of the town with fine views. Juniper Hall (1 mile SE of Mickleham, altered by the Victorians and now a field-study centre) became in the 1790s a haven for French emigrés including Madame de Staël, Talleyrand and General d'Arblay, Fanny's future husband. The couple were married at the parish church of Mickleham, St Michael, in 1793. Camilla Cottage in nearby West Humble, designed by the General and named after the novel whose proceeds made its building possible, unfortunately no longer remains, but the earlier house they rented in Great Bookham does: still called the Hermitage, it stands on the corner of East Street.

When the d'Arblays returned to England after many years in France (1802–15) they went to live in Bath. She had previously visited the fashionable resort, most notably in 1780 when she spent the summer at No. 14 South Parade with the Thrales, friends of Dr Johnson (q.v.). The decision to live in Bath permanently seems natural enough given the elegant and socially alert character of her fiction, but it was partly owing to the money worries that dogged the couple throughout their married life.

> There is no place I have yet seen where the inconveniences of a limited fortune are so lightly felt, nor where the people at large are so civilised . . . Equipage, servants, Table, Jewels, though *here* as everywhere, very desirable, are not *here* requisite. *Respect* does not hang either upon the lackey or the attire; and admission is as easy without the one, as reception is good or bad without the other. There is something nearer to independence from the shackles of fortuitous circumstances in the society of *Bath* than I have ever witnessed elsewhere.

Their home was at No. 23 Great Stanhope Street. The general, who died in 1818, was buried in the cemetery of St Swithin's on Walcot Street; his epitaph was written by his wife.

Fanny Burney was also buried at St Swithin's but she spent her long years of widowhood in London. Her home from 1818 until 1828, No. 11 Bolton Street north of Piccadilly in Mayfair, is marked by a plaque.

Windsor Castle (DoE). Precincts open mid March to 30 April & 1 Sept to late Oct, daily 10–5.15; May to end Aug, daily 10–7.15; late Oct to mid March, daily 10–4.15. State apartments open Mon to Sat from 10.30, Sun from 1.30. Fee for State apartments.

Kew Palace (DoE). Open April to Sept, daily 11–5.30. Fee.

Westminster Hall. Open Mon to Sat, 10–1.30 provided neither House is sitting, and during Recess Mon to Fri 10–4, Sat 10–5.

Robert Burns

b. Alloway, Strathclyde, 1759; d. Dumfries, Dumfries and Galloway, 1796. *Poems, chiefly in the Scottish Dialect* (1786; enlarged editions, 1787 and 1793); contributions to *The Scots Musical Museum*, edited by James Johnson (1787–1803).

Burns' unofficial position as Scotland's national poet is not without its dangers. His formal schooling has often been ignored as detracting from the legend of the 'heaven-taught ploughman'; his sexual adventures, tangled and fascinating though they admittedly are, have been stressed and his political radicalism almost forgotten; and his early death has been proffered as an example of the dangers of drink, when it was really due to rheumatic fever aggravated by the wrong medical treatment. To a modern Scottish poet like Hugh MacDiarmid the Burns cult could seem a distraction from the writer's real achievement and, indeed, from the real potentialities of Scottish poetry: 'It has denied his spirit to honour his name . . . It has preserved his furniture and repelled his message.' Yet this very full commemoration of scenes connected with Burns' life and poetry still offers the patient, and slightly sceptical, visitor a series of rewarding tours.

His early life was spent near the west coast of Scotland in the former county of Ayrshire, now assimilated into Strathclyde Region. We begin our first tour at Alloway, then an independent village but since overtaken by the suburbs of Ayr itself. The chief attraction is Burns Cottage, the low dwelling with whitewashed walls and thatched roof rebuilt by William Burnes (as the family name was spelled) when he came to live here in 1756. Robert, his eldest child, was born in it some three years later. In 1766 William moved south of the village to Mount Oliphant, where he established a family tradition of unsuccessful farming ventures that his son was later to maintain. The museum adjoining Burns Cottage displays a collection of relics.

Continuing south through the village we reach Alloway Kirk, already a ruin in Burns' time, where his most famous character, Tam o'Shanter, witnessed the witches' orgy. William Burnes, who died in 1784, is buried in the churchyard; the present headstone is the third on the site, the original one erected by the poet having been dismantled piecemeal by souvenir-hunting tourists. The modern Land o'Burns Centre opposite the church has an agricultural museum and an audio-visual show illustrating the poet's life; it is a recommended starting-point for the Burns Heritage Trail devised by the Scottish Tourist Board. Nearby is the Burns Monument of 1820, inappropriate in both its size and its Grecian style. Its gardens, where figures by the local self-taught sculptor James Thom depict characters from Burns' work, offer a good view of the Brig o'Doon, across which Tam o'Shanter escaped the pursuing witches.

B7024 leads south from Alloway to Maybole (6 miles), home of Burns' mother Agnes Broun, where A77 is taken an additional 6 miles to Kirkoswald. The poet came here to study mathematics and surveying under Hugh Rodger in 1775, though he later remembered the town in another light: 'The contraband trade was at the time very successful; scenes of swaggering riot and roaring dissipation were as yet new to me; and I was no enemy to social life.—Here . . . I learned to look unconcernedly on a large tavern-bill, and mix without fear in a drunken squabble.' Its main surviving monument is the home of John Davidson, now called Souter Johnnie's Cottage after the name he is given in 'Tam o'Shanter.' It contains items from the time of Davidson's occupancy and a set of the tools used by a souter, or cobbler; in the garden we find more sculptures by James Thom, representing characters from Burns' poem. Davidson, Douglas Graham (the original for Tam o'Shanter) and relatives of Burns' mother, the Brouns, are buried in the church nearby.

From Kirkoswald we cross to the coastal A719 and make the 14-mile journey to the centre of Ayr, where Burns attended grammar school and which was, according to 'Tam o'Shanter,' unsurpassed 'For honest men and bonny lasses' (line 16). A walking tour begins outside the railway station, where he is commemorated by a statue of 1891.

Alloway Street leads to the High Street where, on the right, we find the former Tam o'Shanter Inn, now a museum. In Burns' day it was a brewhouse, supplied by Douglas Graham and so has commonly been identified as the starting point of Tam o'Shanter's ride. Further up the High Street the little Kirk Close leads (right) to the 17C Auld Kirk, interesting in its own right but notable for the present purpose as the scene of Burns' baptism. From its churchyard we have a good view of the 13C Auld Brig and, beyond, the New Bridge of 1788 (rebuilt 1877); they are the speakers in Burns' dialogue poem, 'The Brigs of Ayr.'

We leave Ayr on A719 and A758 to the NE, turning left for Tarbolton (9 miles). The poet's connection with the town and its surrounding area began in 1777, when his father took the lease of Lochlea (or Lochlie) farm nearby, and was continued after William Burnes' death in 1784 when he and his brother Gilbert took the lease of Mossgiel farm, near Mauchline. In Tarbolton itself the main point of interest is the Bachelors' Club, originally a hall attached to the local inn. It was the meeting place for a debating and social society, formed in 1780, of which Burns was founder member and first president. According to the prospectus drafted by the poet, its purpose was 'to unite ourselves into a club or society under such rules and regulations that while we should forget our cares and labours in mirth and diversion, we might not transgress the bounds of innocence and decorum.' The Bachelors' Club was also probably the scene of Burns' initiation as a freemason.

Returning to A758 and continuing NE we come after 4 miles to the village of Failford. A monument near the bridge over the Ayr marks the place where Burns is reputed to have parted from his fiancée, Mary Campbell, in May 1786, only a few months before her death. She is the Highland Mary of 'The Highland Lassie O' and 'Will ye go to the Indies, my Mary?,' while Burns remembered their last meeting in the lyric beginning 'Thou lingering Star with lessening ray.'

The little town of Mauchline, another 3 miles up A758, is particularly rich in its connections with Burns, who knew it well during his tenancy of Mossgiel farm and returned to it briefly in 1788 after his stay in Edinburgh. Most interesting perhaps is the house then owned by Gavin Hamilton, next to Mauchline Tower. Hamilton was Burn's landlord and a leading supporter of the New Licht faction in its clashes with the traditional Calvinist beliefs of the Kirk; the poet's agreement with his views is shown by several vigorous satires, of which 'Holy Willie's prayer' is the most famous. Mary Campbell worked as a nursemaid in Hamilton's household. Burns House in Castle Street was the writer's home after his long-delayed marriage in 1788 to Jean Armour, who had already borne his children. It is now a small museum with furnishings of the period. Mauchline's church has been rebuilt since the time when Burns was censured for his relations with Jean Armour and eventually celebrated his wedding to her, but its churchyard still contains the graves of four of his children, as well as the graves of Gavin Hamilton and William Fisher, the original Holy Willie. Poosie Nansie's Tavern opposite, still a pub, was 'well known to and much frequented by the lowest orders of Travellers and Pilgrims' and by Burns himself, as his superbly extravagant cantata, 'The Jolly Beggars,' testifies.

North of Mauchline on A76 we find the Burns Memorial Tower.

Mossgiel farm lies to the west.

A76 continues to Kilmarnock (6 miles) where Burns' first collection of poems was published by John Wilson in 1786. The event is remembered by the massive and regrettable Kay Park Monument of 1879, whose museum displays a copy of the Kilmarnock edition among other items.

The industrial town of Irvine, 8 miles west on A71, was the scene of Burns' brief career as a flax-dresser, which ended in 1782 when his premises burned down during New Year celebrations. The site of his lodgings on Glasgow Vennel is marked by a plaque put up by the Irvine Burns Club on its foundation in 1826. The Club's building in Eglinton Street contains a museum of relics and a mural depicting the poet's life in the town. Near the river on the northern part of the town moor we find a bronze statue by J. Pittendreigh MacGillvray, unveiled by the Poet Laureate, Alfred Austin, in 1896.

Encouraged by the strongly favourable reception of the Kilmarnock edition, Burns came to Edinburgh in 1786. Apart from the Highland travels on which he gathered traditional songs for James Johnson's *The Scots Musical Museum*, he remained there until 1788. He was lionised by the literary society of the day, impressing the young Sir Walter Scott (q.v.) by his 'dignified plainness and simplicity,' but was sceptical of such passing popularity and did not find the atmosphere of the city conducive to poetry. The opening of his address to the capital, 'Edina! *Scotia*'s darling seat!,' shows how uncongenial he found its conventional literary language.

A walking tour begins on Lawnmarket. At the junction with Lady Stair's Close a plaque marks the site of his first lodgings, on what was then Baxter's Close. The 17C Lady Stair's House is now a museum devoted to Burns, Sir Walter Scott and Robert Louis Stevenson (qq.v.). Its Burns memorabilia include the stool from the office of his publisher, Smellie, which he used while correcting proofs for the second edition of his poems. Lawnmarket continues eastward, becoming High Street and then Canongate. Canongate Cemetery has the grave of the Scots poet Robert Fergusson (1750–74), whose last Edinburgh years were spent in depression, drinking and madness; Burns' commemorative poem calls him 'my elder brother in Misfortune,/ By far my elder Brother in the muse.' Burns was also responsible for erecting Fergusson's monument in 1787, though he was unable to pay the bill until 1792. The tour ends by following Tollbooth Wynd at the side of the cemetery to Regent Road. On its southern side we find the Burns Monument of 1830.

For the last years of his life Burns lived in the Dumfries area, south of his native Ayrshire. In 1788 he leased Ellisland farm off A76 4½ miles NW of Dumfries but ran into financial difficulties, worsened by his refusal to accept payment for the contributions he was continuing to make to Johnson's *Scots Musical Museum*. He was forced to take on part-time work as an exciseman and then, in 1791, to give up the farm altogether. Ellisland has been preserved as a museum of Burns relics and farming life.

After the failure at Ellisland, Burns and his wife moved to the busy town of *Dumfries, where he worked as an exciseman, offending local opinion by his radical sympathies with the French Revolution and leaving behind him a reputation, much exaggerated, for heavy drinking. A convenient tour begins at the Burns statue on the northern part of the High Street near Greyfriars Church. Walking south, we pass on our right the turning for Bank Street, formerly Wee Vennel but called 'Stinking Vennel' by Burns when he lodged there in a three-room flat from 1791 to 1793. Near Midsteeple in the town centre a passage leads to the charming Globe Inn. Its attractions and those of its barmaid, Helen Ann Park, by whom Burns had a daughter, are celebrated in the lyric beginning:

> Yestreen I had a pint o' wine,
> A place where body saw na;
> Yestreen lay on this breast o'mine
> The gowden locks of Anna.—
> The hungry Jew in wilderness
> Rejoicing o'er his manna,
> Was naething to my hiney bliss
> Upon the lips of Anna.—

His favourite chair is preserved in the howff, or snuggery, at the back of the ground floor, and window panes he incised with verses may be seen upstairs. In Burns Street, then Mid Vennel, beyond the Globe we find the house where the poet lived for the last three years of his life; it is now a museum. A short walk to the left from the end of Burns Street brings us to St Michael's Church, the final point of interest in Dumfries. Inside, Burns' customary pew is indicated by a tablet. Outside, his body was moved from its original grave, visited by Wordsworth (s.v. Lake Poets, Rte 14) in 1803 and remembered in a poem of tribute, to its present mausoleum in 1815. Keats (q.v.), whose visit in 1818 led to an undistinguished poem, found the monument 'not very much to my taste, though on a scale, large enough to show they wanted to honour him.'

Although he had no connection with London in his lifetime, Burns is now remembered there by a monument in Poets' Corner (fee) of Westminster Abbey and by a statue in the Victoria Embankment Gardens near Embankment Underground Station (Northern, Bakerloo, Circle and District Lines).

Burns Cottage, Alloway. Open Apr to Oct, Mon to Sat 9–7, Sun 2–7 (June to Aug, Sun 10–7); Nov to March, Mon to Sat, 10–dusk. Fee includes entry to Burns Monument.

Land o'Burns Centre, Alloway. Open daily spring & autumn, 10–6, summer 10–9, winter 10–5. Fee.

Burns Monument, Alloway. Open Apr to mid Oct, daily 9–7. Fee includes entry to Burns Cottage.

Souter Johnnie's Cottage, Kirkoswald (NTS). Open 1 Apr to 30 Sept, daily except Fri. 12–5 or by appointment. Fee.

Tam O'Shanter's Inn, Ayr. Open Apr to Sept, Mon to Sat 9.30–5.30 & June to Aug, Sun 2.30–4; Oct to March, Mon to Sat 2–4. Fee.

Bachelors' Club, Tarbolton (NTS). Open 1 Apr to 31 Oct, daily 10–6. Fee.

Burns House, Mauchline. Open Easter to 31 Oct, Mon to Sat 11–12.30 & 1.30–5.30, Sun 1.30–5.30, or by arrangement. Fee.

Kay Park Monument, Kilmarnock. Open by appointment with the Curator, Dick Institute, Kilmarnock.

Burns Club, Irvine. Open Sat afternoon and by arrangement.

Lady Stair's House, Edinburgh. Open Mon to Sat 10–5 (June to Sept, 10–6).

Ellisland Farm. Open at all reasonable times.

Burns House, Dumfries. Open Apr to June, & Sept, Mon & Wed to Sat 10–1 &

2–5, Sun 2–5; July & Aug, daily 10–5; Oct to March, Mon & Wed to Sat 2–5. Fee.

Robert Burton

b. Lindley, Leicestershire, 1577; d. Oxford, 1640. *The Anatomy of Melancholy* (1621).

Burton spent his entire adult life in Oxford. He entered Brasenose College in 1593 and became a Student (ie. a Fellow) of Christ Church in 1599. In 1616 he also acquired the living of St Thomas, now much altered and restored, on Becket Street near the railway station and was apparently responsible for building the south porch. We know little more about Burton, beyond the occasional facts he let drop in the splendidly digressive course of his *Anatomy* and these brief remarks by Bishop Kennett in his *Register and Chronicle* (1728):

> The Author is said to have labour'd long in the Writing of this Book to suppress his own Melancholy, and yet did but improve it: And that some Readers have found the same Effect. In an interval of Vapours he would be extremely pleasant, and raise Laughter in any Company. Yet I have heard that nothing at last could make him laugh, but going down to the Bridge-foot in *Oxford*, and hearing the Barge-men scold and storm and swear at one another, at which he would set his Hands to his Sides, and laugh most profusely: Yet in his College and Chamber so mute and mopish that he was suspected to be *Felo de se*.

The Latin Chapel of Christ Church Cathedral has a monument with a bust and an inscription mentioning melancholy.

George Gordon, Lord Byron

b. London, 1788; d. Missolonghi, Greece, 1822. *Fugitive Pieces* (1806); *Poems on Various Occasions* (1807); *Hours of Idleness* (1807); *Poems Original and Translated* (1807); *English Bards and Scotch Reviewers* (1809); *Childe Harold's Pilgrimage* (1812–18); *The Giaour* (1813); *The Bride of Abydos* (1813); *The Corsair* (1814); *Hebrew Melodies* (1815); *The Siege of Corinth* (1816); *Parisina* (1816); *The Prisoner of Chillon and Other Poems* (1816); *Manfred* (1817); *Beppo: A Venetian Story* (1818); *Mazeppa* (1819); *Ode on Venice* (1819); *Don Juan* (1819–24); *Sardanapalus* (1821); *The Two Foscari* (1821); *Cain: A Mystery* (1821); *The Vision of Judgment* (1821); *Werner* (1823); *The Island* (1823); *The Age of Bronze* (1823); *The Deformed Transformed* (1824).

The most famous part of Byron's life is probably its close, and that belongs not to England but to the Continent. When he left his native country for good in 1816 he did not fade into the obscurity that sometimes awaits exiles. Stories of his Italian mistress, illegitimate English daughter, menagerie of animals, friendship with Shelley (q.v.), verse that shocked his publisher and, finally, death in the Greek war for independence all served to magnify a scandalous reputation into an enduring legend. So the places we most readily associate with him—the Villa Diodati near Geneva, the Palazzo Mocenigo in Venice and, above all, Missolonghi—are not English and, when his poetry has a local atmosphere, it is the atmosphere of

Switzerland, Italy or Greece. At the same time, however, the English scenes of Byron's life are well commemorated— he may often have been misunderstood but he has never been neglected—and, because less exotic, can help us penetrate the façades with which he delighted to obscure his complex personality. It is, after all, instructive to trace the hero of Missolonghi to Marylebone and the lover of Teresa Guiccioli to Aberdeen, to find Childe Harold in Nottingham.

For someone who later became an ornament, and sometimes a scandal, to the fashionable society of London, Byron started his life in the capital among very drab surroundings. He was born in Marylebone, in a rented back room at No. 16 Holles Street, which connects Oxford Street with Cavendish Square. The house was destroyed by bombs during the war but the department store that succeeded it has a sculpture by Barbara Hepworth remembering him. His baptism took place at Marylebone Parish Church in the absence of his father, Captain John Byron, who was hiding from creditors. This building, too, has vanished, though its site near the northern end of Marylebone High Street is marked by a garden of rest.

In 1789 Byron's mother took him to Aberdeen, on the east coast of her native Scotland. Captain Byron followed, quarrelled with his wife, and left again with what little money the couple possessed. Today the city has only a statue outside the Grammar School on Skene Street to remind the visitor of Byron; the building he attended (1794–98) stood closer to the centre in the Schoolhill. Yet this Scottish episode should not be forgotten, if only because it emphasised the crucial, early influence of Calvinism on his character.

Byron's circumstances changed when he inherited the title from his grandfather in 1798. He travelled south with his mother to claim the family home and estate, •Newstead Abbey, 10 miles north of Nottingham, reached from A60 to Mansfield. The 12C Augustinian Priory had been bought by Sir John Byron from Henry VIII in 1540 but, despite additions over the centuries, it was a scarcely habitable ruin when the poet and his mother first saw it: the deer had gone from the park, the oaks had been felled and even the furniture had been claimed by the fifth lord's creditors. The opening of Byron's early poem, 'On Leaving Newstead Abbey,' hardly exaggerates: 'Through thy battlements, Newstead, the hollow winds whistle.' Such melancholy decay has its romantic charm and this may explain why Byron's fitful expenditures on the building did little more than create living quarters for himself; even these were not ready until 1808. Charles Skinner Matthews, a friend from Cambridge and a guest at Newstead, described a typical day there:

> Our average hour of rising was one. I, who generally got up between eleven and twelve,—even when an invalid,—the first of the party, and was esteemed a prodigy of early rising. It was frequently past two before the breakfast party broke up. Then, for the amusements of the morning, there was reading, fencing, single-stick, or shuttlecock, in the great room; practising with pistols in the hall; walking—riding—cricket—sailing on the lake, playing with the bear, or teasing the wolf. Between seven and eight we dined; and our evening lasted from that time till one, two, or three in the morning. The evening diversions may be easily conceived.
>
> I must not omit the custom of handing round, after dinner, on the removal of the cloth, a human skull filled with burgundy . . . A set of monkish dresses, which had been provided, with all the proper apparatus

of crosses, beads, tonsures, etc., often gave a variety to our appearance and to our pursuits.

The present condition of the Abbey is owing largely to tactful repairs undertaken by Colonel Thomas Wildman, who bought it in 1818. The cloister and chapter house survive, the Great Hall has been restored, while Byron's apartments now contain the Roe-Byron library and a collection of relics. Near the NE angle of the house is the monument Byron erected in 1808 to his dog, Boatswain, complete with elegiac poem. It was placed with deliberate blasphemy on the spot where the high altar of the Abbey church presumably stood.

In the surrounding area we may visit several other places of interest. Annesley Hall, 3 miles SW of Newstead, was the home of Mary Chaworth, with whom the poet fell in love while still a schoolboy; her attractions were no doubt increased in his eyes by the fact that his grandfather had killed one of her ancestors in a duel. From 1803 to 1808 Byron and his mother lodged in Southwell, 12 miles east of Newstead and south of A617. According to Byron, they found in the cathedral town 'the advantage of very genteel society, without the hazard of being annoyed by mercantile affluence.' Burgage Manor, the Georgian house they rented, stands on the Green north of the picturesque Saracen's Head Inn. Opposite were the Pigot family, whose daughter Elizabeth became Byron's close friend, though her first impression was of 'a fat, bashful boy with his hair combed straight over his forehead.' An earlier lodging in Nottingham is marked by a plaque at No. 76 St James Street, between Maid Marian Way and the Old Market Square. Byron's familiarity with the city helps explain the sympathetic understanding he showed towards industrial unrest in his speeches to the House of Lords. Finally, on A611 north of Nottingham, we find the colliery town of Hucknall Torkard (usually abbreviated to Hucknall) and the church where Byron, his mother and daughter were buried.

From 1801 to 1805 Byron attended Harrow School in NW London, on the hill south of the modern centre of Harrow. Visitors can see the poet's name carved on a panel from the old Fourth Form Room. The *churchyard of St Mary at the top of the hill was a favourite spot of Byron's during his schooldays, as an early poem, 'Lines Written Beneath an Elm in the Churchyard of Harrow,' bears witness. The elm has gone but the tombstone of John Peachey where Byron used to sit is still there, now protected by railings. Byron's illegitimate daughter by Claire Clairmont is buried somewhere nearby. She was refused burial inside the church and her grave outside was never marked with the inscription her father wrote: 'In Memory of Allegra, daughter of G.G. Lord Byron, who died at Bagnacavallo, in Italy, April 20th 1822, aged five years and three months.'

When Byron entered university in 1805 he was, he complained, 'wretched at going to Cambridge instead of Oxford.' But he had to make do with *Trinity College rather than Christ Church, and was soon content with his lodging in the SE corner of Great Court: 'I am now most pleasantly situated in Superexcellent Rooms flanked on one side by my Tutor, upon the other by an old Fellow, both of whom are rather checks upon my vivacity.' They did not check his vivacity completely, and the main features of his undergraduate life suggest the Regency nobleman rather than the apprentice poet: 'between ourselves,' he confessed to a friend, 'College is not the place to improve either Morals or Income.' He boxed and swam (the mill pond in the nearby village of Trumpington is still called Byron's Pool), and at one point housed a bear in the hexagonal tower above his rooms, announcing that it would '*sit for a fellowship.*' Yet we should not be completely beguiled by this 'routine of dissipation,' as he called it—anymore than by the title of the volume he published during these years, *Hours of Idleness*—for he was always careful to hide a hard-working, ambitious temperament under a guise of aristocratic laziness. He is now commemorated in the College by Thorvaldsen's

Lord Byron at Cambridge, engraved by F.W. Hunt, after Gilchrist. Courtesy of Nottinghamshire Public Libraries

statue (1829) in the fine Wren Library on the west side of Nevile's Court. It is hardly surprising that the seated figure of the poet should seem inappropriately large for its surroundings, since it was originally intended for Westminster Abbey but refused a place there.

After he left Cambridge Byron spent two years abroad, returning in 1811 to England, London and literary fame. Byron House on St James's Street, south of Piccadilly, occupies the site of the lodgings where he awoke and found himself famous after *Childe Harold's*

Pilgrimage began publication in 1812. He later lived (1814–15) in the secluded and distinguished Albany, north of Piccadilly, where the novelist 'Monk' Lewis (q.v.) was a neighbour. His popularity gained him the *entrée* to Holland House in Holland Park, made the centre of Whig literary circles by the wife of the third Lord Holland. It was here he first met Lady Caroline Lamb, wife of the politician who became Lord Melbourne; with eager relish she judged him 'mad—bad—and dangerous to know,' and they enjoyed an affair which struck even Regency society as indiscreet. Only the park and east wing of the Tudor mansion remain, their appearance changed for the worse by the addition of the King George VI Memorial Hostel.

When Byron's body was returned from Missolonghi, embalmed almost beyond recognition, it was refused burial in Westminster Abbey and so his funeral cortège, watched by thousands, proceeded north to Hucknall where he had anyway wished to be buried. Thorvaldsen's statue was later excluded from the building and the rejection in 1924 of yet another petition that Byron be remembered in the Abbey provoked an amusing doggerel poem, 'A Refusal,' from Thomas Hardy (q.v.). The present simple memorial slab in Poets' Corner (fee) was unveiled as recently as 1969.

Newstead Abbey. Park open daily 10–dusk, except last Fri in Nov. Fee. Buildings open Good Fri to end Sept, daily 2–6. Fee.

Harrow School. Visits by prior arrangement with the Custos of the Old Schools.

Trinity College Library, Cambridge. Open Mon to Fri 12–2, and also Sat 10.30–12.30 during Full Term.

Thomas Carlyle

b. Ecclefechan, Dumfries and Galloway, 1795; d. London, 1881. *Sartor Resartus* (1833–34); *The French Revolution* (1837); *Heroes, Hero-Worship and the Heroic in History* (1841); *Past and Present* (1843); *The Letters and Speeches of Oliver Cromwell* (1845); *Frederick the Great* (1858–65).

Carlyle's hometown of Ecclefechan, between Gretna and Lockerbie, preserves his birthplace, Arched House, spanning a gateway halfway up the street. It is now a museum where visitors may see the room in which he was born and furniture from his Chelsea study. He is buried near his parents in the simple churchyard, and a replica of the Chelsea statue (see below) has been erected at the top of the town. Ecclefechan appears as 'Entepfuhl' in the quasi-autobiographical *Sartor Resartus*, 'standing in "trustful derangement" among the wooded slopes' (Bk 2, Ch. 2). In Annan to the south Carlyle attended the Academy ('Hinterschlag Gymnasium'; now the old Grammar School) where he found the teachers 'hide-bound Pedants, without knowledge of man's nature, or of boy's; or of aught save their lexicons and quarterly account-books' (Bk 2, Ch. 3), before studying at Edinburgh University. After his marriage in 1826 to Jane Welsh he lived (1828–34) at Craigenputtock, a large remote farm to the NW of Dumfries and reached by following Glenesslin west from Dunscore. *Sartor Resartus* was written here.

During a first brief stay in London (1831–32) the Carlyles lodged at No. 33 (then No. 4) Ampton Street, off Gray's Inn Road, marked with a plaque. A more famous residence is ••Carlyle's House in

Cheyne Row, running north from Cheyne Walk and the river in Chelsea. Carlyle and his wife lived in this modest Georgian terraced house—though not always in perfect concord—from 1834 until their deaths, Jane dying before him in 1866. In a spontaneous and unassuming fashion it became one of the most important literary gathering places in Victorian London. Distinguished visitors, often the subject of penetrating character sketches by their host, included: Dickens (q.v., Rte 5), who remained an admirer rather than intimate friend; Ralph Waldo Emerson, the American philosopher with whom Carlyle conducted a lengthy correspondence; Leigh Hunt (q.v.), poet, critic and neighbour, inspired by Mrs Carlyle's reception of him on one occasion to write 'Jenny Kissed Me'; Ruskin (q.v.), who found a common bond in Carlyle's Scottish ancestry and derived consolation from the older man's approval of his controversial views on political economy; and Tennyson (q.v.), who shared with Carlyle a passion for consuming 'infinite tobacco.'

Today it is perhaps the richest and best preserved writer's house in England, its rooms still filled with pictures, furniture and mementoes from the couple's long residence and still radiating the atmosphere captured in R.S. Tait's painting, 'A Chelsea Interior' (1858), which is on display. Of particular interest is the attic study, sound-proofed in 1853 for protection against the noise of the 'demon fowls' next door. To Carlyle's morbidly sensitive ears at least, the remedy was inadequate and the distracting sound was offered as one reason for the delays attending the writing of *Frederick the Great*.

A statue of Carlyle by Boehm (1882) stands in the garden between the end of Cheyne Walk and the Embankment.

Carlyle's tour of Eastern England in 1842, prompted in part by his interest in Cromwell, included a visit to Bury St Edmunds, Suffolk,

'A Chelsea Interior,' by Robert Tait (c. 1857). Courtesy of the Marquess of Northampton

which he found

> a prosperous brick Town; beautifully diversifying, with its clean brick houses, ancient clean streets, and twenty or fifteen thousand souls busy, the general grassy face of Suffolk; looking out right pleasantly, from its hill-slope, towards the rising sun: and on the eastern edge of it, still runs, long, black and massive, a range of monastic ruins; into the wide internal spaces of which the stranger is admitted on payment of one shilling. (*Past and Present*, Bk 2, Ch. 2)

In *Past and Present* the *Abbey becomes a symbol of ideal order, presented in rebuke to the turbulence, competitiveness and lack of spiritual purpose Carlyle saw around him in 19C England.

The Arched House, Ecclefechan (NTS). Open 20 Apr to 31 Oct, Mon to Sat 10–6. Fee.

Carlyle's House, Chelsea (NT). Open Apr to end Oct, Wed to Sun & BH Mon 11–5. Closed Good Fri. Fee.

Bury St Edmunds Abbey (English Heritage). Open Apr to Sept, Mon to Sat 9.30–6.30, Sun 2–6.30; Oct to March, 9–4.

'Lewis Carroll' (pseud. of Rev. Charles Lutwidge Dodgson)

b. Daresbury, Cheshire, 1832; d. Guildford, Surrey, 1898. *Alice's Adventures in Wonderland* (1865); *Through the Looking-Glass and What Alice Found There* (1872); *The Hunting of the Snark: An Agony in Eight Fits* (1876); *Sylvie and Bruno* (1889); *Sylvie and Bruno Concluded* (1893).

At Daresbury, a village off A56 16 miles NE of Chester, the parsonage where Carroll was born and spent his early childhood has gone but the church now has a memorial window depicting scenes from *Alice in Wonderland*. A more expressive location is Croft-on-Tees, on A167 at the border between North Yorkshire and County Durham, where Carroll's family moved when he was eleven. Although the Old Rectory is now divided into separate dwellings it still exudes the comfortable, affluent gentility in which he was brought up. His shy, fastidious nature did not make him a typical pupil at Rugby School in Warwickshire, which he entered in 1846, and his subsequent life emphasised how little he had in common with old Rugbeians like Thomas Hughes (q.v.).

Christ Church, Oxford was a more congenial environment and became his permanent home. He entered as an undergraduate in 1850, became a Student (Christ Church's term for Fellow) in 1852 and remained until death. The rooms he occupied from 1868 are in the NW corner of Tom Quad. Visitors here included Walter Pater (q.v.) from Brasenose. Carroll's quiet life was the very essence of bachelor donnishness. He overcame his shyness only in the company of young children, when his stutter disappeared, and in the pursuit of famous subjects for his camera. His letters (of which he wrote, by his own tally, 98,721) show a fussy perfectionism in dealings with college servants, colleagues, tradesmen, publishers and illustrators. His only serious intervention in college affairs occurred in 1870, when he protested against the alterations to Christ Church Cathedral made by Sir Gilbert Scott under the supervision of Dean Liddell. The

Library, in Peckwater Quad, has a collection of Carroll memorabilia.

No. 83 St Aldate's Street, opposite Christ Church, is traditionally identified with Sir John Tenniel's illustration of the shop where Alice encounters the sheep in Chapter 5 ('Wool and Water') of *Through the Looking-Glass.* Carroll's career as famous children's author began on a 'golden afternoon' in July 1862 when he and his friend Robinson Duckworth took the three young daughters of Dean Liddell on a boating trip on the upper river of the Thames (or Isis). They left from Folly Bridge, south of Christ Church via St Aldate's, and rowed to Godstow (3¼ miles), with its ruined Benedictine nunnery. In later life Alice Liddell recalled: 'Nearly all of *Alice's Adventures Under Ground* [Carroll's original title for his first Alice book] was told on that blazing summer afternoon with the heat haze shimmering over the meadows where the party landed to shelter for a while in the shadow

Alice in the shop, by Sir John Tenniell. From Through the Looking Glass. *Courtesy of Cambridge University Library*

cast by the haycocks near Godstow.' It was she who urged Carroll to write his story down.

Carroll visited Russia in 1868 but otherwise restricted himself to a less adventurous ambit of movement. In the early 1870s he was several times a guest at the Elizabethan mansion, Hatfield House (off A1 south of Welwyn Garden City in Hertfordshire). The friendship with Lord Salisbury, Chancellor of Oxford and later Prime Minister, had begun when Carroll sought permission to photograph his daughters. Some of the *Sylvie and Bruno* stories, his last and least successful writing for children, were first told at Hatfield. From 1877 onwards Carroll was in the custom of. spending his holidays at Eastbourne on the south coast. The boarding house where he stayed, at No. 7 Lushington Road, is marked with a plaque.

He died in Guildford (SW of London via A3) at the home his sisters had occupied since the death of their father in 1868. The Chestnuts still stands on Castle Hill and is now marked with a plaque. The little Museum and Muniments Room by Castle Archway nearby has letters and relics. His grave is in the New Cemetery on The Mount to the west.

Library, Christ Church. Visitors by appointment.

Hatfield House. House and west gardens open end of March to beginning of Oct, Tues to Sat 12–5, Sun 2–5.30. Closed Good Fri but open BH Mon 11–5. Park open daily 10.30–8. Fee.

Museum and Muniments Room, Guildford. Open Mon to Sat 11–5.

George Chapman

b. Hitchin, Hertfordshire? 1559? d. London, 1634. *Hero and Leander* (continuation of poem by Christopher Marlowe [q.v.]; 1598); *Eastward Hoe* (with Ben Jonson and John Marston [qq.v.]; 1605); *Bussy D'Ambois* (1607); *Iliad* (1611); *Odyssey* (1614–15).

The dramatist and poet whose translation of Homer was celebrated some two centuries later by Keats (q.v.) is today remembered only by scenes connected with the beginning and end of his life.

Chapman was perhaps born and probably spent the early years of his life at Hitchin, 3 miles west of the A1. By following Bucklesbury south from the Market Place the visitor comes to Tilehouse Street, unusually rich in half-timbered and Georgian houses; No. 35 bears a plaque in memory of the writer.

He was buried in London at St Giles-in-the-Fields, on St Giles High Street near St Giles Circus, in the south side of the churchyard. According to the 17C antiquary Anthony à Wood: 'Soon after was a monument erected over his grave, built after the way of the old Romans, by the care and charge of his most beloved friend Inigo Jones.' The monument, damaged and with its inscription recut, now stands in the north aisle of the rebuilt church.

Thomas Chatterton

b. Bristol, Avon, 1752; d. London, 1770. *Poems supposed to have been written at Bristol, by Thomas Rowley and others, in the Fifteenth Century* (edited by Thomas Tyrwhitt; 1777).

Chatterton was born at the old Schoolmaster's House on Redcliffe Way (then Pile Street) in SE Bristol. His widowed mother sent him to Colston's Hospital, a charity school for boys destined to become apprentices; its medieval buildings on Colston Street near the city centre have been replaced by Colston Hall. From the age of fifteen he worked as scrivener for an attorney, John Lambert, at offices, now vanished, on Corn Street north of the Cross.

None of these places was as important to Chatterton as **St Mary Redcliffe near his birthplace, where his uncle was sexton. In this magnificent Perpendicular church he found a striking contrast to the 'dingy piles of brick' that were 18C commercial Bristol and an escape from the frustrating realities of his own life. It became focus and inspiration for that passionate medievalism which led him to write poems he attributed to the fictitious Thomas Rowley, Bristol monk during Edward IV's reign. Of the various lyrics about St Mary Redcliffe itself, 'Onn Oure Ladie's Church' is perhaps the finest. Under the window of the south transept lies the tomb of William Canynge the younger (d. 1474), benefactor of St Mary and Mayor of Bristol, frequently mentioned in the Rowley poems. The muniments room where Chatterton claimed to have discovered his manuscripts is above the north porch. A statue depicting him in the uniform of Colston's Hospital stands in the churchyard.

During his short lifetime Chatterton signally failed to engage the interest of his distinguished contemporary, Horace Walpole (q.v.), and succeeded in deceiving only a handful of local self-styled antiquaries. But in the years of posthumous fame and debate about the authenticity of his forgeries many distinguished literary men visited the scenes of his life. Dr Johnson (q.v.) came with Boswell and, though he left a disbeliever, conceded that Chatterton was 'the most extraordinary young man that has come to my knowledge.' Oliver Goldsmith (q.v.) offered a promissory note for £200 to the owner of the manuscripts, an offer that gentleman prudently declined. William Henry Ireland, whose own Shakespearean forgeries were encouraged by Chatterton's example, made his pilgrimage. In a later generation Robert Southey, a native of Bristol, and Samuel Taylor Coleridge treasured the places associated with Chatterton as part of a growing Romantic legend (s.v. Lake Poets, Rte 5).

In London nothing remains of No. 39 Brooke Street, north of Holborn, the lodgings where Chatterton spent his last months struggling as a hack writer and where, at the age of seventeen years and nine months, he committed suicide. Before its demolition the house enjoyed a vogue as a literary shrine, just as Chatterton's death became a favourite subject for Romantic poets and painters.

Chatterton's Birthplace, Bristol. Visits by application to the Director, City Museum, Queen's Road, Bristol.

Geoffrey Chaucer

b. London, 1340–45; d. London, 1400. *The Book of the Duchess* (1369–70?); *The House of Fame* (1372–80?); *The Parliament of Fowls* (1380–86?); *Troilus and Criseyde* (1380–86?); *The Canterbury Tales* (unfinished, 1387–1400?).

Since Chaucer came from a wealthy family and made a career as court official his life is well documented for a man of his time, as the bulky volume of *Chaucer Life-Records* (1966) initiated by Professor Manly and Miss Rickert amply testifies. His various posts at court required travel and so gave him a wide knowledge of his country; Professor J.A.W. Bennett's elegant *Chaucer in Oxford and Cambridge* (1974) is particularly persuasive in demonstrating the poet's familiarity with the University cities and their ways.

The surviving monuments to Chaucer's life in London centre on Westminster Abbey. His **altar-tomb in Poets' Corner (fee), just outside the entrance to St Benedict's Chapel, was erected in 1556 by Nicholas Brigham, though the tomb chest itself may be work of an earlier date. Yet Chaucer's connections with the Abbey are far deeper than the honour of his burial there, for the building came under his responsibility when he was Clerk of Works between 1389 and 1391. This was the period when the architect Henry Yevele was completing the nave; Yevele's other most notable contributions include the tomb of Archbishop Langham (d. 1376) in the Chapel of St Benedict, and the tombs of Edward III (d. 1377) and Richard II and Anne (d. 1400 and 1395) in St Edward the Confessor's Chapel. During the last year of his life Chaucer leased a house in the Abbey grounds near what is now Henry VII's Chapel at the east end of the building.

In 1390 Chaucer held a special commission as Master of Works at Windsor Castle (west of central London via M4). The St George's Chapel whose repair he supervised is not the present magnificent building of that name but an earlier one on the site of what is now the Albert Memorial Chapel. He is reputed to have stayed in the Winchester Tower by the entrance to the north terrace.

The very title of Chaucer's most famous poem declares its rooted-ness in English geography, yet the references to the pilgrims' journey from London to the shrine of St Thomas (demolished 1538) in Canterbury Cathedral are only spare and generalised. The main features of their journey may be easily summarised. It begins im-mediately south of London Bridge in Southwark where, on the left-hand side of Borough High Street, stood the Tabard, the 'gentil hostelrye' (General Prologue, line 718) whose accommodation Chaucer praised:

> The chambres and the stables weren wyde,
> And wel we weren esed atte beste.

> (lines 28–29)

The inn burnt down in 1676 and its successor was demolished in 1875–76; it is remembered today in the name of Talbot Yard. The 17C wing of its fellow, the George, still stands, doubling as inn and National Trust property.

The route continues down Borough High Street and left on Great Dover Street which, after a large junction, becomes the Old Kent Road. At the corner of Albany Road on the right stood the 'wateryng of Seint Thomas' (line 826) where, at the Host's suggestion, the pilgrims cast lots to decide who shall begin the storytelling—an honour that falls to the Knight.

We then leave central London via New Cross Road, Blackheath Road, Blackheath Hill and Shooter's Hill Road. The journey takes us past Deptford and Greenwich, saluted by the Host in the Prologue to 'The Reeve's Tale':

> Lo Depeford! and it is half-way pryme.
> Lo Grenewych, ther many a shrewe is inne!
>
> (lines 51–52)

We ignore the A2 (Rochester Way) and remain on Shooter's Hill Road, the old Watling Street and now at this point A207, which rejoins the A2 east of Dartford (16 miles). Rochester (28 miles) is mentioned in the Prologue to 'The Monk's Tale' (line 37) and would in the normal course of such pilgrimages have been a stopping place for the first or second night. Sittingbourne (38 miles) appears as 'Sidyngborne' at the end of 'The Wife of Bath's Prologue,' while at Ospringe (45 miles) stands one of the few survivals of the old pilgrims' route, a medieval Maison Dieu. At the Brenley Corner roundabout (48 miles) east of Faversham we ignore the present A2 and follow its previous course via Boughton Street, with Blean Wood to our left and the area of Boughton under Blean to our right, and Dunkirk. It was at 'Boghton under Blee' (Prologue to 'The Canon Yeoman's Tale,' line 3) that the company is joined by the Canon Yeoman.

Chaucer's last topographical reference in the incomplete poem occurs in the Prologue to 'The Manciple's Tale':

> a litel toun
> Which that ycleped is Bobbe-up-and-doun,
> Under the Blee, by Caunterbury waye.
>
> (lines 1–3)

The quaintly named place is usually identified as Harbledown (56 miles), now on the outskirts of the cathedral city and notable for its Hospital of St Nicholas, a medieval leper foundation with an 11C chapel.

Windsor Castle (DoE). Precincts open mid March to 30 Apr & 1 Sept to late Oct, daily 10–5.15; May to end Aug, daily 10–7.15; late Oct to mid March, daily 10–4.15. State apartments open Mon to Sat from 10.30, Sun from 1.30. Fee for State apartments.

Maison Dieu, Ospringe (English Heritage). Open March, Apr & Oct, Mon to Sat 9.30–5.30, Sun from 2; May to Sept, Mon to Sat 9.30–7, Sun from 2; Nov to Feb, Mon to Sat 9.30–4, Sun from 2. Fee.

G.K. Chesterton

b. London, 1874; d. Beaconsfield, Buckinghamshire, 1936. *Greybeards at Play* (1900); *The Wild Knight and Other Poems* (1900); *Robert Browning* (1903); *The Napoleon of Notting Hill* (1904); *The Club of Queer Trades* (1905); *Heretics* (1905); *Charles Dickens* (1906); *The Man Who Was Thursday: A Nightmare* (1908); *Orthodoxy* (1908); *The Ball and the Cross* (1910); *What's Wrong With the World* (1910); *The Innocence of Father Brown* (1911); *The Ballad of the White Horse* (1911); *Manalive* (1912); *The Flying Inn* (1914); *The Wisdom of Father Brown* (1914); *A Short History of England* (1917); *Irish Impressions* (1919); *The Superstition of Divorce* (1920); *The New Jerusalem* (1920); *Eugenics*

and Other Evils (1922); *The Man Who Knew Too Much and Other Stories* (1922);
St Francis of Assisi (1923); *Tales of the Long Bow* (1925); *The Everlasting Man*
(1925); *William Cobbett* (1925); *The Incredulity of Father Brown* (1926); *The
Outline of Sanity* (1926); *The Queen of Seven Swords* (1926); *The Return of
Don Quixote* (1927); *The Secret of Father Brown* (1927); *The Poet and the
Lunatics: Episodes in the Life of Gabriel Gale* (1929); *Four Faultless Felons*
(1930); *St Thomas Aquinas* (1933); *The Scandal of Father Brown* (1935);
Autobiography (1936); *The Paradoxes of Mr Pond* (1937).

Although Kensington in London has no striking monuments to
Chesterton's connection with it, enough places of interest survive to
justify a walking tour. It begins at Notting Hill Gate Underground
Station (Central, and District and Circle Lines) in the neighbourhood
Chesterton used for his earliest novel. After walking south on
Kensington Church Street we turn right on to Sheffield Terrace,
where Chesterton was born at No. 32 to an affluent family of estate
agents and auctioneers. We then return to Kensington Church Street
and follow it south to the junction with Kensington High Street. In
1901 Chesterton married Frances Blogg at the church of St Mary
Abbots on this corner.

To our left lie Kensington Gardens, scene of 'The Last Battle' in
Book 5 of *The Napoleon of Notting Hill*. The main route takes us to
the right. Chesterton was a pupil at St Paul's School in the days when
it was located on Hammersmith Road, Kensington High Street's
western continuation. But before this we turn left on to Warwick
Gardens, where the Chesterton family lived for most of his childhood
and youth at No. 11. Pembroke Gardens leads left from Warwick
Gardens to the charming Edwardes Square. Chesterton and his wife
started their married life at No. 1.

The couple then went to live in Battersea, but the best place to
remember the early years of Chesterton's career is in Fleet Street.
His burly figure, made the more distinctive by the cloak and
swordstick that soon became his trademarks, was a familiar sight in
several of the street's taverns: the Cock near Temple Bar, El Vino's
on the south side near the junction with Fetter Lane, and the Cheshire
Cheese, by Wine Office Court on the north side. Chesterton's
flamboyant manner, relentless energy and decided opinions that
combined the conservative and the radical in almost equal proportions
soon attracted attention in literary and journalistic circles. His close
association with Hilaire Belloc (q.v.), a frequent companion in the
Fleet Street pubs and restaurants, made Shaw (q.v.) view the pair as
a pantomime beast, the 'Chesterbelloc.' Shaw himself, though he
never agreed with Chesterton, remained an admirer and close friend.

In 1909 Chesterton and his wife moved to Beaconsfield (west of
London on A40 near High Wycombe), renting Overroads on Grove
Road near the railway station and later building themselves a new
house, Top Meadow, opposite. At first sight the town was a surprising
choice of home for a man who seemed to belong to London and Fleet
Street as thoroughly as Dr Johnson (q.v.) had done, but Chesterton
himself vigorously defended suburban life. At any rate, his
Beaconsfield years brought no slackening of his formidable output
or of the reputation he had made. He created his popular detective,
Father Brown, and increased his audience by lecture tours, public
debates and, at the end of his life, radio broadcasts. In 1922 he was
received into the Roman Catholic church, a logical progression from
the High Anglicanism he had adopted in early manhood, and he is

now remembered in St Teresa's church in Beaconsfield.

John Clare

b. Helpston, Cambridgeshire, 1793; d. Northampton, 1864. *Poems Descriptive of Rural Life and Scenery* (1820); *The Village Minstrel* (1821); *The Shepherd's Calendar* (1827); *The Rural Muse* (1835); *Sketches in the Life of John Clare Written by Himself* (edited by Edmund Blunden; 1931).

Clare's career followed a pattern all too familiar in the lives of the so-called 'peasant poets' of the late 18C and early 19C. After a childhood and youth spent in manual work he managed to achieve popularity with a volume of poetry reflecting his background; later volumes were less successful, undeservedly so in his case, and his life became overshadowed by first financial and then mental problems. In the poetry of his madness he sometimes insisted that he was a man unbounded by time and space, yet the real strength of his writing lies in its local character: its precise observation of the manners, speech and changing social conditions of the agrarian poor, as well as the countryside where his life was passed.

Clare's countryside is found on the border of Eastern and Central England, where the modern counties of Cambridgeshire, Lincolnshire, Leicestershire and Northamptonshire meet. Its centre is Helpston (then Helpstone and in Northamptonshire) on B1443 6 miles NW of Peterborough, 'a gloomy village' but the occasion for much of his best poetry. He is remembered by a Gothic memorial of 1869 on the green. The cottage on Woodgate where he was born and lived for much of his life is marked with a plaque. In his boyhood he worked as a servant at the Bluebell Inn next door. He is buried in the churchyard of St Botolph.

Like other literary men, Clare had connections with the Renaissance mansion of Burghley House, 4 miles west of Helpston on B1443. As a child he climbed over the wall of the estate to read a newly purchased copy of Thomson's *The Seasons* among the 'uncommonly beautiful' scenery. In 1809 he was apprenticed as an under-gardener but his companions introduced him to 'irregular habits' and he stayed at Burghley only nine months. After the success of his first collection of verse in 1820 the house's owner, the Marquis of Exeter, granted him a small annuity for life. In Stamford, 2 miles further west, he bought books and the precious stock of pencils with which he started writing, and later attracted the notice of influential residents who helped him to publication. In 1817 he was working at a lime-kiln in the village of Pickworth, 4 miles to the NW and reached by following B1081 to Great Casterton and then taking a right. Its old church is remembered in 'On a Sunday Morning'; only a fragment remains as the outer entrance to the south porch of the present building.

Clare's move from Helpston to Northborough in 1832, made with the help of his patrons, took him only some 3 miles NE of his birthplace. Yet, as 'The Flitting' shows, it came as a wrench to someone of his minutely local sensibility:

> The ivy at the parlour end
> The woodbine at the garden gate
> Are all and each affections friend

> That renders parting desolate
> But times will change and friends must part
> And nature can still make amends
> Their memory lingers round the heart
> Like life whose essence is its friends

(lines 201–208)

His cottage, now greatly modernised, stands east of the church and manor house. Shyness of the visitors whom his fame was attracting caused him to have it built back from the road with its front door facing the rear garden. Although his Northborough years began by being among his most productive, a 'mild derangement' in 1837 caused him to enter a private asylum near Ponders End in Epping Forest. He escaped in July 1841 and, advised of the route by gipsies, walked back to his Northborough home.

The episode led to permanent commitment in the county asylum at Northampton, where he continued to write but also to suffer insane delusions. According to the medical superintendent, 'he would maintain that he had written the works of Byron, and Sir Walter Scott, that he was Nelson and Wellington, that he had fought and won the battle of Waterloo, that he had had his head shot off at this battle, whilst he was totally unable to explain the process by which it had again been affixed to his body.' The modern visitor can still see the Ionic portico (1701) of All Saints' Church on George Row where Clare delighted to sit when he was allowed out of the asylum.

Burghley House, near Stamford. Open 1 Apr to 7 Oct, Sat & BH 11–5, Sun & Good Fri 2–5. Fee.

Arthur Hugh Clough

b. Liverpool, Merseyside, 1819; d. Florence, Italy, 1861. *The Bothie of Toberna-Vuolich: A Long-Vacation Pastoral* (1848); *Ambarvalia* (1849); *Amours de Voyage* (1858); *Poems, With a Memoir* (edited by Francis Turner Palgrave; 1862).

No. 9 Rodney Street, the poet's birthplace in a row of dignified 18C houses in Liverpool, is marked with a plaque.

His family emigrated to South Carolina while he was still an infant. When he was sent back to England to be educated Clough attended exactly the same institutions as his contemporary, Matthew Arnold (q.v.). He studied at Rugby (1829–37) and left school as the ideal product of Dr Thomas Arnold's system. Yet Clough's years as an undergraduate at Balliol College, Oxford (1837–41) and as fellow and tutor at Oriel College (1842–48) did not fulfil his early promise. Arnold's elegy, 'Thyrsis,' sadly addressed him as 'too quick despairer' (line 61). His poetry combined a mastery of classical form that would have cheered Dr Arnold's heart with a doubting and self-doubting tone that was alien to the firm regimen of his old school.

During his Oxford years Clough several times took vacation reading parties of undergraduates to the Lake District. He is remembered there by a memorial in the churchyard of St Oswald at Grasmere, 4 miles north of Windermere on A591.

William Cobbett

b. Farnham, Surrey, 1763; d. Normandy, Surrey, 1835. *The Life and Adventures of Peter Porcupine* (1796); *The Political Censor* (1796–97); *Porcupine's Gazette* (1797–1800); *The Rush-Light* (1800); *The Porcupine* (1800–01); *Cobbett's Political Register* (1802–35); *Paper Against Gold and Glory Against Prosperity* (1810–11); *Mr Cobbett's Address to His Countrymen* (1817); *A Journal of a Year's Residence in the United States* (1818–19); *A Grammar of the English Language* (1818); *The American Gardener* (1821); *The Farmer's Friend* (1822); *The Farmer's Wife's Friend* (1822); *Cottage Economy* (1822); *A History of the Protestant Reformation* (1824–27); *The Poor Man's Friend* (1826); *Advice to Young Men* (1829); *The English Gardener* (1829); *The Emigrant's Guide* (1829); *Rural Rides* (1830; revised and expanded edition by James Paul Cobbett, 1853); *Plan of Parliamentary Reform* (1830); *Cobbett's Twopenny Trash* (1830–32); *A Tour in Scotland* (1832); *Cobbett's Manchester Lectures* (1832); *A Geographical Dictionary of England and Wales* (1832).

Throughout his combative, much-travelled life Cobbett kept a special affection for his native Farnham, between A325 and A31 SW of London. The town was, he told readers of *A Journal of a Year's Residence in the United States,* 'the neatest in England, and, I believe, in the whole world':

> All there is a garden. The neat culture of the hop extends its influence to the fields round about. Hedges cut with shears and every other mark of skill and care strike the eye at Farnham, and become fainter and fainter as you go from it in every direction. (General Preface)

Even if time has diminished its pastoral charms, Farnham today has not forgotten the man who praised it so emphatically. Cobbett mementoes are displayed in the Willmer House Museum at No. 38 West Street and there is a bust in Gostrey Meadow near the river. Two important landmarks commemorate the beginning and end of his life. His birthplace, the former Jolly Farmers Inn in Bridge Square, has now been renamed The William Cobbett. His tomb stands in the churchyard of St Andrew, Cobbett having spent his last years (1831–35) farming at Normandy, a village to the NE.

In his youth he worked as a gardener for the Bishop of Winchester at Farnham Castle, north of A325. Revisiting the region in later life he took his son to Tilford, 3 miles SE of Farnham:

> on the Green we stopped to look at an *oak tree,* which, when I was a little boy, was but a very little tree, comparatively, and which is now, take it altogether, by far the finest tree that I ever saw in my life. The stem or shaft is short; that is to say, it is short before you come to the first limbs; but it is full *thirty feet round,* at about eight or ten feet from the ground. (*Rural Rides,* entry for 27 September 1822)

The tree is still there.

The passage reminds us that Farnham is at the centre of the country traversed in *Rural Rides,* that generous and angry, bigoted and perceptive book which is certainly Cobbett's great achievement and perhaps the finest achievement of English travel literature. From 1822 until 1826 he travelled through Southern England, with excursions into South-Western and Eastern England; his titlepage lists Surrey, Kent, Sussex, Hampshire, Wiltshire, Gloucestershire, Herefordshire, Worcestershire (now amalgamated, of course, into Hereford and Worcester), Somerset, Oxfordshire, Berkshire, Essex,

Suffolk, Norfolk and Hertfordshire. He went by horse and avoided turnpike roads (among his pet hates) since his object was 'to see the *country*; to see the farmers at *home*, and to see the labourers *in the fields*' (entry for 25 September 1822). The result is something more than a document of agrarian life struggling under the first impact of the Industrial Revolution. It remains a living book, an ideal travelling companion. The modern tourist who wishes to gain a foretaste of the changes that have since overtaken the places Cobbett described should consult Laurence Vulliamy's 'photographic exploration,' *Rural Rides Revisited* (1977).

It was ironic, and the irony did not escape Cobbett, that a man so passionately attached to the older rural way of life should have spent most of his working life in London, the 'Wen' denounced in his political journalism. We may remember him in SW London at Kew Gardens; the main entrance is at the west end of Kew Green and there are several entrances on Kew Road near Kew Gardens Underground Station (District Line). At the age of about fourteen Cobbett ran away from Farnham, stopped in Richmond to make his momentous purchase of Swift's *Tale of a Tub* and came to work at Kew. He later recorded, with a touch of pride, that he attracted the attention of the future George IV by the oddity of his dress, for he had arrived still in his country clothes, 'blue smock-frock and my red garters tied under my knees' (*Political Register*, 19 February 1820).

Willmer House Museum, Farnham. Open Tues to Sat 11–5, also Wed 7–9 in May to Sept & BH Mon 2–5. Fee.

Farnham Castle. Keep (English Heritage) open 15 March to 15 Oct, Mon to Sat 9.30–6.30, Sun 2–6.30; 16 Oct to 14 March, Mon to Sat 9.30–4, Sun 2–4. Fee. Domestic buildings (Centre for International Briefing) open Wed 2–4.

Kew Gardens. Open daily except Christmas Day and 1 Jan from 10. Fee.

Wilkie Collins

b. London, 1824; d. London, 1889. *Antonina, or The Fall of Rome: A Romance of the Fifth Century* (1850); *Rambles Beyond Railways: or Notes in Cornwall, Taken A-Foot* (1851); *Mr Wray's Cash Box, or The Mask and the Mystery: A Christmas Sketch* (1852); *Basil: A Story of Modern Life* (1852); *Hide and Seek* (1854); *After Dark* (1856); *The Dead Secret* (1857); *The Queen of Hearts* (1859); *The Woman in White* (1860); *No Name* (1862); *Armadale* (1866); *The Moonstone: A Romance* (1868); *Man and Wife* (1870); *Poor Miss Finch* (1872); *The New Magdalen: A Dramatic Story in a Prologue and Three Acts* (1873); *The Law and the Lady* (1875); *The Two Destinies: A Romance* (1876); *The Haunted Hotel: A Mystery of Modern Venice, to Which is Added My Lady's Money* (1879); *A Rogue's Life: From His Birth to His Marriage* (1879); *The Fallen Leaves* (1879); *Jezebel's Daughter* (1880); *The Black Robe* (1881); *Heart and Science: A Story of the Present Time* (1883); *I Say No* (1884); *The Evil Genius: A Domestic Story* (1886); *Little Novels* (1887); *The Legacy of Cain* (1889); *Blind Love* (1890).

There is little left to remind the visitor of Collins' childhood and youth in London, part of which (1826–30) was spent in Hampstead where his father, distinguished landscape painter and Royal Academician, inhabited a succession of houses. Some indication, however, of the impression that the area made on his imagination is offered by the memorable encounter between Walter Hartright and the mysterious woman in white who provides the title for his first really successful and still probably his best known novel. The incident—which may also owe something to the circumstances of Collins' first meeting in 1859 with Caroline Graves, his future mistress—is located exactly. Hartright is returning late one evening from Hampstead to his chambers in town via Frognal Lane, and reaches the junction with the present Finchley Road.

> There, in the middle of the broad, bright high-road—there, as if it had that moment sprung out of the earth or dropped from the heaven—stood the figure of a solitary Woman, dressed from head to foot in white garments; her face bent in grave inquiry on mine, her hand pointing to the dark cloud over London, as I faced her. (Hartright's Narrative, Ch. 3)

In 1850, some years before the publication of this novel, Collins had taken the walking holiday described in a neglected travel book, *Rambles Beyond Railways, or Notes in Cornwall*, which can still serve as a pleasant introduction to scenes now more frequently visited by tourists. The book is notable for its sympathetic accounts of Cornish people, customs and legends as much as for descriptions of landscape or buildings. Collins' itinerary begins at the fishing town and resort of Looe (on A387 18 miles west of Plymouth), praised for its 'quaint old houses, . . . delightfully irregular streets, and . . . fragrant terrace-gardens' (Ch. 2), and proceeds by a meandering route along the south coast of the Duchy. Liskeard (Ch. 4), 8 miles to the north, is visited not for any intrinsic attractions but because of its proximity to St Cleer's Well, the stone circles known as the Hurlers and the granite pile of the Cheesering, all on Bodmin Moor to the north. From Helston, on A394 and a long stride of 46 miles to the SW, he goes south to Loe Pool and the Lizard (Chs. 5 and 6). After Land's End in Chapter 8, he moves north to Botallack (B3306) near St Just and a fascinating description of a descent into its mine (Ch. 9). The journey ends with visits to the Vale of Mawgan between St Colomb Major and the coast (Ch. 12), and to the dramatic headland of Tintagel with its ruined Castle.

In the 1850s Collins attracted the notice of Dickens (q.v.), his senior by twelve years—an association that led to close friendship, literary collaboration and inevitably, given both men's taste for travel, various holidays in each other's company. An accident-plagued tour of Cumbria in 1857 (see Dickens, Rte 17) resulted in *The Lazy Tour of Two Idle Apprentices* and Collins' decision to locate 'Limmeridge House,' Marion Halcombe and the Fairlies' home in *The Woman in White*, on the coast south of Carlisle. A visit to Clovelly, Devon in 1860 (Dickens, Rte 13) produced another collaborative work, 'A Message from the Sea,' published as the *Household Words* Christmas story for that year.

The most important of Collins' visits to Gad's Hill (Dickens, Rte 11) took place in 1860, when his younger brother Charles was married to Dickens' daughter Kate. Like his mentor, he was also fond of Broadstairs (Dickens, Rte 11 again). His stay in 1859 was made memorable by the discovery of a title for the novel he was writing, under circumstances he later described to a reporter:

> He walked for several hours on the cliffs between Kingsgate and Bleak House, and smoked an entire case of cigars, striving for a title but with barren result. As the sun went down the novelist threw himself on the grass, contemplating the North Foreland lighthouse, and, being hipped and weary, looked by no means lovingly on that hideous edifice. Savagely, biting the end of his last cigar he apostrophised the building, standing

coldly and stiffly in the evening light, 'You are ugly and stiff and awkward; you know you are: stiff and as weird as my white woman. White woman!—woman in white! The title, by Jove!'

Appropriately enough it was Dickens, virtually alone among Collins' acquaintance, who approved the proposed title and did not think it too melodramatic. During a subsequent visit in 1862 Collins occupied Dickens' own former lodging, Bleak House.

The Suffolk coastal town of Aldeburgh, which Collins visited in the spring of 1862, provided locales for *No Name*, another of his successful novels of the 1860s. He notes the Moot Hall, left stranded on the beach by the encroachments of the sea, and reminds the reader of the town's connection with George Crabbe (q.v.). Landscape descriptions like the following show him attempting to emulate the 18C poet:

> It was a dull, airless evening. Eastward, was the gray majesty of the sea, hushed in breathless calm; the horizon line invisibly melting into the monotonous, misty sky; the idle ships shadowy and still on the idle water. Southward, the high ridge of the sea dike, and the grim, massive circle of a martello tower reared high on its mound of grass, closed the view darkly on all that lay beyond. Westward, a lurid streak of sunset glowed red in the dreary heaven, blackened the fringing trees on the far borders of the great inland marsh, and turned its little gleaming water-pools to pools of blood. Nearer to the eye, the sullen flow of the tidal river Alde ebbed noiselessly from the muddy banks; and nearer still, lonely and unprosperous by the bleak water-side, lay the lost little port of Slaughden, with its forlorn wharfs and warehouses of decaying wood, and its few scattered coasting-vessels deserted on the oozy river-shore. No fall of waves was heard on the beach, no trickling of waters bubbled audibly from the idle stream. Now and then the cry of a sea-bird rose from the region of the marsh; and at intervals, from farmhouses far in the inland waste, the faint winding of horns to call the cattle home traveled mournfully through the evening calm. (Fourth Scene, Ch. 1).

Throughout his life Collins was a Londoner, living at various addresses in Marylebone. In 1867 he moved to No. 65 (then No. 90) Gloucester Place, north of Oxford Street, a fine Georgian house now marked with a plaque. He remained there until the year before his death, writing his great contribution to the detective novel, *The Moonstone*, but later suffering a serious decline in both popularity and health. His funeral at Kensal Green Cemetery, opposite Kensal Green Station (Bakerloo Line and British Rail), was attended by Oscar Wilde (q.v.) among other literary figures but marred by scenes which, as his biographer points out, might almost have come from one of his novels:

> There must have been at least a hundred of those unwholesome creatures, who call themselves women, who seem to live in graveyards. When the coffin had been lowered into the bricked grave there was a general rush of these people who craned over into space, and clawed the wreaths of flowers, and pulled about the cards which were attached to the wreaths, and laughed and cried and chattered until they were moved on by the graveyard police.

The grave is No. 31754 in Square 141, north of West Centre Avenue and immediately west of the church. His mistress, Caroline Graves, was buried beside him in 1895, though her presence was not recorded. A petition for a memorial in either St Paul's Cathedral or Westminster Abbey was unsuccessful, the rejection being influenced, according to one report, by 'other considerations than Mr Collins' literary excellence.'

Tintagel Castle (English Heritage). Open 15 March to 15 Oct, Mon to Sat 9.30–6.30, Sun 2–6.30 (from 9.30 Apr to Sept); 16 Oct to 14 March, Mon to Sat 9.30–4, Sun 2–4. Closed Christmas Eve, Christmas Day, Boxing Day & New Year's Day. Fee.

Bleak House (Dickens & Maritime Museum), Broadstairs. Open March to Nov, daily 10–6, until 9 in July, Aug & Sept. Fee.

Kensal Green Cemetery. Open Mon to Sat 9–5.30 (or dusk, if earlier), Sun 2–5.30 (or dusk); Good Fri 2–5.30, Christmas Day 10–2. Closes at 1 on BH.

William Collins

b. Chichester, West Sussex, 1721; d. Chichester, 1759. *Persian Eclogues* (1742); *Odes* (1747).

After attending Winchester College, Collins went to Oxford: first to The Queen's College in 1740 and then the following year to Magdalen College where, according to his contemporary Gilbert White (q.v.), he showed 'too high an opinion of his school acquisitions, and a sovereign contempt for all academic studies and discipline.' On the strength of his *Persian Eclogues* he was emboldened to reject a clerical career and join the literary life of London. He was a frequent visitor to James Thomson's cottage at Richmond (described under the entry for that author) and apparently even took lodgings in the area to be near his friend. Collins is the probable subject of a portrait in Thomson's last poem, *The Castle of Indolence* (1748), as

> a man of special grave remark:
> A certain tender gloom o'erspreads his face,
> Pensive, not sad . . .
>
> (stanza 57)

He repaid the compliment with the fine 'Ode on the Death of Mr Thomson.'

Suffering from financial difficulties and increasing mental disorder, he returned in 1749 to Chichester, the town of his birth and, in the words of Edmund Blunden 'the most intimate relic of the life of William Collins that now exists.' He lived on Westgate, west of the Cathedral, under the care of his sister and later at the Chantry in the cloisters of the Cathedral. Though he was buried at St Andrew Oxmarket (now redundant) off East Street, his best memorial is in the SW tower of the Cathedral. Flaxman's *monument shows him immersed in the New Testament while its inscription records the suffering of his last years:

> He pass'd in madd'ning pain life's feverish dream;
> While rays of genius only serv'd to shew
> The thick'ning horror and exalt his woe.

Winchester College. Open Apr to Sept, Mon to Sat 10–6, Sun 2–6 (guided tours start Mon to Sat 11, 2 & 3.15, Sun 2 & 3.15); Oct to March, Mon to Sat 10–4, Sun 2–4.

William Congreve

b. Bardsey, West Yorkshire, 1670; d. London, 1729. *The Old Bachelor* (1693); *The Double Dealer* (1694); *Love for Love* (1695); *The Way of the World* (1700).

Although Congreve's birthplace in the small village of Bardsey (on A58 between Leeds and Wetherby) does not survive the church where he was baptised, notable for its Saxon tower, is still there.

His father's military career moved the family to Ireland in 1674. Congreve's connections with the country are best remembered by the places where he was educated. He attended Kilkenny College in the county town of Kilkenny; its present buildings are on the north bank of the Nore near John's Bridge, but in Congreve's time the school was apparently in the Cathedral Close. He then studied at Trinity College, Dublin, occupying rooms in the Old Quadrangle. During his university career he enjoyed a reputation for convivial living and strengthened his friendship with Swift (q.v.), who had been a fellow pupil at Kilkenny.

In London there is nothing to commemorate Congreve's brief but distinguished career as a dramatist or his later life as man of leisure and holder of a convenient government sinecure. Instead, three country houses in scattered locations deserve mention. At Stretton Hall in Staffordshire, south of the county town and near the junction between A5 and A449, family home of the Congreves, he began his first play on his return from Ireland in 1689. The original house has been replaced by a fine brick 18C one. Tradition also ascribes the writing of the play to a stay in 1692 at Ilam, in Dovedale and 4 miles NW of Ashbourne, Derbyshire. The present Hall dates from the 19C and now serves as a Youth Hostel but the grounds, where the Manifold emerges from its subterranean course, justify a visit. Most important, Congreve was a guest at Stowe, 2 miles NW of Buckingham. Beginning in 1710 Sir Richard Temple, later Viscount Cobham, made substantial alterations to his 17C mansion and made its grounds perhaps the finest example of 18C landscaping. A monument to Congreve, in the curious form of an obelisk surmounted by a monkey, stands on an island in the Octagonal Lake. It was designed by William Kent and erected in 1736. Stowe is now a public school.

After Congreve's death, partly caused by an accident sustained during a visit to Bath, his body lay in state in the Jerusalem Chamber of Westminster Abbey. He was buried not in Poets' Corner but in the south aisle of the nave, with a monument erected by his friend Henrietta, Duchess of Marlborough, who herself chose to be buried near him.

Ilam Park, near Ashbourne (NT). Park open every day. Information room open Apr to end Oct, daily 10–6; Nov to end March, Sat & Sun 10–5.

Stowe, near Buckingham. Grounds and garden buildings open Easter & summer school holidays, Fri, Sat, Sun & Aug BH Mon, 1–6. Fee.

'Joseph Conrad' (pseud. of Józef Teodor Konrad Korzeniowski)

b. Berdyczów, Poland, 1857; d. Bishopsbourne, Kent, 1924. *Almayer's Folly: The Story of an Eastern River* (1895); *An Outcast of the Islands* (1896); *The Nigger of the 'Narcissus': A Tale of the Sea* (1897); *Lord Jim: A Tale* (1900); *Youth: A Narrative, and Two Other Stories* (includes *Heart of Darkness*; 1902); *Typhoon* (1902); *Romance: A Novel* (with Ford Madox Ford; 1903); *Nostromo: A Tale of the Seaboard* (1904); *The Secret Agent: A Simple Tale* (1907); *Under Western Eyes: A Novel* (1911); *Chance: A Tale in Two Parts* (1913); *Victory: An Island Tale* (1915); *The Shadow-Line: A Confession* (1917); *The Arrow of Gold: A Story Between Two Notes* (1919); *The Rescue: A Romance of the Shallows* (1920); *The Rover* (1923); *Suspense: A Napoleonic Novel* (unfinished; 1925).

Conrad did not visit England until 1878, nor did he give up the sea until the mid 1890s and his marriage to Jessie George. When he did settle down and devote himself to writing, his novels looked backward to earlier adventures abroad and at sea rather than at the English life around him. The only place to have an important connection with his fiction is Greenwich Park in SE London. The former Royal Observatory on top of the hill was the target of an attack in 1894 by the anarchist Martial Bourdin, who succeeded only in blowing himself up. The incident gave Conrad the germ of *The Secret Agent*. At the opening of *Heart of Darkness* the Thames below is evoked as 'the beginning of an interminable waterway' which leads Captain Marlow to the inner reaches of the Congo.

Conrad's years as a writer were spent mainly in Kent, which he was surely right to call 'the very heart of English literary life of that period' since other residents of the south-eastern counties then included Henry James, Rudyard Kipling and H.G. Wells (qq.v.). From 1898 to 1907—the period that produced *Lord Jim*, the *Youth* volume of stories and *Nostromo*—he lived north of Hythe. We reach his home by following B2068 2½ miles north from its junction with A20 and then turning right for Postling. Pent Farm lies on the right before we enter the village. The period 1910–19 was spent near Ashford to the west. From the A20 we take B2068 south to Lympne (1 mile) and then continue west a further 8 miles on B2067, where we follow B2070 north towards Ashford. By turning right for Bonnington after 1 mile we soon reach Capel House, the farmhouse where Conrad wrote *Chance* and *Victory*.

His last home (1919–24) was Oswalds, the Georgian former rectory of Bishopsbourne, a little village off A2 4½ miles SE of Canterbury. By this time he had won international recognition as a novelist, though he had passed the height of his powers. He had also, apparently, transformed himself into an English country gentleman, though in Bertrand Russell's words he still 'thought of civilised and morally tolerable human life as a dangerous walk on a thin crust of barely cooled lava.' A few months before his death he was offered a knighthood but put the letter aside unopened, fearing it came from the Inland Revenue. When the Prime Minister sent a personal messenger to make further inquiry, Conrad declined the honour.

His funeral service was held at the Roman Catholic church of St Thomas in Canterbury, between St George Street and Burgate. His simple tombstone in the Catholic cemetery gives his name only in Polish (with 'Teodor' misspelled), omits any reference to his novels, and quotes the lines from Spenser (q.v.) he had used as the epigraph to his last complete work, *The Rover*:

> Sleep after toyle, port after stormie seas,
> Ease after warre, death after life, does greatly please.

'Marie Corelli' (pseud. of Mary MacKay)

b. place unknown, 1855; d. Stratford-upon-Avon, Warwickshire, 1924. *The Romance of Two Worlds* (1886); *Thelma* (1887); *Ardath* (1889); *Barabbas* (1893); *The Sorrows of Satan*' (1895); *The Mighty Atom* (1896).

The houses where Marie Corelli lived until middle age have followed her once best-selling novels into obscurity. She spent a childhood and youth (1865–83) later romanticised beyond recognition at Mickleham, between Dorking and Leatherhead in Surrey, near Box Hill and the better known residence of George Meredith (q.v.). Her London home (1883–1900) at No. 47 Longridge Road in Earl's Court, south of and parallel to West Cromwell Road, is now owned by the Egyptian Embassy. The plaque that misspelled her name was removed but later replaced at the request of her modern biographer.

Marie Corelli is better, though not always kindly, remembered in Stratford-upon-Avon where she lived at Mason Croft, near the southern end of Church Street, from 1901 until her death. The pleasant 18C house now belongs to the University of Birmingham Shakespeare Institute. Together with the popularity of her novels, her habit of boating on the Avon in a gondola specially imported from Venice and her frequent quarrels with the Trustees of Shakespeare's Birthplace made her a tourist attraction to complement if not rival Shakespeare (q.v., Rte 6) himself. *Punch* satirised the reactions of one such visitor:

> 'Behold,' he cries, 'the actual house
> That Miss Corelli leases,
> In yonder study's restful shade,
> Accepting none but Heaven's aid,
> She makes her masterpieces.'

She made a more lasting contribution to Stratford in 1909 by being instrumental in the purchase, restoration and public opening of Harvard House in the High Street. She is buried in the cemetery on Evesham Road.

A flirtatious but later embittered relationship with the painter Arthur Severn, husband of Ruskin's niece, made her a visitor to the writer's former home of Brantwood, near Coniston in Cumbria.

Harvard House, Stratford-upon-Avon. Open Apr to Oct, Mon to Sat 9–1, 2–6, Sun 2–6; Nov to March, Thurs, Fri, Sat 10–1, 2–4. Closed Christmas Eve, Christmas Day, Boxing Day & 1 Jan. Fee.

Brantwood, near Coniston. Open Good Fri to end Oct, daily except Sat 11–5.30. Fee.

William Cowper

b. Berkhamsted, Hertfordshire, 1731; d. East Dereham, Norfolk, 1800. Contributions to *Olney Hymns* (1779); *John Gilpin* (1785); *The Task* (1785).

Though born in Hertfordshire Cowper was mainly educated in London at Westminster School, which stands in Little Dean's Yard to the south of Westminster Abbey. Without being conspicuously unhappy, his experiences there left him with the life-long dislike of the public school system expressed in his poem 'Tirocinium' (1785). He then studied law, lodging at No. 62 Russell Square, off Southampton Row in Bloomsbury, and in various parts of the Temple, south of Fleet Street near its junction with the Strand: in a house (now demolished) on Inner Temple Lane and in Pump Court nearby. It was in Fig Tree Court that Cowper, faced with the prospect of an examination for a House of Lords clerkship, attempted to hang himself in 1763.

As a result of the experience Cowper left London and the law, 'unwilling to revisit those noisy and crowded scenes, which I never loved, and which I now abhor.' After a period under medical care he went to live in Huntingdon, Cambridgeshire, making regular visits to nearby Cambridge where his brother was a Fellow of Corpus Christi College. The house in Huntingdon's High Street where he lodged with Rev. Morley Unwin and his wife Mary is marked by a plaque.

When Unwin died suddenly in 1767 Cowper moved moved with Mrs Unwin to *Olney, a lace-making town near A428 between Bedford and Northampton but itself in Buckinghamshire. The Olney years were in many ways the most significant of his life and are certainly now the best remembered. He turned seriously to poetry, wrote some of his most charming letters, indulged his compassionate interest in animals and came under the Evangelical influence of the local perpetual curate, John Newton. Yet he still could not escape mental turbulence. In 1773–74 religious delusions, suicidal impulses and anxiety about his forthcoming marriage to Mrs Unwin (never to take place) made him flee his home and seek refuge with Newton.

The house Cowper normally shared with Mrs Unwin, then called Orchard Side and now the Cowper and Newton Museum, stands in the Market Place. Its contents include the sofa which, at the suggestion of his friend Lady Austen, he took as the subject of his poem, *The Task*. The garden, communicating with the parsonage where Newton lived, preserves his summer house. There is a commemorative window in the Memorial Chapel of the church.

In 1786 Cowper and Mrs Unwin moved to *Weston Underwood, 2 miles SW of Olney and in the poet's eyes 'one of the prettiest villages in England.' They lived at the Lodge in the main street until 1795.

In the autumn of 1792 he made an extended visit to William Hayley, friend of good poets though a bad poet himself, at Eartham in West Sussex. On his way back he dined in Richmond with his relative, General Spencer Cowper, at Ham House, a fine 17C mansion with Baroque interiors and with grounds stretching to the Thames.

When he left Weston Cowper wrote on his bedroom window:

Farewell, dear scenes, for ever closed to me;
Oh, for what scenes must I now exchange ye!

His foreboding was justified, for the last years of his life were marked by Mrs Unwin's decline into senility before her death in 1796 and his own decline into the despairing melancholy so poignantly expressed by his poem 'The Castaway.' They were spent in Norfolk at Mundesley (on the coast 7 miles SE of Cromer), where his cousin's house on the High Street has since been renamed Cowper's House, and at East Dereham, 16 miles west of Norwich, again with his cousin John Johnson. The Cowper Memorial Congregational Church now occupies the site of his home in East Dereham's Market Place; a plaque pays tribute to the 'patient friends' who cared for him. He was buried in St Nicholas nearby, which has a stained glass window and a memorial tablet with epitaph by Hayley. George Borrow (q.v.), who spent part of his childhood in the town, was proud that its 'venerable church' should hold 'the mortal remains of England's sweetest and most pious bard':

> Yes, pretty D——, I could always love thee, were it but for the sake of him who sleeps beneath the marble slab in yonder quiet chancel. It was within thee that the long-oppressed bosom heaved its last sigh, and the crushed and gentle spirit escaped from a world in which it had known naught but sorrow. Sorrow! do I say? How faint a word to express the misery of that bruised reed; misery so dark that a blind worm like myself is occasionally tempted to exclaim, Better had the world never been created than that one so kind, so harmless and so mild, should have undergone such intolerable woe! But it is over now, for, as there is an end of joy, so has affliction its termination. (*Lavengro*, Ch. 3)

Cowper and Newton Museum, Olney. Open Tues to Sat 10–12, 2–5. Closed Good Fri, Christmas & 1 Jan. Fee.

Ham House, Richmond. (NT and V&A Museum). Open Apr to Sept, daily except Mon 2–6; Oct to March, daily except Mon 12–4. Open BH Mon; closed Good Fri, May Day & Christmas. Fee.

George Crabbe

b. Aldeburgh, Suffolk, 1755; d. Trowbridge, Wiltshire, 1832. *The Village* (1783); *The Parish Register* (1807); *The Borough* (1810); *Tales* (1812).

Although the various occasions of his life took him to several different regions it is with Eastern England and in particular with the Suffolk coastal town of *Aldeburgh, birthplace, intermittent residence in adult years and stimulus for some of his best poetry, that Crabbe is mainly associated.

Its main point of interest is the church of St Peter and St Paul where he served briefly as curate after his ordination at Norwich in 1781 and whose north chapel contains a memorial of 1847 by Thurlow. The house where he was born and Slaughden Quay, where as boy and young man he did uncongenial work for his father, have been obliterated by the encroachments of the sea—a process to which the present location of the half-timbered Moot Hall, once undoubtedly part of a market centre but now stranded on the beach, offers striking testimony. Crabbe Street, running between the coast and the High Street before converging with the latter, appears to owe its name to a spirit of general tribute rather than to any specific connection with the writer.

According to the poet's son Aldeburgh was 'a poor and wretched place' in the time of Crabbe's youth, a description amply confirmed by the bleakly realistic portrayal of the local inhabitants and their condition in *The Village* and *The Borough*. Despite the fashionable status it has later come to enjoy, its seafront and adjoining coastline still retain the atmosphere recorded in Crabbe's verse and expressed most memorably, perhaps, in his account of the hero's melancholy visits to the shore in 'Peter Grimes' (from *The Borough*):

> Here dull and hopeless he'd lie down and trace
> How sidelong crabs had scrawl'd their crooked race;
> Or sadly listen to the tuneless cry
> Of fishing gull or clanging golden-eye;
> What time the sea-birds to the marsh would come,
> And the loud bittern, from the bull-rush home,
> Gave from the salt-ditch side the bellowing boom . . .
>
> (lines 193–199)

In this century Crabbe's association with the town has been commemorated by the local premiere in 1945 of Benjamin Britten's opera, *Peter Grimes*.

In the surrounding area Bungay and Stowmarket where Crabbe attended school, as well as Wickham Brook and Woodbridge, where he was apprenticed to apothecaries and surgeons, can boast no surviving evidence of his presence there; but the last town (16 miles SW of Aldeburgh via A1094 and A1152), especially that part of it by the Deben estuary, still possesses much of the flavour it would have had in the poet's day. It was at Woodbridge that Crabbe first met his future wife, Sarah Emily.

Crabbe's connection with Central England was owing to the patronage of the Duke of Rutland and began in 1782 with his appointment as chaplain at the Duke's seat of Belvoir Castle, Leicestershire, 7 miles west of A1 near Grantham. His lodging from the time of his marriage in 1783 until 1785 was later destroyed by the fire that led to James Wyatt's extensive rebuilding of 1816. Crabbe later took up the curacy of Stathern (5 miles SW of Belvoir) and, in 1789, the living of Muston (4 miles north of Belvoir), which he held until 1814 with a long record of absenteeism in his native Suffolk. His wife, who died and was buried at Muston, is commemorated by a plaque in the chancel of the church.

Crabbe moved to South-Western England in the later years of his life to occupy the more profitable living of Trowbridge, west of Devizes in Wiltshire but close to the Somerset border, where he remained until his death. He did, however, make several journeys from Wiltshire, most notably an 1817 visit to London which is better documented than his earlier sojourn in the capital (1780–81). He took lodgings at No. 37 Bury Street, to the south of Piccadilly, thus having the poet Thomas Moore as a near neighbour, and gained the *entrée* to Holland House in Holland Park, which the wife of the third Lord Holland had made a fashionable gathering place. Only the park and east wing of this Tudor mansion now survive, their appearance changed for the worse by the addition of the modern King George VI Memorial Hostel. In London circles Crabbe caused remark by his provincial look ('dressed as he was in the rather old-fashioned style of clerical propriety') and his habit of making sugary addresses to the ladies. He spent the autumn of 1822 with Sir Walter Scott (q.v.) in his house at No. 39 Castle Street, Edinburgh.

Crabbe's memory is recorded by a tablet in the chancel of Trowbridge church.

Belvoir Castle. Open late March to Sept, Tues, Wed, Thurs & Sat 12–6, Sun 12–6; BH Mon 11–7, Good Fri, 12–6; also Sun in Oct 2–6. Fee.

Dinah Craik (née Mulock)

b. Stoke-upon-Trent, Staffordshire, 1826; d. London, 1887. *The Ogilvies* (1849); *Olive* (1850); *The Head of the Family* (1851); *Agatha's Husband* (1853); *Avillion and Other Tales* (1853); *John Halifax, Gentleman* (1856); *A Woman's Thoughts About Women* (1858); *A Life For a Life* (1859); *Mistress and Maid* (1863); *Christian's Mistake* (1865); *The Little Lame Prince* (1875); *An Unsentimental Journey Through Cornwall* (1884).

John Halifax, Gentleman, always Mrs Craik's most popular novel and now the only one to be remembered, is set in the attractive Gloucestershire town of Tewkesbury (on A38 9 miles NW of Cheltenham), which she calls 'Norton Bury.' She is commemorated by a marble neo-Renaissance tablet in the south transept of the fine Norman Abbey Church. The picturesque Bell Hotel opposite the churchyard gate becomes the home of Abel Fletcher in the novel. Mill Street leads to the River Avon and the Abbey Mill, renamed Abel Fletcher's Mill and now a restaurant. The Tudor House Hotel on the High Street, a building much altered but of genuine antiquity, is identified with the home of Ursula March.

Mrs Craik spent the later years of her life in Bromley, then in Kent and now absorbed into SE London. She was buried nearby in the churchyard at Keston, by A233 1½ miles south of its junction with A232.

Samuel Daniel

b. near Taunton, Somerset?, 1562; d. Beckington, Somerset, 1619. *Delia* (1592); *Musophilus, or Defence of Learning* (1599); *Defence of Rhyme* (1602).

Daniel was educated at Magdalen College, Oxford. In the early 1590s he became tutor to William, son of Mary Herbert, Countess of Pembroke and sister to Sir Philip Sidney (q.v.), and so joined the impressive list of literary men connected with Wilton House, near Salisbury in Wiltshire. *Delia*, a sonnet cycle in the Petrarchan manner and today better remembered than his Senecan tragedies, court masques and prose treatises, is dedicated to the Countess.

Later the same decade Daniel became tutor to Lady Anne Clifford, daughter of the Countess of Cumberland, at Skipton (22 miles west of Harrogate via A59) in North Yorkshire. Originally medieval but with Tudor additions, •Skipton Castle was later extended by Lady Anne; the pleasingly irregular Conduit Court is particularly notable.

In 1610 Daniel moved to the village of Beckington, at the junction of A36 and A361 between Trowbridge and Frome near the Wiltshire–Somerset border. Its church has a monument erected in his memory by Lady Anne.

Wilton House, near Salisbury. Open mid Apr to mid Oct, Tues to Sat & BH Mon 11–6, Sun 1–6. Fee.

Skipton Castle. Open Mon to Sat 10–6 or sunset, Sun 2–6 or sunset. Fee.

C. Day-Lewis

b. Ballintubbert, Co. Laois, 1904; d. Hadley Common, Hertfordshire, 1972. *Beechen Vigil and Other Poems* (1925); *Country Comets* (1928); *Transitional Poem* (1929); *From Feathers to Iron* (1931); *The Magnetic Mountain* (1933); *A Hope for Poetry* (1934); *A Time to Dance* (1935); *A Question of Proof†* (1935); *Noah and the Waters* (1936); *The Friendly Tree* (1936); *Thou Shell of Death†* (1936); *Starting Point* (1937); *There's Trouble Brewing†* (1937); *Overtures to Death* (1938); *The Beast Must Die†* (1938); *Child of Misfortune* (1939); *The Smiler With the Knife†* (1939); *Malice in Wonderland†* (1940); *The Case of the Abominable Snowman†* (1941); *Word Over All* (1943); *The Poetic Image* (1947); *Minute for Murder†* (1947); *Poems 1943–1947* (1948); *Head of a Traveller†* (1949); *An Italian Visit* (1953); *The Dreadful Hollow†* (1953); *The Whisper in the Gloom†* (1954); *A Tangled Web†* (1956); *Pegasus* (1957); *End of Chapter†* (1957); *A Penknife in My Heart†* (1958); *The Widow's Cruise†* (1959); *The Buried Day* (1960); *The Worm of Death†* (1961); *The Gate* (1962); *The Deadly Joker†* (1963); *The Sad Variety†* (1964); *The Room* (1965); *The Lyric Impulse* (1965); *The Morning After Death†* (1966); *The Private Wound†* (1968); *The Whispering Roots* (1970).

† detective novels published under the pseudonym 'Nicholas Blake.'

Born into an Anglo–Irish family, Day-Lewis left Ireland when still a baby and did not become fully aware of his roots until middle age. 'The House Where I Was Born,' published in 1957, contemplates a family photograph of Ballintubbert House, 'An elegant, shabby, white-washed house/ With a slate roof' (lines 1–2), and finds it a symbol of the old Anglo–Irish order. The building and the tiny village of Ballintubbert are near Windy Gap, off N80 12 miles NW of Carlow in Laois. In Wexford to the SE lies Monart (2 miles west of Enniscorthy) where Day-Lewis paid childhood visits to his uncle, Rev. William Goldsmith Squires, a descendant of Oliver Goldsmith (q.v.). *The Buried Day* remembers these holidays with special fondness: 'Monart did more than any other place for my sensuous education' (Ch. 2).

The adult Day-Lewis detected in himself a love both of putting down roots and of tearing them up again. It is not hard to see the origin of this tendency in the itinerant life he led after he was first brought to England in 1905. The family's movements are best summarised by a list of the churches where his father was either curate or rector: the lovely Priory Church in Great Malvern (8 miles SW of Worcester); Christ Church, a Victorian Gothic building conspicuous for its spire, in Lancaster Gate opposite the north side of Kensington Gardens in London; and the parish church of Edwinstowe (on A6075 7 miles NE of Mansfield in Nottinghamshire).

A degree of fixity was provided by his education (1917–23) at the public school in Sherborne (on A30 in Dorset), where he met another future poet, Louis MacNeice (q.v.). Day-Lewis' marriage in 1928 to a local girl at Sherborne's splendid Abbey is but one aspect of his abiding connection with Dorset.

The friendship with MacNeice was renewed when Day-Lewis went to Wadham College, Oxford in 1923. Both men were drawn into 'The

Gang', the group of young poets gathered round the compelling figure of W.H. Auden (q.v.). Maurice Bowra, then Dean and later Warden of Wadham, introduced him to Lady Ottoline Morrell at Garsington Manor (off B480 4 miles SE of the city). He returned to Oxford as Professor of Poetry (1951–56).

Like many other poets, Day-Lewis slid with reluctance into schoolteaching when he left university, working first in Oxford itself and landing up at the boys' College in Cheltenham (on the Bath Road). Its conservative atmosphere was not suited to a poet who was rapidly gaining a reputation for his left-wing views, and in 1935 Day-Lewis resigned to devote himself full-time to writing. The break was encouraged by his desire to join the Communist Party, and by his new and profitable sideline in detective novels written under the pseudonym of 'Nicholas Blake.' *A Question of Proof*, the first such book, clearly reflects his experience of public schools.

From 1938 to 1950 he lived in south Devon in the village of Musbury (on A358 between Axminster and Seaton). His house, Brimclose, lies in the shadow of a hill crowned by an Iron Age fort. Lyme Regis and its lovely bay (SE of the village) appear at the beginning and end of what is perhaps his finest detective novel, *The Beast Must Die*.

With the breakup of his marriage Day-Lewis went to London and lived in Kensington, where Kensington Gardens are used in the opening scene of *The Whisper in the Gloom*. In 1956, married to the actress Jill Balcon, he made a final move to Greenwich in SE London. From his house at No. 6 Croom's Hill, on the western edge of Greenwich Park, he could watch 'the great cargo-liners rounding the Isle of Dogs, the tugs and their strings of lighters, the wharves, warehouses, power stations, the skyline restless with cranes, the blue-diamond lights of welding and the indigo smoke from tall chimneys—all the river life which, here at Greenwich, overlooked by the palace and the park, enlivens their elegance with a workaday reality' ('Postscript' to *The Buried Day*). This scene and his new home appear in another 'Nicholas Blake' novel, *The Worm of Death*.

Love of Dorset and admiration for Thomas Hardy (q.v.) made him choose to be buried in the churchyard at Stinsford (off A35 1 mile east of Dorchester).

Garsington Manor. Gardens open under NGS. Fee.

Daniel Defoe

b. London, 1660; d. London, 1731. *The True-Born Englishman* (1701); *The Shortest Way with the Dissenters* (1702); *The Life and Strange Surprising Adventures of Robinson Crusoe* (1719); *The Adventures of Captain Singleton* (1720); *The Fortunes and Misfortunes of the Famous Moll Flanders* (1722); *A Journal of the Plague Year* (1722); *The History and Remarkable Life of Colonel Jacque, Commonly Call'd* (1722); *Roxana, or the Fortunate Mistress* (1724); *A Tour through the Whole Island of Great Britain* (1724–27).

It is ironic that so few places reminiscent of Defoe's life and work should survive, for in his novels he obviously appreciates the role geographical precision can play in creating verisimilitude and in his *Tour* he left a major travel book that still deserves reading. Yet the lack of places to visit is not entirely surprising. Defoe led the sort of active life immersed in affairs of the moment that often leaves no permanent mark, being businessman and government agent as well as author of more books than the headnote above can attempt to record.

Though born in the City of London he was educated in Stoke Newington to the north, returning to live there in later life. A plaque marks the site of his former house on Newington Church Street. The original tombstone from his grave (see below) is now on display in the entrance lobby of the Central Library nearby.

He died on Ropemaker Street (then Ropemaker Alley), south of Chiswell Street in Finsbury, and was buried to the north in the Nonconformist cemetery of Bunhill Fields. An obelisk erected in 1870 replaces his original tombstone. He attended worship at St Giles without Cripplegate, at the western end of Chiswell Street and now surrounded by the modern Barbican.

Of the many places visited in his travels the only one to preserve a personal reminder is Bury St Edmunds in Suffolk. He stayed at the *Cupola House, now a pub, on The Traverse after the spell in Newgate and the pillory that the success of his satire, *The Shortest Way with the Dissenters*, had earned him. This fine building of 1693 is made the more noteworthy for having been described in detail by another traveller, Celia Fiennes, several years before:

> this high house is an apothecarys, at least 60 stepps up from the ground and gives a pleaseing prospect of the whole town, that is compact severall streetes but no good buildings; except this the rest are great old houses of timber and mostly in the old forme of the country which are very long peaked roofes of tileing; this house is the new mode of building, 4 roomes of a floor pretty sizeable and high, well furnish'd, a drawing roome and Chamber full of China and a Damaske bed embroyder'd, 2 other roomes, Camlet and Mohaire beds, a pretty deale of plaite in his wives chamber, parlours below and a large shop.

Defoe himself wrote about Bury with special approval in his *Tour*, characteristically paying less attention to its history and Abbey than to 'the present state of the place':

> the beauty of the town consists in the number of gentry who dwell in and near it, the polite conversation among them; the affluence and plenty they live in; the sweet air they breathe in, and the pleasant country they have to go abroad in.

Central Library, Stoke Newington. Open Mon, Tues, Thurs 9–8, Fri 9–6, Wed & Sat 9–5.

Bunhill Fields. Open Mon to Fri 7.30–4, Sat & Sun 9.30–4.

Sir John Denham

b. Dublin, 1615; d. London, 1669. *Coopers Hill* (1642; revised 1650 and 1655).

After studying at Trinity College, Oxford (1631–34)—where Anthony à Wood records that he was 'more addicted to gaming than study'—Sir John Denham inherited his father's estates at Egham, on A30 in Surrey. The parish church is 19C but preserves the remarkable monuments to the elder Sir John Denham (d. 1638) and his two wives; the small kneeling figure at the left of the latter monument is the only contemporary portrait of the poet.

Nearby Cooper's Hill, overlooking Runnymede and surmounted by a Commonwealth Air Forces Memorial, gave its name to the poem that, in the opinion of Samuel Johnson (q.v.), 'confers upon him the rank and dignity of an original author':

> He seems to have been, at least among us, the author of a species of composition that may be denominated *local poetry*, of which the fundamental subject is some particular landscape, to be poetically described, with the addition of such embellishments as may be supplied by historical retrospection, or incidental meditation.

Coopers Hill is usually remembered for its mellifluous invocation to the Thames:

> O could I flow like thee, and make thy stream
> My great example, as it is my theme!
> Though deep, yet clear, though gentle, yet not dull,
> Strong without rage, without ore-flowing full.
>
> (lines 189–192)

In 1642, during the Civil War, Sir John expelled the Puritan poet George Wither from the command of the Castle at Farnham (on A31 20 miles SW of Egham) on behalf of the Royalists, but was himself obliged to abandon its defence later the same year. Perhaps in retaliation, Wither occupied Denham's house at Egham and laid claim to his property. John Aubrey adds a pleasant but unsupported footnote to the story of the poets' rivalry:

> G.W. was taken prisoner, and was in danger of his life, having written severely against the king, &c. Sir John Denham went to the king, and desired his majestie not to hang him, for that whilest G.W. lived he should not be the worst poet in England.

After he returned from the Continent in 1652, deprived of his property, Denham found refuge with the Pembroke family at Wilton House, west of Salisbury in Wiltshire, where Inigo Jones had just completed work on restoration.

In 1634 Denham had married in London, at the predecessor to Wren's St Bride's off Fleet Street. After the Restoration, in 1665, he married Margaret Brooke in Westminster Abbey. She was buried in 1667 at nearby St Margaret's, Westminster, the common gossip of the day being that Denham had poisoned her in revenge for her public infidelity with the Duke of York. He himself was buried in Poets' Corner (fee) of the Abbey.

Farnham Castle. Keep (English Heritage) open 15 March to 15 Oct, Mon to Sat 9.30–6.30, Sun 2–6.30; 16 Oct to 14 March, Mon to Sat 9.30–4, Sun 2–4. Fee. Domestic buildings (Centre for International Briefing) open Wed 2–4.

Wilton House, near Salisbury. Open mid Apr to mid Oct, Tues to Sat & BH Mon 11–6, Sun 1–6. Fee.

Benjamin Disraeli, Earl of Beaconsfield

b. London, 1804; d. London, 1881. *Vivian Grey* (1826–27); *Contarini Fleming: A Psychological Autobiography* (1832); *Henrietta Temple: A Love Story* (1837); *Coningsby: or The New Generation* (1844); *Sybil: or The Two Nations* (1845); *Tancred: or The New Crusade* (1847); *Lothair* (1870); *Endymion* (1880).

Disraeli's early years were spent in London's Holborn. His birthplace at No. 22 Theobald's Road, off the Gray's Inn Road, is marked by a GLC plaque. His father, the writer Isaac D'Israeli, belonged to no organised religion but was persuaded of the need to bring his children up in the Church of England. So when he was twelve Disraeli was baptised at St Andrew, by Holborn Circus, a Wren church now rebuilt after war-time bomb damage. The service was conducted by a nephew of the poet Coleridge (s.v. Lake Poets). In 1824 Disraeli entered Lincoln's Inn to the south of Holborn and kept nine terms, though of course he never followed a legal career. Instead, he established himself as a wit, a dandy and a novelist whose talents were most fully expressed in the 'Young England' trilogy of the 1840s.

His flamboyant, controversial and eventually distinguished career as Tory politician is well remembered in Westminster. Mario Raggi's statue on the lawn of Parliament Square is near the Palace of Westminster, where Disraeli served in the Commons from 1837 and the Lords from 1876. The north transept of Westminster Abbey has a statue by Sir Edgar Boehm.

Disraeli's marriage in 1839 to the wealthy widow Mrs Wyndham Lewis took him to Mayfair. The wedding ceremony was performed in St George's south of Hanover Square. Until his wife's death in 1872, he lived at No. 93 Park Lane. He died just round the corner at No. 19 Curzon Street, now marked with a GLC plaque.

Yet the place most fully reminiscent of Disraeli lies in his Buckinghamshire constituency: *Hughenden Manor, 1½ miles north of High Wycombe and reached from A4128. He bought the property in 1848 and used it as his country estate for the rest of his life, taking considerable pleasure in the role of country gentleman. Originally of very simple design, the late 18C building was remodelled with unfortunate results by the Gothic architect, E.B. Lamb, in 1862–63. Hughenden still has much of Disraeli's furniture and many mementoes.

Although he was assured a place in Westminster Abbey, Disraeli chose to be buried in Hughenden church. Gladstone regarded the gesture with suspicion: 'As he lived so he died—all display without reality or genuineness.' Queen Victoria, who paid a special visit to the grave, took a different view and caused a monument in his memory to be placed in the chancel. Its inscription quotes from the Book of Proverbs: 'Kings love him that speaketh right.'

Hughenden Manor, High Wycombe (NT). Open Apr to end Oct, Wed to Sat 2–6, Sun & BH Mon 12–6; March, Sat & Sun 2–6. Closed Good Fri. Fee.

John Donne

b. London, 1572; d. London, 1631. Metaphysical poet.

A convenient London walking tour begins at St Paul's Cathedral. Donne was Dean of the old Cathedral on this site from 1617 until his death and was buried there. Almost alone among its monuments his **memorial statue by Nicholas Stone survived the fire of 1666 virtually undamaged and is now placed in the south side of the ambulatory. In a striking expression of the same Jacobean sensibility that pervades his poetry, both secular and religious, it shows him standing on an urn dressed for the grave. His friend and first biographer Izaak Walton quotes a contemporary account of Donne ordering and posing for the picture on which the memorial was based:

> Several Charcole-fires being first made in his large study, he brought with him into that place his winding-sheet in his hand, and, having put off all his cloaths, had this sheet put on him, and so tyed with knots at his head and feet, and his hands so placed, as dead bodies are usually fitted to be shrouded and put into their coffin, or grave. Upon this Vrn he thus stood with his eyes shut, and with so much of the sheet turned aside as might shew his lean, pale and death-like face, which was purposely turned toward the East, from whence he expected the second coming of his and our Saviour Jesus.

From St Paul's we descend Ludgate Hill (to the right of which lay the Fleet Prison, where Donne was confined in 1602 for marrying without official permission) and follow its continuation as Fleet Street. Halfway down on the right is St Dunstan in the West, an early 19C church replacing the older building of which Donne was vicar from 1624 to 1631. A right turn on to Chancery Lane shortly beyond leads to Lincoln's Inn, with which he was intimately connected from the time of his first admission in 1592. His 'Epithalamion made at Lincoln's Inn', dating from the early 1590s, may well have been written for a mock-occasion connected with his post as Master of Revels, which he held in 1593. In Old Square, to the right of the main gatehouse, stands the Chapel rebuilt between 1619 and 1623, when Donne was Divinity Reader at the Inn. He is reputed to have laid the cornerstone. By returning to Fleet Street and continuing west as it changes to the Strand, we reach St Clement Danes, a Wren church now restored after war-time damage. Donne's wife Ann (d. 1617) was buried in the previous church on this site.

Another London church important to Donne's life may be found in Chelsea, by the river at the junction of Cheyne Walk and Old Church Street. At All Saints (also known as Chelsea Old Church), now restored after severe war-time damage, he preached the funeral sermon for his friend Lady Magdalen Danvers in 1627. Her son the poet George Herbert (q.v.) and Izaak Walton were among the congregation. The church is also notable for a monument of 1631 to Sara Colville, in the same macabre vein as Donne's own. On Danvers Street nearby stood Danvers House, on the site of a house that had belonged to Sir Thomas More and itself demolished in 1720. Donne was Lady Danvers' guest there in 1625, taking refuge from the plague-ridden City.

Places outside London reminiscent of Donne's life are few and scattered. He studied at Hertford College, Oxford, when it was still Hart Hall. He visited Lady Danvers, then Mrs Magdalen Herbert, at the now-ruined castle of Montgomery, once the county town of Montgomeryshire but now in Powys, Wales. The occasions are remembered in the poems 'The Primrose, being at Montgomery Castle' and 'Good Friday, 1613. Riding Westward.' From 1616 until his death he was pluralist rector of St Nicolas on the High Street of Sevenoaks, Kent; the church contains a memorial. Because of this position, he also preached at the mansion of Knole, seat of the Sackville family, to the SE of the town.

Ambulatory, St Paul's Cathedral. Open Mon to Fri 10–3.15 (4.15 in summer),

Sat 11–3.15 (4.15 in summer). Entrance may be restricted during special services. Fee.

Knole, Sevenoaks (NT), Park open all year to walkers. House open Apr to end Nov, Wed to Sat 11–5, Sun 2–5; Good Fri & BH Mon 11–5. Fee.

Sir Arthur Conan Doyle

b. Edinburgh, 1859; d. Crowborough, East Sussex, 1930. *A Study in Scarlet* (1888); *Micah Clarke* (1889); *The Mystery of Cloomber* (1889); *The Sign of Four* (1890); *The Captain of the Polestar and Other Tales* (1890); *The Firm of Girdlestone: A Romance of the Unromantic* (1890); *The White Company* (1891); *The Doings of Raffles Haw* (1892); *The Great Shadow* (1892); *Beyond the City* (1892); *The Adventures of Sherlock Holmes* (1892); *The Refugees* (1893); *The Memoirs of Sherlock Holmes* (1894); *Round the Red Lamp: Being Facts and Fancies of the Medical Life* (1894); *The Stark Munro Letters* (1895); *The Exploits of Brigadier Gerard* (1896); *Rodney Stone* (1896); *Uncle Bernac: A Memory of the Empire* (1897); *The Tragedy of the 'Korosko'* (1898); *The Hound of the Baskervilles* (1902); *The Adventures of Gerard* (1903); *The Return of Sherlock Holmes* (1905); *Sir Nigel* (1906); *Through the Magic Door* (1907); *Round the Fire Stories* (1908); *The Lost World* (1912); *The Poison Belt* (1913); *The Valley of Fear* (1915); *His Last Bow* (1917); *Memories and Adventures* (1924); *The Land of Mist* (1926); *The History of Spiritualism* (1926); *The Case-Book of Sherlock Holmes* (1927); *The Maracot Deep and Other Stories* (1929).

Of the scenes connected with Doyle's early years only the places where he was educated survive. He attended the Jesuit public school, Stonyhurst College, which lies off B6243 12 miles north of Blackburn in Lancashire. Soon after leaving, however, he abandoned Roman Catholicism (eventually becoming an ardent spiritualist) and later explained why he would not have a son of his own educated by the Jesuits: 'They try to rule too much by fear—too little by love or reason.' In his hometown of Edingburgh he studied medicine at the University, where his teacher Dr Joseph Bell unconsciously sat for the portrait of Sherlock Holmes.

The house in Portsmouth where Doyle created Holmes while waiting for his first patients to come has been demolished, but his career after he moved to London in 1890 is better commemorated. He lived at No. 23 Montague Place, behind the British Museum, and walked westward each day to his surgery at No. 2 Devonshire Place, south of the Marylebone Road and near the more fashionable Harley Street. Both addresses are connected with Holmes, whom Doyle had revived with great success for the series of stories in the *Strand* magazine. In 'The Musgrave Ritual' Holmes tells Dr Watson that his first London lodgings had been on Montague Street, near Montague Place. Devonshire Place, of course, is near Baker Street, where No. 221B is probably the most famous imaginary address in England. It should be remembered that Baker Street was then confined to the stretch between Portman Square in the south and Paddington Street in the north, and that it had not completed its descent to being merely a commercial thoroughfare.

Yet the exact location of Holmes and Watson's lodgings has defied identification even by the dedicated, stubbornly ingenious researchers whom Doyle's work has always attracted. In fact, the visitor who wishes to trace Holmes' footsteps through London (and there are several commercial tours that offer to satisfy this pleasure) will find the great detective curiously elusive. The rich, powerful sense of the metropolis exuded by the stories depends more on atmosphere than exact reference. Sherlock Holmes' London is created out of fog and gaslights and hansom cabs, not specific buildings. The detective's best monument is The Sherlock Holmes pub and restaurant on Northumberland Street, south of the Strand near Charing Cross, which now boasts a recreation of his Baker Street livingroom. The building was formerly the Northumberland Hotel, where Sir Henry Baskerville stayed (and had two odd shoes stolen) in Chapter 4 of *The Hound of the Baskervilles.*

This novel treats Dartmoor in South-Western England with the same generalising touch that Doyle brought to the topography of London. He visited the area with his friend Fletcher Robinson in 1900, but took the writer's customary liberties with fact. His Dartmoor is both larger and wilder than the real thing; its tors and prehistoric huts are too generally described to be identified among the many candidates that the actual terrain offers. However, Grimspound Bog (3 miles NW of Widecombe-in-the-Moor and $1\frac{1}{2}$ miles south of B3212) suggested at least the name of 'Grimpen Mire', in which the criminal Stapleton perishes.

By the time he wrote *The Hound of the Baskervilles* Doyle had moved from London, following the preference common among writers of his generation for South-Eastern England. After his second marriage in 1907 he bought Windlesham Manor in Crowborough, off A26 7 miles SW of Royal Tunbridge Wells. The family nicknamed the house 'Swindlesham' because of the extortionate price he had paid for it. The lovely Groombridge Place, a 17C moated house 5 miles north, must surely have suggested Douglas' home in *The Valley of Fear.* Needing a place where he could conduct spiritualist seances away from gossip and publicity, Doyle later bought a home near Minstead (2 miles NW of Lyndhurst in the New Forest), a village that had earlier featured in his novel, *The White Company.* His body, originally buried in the garden at Windlesham, was later reburied in the churchyard here under the epitaph 'Steel True, Blade Straight.'

Michael Drayton

b. Hartshill, near Atherstone, Warwickshire, 1563; d. London, 1631. *Idea, The Shepheards Garland* (1593); *Poly-Olbion* (1613–22).

A black marble monument to Drayton, erected by the Countess of Dorset, stands in Poets' Corner (fee), Westminster Abbey. Its commemorative verse is sometimes attributed to Ben Jonson (q.v.).

Although he is usually remembered for his sonnet cycle, *Idea,* and particularly for the later individual sonnet beginning 'Since there's no help, come let us kiss and part,' Drayton also made a massive contribution to topographical poetry with *Poly-Olbion.* Divided into two books and thirty songs, the poem deals with the Channel Islands, Wales and virtually every English county. Its subtitle prepares the reader for the expansive nature of Drayton's undertaking, as well as its inevitable longueurs, periodic delights and fanciful digressions: 'A Chorographicall Description of Tracts, Rivers, Mountaines, Forests, and other Parts of this renowned Isle of Great Britain, With intermixture of the most Remarquable Stories, Antiquities, Wonders, Rarityes, Pleasures, and Commodities of the same.' *Poly-Olbion* still makes a pleasant companion for the traveller, especially if it is used in conjunction with the index of placenames provided in Volume 5 of the Tercentenary Edition of his *Works* (revised 1961) by J. William Hebel.

John Dryden

b. Aldwinkle (or Aldwincle), Northamptonshire, 1631; d. London, 1700. *Annus Mirabilis* (1667); *Essay of Dramatick Poesie* (1668); *Aurangzebe* (1676); *All for Love* (1678); *Absalom and Achitophel* (1681); *MacFlecknoe* (1682); *Religio Laici* (1682); *The Hind and the Panther* (1687).

Aldwinkle is a small village west of A605 between Thrapston and Oundle. Dryden's birthplace, the Rectory, still stands opposite the 13C–15C church of All Saints where his father was incumbent. Much of the poet's childhood was spent in Titchmarsh, 3½ miles to the SE, home of his mother's family, the Pickerings. A monument of 1722 in the north chapel of the church, itself notable for a striking tower, commemorates his parents and the poet himself: 'We boast that he was bred and had his first learning here.' Dryden maintained his connection with the area throughout his life. Part of *The Hind and the Panther* may have been written at Rushton Hall, 4 miles NW of Kettering, Renaissance seat of the Tresham family. The building is now a school belonging to the Royal National Institute for the Blind. Of particular interest is Sir Thomas Tresham's fanciful Triangular Lodge in the grounds but reached by a separate entrance on the Desborough Road. In the summer of 1695 Dryden completed the

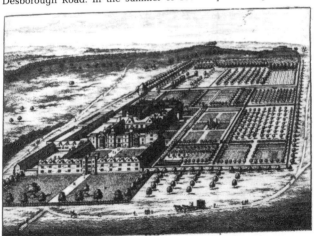

Knole. From James Beeverell, Les Délices de la Grand' Bretagne, et de l'Irlande *(expanded edition, 1727). Courtesy of Cambridge University Library*

seventh book of his translation of Virgil's *Aeneid* at the splendid Renaissance mansion of Burghley House, near Stamford and the A1.

Of his education at Trinity College, Cambridge (1650–54) little record survives save an entry in the 'Conclusion Book' of 1652 noting his punishment for disobedience to the Vice Master.

During the years of his fame as poet and dramatist Dryden enjoyed the *entrée* to several country houses other than those in his native Central England. His father-in-law owned the estate of Charlton Park, 2 miles NE of Malmesbury, Wiltshire; the Jacobean house where Dryden took refuge from London's plague and fire in 1665–66 no longer survives. He also visited the seat of his friend and patron, Charles Sackville, Lord Buckhurst, Earl of Dorset, at Knole near Sevenoaks in Kent. It is reported that on one occasion he was gratified to find a £100 note under his plate when he sat down to dinner.

The majority of Dryden's life, however, was spent in London. He was educated from about 1644 until 1650 at Westminster School, whose buildings stand in Little Dean's Yard to the south of Westminster Abbey. He died at No. 44 Gerrard Street in Soho, parallel to and south of Shaftesbury Avenue; the house has been rebuilt but its neighbour bears a plaque. He was buried in Poet's Corner (fee) of Westminster Abbey. The lack of a proper memorial, which Pope (q.v.) complained about ('Beneath a rude and nameless stone he lies'), was made good by John Sheffield, Duke of Buckingham in 1720. Pope substituted a simple inscription for the epitaph he had originally composed:

> This SHEFFIELD rais'd. The sacred Dust below
> Was DRYDEN once: The rest who does not know?

A bust by Scheemakers was added in 1731.

Rushton Park (Royal National Institute for the Blind school). Grounds open daily in Aug 10–4. House open by telephone arrangement (0536–710506).

Triangular Lodge, Rushton (English Heritage). Open 15 March to 15 Oct, Mon to Sat 9.30–6.30, Sun 2–6; 16 Oct to 14 March, Mon to Sat 9.30–4, Sun 2–4. Fee.

Burghley House, near Stamford. Open 1 Apr to 7 Oct, Sat and BH 11–5, Sun & Good Fri 2–5. Fee.

Knole, Sevenoaks (NT). Park open all year to walkers. House open Apr to end Nov, Wed to Sat 11–5, Sun 2–5; Good Fri & BH Mon 11–5. Fee.

John Dyer

b. Llangathen, Dyfed, 1699; d. Coningsby, Lincolnshire, 1758. *Grongar Hill* (1726); *The Ruins of Rome* (1740); *The Fleece* (1757).

Although he was educated at London's Westminster School, in Little Dean's Yard to the south of Westminster Abbey, and later held various livings in Central and Eastern England, Dyer's most important connection is with his native Wales. He came from the Vale of the Tywi (or Towey), west of Llandeilo, praising its scenery in *Grongar Hill*, the slight but charming landscape poem on which his slender reputation is based. A convenient tour leaves Llandeilo by A40 and passes, all to the left: Llangathen (3½ miles) where Dyer was born and lived at Aberglasney House; Grongar (or Grongaer) Hill itself (4 miles) with its hillfort; and the ruined ancient stronghold of Dryslwyn Castle, also mentioned in the poem, which is reached via B4297 (6 miles).

Maria Edgeworth

b. Black Bourton, Oxfordshire, 1767; d. Edgeworthstown, Co. Longford, 1849. *Letters for Literary Ladies* (1795); *Practical Education* (1798); *Castle Rackrent: An Hibernian Tale* (1800); *Early Lessons* (1801– 25); *Belinda* (1801); *Essay on Irish Bulls* (with Richard Lovell Edgeworth; 1803); *Popular Tales* (1804); *The Modern Griselda: A Tale* (1805); *Leonora* (1806); *Tales of Fashionable Life* (1809); *Patronage* (1814); *Harrington: A Tale* (1817); *Ormond: A Tale* (1817); *Helen: A Tale* (1834).

Nothing significant has survived in England to commemorate the novelist, though she spent her early life here and later gained entry to London literary circles by the popularity of her writings. In Scotland we may remember her connection with a more famous contemporary, Sir Walter Scott (q.v.), who acknowledged the influence of *Castle Rackrent* on his own Highland novels. In 1823 she was his guest at No. 39 Castle Street in Edinburgh and at Abbotsford, by the junction of A7 and A6091 32 miles SE of Edinburgh.

From 1782 until her death she lived in the Irish town that bears her family name, at the meeting of N4 and N55 8 miles SE of the county town of Longford. Edgeworthstown House, where she wrote her novels and took neat, careful charge of the estate, is now a convent. Here she repaid Scott's hospitality in 1825 and was visited by Wordsworth in 1829, though the entry for the Lake Poets (Rte 17) shows that her impressions of the poet were not entirely favourable. She is buried in the churchyard of St John's near her father, whose educational theories derived from Rousseau profoundly shaped her own life.

Abbotsford. Open 19 March to 31 Oct, Mon to Sat 10–5, Sun 2–5. Fee.

'George Eliot' (pseud. of Marian or Mary Ann Evans)

b. Chilvers Coton, Warwickshire, 1819; d. London, 1880. *Scenes of Clerical Life* (consists of 'The Sad Fortunes of the Reverend Amos Barton,' 'Mr Gilfil's Love Story' and 'Janet's Repentance'; 1858); *Adam Bede* (1859); *The Mill on the Floss* (1860); *Silas Marner: The Weaver of Raveloe* (1861); *Romola* (1863); *Felix Holt the Radical* (1866); *The Spanish Gypsy: A Poem* (1868); *Middlemarch: a Study of Provincial Life* (1872); *Daniel Deronda* (1876); *Impressions of Theophrastus Such* (1879).

'A human life,' George Eliot suggested in *Daniel Deronda*, 'should be well rooted in some spot of native land, where it may get the love of tender kinship for the face of earth, for the labours men go forth to, for the sounds and accents that haunt it, for whatever will give that early home a familiar unmistakable difference amidst the future widening of knowledge: a spot where the definiteness of early memories may be inwrought with affection, and kindly acquaintance with all neighbours, even to the dogs and donkeys, may spread not by sentimental effort and reflection, but as a sweet habit of the blood' (Ch. 3). She clearly had the example of herself in mind, since her childhood and youth in Central England provided a solid bedrock for a life that went on to involve complex intellectual pilgrimage, as well as the ambiguous social position brought about by her liaison with George Henry Lewes. And memories drawn from that time and that area provided rich material for her art, especially the early novels. Even today, when the industrialisation of the Midlands—already beginning to happen in her youth and presaged by the coming of the railway in *Middlemarch*—has transformed so much of its landscape, a rich cluster of places associated with her life and work still remains.

A convenient tour of this George Eliot country may begin at Nuneaton in Warwickshire, the market centre round which her earliest years revolved and the original of 'Milby' in *Scenes of Clerical Life*. The fictional town is described as a 'quiet provincial place' ('Amos Barton,' Ch. 4) but George Eliot privately assured her publisher that 'the real town was more vicious.' In College Street we find the former workhouse of 1800, now called Coton Lodge, 'the huge square stone building' (Ch. 2) where Amos Barton conducts services for the inmates. Lacking further surviving reminders of the writer, Nuneaton has a Memorial Garden of 1953 near its public library.

By following A444 south we come after 1 mile to Chilvers Coton, now in fact a suburb of Nuneaton but still a separate village in the nineteenth century. Although the church where George Eliot was baptised had to be rebuilt after wartime bomb damage, the graveyard is still of interest. It contains the tomb of her father, Robert Evans (d. 1849), and her mother, Christiana (d. 1836), Robert's second wife. Here we can also find the grave of Emma Gwyther, whose death suggested the pathetic climax to 'Amos Barton.' The connection between the Bartons and the Gwythers is, in fact, the closest example of a correspondence between George Eliot's fiction and the local life of her native country. Although she did not realise it, John Gwyther, once curate of Chilvers Coton, was still alive when the story was published and recorded his 'pained feelings at the making public my private history.'

A mile further south on A444 we come to Griff House, the substantial home to which George Eliot's family moved when she was only a few months old and where they remained until 1841. It is now a hotel. By turning right at this point we enter the estate of the Newdigates, for whom Robert Evans worked as agent. On the left after 1½ miles is South Farm, called Arbury Farm when the writer was born here in 1819, a picturesque building that is noticeably less grand than Griff House. On the right beyond the lake lies •Arbury Hall itself. This originally Tudor mansion is notable in its own right for the 18C Gothic additions. George Eliot enjoyed the run of its library as a teenager and made it, with virtually no alteration, into the 'Cheverel Manor' of 'Mr Gilfil's Love Story': a 'castellated house of grey-tinted stone' with 'many-shaped panes in the mutilated windows, and a great beech leaning athwart one of the flanking towers, and breaking, with its dark flattened boughs, the too formal symmetry of the front' (Ch. 2).

We now return to A444 and travel the remaining 7 miles south to

Coventry, which some have identified with 'Middlemarch' despite the deliberately generalising name George Eliot chose for her fictional town. On the Foleshill Road, as A444 becomes when it enters the city, stands Robert Evans' home from his retirement until death (1841–49), Bird Grove. Even now, half-demolished and sadly changed, it can still testify to the substantial respectability it once possessed. Evans recorded in his diary for 1841 that when he told Lord Aylesford 'I was going to my new residence this evening for the first night, on the Foleshill road in Coventry parish, he Laphd [sic] and said they would make me Mayor.' For George Eliot, who acted as her father's housekeeper, these years were crucial. As evidence of their effect we may cite Rosehill on the Radford Road (A423) nearby, home of Charles Bray whose bold, unconventional ideas helped liberate her from the strict Evangelicalism in which she had been brought up. Near the city centre, at No. 29 Warwick Row, west of Greyfriars Green, we find Nantglyn, the fashionable school run by the Misses Franklin which George Eliot entered in 1832.

Although the Nuneaton–Coventry area is the centre of the George Eliot country, her connections with the Derbyshire–Staffordshire border to the north should not be forgotten. In fact, *Adam Bede* prevents that. Ashbourne (on A515 and A52) suggested the name 'Oakbourne,' if nothing else. The novel is set in the beautiful stretch of the Dove valley SW of the town:

> That rich undulating district of Loamshire [Derbyshire] to which Hayslope belonged, lies close to a grim outskirt of Stonyshire [Staffordshire], overlooked by its barren hills as a pretty blooming sister may sometimes be seen linked in the arm of a tall, swarthy brother . . . High up against the horizon were the hugh conical masses of hill, like giant moulds intended to fortify this region of corn and grass against the keen and hungry winds of the north; not distant enough to be clothed in purple mystery, but with sombre greenish sides visibly speckled with sheep. (Ch. 2)

Ellastone (5 miles via A52 and B5032), where her father lived in his youth, is identified with 'Hayslope,' Adam Bede's home; Dinah Morris preached on the Green and Mr Irwine in the Church. Norbury (½ a mile further on B5033) is 'Norburne.' Six miles NE of Ashbourne on B5035 we find Wirksworth, presumably 'Snowfield' and certainly the home of Elizabeth Evans (d. 1849), George Eliot's aunt, who suggested the character of Dinah Morris. Her connection with *Adam Bede* is remembered by the memorial tablet of 1873 in the Ebenezer Methodist church.

George Eliot's next novel, *Mill on the Floss*, again breathes the atmosphere of her childhood, but is not set among familiar scenes since its plot required a location that would make the flooding of the river at the end plausible. In 1859, after rejecting Weymouth and Dorchester in South-Western England, she lighted on Gainsborough by the River Trent, 18 miles NW of Lincoln and on the fringes of Central England. The town today is sadly changed from her description of 'St Ogg's' with 'its aged, fluted red roofs and the broad gables of its wharves between the low wooded hill and the river brink' (Ch. 1). Only the 18C church and the 15C Old Hall can remind the visitor of the character that Gainsborough must have possessed in George Eliot's—and Maggie Tulliver's—times.

The 'future widening of knowledge' to which George Eliot refers in *Daniel Deronda* involved in her case a working life spent mainly in London, where she first arrived in 1851. It is unfortunate that so few of the houses she lived in survive; the loss of The Priory by Regent's Canal, where she presided over afternoon teas for famous and aspiring writers, leaves a specially important gap. We may, however, visit No. 31 Wimbledon Park Road (then called Holly Lodge), reached by crossing the Park from Wimbledon Park Underground Station (District Line). During her stay (1859–60) in this 'tall cake, with a low garnish of holly and laurel' she wrote *Adam Bede* but also led a withdrawn life, for the liaison with Lewes—himself married and unable to divorce his wife—still excluded her from respectable society. When Holly Lodge proved inconveniently far from the centre of things the couple moved to Marylebone. They stayed briefly in Harewood Square, now vanished beneath Marylebone Station, before settling round the corner at No. 16 Blandford Square (1860–63).

A visit to Cambridge in 1873 provided a famous and memorable glimpse of George Eliot in the character of Victorian sage she assumed so readily in later life. F.W.H. Myers, her host and a Fellow of Trinity College, walked with her in the Fellows' Garden:

> she, stirred somewhat beyond her wont, and taking as her text the three words which have been used so often as the inspiring trumpet-calls of men,—the words, *God, Immortality, Duty*,—pronounced, with terrible earnestness, how inconceivable was the *first*, how unbelievable the *second*, and yet how peremptory and absolute the *third*. Never, perhaps, have sterner accents affirmed the sovereignty of impersonal and un-recompensing Law. I listened, and night fell; her grave, majestic countenance turned toward me like a sibyl's in the gloom; it was as though she withdrew from my grasp, one by one, the two scrolls of promise, and left me with the third scroll only, awful with inevitable fates. And when we stood at length and parted, amid that columnar circuit of forest-trees, beneath the last twilight of starless skies, I seemed to be gazing, like Titus at Jerusalem, on vacant seats and empty halls,—on a sanctuary with no Presence to hallow it, and heaven left lonely of a God.

The young Bertrand Russell was reminded of the incident when he visited the Garden with Julian Sturgis, who exclaimed: 'Oh yes! This is where George Eliot told F.W.H. Myers that there is no God, and yet we must be good; and Myers decided that there is a God and yet we need not be good.'

In 1876 George Eliot and Lewes brought Rosslyn Court (then The Heights) in the Surrey village of Witley, on A283 4 miles SW of Godalming, though problems with furnishing it prevented them from moving in until the next year. Henry James (q.v.) paid a visit with Mrs Richard Greville on a wet November afternoon in 1878: 'I see again our bland, benign, commiserating hostess beside the fire in a chill desert of a room . . . and I catch once more the impression of . . . their liking us to have come, mainly from a prevision of how they should much more devoutly like it when we departed.' The occasion was made more uncomfortable when Lewes insisted on returning, unread, a copy of the newly published *The Europeans* which James had loaned them. Lewes died the same month, but George Eliot continued to live at The Heights after her marriage to J.W. Cross in April 1880—a marriage whose haste, coupled with the fact that Cross was some twenty years her junior, caused surprise and some disapproval among her friends.

The wedding ceremony took place in London at the fashionable St George's, Hanover Square, SW of Oxford Circus. Later that year the couple acquired a house in Chelsea, No. 4 Cheyne Walk, by the Embankment and the river. It is ironic that this, the only one of George Eliot's homes to be marked with a GLC blue plaque, should have been lived in for so short a period. She moved into the house on 3 December 1880 and died on 25 December.

Given her relationship with Lewes and her views on religion, it could hardly be expected that she would rest in Westminster Abbey. Dean Stanley told her friend Herbert Spencer that he would require 'strong representations' before considering the idea, and the matter was quietly dropped. Instead, she was buried at that magnificent but now decaying expression of Victorian secularity, Highgate Cemetery. It is reached by walking south from Highgate Underground Station (Northern Line) on Southwood Lane, South Grove and Swains Lane. George Eliot lies in the newer part of the cemetery to the east of the lane. After entering through the main gates we take the left fork and then, shortly before Karl Marx's tomb, a small footpath to the left. Beside the plain grey obelisk in her memory is the grave of Elma Stuart (d. 1903); the fulsome reference to the novelist in its inscription is a reminder of the passionate hero-worship she could inspire.

Arbury Hall, near Nuneaton. Open Easter Sun to first Sun in Oct, Sun and BH Mon & Tues 2.30–6. Fee.

Gainsborough Old Hall. Open Mon to Sat 10–5; Easter to Oct, Sun 2–5. Fee.

Highgate Cemetery. Tours leave from Swains Lane daily on the hour, Apr to Sept 10–4, Oct to March 10–3.

T.S. Eliot

b. St Louis, Missouri, USA, 1888; d. London, 1965. *Prufrock and Other Observations* (1917); *The Sacred Wood: Essays on Poetry and Criticism* (1920); *The Waste Land* (1922); *Homage to John Dryden: Three Essays on the Poetry of the Seventeenth Century* (1924); *Poems 1909–1925* (1925); *Journey of the Magi* (1927); *For Lancelot Andrewes: Essays on Style and Order* (1928); *Dante* (1929); *Ash-Wednesday* (1930); *Marina* (1930); *Sweeney Agonistes: Fragments of an Aristophanic Melodrama* (1932); *The Use of Poetry and the Use of Criticism* (1933); *After Strange Gods: A Primer of Modern Heresy* (1934); *The Rock: A Pageant Play* (1934); *Murder in the Cathedral* (1935); *The Family Reunion* (1939); *Old Possum's Book of Practical Cats* (1939); *Four Quartets* (1943); *Notes Towards the Definition of Culture* (1948); *The Cocktail Party: A Comedy* (1950); *On Poetry and Poets* (1957); *The Elder Statesman* (1959); *Collected Poems 1909–1962* (1963); *Knowledge and Experience in the Philosophy of F.H. Bradley* (1964).

Eliot first came to England in 1914 on a travelling fellowship from Harvard, where he had taken his undergraduate degree and was working toward his Ph.D. He studied at Merton College, Oxford. The philosopher F.H. Bradley, subject of Eliot's thesis (eventually published at the end of his life), was then a Fellow at Merton but the two men apparently did not come into contact. In light of his later commitment to the most English of English values, and particularly the famous declaration in *For Lancelot Andrewes* that he was 'classical in literature, royalist in politics, anglo-catholic in religion,' it is interesting to note that Eliot did not fall in love with either Oxford or England at first sight. The university, he wrote to an American friend, 'is very pretty, but I don't like to be dead.'

As Eliot's interest shifted from philosophy to poetry in the years that followed he visited several important gathering places for writers of his time. He was a guest of Lady Ottoline and Philip Morrell at Garsington Manor (off B480 4 miles SE of Oxford). Further contact with the Bloomsbury group was represented by visits to Virginia Woolf (q.v.) at her home in Rodmell.

In fact, he had little in common with these writers and was never a joiner of literary groups. During the aftermath of the First World War the real centre to his life was in the City of London, where he worked as a banker from 1917 onwards. It has often been noted that *The Waste Land* captured the mood of its age but less often remarked that this achievement depended on capturing the mood of a particular place. The poem is dominated by the City, just as the City is dominated by the Thames, once deserving praise by Spenser (q.v.) but now sordid and defiled. A brief tour of scenes in the poem and in Eliot's life during the years of its gestation can fruitfully begin by Bank Underground Station (Central and Northern Lines) at the junction of Lombard Street and King William Street. Eliot was employed in the colonial and foreign department of Lloyds Bank on Lombard Street, where a building of 1931 has replaced the one in which he worked. The critic I.A. Richards paid a call and found him 'a figure stooping, very like a dark bird in a feeder, over a big table covered with all sorts and sizes of foreign correspondence. The big table almost entirely filled a little room under the street. Within a foot of our heads when he stood were the thick, green glass squares of the pavement on which hammered all but incessantly the heels of the passers-by.' In *The Waste Land* the crowds of businessmen on their way to work become modern versions of the damned in Dante's *Inferno*:

> Under the brown fog of a winter dawn,
> A crowd flowed over London Bridge, so many,
> I had not thought death had undone so many,
> Sighs, short and infrequent, were exhaled,
> And each man fixed his eyes before his feet.
> Flowed up the hill and down King William Street,
> To where Saint Mary Woolnoth kept the hours
> With a dead sound on the final stroke of nine.
> (lines 61–68)

The hexagonal clock is still a prominent feature of Hawksmoor's church. We now reverse the route of Eliot's commuters by following King William Street south towards the river. A left turn on to Monument Street and a right on Fish Street Hill bring us to Lower Thames Street, whose fishy atmosphere is well caught near the end of the poem's third section, 'The Fire Sermon.' Almost opposite is Wren's church of St Magnus Martyr, whose interior holds 'Inexplicable splendour of Ionian white and gold' (line 265).

Whilst working in the City Eliot lived near Regent's Park at No. 68 Clarence Gate Gardens, reached by following Melcombe Street from Baker Street Underground Station (Bakerloo, Circle, Metropolitan and Jubilee Lines). After the break-up of his first marriage in 1932 he moved to Kensington and stayed with Father Eric Cheetham, Vicar of St Stephen in Gloucester Road, north of Cromwell Road opposite Gloucester Road Underground Station (Piccadilly, Circle and District Lines). The Victorian church now has a plaque commemorating his service as Vicar's Warden from 1934 to 1959.

Eliot returned to this part of London in later years but during the Second World War his life centred on Bloomsbury, where he had been working for the publishing house of Faber and Faber since the mid 1920s. Throughout the Blitz he slept during the week in his office at No. 24 Russell Square behind the British Museum and served as a firewatcher in the neighbourhood—an experience vividly evoked by the second section of 'Little Gidding' in *Four Quartets*.

From 1948 until 1957 he lived in Chelsea at No. 19 Carlyle Mansions on Cheyne Walk, a block of flats formerly occupied by another Anglo-American writer, Henry James (q.v.). His flatmate was the critic John Hayward, whose editorial help with *Four Quartets* Eliot acknowledged. He left Carlyle Mansions when he married Valerie Fletcher in the church of St Barnabas, east of Chelsea in Pimlico. The mid-19C building lies off Pimlico Road near the junction with Ebury Street.

Where *The Waste Land* locates Eliot's despair firmly in the landscape of London, *Four Quartets* presents the spiritual quest of his later life in topographical terms. The poems describe pilgrimages in the full sense of the term, journeys to both a particular place and a religious revelation. Only one, 'The Dry Salvages,' takes him outside England, back to the Mississippi river and the New England of his youth.

Of the English locations Burnt Norton, subject of the first poem, is the least rewarding. The country house lies 1 mile east of Aston Subedge in the Cotswolds, 13 miles SW of Stratford-upon-Avon via A46, though Eliot visited it by making the 2-mile journey NW from the pleasant town of Chipping Campden. Burnt Norton had been damaged by fire in the 18C—hence its name—but later rebuilt. Now a school, it was derelict when Eliot came and his poem, with its stress on the gardens and the dry pool, evokes the emptiness of a landscape peopled only by fugitive echoes.

Altogether more rewarding is the subject of the second poem in the sequence, *East Coker, a picturesque little Somerset village south of A30 between Yeovil and Crewkerne. Eliot first came here in 1937, approaching East Coker down the narrow, steeply banked roads characteristic of the area :

> Now the light falls
> Across the open field, leaving the deep lane
> Shuttered with branches, dark in the afternoon,
> Where you lean against a bank while a van passes,
> And the deep lane insists on the direction
> Into the village.

(lines 14–19)

He was drawn by the memory of his ancestors, who had left East Coker for America in the 17C, and so in the poem his journey becomes a movement backwards in time, finally challenging a simple linear concept of time itself. The next stage in the cycle came when Eliot was buried in the simple church, his memorial tablet fittingly carved with the words that form the close of his poem: 'In my end is my beginning.'

The subject of the fourth poem is **Little Gidding, a small Cambridgeshire village on an unclassified road off A1 12 miles NE of Huntingdon. In the 17C it had been the site of Nicholas Ferrar's Anglican community, which gave shelter to Charles I when he was a fugitive and which suffered attacks from the Puritans. Eliot approaches it with memories of the 'broken king' (line 27) in mind, and stresses the initial disappointment that the visitor can still feel

> when you leave the rough road
> And turn behind the pig-sty to the dull façade
> And the tombstone.
>> (lines 29–31)

Yet in this 'husk of meaning' (line 32), the simple 17C church of St John the Evangelist with Ferrar's tomb outside its door, he at last achieves the sense of reconciliation for which the *Four Quartets* has strived, an intersection of history and the timeless moment:

> So, while the light fails
> On a winter's afternoon, in a secluded chapel
> History is now and England.
>> (lines 238–240)

East Coker and Little Gidding are undoubtedly the places that bring us closest to the spirit informing his late poetry, but Eliot is also publicly remembered in Poets' Corner (fee) of Westminster Abbey.

St Magnus Martyr, City of London. Usually open Tues to Fri 10.30–4, Sat 2–4, Sun 10.15–1.

Garsington Manor. Gardens open under NGS. Fee.

John Evelyn

b. Wotton, Surrey, 1620; d. London, 1706. Diarist.

Near the beginning of the diary he kept for most of his long life Evelyn proudly described his birthplace and childhood home:

> The house is large and antient, suitable to those hospitable times, and so sweetely environ'd with those delicious streames and venerable Woods, as in the judgment of strangers, as well as Englishmen, it may be compared to one of the most tempting and pleasant seates in the Nation.

Wotton House itself, by A25 3 miles west of Dorking in Surrey, has been largely rebuilt and is now predominantly 19C but part of the grounds Evelyn landscaped survive. Of the surrounding countryside Leith Hill (3 miles south of Wotton), the highest point in south-east England, and its National Trust woodland are particularly notable. Evelyn returned to Wotton in 1694 and inherited the house on the death of his brother in 1699. He is buried in the family chapel in the church—a curious choice of resting place for a man who had earlier agreed with his father-in-law that the practice of burying people inside churches was an 'ill & irreverent example, & prejudicial to the health of the living' (diary entry for 18 February 1683). His lengthy epitaph records the conclusion to which his experience of 'an age of extraordinary events, & revolutions' led him: 'That all is vanity wch is not honest, & that there's no solid Wisdom but in real Piety.'

At the age of five, when the plague came to Surrey, Evelyn was sent to his grandparents in Lewes, 8 miles NE of Brighton. He returned there after the death of his mother to attend the grammar school and live with his grandmother in Southover Grange, an Elizabethan house reached by following Keere Street south from Lewes' High Street. In 1627 he laid the foundation stone for the

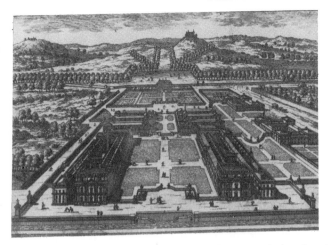

'A Prospect of GREENWICH HOSPITALL for Seamen as designed and advancing Ao. 1699.' From James Beeverell, Les Délices de la Grand' Bretagne, et de l'Irlande (expanded edition, 1727). Courtesy of Cambridge University Library

church at South Malling, 1 mile north on A26, it then being customary for young children to perform the ceremony.

In Oxford Evelyn studied at Balliol College. Returning to the city in the course of a tour round England with his wife in July 1854 he had a memorable dinner at Wadham College, then flourishing under the wardenship of Dr John Wilkins and a congenial port of call for a future Fellow of the Royal Society. Here he met, apparently for the first time, 'that miracle of Youth' Christopher Wren. The Library at Christ Church has the manuscript of Evelyn's diary.

By 1854 Evelyn had completed the Continental travels on which he had prudently embarked during the Civil War and the early years of the Interregnum and had settled at Deptford in south-east London, then a separate village. His skill in gardening and forestation made Sayes Court, the estate belonging to his wife's family, into 'a most beautiful place,' as his friend Samuel Pepys (q.v.) reported. On returning to Wotton House Evelyn leased the Court to Admiral Benbow, who sublet it to Peter the Great with disastrous results. Today the only relic is the little garden off Grove Street, which leads from Evelyn Street (A200) towards the docks. A more substantial reminder of Evelyn's presence in the area is Wren's Greenwich Hospital (now Royal Naval College) to the east. He was one of the commissioners responsible for the building and recorded with triumph in his diary for 30 June 1696:

> I went with a select committee of the Commissioners for the fabrik of Greenewich Hospital, & with Sir Chr: Wren the Surveyor, where with him I laied the first stone of that intended foundation; precisely at 5 a clock in the Evening after we had dined together: Mr Flamsted the Kings Astronomical Professor observing the punctual time by Instruments: Note that one of the workmen in helping to place the stone, being a Corner large stone, grating his fingers against the gravelly banke, some drops of blood fell upon it.

An earlier example of Evelyn's interest in the fate of disabled seamen and soldiers is the Royal Hospital, also by Wren, on the Chelsea Embankment in south-west London. He proposed the idea for such a building to Charles II, though it had to wait for the generosity of Sir Stephen Fox to be realised. Evelyn's diary for 12 May 1691 reported on the result:

> I went to see the Hospital & Infirmarie for Emerited Souldiers lately built at Chelsey, which is indeede a very Magnificent, Compleat & excellent Foundation, the two Cutts from the Thames, Courts, and other accomodations wonderfull fine: The several wards for the souldiers, Infirmary for the sick, Dispensatory, Governors house & other officers, especially the Refectory for 400 men, & Chapell; In the Refectory is a noble picture of heroic argument in honour of Char: 2d painted by Virrio [Antonio Verrio]: also the Kings Statue in Brasee, of the work of Gibbons [Grinling Gibbons] in the Court next the Cloister & c.

It was inevitable that Evelyn, close to the public events of his age but careful not to be damaged by their turbulence, should have had a visitor's acquaintance with the Tower of London. In his youth he witnessed and deplored the execution of the Earl of Strafford, Charles I's Lord Deputy of Ireland, on Tower Hill: 'the fatal Stroake, which sever'd the wisest head in England' (entry for 7 May 1641). In later life, on 4 June 1679, he dined with Samuel Pepys, then imprisoned in the Tower 'but I believe unjustly.'

Evelyn's interest in science, gardening and architecture—his role, in fact, as one of the age's leading connoisseurs—ensured that he travelled widely. His connection with Eastern England is perhaps especially notable. In 1654 he first visited Audley End in Essex, not yet ruthlessly altered by Vanbrugh (q.v.): 'It is a mixt fabric, 'twixt antique & modern, but observable for its being compleately finish'd, & without comparison one of the stateliest palaces of the Kingdome, consisting of two Courts, the first very large, Wingd with Cloisters' (1 September 1654). The house stands east of M11 and B1383 near Saffron Walden. Of Cambridge he wrote in the same diary entry as only a graduate of Oxford could. King's College Chapel was 'altogether answerable to expectation, especially the roof all of stone, which for the flatnesse of its laying & carving may I conceive vie with any in Christendome' but he could find little else to praise:

> the whole Towne situated in a low dirty unpleasant place, the streets ill paved, the air thick, as infested by the fenns; nor are its Churches (of which St *Maries* is the best) anything considerable in comprre to *Oxford* which is doubtlesse the noblest Universitie now in the whole World.

His visit to Norwich in 1671 is described under the entry of Sir Thomas Browne, whom he met there.

Southover Grange, Lewes. Gardens open Mon to Sat 8–dusk, Sun & BH 9–dusk.

Library, Christ Church. Visitors by appointment.

Royal Naval College, Greenwich (Greenwich Hospital). Grounds, Painted Hall and Chapel open Mon to Wed, Fri & Sat 2.30–5, Sun in May to Sept 2.30–5. Sun service in Chapel at 11.

Royal Hospital, Chelsea. Grounds open Mon to Sat 10–dusk, Sun 2–dusk. Buildings open daily 10–12, 2–4 except BH Sun. Museum open daily in summer 10–12, 2–5, in winter 10–12, 2– 4.

Tower of London, (DoE). Open March to Oct, Mon to Sat 9.30–5, Sun 2–5; Nov to Feb, Mon to Sat 9.30–4. Closed Christmas Eve, Christmas Day, Boxing Day,

New Year's Day, Maundy Thurs, Good Fri. Fee.

Audley End, Saffron Walden (English Heritage). Open Apr to Sept, Tues to Sun 1–6.30. Closed Good Fri but open BH Mon except May Day. Fee.

George Farquhar

b. Londonderry, 1678; d. London, 1707. *The Constant Couple* (1699); *The Recruiting Officer* (1706); *The Beaux' Stratagem* (1707).

Though much of Farquhar's childhood in Ireland remains obscure or uncommemorated, he followed a pattern of education common among gentlemen and writers of the age. He received his schooling in the county town of Kilkenny at Kilkenny College, then apparently located in the Close of St Mary's Cathedral; its present buildings, which date from 1780, are on the north bank of the Nore near John's Bridge. In 1694 he entered Trinity College, Dublin as a sizar (or poor student) and enjoyed a rather chequered undergraduate career which seems to have ended the following year.

After university Farquhar was actor and then soldier. In 1705 he was sent as recruiting officer for Marlborough's army to the cathedral city of Lichfield, 16 miles north of Birmingham, and to Shrewsbury, the county town of Shropshire. The experience left its mark on the two genial comedies by which he is usually remembered. *The Recruiting Officer* takes place in Shrewsbury and is dedicated to 'All Friends Round the Wrekin.' *The Beaux' Stratagem* is set in Lichfield and the scene of its first act is an inn obviously modelled on the George, on Bird Street, where Farquhar himself had stayed.

The last years of his short life were spent in poverty in London. He was buried at St Martin's in the Fields by Trafalgar Square.

Henry Fielding

b. Sharpham Park, Somerset, 1707; d. Lisbon, Portugal, 1754. *The Tragedy of Tragedies; or, The Life and Death of Tom Thumb the Great* (1731); *An Apology for the Life of Mrs Shamela Andrews* (1741); *The History of the Adventures of Joseph Andrews, and of his Friend Mr Abraham Adams* (1742); *Jonathan Wild the Great* (1743); *The History of Tom Jones, A Foundling* (1749); *Amelia* (1751); *Journal of a Voyage to Lisbon* (1755).

The parts of South-Western England which played so important a role in Fielding's life and appear so often in his fiction have four main centres: Glastonbury (Somerset), Shaftesbury (Dorset), Salisbury (Wiltshire) and Bath (now in Avon).

Sharpham Park, his birthplace, lies 3 miles SW of Glastonbury and 1 mile north of Walton. The old manor house, once a residence of the Abbots of Glastonbury, has now become Sharpham Park Farm. The main features of the ˙view from Glastonbury Tor correspond to the prospect enjoyed by Mr Allworthy's house in *Tom Jones*:

> Out of this lake, which filled the centre of a beautiful plain, embellished with groupes of beeches and elms, and fed with sheep, issued a river, that, for several miles, was seen to meander through an amazing variety of meadows and woods, till it emptied itself into the sea; with a large arm

of which, and an island beyond it, the prospect was closed.

On the right of this valley opened another of less extent, adorned with several villages, and terminated by one of the towers of an old ruined abbey, grown over with ivy, and part of the front, which remained still entire.

The left hand scene presented the view of a very fine park, composed of very unequal ground, and agreeably varied with all the diversity which hills, lawns, wood, and water, laid out with admirable taste, but owing less to art than to nature, could give. Beyond this the country gradually rose into a ridge of wild mountains, the tops of which were above the clouds. (Bk 1, Ch. 4)

In this description the meandering river is the Brue, the sea is the Bristol Channel, the island Stert Island in Bridgwater Bay and the 'old ruined abbey' Glastonbury Abbey: the 'wild mountains' are, by exercise of poetic licence, the Mendip Hills and the Quantocks.

In early childhood Fielding moved to East Stour, 4 miles west of Shaftesbury on A30, returning to the village in 1734–36 after his marriage. The old rectory his mother had inherited no longer stands and Fielding's fiction remains the best memorial to his connections with the area. Parson Adams of *Joseph Andrews* was based on Rev. William Young, curate of East Stour and several neighbouring parishes, while Mr Peter Pounce in the same novel owes something to a miserly lawyer, Peter Walter, of Stalbridge Park to the SW (now demolished). A local character, Jemmy Tweedle, is the subject of an affectionate mock-heroic tribute in *Tom Jones*:

Him the pleasant banks of sweetly winding Stower had nourished, where he first learnt the vocal art, with which, wandring up and down at wakes and fairs, he cheered the rural nymphs and swains, when upon the green they interweave the sprightly dance; while he himself stood fiddling and jumping to his own music. (Bk 4, Ch. 8)

At Salisbury Fielding met his first wife, Charlotte Cradock, during visits in 1730–34. The house from which she eloped with him is a fine 17C building, still bearing her family name, on The Friary south of Saint Ann Street. Entering the Cathedral Close via Saint Ann's Gate nearby we come to No. 14, the first house on the left, where she and her children lodged in 1737. Rev. Richard Hele, Prebendary of Salisbury and Master of the school in the Close, had the misfortune to sit for the portrait of Thwackum in *Tom Jones*.

The most important reminder of Fielding's connection with South-Western England is *Prior Park, the grand Palladian mansion built by John Wood the elder at Combe Down. About a mile SE of Bath, it is reached from the south of the city via Claverton Street and Prior Park Road. Now a Roman Catholic school, Prior Park has been greatly altered inside but its exterior and grounds (especially the Palladian bridge) remain magnificent. In the 18C it was the seat of Ralph Allen (1693–1764), much-admired philanthropist and improver of Bath. Fielding was a regular and intimate guest, particularly at the time he was at work on *Tom Jones*. He repaid Allen's hospitality with the dedication of *Amelia*, the portrait of Allworthy in *Tom Jones* (though he made the Squire's house Gothic rather than Palladian and, as we have seen, transplanted it south to Glastonbury) and this thinly veiled compliment in *Joseph Andrews*:

I could name a Commoner raised higher above the Multitude by superiour Talents, than is the power of his Prince to exalt him; whose Behaviour to those he hath obliged is more amiable than the Obligation itself, and who is so great a Master of Affability, that if he could divest himself of an inherent Greatness in his Manner, would often make the lowest Acquaintance forget who was the Master of that Palace, in which they are so courteously entertained. (Bk 3, Ch. 1)

In Widcombe (near the route between Bath and Combe Down) Fielding stayed at Widcombe Lodge on Church Street while writing *Tom Jones*.

At Charlcombe, in the hills 2 miles north of Bath, Fielding's runaway marriage to Charlotte Cradock took place in 1734. Unfortunately, St Mary's Church was altered and enlarged by the Victorians.

Two locations in Hereford and Worcester should not be forgotten. On the High Street of Upton-on-Severn, a pleasant town at the junction of B4211 and A4104 10 miles south of Worcester, we find the White Lion, a stuccoed building distinguished by giant pilasters and an effigy of a lion over its porch. It is traditionally identified with the 'house of exceedingly good repute' and scene of a memorable night of errors in Book 9, Chapters 3–5 of *Tom Jones*. Fielding's visits to the area, some of them made in the course of legal duties on the Western Circuit, also took him to the seat of his friend Lord Lyttleton at Hagley Hall. The present building, with its sumptuous interior and elaborately landscaped grounds, dates from the 1750s.

In London—where most of Fielding's working life as dramatist, journalist, lawyer and magistrate was conducted—only two places can be recommended. He married his second wife and former housekeeper, Mary Daniel, in 1747 at the little Wren church of St Benet's on Bennet's Hill, south of Queen Victoria Street. During the period of his Bow Street magistracy (1748–54) he attended services and the christenings of children by his second marriage at St Paul's near Covent Garden Market. The church burned down at the end of the 18C but was rebuilt according to Inigo Jones' original design.

Prior Park (Prior Park College), near Bath. Grounds and chapel open Good Fri to Easter Mon, daily in May & Aug, 10–dusk.

Hagley Hall. Open from Easter Sun, BH Sun, and Mon 12.30–5; 1 July to 2 Sept, daily except Sat 12.30–5. Fee.

Edward FitzGerald

b. Boulge, Suffolk, 1809; d. Merton, Norfolk, 1883. *Rubáiyát of Omar Khayyám, the Astronomer-Poet of Persia, Translated into English Verse* (1859).

FitzGerald's long, unambitious and unusually serene life belonged almost entirely to Eastern England. Its major scenes may conveniently be organised into a tour beginning at Cambridge.

During his undergraduate years at Trinity College (1829–30) and his return visits to Cambridge in the 1830s he lodged on King's Parade opposite King's College Chapel. The building is now marked with a plaque. Vistors here included Thackeray and Tennyson (qq.v.), with whom he formed lifelong friendships. FitzGerald, however, became less and less impressed with the generation of undergraduates who had succeeded him, remarking in a letter of 1839 that 'the hard-reading, pale, dwindled students . . . looked as if they were only fit to have their necks wrung.' *Euphrator* (1837) is a Platonic dialogue criticising the narrowness of English university education.

In Bury St Edmunds (28 miles east via A45) he attended the King Edward VI Grammar School, now housed in Arthur Blomfield's buildings (1883) off Eastgate. The town otherwise retains much of the charming character that made FitzGerald enjoy revisiting it in later years. He once recommended a friend 'to look at the Abbey Gate—from the windows of the Angel Inn just opposite—with a Biscuit and a Pint of Sherry—as I have so often done.'

For most of his adult life he lived near the Suffolk coast in Woodbridge and its surrounding area, 32 miles SE of Bury via A45 and A12. He settled permanently in the town in 1860. Its quiet provincial atmosphere, which still largely survives, could sometimes make him grumble:

> Oh, if you were to hear 'where and Oh where is my Soldier Laddie gone' played every three hours in a languid way by the Chimes of Woodbridge Church, wouldn't you wish to hang yourself? On Sundays we have the 'Sicilian Mariners' Hymn'—very slow indeed. I see, however, by a handbill in the Grocer's Shop that a man is going to lecture on the Gorilla in a few weeks. So there is something to look forward to.

Yet he came to appreciate Woodbridge and became, indeed, a well-known local figure—more for his mildly eccentric dress than for his literary achievements, about which he always remained modest. His favourite pastime was sailing on the Deben estuary in his yacht *Scandal*, named (he said) after 'the staple product of Woodbridge.' His first lodging in the town was a modest two rooms over a shop on the north side of Market Hill. It was conveniently near his favourite inn, the Bull, where friends including Tennyson used to stay when they visited him. In 1864 he bought Little Grange on Pytches Road, reached from Woodbridge's main road, B1438. It is the 'suburb grange' of the poem addressed to FitzGerald which prefaces Tennyson's 'Tiresias.' Yet even after he had enlarged Little Grange FitzGerald was reluctant to live there and did not take up residence until 1874.

Boulge, the traditional home of the FitzGerald family, lies north of Woodbridge and is the name of a parish rather than an actual village. His birthplace, Bredfield Hall, stood to the left of A12 1 mile north of its junction with A1152 but was demolished in 1950. However, to the right of the unclassified road that runs from A12 towards Debach we may still find Boulge Cottage, where FitzGerald lived from 1837 until 1853. In this small house with walls 'as thin as sixpence' and thatched roof 'perforated by lascivious sparrows' FitzGerald began the Persian studies that resulted in his most famous work and led an apparently idle bachelor life that was the envy of his friends. 'His tranquillity,' one remarked, 'is a pirated copy of the peace of God.'

Boulge Hall, his parents' last home, stood opposite the cottage. It has been demolished but in its grounds is the church of St Michael where FitzGerald was buried. On his grave grows a descendant of a rose from the tomb of Omar Khayyám, first planted by members of the Omar Khayyám Club in 1893.

John Ford

b. Ilsington, Devon, 1586; d. place unknown, 1625?. *'Tis Pity She's a Whore* (1633); *The Broken Heart* (1633).

The only building to survive as a reminder of the dramatist's otherwise obscure life is the church of St Michael, where he was baptised, at Ilsington, 3 miles SW of Bovey Tracey and on the south eastern edge of Dartmoor. It has a fine wagon roof.

E.M. Forster

b. London, 1879; d. Coventry, West Midlands, 1970. *Where Angels Fear to Tread* (1905); *The Longest Journey* (1907); *A Room With a View* (1908); *Howards End* (1910); *The Celestial Omnibus and Other Stories* (1911); *A Passage to India* (1924); *Aspects of the Novel* (1927); *The Eternal Moment and Other Stories* (1928); *Goldsworthy Lowes Dickinson* (1934); *Abinger Harvest* (1936); *Two Cheers For Democracy* (1951); *Billy Budd* (libretto for opera by Benjamin Britten; 1951); *The Hill of Devi* (1953); *Marianne Thornton 1797–1887: A Domestic Biography* (1956); *Maurice* (1971).

Although he was born in London, Forster's most important childhood home was in Stevenage (immediately east of A1 in Hertfordshire), where his widowed mother took him in 1883. The town, of course, has expanded and been sadly changed since then but their home, Rook's Nest (on Weston Road in Old Stevenage, NE of St Nicholas' church), remains. To Forster this charming house represented 'my childhood and safety' and his affection for it is demonstrated in his portrait of 'Howards End.'

In Tonbridge (SW of Maidstone, Kent via A26), where he and his mother came to live in 1893, he was not so happy. Even in old age he could not bring himself to view his years at Tonbridge School, off the High Street, with nostalgia and once remarked that if he gave an end-of-term address it would say:

> School was the unhappiest time of my life, and the worst trick it ever played me was to pretend that it was the world in miniature. For it hindered me from discovering how lovely and how delightful and kind the world can be, and how much of it is intelligible. From this platform of middle age, this throne of experience, this altar of wisdom, this scaffold of character, this beacon of hope, this threshold of decay, my last words are: There's a better time coming.

His experience of Tonbridge informed the second section of Forster's most closely autobiographical novel, *The Longest Journey*, in which the hero teaches at 'Sawston School,' and led to his famous criticism that the public school system, whatever it may do for boys' minds and bodies, leaves them with undeveloped hearts. Nearby Tunbridge Wells, where his mother went to live in 1898, was no better than Tonbridge; Forster remembered it as a 'Filthy, self-righteous place.'

After the narrowness of school Cambridge had a liberating and enlarging effect on the young Forster; in old age it again became his home. He first entered *King's College in 1896, when M.R. James (best remembered as a writer of ghost stories) was Dean and the

E.M. Forster in his rooms at King's College, c. 1950, a photograph he used as his Christmas card. Courtesy of King's College, Cambridge

Fellows included Oscar Browning and Goldsworthy Lowes Dickinson, whose biography he later wrote. Like Tennyson (q.v.) before him he was elected to that exclusive intellectual circle, the Apostles, and he visited the Darwin family at Newnham Grange (now assimilated into the buildings of Darwin College on Silver Street). Gwen Raverat's *Period Piece* (1952) captures the atmosphere of the Darwin household in these years, while the first section of *The Longest Journey* poignantly expresses Forster's own sense of what Cambridge meant to him. He came back in 1927 to deliver the Clark lectures, published as *Aspects of the Novel*, and in 1946 was elected to an Honorary Fellowship of his old college. The distinction coincided with his unhappy departure from West Hackhurst (see below) and Forster gratefully seized the chance to return to King's as a resident. He remained, living in rooms on A staircase in the front court, until the end of his life.

In 1904 Forster made a significant visit to *Figsbury Rings (NT), an Iron Age camp NE of Salisbury between A30 and A338. The atmosphere of the place and an accidental meeting with a lame shepherd boy played their part in the genesis of *The Longest Journey*, where the Rings are described as curious rather than impressive. Neither embankment was over twelve feet high, and the grass on them had not the exquisite green of Old Sarum, but was grey and wiry. But Nature (if she arranges anything) had arranged that from them, at all events, there should be a view. The whole system of the country lay spread before Rickie . . . He saw Old Sarum, and hints of the Avon valley, and the land above Stonehenge, and behind him he saw the great wood beginning unobtrusively, as if the down too needed shaving; and into it the road to London slipped, covering the bushes with white dust. Chalk made the dust white, chalk made the water clear, chalk made the clean rolling outlines of the land, and favoured the grass and the distant coronals of trees. Here is the heart of our island: the Chilterns, the North Downs, the South Downs radiate hence. The fibres of England unite in Wiltshire, and did we condescend to worship her, here we should erect our national shrine. (Chapter 13)

In the years between graduating from and returning to Cambridge Forster travelled abroad, his experience of Italy and India enriching his fiction and sharpening his critique of English narrowness. His most important home in England was at Abinger Hammer, a Surrey village on A25 between Guildford and Dorking. Forster's aunt had first leased West Hackhurst here in 1878 and he inherited the house on her death in 1924. Forster regarded the prospect of being gathered into the country gentry with amusement and some irritation but stayed until the lease expired in 1946. His forced departure was a source of great pain, though he retained a permanent stake in Abinger Hammer because he had earlier bought Piney Copse adjoining the house, subject of the wry little essay, 'My Wood.' He left it to the National Trust and it is now usually known as Forster's Wood.

John Galsworthy

b. London, 1867; d. London, 1933. *From the Four Winds* (as 'John Sinjohn'; 1897); *Jocelyn* (as 'John Sinjohn'; 1898); *Villa Rubein* (as 'John Sinjohn'; 1900); *A Man of Devon* (as 'John Sinjohn'; 1901); *The Island Pharisees* (1904); *The Man of Property* (1904); *The Silver Box* (1909); *The Country House* (1907); *Joy* (1909); *Fraternity* (1909); *Strife* (1909); *Justice* (1910); *The Patrician* (1911); *The Dark Flower* (1913); *The Freelands* (1915); *Beyond* (1917); *Saint's Progress* (1919); *In Chancery* (1920); *The Skin Game* (1920); *Awakening* (1920); *To Let* (1921); *The White Monkey* (1924); *The Silver Spoon* (1926); *Two Forsyte Interludes* (1927); *Swan Song* (1928); *On Forsyte 'Change* (1930); *Maid in Waiting* (1931); *Flowering Wilderness* (1932); *Over the River* (1933).

Galsworthy was 'a queer fish, like the rest of us,' thought James Barrie (q.v.): 'So sincerely weighed down by the out-of-jointness of things socially . . . but outwardly a man-about-town, so neat, so correct.' It is the man about town whom the surviving scenes of Galsworthy's life commemorate.

He was educated at the famous public school at Harrow on the Hill in north-west London and at New College, Oxford, where a contemporary remembered him as 'the best dressed man in College.' At Lincoln's Inn he qualified for the Bar and found that he hated the law, a common apprenticeship for writers to serve. In 1904 he married Ada, divorced wife of his cousin, at the Mayfair church of St George's, Hanover Square. From 1913 they lived at No. 1A Adelphi Terrace (now rebuilt), between the Strand and Victoria Embankment Gardens, an elegant and fashionable address shared by Barrie and

Shaw (qq.v.). In later life Galsworthy moved to Hampstead, where the imposing Grove Lodge on Admiral's Walk (off Heath Street near the top of the hill) is now marked by a plaque.

Two places outside London were important in this otherwise urban life. The first is in Devon, the county from which his family originally came and for which Galsworthy always felt a strong affection. From 1907 onwards he leased part of Wingstone, a farmhouse a quarter of a mile NW of the village of Manaton, itself on the edge of Dartmoor 5 miles NW of Bovey Tracey via B3344. In 1926 he bought a rather grander place in the country, the neo-Tudor Bury House in the Sussex village of Bury, on A284 4 miles north of Arundel. At his own request, his ashes were scattered in the surrounding countryside.

Harrow School. Visits by prior arrangement with the Custos of the Old Schools.

Elizabeth Gaskell (née Stevenson)

b. London, 1810; d. Holybourne, Hampshire, 1865. *Mary Barton: A Tale of Manchester Life* (1848); *Ruth* (1853); *Cranford* (1853); *North and South* (1855); *The Life of Charlotte Brontë (1857)*; *Sylvia's Lovers* (1863); *Cousin Phillis* (1865); *Wives and Daughters: An Everyday Story* (1866).

Mrs Gaskell was born in that part of Cheyne Walk then known as Lindsey Row, west of Battersea Bridge in Chelsea. The house, now No. 93, is marked with a GLC plaque.

She left London in infancy after the death of her mother and spent her childhood and youth in the pleasant little Cheshire town of *Knutsford, 16 miles SW of Manchester at the junction of A50 and A537. Her precise and tender recollections of Knutsford transformed it into 'Cranford' and the 'Hollingford' of her last, incomplete novel, *Wives and Daughters*. The town today retains enough atmosphere and boasts enough memorials of the writer to deserve a walking tour. This naturally begins south of the Heath on Gaskell Avenue, the name itself a sign of local pride in the writer. The house where she was brought up by her aunt, Mrs Lumb, is marked with a plaque. After following the Avenue towards the town centre we turn right on to Princess Street. By taking Adam's Hill to the left we find the Brook Street Unitarian Chapel of 1689 which Mrs Gaskell attended. This charming building was made the subject of an equally charming description in *Ruth*:

> The chapel had a picturesque and old-world look, for luckily, the congregation had been too poor to rebuild it, or new-face it in George the Third's time. The staircases which led to the galleries were outside, at each end of the building, and the irregular roof and worn stone steps looked grey and stained by time and weather. The grassy hillocks, each with a little upright headstone, were shaded by a grand old wych-elm. A lilac-bush or two, a white rose-tree, and a few laburnums, all old and gnarled enough, were planted round the chapel yard; and the casement windows of the chapel were made of heavy-leaded, diamond-shaped panes, almost covered with ivy, producing a green gloom, not without its solemnity, within . . . The interior of the building was plain and simple . . . when it was fitted up, oak-timber was much cheaper than it is now, so the wood-work was all of that description. . . . The walls were whitewashed and were recipients of the shadows of the beauty without;

on their 'white plains' the tracery of the ivy might be seen, now still, now stirred by the sudden flight of some little bird. (Ch. 14)

Mrs Gaskell was buried in the graveyard; her husband, Rev. William Gaskell (d. 1884), lies beside her.

At the end of Adam's Hill we turn left, cross the railway bridge and follow King Street, the town's main thoroughfare. A left turn on Church Hill brings us to St John Baptist, a brick church of the 1740s, where the novelist was married in 1832. Returning to King Street and continuing north we pass the grandiose, eccentric Gaskell Tower of 1907, with a medallion bust of the novelist on one side and a profuse inscription. Like its neighbour, The King's Coffee House, it is one of several remarkable additions to Knutsford by Richard Harding Watt.

From the top of King Street Knutsford Lodge and Knutsford Drive give access to Tatton Park (3½ miles). Once the seat of the Egerton family, this early 19C mansion set in its large park and fine gardens appears as 'Cumnor Towers' in *Wives and Daughters*.

After her marriage Mrs Gaskell moved to Manchester, showing her compassionate knowledge of its industrial workers in *Mary Barton*. Today neither her first two homes nor the old Cross Street Chapel where her husband preached survive. Her last and most famous home, however, still stands: No. 84 Plymouth Grove, a street running SE from the main buildings of the University. She moved into this large early 19C house in 1850 and turned it into a salon visited by distinguished contemporaries, whom the fame of her writing and the charm of her personality readily attracted. Of these, the closest and most important friend was Charlotte Brontë (q.v.), who came to stay in 1851 and again in 1853. Mrs Gaskell, in turn, visited Haworth and attended Charlotte's wedding in 1854, as well as writing the controversial biography of her fellow-novelist in 1857. The Plymouth Grove house is now the University Overseas Centre.

In November 1859 Mrs Gaskell visited Whitby, 18 miles NW of Scarborough on Yorkshire's east coast, to gather material for *Sylvia's Lovers*, which is set in a whaling port at the end of the 18C. Whitby's harbour and old fishing town still preserve some of the flavour Mrs Gaskell captured in her portrait of 'Monkshaven'.

In the last year of her life she resolved to buy a second home, keeping its purchase as a surprise for her husband, and chose The Lawn, a Georgian building 'in the middle of a pretty rural village,' Holybourne. The village lies immediately NE of Alton, off A31 between Farnham and Winchester in Hampshire. Yet she had barely moved in and had not revealed the secret to her husband before she died, quite unexpectedly and peacefully, of a heart attack over tea one afternoon.

Tatton Park, Knutsford (NT and Cheshire County Council). Open Apr to mid May & Sept to end Oct, house Mon to Sat 1–4, Sun & BH Mon 1–5, garden 12–4.30, Sun & BH Mon 11–5, park Mon to Sat 9–7 (pedestrians), 11–6 (others), Sun & BH Mon 10–6; mid May to end Aug, house Mon to Sat 1–5, Sun & BH Mon 12–5, garden Mon to Sat 11–5.30, Sun & BH Mon 11–6, park Mon to Sat 9–8 (pedestrians), 10.30–7 (others), Sun & BH Mon 10–7; Nov to March, garden Mon to Sat 1–4, Sun & BH Mon 12–4, park daily 9–dusk (pedestrians), 11–dusk (others). Closed Christmas Day. Fees.

The 'Gawain' Poet

Sir Gawain and the Green Knight; *Pearl*; *Purity* (or *Cleanness*); *Patience* (all c. 1375–c. 1400).

Virtually all that is known about these poems stems from the unique manuscript of c. 1400 in the Cotton Collection at the British Museum. Their author's identity has not been established and, indeed, the attribution of all four works to the same poet remains likely supposition rather than proven fact.

For a medieval romance *Sir Gawain and the Green Knight* shows an unusually precise interest in topography, as well as one that accords with expert attribution of its dialect to Cheshire or Lancashire. Sir Gawain's journey may start from the fabulous Camelot but its terrain quickly becomes recognisable. He rides through 'the ryalme of Logres' (line 691)—that is, the land south of the River Humber—and almost into north Wales, keeping 'Alle the iles of Anglesay [Anglesey, Gwynedd] on lyft half' (line 698). He fords the River Dee into 'the wyldrenesse of Wyrale' (line 701), the Wirral peninsula formed by the Dee and the Mersey, and now part of the Merseyside area; amid its formerly wild scenery he undergoes the hardships narrated in lines 713–739 before his arrival at Bercilak's Castle and the Green Chapel.

The chapel, sinister natural setting for Gawain's final encounter with the Green Knight, is described in specific terms:

> Hit hade a hole on the ende and on ayther syde,
> And overgrowen with gresse in glodes aywhere;
> And al was holw [hollow] inwith, nobot [nothing but] an olde cave
> Or the crevisse of an olde cragge . . .

> (lines 2180–2183)

It is understandable that readers should have assumed the poet to have an actual place in mind and that its whereabouts should have attracted scholarly speculation. An older view advanced by Sir Frederic Madden identified it with the now-vanished Chapel of the Grune, near Skinburness (west of Carlisle on the Cumbrian coast). Later and better supported theories assign it to two locations further south, in the Peak District. Both possible sites are well worth visiting but both require an aptitude for country walking as hardy as Gawain's own. The first candidate is *Wetton Mill, Staffordshire; it lies 8 miles NW of Ashbourne, Derbyshire in a valley at the junction of Hoo Brook and the River Manifold, and is best reached either from Butterton to the west or Wetton to the east. The large stone outcrop, on the side of a hill and with a large hole leading into a chamber that once had a natural roof, agrees well with the main features in the poem; the Manifold, narrowed almost to a stream at this point, corresponds to the water that the Green Knight 'hypped over on hys ax' (line 2233).

The second candidate is nearby *Lud's Church, 9 miles NW and west of the A53 Leek to Buxton road: a dramatic rock fissure some 100ft long and reaching a height of 50ft, entered by a cave-like opening. An interesting approach which would seem to duplicate Gawain's route begins at Swythamley Hall (near Wincle). It leads east with a climb towards Roach End and then veers sharply north for a descent to the junction of Black Brook and the River Dane. Lud's Church is on the wooded southern bank of the river.

John Gay

b. Barnstaple, Devon, 1685; d. London, 1732. *The Shepherd's Week* (1714); *Fables* (1727–28); *The Beggar's Opera* (1728); *Polly* (1729).

In Barnstaple on the north coast of Devon, the 'happy native land' he praised in 'A Journey to Exeter,' Gay was educated at the free grammar school. Its 14C building, St Anne's Chapel, now houses a local museum.

Throughout his life Gay's charm readily won the affection of others, while his habits of mismanagement ensured that friends adopted a protective role. He was particularly close to Swift and Pope (qq.v.), frequently visiting the latter's Villa at Twickenham and becoming an intimate, at times a household pet, of various members of Pope's circle: Mrs Howard (later Lady Suffolk), the Dormer family of Rousham Hall, and Lords Bathurst, Burlington and Harcourt. The houses where he visited them are described under the entry for his better known contemporary.

After 1720, when he lost money by a characteristically ill-timed investment in the South Sea Bubble, Gay fell under the protection of the Duke and Duchess of Queensberry. He stayed with them at Douglas House, near Ham House in Richmond, and at Amesbury Abbey in Wiltshire, 14 miles west of Andover via A303, where in 1727 he wrote *The Beggar's Opera*. The 17C building was demolished in the 19C but replaced by one closely following the original design; the gardens by Charles Bridgeman have gone.

Gay was buried in Westminster Abbey and honoured with a monument in Poets' Corner (fee) erected by the Duke and Duchess of Queensberry. Pope's epitaph, which greatly annoyed Dr Johnson (q.v.), remembers him as being 'Of manners gentle, of affections mild,/ In wit a man, simplicity a child.' To it is added the light-hearted epitaph Gay had written for himself:

> Life is a jest, and all things show it,
> I thought so once, but now I know it.

St Anne's Museum, Barnstaple. Open Whitsun to Michaelmas, Mon to Sat 10–4. Fee.

Sir William Schwenk Gilbert

b. London, 1836; d. London, 1911. *The 'Bab' Ballads: Much Sound and Little Sense* (1869); *More 'Bab' Ballads* (1873); and the Savoy operas in collaboration with Sir Arthur Sullivan.

Gilbert's rise to fame and affluence with the success of the Savoy operas was charted by a progression of splendid London homes. In the 1870s he lived at No. 24 The Boltons, an elegant row of houses running south from the Old Brompton Road in South Kensington, where his neighbours included the singer Jenny Lind. In 1883 he moved to No. 39 Harrington Gardens (GLC plaque), north of the Old Brompton Road via Bolton Gardens. Gilbert himself played a part in designing the brick neo-Renaissance house with its elaborate terracotta decorations. In 1890 he bought Grim's Dyke on Harrow Weald Common (west of A409), then in Middlesex but now in north-west London. The neo-Tudor building had been designed by Norman Shaw for the artist Frederick Goodall in 1872. While Gilbert was owner its grounds harboured unmolested pheasants and foxes, for he greatly disliked blood sports, once remarking: 'Deer-stalking would be a very fine sport if only the deer had guns.' He died of a heart attack after rescuing a young lady from drowning in his lake, and was buried in the churchyard at Great Stanmore, near the junction of A410 (Stanmore Hill) and A4140 to the SE.

In Central London Gilbert is commemorated by a bas-relief plaque on the wall of the Victoria Embankment near Charing Cross Pier and Embankment Underground Station (Northern, Bakerloo, Circle and District Lines). Across the road the Victoria Embankment Gardens have a statue of Sir Arthur Sullivan (1842–1900). On the Strand to the north is a rebuilt version of the Savoy Theatre, opened by Richard D'Oyly Carte in 1881, where Gilbert and Sullivan's operas from *Iolanthe* onwards were first staged.

George Gissing

b. Wakefield, West Yorkshire, 1857; d. St Jean de Puz, France, 1903. *Workers in the Dawn* (1880); *The Unclassed* (1884); *Isabel Clarendon* (1886); *Demos* (1886); *Thyrza* (1887); *A Life's Morning* (1888); *The Nether World* (1889); *The Emancipated* (1890); *New Grub Street* (1891); *Denzil Quarrier* (1892); *Born in Exile* (1892); *The Odd Women* (1893); *In the Year of Jubilee* (1894); *Eve's Ransom* (1895); *The Paying Guest* (1895); *Sleeping Fires* (1895); *The Whirlpool* (1897); *Charles Dickens: A Critical Study* (1898); *The Town Traveller* (1898); *The Crown of Life* (1899); *Our Friend the Charlatan* (1901); *By the Ionian Sea* (1901); *The Private Papers of Henry Ryecroft* (1903); *Veranilda* (1904); *Will Warburton* (1905).

Gissing's early years were spent in Northern England. At Wakefield, 8 miles south of Leeds, his birthplace is marked by a tablet on No. 30 Westgate in the market place, where his father kept a chemist's shop. At the age of fourteen, after his father's death, he was sent to school in Alderley Edge, 12 miles south of Manchester. Lindow Grove School, no longer a school and since renamed College Flats, stands to the left of A34 as one approaches the town from Mancester and Wilmslow. Academic promise won Gissing a place at Owens College, founded in 1851 and later to grow into Manchester University. His student days spanned the move from the College's old building on Quay Street, west of St Peter's Square and now the County Court, to the first of Alfred Waterhouse's new university buildings, the west wing of 1873, in Oxford Road 1 mile SE of St Peter's Square. Yet his career ended in disgrace when he was caught stealing from fellow students: he was stripped of his prizes and distinctions, and sentenced to a month's imprisonment.

Prison was followed by a spell as a clerk in Liverpool and a visit to America before, in 1878, Gissing arrived in London to occupy the first of a series of shabby, fugitive lodgings. His experiences are powerfully evoked in his fiction, where London becomes a city of struggling writers and 'odd women' leading lives of quiet desperation amid the trappings of modern commerce and advertising. It is a compelling achievement, too little noticed until recently, which creates a vital link between the London of Dickens (q.v.) and the London of George Orwell (q.v.).

In 1879–80, after his disastrous first marriage to Nell Harrison, he was lodging at No. 22 Colville Place, which is reached by following Goodge Street west from Tottenham Court Road and turning left into Charlotte Street. The house does not survive but the alley retains much of its atmosphere. In the quasi-autobiographical *Private Papers of Henry Ryecroft* he remembered this gloomy period:

> I see that alley hidden on the west side of Tottenham Court Road, where after living in a back bedroom on the top floor, I had to exchange for the front cellar; there was a difference, if I remember rightly, of sixpence a week, and sixpence, in those days, was a very great consideration—why, it meant a couple of meals . . . Here I lived; here I *wrote*. Yes, 'literary work' was done at that filthy deal table, on which, by the by, lay my Homer, my Shakespeare, and the few other books I then possessed. At night, as I lay in bed, I used to hear the tramp, tramp of a *posse* of policemen who passed along the alley on their way to relieve guard; their heavy feet sometimes sounded on the grating above my window. ('Spring,' Ch. 10)

In *Workers in the Dawn*, which belongs to these years, Mr Tollady has his printing shop on Charlotte Place, the next alley to run south from Goodge Street after we pass the junction with Charlotte Street.

Gissing, of course, spent much of his time in the British Museum and Library, east of Tottenham Court Road and reached via Great Russell Street. Marian Yule is one of several characters in *New Grub Street* who work in the domed, circular Reading Room:

> The fog grew thicker; she looked up at the windows beneath the dome and saw that they were a dusky yellow. Then her eye discerned an official walking along the upper gallery, and in pursuance of her grotesque humour, her mocking misery, she likened him to a black, lost soul, doomed to wander in an eternity of vain research among endless shelves. Or again, the readers who sat here at these radiating lines of desks, what were they but helpless flies caught in a huge web, its nucleus the great circle of the Catalogue? Darker, darker. From the towering wall of volumes seemed to emanate visible motes, intensifying the obscurity; in a moment the book-lined circumference of the room would be but a featureless prison-limit. (Ch. 8)

Two later London addresses are worth noting. In 1883, freed from Nell Harrison, Gissing lived at No. 33 Oakley Gardens in Chelsea, now marked by a plaque. The tiny square is found by following Oakley Street north from Albert Bridge and then taking a right on Phene Street. He made a longer stay in Marylebone (1884–91) at No. 7K Cornwall Terrace Mansions, between Baker Street Underground Station (Bakerloo, Metropolitan, Circle and Jubilee Lines) and Regent's Park.

By the mid-1890s Gissing had won a reputation that relieved the worst of his poverty. In July 1895 he was a guest at a literary dinner of the Omar Khayyám Club at the Burford Bridge Hotel in Surrey, near the foot of Box Hill some 1½ miles north of Dorking of A24. George Meredith (q.v.), who lived nearby, and Thomas Hardy (q.v.) also attended and press reports bracketed the three writers together. Gissing later moved to Dorking itself, living from 1898 to 1899 at No.

7 Clifton Terrace, separated from his second wife but unable to get a divorce. It was here that he met Gabrielle Fleury, with whom he spent his last years in France.

British Museum & Library. Museum open Mon to Sat 10–5, Sun 2.30–6; closed Christmas Eve, Christmas Day, Boxing Day, New Year's Day, Good Fri & BH. Admission to the Library's Reading Room is by ticket only, for which written application accompanied by a letter of recommendation is required.

Oliver Goldsmith

b. Pallas, Longford or Elphin, Roscommon, 1730?; d. London, 1774. *The Citizen of the World* (1762); *The Life of Richard Nash, Esq* (1762); *The Vicar of Wakefield* (1766); *The Good-Natured Man (1768)*; *The Deserted Village* (1770); *She Stoops to Conquer* (1773).

Very little survives to remind the tourist of Goldsmith's early years in Ireland, though the scene of his poem *The Deserted Village* is identified as Lissoy, Westmeath, off N55 8 miles NE of Athlone and near the area where he spent his childhood. Trinity College, Dublin, which he attended in the humiliating capacity of sizar (or poor student), has a statue (1863) outside its main front on College Green.

He completed his training as a doctor at Edinburgh University. Its mean huddle of buildings on Chambers Street, sometimes mistaken by strangers for almshouses, was replaced by Robert Adam's fine Old University of 1789.

After his arrival in England (1756) Goldsmith's life and career is rather better commemorated. His friendship with Robert Nugent, later Lord Clare, made him a visitor to Gosfield Hall, off A1017 4 miles north of Braintree in Essex. The Hall's exterior is a remarkable medley of different periods but the tour of the interior includes some fine 18C state rooms. Goldsmith was also a guest at Lord Clare's house in Bath, No. 11 North Parade, though with his ungainly appearance and proneness to social blunders he must surely have cut a strange figure in that fashionable city.

An unproved, tantalising tradition connects the best-known character in his best-known play with the Anthony Lumpkin whose grave is to be found in the churchyard at Leverington, off A1101 2 miles NE of Wisbech in Cambridgeshire.

Most of Goldsmith's working life was spent in London. Thanks to the help of a kindly publisher, John Newbery, he lived (1764–67) at Canonbury Tower, facing Canonbury Place SE of Highbury and Islington Station (British Rail and Victoria Underground Line). The fine building is now occupied by the Tower Theatre.

His usual haunts were in the City near Fleet Street. Like so many other literary men of his age he is supposed to have frequented the Cheshire Cheese on Wine Office Court. His lodgings at No. 6 nearby have gone, though Nos 1–3, apparently of the same period, still stand. In 1762 Dr Johnson (q.v.) found him here on the verge of financial ruin and despair—disasters Johnson sensibly averted by selling the manuscript of *The Vicar of Wakefield* to a publisher. From 1767 until his death Goldsmith lived at No. 2 (demolished) Brick Court off Middle Temple Lane, where his loudly sociable habits irritated his neighbour, the legal historian William Blackstone. A stone in the raised part of the churchyard north of the Temple Church marks the approximate site of his grave.

Poets' Corner (fee) in Westminster Abbey has a monument of 1776 by Joseph Nollekens with a Latin epitaph by Johnson, who stuck to his choice of language despite a good-humoured protest from fellow members of the Literary Club:

> But if we might venture to express our wishes, they would lead us to request, that he would write the Epitaph in English rather than in Latin. As we think that the Memory of so eminent an English Writer ought to be perpetuated in the Language to which his Works are likely to be so lasting an Ornament, Which we also know to have been the opinion of the late Doctor himself.

In fact, Johnson also paid a magnificent vernacular tribute to Goldsmith in a letter to Bennet Langton: 'let not his frailties be remembered; he was a very great man.'

Gosfield Hall. Open 1 May to 30 Sept, Wed & Thurs 2–4. Fee.

Canonbury Tower (Tower Theatre). Tours by arrangement, and for parties after Sat evening performance.

John Gower

b. place unknown, 1325?; d. London, 1408. *Speculum Meditantis* (n.d.); *Vox Clamantis* (n.d.); *Confessio Amantis* (n.d.).

The obscurity that has overtaken the life and writings of Gower, poet and near-contemporary of Chaucer (q.v.), is more than compensated for by the survival of his splendid, well restored **✶✶tomb** in the north aisle of Southwark Cathedral (at the south end of London Bridge). Wearing Henry IV's emblem of the swan on the collar round his neck, his effigy rests on copies of his three main works, beneath an arched canopy. The inscription, more charitable than posterity, remembers him as 'Angl. poeta celeberrimus.' Gower was a benefactor of the Augustinian Priory of St Mary Overie, of which the Cathedral was then part, and may have been resident there at the time of his death.

Thomas Gray

b. London, 1716; d. Cambridge, 1771. *Ode on a Distant Prospect of Eton College* (1747); *Elegy Written in a Country Churchyard* (1751); *The Progress of Poesy* (1757); *The Bard* (1757).

Gray's connection with Cambridge spanned his entire adult life. He entered **✶Peterhouse** as an undergraduate in 1734 and left without taking a degree in 1738. After a continental tour in the company of Horace Walpole (q.v.), later perhaps the most vocal advocate of Gray's literary talent, he returned to his old college as a fellow-commoner studying civil law. The second floor rooms he occupied in the Fellows' Building overlook Trumpington Street and the churchyard of St Mary the Less.

A man of quiet and finicky temperament ('dull in company, dull in his closet, dull everywhere,' according to Dr Johnson [q.v.]), he pursued the noiseless tenor of his way far from the ignoble strife of social and academic politics. The only serious interruption of its calm occurred in 1756 and resulted from a morbid fear of fire that had led him to equip his room with a rope ladder and his windows with iron bars (still visible from Trumpington Street). Such nervous precautions invited an undergraduate practical joke:

> The other morning Lord Percival and some Petrenchians, going a hunting, were determined to have a little sport before they set out, and thought it would be no bad diversion to make Gray bolt, as they called it, so ordered their man Joe Draper to roar out fire. A delicate white nightcap is said to have appeared at the window; but finding the mistake, retired to the couch. The young fellows, had he descended, were determined, they said, to have whipped the butterfly up again.

This contemporary account by the Reverend John Sharp of Corpus Christi is undoubtedly more accurate than later embellished versions which have the poet climbing down his rope and landing in a tub of water. But even the modest actuality of the incident greatly distressed him and, when the Master of Peterhouse failed to take his complaint seriously, Gray moved across Trumpington Street to Pembroke. 'This may be look'd upon as a sort of Aera in a life so barren of events as mine,' he wrote to a friend.

Save for a brief period in London (1759–61) Gray remained at Pembroke for the rest of his life, quietly enjoying the substantial reputation his poetry had won, penning the letters that distinguish him even in an age of great correspondents, and assuming the Regius Professorship of Modern History in 1768. His rooms were in Ivy Court (or Second Court) above what is now the Senior Parlour on I staircase of the *Hitcham Building.

Though his connection with Cambridge was the most enduring of Gray's life, the most poignant is to be found at Stoke Poges, north of A4 and Slough in Buckinghamshire. His mother retired from London to Stoke after the death of her husband in 1741, living at West End House (now Stoke Court) with her two sisters. In the course of his many visits over the years Gray formed the friendship with Viscountess Cobham and Miss Speed celebrated in the comic poem 'A Long Story' and wrote the *Ode on a Distant Prospect of Eton College* (his old school, south of A4 and M4). Most importantly, it was at Stoke Poges that he began (c. 1742) and finished (1750) his *Elegy Written in a Country Churchyard*, that finely measured reflection on death on which his fame still depends. The *churchyard (near junction of B416 and B473), where Gray was buried, has a monument of 1799 (NT) bearing quotations from his poem. The grave of his mother (d. 1753) near the east wall of the church carries an epitaph by Gray that remembers her as 'the careful mother of many children, one of whom alone had the misfortune to survive her.'

Eton College. Open daily 2–5 during term, 10.30–5 during spring holiday, 9–5 during summer holiday. Fee.

Sir Fulke Greville, Lord Brooke

b. Beauchamp Court, Warwickshire, 1554; d. London, 1628. *The Tragedy of Mustapha* (1609).

Although Sir Fulke Greville's rather slender literary reputation today depends more on his Senecan closet drama *Mustapha* than the sometimes laboured poetry he wrote in imitation of Sir Philip Sidney (q.v.), it is in fact that friendship with Sidney which provides a major theme in his life and its surviving reminders. Greville was an exact contemporary of the better known poet at Shrewsbury School, Shropshire; now a Library, the School's old buildings stand on Castle Gates opposite the Castle. After studying at Jesus College, Cambridge Greville again joined Sidney at court in 1577.

Of the several grants of land and property that rewarded his services to Queen Elizabeth and King James the most important was the acquisition in 1605 of Warwick Castle. He made extensive repairs and embellishments to the interior of the medieval building. After his death in London—where he was stabbed by a servant whom he had omitted from his will—Greville was buried at the church of St Mary, in Warwick to the north of the Castle. His oversize black and white marble monument stands in the chapter house, bearing this inscription: 'Fulke Greville, servant to Queen Elizabeth, councillor to King James, and friend to Sir Philip Sidney. Trophaeum Peccati.'

Shrewsbury Library. Open Mon & Wed 9.30–6, Tues & Fri 9.30–2, Sat 9.30–5.

Warwick Castle. Open 1 March to end Oct daily 10–5.30; 1 Nov to end Feb daily 10–4.30. Fee.

R.S. Hawker

b. Plymouth, Devon, 1803; d. Plymouth, 1875. *Records of the Western Shore* (1832); *Ecclesia* (1840); *Reeds Shaken in the Wind* (1843); *Echoes from Old Cornwall* (1846); *The Quest of the Sangraal: Chant the First* (1864); *Cornish Ballads and Other Poems* (1869).

This eccentric Victorian poet and clergyman is usually remembered, when he is remembered at all, for 'The Song of the Western Men' (1825) and particularly for the rousing lines from its second stanza:

> And shall Trelawny die?
> Here's twenty thousand Cornish men
> Will know the reason why!

Modern churchgoers are in his debt, even if they do not commonly realise it, for Hawker has the best claim to have originated the Harvest Festival service.

Most of his working life was spent as vicar (1834–75) of the scattered parish of Morwenstow near Bude on the north Cornish coast. Bounded by cliffs on one side and bleak moorland on the other, the village is reached from A39 via unclassified roads. If it seems remote to the modern visitor we have Hawker's reminder, in a letter of 1862, of its state in the 19C: 'Did you ever hear that for every 100 miles you live from London, you must reckon yourself a century back from your own date? We, therefore, who are 250 miles off, are now in the year 1610 in all that relates to agriculture and civilisation.'

The most prominent memorial to his years at Morwenstow is the Gothic *vicarage built to his own design in 1837. Its chimneys are shaped in imitation of church towers, while the one over the kitchen is modelled after his mother's tomb. Over the front door we find this verse:

A House, a Glebe, a Pound a Day,
A pleasant Place to Watch and Pray.
Be true to Church—Be kind to poor,
O Minister, for ever more.

When Tennyson (q.v.) dined here in 1848 Hawker was struck by the oddity of his famous hat and cloak, a curious reaction from a man who usually dressed in brimless hat, purple cassock and fisherman's jersey. He helped another visitor, Charles Kingsley (q.v.), with the topography of *Westward Ho!*, though he liked neither the novelist nor the novel.

Nearby is the church that Hawker restored—he is said to have destroyed one private pew with an axe himself—but did not take pains to keep clean. A visitor noted with distaste: 'The church floor was strewn with sweet-smelling herbs,—in fact carpeted with them, which however caused it to be always dirty. In fact *dirt* was over everything, vestry and pulpit very dirty. He said his cat always went with him to church, and sometimes into the pulpit.' There is now a window in Hawker's memory. In the churchyard is the grave of his first wife, Charlotte (d. 1863), and the figurehead from the ship *Caledonia*, a reminder of how many drowned sailors Hawker buried. On Vicarage Cliff (NT) to the west is the little hut he built from driftwood and used as an outdoor study.

In the last year of his life Hawker returned to his native Plymouth on the south Devon coast. He was received into Roman Catholicism on his deathbed. His grave in the Cemetery off Ford Park Road bears an epitaph from his most ambitious poem, *The Quest of the Sangraal*: 'I would not be forgotten.'

George Herbert

b. Montgomery, Powys, 1593; d. Bemerton, Wiltshire, 1633. *The Temple* (1634).

The castle of Montgomery in Wales (formerly the county town of Montgomeryshire) where George Herbert was born is now ruined, but the local church contains the fine tomb of his father, Sir Richard Herbert (d. 1600). The burial of his mother, who became Lady Margaret Danvers, is described under the entry of John Donne, who preached the funeral sermon.

Herbert's admission to Trinity College, Cambridge in 1609 began a connection with the university that continued with a College Fellowship in 1616 and his appointment as Public Orator (1619–27). His duties in the second post included delivering addresses in the fine church of Great St Mary's opposite the Senate House on King's Parade. In 1626 Herbert also became prebend of **St Mary's in Leighton Bromswold, 9 miles west of Huntingdon via A604 and now in Cambridgeshire. There is no evidence that Herbert ever set foot in the parish but he certainly supervised the repairs to its church with great care. St Mary's 17C tower (perhaps designed by Inigo Jones), spacious aisles and fine woodwork exude a dignified simplicity that is perfectly expressive of Herbert's sensibility. Of special note are the two pulpits, apparently a unique feature in an English parish church, embodying his belief in the equal importance of praying and preaching. At Little Gidding 5 miles NE his friend Nicholas Ferrar organised a religious community which also attracted the interest of Herbert's fellow poet and Cambridge don, Richard Crashaw, and whose fame has been revived in our own century by the work of T.S. Eliot (q.v.). It was Ferrar to whom Herbert entrusted the publication of his poems, *The Temple*, on his death. Ferrar's tomb (d. 1637) stands outside the church of St John the Evangelist, a much-restored little building that still manages to retain its character and atmosphere.

In 1630 Herbert was appointed rector of Bemerton in Wiltshire, then a distinct village but now absorbed into the suburbs of Salisbury. In the words of John Aubrey, he found the church of St Andrew 'a pittifull little chappell of ease.' His restoration of it was largely obliterated by the work of T.H. Wyatt in 1866 but Aubrey's complaint about the lack of a proper memorial ('He lyes in the chancell, under no large, nor yet very good, marble grave-stone, without any inscription') has been remedied by a plaque. The 'very ruinous' Rectory which Herbert also needed to repair and whose garden gave him particular delight still stands and is to the south of the church.

Robert Herrick

b. London, 1592; d. Dean Prior, Devon, 1674. *Hesperides* (1648).

None of the London scenes of Herrick's life survives unaltered. The original Wood Street where he was born and nearby St Vedast's church where he was baptised, both off Cheapside, were destroyed in the fire of 1666; while St Anne Street (formerly Lane) between Great Peter and Great Smith Streets in Westminster, where he lived from 1647 to 1662, has been demolished and rebuilt. Cambridge, however, is more fortunate: Herrick entered St John's College in 1613 and moved, apparently for financial reasons, to Trinity Hall in 1616.

Herrick is best remembered at Dean Prior, a village on A38 south of Ashburton in Devon and near the picturesque scenery of the Dean Burn Valley. He acquired the living of St Mary's in 1629 and held it until his death except for the London interlude, when he had been deprived of his position because of Royalist sympathies. The rural setting seems appropriate to the often delicately pastoral character of the verses collected in *Hesperides*, yet the robust epigrams directed at neighbours and members of his congregation are reminders of Herrick's discontent with country life and his preference for the city. There is a monument of 1857 in the church.

James Hogg

b. Ettrick, Borders, 1770; d. Altrive Lake, Borders, 1835. *The Mountain Bard* (1807); *The Forest Minstrel* (1810); *The Queen's Wake: A Legendary Poem* (1813); *The Private Memoirs and Confessions of a Justified Sinner* (1824); *Altrive Tales: Collected Among the Peasantry of Scotland and from Foreign Adventurers* (1832); *The Domestic Manners and Private Life of Sir Walter Scott* (1834).

Although he is now remembered as the author of a powerful exercise in psychological Gothic, *Confessions of a Justified Sinner*, Hogg was known in his own day as a poet and peasant bard, discovered by Sir Walter Scott (q.v.) in the course of his researches for *Minstrelsy of the Scottish Border* and achieving a fame like that of his fellow countryman Robert Burns (q.v.). He clung to a title 'the Ettrick Shepherd,' proclaiming his humble origins and appeared under this name, though usually caricatured as a 'boozing buffoon,' in *Noctes Ambrosianae*, the long-running series of articles by John Wilson ('Christopher North') in *Blackwood's Edinburgh Magazine*.

In Ettrick, a village on B709 SW of Selkirk, the site of Hogg's birthplace is marked by a monument; he is buried in the churchyard. Altrive Lake, the farm granted to him rent free by the Duke of Buccleuch in 1815, and Mount Benger, the farm he acquired in 1821 with disastrous financial results, lay north of Ettrick in the valley of the Yarrow near the junction with A708. Hogg was a regular patron of Tibbie Shiel's Inn, now a hotel, off A708 near the southern end of St Mary's Loch. Nearby is a statue that depicts him seated with his dog. The occasion in 1814 when he showed Wordsworth (s.v. Lake Poets, Rte 14) the sights of the Yarrow is remembered in the latter's 'Extempore Effusion Upon the Death of James Hogg'.

Gerard Manley Hopkins

b. London, 1844; d. Dublin, 1889. *Poems* (edited by Robert Bridges; 1918).

After an unhappy but distinguished career at London's Highgate School, whose old buildings were replaced shortly after he left, Hopkins found a more congenial environment at Oxford. During his undergraduate years at Balliol College (1863–67) he was influenced both by Walter Pater (q.v.) and the Oxford Movement. As an undergraduate he dedicated two sonnets to Oxford and, when he returned in 1878–79 as curate of the Roman Catholic church of St Aloysius on Woodstock Road near its junction with St Giles, hailed it in 'Duns Scotus's Oxford' as a

> Towery city and branchy between towers;
> Cuckoo-echoing, bell-swarmèd, lark-charmèd, rook-racked, river-
> rounded.

(lines 1–2)

Hopkins had been received into the Catholic faith by John Henry Newman in 1866, and after Oxford he spent six months in Birmingham at the Oratory of St Philip Neri which Newman had founded in 1847. It lies on the Hagley Road in the south-western suburb of Edgbaston.

Instead of remaining with Newman's Benedictine order Hopkins chose to enter the Society of Jesus and passed the rest of his short life at a long succession of its foundations. 'Permanence with us,' he told a friend, 'is ginger-bread permanence; cob-web, soapsud, and frost-feather permanence.'

He served his novitiate at Manresa House, a fine 18C building in south-west London's Roehampton, south of A205 (Richmond Road) between Roehampton Lane and Richmond Park. He returned several times before entering his tertianship in 1881. After Manresa House he went north to Stonyhurst College, first as a student in 1870–73 and later to teach Greek and Latin in 1882–84. The College, whose nucleus is Sir Richard Shireburn's Elizabethan mansion, lies off B6243 12 miles north of Blackburn in Lancashire. The surrounding landscape of Pendle Forest appealed greatly to Hopkins' love of nature. So, too, did the Vale of Clwyd in north Wales, where he studied at St Beuno's College, 1 mile north of Tremeirchion. 'Looking all around but most in looking far up the valley,' he wrote in his journal a few weeks after he arrived in 1873, 'I felt an instress and charm in Wales.'

In these surroundings he turned again to the poetry he had abandoned on becoming a Jesuit, writing 'The Wreck of the Deutschland' at a hint from his rector. The well in the much-restored St Winifred's Chapel at Holywell, on A55 8 miles NE of St Beuno's and a traditional object of pilgrimage, suggested the idea for his incomplete tragedy 'St Winefred's Well'; his lyric, 'The Leaden Echo and the Golden Echo,' is a fragment from this drama. Yet, though he continued to write until the end of his life, Hopkins pursued a lonely and unrecognised career as poet. His dedication to the Society of Jesus and his awareness of the radically innovative character of his work made him shrink from publication, and he was supported only by his correspondence with Robert Bridges and Richard Watson Dixon. Even his connection with Coventry Patmore (q.v.), whom he visited at Hastings, was the friendship more of priest and devout layman than of two fellow poets.

Not all Hopkins' subsequent postings were as congenial as St Beuno's, and his last appointment as Professor of Classics at University College, Dublin in 1884 was particularly trying. The years at Newman House, on the south side of St Stephen's Green, were 'hard wearing wasting wasted'; it was the period of his 'terrible' sonnets. To the young W.B. Yeats (q.v.), who met him in Dublin, he seemed only a 'querulous, sensitive scholar.' Hopkins died of typhoid and was buried in the Jesuit section of Prospect (or Glasnevin) Cemetery in the north of the city.

He is remembered by a plaque in Poets' Corner (fee) of Westminster Abbey and a window in the church at Haslemere (off A3 in Surrey), where his parents lived in their later years.

St Winifred's Chapel, Holywell (DoE/Welsh Office). Open Apr to Sept, Fri & Sat 11–7.

A.E. Housman

b. Fockbury, Hereford and Worcester, 1859; d. Cambridge, 1936. *A Shropshire Lad* (1896); *Last Poems* (1922); *The Name and Nature of Poetry* (1933); *More Poems* (edited by Laurence Housman; 1936).

Housman spent his childhood in the Bromsgrove area south-west of Birmingham. He was born in the parish of Fockbury, 2 miles NW of Bromsgrove and immediately west of the M5, at Valley House, a Georgian farmhouse since renamed Housmans. After his mother's death the family returned in 1872 to live at Clock House nearby. Housman himself was baptised and his mother buried at the early Victorian church in Catshill, on B4091 2 miles north of Bromsgrove. In Bromsgrove itself the Housmans lived from 1859 until 1872 at Perry Hall, now a hotel, on Kidderminster Road. The poet attended Bromsgrove School in its late 17C building with 19C additions on Worcester Road.

Housman entered St John's College, Oxford in 1877. Despite his obvious brilliance as a classical scholar, he made a disappointing performance in his exams and succeeded in obtaining only a pass degree.

The failure overshadowed his life in London for the next few years. He did unglamorous work for the Patent Office in Southampton Buildings, which connects High Holborn and Chancery Lane. His own office was in the little Quality Court off Chancery Lane nearby. He continued classical studies in his spare time and in 1892 redeemed his earlier disgrace by being appointed Professor of Latin at University College, on Gower Street near the British Museum and Library. Since 1885 he had been living in Highgate at No. 17 North Road, a Georgian row of houses running north from Highgate High Street. It was here that he wrote *A Shropshire Lad*.

In 1911 Housman was elected to the Kennedy Chair of Latin at Cambridge and a fellowship at Trinity College. He lived in the Victorian Whewell's Court opposite the College's main buildings, occupying rooms in the tower by the Sidney Street entrance. He spent the remainder of his life here, striking undergraduates more as a retiring don than as a popular poet.

Fittingly, he was buried in the county that had been the subject of his most famous work. His grave lies near the north wall of the churchyard in the charming town of Ludlow, overlooking the Shropshire hills. Wenlock Edge, mentioned in the famous lyric 31 of *A Shropshire Lad*, lies off B4368 11 miles to the north. Yet the poem is less local than its free use of Shropshire placenames would suggest. It grew from childhood memories of the hills that had formed 'our western horizon' when he was at Bromsgrove and from a generalised longing for the English countryside, not from intimate knowledge of Shropshire. Nor did Housman hesitate to take liberties with the real geography of the area. The vane on the church steeple at Hughley (off B4371 north of Wenlock Edge) is by no means the 'far-known sign' that lyric 61 proclaims, for the village lies in a valley.

Thomas Hughes

b. Uffington, Oxfordshire, 1822; d. Brighton, East Sussex, 1896. *Tom Brown's School Days, By an Old Boy* (1857); *The Scouring of the White Horse: or the Long Vacation Ramble of a London Clerk* (1859); *Tom Brown at Oxford* (1861).

Hughes was brought up in the beautiful Vale of the White Horse, then in Berkshire but now in Oxfordshire, and remained attached in imagination to the area throughout his life. At the village of Uffington (2 miles north of B4507 between Wantage and Swindon) the fine church where his grandfather was vicar now has a plaque in his memory. The 17C Uffington School building nearby was attended by his most famous creation, Tom Brown. In fact, the first chapter of *Tom Brown's School Days* is an enthusiastic travelogue of Hughes' native region, while *The Scouring of the White Horse* is less a novel than a collection of local legends. The White Horse itself is carved on the chalk downs that rise to the south of B4507 near the turning for Uffington. On the downs to the south-west, enjoying a fine view, is Uffington Castle: 'a magnificent Roman camp, and no mistake . . . all as complete as it was twenty years after the strong old rogues left it' (*Tom Brown's School Days*, Ch. 1).

Yet in the popular mind Hughes is best remembered for his connection with the school at Rugby (on A428 4 miles west of M1 junction 18 and 12 miles east of Coventry). His career there (1834–41) lacked the academic distinction gained by his contemporaries Matthew Arnold and Arthur Hugh Clough (qq.v.), and his best-known novel dramatised a hearty, athletic ideal of public-school life that immediately found favour with Victorian readers. Hughes is com-

The Vale of the White Horse, by Richard Doyle. From The Scouring of the White Horse. *Courtesy of Cambridge University Library*

memorated with a statue by Brock, but otherwise the school's buildings bear the imprint of a later Victorian architect, William Butterfield. The chapel where Tom visited the grave of Dr Thomas Arnold in the last chapter of the novel has gone; a monument to the headmaster (1844) may be found in Butterfield's building of 1872.

Like so many old Rugbeians of his generation, Hughes was an undergraduate at Oriel College, Oxford (1841–45). *Tom Brown at Oxford*, in which Oriel becomes 'St Ambrose,' lacks the power of its predecessor and has never enjoyed the same popularity.

After Oxford Hughes went to London to study the law and lived in Lincoln's Inn, off Chancery Lane in Holborn. His first lodging was on the north side of Lincoln's Inn Fields near Sir John Soane's Museum. After his marriage in 1848 he kept chambers at No. 3 Old Buildings, to the left of the Inn's main entrance from Chancery Lane. During these years he was an active Christian Socialist, first encountering its ideals in the sermons delivered by F.D. Maurice in Lincoln's Inn Chapel, opposite Old Buildings. The effect on his view of the city around him is shown by this passage of reminiscence:

> I passed daily, twice at least, through the horrible nests of squalor and vice which then stood on the site of the New Law Courts [G.E. Street's Gothic building of 1874–82 on the north side of the Strand]. I soon found that (with the exception of thieves and beggars) these nests were peopled by shop workers—poor men, women and children, who if their employers could have flogged them, would have been in a far worse case than any negro slave. I say that the competitive struggle for life had brought them to this pass; and yet the most approved teachers, in reviews and newspapers, which I had begun to read, and even in Parliament, were insisting on 'free competition' as a corollary to 'free trade,' and a necessary pillar of industrial prosperity.

From 1859 to 1882 he lived at a succession of addresses in Park Street, which runs south from Oxford Street and parallel to Park Lane.

In later life his appointment as a circuit judge took him to Chester. Here in 1885 he built himself a home and named it, predictably, Uffington House. It stands east of the city centre in Dee Hills Park, overlooking the River Dee. Hughes wrote to a friend, the American poet James Russell Lowell:

> Out of the windows of my den I look right over the Cheshire vale to the Packforten hills on the East & the lordly castle of the Tollemaches perched on the spur; & over the gleaming Dee and green water meadows to the woods & spire of Eaton on the South; while to the west (which I must go out on to the stair-case to contemplate) lie Chester Castle & Cathedral with the Welsh Moels on the horizon—there is nothing more delightful in the way of an all round view anywhere that I know, & it don't seem to me that the democratic republic will have an easy task in remaking it all.

The Moels are the peaks of the Clwydian Hills which rise beyond Mold, 10 miles west of Chester. The 'lordly castle of the Tollemaches' is the 19C Peckforton Castle, masterpiece of the architect Anthony Salvin, on a red sandstone crag rising from the Cheshire Plain. It is 14 miles SE of Chester, on unclassified roads leading south from Taporley on A49 to Nantwich. On the adjoining hill stand the fine ruins of the medieval Beeston Castle.

White Horse, Uffington (English Heritage). Open at all reasonable times.

Uffington Castle (English Heritage). Open at all reasonable times.

Beeston Castle, near Taporley (English Heritage). Open 15 March to 15 Oct, Mon to Sat 9.30–6.30, Sun 2–6.30 (Apr to Sept, Sun 9.30–6.30); 16 Oct to 14 March, Mon to Sat 9.30–4, Sun 2–4. Closed Christmas Eve, Christmas Day, Boxing Day and New Year's Day. Fee.

Victor Hugo

b. Besançon, France, 1802; d. Paris, 1885. Works written in exile: *Histoire d'un Crime* (1852–77); *Les Châtiments* (1853); *Les Contemplations* (1856); *La Légende des Siècles* (1859–83); *Les Misérables* (1862); *William Shakespeare* (1864); *Les Chansons des Rues et des Bois* (1865); *Les Travailleurs de la Mer* (1866); *L'Homme Qui Rit* (1869).

Victor Hugo fled France in 1851 after the *coup d'état* which established the Second Empire and exalted Louis Napoleon to the rank of Emperor. He did not return until the fall of Napoleon III in 1870. Most of his years in exile were spent on the Channel Islands. He brought his family and mistress, Juliette Drouet, to Jersey in 1853 and lived in St Clement's, SE of St Helier, where his home at No. 3 Marine Terrace is now part of the Victor Hugo Hotel. When he was expelled for attacking Queen Victoria's friendliness towards Napoleon III he took refuge on the neighbouring island of Guernsey. In 1856 he bought Hauteville House, near the Castle Pier in the south of St Peter Port. Its generous proportions offered ideal scope to his lavish taste in furnishing, and the main rooms of Hauteville House today still preserve the sumptuous appearance he gave them. They are in contrast to his stark bedroom and the simple study overlooking the sea where he maintained a demanding regimen of work each day. Hugo's work at Hauteville included his most successful novel, *Les Misérables*, and *Les Travailleurs de la Mer*, set on Guernsey. There is a statue of Hugo near the Guernsey Museum and Art Gallery in Candie Gardens to the north.

Hauteville House, St Peter Port. Open 1 April to 30 Sept, Mon to Sat 10–11.30, 2–4.30; 1 Oct to 31 March, Mon to Sat guided tour at 10.30. Closed BH. Fee.

Leigh Hunt

b. London, 1784; d. London, 1859. *The Descent of Liberty: A Mask* (1815); *The Story of Rimini* (1816); *Lord Byron and Some of His Contemporaries* (1828); *Sir Ralph Esher; or Adventures of a Gentleman of the Court of Charles II* (1832); *The Autobiography* (1850); *Table Talk* (1851).

Though he was a prolific and in his own day a controversial writer, Hunt is now usually remembered for his friendships with more famous contemporaries.

All the surviving buildings connected with him are in London. From 1816 to 1822 he lived at Hampstead in the Vale of Health, reached from East Heath Road, though perhaps not in the cottage that now bears his name. It was here that he introduced Keats, another Hampstead resident, and Shelley (qq.v.) to each other, but without conspicuous success. After his return from Italy—where he had travelled with Byron (q.v.)—he lived in Chelsea (1833–40) at No. 22 Upper Cheyne Row, which has a GLC plaque. His *Autobiography* indulged in fond reminiscence of the house and its then rural surroundings:

> I know not whether the corner I speak of remains as quiet as it was. I am afraid not; for steamboats have carried vicissitude into Chelsea, and Belgravia threatens it with her mighty advent. But to complete my sense of repose and distance, the house was of that old-fashioned sort which I have always loved best, familiar to the eye of my parents, and associated with childhood. It had seats in the windows, a small third room on the first floor, of which I made a *sanctum*, into which no perturbation was to enter, except to calm itself with religious and cheerful thoughts (a room thus appropriated in a house appears to me an excellent thing); and there were a few lime trees in front, which, in their due season diffused a fragrance.

Carlyle (q.v.) was a neighbour on Cheyne Row and it was Mrs Carlyle's uncharacteristically warm greeting on one visit that prompted a well-known poem, 'Jenny Kissed Me.'

In later life (1840–51) he lived at No. 32 of the charming Edwardes Square, south of Kensington High Street. His last years (1853–59) were spent in Hammersmith, to the west of Kensington. His home at No. 16 Rowan Road (then No. 7 Cornwall Road), which connects Brook Green and Hammersmith Road, is marked with a plaque. Visits from Dickens (q.v.) led to the caustic portrait of Hunt as Harold Skimpole in *Bleak House.*

He was buried in Kensal Green Cemetery, on Harrow Road opposite Kensal Green Station (Bakerloo Line and British Rail). His tomb (No. 13650 in Square 121) lies near the canal and is marked by a quotation from his poem 'Abou-ben-Adhem.'

Kensal Green Cemetery. Open Mon to Sat 9–5.30 (or dusk, if earlier), Sun 2–5.30 (or dusk); Good Fri 2–5.30, Christmas Day 10–2. Closes at 1 on BH .

Aldous Huxley

b. Godalming, Surrey, 1894; d. Los Angeles, California, USA, 1963. *Limbo* (1920); *Crome Yellow* (1921); *Mortal Coils* (1922); *Antic Hay* (1923); *On the Margin: Notes and Essays* (1923); *Little Mexican, and Other Stories* (1924); *Those Barren Leaves* (1925); *Along the Road: Notes and Essays of a Tourist* (1925); *Jesting Pilate: The Diary of a Journey* (1926); *Point Counter Point* (1928); *Vulgarity in Literature: Digressions from a Theme* (1930); *Music at Night, and Other Essays* (1931); *Brave New World* (1932); *Eyeless in Gaza* (1936); *Ends and Means* (1937); *After Many a Summer* (1939); *Grey Eminence: A Study in Religion and Politics* (1941); *The Art of Seeing* (1942); *Time Must Have a Stop* (1944); *The Perennial Philosophy* (1945); *Science, Liberty and Peace* (1946); *Ape and Essence* (1948); *Themes and Variations* (1950); *The Devils of Loudon* (1952); *The Doors of Perception* (1954); *The Genius and the Goddess* (1955); *Heaven and Hell* (1956); *Brave New World Revisited* (1958); *Island* (1962).

The novelist was sent to Eton in 1908 but developed the eye disease, a violent inflammation of the cornea, from which he suffered for most of his life and was forced to leave abruptly in 1911. He returned, however, as a teacher in 1917–19. The College is south of M4 near Windsor.

Despite problems with his eyesight Huxley went up to Balliol

College, Oxford in 1913. The novelist L.P. Hartley was a contemporary and friend. Huxley gained a First in English and left, in his own phrase, 'crowned with the artificial roses of academic distinction.'

During his Oxford years he was first introduced by the critic Desmond MacCarthy to Garsington Manor (off B480 4 miles SE of the city), home of Lady Ottoline and Philip Morrell, and at this time a centre for the younger generation of writers and intellectuals. Huxley's descent from the distinguished scientist T.H. Huxley on his father's side and from Matthew Arnold (q.v.) on his mother's side made him a welcome guest and he quickly became an intimate of the Garsington circle, meeting T.S. Eliot, Virginia Woolf (qq.v.), Bertrand Russell, Clive Bell and Katherine Mansfield, among others. After graduating from Oxford in 1916 he went briefly to work on Philip Morrell's farm. His experiences gave him material for his first novel, in which Crome, the country house of the title, is clearly a satirical version of Garsington.

In London Huxley and his wife lived from 1917 to 1920 at No. 18 Hampstead Hill Gardens, connecting Rosslyn Hill and Pond Street south of the Heath. From 1934 until 1937 they were tenants on the ground floor of the Albany, the exclusive block of flats north of Piccadilly which had numbered Byron (q.v.) among its previous tenants. Huxley found its genteel atmosphere little to his taste, and the management allowed him to use his typewriter only after being assured that he would write just poetry on it. In fact, he was producing a rapid succession of novels and travel books, and interspersing his residence in London with tours abroad in the company of D.H. Lawrence (q.v.), among others. In 1937 he left permanently for California, where he ended his days.

In 1971 his ashes were returned to England and buried in his parents' grave at Compton, off A3 between Guildford and Godalming. The cemetery is NE of the village.

Eton College. Open daily 2–5 during term, 10.30–5 during spring holiday, 9–5 during summer holiday. Fee.

Garsington Manor. Gardens open under NGS. Fee.

Henry James

b. New York, USA, 1843; d. London, 1916. *Roderick Hudson* (1876); *The American* (1877); *The Europeans* (1878); *Daisy Miller* (1879); *Washington Square* (1881); *The Portrait of a Lady* (1881); *The Art of Fiction* (1885); *The Bostonians* (1886); *The Princess Casamassima* (1886); *The Reverberator* (1888); *The Aspern Papers* (1888); *The Tragic Muse* (1890); *The Lesson of the Master* (1892); *Terminations* (1895); *The Spoils of Poynton* (1897); *What Maisie Knew* (1898); *In the Cage* (1898); *The Turn of the Screw* (1898); *The Awkward Age* (1899); *The Sacred Fount* (1901); *The Wings of the Dove* (1902); *The Ambassadors* (1903); *The Golden Bowl* (1904); *English Hours* (1905); *Italian Hours* (1909); *The Ivory Tower* (1917).

Although he had several times visited England during his youth, James did not settle in London until 1876. An essay in *English Hours* later recorded his first impressions of 'the dreadful, delightful city' and his conclusion that 'for the real London-lover the mere immensity of the place is a large part of its savour.' His first lodging, where he

Henry James at Lamb House. Courtesy of British Information Service, New York

remained until 1885, was at No. 3 Bolton Street, north of Piccadilly opposite Green Park. Of these crucial years when he established himself in London society and literary life he wrote in his journal: 'I have *lived* much there, felt much, thought much, learned much, produced much; the little shabby furnished apartment ought to be sacred to me. I came to London as a complete stranger, and today I know much too many people. *J'y suis absolumment comme chez moi.*' In 1886 he moved to Kensington and a much grander flat on the fourth floor of No. 34 De Vere Gardens, now marked with a plaque, south of Kensington High Street almost opposite the Palace Gate to Kensington Gardens. He stayed here until 1896, taking slightly ironic pleasure in the conventional way he furnished his rooms: 'expectedness everywhere.' In 1887–89 Robert Browning (q.v.) was a neighbour at No. 29 and so became a friend.

James' last London home (1912–16) was in Chelsea: No. 21 Carlyle Mansions, at the junction of Lawrence Street and Cheyne Walk. After his death here the funeral service was held at Chelsea Old Church, on the corner of the Walk and Old Church Street, though his ashes were buried in the family cemetery at Cambridge, Massachusetts. The church has a memorial tablet. A memorial stone was recently added to Poets' Corner (fee) in Westminster Abbey.

A gloomy visit to George Eliot at Witley, Surrey is described under the entry for that novelist.

For all his relish of London, James hankered after a quiet, picturesque corner of England where he could comfortably root himself. The need was magnificently answered by *Lamb House in the coastal town of Rye, 12 miles NE of Hastings in East Sussex. He first leased the Georgian house, found near the church at the top of West Street, in 1898 and used it as a summer residence for the rest of his life. Though the garden room where he did much of his writing in good weather was destroyed by a bomb during the Second World War, the grounds otherwise have all the typically English charm he evoked in *English Hours*:

> a dear old garden—a garden brown-walled, red-walled, rose-covered, . . . divided by the width of a quiet street of grass-grown cobbles from the house of its master, and possessed of a little old glass-fronted, panelled pavilion . . . There is not much room in the pavilion, but there is room for the hard-pressed table and the tilted chair—there is room for a novelist and his friends.

In London, James was always keenly aware of the spirit of Thackeray (q.v.). His residence on the Sussex coast made him particularly appreciative of his predecessor's last novel, whose connection with the area is celebrated by a fine essay in *English Hours*, 'Winchelsea, Rye and "Denis Duval".'

Lamb House, Rye (NT). Open Apr to end Oct, Wed & Sat 2–6. Fee.

Richard Jefferies

b. Coate, Wiltshire, 1848; d. Goring-by-Sea, West Sussex, 1887. *The Gamekeeper at Home* (1878); *Wild Life in a Southern County* (1879); *The Amateur Poacher* (1879); *Greene Ferne Farm* (1880); *Hodge and His Masters* (1880); *Round About a Great Estate* (1880); *Wood Magic: A Fable* (1880); *Bevis: The Story of a Boy* (1882); *Nature Near London* (1883); *The Story of My Heart: My Autobiography* (1883); *The Dewy Morn* (1884); *The Life of the Fields* (1884); *Red Deer* (1884); *After London: Or Wild England* (1885); *The Open Air* (1885); *Amaryllis at the Fair* (1887); *Field and Hedgerow: Being the Last Essays of Jefferies, Collected by His Widow* (1889).

Jefferies spent the first twenty-nine years of his short life in the region near Swindon (north of M4 in Wiltshire), countryside he described in *Wild Life in a Southern County*, the semi-autobiographical *Bevis* and the openly autobiographical *Story of My Heart* among other works. In the village of Coate, 2 miles SE of Swindon on A345, his family home at Coate Farm is now the Jefferies Museum. The farm is portrayed as 'Coombe Oaks' in *Amaryllis at the Fair*, where his parents also appear as the Idens. Coate itself is the subject of 'My Old Village' in *Field and Hedgerow*. Immediately to the south lies Coate Water, a 72-acre artificial lake created in 1822 and one of his favourite haunts in boyhood and youth. A contemporary described his shy, solitary ways:

> Supplied with his books—whether on history or fable, on astrology or Euclid, it mattered not—he was wont to launch his boat, rigged by his own hands, and, having placed his gun and a scrap of food therein, to cruise about the neighbouring lake. Thus alone all day, he was thrown upon himself and his own resources. He got to learn the ways of fish, of birds, and of all the denizens of nature. Then he would read his books, and having shut them up after a while, he would lie back in his boat, and dream long wakeful dreams such as rarely visit lads of his few years.

By A345 2 miles south of Coate is Chiseldon, where he attended the parish church and was married in 1874.

From Chiseldon we may continue SW into the open downland that was Jefferies' special love. The main object of such a journey should be Barbury Castle, an Iron Age hill fort which gives magnificent views of the surrounding countryside. It can be reached by taking B4005 west and then following an unclassified road south (4 miles), but it is much better to walk directly from Chiseldon along the Ridgeway (3½ miles). This ancient track originates to the north east in Buckinghamshire, at Ivinghoe Beacon near Tring, and follows the line of the Chiltern Hills; at Streatley in Berkshire it heads west, following the Downs along the Vale of the White Horse, and, after Barbury Castle, continues south across the Marlborough Downs into the Vale of Pewsey. Much of its course is traced by the Ridgeway Path, devised and established by the Countryside Commission. Of Jefferies' many references to the Ridgeway, his essay in *Wild Life in a Southern County* may be recommended as an introduction.

In 1877 he left the countryside of his childhood, though he continued to write about it until the end of his life. His connection with Wiltshire is commemorated by a bust in Salisbury Cathedral (40 miles south of Swindon via A345). He lived first near London and then, after the onset of illness in 1882, at a series of places in South-Eastern England. In 1885–86 he was at Crowborough (on A26 between Royal Tunbridge Wells and Lewes); his home, The Downs, stands on the northern continuation of the High Street as London Road. From there he went to Goring-by-Sea on the coast west of Worthing via A259. The house and street where he lived have both since been renamed after him; they can be found off Sea Lane as it runs south from A259 near St Mary's Church. He was buried in the Broadwater and Worthing Cemetery in the northern part of Worthing. W.H. Hudson (1841–1922), author of *Green Mansions* and another sensitive observer of nature, chose to be buried near him.

Jefferies Museum, Coate. Open Wed, Sat & Sun 2–6. Fee.

Jerome K. Jerome

b. Walsall, West Midlands, 1859; d. Northampton, 1927. *On Stage and Off* (1888); *Idle Thoughts of an Idle Fellow* (1889); *Three Men in a Boat (To Say Nothing of the Dog)* (1889); *The Second Thoughts of an Idle Fellow* (1898); *Three Men on the Bummel* (1900); *Paul Kelver* (1902); *The Passing of the Third-Floor Back, and Other Stories* (1907); *My Life and Times* (1926).

Though it was distinguished by a plaque during his lifetime, Jerome K. Jerome's birthplace in Walsall has since been demolished. *Paul Kelver*, the autobiographical novel which he himself thought his best book, reflects his early struggle after leaving school at the age of fourteen and his progress from railway clerk to actor and eventually to journalist.

The region we most readily associate with Jerome lies along the course of the Thames from London to Oxford, celebrated in his amiable compilation of anecdotes and reflections about city dwellers on holiday, *Three Men in a Boat*. In fact, he first conceived the book as a serious historical guide, and in its final form it still bears enough marks of its origin to make it a useful as well as a pleasant travellers' companion. Fittingly, Jerome wrote it at his flat overlooking the river, in Chelsea Gardens at the junction of Chelsea Bridge Road and Ebury Street.

The fictional journey of *Three Men in a Boat* begins at the bridge in Kingston-upon-Thames, south-west London, from which modern travellers who wish to avoid the misadventures of Jerome and his party can take a steamer upriver to Oxford. The sight of Hampton Court (2½ miles) prompts Harris to remember his embarrassing time in the Maze (Ch. 6). Despite the fact that he 'revels in tombs, and graves, and epitaphs, and monumental inscriptions' (Ch. 7), he is not allowed the chance to see the elaborate 18C tomb of Mrs Thomas in the church at Hampton (4 miles). In Chapter 8 Jerome mentions the tombs and scolds' bridle in Walton church (7½ miles), though since he wrote the bridle has been replaced by a modern replica. After being joined at Weybridge by George, the party camps for the night near Runnymede (18 miles), and Jerome recreates the scene when Magna Carta was signed in Chapter 11. After lunching the next day at the popular Monkey Island (27½ miles), they pass Cliveden woods, part of the estate where Charles Barry's 19C mansion (later owned by the Astor family) stands: 'In its unbroken loveliness this is, perhaps, the sweetest stretch of the river' (Ch. 12). Marlow (37 miles) is 'one of the pleasantest river centres I know of' (Ch. 13), and so makes an appropriate resting place for the night. The town's connection with Shelley (q.v.) is noted and the Hoby monuments in Bisham church on the opposite bank recommended to the visitor. Medmenham Abbey (40 miles), a mansion built on the site of a monastery, provokes memories of the 18C 'Hell Fire Club.' Sonning (48 miles) is praised as 'the most fairy-like little nook on the whole river. It is more like a stage village than one built of bricks and mortar' (Ch. 14). On the other hand, 'One does not linger in the neighbourhood of Reading' (Ch. 16). In fact, though he describes a two-day rest at Streatley (Chs 16 and 17) and praises Dorchester in Chapter 18, Jerome deals briskly with the last stages of the journey to Oxford (91½ miles), reached in Chapter 19. When it begins to rain on the way back, the three friends abandon their boat for the comfort of a railway train.

To the modern tourist the chief interest of the Thameside region near Oxford is Ewelme (off B4009 2 miles NE of Wallingford on the river and 12 miles SE of Oxford). Jerome is buried in the churchyard of this pretty Chiltern village.

Hampton Court Palace (DoE). Open May to Sept, Mon to Sat 9.30–6, Sun 11–6; March, Apr & Oct, Mon to Sat 9.30–5, Sun 2–5; Nov to Feb, Mon to Sat 9.30–4, Sun 2–4. Entrance to grounds and courtyards free; charge for State Apartments and Great Hall, as well as for Maze.

Cliveden (NT). Grounds open March to end Dec, daily (including Good Fri) 11–6 or sunset if earlier. Fee. House (only two rooms shown) open Apr to end Oct, Sat & Sun 2–6. Fee.

Samuel Johnson

b. Lichfield, Staffordshire, 1709; d. London, 1784. *London* (1738); *The Life of Richard Savage* (1744); *The Vanity of Human Wishes, being the Tenth Satire of Juvenal Imitated* (1749); *Irene* (1749); *The Rambler* (1750–52); *A Dictionary of the English Language* (1755); *The Idler* (1758–60); *Rasselas, Prince of Abyssinia* (1759); *A Journey to the Western Islands of Scotland* (1775); *Lives of the Poets* (1779–81).

Related works: James Boswell, *Journal of a Tour to the Hebrides with Samuel Johnson, LL.D.* (1785) and *The Life of Samuel Johnson, LL.D.* (1791).

*Lichfield, 16 miles north of Birmingham, is more than just the city of Johnson's birth, childhood and youth, though this fact alone would lend it great interest. Here he formed friendships whose influence lasted throughout his life and was maintained by long, frequent visits. Its inhabitants, he loyally declared, were 'the most sober, decent people in England—the genteelest, in proportion to their wealth, and spoke the purest English' (Boswell's *Life*, Aetat. 67). Lichfield today, though greatly expanded beyond the community of three thousand people Johnson knew, has preserved much of the atmosphere of his time and enough specific buildings associated with him to reward a walking tour.

It begins in the market place where Johnson is commemorated by Richard Cockle Lucas' statue of 1838 with bas-reliefs around its base depicting episodes from the subject's local life. These include the infant Johnson sitting on his father's shoulders to hear the Tory Dr Sacheverell preach in the Cathedral, a story repeated by Boswell in his *Life* (Aetat. 3) but unsubstantiated by modern research, and the adult Johnson doing penance at Uttoxeter market (see below). Percy Fitzgerald's statue of Boswell (1908) is nearby.

Johnson's birthplace stands at the corner of Breadmarket Street. The tall, steep-roofed house was built in 1707 by Michael Johnson, from whom his son inherited a tendency to 'vile melancholy' (*Life* for 1709), and used by him as both home and bookshop. After Michael died and Johnson went to London, Johnson's mother, his step-daughter Lucy Porter, and a servant, Catherine Chambers, remained to run the business. The house is now the Samuel Johnson Birthplace Museum, rich in relics of Johnson, his relatives and his circle of friends in Lichfield. A plaque on the building next door marks the former Three Crowns Inn where Johnson and Boswell stayed on later visits.

From Market Street we follow St John Street south. Opposite St John's Hospital stood the Grammar School, a large oak-panelled room attended by Johnson from the age of seven to seventeen, as well as by his younger contemporary, the actor David Garrick. The only part to survive is the 17C Headmaster's House (now Council offices), then inhabited by John Hunter, whom the writer remembered for the brutal efficiency with which he taught Latin: 'My master whipt me very well' (*Life*, Aetat. 10–16). By retracing our steps north on St John Street and continuing on Bird Street we find, on our left, the fine 18C Swan Inn where Johnson and the Thrales stayed in 1774 on their way to Wales (see below).

As we enter the Cathedral Close by turning right from Beacon Street we notice on our left a plaque marking the house of Dr Erasmus Darwin (1731–1802), scientist and grandfather of a more famous scientist. Johnson and the elder Darwin were acquainted but of sufficiently similar temperaments that Lichfield friends found it unwise to invite them both to the same gathering. On the north side of the Close is the splendid 17C Bishop's Palace, now the Cathedral Choir School. Its tenant in Johnson's youth was Gilbert Walmesley, Registrar of the Ecclesiastical Court of Lichfield and the first man to give serious recognition to his talents. The account of Edmund Smith in *Lives of the Poets* turns aside from its subject to indulge in affectionate reminiscence of Walmesley: 'Such was his amplitude of learning and such his copiousness of communication that it may be doubted whether a day now passes in which I have not some advantage from his friendship.' Johnson also knew the Palace's later

Samuel Johnson, unfinished oil painting by James Barry (c. 1777). Courtesy of National Portrait Gallery

tenants, the Seward family, of whom the best remembered is Anna Seward (1747–1809), poetess and 'Swan of Lichfield.'

The Cathedral, where Johnson may or may not have heard Dr Sacheverell preach, has monuments to Erasmus Darwin (by the S transept), Anna Seward and Gilbert Walmesley (in the NW chapel near the font). Busts of Johnson and Garrick by Westmacott are next to each other in the south transept.

We leave the Cathedral Close by Dam Street to the south and take a path left to St Chad's Church (1 mile). The route takes us past Johnson's Willow, beyond which lay the unsuccessful parchment works run by Michael Johnson. St Chad's is the burial place of Lucy Porter and Catherine Chambers; a plaque can be found on the north side of the chancel. Returning to the picturesque Dam Street, we head south towards the market. A plaque remembers the probable scene of Johnson's earliest education, Dame Oliver's School.

St Michael's Church, on a hill by the road to Burton-upon-Trent, has the graves of Johnson's parents and his brother, Nathaniel. The Latin epitaph he composed on a last visit to Lichfield just before his own death is by the chancel steps. At Edial Hall, 3 miles SW on A5190 to Burntwood, Johnson tried unsuccessfully to establish a school after his marriage. The attempt ended in 1737 when he left for London with Garrick, one of the few pupils he had been able to attract.

The area north of Lichfield extending into Derbyshire is rich in Johnsonian associations. Uttoxeter (20 miles north via A515 and A50) was the scene of a famous and moving episode, best described by Johnson himself as reported in Boswell's *Life*. Recalling his conduct as a child, he confessed:

> Once, indeed, . . . I was disobedient; I refused to attend my father to Uttoxeter-market. Pride was the source of that refusal, and the remembrance of it was painful. A few years ago I desired to atone for this fault; I went to Uttoxeter in very bad weather, and stood for a considerable time bareheaded in the rain, on the spot where my father's stall used to stand. In contrition I stood, and I hope the penance was expiatory. (*Life*, Aetat. 75)

A replica of Lucas' bas-relief of the incident on the Lichfield statue now decorates the conduit in the market, though there is some reason to suppose that Michael Johnson kept his stall near the gate to the churchyard.

At Ashbourne, 10 miles north of A50 on A515, Johnson frequently visited Dr John Taylor, a fellow-pupil at Lichfield Grammar School who grew into a worldly Whig clergyman. His house, The Mansion, stands on Church Street opposite the Tudor Grammar School. During a visit of 1777 Boswell stayed at the Green Man and Black's Head, whose sign still straddles the road, and attended Sunday service with Johnson at the fine church of St Oswald, which he reported 'one of the largest and most luminous that I have seen in any town of the same size.'

Johnson greatly admired nearby Dovedale ('He that has seen Dovedale has no need to see the Highlands') and some have supposed it the original of the 'Happy Valley' at the beginning of *Rasselas*. During their visit of 1777 he took Boswell 4 miles NW from Ashbourne to Ilam Hall, which has been replaced by a Victorian building (now a youth hostel) though the fine grounds where the Manifold emerges from its subterranean course survive. Johnson was stubbornly sceptical of this natural curiosity, but both men took pleasure in the place's association with Congreve (q.v.).

At Derby (24 miles NE of Lichfield on A38; 14 miles SE of Ashbourne on A52) Johnson was married in 1735 to Elizabeth ('Tetty') Porter, a widow some twenty years his senior. Boswell's *Life* (Aetat. 26) tells the story of how Johnson turned the walk from Birmingham to Derby into a demonstration of the 'manly firmness' he intended to adopt towards his wife. St Werburgh's Church on Friargate, where the ceremony took place, is now greatly altered.

In 1764 he visited Thomas Percy, who published his influential *Reliques of Ancient English Poetry* the next year, at the Old Rectory in the village of Easton Maudit, off A509 9 miles east of Northampton. A plaque on the front pew of the church commemorates his worship here.

A visit to Oxford completes the review of Johnson's connections with Central England. He entered Pembroke College in 1728, having second-floor rooms over the main gateway, but stayed only four terms and left without a degree. He was, however, fond of his old college, revisiting it and proudly calling it 'a nest of singing birds' (*Life*, Aetat. 21), though the only other Pembroke writer of this period to be remembered is William Shenstone (q.v.), whom 'he would not allow . . . to approach excellence as a poet.' The award of an M.A. in 1755 came just in time for him to place the initials after his name on the titlepage of his *Dictionary*. 'It is in truth doing ourselves more honour than him, to have such a work done by an Oxford hand,' remarked one of the dons responsible. A Doctorate of Civil·Law followed in 1775, though Oxford had been anticipated by Trinity College, Dublin in entitling Johnson to the 'Dr' by which the world came to know him but he himself rarely used.

Johnson's famous dictum that 'when a man is tired of London, he is tired of life' (*Life*, Aetat. 68) illustrates with characteristic hyperbole the central role that the city played in his life and he, indeed, came to play in the life of London. His poverty during the early years after his arrival in 1737 assured that familiarity with its variety which he later recommended to Boswell. Toward the end of his life he listed for his future biographer's benefit some thirteen addresses where he had lived, most of them near Fleet Street and the Strand, and several in the Inns of Court.

The only one to remain is ·No. 7 Gough Square, a pleasant backwater reached from the north side of Fleet Street via Johnson's Court (not named after him, but another of his addresses). It was his home from 1749 to 1758, the years when he was working on his *Rambler* essays and the *Dictionary*. His household included the blind Mrs Anna Williams, sometime poetess and housekeeper for much of his life, and Frank Barber, the black servant whom he educated. Tetty Johnson died here in 1752. Johnson's House is now a museum. Its contents include manuscripts, relics of Johnson and his circle, and portraits—of which James Barry's oil sketch (c. 1777) over the fireplace in the dining room is the most striking. At the top of the house is the garret where he and his six assistants laboured on the completion of the *Dictionary*.

St Clement Danes, in the middle of the Strand just beyond Temple Bar, was Johnson's parish church for many years. It has a statue by Percy Fitzgerald outside its east end.

Johnson also has the distinction of being remembered in both

Westminster Abbey and St Paul's Cathedral. In Poets' Corner (fee) at the Abbey we find his grave with a bust by Nollekens near his lifelong friend, Garrick. St Paul's is less lucky. Beneath the dome is John Bacon's statue (1795) of an improbably athletic figure draped in a toga.

Nothing remains in either Southwark or Streatham to recall Johnson's long, significant intimacy with Hester Thrale and her husband. The only surviving memento of the association has found its way to Hampstead, where the summer house Johnson used at Thrale Place has been re-erected in the grounds of Kenwood House on Hampstead Lane.

Greenwich Park, in south-east London by the Thames, was a favourite retreat of Johnson's while he was composing *Irene*, the tragedy he had brought half-finished with him to London. He took Boswell to the Park in the early days of their acquaintance:

> He asked me, I suppose, by way of trying my disposition, 'Is not this very fine?' Having no exquisite relish of the beauties of Nature, and being more delighted with 'the busy hum of men,' I answered, 'Yes, Sir; but not equal to Fleet-street.' JOHNSON. 'You are right, Sir.' (*Life*, Aetat. 54)

On the same occasion he also made a curious criticism of Wren's Greenwich Hospital (now the Royal Naval College), thinking that it 'was too magnificent for a place of charity, and that its parts were too much detached, to make one great whole.'

With the Thrales Johnson several times visited Brighton on the Sussex coast, in the days when it was still Brighthelmston and had not fully achieved the fashionable status it enjoyed after the Prince Regent had chosen to build his Pavilion here. He worshipped in the Thrale pew at the church of St Nicholas on Dyke Road, which leaves the town to the NW; there is a plaque on the north wall. From Brighton Johnson went to 'see how our ancestors lived' (*Life*, Aetat. 73) at the magnificent late 17C Petworth House (24 miles NW via A283) and at Cowdray House in Cowdray Park, Midhurst (6 miles further west via A272), now ruined but still impressive.

Langton Hall in Lincolnshire, where Johnson stayed with his friend Bennet Langton in 1764, has gone but his connection with the area is remembered at Tetford in the Wolds 5 miles NE of Horncastle. He addressed the Tetford Club at the pleasant White Hart Inn, which still has a fine oak settle from the period.

Even these fragmentary reminders of Johnson's travels outside London, together with his more important connections with Lichfield, go some way towards challenging Macaulay's famous judgement:

> He had studied, not the genus man, but the species Londoner. Nobody was ever so thoroughly conversant with all the shades of moral and intellectual character which were to be seen from Islington to the Thames and from Hyde Park Corner to Mile-End Green. But his philosophy stopped at the first turnpike-gate.

The best rebuttal—or perhaps the most intriguing test—of Macaulay's opinion is the Scottish tour Johnson made with Boswell in autumn 1773: 'He always said, that he was not come to Scotland to see fine places, of which there were enough in England; but wild objects,—mountains,—waterfalls,—peculiar manners; in short, things which he had not seen before' (Boswell's *Journal*, 26 August). It would not be possible to describe the trip in full detail here nor, in fact, is it necessary since Johnson's own *Journey to the Western Islands* and

Boswell's *Journal of a Tour to the Hebrides* provide far better accounts than any modern guidebook could hope to offer. Of these works, Johnson's is the more precisely topographical and Boswell's the more entertaining, for it enjoys the great advantage of having Johnson as well as Scotland for its subject.

The main surviving points, at least, of their itinerary may briefly be noted. It began and ended in Edinburgh, where Boswell was able to exult in his *Journal* entry for 14 August: 'I now actually had him in Caledonia.' In the course of touring the major sights of the capital Johnson was unpleasantly surprised by the dirty and neglected state of St Giles Cathedral, then divided into four Presbyterian churches, on the High Street but Boswell's *Journal* (16 August) assured readers: 'It is now very elegantly fitted up.'

After crossing the Firth of Forth the pair travelled up the east coast to St Andrews (on A915, 48 miles NE of Edinburgh), site of Scotland's oldest university, which Johnson's *Journey* judged 'a place eminently adapted to study and education, being situated in a populous, yet a cheap country, and exposing the minds and manners of young men neither to the levity and dissoluteness of a capital city, nor to the gross luxury of a town of commerce.' Boswell (18 August) offers a pleasant account of an evening walk round the former buildings of St Leonard's College off Abbey Street, then a private house and now St Leonard's School. From New Slains Castle (26 miles north of Aberdeen), now an impressive ruin overlooking Cruden Bay, they visited the Bullers of Buchan (2 miles north on A975 and A952), a dramatic rock chasm 'which' (wrote Johnson) 'no man can see with indifference, who has either sense of danger or delight in rarity.'

The westward route they then followed across the Highlands included two places of special interest: the magnificent ruins of Elgin Cathedral (on A96 8 miles south of Lossiemouth) and Cawdor Castle, successor to the building supposedly occupied by the historical Macbeth, on B9090.10 miles SW of Nairn.

From Glenelg on the west coast they crossed to the island of Skye in the Inner Hebrides. Their month's stay included visits to Flora MacDonald, who had helped Bonnie Prince Charlie escape after the defeat of the 1745 rebellion, at Kingsburgh (now rebuilt; off A856 near Loch Snizort Beag) and the Macleods of Dunvegan Castle (A850 on Loch Dunvegan). The 15C–18C castle now displays a portrait of Johnson.

From the island of Mull to the south they reached Iona, with its relics of Britain's earliest Christianity. Johnson admitted that he was 'less eager' than his companion to make the pilgrimage and left it to Boswell to record his famous extempore praise: 'That man is little to be envied, whose patriotism would not gain force upon the plains of *Marathon*, or whose piety would not grow warmer among the ruins of *Iona*!' (19 October).

Returning to the mainland at Oban, Boswell and Johnson then continued south, visiting Inverary Castle on the north shore of Loch Fyne. Johnson was 'much struck by the grandeur and elegance of this princely seat' (*Journal*, 25 October) and gratified by the cordial welcome he received from the Duke of Argyll, while Boswell found more than architecture to delight the eye: 'I shall never forget the impression made upon my fancy by some of the ladies' maids tripping about in neat morning dress.' The 18C building, altered since that time, is mainly notable for its collection of treasures and paintings.

Four miles NW of Dumbarton and on the southern tip of Loch Lomond they stopped at Cameron House, where Johnson gave advice on Smollett's epitaph to the writer's cousin; both the house and the epitaph are described under the entry for that author.

After an unmemorable visit to Glasgow they made their last stop before Edinburgh at Auchinleck, 12 miles SE of Kilmarnock on A76, the family home of Boswell. A clash between his father, the Whig and Presbyterian Lord Auchinleck, and Johnson, Tory and Anglican, was almost inevitable:

> They became exceedingly warm, and violent, and I was very much distressed by being present at such an altercation between two men, both of whom I reverenced; yet I durst not interfere. It would certainly be very unbecoming in me to exhibit my honoured father, and my respected friend, as intellectual gladiators, for the entertainment of the publick; and therefore I suppress what would, I dare say, make an interesting scene in this dramatick sketch. (6 November)

Boswell (d. 1795) and his wife are buried in the family mausoleum adjoining Auchinleck church, which is now a small museum.

Because it produced no comparable literary record Johnson's visit to north Wales the following summer (1774) with Hester Thrale and her husband is less well remembered. The first object of their journey

'Scottifying the Palate,' by Thomas Rowlandson. From The Picturesque Beauties of Boswell *(1786). Courtesy of Cambridge University Library*

'I bought some speldings, *fish (generally whitings) salted and dried in a particular manner, being dipped in the sea and dried in the sun, and eaten by the Scots by way of a relish. He had never seen them, though they are sold in London. I insisted on* scottifying *his palate; but he was very reluctant. With difficulty I prevailed with him to let a bit of one of them lie in his mouth. He did not like it.' Entry for 18 August in Boswell's* Journal of a Tour to the Hebrides

was Tremeirchion, a village on B5429 overlooking the Vale of Clwyd. Mrs Thrale had inherited the family home of Bach-y-Graig here (now gone) and returned after her marriage to Gabriel Piozzi (1784), of which Johnson violently disapproved, to build the house Brynabella to the south. She is commemorated by a plaque in the north chancel of the church. From Tremeirchion Johnson visited Denbigh Castle, 4½ miles south via A543. Two other impressive castles were included in the route across Wales: the ruins of Beaumaris on south-east Anglesey, reached from the mainland by the Menai Bridge and A545, and the shell at Caernarvon on A487 and the south shore of the Menai Strait. The party's final destination was near Pwllheli, on A499 and the southern shore of the Lleyn Peninsula. Mrs Thrale was born at Bodvel Hall, 2 miles NW of the town on A497.

Samuel Johnson Birthplace Museum, Lichfield. Open May to Sept, Mon to Sat 10–5, Sun 2.30–5; Oct to Apr, Mon to Sat 11–5.30. Fee.

Headmaster's House (Council Offices), Lichfield. Visitors by appointment.

Bishop's Palace (St Chad's Cathedral Choir School), Lichfield. Visitors by appointment.

Edial Hall, near Lichfield. Visitors by appointment.

Ilam Park, near Ashbourne (NT). Park open every day. Information room open Apr to end Oct, daily 10–6; Nov to end March, Sat & Sun 10–5.

Old Rectory, Easton Maudit. Visitors by appointment.

Dr Johnson's House, Gough Square. Open May to Sept, Mon to Sat 11–5.30; Oct to Apr, Mon to Sat 11–5. Fee.

Kenwood House, Hampstead (GLC). Open Apr to Sept, daily 10–7; Oct, Feb & March, daily 10–5; Nov to Jan, daily 10–4. Closed Christmas Eve, Christmas Day & Good Fri.

Royal Naval College, Greenwich (Greenwich Hospital). Grounds, Painted Hall and Chapel open Mon to Wed, Fri & Sat 2.30–5, Sun in May to Sept 2.30–5. Sun service in chapel at 11.

Petworth House (NT). Open Apr to end Oct, Tues (except after BH), Wed, Thurs, Sat, Sun, BH Mon 2–6. Fee.

Cowdray House, Midhurst. Open 1 Apr to 1 Oct, daily except Wed 10–6.

Cawdor Castle. Open 1 May to 30 Sept, daily 10–5.30. Fee.

Dunvegan Castle. Open early Apr to mid May & 1 Oct to 27 Oct, daily 2–5; mid May to end Sept, daily 10.30–5. Fee.

Inverary Castle. Open 7 Apr to end June, 1 Sept to end Oct, Mon to Thurs 10–1, 2–6, Sun 1–6; July & Aug, Mon to Sat 10–6, Sun 1–6. Fee.

Auchinleck Boswell Museum and Mausoleum. Apply to Mr G.P. Hoyle, No. 131 Main Street, Auchinleck. Prior notice is appreciated.

Denbigh Castle (DoE/Welsh Office). Open 15 March to 15 Oct, Mon to Sat 9.30–6.30, Sun 2–6.30 (Apr to Sept, Sun 9.30–6.30); 16 Oct to 14 March, Mon to Sat 9.30–4, Sun 2–4. Closed Christmas Eve, Christmas Day, Boxing Day & New Year's Day. Fee.

Beaumaris Castle (DoE/Welsh Office). Open 15 March to 15 Oct, daily 9.30–6.30; 16 Oct to 14 March, Mon to Sat 9.30–4, Sun 2–4. Closed Christmas Eve, Christmas Day, Boxing Day & New Year's Day. Fee.

Caernarvon Castle (DoE/Welsh Office). Open 15 March to 15 Oct, daily 9.30–6.30; 16 Oct to 14 March, Mon to Sat 9.30–4, Sun 2–4. Closed Christmas Eve, Christmas Day, Boxing Day & New Year's Day. Fee.

Ben Jonson

b. London, 1572; d. London, 1637. *Every Man in His Humour* (1601); *Eastward Hoe* (with George Chapman and John Marston [qq.v.]; 1605); *Volpone, or The Fox* (1607); *Epicoene, or The Silent Woman* (1609); *The Alchemist* (1612); *The Forest* (1612); *Bartholomew Fayre* (1614).

Very little survives in London to recall the memory of Jonson's lifetime residence or his long theatrical career, though some account of the areas connected with the Renaissance drama is offered under the entry for Shakespeare. He was educated at Westminster School, in Little Dean's Yard to the south of Westminster Abbey. A poem later celebrated his master, William Camden, as him 'to whom I owe/ All that I am in arts, all that I know.' His grave is marked by a slab in the north aisle of Westminster Abbey with the magnificently simple epitaph: 'O rare Ben Jonson.' Poets' Corner (fee) has an 18C monument by Gibbs and Rysbrack.

Jonson's main connections outside London are with the country houses where the spectacular entertainments, masques and antimasques of his later career were performed. The chief surviving places may be listed briefly with their opening hours:

Belvoir Castle, Leicestershire, west of A1 near Grantham. Rebuilt since the performance of *A Masque of the Metamorphosed Gypsies* (1621). Open late March to Sept, Tues, Wed, Thurs & Sat 12–6; Sun 12–6; BH Mon 11–7, Good Fri 12–6; also Sun in Oct 2–6. Fee.

Kenilworth Castle, now ruined, north of Warwick. *The Masque of Owls* (1624). English Heritage. Open 15 March to 15 Oct, Mon to Sat 9.30–6.30, Sun 2–6.30 (Apr to Sept, Sun 9.30–6.30); 16 Oct to 14 March, Mon to Sat 9.30–4, Sun 2–4. Closed Christmas Eve, Christmas Day, Boxing Day & New Year's Day. Fee.

Althorp, 16C–18C mansion 6 miles NW of Northampton, off A428. Entertainment in 1603 for Queen Anne, to celebrate James I's accession to the throne. Open Tues, Wed, Thurs, Sat & Sun 2.30–5.30, BH 11.30–6.30. Fee.

Welbeck Abbey, early 17C mansion, off A60 10 miles north of Mansfield in Nottinghamshire. *Love's Welcome* (1633), in the presence of Charles I. Welbeck is now an Army training school.

Bolsover Castle, on A632 7 miles NW of Mansfield. A second version of *Love's Welcome*, in 1634, again in the presence of Charles I. English Heritage. Open 15 March to 15 Oct, Mon to Sat 9.30 6.30, Sun 2–6.30 (Apr to Sept, Sun 9.30–6.30); 16 Oct to 14 March, Mon to Sat 9.30–4, Sun 2–4. Closed Christmas Eve, Christmas Day, Boxing Day & New Year's Day. Fee.

A more important connection links Jonson and ****Penshurst Place** (SW of Tonbridge in Kent), birthplace of Sir Philip Sidney (q.v.) and home of the Sidney family. In 'To Penshurst' (published in *The Forest*), progenitor of a series of 17C poems about country houses, it is celebrated for its architectural modesty, hospitality to guests and benevolent relations with the community around. The poem concludes:

> Now, *Penshurst*, they that will proportion thee
> > With other edifices, when they see
> Those proud, ambitious heaps, and nothing else,
> > May say, their lords have built, but thy lord dwells.

Penshurst Place. Open Apr to end Oct, Tues (except after BH), Wed, Thurs, Sat, Sun, BH Mon 2–6. Fee.

John Keats

b. London, 1795; d. Rome, 1821. *Poems* (1817); *Endymion: A Poetic Romance* (1818); *Lamia, Isabella, The Eve of St Agnes and Other Poems* (1820).

London still offers significant reminders of the poet's brief life. A plaque at No. 85 Moorgate near its junction with London Wall in the City marks the site of his birthplace, a livery stable run by his father. He was baptised at the early 18C church of St Botolph on Bishopsgate to the east. From 1815 he studied medicine at Guy's and St Thomas's Hospitals on the east side of Borough High Street in Southwark, reached by following London Bridge south over the river. Guy's of course, is vastly changed since then and St Thomas's buildings have virtually disappeared, but on St Thomas Street—where Keats was lodging when he wrote 'On First Looking into Chapman's Homer'—we find a fascinating survival of the medical conditions he knew. The Chapter House of Southwark Cathedral contains the Old Operating Theatre of St Thomas's. It dates from 1821, was rediscovered in 1956 and has been carefully restored; the cramped stalls from which medical students like Keats could watch operations are of special interest. A further reminder of the poet's medical career

Keats in the sitting room of Wentworth Place, now Keats Memorial House, by Joseph Severn (1821). Courtesy of National Portrait Gallery

is the charming 17C–18C Apothecaries Hall on Blackfriars Lane, north of Queen Victoria Street in Blackfriars. Keats took and passed his exam for an apothecary's licence here in 1816.

In 1817 he moved north to Hampstead, which still preserves some of the rural atmosphere that delighted him and is still the London borough most closely linked with his name. His first lodging was on Well Walk, the picturesque continuation of Flask Walk from Hampstead High Street, next to the pub at the present No. 30. Here he nursed his consumptive younger brother, Tom, who died in December 1818.

It was partly to escape the associations of Well Walk after Tom's death that Keats moved to what is now the major landmark for his admirers: the *Keats Memorial House in Keats Grove near the southern tip of the Heath and Hampstead Ponds. Wentworth Place, to use its original name, was built in 1815–16 by two friends of the poet, Charles Wentworth Dilke and Charles Armitage Brown, as a pair of semi-detached houses sharing the same garden. Keats came in December 1818 to share the eastern half with Brown. From April 1819 the western half was let to Mrs Brawne and her daughters; Fanny, the eldest, became Keats' fiancée in the autumn. Returning to his bedroom one evening in February 1820, he coughed blood into his handkerchief and told Brown: 'I know the colour of that blood; it is arterial blood. I cannot be deceived in that colour. That drop of blood is my death warrant. I must die.' He left Wentworth Place in September and died in Rome early the following year. The house today, restored in a rather harsh and clinical manner, displays a large collection of Keats relics. In the pleasant garden, where he heard the nightingale that suggested the famous 'Ode,' we find a successor to the plum tree he knew. The public library next door has a collection of early Keats editions.

Keats was a frequent visitor to Leigh Hunt (q.v.) at his cottage in the Vale of Health, reached from East Heath Road. He first met Shelley (q.v.) here, though their host later recalled: 'Keats did not take to Shelley as kindly as Shelley did to him ... Keats, being a little too sensitive on the score of his origin, felt inclined to see in every man of birth a sort of natural enemy.' His meeting (1819) on Hampstead Heath with Coleridge, then living in Highgate, is described under the entry for the Lake Poets (Rte 3). Hampstead Parish Church on Church Row has a bust of the poet donated by his American admirers in 1894.

Westminster Abbey always regarded the Romantic poets with suspicion and its joint memorial to Keats and Shelley in Poets' Corner (fee) was not unveiled until 1954.

Although most of Keats' life was passed in London, his several tours outside the capital are worth noting. They occasionally cast light on his poetry, and they show the writer who praised Shakespeare and Homer in memorable sonnets as an ardent seeker of literary shrines.

His trip with Brown to the Lake District and Scotland in the summer of 1818—the trip from which he returned with the sore throat presaging his fatal illness—was a combination of demanding walking tour and literary pilgrimage. From Ambleside near the head of Lake Windermere he walked to Dove Cottage, Rydal Mount and other scenes connected with Wordsworth; they are described in detail under the entry for the Lake Poets (Rte 12C). He was disgusted by the crowds of tourists and by local reminders of Wordsworth's Tory allegiances, but profoundly moved by Windermere itself:

> the two views we have had of it are of the most noble tenderness—they can never fade away—they make one forget the divisions of life; age, youth, poverty and riches; and refine one's sensual vision into a sort of north star which can never cease to be open lidded and stedfast over the wonders of the great Power.

In Scotland he went to Alloway, the Brig o'Doon and other sights described in connection with Robert Burns; his visit to the poet's grave in Dumfries prompted a rather undistinguished tribute in verse.

In November 1819 he stayed at the Burford Bridge Hotel in Surrey, near the foot of Box Hill some $1\frac{1}{2}$ miles north of Dorking on A24. From here he wrote the famous letter to his Oxford friend, Benjamin Bailey, which declared:

> I am certain of nothing but of the holiness of the Heart's affections and the truth of Imagination—What the Imagination seizes as Beauty must be truth—whether it existed before or not—for I have the same Idea of all our Passions as of Love they are all in their sublime, creative of essential Beauty . . .—The Imagination may be compared to Adam's dream—he awoke and found it truth.

During the winter of 1818–19 he went with Brown to Chichester in West Sussex. They stayed with Dilke's parents at No. 11 Eastgate Square (now marked with a plaque) by the junction of East Road and The Hornet. Keats began 'The Eve of St Agnes' during the visit and scholars have suggested that the poem's medieval setting owes something to his impressions of Chichester Cathedral and its precincts. He was particularly struck by Vicars Close, a narrow street of 15C house with 18C frontages, off Canon Lane south of the Cloisters.

In January 1819 he and Brown travelled west from Chichester to attend the consecration of Stansted Chapel on the estate of Lewis Way, an ardent campaigner for the conversion of the Jews. He was not impressed by the ceremony, which made him 'begin to hate Parsons.' Yet the chapel's delightful Regency Gothic, and particularly the armorial glass of its nave, must surely have helped the rich descriptions in 'The Eve of St Agnes':

> A casement high and triple-arch'd there was,
> All garlanded with carven imag'ries
> Of fruits, and flowers, and bunches of knot-grass,
> And diamonded with panes of quaint device,
> Innumerable of stains and splendid dyes,
> As are the tiger-moth's deep-damask'd wings;
> And in the midst, 'mong thousand heraldries,
> And twilight saints, and dim emblazonings,
> A shielded scutcheon blush'd with blood of queens and kings.
>
> (stanza 24)

The modern traveller can reach the chapel by going 9 miles west of Chichester on A27 to Emsworth, then turning right through Westbourne and continuing on sideroads towards Forestside until the turning for the estate (3 miles).

From Chichester we may also reach the Isle of Wight, off Portsmouth to the SW. During a visit in 1817 Keats saw Carisbrooke Castle in the centre of the island:

> I have not seen many specimens of Ruins—I dont think however I shall ever see one to surpass Carisbrooke Castle. The trench is o'ergrown with the smoothest turf, and the walls with ivy—The Keep within side is one

Bower of ivy—a Colony of Jackdaws have been there many years—I dare say I have seen many a descendant of some old cawer who peeped through the Bars at Charles the first, when he was there in Confinement.

During the summer of 1819 he stayed at Shanklin on the south-eastern coast, writing 'Lamia,' beginning the disastrous *Otho the Great* in hope of making money and sketching the church in his spare time. His lodging was in Eglantine Cottage at the south end of the High Street:

Our window looks over house tops and Cliffs onto the Sea, so that when the Ships sail past the Cottage chimneys you may take them for Weathercocks. We have Hill and Dale forest and Mead and plenty of Lobsters.

From the Isle of Wight he moved north to Winchester, where he spent the autumn months of 1819 just before his final departure from England and where he wrote his 'Ode to Autumn.' His lodging near the Cathedral does not survive, but the modern visitor can still find some of the atmosphere which led Keats to tell his younger sister that Winchester was 'the pleasantest Town I ever was in':

There is a fine Cathedral which to me is always a sourse of amusement; part of it built 1400 years ago; and the more modern by a magnificent Man, you may have read of in our History, called William of Wickham. The whole town is beautifully wooded—From the Hill at the eastern extremity you see a prospect of Streets, and old Buildings mixed up with Trees . . . And what improves it all is, the fashionable inhabitants are all gone to Southampton.

Old Operating Theatre, Southwark. Open Mon & Wed 12.30–4, and by arrangement at other times except Sat; closed Christmas Eve, Christmas Day, New Year's Day, Good Fri, Easter Mon, spring and later summer BH. Fee.

Keats Memorial House, Hampstead. Open Mon to Sat 10–1, 2–6, Sun & BH 2–5. Closed Christmas Day, Boxing Day, New Year's Day, Good Fri, Easter Eve, May BH.

Carisbrooke Castle (English Heritage). Open 15 March to 15 Oct, Mon to Sat 9.30–6.30, Sun 2–6.30 (Apr to Sept, Sun 9.30–6.30); 16 Oct to 14 March, Mon to Sat 9.30–4, Sun 2–4. Closed Christmas Eve, Christmas Day, Boxing Day & New Year's Day. Fee.

Charles and Henry Kingsley

Charles Kingsley: b. Holne, Devon, 1819; d. Eversley, Hampshire. 1875. *Alton Locke, Tailor and Poet: An Autobiography* (1850); *Yeast: A Problem* (1851); *Hypatia: or New Foes With an Old Face* (1853); *Westward Ho! or The Voyages and Adventures of Sir Amyas Leigh, Knight* (1855); *Two Years Ago* (1857); *The Water-Babies: A Fairy Tale for a Land-Baby* (1863); *The Roman and the Teuton* (1864); *Hereward the Wake: 'Last of the English'* (1866).

Henry Kingsley: b. Barnack, Cambridgeshire, 1830; d. Cuckfield, West Sussex, 1876. *The Recollections of Geoffrey Hamlyn* (1859); *Ravenshoe* (1862); *Austin Elliott* (1863); *The Hillyars and the Burtons: A Story of Two Families* (1865).

The most important place in Charles Kingsley's life was always Devon. He was born on the edge of Dartmoor at Holne, an attractive village where his father was curate, 2½ miles west of Ashburton. The rectory, then badly dilapidated, stands a few hundred yards west of the church. The family moved away from Holne when Charles was only six weeks old but renewed their connection with the county in 1831 when Rev. Kingsley was appointed curate of *Clovelly, on the north coast 12 miles west of Bideford. He became rector the following year and remained until 1836. In later years Kingsley returned to the home of his boyhood, finding both a relief from the pressures of his busy, combative adult life and a stimulus to his novelist's imagination. The adjoining coastline became the setting for *Westward Ho!*, his hugely patriotic and hugely popular novel about England at the time of the Armada; Clovelly itself reappeared as 'Aberalva' in *Two Years Ago*, which takes place during the Crimean War. Indeed, Kingsley may be said to have drawn his contemporaries' attention to the little village, ensuring it a popularity that continues today. If at all possible, Clovelly should be avoided during the summer months, especially the weekends, when its charm often disappears beneath the burden of visitors.

To the side of B3237, which leads to Clovelly's car park, lie the church, the rectory where the Kingsleys lived and the surviving wing of Clovelly Court. In the Kingsleys' time the owner of the Court was Sir James Hamlyn-Williams, patron of the living, responsible for Hobby Drive, which stretches along the cliff to the east offering fine walks and views. In *Westward Ho!* Will Cary lives at Clovelly Court (Ch. 5), while in *Two Years Ago* it becomes 'Pentalva Court,' home of the morbid poet Elsley Vavasour, whom Tennyson (q.v.) mistakenly supposed to be a likeness of himself. In the church we find a memorial to Kingsley, a fine Jacobean pulpit carved with Will Cary's initials and later monuments to the Cary family. From the car park we walk down the cliff to the steep main street—too steep to admit traffic—flanked with neat fishermen's cottages. Kingsley lodged here on a visit in 1849. There is a magnificent view of Barnstaple or Bideford Bay.

The best way to explore the coastline, rich in scenery and points of interest from *Westward Ho!*, is by walking the coastal footpaths as Kingsley did. The following list is merely a summary and, for convenience's sake, locates places in relation to the nearest road accessible by car. 6 miles west via A39, B3248 and an unclassified road we find the fine 14C church of Hartland parish at Stoke, where Kingsley preached. On the coast to the south lies Marsland Mouth, one of a series of dramatic coves Kingsley described in *Westward Ho!*: 'To landward, all richness, softness, and peace; to seaward, a waste and howling wilderness of rock and roller, barren to the fisherman, and hopeless to the shipwrecked mariner' (Ch. 6). Rose Salterne's moonlight bathing here is interrupted by Eustace Leigh and the Jesuits. To reach the Mouth we follow A39 south from the B3248 turning to Eastcott (6 miles) and then follow unclassified roads $2\frac{1}{2}$ miles through Gooseham; a footpath ($\frac{1}{2}$ mile) finally brings us to the coast. From Eastcott, too, we may take unclassified roads to the parish of Morwenstow (4 miles) where Kingsley visited the eccentric poet-parson R.S. Hawker (q.v.). It was Hawker who helped Kingsley discover the countryside south of Morwenstow, though he did not approve the novelist's use of history or topography in *Westward Ho!*: 'The whole Book is an assumption—and *me judice* a failure.' The fine medieval manor of Tonacombe, on the cliff near the road leading to Coombe, became 'Chapel.' Hawker and Kingsley also went beyond Coombe to Stowe Barton (NT; $3\frac{1}{2}$ miles from Morwenstow), where they inspected the site of Sir Richard Grenville's mansion, resurrected in the novel as a 'huge rambling building, half castle, half dwelling-house' (Ch. 7). From Stowe Barton we may regain A39 by following unclassified roads east through the Coombe Valley to Kilkampton (4 miles). The church's 'lofty tower' and 'monuments and offerings of five centuries of Grenviles' are briefly noted in Chapter 7 of Kingsley's novel.

Kilkampton ends the journey west and south of Clovelly. The sites to the east are more simply described, for they are concentrated in Bideford. Kingsley's introduction of the town at the beginning of his book can hardly be bettered:

> All who have travelled through the delicious scenery of North Devon must needs know the little white town of Bideford, which slopes upwards from its broad tide-river paved with yellow sands, and many-arched old bridge where salmon wait for autumn floods, toward the pleasant upland in the west. Above the town the hills close in, cushioned with deep oak woods, through which juts here and there a crag of fern-fringed slate; below they lower, and open more and more in softly rounded knolls, and fertile squares of red and green, till they sink into the wide expanse of hazy flats, rich salt-marshes and rolling sandhills, where Torridge joins her sister Taw, and both together flow quietly toward the broad surges of the bar, and the everlasting thunder of the long Atlantic swell. (Ch. 1)

Near the junction with Kingsley Road on the Quay is a statue of the writer commemorating his connection with Bideford. Just south of the bridge stands the church of St Mary, scene of the thanksgiving service held after Amyas Leigh's return from his journey round the world (Ch. 2). It was substantially rebuilt in 1864. In East-the-Water at the other end of the bridge is the Royal Hotel, whose unremarkable facade conceals a merchant's house of 1688. Tradition maintains that Kingsley lodged here at the start of his 1854–55 stay in Bideford when *Westward Ho!* was written.

B3236 leads NW to Westward Ho! (3 miles), an unattractive resort developed in the 1870s and named after the novel. From Ilfracombe, 21 miles NE of Bideford via A39 and A361, a steamer makes the crossing (via Clovelly) to the tiny island of Lundy (NT) in the Bristol Channel. In Chapter 32 of *Westward Ho!* the Spanish galleon *Santa Catharina* is wrecked on the Shutter Rock off its south-west coast: 'a huge black fang . . ., waiting for its prey' (Ch. 32).

Though the most important, Devon is far from being the only scene of Kingsley's life and writing. Part of his childhood (1824–30) was spent in the village of Barnack, then in Northamptonshire but now in Cambridgeshire, 4 miles SE of Stamford. Henry Kingsley, younger brother and less famous novelist, was baptized at the fine font in the church. The building has a striking Saxon tower and Charles' last novel, *Hereward the Wake*, returned to the Saxon history and legends of the nearby Fens. He followed tradition and located the opening scenes at Bourne, Hereward's reputed birthplace and a typical market town 11 miles NE of Stamford via A6121 and A151. A major setting later in the book is Crowland Abbey (14 miles SE of Bourne via A15 and B1166): 'a vast range of high-peaked buildings founded on piles of oak and alder driven into the fen' (Bk 2, Ch. 1). The Saxon foundation dedicated to St Guthlac has of course disappeared and the present remains date from the Norman period onwards. The Danish sacking of the Cathedral at Peterborough to the south is described in Bk 2, Ch. 7, while the fall of Ely further SE occurs in Bk 2, Ch. 14.

The Rev. Kingsley's last clerical appointment brought his children to London and St Luke's Church in Chelsea. The early Gothic Revival building of which he was rector from 1836 until his death stands on Sydney Street north of King's Road. The old Rectory is at No. 56 Old Church Street, west of and parallel to Sydney Street. The neighbourhood was remembered not by Charles but by Henry in his unjustly neglected novel *The Hillyars and the Burtons*. It contains some fine early episodes in Chelsea, especially All Saints by the Embankment, which St Luke's replaced as parish church:

> Four hundred years of memory . . . are crowded into that dark old church, and the great flood of change beats round the walls, and shakes the door in vain, but never enters. The dead stand thick together there, as if to make a brave resistance to the moving world outside, which jars upon their slumber. (Vol. 1, Ch. 13)

From London Charles Kingsley went in 1838 to Cambridge, where he studied at Magdalene College. His lodging was at the top of C staircase in the First Court. His vigorous and earnest piety does not seem to have been in sympathy with the college's atmosphere, for Magdalene was then known as 'a favourite home for young men who are of the opinion, either from conjecture or experience, that other colleges are too strict for them.' In 1860–69 Kingsley was back in Cambridge as Regius Professor of Modern History, a surprising appointment given that he had neither the equipment nor the temperament of a scholar. In fact, he owed it to royal patronage and acted as tutor to the Prince of Wales, the future Edward VII, then in residence at Madingley Hall (3½ miles NW via A1303; now a study centre). Kingsley's own Cambridge base during the early years of his Professorship was at No. 3 St Peter's Terrace, an elegant mid 19C row that stands back from Trumpington Street immediately south of the Fitzwilliam Museum.

Social contacts made during his years as Professor took him to Yorkshire and Monk Fryston Hall (now a hotel; 2 miles east of A1 on A63 towards Selby), the home of Richard Monckton Milnes, Lord Houghton, described under the entry for Swinburne (q.v.). Given their differences in character and views, it is fortunate that the poet and the novelist never coincided as guests. Another and more important Yorkshire connection was formed in 1858 when he visited the limestone country near Settle (36 miles NW of Harrogate via A59 and A65). Kingsley stayed at Tarn House on the north shore of Malham Tarn (NT; 5 miles NW of Settle via an unclassified road and footpath). Taking his cue from the building's curious combination of neo-classical with Italian Gothic, he made it into 'Harthover House' in his fantasy for children, *The Water-Babies*: 'built at ninety different times, and in nineteen different styles, . . . as if somebody had built a whole street of houses of every imaginable shape, and then stirred them together with a spoon' (Ch. 1). 2½ miles south and near the unclassified road leading to Malham is Malham Cove, a natural amphitheatre of rock 'just like ill-made pavements with deep cracks between the stones and ledges' (Ch. 2), where the Aire emerges from the subterranean course it has followed since the Tarn. It is here that Tom, the chimney-sweeper hero of Kingsley's story, enters his underwater world.

Despite his busy career as writer and the public preferments which fame brought him Kingsley always regarded himself as first and foremost a country clergyman. He fulfilled this role with great conscientiousness for his entire adult life in the parish of Eversley, 8 miles SE of Reading on A327. The rectory and 18C church lie about a mile south of the main village on an unclassified road. He first came here as curate in 1842, immediately after leaving Cambridge and taking holy orders. In 1844 he became rector when his predecessor fled with the parish funds rather than answer 'a formal charge of a most revolting nature' about his conduct with a local married woman. The battle to reform a parish where the reputation of the clergy had sunk so low brought him into conflict with the patron of the living, Sir John Cope, who lived in the Jacobean mansion at Bramshill Park (2½ miles west of the church; now a police training college). Kingsley is remembered in Eversley church and buried in its churchyard.

In Westminster Abbey, of which he was appointed a Canon in 1873, the Chapel of St George near the west entrance has a bust by Thomas Woolner.

The adult life of Henry Kingsley took a very different course from his brother's. His career at Worcester College, Oxford was cut short in 1835. Although he apparently left on his own will Chapter 7 of his best novel, *Ravenshoe*, shows him familiar with the attitude adopted by Oxford colleges towards overly high-spirited undergraduates. He returned from Australia in 1858 without a fortune but with the partly completed manuscript of *Geoffrey Hamlyn* and with a stock of experience that served him in later novels. His final years were spent in Cuckfield (16 miles N of Brighton in West Sussex via A23 and A272), where he is buried in the churchyard.

Rudyard Kipling

b. Bombay, India, 1865; d. London, 1936. *Departmental Ditties and Other Verses* (1886); *Plain Tales from the Hills* (1888); *Soldiers Three* (1888); *The Story of the Gadsbys* (1888); *In Black and White* (1888); *Under the Deodars* (1888); *The Phantom Rickshaw and Other Tales* (1888); *Wee Willie Winkie and Other Tales* (1888); *Departmental Ditties, Barrack-Room Ballads and Other Verses* (1890); *The Courting of Dinah Shadd and Other Stories* (1890); *The Light That Failed* (1890); *American Notes* (1891); *Mine Own People* (1891); *The Jungle Book* (1894); *The Second Jungle Book* (1895); *The Seven Seas* (1896); *'Captains Courageous': A Story of the Grand Banks* (1897); *The Day's Work* (1898); *Stalky & Co.* (1899); *Puck of Pook's Hill* (1906); *Rewards and Fairies* (1910); *Something of Myself* (unfinished; 1937).

Like most sons of Anglo-Indian parents, Kipling was sent back to England for his schooling. He attended the United Services College at Westward Ho!, the dreary North Devon coastal resort (3 miles NW of Bideford) named after the novel by Charles Kingsley (q.v.). Even if the story of Kipling's miserable childhood has sometimes been exaggerated, the college was still not a fortunate choice. Its most useful consequence was *Stalky & Co.*, a book that describes schoolboys with a realism that shocked contemporaries used to the work of Thomas Hughes (q.v.).

After leaving the United Services College Kipling did not return to England until 1889, when his Indian stories and verses were already beginning to attract the attention of the literary world. He quickly confirmed his reputation. His lodgings in London were at No. 43 Villiers Street, south of the Strand near Charing Cross, now marked by a GLC blue plaque.

After his marriage to Caroline Balestier in 1892 Kipling spent several years in her native America. They returned in 1896 to live in SW England, moving the next year to Rottingdean, a charming little village on the Sussex Downs 4 miles east of Brighton. At first they stayed at North End House, the summer home of his uncle, the painter Edward Burne-Jones. Here Kipling wrote 'Recessional,' the poem that typified his role as poet of the Empire. Later in 1897 the Kiplings moved across the green to The Elms. Rottingdean Grange, now a public library and museum, has a small collection of Kipling relics.

'What should they know of England who only England know?' Kipling asked. His Rottingdean years were spent getting to know England itself properly for the first time, and in particular they were spent exploring Sussex in an early steam-driven motor car. When they decided that Rottingdean was becoming 'too populated,' the main purpose of the Kiplings' drives was to find a more suitable home. In 1902 they bought *Bateman's, a 17C ironmaster's house in the village of Burwash, on A265 27 miles NE of Brighton and near the Kent border. He wrote enthusiastically to a friend:

> Behold us lawful owners of a grey stone lichened house—A.D. 1634 over the door—beamed, panelled, with old oak staircase, and all untouched and unfaked. Heaven looked after it in the dissolute times of mid-victorian restoration and caused the vicar to send his bailiff to live in it for 40 years, and he lived in peaceful filth and left everything as he found it.
>
> It is a good and peaceable place standing in terraced lawns nigh to a walled garden of old red brick, and two fat-headed oasthouses with red brick stomachs, and an aged silver-grey dovecot on top. There is what they call a river at the bottom of the lawn. It appears on all maps and that, except after very heavy rains, is the only place where it puts in any appearance . . . Its name is the Dudwell, and it is quite ten feet wide.

Between the river and Burwash Common on A265 is the countryside of *Puck of Pook's Hill*, the book most completely expressive of his love for Sussex. Kipling lived at Bateman's until death and, when his widow died in 1939, the house was bequeathed to the National Trust.

Kipling unveiled the First World War memorial in Burwash, remarking that it 'occupied the very place it should do, right in the centre of the church approach—for surely it was a small thing that as they approached the House of God, they should pause awhile and remember the sacrifice.' The church and the inn opposite appear in 'Hal o' the Draft' in *Puck of Pook's Hill*.

Kipling died at the Middlesex Hospital in London and was given a grand funeral in Poets' Corner (fee) of Westminster Abbey.

Mrs Elsie Bambridge, Kipling's daughter, lived for many years at Wimpole Hall, perhaps the finest 18C mansion in Cambridgeshire and notable for its landscaped grounds. It stands 8 miles SW of Cambridge off A603.

Rottingdean Grange. Open Mon, Thurs, Sat 10–5, Tues & Fri 10–1, 2–5, Sun 2–5.

Bateman's, Burwash (NT). Open Apr to end Oct, Mon to Wed, Sat & Sun 11–6. Open Good Fri. Fee.

Wimpole Hall, Orwell (NT). Open 31 March to 4 Nov, daily except Fri but including BH, 2–6; closed Good Fri. Fee.

William Langland

b. place uncertain, 1332?; d. place unknown, 1400? *The Vision Concerning Piers the Plowman* (n.d.).

Although *Piers Plowman* is cast in the form of an autobiographical dream-vision and contains topographical references (most notably to Cornhill in London), both the poet and the places he frequented have eluded precise identification. Examination of the poem's dialect agrees with its author's own reference to the Malvern Hills. The claim of Cleobury Mortimer, a village on A4117 12 miles east of Ludlow in Shropshire, to be his birthplace is advanced by an inscription in the church porch and, inside the church, by an east window of 1875 depicting scenes from the poem. But rival and more plausible claims have been made on behalf on Ledbury (16 miles SW of Worcester on A449), strengthened by the presence of a large field still called Longland or the Longlands nearby. The site of the poet's dream-vision would thus be the Pewtress Spring, about 4 miles NE between Chance's Pitch and the Herefordshire Beacon. Langland may have been educated at the Priory of Great Malvern, whose fine church survives.

D.H. Lawrence

b. Eastwood, Nottinghamshire, 1885; d. Vence, France, 1930. *The White Peacock* (1911); *The Trespasser* (1912); *Love Poems, and Others* (1913); *Sons and Lovers* (1913); *The Widowing of Mrs Holroyd* (1914); *The Prussian Officer, and Other Stories* (1914); *The Rainbow* (1915); *Twilight in Italy* (1916); *Amores: Poems* (1916); *Look! We Have Come Through* (1917); *New Poems* (1918); *Bay: A Book of Poems* (1919); *Touch and Go* (1920); *Women in Love* (1920); *The Lost Girl* (1920); *Movements in European History* (as 'Lawrence H. Davison'; 1921); *Psychoanalysis and the Unconscious* (1921); *Sea and Sardinia* (1921); *Aaron's Rod* (1922); *Fantasia of the Unconscious* (1922); *England, My England, and Other Stories* (1922); *The Ladybird, The Fox, The Captain's Doll* (1923); *Studies in Classic American Literature* (1923); *Kangaroo* (1923); *Birds, Beasts and Flowers: Poems* (1923); *The Boy in the Bush* (with M.L. Skinner; 1924); 'Introduction' to *Memoirs of the Foreign Legion* by Maurice Magnus (1924); *St Mawr, Together with The Princess* (1925); *Reflections on the Death of a Porcupine, and Other Essays* (1925); *The Plumed Serpent* (1926); *David* (1926); *Mornings in Mexico* (1927); *The Woman Who Rode Away, and Other Stories* (1928); *Lady Chatterley's Lover* (privately printed, 1928; expurgated edition, 1932; unexpurgated edition, 1960); *Collected Poems* (1928); *Pansies: Poems* (1929); *A Propos of Lady Chatterley's Lover* (1930); *The Virgin and The Gypsy* (1930); *Love Among the Haystacks, and Other Pieces, With a Reminiscence by D. Garnett* (1930); *Apocalypse* (1931); *Etruscan Places* (1932); *Phoenix: The Posthumous Papers* (edited by E.D. McDonald; 1936); *Phoenix II: Uncollected, Unpublished and Other Prose Works* (edited by F.W. Roberts and H.T. Moore; 1968); *Mr Noon* (1984).

One could not hope to better Lawrence's own description of his native corner of Central England and his hometown, *Eastwood, as he remembered them from boyhood: 'a mining village of some three thousand souls, about eight miles from Nottingham, and one mile from the small stream, the Erewash, which divides Nottinghamshire from Derbyshire. It is hilly country, looking west towards Crich and towards Matlock, sixteen miles away, and east and north-east towards Mansfield and the Sherwood Forest district. To me it seemed, and still seems, an extremely beautiful countryside, just between the red sandstone and the oak-trees of Nottingham, and the cold limestone, the ash-trees, the stone fences of Derbyshire. To me, as a child and a young man, it was still the old England of the forest and the agricultural past; there were no motor-cars, the mines were, in a sense, an accident in the landscape, and Robin Hood and his merry men were not very far away' ('Nottingham and the Mining Countryside,' *Phoenix*). On his last visit, made in 1926, he found disconcerting physical changes and depressing social ones in Eastwood but he also renewed a sense of kinship, however anguished:

> I feel I hardly know any more the people I come from, the colliers of the Erewash valley district. They are changed, and I suppose I am changed. I find it so much easier to live in Italy. And they have got a new kind of shallow consciousness, all newspaper and cinema, which I am not in touch with. At the same time, they have, I think, an underneath ache and heaviness very much like my own. It must be so, because when I see them, I feel it so strongly.
>
> They are the only people who move me strongly, and with whom I feel myself connected in deeper destiny. It is they who are, in some peculiar way, 'home' to me. I shrink away from them, and I have an acute nostalgia for them. ('Return to Bestwood,' *Phoenix II*)

Modern Eastwood shows the effect of further change—its population has quadrupled since Lawrence's day—but has at last recovered from its previous attitude of embarrassed neglect towards its native son. The visitor will now find Lawrence conspicuously remembered, and the town thoroughly deserves a walking tour.

The obvious place to start is at the Library on Eastwood's main street, Nottingham Road. The collection includes books by Lawrence and the headstone, decorated with a phoenix, from his grave at Vence; his body was later removed, cremated and reburied at the New Mexican ranch where he had lived with Frieda in the 1920s. From the Library we walk west along Nottingham Road and turn left for Queen's Square. Bromley House, on its western side, was the home of Lawrence's relatives after the death of his mother. From the same side of the square we can quickly reach Alexander Street, which leads back towards Nottingham Road. Before this, however, we take a left on Devonshire Drive. The second house on the right was the home of W.E. Hopkin, friend and mentor to Lawrence when he was in his teens. Lawrence attended Hopkin's Friday and Saturday night gatherings, and seems to have had the house in mind as the final home of Will and Anna Brangwen in *The Rainbow*. We may thus think of it as the setting for the opening chapter of *Women in Love*.

Returning to Nottingham Road we continue west and find, on our right, the entrance to Victoria Street. No. 8A is now the Lawrence Birthplace Museum, its interior carefully recreating a Victorian atmosphere. Arthur and Lydia Lawrence moved here in the 1880s shortly before the birth of their fourth child, the writer. The little house's shopfront is a reminder of Mrs Lawrence's brief and unsuccessful venture into the haberdashery business, one sign of her determination to cling to middle-class respectability in reaction against the working-class culture of her collier husband.

From the birthplace we return to Nottingham Road, which is followed a short way right to the Market Place. To the south on

Church Street we find the parish church of St Mary's and, beyond, the Lawrence family grave with an inscription mentioning the writer. North of the Market Place on the right-hand side of Mansfield Road stand the former offices of Arthur Lawrence's employers, Barber, Walker & Co. Readers of *Sons and Lovers* will remember the scene in Chapter 4 when the young Paul Morel is sent to the 'new, red-brick building, almost like a mansion' to collect his father's wages.

Brinsley Colliery, where Mr Lawrence worked, lay further north off the Mansfield Road but we now turn right on Greenhills Road. To our right, and opposite the cricket ground, is the development known as The Breach, 'The Bottoms' of *Sons and Lovers*: 'blocks of miners' dwellings . . . like the dots on a blank-six domino' (Ch. 1). The end-of-terrace house where the Lawrences lived from 1887 to 1891 is now No. 28 Garden Road and is open to the public. Though Lawrence's description in *Sons and Lovers* goes on to note that the house was 'substantial and very decent' Mrs Lawrence hated it, and it became the scene of the marital conflict fictionalised in the early episodes of *Sons and Lovers*.

From the east end of Garden Road we walk right on Lynncroft and take another right on Walker Street. No. 8 (then No. 3) on the left after the junction with Percy Street was the Lawrence family home when they left Garden Road. Lawrence nicknamed it 'Bleak House' because of its high, exposed situation but in 'Return to Bestwood' described the view with relish:

> one looks across at the amphitheatre of hills which I still find beautiful, though there are new patches of reddish houses, and a darkening of smoke. Crich is still on the sky line to the west, and the woods of Annesley to the north, and Coney Grey Farm still lies in front. And there is still a certain glamour about the country-side.

Behind the house and reached from Three Tuns Road is the pub which Arthur Lawrence used as his local and which appears in *Sons and Lovers* as 'The Moon and Stars.'

We now retrace our steps along Walker Street back to Lynncroft, which is followed to the right. No. 97, on the right-hand side near the end, was the family home from 1902 onwards, and appears as Aaron Sisson's home in *Aaron's Rod*. Mrs Lawrence died of cancer here in 1910, living just long enough to hold an advance copy of her son's first novel, *The White Peacock*, in her hands. From Lynncroft, Dovecote Road leads left to the junction with Mill Road, where we find Beauvale School, the former Board School which Lawrence attended for five not very happy years. He left in 1898 to take up a scholarship at Nottingham High School.

The surrounding countryside is richly associated with Lawrence. Of the nearby places to visit, Underwood (2 miles) is reached by following Dovecote Road and then branching left on B600. To the right we pass the village of Greasley, from which New Road leads north to the ruins of Beauvale Priory, scene of the short story 'A Fragment of Stained Glass.' Also to the right of B600 we see Moorgreen Reservoir, the 'Nethermere' of *Sons and Lovers* and, most memorably, the 'Willey Water' where the drowning takes place in *Women in Love* (Ch. 14). B600 joins A608, which is followed briefly north to the turning for Felley Mill Lane on the right. South of the lane lies Haggs Farm, home of Lawrence's friend Jessie Chambers. It appears in *Sons and Lovers* as 'Willey Farm' and Lawrence's relations with Jessie Chambers are used as the basis for Paul's romance with Miriam.

The village of Cossall (off A6096 4 miles SE of Eastwood) is the 'Cossethay' of *The White Peacock* and *The Rainbow*. Church Cottage was the home of Alfred Burrows and his daughter Louisa, to whom Lawrence was briefly engaged. Burrows' interest in woodcarving, represented in the rebuilt Victorian church, left its mark on the portrait of Will Brangwen in *The Rainbow*. Marsh Farm, which stood near the canal bridge, has gone.

Over the Derbyshire border NW of Eastwood, two places are of particular note. Wingfield Manor, a ruined 15C manor house where Mary Queen of Scots was imprisoned, is visited by Paul and Miriam in *Sons and Lovers* (Ch. 7). It lies 6 miles SE of Matlock, near the village of South Wingfield and south of B5035. Middleton (on B5023 4½ miles SW of Matlock) was Lawrence's home in 1918–19, shortly before he quitted England for good. At Mountain Cottage, with magnificent views of the Via Gellia, he worked on the book that eventually became *Studies in Classic American Literature*.

East of Lawrence's hometown three widely dispersed places demand a visit. Nottingham, of course, was well known to him as the urban centre nearest Eastwood. The High School he attended from 1898 to 1901, its Victorian buildings since greatly enlarged, can be found on Arboretum Street north of the Arboretum. On Shakespeare Street to the south are the former buildings of University College, now housing a polytechnic. Lawrence studied for his Teacher's Certificate here in 1906–08 and in Chapter 15 of *The Rainbow* he endowed Ursula Brangwen with some of his own reactions to the place. She moves from initial delight with the college ('Its rather pretty, plaything, Gothic form was almost a style in the dirty, industrial town') to disillusionment: 'the whole thing seemed sham, spurious; spurious Gothic arches, spurious peace, spurious Latinity, spurious dignity of France, spurious naïveté of Chaucer.' Southwell (on A612 12 miles NE of Nottingham) appears in Chapter 23 of *Women in Love*, when Ursula and Birkin view what Lawrence uncharitably calls its 'rigid, sombre, ugly cathedral' before having tea in the nearby Saracen's Head. *Lincoln Cathedral (A46, 23 miles NE of Southwell) is memorably evoked in *The Rainbow*. The description of Will and Anna's visit in Chapter 7 has an important place in the tradition of writing about Gothic architecture which stems from Ruskin (q.v.).

Elsewhere in England we can find reminders of the unsettled years between 1908, when Lawrence left the region of his birth, and 1919, when he and his wife Frieda finally left the country for a widening circle of travel that embraced the Continent, Australia, America and Mexico. His first teaching post (1908–12) was at Croydon in south London. The Davidson School, then newly opened, stands on Davidson Road as it leads north from Lower Addiscombe Road (A222), following the route of the railway line between East Croydon and Norwood Junction (British Rail). For portraits of Lawrence's fellow teachers we should turn to his second novel, *The Trespasser*. His Croydon lodgings were at No. 12 Colworth Road, south of Lower Addiscombe Road near Bingham Road station (British Rail). In 1915, the bitter period that saw the prosecution of *The Rainbow*, he returned to live in London. The Hampstead lodgings he shared with Frieda were at No. 1 Byron Villas, in The Vale of Health near North End Way, and are now marked by a plaque.

1915, too, saw Lawrence's first visit to Lady Ottoline and Philip Morrell at Garsington Manor (off B480 4 miles SE of Oxford). It was inevitable that he should at some point have come to this gathering place for the hopeful, promising or distinguished writers of his generation, and appropriate that he should have come during the First World War, when Garsington served as a centre for the disaffected. Yet it is surprising that Garsington, with its elegant and mildly aristocratic tone, should have played so important a part in Lawrence's development. With a fellow guest, Bertrand Russell, he formed an energetic if short-lived friendship and with Lady Ottoline herself an intimate and confidential friendship superbly captured in his letters during the years that followed. The conversations in *Women in Love* owe much to the intellectual atmosphere of Garsington and in the character of Hermione Roddice we may detect a sharp, though not entirely dismissive, portrait of its hostess.

That novel was finished in Cornwall, where Lawrence went from Hampstead in early 1916. He and Frieda first stayed with J.D. Beresford at St Merryn, 2 miles west of Padstow on the Camel estuary. At the end of February they moved SW to Zennor (on B3306 4 miles west of St Ives) where they rented Higher Tregerthen, a cottage by the coast NE of the village. Lawrence, whose mind was much occupied by schemes for removing himself from the decadence of Europe and the horrors of the First World War, at first believed that he had made a significant step in that direction. He told Katherine Mansfield, who visited him with John Middleton Murry, in a letter:

> I love being here in Cornwall—so peaceful, so far off from the world. But the world has disappeared for ever—there is no more world any more: only here, and a fine thin air which nobody and nothing pollutes.

But the world does not leave Utopian writers to their own devices, and the Lawrences' stay turned into a nightmarish version of Wordsworth and Coleridge's stay at Nether Stowey (s.v. Lake Poets, Rte 5). First Lawrence had to undergo 'the loathsome performance' of medical examination—and rejection—by the Army. Then local suspicion was aroused by the fact that Frieda was German and by a light accidentally shining in a window that overlooked a bay where German submarines prowled. In October 1917 the police came, searched the house and ordered Lawrence to leave Cornwall. He reported, rather mildly, to Lady Cynthia Asquith that the behaviour of the authorities was 'very sickening, and makes me very weary' but Frieda afterwards said that his Cornish experience changed something in him permanently. He was to remain in England for another two years, but faith in his native land had been extinguished.

Eastwood Library. Open Mon, Tues, Thurs 9.30–1, 2–7.30, Fri 9.30–7.30, Sat 9.30–1.

Lawrence Birthplace Museum, Eastwood. Open Mon, Tues, Thurs, Fri & Sun 1.30–4, Wed 9.30–12, Sat 9.30–4. Closed 24 Dec to 1 Jan. Fee.

D.H. Lawrence 'Breach' House, Eastwood. Open all year at similar times to Birthplace Museum. Fee.

Garsington Manor. Gardens open under NGS. Fee.

T.E. Lawrence

b. Tremadog, Gwynedd, 1888; d. Bovington, Dorset, 1935. *Seven Pillars of Wisdom* (privately printed, 1926; publicly issued, 1935); *Revolt in the Desert* (1927); *Crusader Castles* (1936); *The Mint: Notes Made in the RAF Depot Between August and December 1922, and at Cadet College in 1925 by 352087 A/C Ross* (privately printed, 1936; publicly issued, 1955).

The soldier, scholar and writer was born at Tremadog, a 19C town developed by W.A. Madocks, at the junction of A498 and A487 south of Snowdon and near the Welsh coast. His birthplace, Woodlands, is now marked by a plaque.

Lawrence's mother and father were not married (she was the governess for whom he had deserted wife and children) and their embarrassment about this irregular liaison made Lawrence's early childhood itinerant. By the time he was eight his parents had finally settled in Oxford and in 1907 he entered Jesus College with an Exhibition in History. During his undergraduate years he abandoned his interest in medieval culture, inspired by the example of William Morris (q.v.), in favour of Middle Eastern archaeology. An expedition to Syria in 1909 resulted in the thesis that gained him a First, later published as *Crusader Castles*. After the First World War he returned to Oxford a national celebrity, one of the few romantic legends to have emerged from an unromantic war. He took up a Fellowship at All Souls in 1919 and worked on the book which, after much rewriting, became *Seven Pillars of Wisdom*.

Always made uneasy by his reputation as 'Lawrence of Arabia,' he spent much of his subsequent life in an attempt to retire from publicity. In 1922 he joined the RAF as an aircraftman under the name 'John Hume Ross' but was forced to leave the next year when the press discovered his identity. As 'T.E. Shaw' he joined the Tank Corps and was posted to Bovington Camp, north of A352 between Wareham and Dorchester in south Dorset. He was a frequent and welcome visitor to Thomas Hardy (q.v.) at his Dorchester home. The little cottage of *Clouds Hill, on an unclassified road north of the camp, became an important refuge from the Army life he hated. Lawrence repaired the building and spent his evenings here writing. It remained his closest approach to a real home in the unsettled years that followed, when he left the Army to rejoin the RAF. When he was discharged in 1935 he returned here with plans to start a small printing press. Clouds Hill is still, as E.M. Forster (q.v.) said, 'the real framework, the place which his spirit will never cease to haunt.'

A few months after his discharge Lawrence died in a motorcycle accident on the road between Clouds Hill and Bovington Camp, and he was buried in the cemetery opposite the church at Moreton, west of the camp. His friend Winston Churchill attended the funeral and mourned a man whom he had hoped would 'quit his retirement and take a commanding part in facing the dangers which now threaten the country.' St Martin's church at Wareham has an effigy of Lawrence in Arab costume by Eric Kennington.

The same artist was responsible for the bust in the crypt of St Paul's Cathedral in London.

Clouds Hill, Wareham (NT). Open Apr to Sept, Wed, Thurs, Fri, Sun, BH Mon 2–5; Oct to March, Sun 1–4. Fee.

Crypt, St Paul's Cathedral. Open Mon to Fri 10–3.15 (4.15 in summer), Sat 11–3.15 (4.15 in summer). Entrance may be restricted during special services. Fee.

Edward Lear

b. London, 1812; d. San Remo, Italy, 1888. *A Book of Nonsense* (1846; enlarged edition, 1861); *Illustrated Excursions in Italy* (1846); *Journal of a Landscape Painter in Greece and Albania* (1852); *Journal of a Landscape Painter in Southern Calabria and the Kingdom of Naples* (1852); *Views of the Seven Ionian Islands* (1863); *Journal of a Landscape Painter in Corsica* (1870); *Nonsense Songs, Stories, Botany and Alphabets* (1871); *More Nonsense, Pictures, Rhymes, Botany etc.* (1872); *Laughable Lyrics* (1877).

Lear's most memorable contribution to literary topography, of course, was to people the English landscape with figures like the 'imprudent old person of Slough,' the 'romantic old person of Putney' and the 'uncommon old man of Blackheath.' By comparison to this surreal abundance his real connections with English places are few and inexpressive.

In 1831 he took rooms at No. 124 Albany Street in London to be near the Zoological Gardens in Regent's Park (west), where he was drawing life studies of the parrots.

Between 1832 and 1837 he stayed at Knowsley Hall, 6 miles east of Liverpool and east of M57, drawing the animals in the Earl of Derby's menagerie. The nonsense verses and sketches for which he became famous started as a means of entertaining the children in the household, whose company he seems to have preferred to the 'uniformly apathetic tone' of adult society at Knowsley. The Hall is not open to the public but its grounds contain a Safari Park.

After the work at Knowsley was finished he mainly lived abroad, leaving a record of his travels in books and landscape paintings that waited too long for proper recognition. Return visits to England several times took him to the Isle of Wight. In the summer of 1846 he acted as drawing master to the young Queen Victoria at Osborne House, by A3021 SE of East Cowes. Her diary records that he taught 'remarkably well.' He was also a guest of Tennyson (q.v.) at Farringford near Freshwater on the western tip of the island.

During visits to London in 1857–59 he stayed just north of Marble Arch at No. 30 Seymour Street (reached via Great Cumberland Place; then No. 16 Upper Seymour Street and now marked with a GLC plaque). His letters from this address are headed 'Hupper Seemore Street.'

Knowsley Safari Park, near Liverpool. Open daily 1 March to 31 Oct 10–4. Fee.

Osborne House, East Cowes (DoE). Open 4 Apr to end Aug, Mon to Sat 10–5; Sept to early Oct, Mon to Sat 11–5. Fee.

Sheridan Le Fanu

b. Dublin, 1814; d. Dublin, 1873. *The Cock and the Anchor: Being a Chronicle of Old Dublin City* (1845); *Ghost Stories and Tales of Mystery* (1851); *The House* by the Churchyard (1863); *Wylder's Hand* (1864); *Uncle Silas: A Tale of Barham-Haugh* (1864); *In A Glass Darkly* (1872).

Sheridan Le Fanu spent his whole life in Dublin. The supernatural tales and novels for which he is remembered belong to the years of seclusion after his wife's death in 1850, when he was living at No. 70 (then No. 18) Merrion Square, SE of Trinity College (where he had been a student). *The House by the Churchyard* is set in Chapelizod, west of Dublin. Le Fanu is buried in Mount Jerome Cemetery for Protestants in the suburb of Harold's Cross, about 2 miles south of the city centre.

Matthew Gregory ('Monk') Lewis

b. London, 1775; d. at sea, 1818. *Ambrosio, or The Monk* (1796); *The Castle Spectre* (1798).

For a man whose writing has much to do with the horrors of the charnel house, 'Monk' Lewis still managed to spend his life at a succession of unimpeachably respectable places. From the age of eight to fifteen he attended London's Westminster School, in Little Dean's Yard to the south of Westminster Abbey. During the years 1790–94 he studied at Christ Church, Oxford, though without great application and with frequent Continental interludes. In 1809 he bought—for 600 guineas—London chambers in the exclusive Albany, north of Piccadilly. After dining with him Byron (q.v.), himself also a resident of the Albany, noted contemptuously that he had 'looking-glass panels to his book-cases.'

Like many literary men of the time he was a guest, if not always a welcome one, at Holland House in Holland Park, where only the grounds and east wing of the original Tudor mansion now remain. After their first meeting in 1797 the fashionable Lady Holland reported: 'He is little in person, rather ugly and shortsighted; upon the whole not engaging, though better than I expected.' The two never agreed. Toward the end of one quarrel Lewis protested at her rudeness to him: 'She replied that when people forc'd themselves into a House against the will of its owners, they must take the consequence. He said he would remain no longer: she, the sooner he went the better.'

He found more romantic surroundings and less stormy hospitality at the Duke of Argyll's seat, Inverary Castle, on the northern shore of Loch Fyne in Strathclyde. When he met Sir Walter Scott (q.v.) here in 1798 he paid flattering attention to his poetry, then unknown. The castle is notable for its sumptuous interiors and collection of art.

Lewis was buried at sea after dying of fever on the way back from his Jamaican plantations.

Inverary Castle. Open 7 Apr to end June, 1 Sept to end Oct, Mon to Thurs 10–1, 2–6, Sun 1–6; July & Aug, Mon to Sat 10–6, Sun 1–6. Fee.

Richard Lovelace

b. London, 1618; d. London, 1658. Cavalier poet.

Of Lovelace's life there are only scanty topographical reminders. In the City of London the fine 16C–18C buildings formerly used by his old school, Charterhouse, survive on Charterhouse Square near the Central Meat Market and have been well restored. In Westminster Abbey Gatehouse, where he was imprisoned because of his Royalist sympathies in 1642, he wrote perhaps his best known poem, 'To Althea, from Prison,' whose last stanza begins: 'Stone Walls doe not a Prison make,/ Nor Iron bars a Cage.' The poem remains while the stone walls, which stood near the main entrance to the Abbey, do not. This 'handsome man, but prowd,' as John Aubrey described him, spent his impoverished last years on Shoe Lane (formerly Gunpowder Alley) leading north from Fleet Street, and on Rose Street off Long Acre and north of the Strand ('in a cellar,' specifies Aubrey with a typically colourful flourish). He was buried in the church preceding Wren's St Bride's, south of Fleet Street.

Lovelace inherited land in Kent, part of a patrimony spent on the Royalist cause, and lived for a time in Canterbury at Greyfriars. Originally part of England's first Franciscan Friary, it is pleasantly situated in a garden by the river, off Stour Street.

Charterhouse, City of London. Visitors by written appointment only.

Greyfriars, Canterbury. Visitors should apply to the Chapter Office, No. 8 The Precincts, for the key.

John Lydgate

b. Lidgate, Suffolk, 1370?; d. place uncertain, 1451? Poet.

This prolific but largely neglected writer, self-proclaimed disciple and on occasion imitator of Chaucer (q.v.), derived his name from the small village of his birth, on B1085 7 miles SE of Newmarket in Suffolk. The Tudor half-timbered Suffolk House on the village street stands on the site of an earlier building in which he may have been born. The small 15C brass of a priest (head replaced) in the church of St Mary is said to represent him. His education and admission into holy orders associated him with the Abbey at Bury St Edmunds (to the NE), which enjoys a rival claim to Lidgate as his final resting place. In *The Worthies of England* (1662) the antiquary Thomas Fuller, though vague about the location of Lydgate's grave, quotes his Latin epitaph and renders it into English:

> Dead in this world, living above the sky,
> Intombed within this urn doth Lydgate lie,
> In former time famed for his poetry,
>   All over England.

At Long Melford, 12 miles south of Bury St Edmunds via A134, the magnificent *Clopton Chantry of the church has its ceiling decorated with verses ascribed to Lydgate.

Bury St Edmunds Abbey (English Heritage). Open Apr to Sept, Mon to Sat 9.30–6.30, Sun 2–6.30; Oct to March, 9–4.

John Lyly

b. place unknown in Kent, 1554?; d. London, 1606. *Euphues, the Anatomy of Wit* (1578); *Euphues and his England* (1580); *Alexander and Campaspe* (1584); *Endimion* (1591).

Lyly was educated at Magdalen College, Oxford between 1569 and 1573. He also received an M.A. from Cambridge in 1579, though it is not known to which college he was attached, and later paid tribute to both universities in the courtly, balanced language that gave the word 'euphuism' to the history of English prose style:

> I meane not in the way of controuersie to preferre any for the better in Englande, but both for the best in the world, sauing this, that Colledges in *Oxenford* are much more stately for the building, and *Cambridge* much more sumptuous for the houses in the towne, but the learning neither lyeth in the free stones of the one, nor the fine streates of the other, for out of them both do dayly proceede men of great wisedome, to rule in the common welth, of learning to instruct the common people, of all singuler kinde of professions to do good to all. (*Euphues and his England*)

He was buried in the City of London at St Bartholomew-the-Less. The church, which has a 15C tower and a 19C octagonal addition of considerable charm, stands in the precincts of St Bartholomew's Hospital, north of Newgate Street.

Edward Bulwer-Lytton, First Baron Lytton

b. London, 1803; d. Torquay, Devon, 1873. *Falkland* (1827); *Pelham* (1828); *Paul Clifford* (1830); *Eugene Aram* (1832); *Godolphin* (1833); *England and the English* (1833); *Pilgrims of the Rhine* (1834); *The Last Days of Pompeii* (1834); *Rienzi* (1835); *Ernest Maltravers* (1837); *Zanoni* (1842); *The Last of the Barons* (1843); *The Caxtons* (1850); *My Novel* (1853).

The list above provides only a partial record of the long and industrious career that earned Lytton a place among the most popular novelists of his age. His most important memorial is Knebworth House in Hertfordshire, ½ a mile west of A1(M) and reached from the junction north of Welwyn Garden City via B656. During Lytton's childhood his widowed mother altered the Tudor mansion by pulling down three of its wings and Gothicising the fourth. Lytton further elaborated its appearance after he inherited Knebworth in 1843. Externally, the result is not one of the century's happiest exercises in medievalism, though the *State Drawing Room inside is a spirited example of Victorian Gothic. Dickens (q.v., Rte 14) used the largely 17C Great Hall for amateur theatricals in 1850 and Swinburne (q.v.) was a guest in 1866.

In London the novelist lived at No. 36 Hertford Street, near the southern end of Park Lane, from 1829 until 1835. These were the years of his marriage to the unstable and eccentric Rosina; their son, who published poetry under the pseudonym of 'Owen Meredith,' was born here in 1831. After he separated from his wife Lytton kept an apartment in the secluded and exclusive Albany, north of Piccadilly and a fitting address for a writer who had to some extent modelled himself on Byron (q.v.). He apparently owed the honour of burial in Westminster Abbey more to his ancestry and political career than to his literary achievements, for he lies not in Poets' Corner but in the Chapel of Saints Edmund and Thomas the Martyr on the south side of the ambulatory.

Knebworth House, near Stevenage. Open 1 Apr to 21 May, Sun & BH Mon 11.30–4.30; 1 June to 15 Sept, Tues to Sun & BH Mon 11.30–4.30; 15 Sept to 30 Sept, Sun 11.30–4.30. Fee.

Louis MacNeice

b. Belfast, 1907; d. London, 1963. *Blind Fireworks* (1929); *Poems* (1935); *The Agamemnon of Aeschylus* (1936); *Out of the Picture* (1937); *Letters from Iceland* (with W.H. Auden [q.v.]; 1937); *I Crossed the Minch* (1938); *Zoo* (1938); *Modern Poetry: A Personal Essay* (1938); *The Earth Compels, Poems* (1938); *Autumn Journal* (1939); *Poems 1925–40* (1940); *Plant and Phantom* (1941); *The Poetry of W.B. Yeats* (1941); *Springboard, Poems 1941–1944* (1944); *Christopher Columbus* (1944); *The Dark Tower and Other Radio Scripts* (1947); *Holes in the Sky, Poems 1944–1947* (1948); *Collected Poems 1925–1948* (1949); *Goethe's Faust, Parts I and II* (with E.L. Stahl; 1951); *Ten Burnt Offerings* (1952); *Autumn Sequel* (1954); *The Other Wing* (1954); *Visitations* (1957); *Eighty-Five Poems* (1959); *Solstices* (1961); *The Burning Perch* (1963); *Astrology* (1964); *The Strings Are False* (1965).

The poet was born in Belfast but brought up in Carrickfergus, 10 miles NE of the city on Belfast Lough. Its days as a bustling port with a 'bottle-neck harbour' are remembered in the autobiographical poem 'Carrickfergus.'

At the age of ten MacNeice was sent to England and the public school at Sherborne (on A30 in Dorset), where another future poet, C. Day-Lewis (q.v.), was also a pupil. In 1921 he moved to Marlborough College in Wiltshire and, always lucky in his schoolfellows, met John Betjeman (q.v.).

Both these friendships continued when MacNeice entered Merton College, Oxford in 1926. To them was added a close association with W.H. Auden (q.v.), the most commanding figure in the circle of young Oxford poets. Otherwise, if we accept his own self-deprecating account in *The Strings Are False*, his years at Merton were depressing. He soon tired of 'watching the Jacobean buildings turn plum-coloured at tea-time' and discovered that 'in Oxford homosexuality and "intelligence," heterosexuality and brawn, were almost inexorably paired. This left me out in the cold and I took to drink' (Ch. 19).

Drink did not prevent him getting the First in Classics which launched his career as a university teacher, first at Birmingham University, where he was alerted to the economic miseries of the 1930s, and then at Bedford College in London. He left academics in 1941 to begin a twenty-year stint as producer and script editor in the features department of the BBC, work that led to his distinguished radio play, *The Dark Tower*, and brought him into contact with Dylan Thomas (q.v.).

Christopher Marlowe

b. Canterbury, Kent, 1564; d. London, 1593. *Tamburlaine* (1590); *The Tragedy of Dr Faustus* (1604); *The Jew of Malta* (1633); *Edward II* (1594); *The Massacre at Paris* (1600); *Hero and Leander* (later continued by George Chapman [q.v.]; 1593).

A profitable walking tour of Canterbury, the city of Marlowe's birth and education, begins near the southern end of St George's Street at the church of St George the Martyr, where he was baptised in February 1564. The building suffered heavy bomb damage during the Second World War and only the shell of its tower remains. The same war-time raid destroyed the dramatist's reputed birthplace on the corner of St George's Street and St George's Lane nearby. We then follow St George's Street NW towards the city centre until, shortly after it becomes Parade Street, a right turn on Mercery Lane leads via Christ Church Gate to the Cathedral, where Marlowe regularly attended services during his schooldays. Of particular interest is the tomb (1625) of his fellow pupil at Canterbury and fellow student at Cambridge, John Boys, in the Lady Chapel. An extreme example of Jacobean realism, it shows Boys looking towards the altar and seated by a table with an open book; the sides and back of the monument are carved to represent bookcases. The NW transept of the Cathedral gives access to the Cloister where, in the NE corner, the modern library of the Chapter House contains a collection including Renaissance editions of books Marlowe knew as well as the octagonal base of the Early English font from St George. By following the passage between the Chapter House and its library and continuing through the Infirmary Cloister we reach the buildings of King's School, where Marlowe was a pupil. The Norman exterior staircase in the NW corner of Green Court is worth special attention.

As an addition to this tour the visitor may take Rose Lane, which runs from the junction of Parade Street and St George's Street, becomes Marlowe Avenue and leads to the gardens of the Dane John. They contain a late 19C memorial to the dramatist in the form of a statue, the Muse of Poetry, by Onslow Ford.

At Hackington, immediately north of the city and reached via St Peter's Lane, The Causeway and St Stephen's Pathway, the church of St Peter has a striking monument to Sir Roger Manwood (d. 1592), Marlowe's earliest patron and subject of an elegy. It combines a waist-high coloured bust of Sir Roger with a skeleton.

Marlowe entered Corpus Christi College, Cambridge in 1581, receiving his B.A. in 1583 and M.A. in 1587. The 14C 'Old Court, the oldest in Cambridge and then the only court of the College, has a plaque on its north side commemorating his residence there. A portrait of 1585 almost certainly depicting Marlowe hangs in the Hall; it bears a motto entirely appropriate to his life, 'Quod me nutruit me destruit' ('What nourishes me destroys me').

London retains nothing to remind the visitor of Marlowe's short but highly successful career as a dramatist, though some account of the areas connected with the Renaissance theatre may be found under the entry for Shakespeare. The only place to attract the visitor is in SE London at Deptford, where Marlowe met his early, violent death as the result of either a drunken quarrel or the political intrigues in which he was undoubtedly involved. He was buried at the parish church of St Nicholas—north of Deptford Church Street, itself reached from Deptford Broadway—in a spot which tradition places near the north wall of the 15C tower. The interior, badly damaged by war-time bombing, has a modern tablet replacing an older one in his memory. Its inscription concludes by quoting from the Epilogue to his best-known play, *Dr Faustus*: 'Cut is the branch that might have grown full straight.'

Captain Frederick Marryat

b. London, 1792; d. Langham, Norfolk, 1848. *The King's Own* (1832); *Peter Simple* (1834); *Jacob Faithful* (1834); *Japhet In Search of a Father* (1836); *Mr Midshipman Easy* (1836); *Snarleyyow: or the Dog Fiend* (1837); *The Phantom Ship* (1839); *Masterman Ready* (1841–42); *The Children of the New Forest* (1847).

In 1830 Captain Marryat retired from the Navy, which he had entered when he was fourteen, and devoted himself to writing novels drawn largely from his experience of the sea. From 1843 until his death he lived on his small estate at Langham, a village near the Norfolk coast, 14 miles west of Cromer via A149 and B1388. The house where he wrote his famous children's story, *The Children of the New Forest*, has gone but he is remembered in the church and buried in the churchyard.

John Marston

b. Coventry, West Midlands?, 1576; d. London, 1634. *The Metamorphosis of Pigmalion's Image and Certain Satyres* (1598); *The Scourge of Villanie* (1598); *Antonio's Revenge* (with John Webster; 1602); *The Malcontent* (1604); *Eastward Hoe!* (with George Chapman and Ben Jonson [qq.v.]; 1605); *The Dutch Courtesan* (1605).

Marston was educated at Brasenose College, Oxford between 1591 or 1592 and 1594. He may have lived in Oxford again sometime between 1606 and 1609; he was certainly ordained deacon in the latter year at the pleasant village of Stanton Harcourt, 5 miles west of the city.

The intervening period, when Marston gained his often controversial reputation as satirist and dramatist, was spent in London. He was closely connected with that fertile breeding ground of Renaissance literary talent, the Middle Temple, which lies between Fleet Street and the Victoria Embankment. His father was Reader there and he himself was in residence by 1595, though he appears to have shown no very strong interest in the law. He was buried in the Temple Church, one of England's few remaining round churches, reached from Fleet Street via Inner Temple Lane. His gravestone, marked by the inscription 'Oblivioni Sacrum,' has since vanished.

Between 1616 and 1631 he was Rector of Christchurch, Dorset, a harbour town to the east of Bournemouth and notable for its lovely Priory Church.

Andrew Marvell

b. Winestead, Humberside, 1621; d. London, 1678. Metaphysical poet.

Marvell was born at the Old Rectory (since rebuilt) in Winestead, 14 miles west of Kingston-upon-Hull on A1033. His family moved to Hull in 1624 when his father became vicar of the fine Church of the Holy Trinity, by the Market Place and near the confluence of the Hull and the Humber; the poet himself was educated at the Old Grammar School, a 16C building to the south of the church. He was MP for Hull from 1658 until his death.

Between 1650 and 1652 Marvell was tutor to Mary, daughter of General Fairfax at Nun Appleton House in Appleton Roebuck, 7 miles south of York. To this period and place belong several of his best poems, 'The Mower,' 'The Garden' and, of course, 'Upon Appleton House,' a work whose importance to the tradition of country house poetry makes the subsequent rebuilding of Nun Appleton all the more regrettable. A better relic of the period is at Bilbrough, 3 miles NW and by the A64: the magnificent tomb of General Fairfax (d. 1671) in the Victorian church of St James. Marvell's own familiarity with the area is shown by his 'Upon the Hill and Grove at Bill-borow.' He was buried in London at an earlier church on the site of St Giles-in-the-Fields, on St Giles High Street, near St Giles Circus. The present church, dating from the early 18C, has a memorial tablet in the north aisle.

John Masefield

b. Ledbury, Hereford and Worcester, 1878; d. Clifton Hampden, Oxfordshire, 1967. *Salt-Water Ballads* (1902); *Ballads* (1903); *The Tragedy of Nan and Other Plays* (1909); *The Tragedy of Pompey the Great* (1910); *Ballads and Poems* (1910); *Lost Endeavour* (1910); *The Everlasting Mercy* (1911); *The Widow in the Bye Street* (1912); *Good Friday: A Dramatic Poem* (1916); *Reynard the Fox: Or the Ghost Heath Run* (1919); *Sard Harker* (1924); *The Trial of Jesus* (1926); *The Midnight Folk* (1927); *The Coming of Christ* (1928); *The Bird of Dawning* (1933); *The Box of Delights* (1933).

Masefield spent his childhood in Ledbury, on A449 8 miles SW of Great Malvern. His birthplace, The Knapp, is a big Victorian house in the north of the little town. Local tales and the beautiful surrounding countryside of the Malvern Hills appear frequently in his verse, especially *The Everlasting Mercy*, *The Widow in the Bye Street* and the Chaucerian *Reynard the Fox*.

He enrolled as a sea cadet at the age of thirteen, later deserting the merchant service for a roving life, before arriving in London in 1897 to start his career as journalist and writer. In 1912 he and his wife went to live in Hampstead at No. 13 Well Walk, the picturesque street reached from the top of Hampstead High Street via Flask Walk. In these years, when his poetry was first attracting notice, he was an intimate of Yeats (q.v.), visiting the Irish poet at his London home in Woburn Walk and at Lady Gregory's estate in Ireland. Masefield was one of many writers to carve his initials on the famous Autograph Tree in the grounds of Coole Park, described in the entry for Yeats. In later life Masefield left London to be near countryside reminiscent of the scenes of his childhood. His writing celebrated England as 'A land of downs inestimably fair,/ With cornfields, apple-orchards, fruits and spires' ('On England,' lines 10–11). From 1919 until 1933 he lived at Boar's Hill, beyond A34 SW of Oxford. His house, Hill Crest, has since been renamed Masefield House. From 1939 until his death he lived in Clifton Hampden, a village 10 miles south of the city via A34 and A415. His home, Burcote Brook, burned down shortly after his death and the Masefield Leonard Cheshire Home for the disabled now stands on its site.

Masefield, who had been Poet Laureate since 1930, was buried in Poets' Corner (fee) of Westminster Abbey.

Philip Massinger

b. Salisbury, Wiltshire, 1583; d. London, 1640. *A New Way to Pay Old Debts* (1633).

This prolific dramatist, best remembered for the comedy named above, was baptised in Salisbury at the 15C church of St Thomas, north of the Cathedral and near the junction of High Street, Bridge Street and Silver Street. His father was confidential servant to the second Earl of Pembroke and so Massinger was probably brought up at the fine mansion of Wilton House, west of Salisbury. He studied at St Alban Hall, later incorporated into Merton College, Oxford between 1602 and 1606, when he left without taking a degree. He was buried in London at Southwark Cathedral (then St Saviour's), immediately south of London Bridge and at the head of Borough High Street, supposedly in the same grave as another dramatist, John Fletcher (q.v.).

Wilton House, near Salisbury. Open mid Apr to mid Oct, Tues to Sat & BH Mon 11–6, Sun 1–6. Fee.

Charles Robert Maturin

b. Dublin, 1782; d. Dublin, 1824. *Bertram, or the Castle of St Aldobrand* (1816); *Women, or Pour et Contre* (1818); *Melmoth the Wanderer* (1820); *The Albigenses* (1824); *Five Sermons on the Errors of the Roman Catholic Church* (1824).

Except for a brief period in London when his Gothic play, *Bertram*, succeeded at Drury Lane and its successors flopped, Maturin's life belonged almost wholly to Dublin. He studied at Trinity College (1795–1800) and later supplemented his income as curate of St Peter's by running a school at his home, No. 37 York Street, west of St Stephen's Green.

Somerset Maugham

b. Paris, France, 1874; Cap Ferrat, France, 1965. *Liza of Lambeth* (1897); *The Making of a Saint: A Romance of Medieval Italy* (1898); *Orientations: Short Stories* (1899); *The Hero* (1901); *Mrs Craddock* (1902); *A Man of Honour* (1903); *The Merry-Go-Round* (1904); *The Explorer* (1908); *The Magician* (1908); *Lady Frederick* (1912); *Jack Straw* (1912); *Mrs Dot* (1912); *Penelope* (1912); *Smith* (1913); *The Tenth Man* (1913); *Landed Gentry* (1913); *The Land of Promise* (1913); *Of Human Bondage* (1915); *The Moon and Sixpence* (1919); *The Unknown* (1920); *The Trembling of a Leaf: Little Stories of the South Sea Islands* (1921); *The Circle* (1921); *Caesar's Wife* (1922); *East of Suez* (1922); *On a Chinese Screen* (1922); *The Unattainable* (1923); *Our Betters* (1923); *Home and Beauty* (1923); *Loaves and Fishes* (1924); *The Painted Veil* (1925); *The Constant Wife* (1927); *The Letter* (1927); *The Sacred Flame* (1928); *Ashenden: Or The British Agent* (1928); *Cakes and Ale: Or The Skeleton in the Cupboard* (1930); *The Breadwinner* (1930); *The Gentleman in the Parlour: A Record of a Journey from Rangoon to Haiphong* (1930); *The Narrow Corner* (1932); *For Services Rendered* (1932); *Sheppey* (1933); *Ah King: Six Stories* (1933); *The Judgment Seat* (1934); *Don Fernando: Or Variations on Some Spanish Themes* (1935); *Cosmopolitans* (1936); *Theatre* (1937); *The Summing Up* (1938); *The Mixture As Before: Short Stories* (1940); *Up At the Villa* (1941); *The Hour Before Dawn* (1942); *The Razor's Edge* (1944); *Then and Now* (1946); *Creatures of Circumstance: Short Stories* (1947); *Catalina: A Romance* (1948); *A Writer's Notebook* (1949); *The Vagrant Mood: Six Essays* (1952); *Points of View* (1959); *Looking Back* (1962).

Most of Maugham's long life was spent abroad, from his birth in Paris at the British Embassy (where his father was a solicitor) to his later years in the south of France. When his father died in 1884 he was sent back to England and to the King's School in the precincts of the cathedral at Canterbury. Early scenes in *Of Human Bondage* suggest that his schooldays were unhappy, an impression confirmed by his description of the masters as 'frightening bullies' in *Summing Up* (Ch. 18). Yet Maugham made substantial benefactions to the King's School and returned in old age for the opening of its Maugham Library, which houses manuscripts and relics of him. His ashes were buried at the school.

Liza of Lambeth, the harshly realistic product of his observation of slum life while a medical student, was written in his London lodgings at No. 11 Vincent Square (off Vauxhall Bridge Road). A plaque now distinguishes No. 6 Chesterfield Street (off Curzon Street near Park Lane), the house he bought in 1909 when his plays first became hits on the London stage.

George Meredith

b. Portsmouth, Hampshire, 1828; d. Box Hill, Surrey, 1909. *Poems* (1851); *The Shaving of Shagpat: An Arabian Entertainment* (1856); *Farina: A Legend of Cologne* (1857); *The Ordeal of Richard Feverel* (1859); *Evan Harrington; or, He Would Be a Gentleman* (1860); *Modern Love and Poems of the English Roadside* (1862); *Emilia in England* (1864); *Rhoda Fleming: A Story* (1865); *Vittoria* (1867); *The Adventures of Harry Richmond* (1871); *Beauchamp's Career* (1876); *The Egoist: A Comedy in Narrative* (1879); *The Tragic Comedians: A Study in a Well-Known Story* (1880); *Poems and Lyrics of the Joy of Earth* (1883); *Diana of the Crossways* (1885); *One of Our Conquerors* (1891); *Lord Ormont and His*

Aminta: A Novel (1894); *The Amazing Marriage* (1895); *An Essay on Comedy and the Uses of the Comic Spirit* (1897).

Perhaps out of embarrassment at coming from a family of well-to-do tailors, Meredith was vague in later life about his birthplace, describing it as 'near Petersfield' and making one obituary writer suppose it to be Winchester. But it was Portsmouth, which appears—together with portraits of several relatives—as the 'prosperous town' (Ch. 1) of 'Lymport' in *Evan Harrington*. The novel is the best memorial to the writer's early years, for his birthplace at No. 73 High Street in Old Portsmouth has gone and all that survives is St Thomas, the church of his baptism, now incorporated into the Cathedral nearby.

Though never really a Londoner, Meredith had connections with London for most of his life. He was married in 1849 to Mary Ellen Peacock, daughter of the novelist, at St George's, Hanover Square, SW of Oxford Circus. He later lived in Chelsea. In 1858–59, when he was writing his first major novel, *The Ordeal of Richard Feverel*, he lodged at No. 8 Hobury Street, which runs north of King's Road between its junctions with Beaufort Street and Edith Grove. In 1862 he took as his London *pied à terre* a room in Tudor House on Cheyne Walk, the home of Dante Gabriel Rossetti (q.v.). The poet-painter's easygoing domestic habits were not to Meredith's taste and stories about the immediate cause of his departure abound. It is said that his fellow lodger Swinburne (q.v.) threw a poached egg at him for criticising Victor Hugo (q.v.), that Rossetti flung a cup of tea in his face during a quarrel over breakfast, and that Meredith took exception to the presence in the house of Fanny Cornforth, Rossetti's model and mistress.

His real homeland was in Surrey. After living in Weybridge he and his wife went in 1853 to join her father, Thomas Love Peacock (q.v.), at Lower Halliford, now part of Shepperton, on the Thames between Chertsey and Sunbury. The older writer's house, Elmbank, stands at the head of Walton Lane. When the arrangement proved unsatisfactory Meredith and his wife moved to Vine Cottage nearby on Russell Road. These were the years of *The Shaving of Shagpat* but also of the marital problems later recorded in his sonnet cycle, *Modern Love*. The marriage and Meredith's stay at Vine Cottage ended in 1858, when Mary Ellen went to the Continent with Henry Wallis, the Pre-Raphaelite painter. She died in 1861 and was buried in Shepperton churchyard. Shepperton Lock, reached via Ferry Lane from Chertsey Road, is made the meeting place of the hero and Lucy Desborough in *The Ordeal of Richard Feverel*.

Meredith remarried in 1864 in the church at Mickleham, off A24 between Dorking and Leatherhead. And in 1867 he moved to Flint Cottage, a little above Burford Bridge on Box Hill; the garden chalet where he wrote and sometimes slept was added in 1876. Flint Cottage remained his home for the rest of his long life and, when he achieved his position as a grand old man of English letters, it became a place of pilgrimage for distinguished contemporaries and aspiring younger writers. Visits from Robert Louis Stevenson (q.v.) were particularly important. Meredith's love of nature made him relish the splendid scenery of Box Hill (NT): 'I am every morning at the top of Box Hill—as its flower, its bird, its prophet. I drop down the moon on one side, I draw up the sun on t'other. I breathe fine air. I shout ha ha to the gates of the world. Then I descend and know myself a donkey for doing it.' He also took pleasure in the area's literary associations with Jane Austen, Fanny Burney and Keats (qq.v.) and added some of his own: Box Hill is the countryside of his masterpiece, *The Egoist*, and *Diana of the Crossways* makes use of Crossways Farm, to the left of A25 4 miles west of Dorking and near the village of Wotton. Meredith was buried in Dorking cemetery after Westminster Abbey refused him a place because of his attacks on conventional religion. The snub caused Hardy (q.v.) to wonder if the Abbey might not need a 'heathen annexe.'

In his later years Meredith had been a visitor to Eastern England. The sea by the esplanade at Felixstowe, 12 miles SE of Ipswich, is the scene for Matie and Browny's swin in *Lord Ormont and His Aminta*. He stayed several times in the quiet coastal town of Aldeburgh to the north: 'a place without charm, like Crabbe's poetry; only grandeur of Sea.'

John Milton

b. London, 1608; d. London, 1674. *On the Morning of Christ's Nativity* (1629); *L'Allegro* (1632); *Il Penseroso* (1632); *Comus* (1637); *Lycidas* (1637); *The Doctrine and Discipline of Divorce* (1643); *Areopagitica* (1644); *Paradise Lost* (1667); *Paradise Regained* (1671); *Samson Agonistes* (1671).

The many architectural records of Milton's near-lifetime residence in London have been obliterated. His birthplace in Bread Street off Cheapside (already a tourist attraction during his own life, according to Aubrey) was swept away by the Great Fire, together with the old buildings of St Paul's School, which he attended from 1620 or 1621 until 1624, and the other City houses associated with later periods of his life. The process of destruction has continued with the disappearance of his various residences in the Westminster area during the Commonwealth and his tenure as Secretary for Foreign Tongues to Cromwell's Council of State (1649–59).

St Margaret's, Westminster (near the Abbey) has a memorial window of 1888 at the west end of its north aisle, with verses by the American poet John Greenleaf Whittier. The address given by Matthew Arnold (q.v.) at its unveiling was later published in the Second Series of his *Essays in Criticism*. The common tradition that Milton married his second wife, Katherine Woodcock, here in 1656 is certainly wrong; the ceremony was a civil one and probably took place at the Guildhall in the City. Katherine, however, was buried in the church in 1658 with her infant daughter. In Poets' Corner (fee) of Westminster Abbey itself there is a bust to Milton, though his views on politics and religion delayed its erection until some sixty years after his death. He was buried in the same grave as his father at St Giles without Cripplegate, a much damaged and much restored medieval church in the modern Barbican; a memorial can be found at the west end of the south aisle. In 1790 the antiquary Philip Neve described the opening of what was taken to be the poet's coffin, a proceeding that was more desecration than exhumation. A local publican took some of the corpse's teeth and a pawnbroker the hair, while the gravedigger charged sixpence for a sight of the plundered remains. William Cowper (q.v.) wrote a poem in protest, 'On the Late Indecent Liberties Taken with the Remains of Milton.'

Cambridge, where Milton entered Christ's College in 1629, has happier memories to offer. Tradition points to N staircase in the College's First Court as the site of his undergraduate rooms. The identification was accepted by Wordsworth (s.v. Lake Poets, Rte 10) and *The Prelude* (Bk 3, lines 239–321) records a visit of homage in 1787, when he was an undergraduate at St John's, during which he succumbed to 'the weakness of that hour' and became uncharacteristically drunk with wine. A pleasant but unsupported story has it that Milton planted the mulberry tree at the far end of the lovely Fellows' Garden.

His first major poem, 'On the Morning of Christ's Nativity,' was written during his Cambridge years but two lesser poems belonging to the same period, 'On the University Carrier' and 'Another on the Same,' have more precise local associations. They are comic epitaphs to William Hobson, who died in 1631 after having acted as London–Cambridge coachman and letter carrier for many years. Hobson is also remembered in the phrase 'Hobson's choice,' from his habit of insisting that customers take the horse nearest the door of his livery stable or settle for no horse at all. He was buried at St Bene't's Church, the oldest in Cambridge, on Bene't Street near King's Parade.

Il Penseroso, written after Milton had left the university, remembers its atmosphere with a grave dedication that sorts ill with the traditional stories of his being badly treated as a student at Christ's:

> But let my due feet never fail
> To walk the studious Cloysters pale,
> And love the high embowed Roof,
> With antick Pillars massy proof,
> And storied Windows richly dight,
> Casting a dimm religious light.

(lines 155–160)

In *Lycidas*, an elegy for his undergraduate friend Edward King who drowned in 1637, the University appears personified as Camus, god of the river Cam: 'His mantle hairy, and his bonnet sedge,/ Inwrought with figures dim . . . ' (Lines 104–105).

Comus was first performed on 29 September 1634 in the Great Hall, now partly ruined and roofless, of *Ludlow Castle, Shropshire. The occasion marked the appointment of the Earl of Bridgewater as Lord President of Wales, as the masque's opening speech makes clear:

> And all this tract that fronts the falling sun
> A noble peer of mickle trust and power
> Had in his charge, with temper'd aw to guide
> An old and haughty nation proud in Arms.

(lines 30–34)

Henry Lawes, music tutor to the family, provided the music and acted as producer, as well as playing the part of Thyrsis, who speaks the lines just quoted. The Lady, whose survival of danger enacts virtue's triumphant resistance against evil, was played by the Earl's fifteen-year old daughter, Lady Alice Egerton; her two younger brothers were also in the cast.

At Tewkesbury Abbey (on A38 between Worcester and Gloucester) the old organ in the choir stalls is known as the 'Milton Organ' because the poet is believed to have played it when it was in Hampton Court Palace during the Commonwealth.

In 1665 plague forced Milton and his family to flee London for

Chalfont St Giles in Buckinghamshire (off A413 west of Rickmansworth). In the *'pretty box' at the end of the main street where the local Quaker Thomas Ellwood arranged accommodation for him Milton finished *Paradise Lost* and began *Paradise Regained*—a poem that Ellwood naively attributed to his own suggestion. The small building, the only surviving house Milton lived in, is now a museum and library; its collection includes first and rare editions of his poetry.

The Guildhall, City of London. Open Mon to Sat 10–5; also May to Sept, Sun (including BH) 10–5. Closed Christmas, Boxing Day, New Year's Day, Good Fri, Easter Mon.

Fellows' Garden, Christ's College, Cambridge. Open Mon to Sat 2–4.

Ludlow Castle. Open May to Sept, daily 10.30–6; Oct to Apr, Mon to Sat 10.30–4. Fee.

Milton's Cottage, Chalfont St Giles. Open Feb to Oct, Tues to Sat 10–1 & 2–6, Sun 2–6; spring and summer BH Mon 10–1 & 2–6. Fee.

Hannah More

b. Bristol, Avon, 1745; d. Bristol, 1833. *Village Politics* (1792); *Cheap Repository Tracts* (with Sarah More; 1795–98); *Coelebs in Search of a Wife* (1809).

It is convenient to begin by considering Hannah More's connections with London, since they belong to a distinct phase of her long career. On her visits from 1774 onwards she enjoyed great success in intellectual circles, winning the friendship of Sir Joshua Reynolds and Dr Johnson (q.v.), who regretted that she had not married her fellow Bristolian, Thomas Chatterton (q.v.), 'that posterity might have seen a propagation of poets.' David Garrick encouraged her play-writing career, today mercifully forgotten, and in 1776 she paid the first of several visits to his Villa (now flats) on Hampton Court Road west of the Palace, which Robert Adam had just finished modernising. She was also a guest of Horace Walpole (q.v.) at Strawberry Hill in Twickenham.

Most of her life was spent in Bristol and its surrounding area. The city preserves few reminders of her presence there. The Trinity Street school she ran with her four sisters does not survive, though the probable site of its successor at No. 43 Park Street, which runs NW of College Green, is marked by a plaque. South-east of the centre, the magnificent church of St Mary Redcliffe preserves her epitaph on Mrs Patience Little, greatly admired by Edmund Burke on one of his infrequent visits to his constituency.

After selling their school the sisters bought a house at No. 76 Great Pulteney Street in Bath, 11 miles SE of Bristol, which they used as a winter residence from 1790 until 1802. Hannah, however, thought the fashionable centre a 'foolish frivolous place.'

That judgement is a reminder of the Evangelical turn of mind for which she is chiefly remembered and which led to her later career as educator, pamphleteer and author of improving tracts. These years were largely spent SW of Bristol near the Mendip Hills. She moved in 1784 to Cowslip Green, a small village about ten miles SW of Bristol on A38, where the house praised by Walpole as 'first cousin at least to Strawberry Hill' is now Brook Lodge. When William Wilberforce visited in 1789 he was taken over the Mendips to the Cheddar Gorge and Caves but was less struck by the scenery than by the depressed condition of the local poor. Miss More and her sisters were inspired to begin a school, now the Hannah More Cottage, at Cheddar on the southern edge of the Hills. Their experiment in education grew to some twelve schools in the area before it became enmired in the so-called Blagdon Controversy (1800–03), which forced her to defend herself against the charge of Methodism.

In 1802 she moved to Barley Wood (now greatly altered), about ½ a mile NE of Wrington off A38. Her visitors included Coleridge (s.v. Lake Poets, Rte 5) and Thomas De Quincey, representatives of a younger generation unsympathetic to her Tory piety. Rather surprisingly, the poet Wordsworth 'made a conquest of Holy Hannah,' as De Quincey irreverently put it. In 1828 problems with dishonest and unruly servants forced Miss More to retire to Bristol, but she was buried with her sisters in Wrington churchyard.

William Morris

b. London, 1834; d. London, 1896. *The Defence of Guinevere and Other Poems* (1858); *The Life and Death of Jason* (1867); *The Earthly Paradise* (1868–70); *The Story of Sigurd the Volsung, and the Fall of the Niblungs* (1877); *Art and Socialism: A Lecture* (1884); *A Dream of John Ball and A King's Lesson* (1888); *News from Nowhere, or An Epoch of Rest* (1891); *The Wood Beyond the World* (1894); *The Well at the World's End* (1896); *How I Became a Socialist* (1896).

William Morris, who did so much to stimulate his countrymen's awareness of their environment in an age of mass production, rapid urban expansion and misguided restoration of Gothic buildings, deserves to be remembered by the modern traveller. The various places where he lived and worked, too scattered to be organised into a single tour, together form a powerful reminder of both his taste and the influence it has exercised on our own.

It is true that Walthamstow, where he was born and grew up, has changed in exactly the ways he deplored, its transformation from an Essex village into a suburb of NE London being now complete. Morris himself lived to mourn it as 'once a pleasant place enough, but now terribly cocknified and choked up by the jerry builder.' Yet Walthamstow has one rewarding memorial. The Water House, his childhood home from 1848 to 1856, has been converted into The *William Morris Gallery. It lies in Lloyd Park on Forest Road (A503), which runs west from A104 just south of its junction with the North Circular Road (A406). The collection offers a useful introduction to Morris' life and work. Its contents include: designs by Morris, Edward Burne-Jones and Rossetti (q.v.) for Morris and Co.; specimens of the firm's work in various media (tiles, stained glass and wallpaper); Morris furniture; books printed at the Kelmscott Press; and a rotating exhibition of Pre-Raphaelite and later paintings from the gift of the artist Sir Frank Brangwyn.

To discover the scenes that stimulated Morris' childhood imagination we need to travel north from Walthamstow into Epping Forest. By following A104 3 miles beyond its junction with the North Circular

Road and then turning left on Rangers Road (A1069) for a further 2½ miles, we reach on our right Queen Elizabeth's Hunting Lodge (now the Epping Forest Museum). Morris's lecture on 'The Lesser Arts of Life' (1882) recalled 'the impression of romance' this fine half-timbered building made upon him. Waltham Abbey, another childhood haunt, lies further north. We follow A104 from the turning for Rangers Road to the Wake Arms roundabout at 8½ miles and take A121 west for 3 miles. The fine early Norman building has a Victorian extension with a window by Burne-Jones.

Marlborough College in Wiltshire, to which Morris was sent in 1848, proved a fortunate choice. The public school's lack of regimentation or emphasis on athletics allowed him the time to explore the surrounding countryside. He came to know Savernake Forest, SE of Marlborough between the A4 and A346, and the magnificent stone circles at Avebury, 7 miles west of Marlborough on A4 and A361.

When Morris entered Exeter College, Oxford in 1853 he found the university in a crucial period of change. Its appearance was still powerfully reminiscent of the medieval city we glimpse in *The Dream of John Ball*: 'A vision of grey-roofed houses and a long winding street and the sound of many bells' (Ch. 2). Yet the present largely Victorian look of his own college was already being set by Sir Gilbert Scott's massive and gloomy Chapel (1854–60), very much the sort of exercise in Victorian Gothic from which Morris' subtler appreciation of Gothic would help to liberate English architecture. The Chapel now has a tapestry, 'The Adoration of the Magi,' designed by Burne-Jones and made by Morris. Burne-Jones' undergraduate years at Exeter coincided with Morris' own, so beginning their lifelong friendship and artistic collaboration. In their first year they had rooms overlooking the small but very pleasant Fellows' Garden.

Morris revisited Oxford in 1857 with Rossetti and Burne-Jones to decorate the Oxford Union building on St Michael's Street with frescoes depicting Arthurian romance. Their work quickly faded from the unprepared walls and the most permanent legacy of what Rossetti called 'The Jovial Campaign' was Morris' meeting with Jane Burden, whose heavy enigmatic beauty appears in so many Pre-Raphaelite paintings. They were married in 1859 at St Michael at the North Gate on Cornmarket Street, a little medieval church then just restored by G.E. Street (for whom Morris worked) and now restored again after a fire in 1953.

In November 1856 Morris and Burne-Jones took over Rossetti's old rooms in London at No. 17 Red Lion Square, south of Theobald's Road near its junction with Southampton Row. The house, on the south side of the square, is now marked with a GLC plaque. Morris' career as an interior designer began informally when he furnished the lodging to his own taste with the aid of a local carpenter—'rather doing the magnificent,' as Rossetti commented. It began formally with the creation of Morris and Co. in 1861, first housed at No. 7 nearby. Here Morris used to greet his customers in a round hat and workman's blouse that hardly suggested the gentleman, often treating their tastes and specifications with a contempt that hardly suggested the tradesman.

To gain some idea of the interiors Morris created we need to visit the Victoria and Albert Museum at the junction of Exhibition Road and Cromwell Road in South Kensington. Its •Green Dining Room or Morris Room, off Room 13 on the ground floor, was commissioned from the firm in 1866—a surprisingly early date which says much for the Museum's foresight. The panels depicting the seasons (by Burne-Jones) are especially fine. On the upper first floor Room 119 has wallpaper, carpet and tiles by Morris, as well as a wardrobe designed by Philip Webb and decorated by Burne-Jones for Morris' wedding present.

In 1860 Morris collaborated with Philip Webb in building a new home, The *Red House, at what is now Bexleyheath in SE London. The result—L-shaped, with a distinctive high-pitched roof of red tiles and deeply recessed Gothic porches—embodies a revealing paradox. Its contours look lovingly back to the simplicity of domestic Gothic, while its red brick proclaims brashness and experimentation. The Red House is reached from A2 (Rochester Way) by taking A221 (Danson Road) north and then turning right on Bean Road, which quickly leads to Red House Lane.

Morris left The Red House in 1865. Another epoch in his life, more mellow in its nostalgia for the past, was announced by a letter of 1871 to his business partner, Faulkner: 'I have been looking about for a house for the wife and kids, and whither do you guess my eye is turned now? Kelmscott, a little village about two miles above Radcot Bridge—a heaven on earth; an old stone Elizabethan house . . ., and such a garden! close down by the river, a boathouse and all things handy.' *Kelmscott Manor lies by the Thames north of Swindon and is best reached from Lechlade, at the junction of A417 and A361, via an unclassified road leading east (2 miles). Morris' daughter left it to Oxford University in 1939 and it is now owned by the Society of Antiquaries.

Although his choice of the house, which fully deserves his first enthusiastic praise, announced Morris' belief in the quieter values of a pre-industrial age, his early years at Kelmscott were not entirely peaceful. Rossetti came for a series of extended visits meant to restore the health and peace of mind which his habit of combining chloral and whisky had damaged, but his presence soon created problems. He himself was no countryman and no lover of draughty houses, however picturesque, while Morris disliked the dogs which he insisted on bringing. Rossetti's love for Jane Morris stirred deeper tensions, though the question of its fulfilment—or of Morris' attitude to that eventuality— remains a puzzle to scholars. After the final break with Rossetti in 1875 Morris continued to use the Manor as his country home until his death, making it the subject of his essay, 'Gossip About an Old House on the Upper Thames,' and the destination of the narrator's journey in News from Nowhere (Ch. 31).

He died in London but was buried at Kelmscott. The ceremony was appropriately simple and free from the commercial paraphernalia that often marred Victorian funerals, his body being brought to the church on a hay cart escorted by four countrymen. It was, remarked W.R. Lethaby, 'the only funeral I have ever seen that did not make me ashamed to have to be buried.' The gravestone in the local Cotswold style was designed by Philip Webb.

Nearby at Great Coxwell (8 miles SE of Lechlade via A417 and B4019) stands the magnificent 13C Tithe Barn which perfectly exemplifies the architectural values Morris admired and advocated. It is, as he said, 'unapproachable in its dignity, as beautiful as a cathedral, yet with no ostentation of the builder's art.'

It is understandable that Morris should have felt the need for a

London base in his later years, the period of his Socialist campaigning and of the Kelmscott Press (founded 1890). It is understandable, too, that he should have chosen Hammersmith by the Thames in SW London and remote from the fashionable West End. Yet No. 26 Upper Mall, bought from the novelist George MacDonald in 1878 and renamed Kelmscott House, is a surprising addition to the list of homes that had begun with The Red House and continued with Kelmscott Manor. The plain late eighteenth-century building hardly agrees with his taste and this, perhaps, is why the narrator of his futuristic and Utopian fantasy *News from Nowhere* finds it has been replaced by a house of more Gothic appearance:

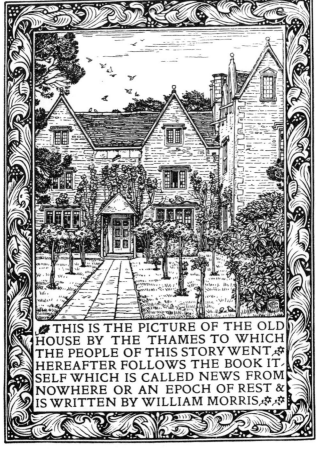

THIS IS THE PICTURE OF THE OLD HOUSE BY THE THAMES TO WHICH THE PEOPLE OF THIS STORY WENT. HEREAFTER FOLLOWS THE BOOK IT-SELF WHICH IS CALLED NEWS FROM NOWHERE OR AN EPOCH OF REST & IS WRITTEN BY WILLIAM MORRIS.

Kelmscott Manor, by William Morris. From the Kelmscott Press edition of News from Nowhere. *Courtesy of Cambridge University Library*

It was a longish building with its gable end turned away from the road,
and long traceried windows coming rather low down set in the wall that
faced us. It was very handsomely built of red brick with a lead roof; and
high up above the windows there ran a frieze of figure subjects in baked
clay, very well executed, and designed with a force and directness which
I had never noticed in modern work before. (Ch. 3)

Yeats (q.v.)—like several members of the rising literary generation,
a frequent visitor in the late 1880s and 1890s—concluded that Morris
'was an ageing man content at last to gather beautiful things rather
than to arrange a beautiful house.' Kelmscott House is now owned
by the William Morris Society. The Kelmscott Press was located first
at No. 16 and then at No. 14 on the same street.

William Morris Gallery, Walthamstow. Open Tues to Sat 10–1, 2–5 or dusk, if
earlier; also first Sun in each month 10–12, 2–5 or dusk, if earlier.

Epping Forest Museum (Queen Elizabeth's Hunting Lodge), Chingford. Open
Wed to Sun 2–6 or dusk in winter. Closed BH. Fee.

Avebury Stone Circles (English Heritage). Open at all reasonable times.

Victoria and Albert Museum, South Kensington. Open Mon to Thurs & Sat
10–5.50, Sun 2.30–5.50. Closed Christmas Eve, Christmas Day, Doxing Day,
New Year's Day & May BH.

The Red House, Bexleyheath. Visitors by written appointment (enclosing
stamped self-addressed envelope) with the owner for guided tours at 2.30 and
3.15 on first Sat and Sun of each month. Fee.

Kelmscott Manor. Open Apr to Sept, first Wed in each month 11–1, 2–5. Fee.

The Great Barn, Great Coxwell (NT). Open daily, at all reasonable hours.

Thomas Nashe (or Nash)

b. Lowestoft, Suffolk, 1567; d. place unknown, 1601?. *Pierce Penilesse his
Supplication to the Divell* (1592); *The Unfortunate Traveller, or the Life of Jacke
Wilton* (1594); *Lenten Stuffe* (1599); *Summers Last Will and Testament* (1600).

London today can boast nothing by which to remember the adult life
and career of Thomas Nashe, pamphleteer, playwright, poet and, in
The Unfortunate Traveller, proto-novelist.
   Eastern England has fared a little better. He was born at Lowestoft
on the Suffolk coast, being baptised in the parish church of St
Margaret on the NW edge of the town. In 1573 his father became
rector at West Harling, Norfolk, on the heath east of Thetford. The
small and remote village church of All Saints is best reached by
taking the A11 north from Thetford, turning right for East Harling
and Middle Harling, and then following progressively minor roads.
The seaside town of Great Yarmouth, 10 miles north of Lowestoft,
has changed greatly since the winter of 1597–98 when Nashe stayed
there to avoid the fracas caused by *The Isle of Dogs*, a play written
in collaboration with Ben Jonson (q.v.) but now lost. A vigorous
satirical description of the town, as well as a whimsical extravaganza
in praise of its local herring, appears in *Lenten Stuffe*.
   Between 1582 and 1586 he was an undergraduate at St John's
College, Cambridge, apparently remaining in the city for some time
after his graduation. His preface to *Menaphon* (1590) by Robert
Greene speaks of his old college in terms of the highest respect as

an university within itself, shining so far above all other houses, halls and hospitals whatsoever, that no college in the town was able to compare with the tithe of her students; having (as I have heard grave men of credit report) more candles lit in it every winter morning before four of the clock than the four-of-the-clock bell gave strokes.

A pamphlet entitled *The Trimming of Thomas Nashe Gentleman* (1597) and sometimes attributed to the don Gabriel Harvey, with whom Nashe engaged in a prolonged literary feud, offers a very different but probably untrustworthy account of his relations with Cambridge:

(being distracted of his wits) he fell into diuers misdemeanors . . . As namely in his fresh-time how he flourished in all impudencie toward Schollers, and abuse to the Townsmen; insomuch, that to this daye the Townes-men call euerie vntoward Scholler of whome there is great hope, *a verie Nashe.*

Nashe's connection with Sir George Carey or Carew, unique in a literary career otherwise lacking friends and patrons among the great, took him to the Isle of Wight for the winter of 1593–94. He stayed at Carisbrooke Castle, held by Sir George in his capacity as Captain General of the Isle.

Carisbrooke Castle (English Heritage). Open 15 March to 15 Oct, Mon to Sat 9.30–6.30, Sun 2–6.30 (Apr to Sept, Sun 9.30–6.30); 16 Oct to 14 March, Mon to Sat 9.30–4, Sun 2–4. Closed Christmas Eve, Christmas Day, Boxing Day & New Year's Day. Fee.

Sean O'Casey

b. Dublin, 1880; d. Torbay, Devon, 1964. *The Shadow of a Gunman* (1925); *Juno and the Paycock* (1925); *The Plough and the Stars* (1926); *The Silver Tassie* (1928); *Within the Gates* (1933); *I Knock at the Door* (1939); *The Star Turns Red* (1940); *Pictures in the Hallway* (1942); *Red Roses For Me* (1942); *Drums Under the Windows* (1945); *Oak Leaves and Lavender* (1946); *Inishfallen, Fare Thee Well* (1949); *Cock-a-Doodle Dandy* (1949); *Rose and Crown* (1952); *Sunset and Evening Star* (1954); *The Bishop's Bonfire* (1955); *The Green Crow* (1956); *The Drums of Father Ned* (1960); *Behind the Green Curtains* (1961).

A plaque now marks the site of No. 85 Upper Dorset Street (north of Grattan Bridge and Capel Street) in Dublin where O'Casey was born, thirteenth child of a poor Protestant family. An eye disease restricted his schooling and he went to work as a labourer. He was still doing manual work in the early 1920s when his plays were first performed at the Abbey Theatre. (The original theatre on Lower Abbey Street near the Custom House has been replaced by a modern building.) O'Casey's ironic view of Irish Nationalism in *The Plough and the Stars* caused a furore like that which had greeted the plays of Synge (q.v.) in the same theatre and, as on the earlier occasion, Yeats (q.v.) spoke out strongly in defence. Friendship with the older poet, then the most powerful figure in his country's letters, made O'Casey a visitor to Lady Gregory at Coole Park. His initials are among those carved on the Autograph Tree in the grounds, described in the entry for Yeats.

O'Casey first came to England in 1926. His decision to remain in exile was encouraged by his public quarrel with Yeats after the

Abbey Theatre rejected *The Silver Tassie*. The increasingly experimental direction his writing took found little favour with audiences in the commercial theatre but O'Casey played a vigorous, combative role in English literary life to the end of his days. In 1938 he moved from London to the pleasant town of Totnes (on A385 and A381 in south Devon), living at Tingrith on Ashburton Road and sending his children to school at Dartington Hall, 2 miles north. In 1954 he moved to Torquay (on the coast 9 miles NE of Totnes), where he had a flat in Villa Rosa at No. 40 Trumlands Road, St Marychurch, near the Teignmouth road.

He died in a Torbay clinic. His ashes were scattered in the Garden of Remembrance at the Golders Green Crematorium, off Finchley Road in NW London.

'George Orwell' (pseud. of Eric Blair)

b. Motihari, India, 1903; d. London, 1950. *Down and Out in Paris and London* (1933); *Burmese Days* (1934); *A Clergyman's Daughter* (1935); *Keep the Aspidistra Flying* (1936); *The Road to Wigan Pier* (1937); *Homage to Catalonia* (1938); *Coming Up for Air* (1939); *Inside the Whale, and Other Essays* (1940); *The Lion and the Unicorn: Socialism and the English Genius* (1941); *Animal Farm: A Fairy Story* (1945); *Critical Essays* (1946); *James Burnham and the Managerial Revolution* (1946); *The English People* (1947); *Politics and the English Language* (1947); *Nineteen Eighty-Four* (1949); *Shooting an Elephant, and Other Essays* (1950); *England, Your England, and Other Essays* (1953).

In infancy George Orwell was brought home from India, where his father was a Civil Servant, to Henley-on-Thames (on A423 and A4155 west of London) which he later made the 'Lower Binfield' of *Coming Up for Air*. He was educated at nearby Eton College (south of M4), though he recalled: 'I did no work there and learned very little, and I don't feel that Eton has been much of a formative influence in my life.' It was left to his friend and contemporary Cyril Connolly to describe the school's life during this period in *The Enemies of Promise*, while Orwell reserved his energies for 'Such, Such Were the Joys,' an attack on the Eastbourne preparatory school (now vanished) he had earlier attended. For much of his youth and early manhood his parent's home, to which he periodically returned after his tramping expeditions, was the genteel Suffolk coastal resort of Southwold. Their house was No. 31 High Street.

In 1934, just after the publication of his first book, Orwell went to work and lodge at Booklovers' Corner in London's Hampstead. The building (now a café) stands at the corner of Pond Street and South End Road, south of Hampstead Heath and Parliament Hill. His impressions of the area, to which he returned towards the end of the Second World War, appear in *Keep the Aspidistra Flying*.

Two rural interludes played an important part in Orwell's life. The first (1936–40) was at Wallington, 4 miles east of Baldock and A1 in Hertfordshire. He came to the village after his momentous journey to the depressed industrial north recorded in *The Road to Wigan Pier*, married his first wife Eileen in the parish church and set out from Wallington to join the Spanish Civil War. In 1946 he chose a far more isolated home on the northern end of Jura, south of Mull in the Inner Hebrides. *Nineteen Eighty-Four*, his last and most famous novel, was written here.

Though never a regular churchgoer, Orwell wished to lie in a churchyard—a final expression, perhaps, of that yearning for traditional Englishness which permeates his writing. The intervention of his friend David Astor made it possible for him to be buried at All Saints in Sutton Courtenay, a charming village 2 miles SW of Abingdon in Oxfordshire.

Eton College. Open daily 2–5 during term, 10.30–5 during spring holiday, 9–5 during summer holiday. Fee.

Thomas Otway

b. Trotton, West Sussex, 1652; d. London, 1685. *Venice Preserv'd* (1682).

Otway's father was curate of Trotton, a small village off A272 3 miles west of Midhurst; an 18C tablet in the church commemorates the writer's birth. Shortly afterwards the family moved to Woolbedding, by the A286 north of Midhurst, where the father became rector. Otway was educated at Winchester College and Christ Church, Oxford. After a career in London as a dramatist, remembered only for the tragedy *Venice Preserv'd*, he died in obscure circumstances —'in an alehouse unlamented,' according to one contemporary. He was buried at St Clement Danes in the Strand, a Wren church completed only a few years before.

Winchester College. Open Apr to Sept, Mon to Sat 10–6, Sun 2–6 (guided tours start Mon to Sat 11, 2 & 3.15, Sun 2 & 3.15); Oct to March, Mon to Sat 10–4, Sun 2–4. Fee.

Walter Pater

b. London, 1839; d. Oxford, 1894. *Studies in the History of the Renaissance* (1873); *Marius the Epicurean: His Sensations and Ideas* (1885); *Imaginary Portraits* (1887); *Appreciations, With An Essay on Style* (1889); *Plato and Platonism* (1893); *Greek Studies* (1895); *Miscellaneous Studies* (1895).

Pater's entire adult life was spent in Oxford. He was an undergraduate at The Queen's College (1858–62) and became a Fellow of Brasenose College in 1864. Though he lived with his sisters first on Bradmore Road and later on St Giles the true centre of his world was his rooms in the College's Old Quad on staircase No. 7. His friends in Oxford included Lewis Carroll (q.v.), but Pater remained modest and reclusive even when his work, with its stress on 'aesthetic' values, was exercising a strong influence over the writers of the 1880s and 1890s. The ante-chapel in Chapel Quad has a medallion showing him surrounded by Plato, Dante, Michaelangelo and Leonardo da Vinci. He is buried in the cemetery of St Cross, reached from the High Street via Longwall and Saint Cross Road.

'Emerald Uthwart,' an 'imaginary portrait' posthumously collected in *Miscellaneous Studies*, includes a lightly fictionalised reminiscence of his schooldays at the King's School, Canterbury. Among other things Pater remembers attending services in the Cathedral nearby:

> On Saturday half-holidays the scholars are taken to church in their surplices, across the court, under the lime-trees; emerge at last up the dark winding passages into the melodious, mellow-lighted space, always three days behind the temperature outside, so thick are the walls;—how warm and nice! how cool and nice! The choir, to which they glide in order to their places below the clergy, seems conspicuously cold and sad. But the empty chapels lying beyond it all about into the distance are a trap on sunny mornings for the clouds of yellow effulgence. The Angel Steeple [ie. the central tower, Bell Harry] is a lantern within, and sheds down a flood of the like just beyond the gates. You can peep up into it where you sit, if you dare to gaze about you. If at home there had been nothing great, here, to boyish sense, one seems diminished to nothing at all, amid the grand waves, wave upon wave, of patiently-wrought stone; the daring height, the daring severity, of the innumerable, long, upward, ruled lines, rigidly bent just at last, in due place, into the reserved grace of the perfect Gothic arch; the peculiar daylight which seemed to come from further than the light outside.

Coventry Patmore

b. London, 1823; d. Lymington, Hampshire, 1896. *The Angel in the House* (1854–62); *The Unknown Eros and Other Odes* (1871); *The Rod, the Root and the Flower* (1895).

Patmore's marriage to Emily Andrews—the subject of his best known poem, *The Angel in the House*—took place in 1847 at Hampstead Parish Church. St John's, an 18C building that now conspicuously remembers its connection with Keats (q.v.), stands at the end of Church Row. Their married life was mainly spent in Hampstead and adjoining Highgate.

After Emily's death in 1862 Patmore lodged at No. 14 Percy Street (now marked with a GLC plaque), which runs west from Tottenham Court Road. Visitors included Tennyson (q.v.) and various members of the Pre-Raphaelite group of painters with whom Patmore was associated. Percy Street was conveniently near the British Museum, reached from Tottenham Court Road via Great Russell Street, where he worked in the printed books department. His appointment by the Museum in the winter of 1846–47 had coincided with the completion of Robert Smirke's distinctive facade of columns. During his time there the domed Reading Room was added, built by Sydney Smirke to a plan by Patmore's superior, Sir Anthony Panizzi.

In 1864 Patmore took leave from his work to visit Rome, where he was converted to Catholicism and met his second wife, Marianne. They were married in London at the recently completed St Mary of the Angels on Moorhouse Road in Bayswater. It is reached from Westbourne Park Station (British Rail and Metropolitan Line) by taking Great Western Road south to Westbourne Park Road, which is followed to the left; we then make a right turn on to Chepstow Road and a second right on Artesian Road.

His second wife's fortune relieved Patmore from the need to return to his job at the British Museum. After several years spent enjoying the role of country gentleman he fulfilled a childhood ambition by moving to Hastings on the Sussex coast in 1875. His home was Old Hastings House (then The Mansion House), a fine Queen Anne building on the High Street of the old town. Among his visitors was Gerard Manley Hopkins (q.v.), with whom he corresponded freely, though the two poets rarely met. After Marianne's death in 1880 Patmore endowed the Roman Catholic church of St Mary Star of the Sea, also on the High Street. It was designed by his friend and future biographer, Basil Champneys.

In 1891 Patmore, already married a third time, was compelled to leave Hastings for Lymington. His last years passed in relative obscurity, though he formed a close friendship with Alice Meynell. Visits to her Bayswater home at No. 47 Palace Court (which runs north from Bayswater Road near its continuation as Notting Hill Gate) brought him into contact with her *protégé*, the poet Francis Thompson (q.v.).

British Museum & Library. Museum open Mon to Sat 10–5, Sun 2.30–6; closed Christmas Eve, Christmas Day, Boxing Day, New Year's Day, Good Fri & BH. Admission to the Library's Reading Room is by ticket only, for which written application accompanied by a letter of recommendation is required.

Thomas Love Peacock

b. Weymouth, Dorset, 1785; d. Lower Halliford, Surrey, 1866. *The Genius of the Thames* (1810); *The Philosophy of Melancholy* (1812); *Sir Hornbrook, or Childe Launcelot's Expedition: A Grammatico-Allegorical Ballad* (1813): *Sir Proteus: A Satirical Ballad* (1814); *Headlong Hall* (1816); *Melincourt* (1817); *Nightmare Abbey* (1818); *The Four Ages of Poetry* (1820); *Maid Marian* (1822); *The Misfortunes of Elphin* (1829); *Crotchet Castle* (1831); *Gryll Grange* (1860).

Although he was born on the Dorset coast Peacock spent most of his life by the banks of the Thames west of London, the stretch of countryside celebrated in his most ambitious early poem. It was an appropriately peaceful setting for a gentle poet and elegantly precise satirist, 'an idly inclined man . . . professedly so in the summer.'

We cannot be sure when he first came to live at Marlow, on A4155 between Slough and Reading, but he played host to Shelley (q.v.) at his house on West Street in 1816. The friendship was strengthened when Shelley bought Albion House on the same street, and the two writers together explored 'woody Marlow's winding vale' (*The Genius of the Thames*, Part 2, Stanza 24). They walked in Bisham Woods, over Marlow Bridge and south of A404, and boated upriver to Lechlade, at the junction of A417 and A361 10 miles NE of Swindon.

In 1823 Peacock moved to Lower Halliford, which remained his home until death; the little village has now been absorbed into Shepperton, between Chertsey and Sunbury. Elmbank, the house he converted from two cottages, stands at the head of Walton Lane with its garden reaching down to the river. George Meredith (q.v.) joined the household briefly in 1853 after his marriage to Peacock's daughter, Mary, but the arrangement was not a happy one, as the rather malicious portrait of Peacock as Dr Middleton in *The Egoist* testifies. The young couple moved to Vine Cottage on Russell Road nearby.

The ruins of the 13C Newark Priory (13 miles south off A3 near Ripley) are associated with both Peacock's youth and his old age. He came here with Fanny Falkner during their mysteriously short-lived engagement in 1807 and returned in 1842, fondly remembering her

Who, on that long-past August day,
Beheld with me these ruins gray.

('Newark Abbey,' lines 23–24)

Samuel Pepys

b. London, 1633; d. London, 1703. Diarist.

Although he was born in London Pepys came from a family whose
real roots were in Eastern England. This is now the region where he
is best remembered. He apparently attended the *grammar school
at Huntingdon, east of A1 and now in Cambridgeshire, in 1644–45
or a little earlier. The charming little building, once part of a medieval
Hospital of St John, has now been renamed the Cromwell Museum
in honour of another famous pupil, whom Pepys admired; it stands
on the High Street side of the Market Square. While being educated
here he presumably lived with his uncle Robert in Brampton, 2 miles
west of Huntingdon. Pepys House, a late 16C building by A604 near
the roundabout leading to the village, was inherited by Pepys' father,
who retired to it in 1661, and by Pepys himself in 1680.

Of all the scenes in the diarist's life Magdalene College, Cambridge
is, as his biographer Richard Ollard reminds us, 'the one that we can
most nearly share with him.' Pepys entered the college in 1651, when
he moved from Trinity Hall, and received his B.A. in 1653. Little is
known about his undergraduate years except that he was formally
admonished for being 'scandalously overseene in drink.' He
frequently returned to Magdalene, usually in the course of visits to
Brampton, as on the occasion when he went 'into the Buttery as a
stranger and there drank my bellyful of their beer, which pleased
me as the best I ever drank' (diary entry for 25 May 1668). His
magnificent library was left to his nephew John Jackson for life and
to Magdalene in 1726; in 1742 the college housed it in the eclectic
17C building that forms one side of Second Court. The *Pepys Library
is notable for the original bookcases from Pepys' home in London,
the manuscript of his diary and the manuscript translation of Ovid's
Metamorphoses made for Caxton. Pepys bought the first part and
the second part was acquired by Magdalene in 1966.

Elsewhere in Cambridge, Pepys attended service at the little church
of St Botolph on Trumpington Street on 26 February 1660. In 1668
he walked to the fine church of St Andrew south of the High Street
in Chesterton, NE of the city, 'and saw the place I used to sit in'
(entry for 25 May). Further abroad, he visited relatives at Impington
(2 miles north via B1049). Pepys' diary for 4 August 1661 records that
he attended Sunday service with his great-uncle Talbot at the church
of St Andrew: 'And at our coming in, the country-people all rise, with
so much reverence. And when the parson begins, he begins "Right
Worshipfull and dearly beloved" to us.'

Pepys was naturally familiar with the major sights on the various
routes between London and Eastern England. He called several times
at Audley End, 13 miles south of Cambridge east of B1383, before
the mansion was altered by Vanbrugh (q.v.). His diary for 17 February
1660 describes how

the housekeeper showed us all the house; in which the stateliness of the ceilings, chimney-pieces, and form of the whole was exceedingly worth seeing. He took us into the cellar, where we drank most admirable drink, a health to the King. Here I played on my Flagelette, there being an excellent Echo.

Yet a later visit left him disappointed: 'Perticularly, the ceilings are not so good as I alway took them to be' (entry for 8 October 1667). At Baldock, by A1 and 20 miles SW of Cambridge via A10 and A505, he found the church of St Mary Virgin 'very handsome' (entry for 6 August 1661). The next day he reported a visit to Hatfield House: 'we bayted and walked into the great House through all the Courts; and I would fain have stolen a pretty dog that followed me, but I could not, which troubled me.' The Elizabethan mansion is 17 miles south of Baldock via A1.

If Eastern England is still rich in landmarks reminiscent of Pepys London, inevitably, has changed too greatly to offer more than a handful of isolated buildings to visit. He was married in 1655 at St Margaret's next to Westminster Abbey. Axe Yard nearby, where he was living when he began his diary in 1660, has long since been swept from the map; it lay south of Downing Street off Whitehall. Two later addresses do survive, both on Buckingham Street, south of the Strand near Charing Cross. The street and its neighbours were built in 1672 on the site of York House, the Duke of Buckingham's mansion. Pepys lived at No. 12 (1679–88), and then at No. 14 (1688–1700), now rebuilt.

To find the most expressive reminder of Pepys in London, we need to visit the City. In 1679 he fell under suspicion of complicity in the Popish Plot and was detained in The Tower of London, where his friend and fellow diarist John Evelyn (q.v.) visited him. From the brick tower of All Hallows nearby he watched the progress of the great fire. On Hart Street to the north we find St Olave's, a church which survived the Great Fire, though it did need substantial restoration after bomb damage in the Second World War. Pepys worshipped here when he lived on adjacent Seething Lane and worked as Secretary of the Admiralty at the Navy Office, which stood on Hart Street's eastern extension, Crutched Friars. He and his wife Elizabeth (d. 1669) were buried beneath the high altar. Pepys' charming *memorial to Elizabeth on the north side of the chancel was complemented in 1883 by a memorial to himself on the south wall of the nave.

Cromwell Museum, Huntingdon. Open Tues to Fri 11–1, 2–5; Sun 11–1, 2–4. Fee.

Pepys House, Brampton. Visitors by appointment for Mon to Sat.

Pepys Library, Magdalene College, Cambridge. Open beginning of Easter Term to end Aug, Mon to Sat 11.30–12.30 & 2.30–3.30; Michaelmas and Lent Terms, Mon to Sat 2.30–3.30.

Audley End (English Heritage). Open Apr to Sept, Tues to Sun 1–6.30. Closed Good Fri but open BH Mon except May Day. Fee.

Hatfield House. House and west gardens open end of March to beginning of Oct, Tues to Sat 12–5, Sun 2–5.30. Closed Good Fri but open BH Mon 11–5. Park open daily 10.30–8. Fee.

Tower of London (DoE). Open March to Oct, Mon to Sat 9.30–5, Sun 2–5, Nov to Feb, Mon to Sat 9.30–4. Closed Christmas Eve, Christmas Day, Boxing Day, New Year's Day, Maundy Thurs, Good Fri. Fee.

Sir Arthur Pinero

b. London, 1855; d. London, 1934. *The Magistrate: A Farce* (1885); *Dandy Dick: A Farce* (1887); *The Second Mrs Tanqueray* (1893); *Trelawny of the 'Wells': A Comedietta* (1898); *The Gay Lord Quex* (1898).

In later life, when his once popular plays had been dislodged from the stage by the work of Ibsen and Shaw (q.v.), Pinero lived at No. 115A Harley Street, south of Marylebone Road, in London. The house is now marked with a GLC plaque. His memorial service was held at St Marylebone Parish Church opposite York Gate, a church more famous for its link with the Brownings (q.v.).

Alexander Pope

b. London, 1688; d. London, 1744. *An Essay in Criticism* (1711); *Windsor-Forest* (1713); *The Rape of the Lock* (1714); *The Iliad of Homer* (1715–20); *The Odyssey of Homer* (1725–26); *The Dunciad* (1728); *Moral Essays* (1731–35); *An Essay on Man* (1733–34); *Imitations of Horace* (1733–37); *Epistle from Mr Pope, to Dr Arbuthnot* (1735).

Scenes associated with an early period of Pope's life may be found at Chiswick in west London. From 1716–19 he lived with his parents on Mawson Row (then Mawson's New Buildings), a group of early 18C houses on Chiswick Lane South just off the delightful Mall. One of his reasons for choosing the area was the desire to be near *Chiswick House, estate of his friend and patron, Lord Burlington, to whom the fourth of his *Moral Essays* is dedicated. In these years the house was a Jacobean building, finally demolished in the late 18C. The present Palladian mansion, where Pope was a frequent guest, was begun in the 1720s. It has recently been stripped of James Wyatt's additions and so has fared rather better than the peer's town residence, Burlington House in Piccadilly, which is encrusted with the work of later architects. The rich interior of Chiswick House includes *trompe l'oeil* paintings of Hercules, Venus and Apollo from Pope's Villa at Twickenham in the Summer Parlour, and portraits of Pope by William Kent (1685–1748) in the Blue Velvet Room and the Bedchamber. Of particular interest are Kent's *gardens—an early specimen of the Picturesque style, which broke away from the symmetry previously fashionable but can still look highly formalised to the modern eye.

Pope is in fact the supreme example of an 18C poet whose life and writings are everywhere linked to the age's taste in architecture and, particularly, landscape gardening. This makes the loss of the Villa at Twickenham, SW of Chiswick, where he lived from 1719 until his death, all the more saddening. The modest house and its plot of land on Crossdeep overlooking the Thames were an endless delight to him; the final form they assumed was a creation as important as any of his poems during these years. Indeed, it is to the poetry that we turn for an account and justification of the principles which dictated the Picturesque laying-out of his garden:

To build, to plant, whatever you intend,
To rear the Column, or the Arch to bend,
To swell the Terras, or to sink the Grot;
In all, let Nature never be forgot.
But treat the Goddess like a modest fair,
Nor over-dress, nor leave her wholly bare;
Let not each beauty ev'rywhere be spy'd,
Where half the skill is decently to hide.
He gains all points, who pleasingly confounds,
Surprizes, varies, and conceals the Bounds.
    (*Moral Essays*, Epistle 4, lines 47–56)

Pope in his Grotto at Twickenham, by William Kent or Dorothy Boyle, Lady Burlington. Courtesy of Courtauld Institute of Art

The poem has proved more durable than the garden. John Serle, Pope's gardener, published a description the year after the poet's death but by 1760 Horace Walpole (q.v.) was writing to Horace Mann in horror at the changes wrought by Sir William Stanhope, brother to Lord Chesterfield and new owner of the property:

> it was a little bit of ground of five acres, enclosed with three lanes and seeing nothing. Pope had twisted and twirled and harmonized this, till it

appeared two or three sweet little lawns opening and opening beyond one another, and the whole surrounded with thick impenetrable woods. Sir William has hacked and hewed these groves, wriggled a winding gravel walk through them with an edging of shrubs, in what they call the modern taste, and in short, has desired the three lanes to walk in again.

The Villa itself has been replaced by a Victorian neo-Tudor building, now a school. The only surviving fragment of Pope's achievement is his famous Grotto. Really a passage beneath the road connecting the house and its riverside gardens, it quickly transcended this simple function and became a favourite retreat of Pope's 'from which,' Dr Johnson (q.v.) observed disapprovingly, 'he endeavoured to persuade his friends and himself that cares and passions could be excluded.' A *camera obscura* reflected the outside world on to walls lined with minerals:

> Thou who shalt stop, where *Thames*' translucent Wave
> Shines a broad Mirrour thro' the shadowy Cave;
> Where lingering Drops from Mineral Roofs distill,
> And pointed Crystals break the sparkling Rill,
> Unpolish'd Gemms no Ray on Pride bestow,
> And latent Metals innocently glow:
> Approach. Great NATURE studiously behold!
> ('Verses on a Grotto by the River Thames at Twickenham')

North of Crossdeep and in the centre of Twickenham's original

Marble Hill House, home of Henrietta Howard, later Countess of Suffolk, friend of Gay and Walpole (qq.v.) as well as Pope. From Colin Campbell, Vitruvius Britannicus *(1715-25). Courtesy of Cambridge University Library*

village we find the parish church of St Mary. Pope's parents, his nurse Mary Beach (her tablet is on the outside wall), and the poet himself were all buried here. A monument erected by Pope's *protégé*, William Warburton, remembers him in his own words as 'one who would not be buried in Westminster Abbey.'

In the park NE of St Mary's is *Marble Hill House. This fine Palladian building was in Pope's time the home of Mrs Howard (later Lady Suffolk), mistress to George II, celebrated in 'On a Certain Lady at Court' as 'a Reasonable Woman,/ Handsome and witty, yet a Friend' but also, perhaps, portrayed as the heartless Cloe in the second of the *Moral Essays*. The grounds of Marble Hill were laid out by Charles Bridgeman, with Pope and later Horace Walpole advising.

In Central England, and especially in a wide radius of Oxford, we may visit a rich list of places connected with Pope's life, reminding us both of people mentioned in his poems and of his taste in landscape gardening.

At Mapledurham House, off A4074 24 miles SE of Oxford and on the fringes of Reading, Pope visited his friends, the Blount sisters, in their Elizabethan manor and the charming village where it is set. His poem, 'Epistle to Miss Blount, on her leaving the Town, after the Coronation,' addressed to his special friend Martha, gives a playfully cynical account of the life she led in the country: 'Old fashion'd halls, dull aunts, and croaking rooks' (line 13).

Inevitably, Pope also knew Stowe, 20 miles NE of Oxford and near Buckingham, where Richard Temple, Viscount Cobham had his house (now a public school) in *grounds that remain perhaps the most complete demonstration of 18C taste in landscaping. The temples are by Vanbrugh (q.v.), Gibbs and Kent, while the gardens were begun by Bridgeman and continued by Kent, with final additions by 'Capability' Brown. Pope's admiration is expressed in the fourth of his *Moral Essays*:

> Still follow Sense, of ev'ry Art the Soul,
> Parts answ'ring Parts, shall slide into a whole,
> Spontaneous beauties all around advance,
> Start ev'n from Difficulty, strike from Chance;
> Nature shall join you, Time shall make it grow
> A Wonder to work at—perhaps a STOW.
>
> (lines 65–7)

Rousham Park, east of A423 14 miles north from Oxford, preserves mementoes of Pope's friendship with the Dormer family. In a letter of 1728 he praised the **grounds through which the Cherwell runs, laid out by Kent, as 'the prettiest place for water-falls, jetts, ponds inclosed with beautiful scenes of green and hanging woods, that ever I saw.' With Chiswick House, they offer probably the best surviving reminder of the type of effect Pope himself created in his vanished garden at Twickenham.

Further north on A423 at Adderbury, 20 miles from Oxford, is the house that once belonged to John Wilmot, Earl of Rochester, described in more detail under the entry for the Restoration poet. In 1739 Pope wrote a poem complimenting Adderbury's then owner, the Duke of Argyll, and recording the disappointing results of sleeping in Rochester's bed:

> With no poetick ardors fir'd,
> I press the bed where *Wilmot* lay:

> That here he lov'd, or here expir'd
>   Begets no numbers grave or gay.

At the pleasant village of Stanton Harcourt (10 miles west of Oxford via A420, B4044 and B4496) Pope stayed for the autumn of 1718 as a guest of Lord Harcourt, frequently host to writers of the period. The poet was clearly charmed by the 15C half-ruined manor house where he was accommodated:

> A Stranger would be grievously disappointed, who should ever think to get into this house the right way. One would expect, after entring thro the Porch, to be let into the Hall: Alas nothing less—you find yourself in a Brewhouse. From the Parlour you step into the Drawing-room, but opening the iron-nailed door, you are convinced by a flight of birds about your ears & a cloud of dust in your eyes, that 'tis the Pigeon-house.

Most of the building was demolished in 1750 and only a few fragments survive. The most interesting are the kitchen and *Pope's Tower, by the church, where he worked on his translation of Homer's *Iliad*. There is a lovely view from the top.

The poet's delight in the decrepit irregularity of his surroundings at Stanton Harcourt has been cited as evidence of the romantic side to his otherwise Augustan sensibility. So has his interest in John Hewet and Sarah Drew, a local pair of devoted lovers killed by lightning during his stay, an interest shared by his friend and companion, John Gay (q.v.). Pope wrote the epitaph for their tomb in the churchyard and gave several accounts of their death in letters to friends. This is the version he sent to Martha Blount:

> Sarah frighted, & out of breath, sunk down on a heap of Wheatsheaves; & John, who never separated from her, rak'd two or three heapes together, to protect her, & sate down by her. Immediately there was heard so loud a crack that Heaven seemd burst asunder: every one was sollicitous for the safety of his next neighbor, & called to one another. Those who were nearest our Lovers hearing no Answer, stept to the Sheaves. They first spy'd a little Smoke, and then saw this faithful Pair, John with one Arm about her neck, & the other extended over her face, as to shield her from the Lightning; both stiff & cold in this tender posture: no mark or blemish on the Bodies; except the left Eyebrow of Sarah a little sing'd and a small Spot between her Breasts.

The age's reaction to such events was not uniformly sentimental. Lady Mary Wortley Montagu, to whom Pope also related the episode, answered in verse:

> Who knows if 'twas not kindly done?
> For had they seen the next year's sun,
> A beaten wife and cuckold swain
> Had jointly curs'd the marriage chain;
> Now they are happy in their doom,
> FOR POPE HAS WROTE UPON THEIR TOMB.

Pope himself privately composed an epitaph of rather different character from the public one to which Lady Mary referred:

> Here lye two poor Lovers, who had the mishap
> Tho very chaste people, to die of a Clap.

He visited *Cirencester Park in Gloucestershire several times, returning to assist and admire Lord Bathurst's ambitious transformation of his estate. His admiration of the peer's use of riches was expressed by the dedication of his third *Moral Essay* and by a famous couplet in the fourth, where Bathhurst's name is linked with Burlington's:

> Who then shall grace, or who improve the Soil?
> Who plants like BATHURST, or who builds like BOYLE.
>> (lines 177–178)

Pope's Seat, a rusticated stone temple in the neo-classical manner, recalls his connection with the place. The 'pleasant prospect' of the charming Cotswold village of Bibury (8 miles NE of Cirencester on A433), viewed on a visit to Bathurst, remained in his memory.

Like other famous literary men he also came to *Prior Park, at Combe Down 1 mile SE of Bath and reached from the south of the city via Claverton Street and Prior Park Road. John Wood the Elder built the grand Palladian mansion for Ralph Allen (1693–1764), the celebrated 'Man of Bath,' and Pope headed the list of writers who paid tribute to Allen as the model of that benevolent philanthropy which the age so admired:

> Let humble ALLEN, with an awkward Shame,
> Do good by Stealth, and blush to find it Fame.
>> ('Epilogue to the Satires,' Dialogue 1, lines 135–136)

Few of Pope's friendships, however, kept an entirely even course. His final visit in 1742, when he was accompanied by Martha Blount, led to a lasting coldness between the two men. Now a Roman Catholic school, Prior Park is greatly reduced from its former glory inside, but its exterior and grounds remain magnificent. The Palladian Bridge is particularly notable.

Chiswick House (English Heritage). House open 15 March to 15 Oct, daily 9.30–6.30; 16 Oct to 14 March, Wed to Sun 9.30–4. Closed Christmas Eve, Christmas Day, New Year's Day & May BH. Fee. Grounds open daily throughout the year.

Pope's Grotto, Pope's Villa, (St Catherine's Convent of Mercy), Twickenham. Visitors by appointment.

Marble Hill House, Twickenham (GLC). Open daily except Fri 10–5 (closes at 4 in Nov to Jan).

Mapledurham House. Open Easter Sun to end Sept, Sat, Sun & BH 2.30–5.30. Fee.

Stowe, near Buckingham. Grounds and garden buildings open Easter and summer school holidays, Fri, Sat, Sun & Aug BH Mon 1–6. Fee.

Rousham Park, Steeple Aston. Gardens open all year, daily 10–6. House open Apr to Sept, Wed, Sun & BH 2–5.30. Fee.

Pope's Tower, Stanton Harcourt. Open BH Sun & Mon in Apr and May, also selected Sun & Thurs in Apr & June to Sept, 2–6. Fee.

Cirencester Park. Open daily 9–dusk.

Prior Park (Prior Park College), near Bath. Grounds and chapel open Good Fri to Easter Mon, daily in May & Aug, 10–dusk.

Beatrix Potter (Mrs Heelis)

b. London, 1866; d. Near Sawrey, Cumbria, 1943. *The Tale of Peter Rabbit* (1901); *The Tailor of Gloucester* (1902); *The Tale of Squirrel Nutkin* (1903); *The Tale of Benjamin Bunny* (1904); *The Tale of Two Bad Mice* (1904); *The Tale of Mrs Tiggy-Winkle* (1905); *The Tale of Jeremy Fisher* (1906); *The Story of a Fierce Bad Rabbit* (1906); *The Story of Miss Moppet* (1906); *The Tale of Tom Kitten* (1907); *The Tale of Jemima Puddle-Duck* (1908); *The Roly-Poly Pudding*

(1908; republished as *The Tale of Samuel Whiskers*, 1926); *The Tale of the Flopsy Bunnies* (1909); *Ginger and Pickles* (1909); *The Tale of Mrs Tittlemouse* (1910); *The Tale of Timmy Tiptoes* (1911); *The Tale of Mr Tod* (1912); *The Tale of Pigling Bland* (1913); *Appley Dapply's Nursery Rhymes* (1922); *The Fairy Caravan* (1929); *The Tale of Little Pig Robinson* (1930).

No. 2 Bolton Gardens, just north of the Old Brompton Road in South Kensington, was destroyed by a bomb in the Second World War. The disappearance of this 'unloved birthplace' where she had remained with her parents until middle age caused Beatrix Potter little regret, for her life there had been enclosed and isolated. Her only outlets were the journals she wrote in code (deciphered by Leslie Linder and published in 1966), the letters to children that grew into published stories and her drawing. The search for objects and specimens for her delicate, precise sketches took her to the Natural History Museum and the Victoria and Albert Museum, both in the Cromwell Road to the north. The coat in *The Tailor of Gloucester* required special study of the Victoria and Albert Museum embroidery collection. On Kensington Church Street near its junction with Kensington High

Beatrix Potter, by D. Banner. Courtesy of National Portrait Gallery

Street is the 19C church of St Mary Abbots where she married William Heelis, a solicitor from the Lake District, in 1913.

The marriage effectively brought her career as children's writer to an end. It also completed her escape from her parents' restrictive way of life and made her attachment to the Lake District permanent. She had first visited the area for holidays in childhood. On several occasions her parents rented the 19C Wray Castle (now a training college for Merchant Navy cadets) on the western shore of Windermere. In 1905 she bought *Hill Top Farm in the little village of Near Sawrey on B5285 by Esthwaite Water 2 miles SE of Hawkshead. Though she never intended or used it as a permanent home, she lavished care and money on it during the following years. It appears in her illustrations for *Tom Kitten* and, with other parts of Sawrey, in *Jemima Puddle-Duck*. On her death she bequeathed the farm to the National Trust, together with some four thousand acres of land in the Lake District. Her married life was spent at Castle Farm nearby in the village, taking an active interest in farming and conservation, and regarding the arrival of tourists attracted by the fame of her books with some surprise. She found the English visitors 'very inquisitive and completely uninteresting. However it happens, the class of Americans who take the trouble to call, are quite different.'

Natural History Museum, South Kensington. Open Mon to Sat 10–6, Sun 2.30–6. Closed Christmas Eve, Christmas Day, Boxing Day, Good Fri & 4 May.

Victoria & Albert Museum, South Kensington. Open Mon to Thurs & Sat 10–5.50, Sun 2.30–5.50. Closed Christmas Eve, Christmas Day, Boxing Day, New Year's Day & May BH.

Hill Top, Near Sawrey (NT). Open Apr to end Oct, Mon to Thurs & Sat 10–5.30, Sun 2–5.30. Fee.

John Cowper, Llewelyn and T.F. Powys

John Cowper Powys: b. Shirley, Derbyshire, 1872; d. Blaenau Ffestiniog, Gwynedd, 1963. *Visions and Revisions: A Book of Literary Devotions* (1915); *Wood and Stone: A Romance* (1915); *Confessions of Two Brothers* (with Llewelyn Powys; 1916); *Wolf's Bane: Rhymes* (1916); *Rodmoor: A Romance* (1916); *Mandragora: Poems* (1917); *The Complex Vision* (1920); *Samphire* (1922); *Ducdame* (1925); *The Religion of a Sceptic* (1925); *Wolf Solent* (1925); *In Defence of Sensuality* (1930); *A Glastonbury Romance* (1932); *A Philosophy of Solitude* (1933); *Autobiography* (1934); *Weymouth Sands* (1934); *Maiden Castle* (1936); *Morwyn: Or The Vengeance of God* (1937); *Owen Glendower: An Historical Novel* (1940); *The Art of Growing Old* (1944); *Pair Dadeni: Or, 'The Cauldron of Rebirth'* (1946); *Porius: A Romance of the Dark Ages* (1951); *The Inmates* (1952); *In Spite Of: A Philosophy for Everyman* (1953); *Atlantis* (1954); *Lucifer: A Poem* (1956); *The Brazen Head* (1956); *All or Nothing* (1960).

Llewelyn Powys: b. Dorchester, Dorset, 1884; d. Davos Platz, Switzerland, 1939. *Confessions of Two Brothers* (with John Cowper Powys; 1916); *Ebony and Ivory* (1923); *Thirteen Worthies* (1923); *Honey and Gall* (1924); *Cup Bearers of Wine and Hellebore* (1924); *Black Laughter* (1924); *Skin for Skin* (1925); *The Verdict of Bridlegoose* (1926); *Henry Hudson* (1927); *The Cradle of God* (1929); *An Hour on Christianity* (1930); *Apples Be Ripe* (1930); *A Pagan's Pilgrimage* (1931); *Impassioned Clay* (1931); *Now That the Gods Are Dead* (1932); *The Life and Times of Anthony à Wood* (1932); *The Glory of Life* (1934); *Earth's Memories* (1934); *Dorset Essays* (1935); *Damnable Opinions* (1935); *The Twelve*

Months (1936); *Somerset Essays* (1937); *Rats in the Sacristy* (1937); *Love and Death* (1939); *A Baker's Dozen* (1939); *Swiss Essays* (1947); *Advice to a Young Poet* (1949).

T.F. Powys: b. Shirley, Derbyshire, 1875; d. Mappowder, Dorset, 1953. *The Left Leg* (1923); *Black Bryony* (1923); *Mark Only* (1924); *Mr Tasker's Gods* (1924); *Mockery Gap* (1925); *Innocent Birds* (1926); *Mr Weston's Good Wine* (1927); *The House With the Echo* (1928); *Kindness in a Corner* (1930); *The White Paternoster* (1930); *Unclay* (1931); *The Two Thieves* (1932); *Captain Patch* (1935); *Make Thyself Many* (1935); *Goat Green* (1937); *Bottle's Path* (1946).

John Cowper and T.F. Powys, the elder of the three literary brothers, were born at Shirley, off A52 4 miles SE of Ashbourne in Derbyshire. Neither the village nor the county subsequently played an important part in the life of a family which, despite the far-flung travels of its various members, was rooted in Somerset and Dorset.

Montacute, 4 miles west of Yeovil on A3088, is an important shrine for the Powys' readers. Rev. Charles Francis Powys brought his family to the village in 1885 and remained until his death in 1923. Montacute may not be the 'King's Barton' of *Wolf Solent* but Mr Urquhart's residence in the novel owes something to John Cowper's childhood memories of its wonderful Elizabethan mansion, Montacute House. His first novel, *Wood and Stone*, describes the village as 'Nevilton' and nearby Ham Hill, to the west, as 'Leo's Hill.' Sherborne, on A30 beyond Yeovil to the east of Montacute, is the 'Ramsgard' of *Wolf Solent*. John Cowper and Llewelyn attended its public school, while another brother, Littleton Charles, became headmaster of Sherborne Preparatory School. Ilchester, on A303 and A37 4 miles north of Montacute, was the birthplace of Roger Bacon, medieval philosopher and inspirer of the necromantic legends recalled in *The Brazen Head*. The historic town of Glastonbury, 11 miles north of Ilchester via B3151 and A39, is the setting for another of John Cowper's works.

Dorchester and its surrounding countryside are also deeply connected with the Powys family. They lived in the county town from 1879 to 1885, when Rev. Charles was curate of the fine church of St Peter's. Llewelyn was born during these years and, like his brothers, was taken to tea with the elderly William Barnes (q.v.). The town is the setting for much of *Maiden Castle*, the novel which takes its title from the prehistoric fort some 2½ miles SW. Weymouth, on the coast 8½ miles south, gives its name to another of John Cowper's novels.

Of particular importance is the little village of East Chaldon or, more picturesquely, Chaldon Herring, some 8 miles SE via A352 and an unclassified road leading towards the coast. Though both John Cowper and Llewelyn lived here, it is mainly associated with T.F. Powys, who came in 1905 and stayed until 1940. His home was Beth Car, a brick house built by Henry Hardy, brother of Thomas Hardy (q.v.). East Chaldon is thus the model for the village that appears so often and under various names in his novels and stories, most memorably as the 'Folly Down' of *Mr Weston's Good Wine*. On the cliff top to the south is a stone memorial to Llewelyn, who died in Switzerland.

T.F. Powys left East Chaldon for another Dorset village, Mappowder (east of B3143), where he is buried in the churchyard. John Cowper spent his last years in Wales, a country that exerted an obvious influence over his work, but his ashes were scattered in the Channel off Chesil Bank near Abbotsbury (on B3157 8 miles NW of Weymouth).

In their youth John Cowper and Llewelyn followed the family

tradition and attended Corpus Christi College, Cambridge, though John Cowper was speaking for both of them when he remarked that the university 'had not the least influence upon my taste, my intelligence, my philosophy or my character.'

Montacute House (NT). Open Apr to end Oct, daily except Tues 12.30–6. Fee.

Maiden Castle, near Dorchester (English Heritage). Open at all reasonable times.

Matthew Prior

b. Wimborne, Dorset, 1664; d. Wimpole Hall, Cambridgeshire, 1721. *Carmen Seculare* (1700); *Solomon on the Vanity of the World* (1718); *Down-Hall, a Ballad* (1723).

After attending London's Westminster School in Little Dean's Yard to the south of Westminster Abbey, Prior studied at St John's College, Cambridge (1683–86). His rooms were apparently in the handsome late 16C Second Court. Although he went on to enjoy a career as diplomat in London and elsewhere, Prior maintained his connection with St John's and left part of his library to the College in his will. The other surviving places associated with his life are all within convenient reach of Cambridge.

In 1688–89 he was tutor to the Earl of Exeter's son at the fine Renaissance mansion of Burghley House near Stamford, Lincolnshire. His 'Epistle to Fleetwood Shepherd, Esq.,' an early example of the Horatian style he aspired to in his poetry, gives a light-hearted account of his recreations there:

> Sometimes I climb my Mare, and kick her
> To bottl'd ale, and neighb'ring vicar;
> Sometimes at STAMFORD take a quart . . .

The house stands 42 miles north of Cambridge via A604 and A1.

In 1719 a gift of £4000 from Edward Harley, Earl of Oxford, made it possible for Prior to buy a country house in Essex, Down Hall, which he improved and landscaped as well as making the subject of a pleasantly ironic poem. Down Hall has been replaced by a 19C building and Prior is better remembered at the Earl of Oxford's country seat, Wimpole Hall, 8 miles SW of Cambridge via A603. The 17C mansion was then being extended by James Gibbs. Prior was a frequent guest and died during a visit to Wimpole in 1721.

He was buried near his old school, in Poets' Corner (fee) of Westminster Abbey, the grave being at his request near that of Spenser (q.v.). His will made provison for the striking monument, though he had earlier offered a humbler memorial to himself in 'Epitaph Extempore':

> Nobles and Heralds, by your leave,
> .   Here lies what once was Matthew Prior;
> The son of Adam and Eve,
>   Can Bourbon or Nassau claim higher?

Burghley House, near Stamford. Open 1 Apr to 7 Oct, Sat & BH 11–5, Sun & Good Fri 2–5. Fee.

Wimpole Hall, Orwell (NT). Open 31 March to 4 Nov, daily except Fri but including BH, 2–6; closed Good Fri. Fee.

Sir Walter Ralegh

b. near Budleigh Salterton, Devon, 1552?; d. London, 1618. Poet and author of *The History of the World* (1614).

Hayes Barton, the E-shaped Tudor farmhouse that was Ralegh's birthplace, lies among wooded scenery north of the Devon coastal resort of Budleigh Salterton and west of East Budleigh.

After attending Oriel College, Oxford Ralegh embarked on the adventurous career which elevated him from relative obscurity to a position as favourite at Queen Elizabeth's court and to fame as one of the best travelled figures of his age.

During his stay in Ireland he took part in the 1580 massacre of the Spanish garrison at Forte del Oro, near the harbour town of Smerwick, County Kerry on the picturesque Dingle peninsula. In 1586 he acquired an estate including Youghal, a fishing town 40 miles east of Cork on N25. The tradition that he lived at Myrtle Grove, to the north of St Mary's Church, should be regarded sceptically. Better documented is his visit in 1589 to a neighbouring poet, Edmund Spenser, which is described under the entry for that author. In 1589 he was also granted the Castle at Lismore, north of Youghal, which remained in his possession until 1602. The 12C building, with good views of the River Blackwater, was rebuilt and remodelled in the 19C; it has a pleasant garden with an attractive Yew Walk.

In 1592 Ralegh acquired property at Sherborne in Dorset. After attempting to renovate the 12C Castle, which lies to the south of the town and its River Yeo, he built himself a new house in 1594, calling it The Lodge. The original castle was damaged during the Civil War, though its Norman gatehouse and keep still stand, while Ralegh's addition was much altered by 19C interiors in the Jacobean style.

In 1603 he was arraigned at Winchester on slender charges of involvement in a plot against James I. His hearing took place in the magnificent *Great Hall of the Norman castle, near West Gate and the west end of the High Street. As a result he was committed for the second time in his life to the Tower of London. His first stay in 1592 had arisen from allegations of a liaison with Elizabeth Throgmorton, maid of honour to Queen Elizabeth, and had occasioned a poem, 'As You Come from the Holy Land,' flattering his sovereign. His second and far longer period of imprisonment was spent in the Bloody Tower and is remembered by the naming of Ralegh's Walk nearby. He passed the time writing the ambitious *History of the World* and a body of poetry, often religious in character, that deserves attention for more than the romantic circumstances of its composition.

He secured his release in 1616 by his plan for the Orinoco expedition in search of gold and silver but was re-arrested on his return to England after its failure. He was probably held in the vanished gatehouse outside the main entrance to Westminster Abbey, but tradition points to a small cell in the White Tower at the Tower of London. His execution took place in 1618 at Old Palace Yard, the space of land between the Abbey and the Palace of Westminster now largely occupied by a car park. He was apparently buried at St Margaret's, Westminster nearby, where a window of 1882 with an inscription by the American poet James Russell Lowell commemorates him. A statue (1959) stands on the lawn in front of the Ministry of Defence in Whitehall.

Lismore Castle. Gardens open 7 May to 14 Sept, daily except Sat 1.45–4.45. Fee.

Sherborne Old Castle (English Heritage). Open 15 March to 15 Oct, Mon to Sat 9.30–6.30, Sun 2–6.30 (Apr to Sept, Sun 9.30–6.30); 16 Oct to 14 March, Mon to Sat 9.30–4, Sun 2–4. Closed Christmas Eve, Christmas Day, Boxing Day & New Year's Day. Fee.

Sherborne Castle. Open Easter Sat to end Sept, Thurs, Sat, Sun, BH Mon 2–6. Fee.

Great Hall, Winchester. Open Apr to Sept, Mon to Fri 10–5, Sat & BH 10–6, Sun 2–6; Oct to March, Mon to Fri & BH 10–5, Sat & Sun 2–5. Closed Christmas Day & Good Fri.

Tower of London (DoE). Open March to Oct, Mon to Sat 9.30–5, Sun 2–5; Nov to Feb, Mon to Sat 9.30–4. Closed Christmas Eve, Christmas Day, Boxing Day, New Year's Day, Maundy Thurs, Good Fri. Fee.

Samuel Richardson

b. Mackworth, Derbyshire?, 1689; d. London, 1761. *Pamela, or Virtue Rewarded* (1740–41); *Clarissa Harlowe* (1747–48); *The History of Sir Charles Grandison* (1753–54).

'I know nothing of Situations of Places, Distances, Contiguities,' confessed Richardson when he was preparing a revised edition of *A Tour through the Whole Island of Great Britain* by his fellow novelist, Defoe (q.v.). There can, in fact, have been few English writers who travelled less than he did.

During visits to Bath in the 1740s he dined with the philanthropist Ralph Allen at Prior Park, the magnificent Palladian mansion built by John Wood the elder at Combe Down, 1 mile SE of the city. Richardson accepted the invitation with a certain naive complacency as evidence of the position his writing had won him: 'Twenty years ago I was the most obscure man in Great Britain, and now I am admitted to the company of the first characters in the kingdom.' Somewhat diminished from its former glory, Prior Park is now a Roman Catholic school.

In London, *Clarissa* may be remembered by a visit to the charming Flask Walk off Hampstead High Street. Richardson's heroine took refuge here, lodging with a Mrs Moore, but was soon discovered by Lovelace and again harassed by his attentions. Mrs Barbauld, editor of the novelist's correspondence, tells of a Frenchman who visited Hampstead in search of the exact house on Flask Walk 'and was surprised at the ignorance or indifference of the inhabitants on that subject.' She concludes that 'constant residence soon destroys all sensibility to objects of local enthusiasm.'

Richardson was buried at St Bride's off the south side of Fleet Street, whose interesting Crypt Museum now details the church's connection with the printing trade. Richardson's own print shops in Fleet Street and Salisbury Court nearby, like his later homes in

Fulham, have long since vanished.

Prior Park (Prior Park College), near Bath. Grounds and chapel open Good Fri to Easter Mon, daily in May & Aug, 10–dusk.
St Bride's Crypt Museum. Open daily 9–5.

John Wilmot, Earl of Rochester

b. Ditchley, Oxfordshire, 1647; d. Woodstock, Oxfordshire, 1680. *A Satire Against Mankind* (1675).

Much of Rochester's short and dissolute life, during which he nevertheless maintained a reputation as satirist and wit, was spent at court, where he was a special favourite of Charles II. But his deepest connections are with Oxfordshire, of which the following tour may be recommended.

It begins in Oxford, where Rochester attended Wadham College as a fellow commoner from 1660 to 1661. The College still has the four silver pint pots he presented. The traveller may then take A423 north to Adderbury (20 miles) where at Adderbury House, east of The Green, Rochester lived after his marriage in 1667. Pope (q.v.) came here in 1739 and left a permanent reminder of his visit in the poem, 'On Lying in the Earl of Rochester's Bed at Atterbury.' The building was extended in the 18C but reduced in size again in the next century. More fruitfully, A34 leads NW from Oxford to Woodstock (8 miles). The High Lodge that Rochester occupied from 1674 after his appointment as Keeper of Woodstock Park was later assimilated into the grounds of Blenheim Palace. It was remodelled in the Gothic style in the 18C. Rochester here acquired a reputation for scandalous living but also underwent the death-bed conversion recorded by Bishop Burnet. To the left of A34 beyond Woodstock lies Ditchley Park, Rochester's birthplace. A print of the 'low antient timber house, with a pretty bowling greene' (as the diarist John Evelyn [q.v.] described it) is displayed in the present building, which is by James Gibbs and dates from the 1720s. At the nearby village of Spelsbury on B4026 (15 miles) Rochester is buried in the churchyard in an unmarked family vault. From Spelsbury the tourist may continue SW via Charlbury to the charming Cotswold town of Burford (23 miles) at the junction of A361 and A40. Rochester attended the Grammar School in Church Lane; despite Victorian alteration and enlargement traces of the original 16C building are still apparent.

Two surviving sites in London together give an apt indication of Rochester's life there. He was briefly detained in the Tower of London for a few days of 1665 on a charge of abducting the heiress Elizabeth Malet, whom he subsequently married. In 1675 or 1676, again apparently in disgrace, he posed as a quack doctor and set up a stall on nearby Tower Hill.

Blenheim Palace. Park open all year 9–5. Fee. House open 15 March to 31 Oct, daily 11–6. Fee.
Ditchley Park. Open for about ten days each year in late July/early Aug. Fee.
Tower of London (DoE). Open March to Oct, Mon to Sat 9.30–5, Sun 2–5; Nov

to Feb, Mon to Sat 9.30–4. Closed Christmas Eve, Christmas Day, Boxing Day, New Year's Day, Maundy Thurs, Good Fri. Fee.

Dante Gabriel Rossetti

b. London, 1828; d. Birchington, Kent, 1882. *Poems* (includes 'The House of Life'; 1870); *Ballads and Sonnets* (includes expanded version of 'The House of Life'; 1881).

A GLC plaque at No. 17 Red Lion Square in London, south of Theobald's Road near its junction with Southampton Row, marks the lodgings Rossetti briefly shared with the artist Walter Deverell in 1851. It was Deverell who first discovered Lizzie Siddal and introduced her to the Pre-Raphaelite Brotherhood; she became Rossetti's favourite model and later his mistress. The lodgings were later occupied by William Morris (q.v.) and Edward Burne-Jones.

In the 1850s Rossetti and Lizzie Siddal visited Hastings on the Sussex coast. They returned in 1860 to be married in the church of St Clement's at the south end of the High Street. It was far from being a romantic occasion: the couple had known each other for ten, not always happy, years, while she was already gravely ill from tuberculosis and he approached marriage in the spirit of reluctant obligation.

On her death in 1862—from an overdose of laudanum, not tuberculosis—she was buried in the Rossetti family plot at Highgate Cemetery in London, where Rossetti's sister Christina (1830–94), author of *Goblin Market*, also lies. The cemetery is reached by walking south from Highgate Underground Station (Northern Line) on Southwood Lane, South Grove and Swains Lane. The Rossetti plot is in the western part, on the far side of the oval walk.

The widowed Rossetti moved to Tudor House, No. 16 Cheyne Walk by the Chelsea Embankment. Except for an important and stormy period at Kelmscott Manor (described under the entry for William Morris) Tudor House remained his home until death. Its survival more than compensates for the disappearance of his earlier London homes. In the first year of his tenancy George Meredith and Swinburne (qq.v.) were lodgers but the arrangement proved fragile. Swinburne was in the habit of sliding naked down the banisters when drunk, which happened quite often; this and other manifestations of domestic chaos were offensive to Meredith. Rossetti himself indulged a passion for filling the house with china and bric-à-brac, and its garden with a progressively exotic menagerie of animals: peacocks, armadillos, gazelles, kangaroos, salamanders, wombats and an Indian bull which took his fancy, he said, because it had eyes like Jane Morris. He even toyed with the idea of keeping an elephant on the grounds it could clean his windows and, by arousing the curiosity of passersby, help attract buyers for his paintings. Ruskin (q.v.) was undoubtedly wise not to pursue his plan of joining the household, though he was a visitor to Cheyne Walk.

In the shrubbery between the Walk and the Embankment is a drinking fountain surmounted by a bronze medallion of Rossetti, designed by his friend Ford Madox Brown. It was unveiled in 1887 by the painter William Holman Hunt, whose speech on that occasion

Rossetti reading to Theodore Watts-Dunton (s.v. Swinburne) in the parlour of Tudor House, by H.T. Dunn (1882). Courtesy of National Portrait Gallery

showed his lingering resentment at the greater publicity Rossetti's role in the Pre-Raphaelite Brotherhood had received.

In early 1882, his health badly damaged by chloral addiction, Rossetti was taken by the young novelist Hall Caine to convalesce at Birchington, on A28 3 miles SW of Margate by the Kent coast. Although the ugly little bungalow where he died on Easter Sunday has been demolished, Birchington is otherwise rich in memorials. The opening stanzas of Christina's poem, 'Birchington Churchyard,' describe the scene of his burial:

> A lowly hill which overlooks a flat,
>> Half sea, half country-side;
>> A flat-shored sea of low-voiced creeping tide
> Over a chalky weedy mat.
>
> A hill of hillocks, flowery and kept green
>> Round crosses raised for hope,
>> With many-tinted sunsets where the slope
> Faces the lingering western sheen.

The south aisle of the church has a window of 1884 by Frederick James Shields. Its left light was intended to carry an adaptation of Rossetti's 'Magdalene at the Door of Simon' but the local vicar objected that the picture was unlikely 'to inspire devotional thoughts and feelings, and . . . in some cases it might rather do the reverse.' Shields made a copy of Rossetti's 'Passover in the Holy Family' instead. Outside the south door is a *Celtic cross by Ford Madox Brown, its surface elaborately carved with symbolic motifs that repay study. Among them we note an Assyrian bull, reminiscent of 'The

Burden of Nineveh,' and a curious wedding ceremony in which the priest is blindfolded and the groom carries a book—perhaps Rossetti's 'House of Life' sonnets, originally buried with Lizzie Siddal but later exhumed at his request.

Highgate Cemetery. Tours leave from Swains Lane daily on the hour, Apr to Sept 10–4, Oct to March 10–3.

John Ruskin

b. London, 1819; d. Coniston, Cumbria, 1900. *Modern Painters* (1843–60); *The Seven Lamps of Architecture* (1849); *The Stones of Venice* (1851–53); *Unto This Last* (1862); *Munera Pulveris* (1862–63); *Sesame and Lilies* (1865); *The Crown of Wild Olive* (1866); *Fors Clavigera* (1871–78); *Praeterita* (unfinished; 1885–89).

We associate Ruskin's name less readily with Britain than with the Continent—with the landscape of the Alps and the architecture of Venice. In large measure this is perfectly just, and Ruskin himself could on occasion find it necessary to excuse an apparent neglect of his native land and culture. In the Preface to *The Seven Lamps of Architecture* he wrote, perhaps a little lamely: 'I could have wished to have given more examples from our early English Gothic; but I have always found it impossible to work in the cold interior of our cathedrals.' Yet his British roots, admittedly less conspicuous than his joyous, repeated discovery of Switzerland and Italy, still go deep. His life and works bear witness to the importance of his Scottish heritage, his connections with Oxford and, above all, his abiding love of the Lake District.

None of Ruskin's London homes any longer stands. The Georgian terrace house at No. 54 Hunter Street, Brunswick Square where he was born, once marked by a Society of Arts plaque, was demolished in 1969. His two homes in the Camberwell area, then a newly fashionable and pleasantly rural suburb appropriate to a rising business family like the Ruskins, have suffered the same fate. Ruskin's idyllic account of No. 28 Herne Hill, the semi-detached villa where his family lived from 1823 to 1842, makes its disappearance (in 1906) and the radical changes that have since overtaken its neighbourhood all the more regrettable. According to *Praeterita* the house

> commanded, in those comparatively smokeless days, a very notable view from its garret windows, of the Norwood hills on one side, and the winter sunrise over them; and of the valleys of the Thames on the other, with Windsor telescopically clear in the distance, and Harrow, conspicuous always in fine weather to open vision against the summer sunset. It had front and back garden in sufficient proportion to its size; the front, richly set with old evergreens, and well-grown lilac and laburnum; the back, seventy yards long by twenty wide, renowned all over the hill for its pears and apples, which had been chosen with extreme care by our predecessor . . .—and possessing also a strong old mulberry tree, a tall white-heart cherry tree, a black Kentish one, and an almost unbroken hedge, all round, of alternate gooseberry and currant bush; decked, in due season, (for the ground was wholly beneficent,) with magical spendour of abundant fruit: fresh green, soft amber, and rough-bristled crimson bending the spinous branches; clustered pearl and pendant ruby joyfully discoverable under the large leaves that looked like vine. (Vol. 1, Ch. 2)

The house remained in the family's possession after they moved and

Ruskin sometimes used it in later years: the passage just quoted was written in his old nursery. The move in 1842 took him and his parents only a short distance north to a larger villa, No. 163 Denmark Hill, where he remained until 1872, the year after his mother's death. *Modern Painters* and *The Stones of Venice* were written in it, for he retained his study even during 1852–54, the period of his marriage when he and his wife lived at No. 30 Herne Hill, next door to his old home. No. 163 was demolished in 1947 but Ruskin's connection with the area is commemorated by Ruskin Park almost opposite the site.

Several London houses where he was a visitor do survive. His close and admiring friendship with Thomas Carlyle (q.v.) brought him frequently to Carlyle's House in Cheyne Row, Chelsea. Dante Gabriel Rossetti (q.v.), whose Pre-Raphaelite paintings he championed, lived at Tudor House, No. 16 Cheyne Walk nearby from 1862 to 1882. Ruskin even debated lodging with Rossetti but rejected the idea, a wise decision given the contrast between his own rather finicky temperament and the painter-poet's notoriously eccentric domestic habits. George MacDonald—novelist, poet and Ruskin's adviser during the emotional turmoil of his middle life—lived from 1868 to 1878 at Kelmscott House (then The Retreat), No. 26 Upper Mall, close to the river in Hammersmith. The house later belonged to William Morris (q.v.).

The Ruskins' Scottish ancestry ensured that he made several

Ruskin's sketch of his childhood home on Herne Hill. Courtesy of Ruskin Galleries, Bembridge

childhood visits to 'the good town of Perth,' as he remembers it in *Praeterita* (Vol. 1, Ch. 3). Bridgend, his aunt and uncle's home, has gone but No. 10 Rose Terrace on the west side of North Inch Park, where his aunt lived after her husband's death, remains. Ruskin returned to Perth in 1848 to marry Euphemia Gray at her home, Bowerswell, east of the Tay and reached by following the Bowerswell Road towards Kinnoull Hill. His parents' absence from the ceremony may have been because the house, formerly owned by the Ruskin family, held unpleasant memories of the suicide of Ruskin's paternal grandfather in 1818. Bowerswell is now an old peoples' home. returned to Perth in 1848 to marry Euphemia Gray at her home, Bowerswell, east of the Tay and reached by following the Bowerswell Road towards Kinnoull Hill. His parents' absence from the ceremony may have been because the house, formerly owned by the Ruskin family, held unpleasant memories of the suicide of Ruskin's paternal grandfather in 1818. Bowerswell is now an old peoples' home.

Ruskin's marriage again brought him north in 1853 with Effie, his *protégé* the Pre-Raphaelite painter John Everett Millais and Millais' brother, William. The party first stayed with his close friend Lady Pauline Trevelyan at the 17C family home of the Trevelyans, •Wallington Hall in Northumberland (20 miles NW of Newcastle upon Tyne via A696 and B6342). Ruskin's unfinished contribution to William Bell Scott's decoration of the central hall, made on a later visit in 1857, can still be seen. On this occasion he also first met Swinburne (q.v.), a man whose morals he deplored and whose poetry he greatly admired. The 1853 trip continued to remote Glenfinglas (or Finglas Water) north of The Trossachs in Central Scotland, where Millais undertook his famous portrait of Ruskin posed against suitably wild scenery.

Two English country houses, in very different locations, are associated with the years following the annulment of his marriage to Effie (who quickly married Millais) and the years of his unhappy attachment to Rose La Touche. Ruskin first visited Winnington Hall, NW of Northwich, Cheshire in 1859 when it was a school for girls run on advanced lines by Margaret Alexis Bell. He reported to his father that it was 'an enormous old-fashioned house—full of galleries and up and down stairs—but with magnificently large rooms where wanted . . . The house stands in a superb park, full of old trees & sloping down to the river; with a steep bank of trees on the other side.' His return visits, usually made in the course of lecturing tours through the Midland industrial cities ('miserable and abysmal places'), were attracted not so much by its architecture as by the pleasure of seeing his 'pets' and 'birds,' as he came to call Miss Bell's pupils. His interest in the school led to *The Ethics of the Dust* (1865). Winnington is now the property of ICI. Broadlands, off A31 south of Romsey in Hampshire—once the home of Lord Palmerston and later in the Mountbatten family—was in Ruskin's time the seat of Lord and Lady Mount-Temple. She became his close confidante, and it was to Broadlands that he went to recover from the shock of Rose La Touche's death in 1875.

Ruskin's connection with Oxford was renewed in 1869 with his appointment as the first Slade Professor of Art, a post he held until 1877 and again, though with unhappy results, from 1883 to 1885. The connection had begun in 1837 when he entered •Christ Church as a gentleman commoner, being received by the young aristocrats who enjoyed that exclusive undergraduate status as 'a good-humoured and inoffensive little cur' (*Praeterita*, Vol. 1, Ch. 11) and graduating in 1842 after delays caused by illness. During this period his overprotective mother took lodgings in the High Street. He found the neo-classical architecture of Peckwater Quad, where he had rooms, not to his taste, though he could praise the chapel (Oxford Cathedral) for being, despite crudities, 'true, and of its time—not an accursed sham of architect's job' (Vol. 1, Ch. 11). Christ Church's magnificent dining hall, completed by Wolsey in 1529, made him uncomfortable, but for social rather than aesthetic reasons: 'in Cardinal Wolsey's dining-room, I was, in all sorts of ways at once, less than myself, and in all sorts of wrong places at once, out of my place' (Vol. 1, Ch. 11). His interest in Oxford was rekindled by the building in 1855–60 of the University Museum (originally called the Oxford Museum of Natural History) on Parks Road opposite Keble College. He enthusiastically approved the Gothic design by Benjamin Woodward, lectured the workman employed on the project and even, according to tradition, built a brick column that afterwards needed discreet relaying, before he became disillusioned with the progress of the building.

In the later years of his professorial appointment Ruskin had rooms in Corpus Christi College but in early 1871 he lodged at the Crown and Thistle, an inn with courtyard on Bridge Street in Abingdon, south of Oxford. His route into the University allowed him to admire 'the wild hyacinths opening flakes of blue fire in Bagley Wood' (*Fors Clavigera*, Letter 6) and also inspired his famous road-building experiment of 1874. Noticing that the lack of a proper road forced carts to cross and so to damage the village green at North (or Ferry) Hinksey, he took lessons in stone-breaking and organised a working party of undergraduates, including Oscar Wilde (q.v.), to make good the deficiency. The scheme provoked much laughter, both locally and nationally, and Ruskin himself later admitted privately that the road his pupils constructed was 'about the worst in the three kingdoms.'

The 1870s also reaffirmed Ruskin's deep and loving connections with the Lake District that had begun with tours in childhood. Friar's Crag (NT, with a memorial to Ruskin) on the eastern shore of Derwentwater had left the most lasting impression:

> The first thing which I remember, as an event in life, was being taken by my nurse to the brow of Friar's Crag on Derwent Water; the intense joy, mingled with awe, that I had in looking through the hollows in the mossy roots, over the crag, into the dark lake, has associated itself more or less with all twining roots of trees ever since. (*Modern Painters*, Vol. 3, Ch. 17)

In 1871 he bought sight unseen the house and estate of Brantwood on the eastern shore of Coniston Water. He lived there first during his Oxford vacations and then permanently, under the care of his niece Joan Severn, as he sank into old age and engulfing insanity. Brantwood itself, badly dilapidated when he bought it, is not of architectural interest—though he was able to enrich its interior with his collection of paintings that included works by Titian, Tintoretto, Sir Edward Burne-Jones and, of course, his idol since youth, Turner. Though most of its contents were dispersed by the Severns after Ruskin's death, Brantwood still contains portraits, remnants of his library and some of the furniture he transported from his parents' home in Denmark Hill. The chief attraction remains the *grounds and the views they offer of Coniston Water and the Coniston Old Man (2635ft) beyond. *The Jumping Jenny*, the boat he designed, and the harbour by the lake whose construction he supervised are also noteworthy.

In the nearby village of Coniston, on the western shore of the Water, the Ruskin Museum houses early mss., mineral specimens, a stone harmonica and other relics from Brantwood. Ruskin's grave in the NE corner of the churchyard is marked by a monument, the work of his disciple Collingwood, featuring emblems of his life and

Study of Gneiss Rock at Glenfinlas, by Ruskin (1853). Courtesy of Ashmolean Museum

work—most notably, a figure of St George on the side facing the Old Man and, on one edge, wild roses in remembrance of Rose La Touche.

He is also commemorated in Poets' Corner (fee) of Westminster Abbey, suitably close to the tablet honouring a favourite writer, Sir Walter Scott (q.v.).

Though not directly connected with Ruskin in his lifetime, one final location should be mentioned. At Bembridge School on the eastern tip of the Isle of Wight the Ruskin Galleries contain a collection of private papers and drawings formerly at Brantwood.

Carlyle's House, Chelsea (NT). Open Apr to end Oct, Wed to Sun & BH Mon 11–5. Closed Good Fri. Fee.

Wallington Hall (NT). Grounds open all year during daylight hours. House open Apr to end Sept, every day except Tues 1–6; Oct, Wed, Sat & Sun 2–5. Walled garden open Apr to end Sept, every day 10–7; Oct, 10–6; Nov to end March 10–4. Fee.

Winnington Hall, Northwich. Visitors by appointment with the Secretary, Winnington Hall Club.

Broadlands, Romsey. Open 1 Apr to 30 Sept, Tues to Sun, also Mon in Aug & Sept & BH Mon 10–6. Fee.

University Museum, Oxford. Open Mon to Sat, 2–5.

Brantwood. Open Good Fri to end Oct, daily except Sat 11–5.30. Fee.

Ruskin Museum, Coniston. Open Easter to end Oct, daily 10–dusk. Fee.

Ruskin Galleries, Bembridge. Visitors by appointment with the Curator.

Sir Walter Scott

b. Edinburgh, 1771; d. Abbotsford, Borders Region, 1832. *The Eve of Saint John: A Border Ballad* (1800); *Minstrelsy of the Scottish Border* (1802); *The Lay of the Last Minstrel* (1805); *Ballads and Lyrical Pieces* (1806); *Marmion: A Tale of Flodden Field* (1808); *English Minstrelsy* (1810); *The Lady of the Lake: A Poem* (1810); *The Vision of Don Roderick: A Poem* (1811); *Rokeby: A Poem* (1813); *The Bridal of Triermain: Or The Vale of St John in Three Cantos* (1813); *Waverley: Or 'Tis Sixty Years Since* (1814); *Guy Mannering: Or The Astrologer* (1815); *The Lord of the Isles: A Poem* (1815); *The Field of Waterloo: A Poem* (1815); *The Antiquary* (1816); *Tales of My Landlord, Collected and Arranged by Jedediah Cleishbotham* (*The Black Dwarf* and *Old Mortality*; 1816); *Harold the Dauntless: A Poem* (1817); *Rob Roy* (1818); *Tales of My Landlord: Second Series* (*The Bride of Lammermoor* and *A Legend of Montrose*; 1819); *Ivanhoe: A Romance* (1820); *The Monastery: A Romance* (1820); *Kenilworth: A Romance* (1821); *The Pirate* (1822); *The Fortunes of Nigel* (1822); *Halidon Hill: A Dramatic Sketch* (1822); *Peveril of the Peak* (1822); *Quentin Durward* (1823); *St Ronan's Well* (1824); *Redgauntlet: A Tale of the Eighteenth Century* (1824); *Tales of the Crusaders* (*The Betrothed* and *The Talisman*; 1825); *Woodstock: Or The Cavalier* (1826); *Chronicles of the Canongate* (*The Highland Widow, The Two Drovers* and *The Surgeon's Daughter*; 1827); *The Life of Napoleon Buonaparte* (1827); *Tales of a Grandfather: Being Stories Taken from Scottish History* (1828); *Chronicles of the Canongate: Second Series* (*Valentine's Day, Or The Fair Maid of Perth*; 1828); *Tales of a Grandfather, Being Stories Taken from Scottish History: Second Series* (1829); *Anne of Geierstein; Or The Maiden of the Mist* (1829); *Tales of a Grandfather, Being Stories Taken from the History of Scotland: Third Series* (1830); *The History of Scotland* (1830); *Letters on Demonology and Witchcraft* (1830); *Tales of a Grandfather, Being Stories Taken from the History of France: Fourth Series* (1831); *Tales of My Landlord: Fourth Series* (*Count Robert of Paris* and *Castle Dangerous*; 1832).

Today, when Scott's poetry is usually forgotten and most of his novels are on the way to oblivion, it is hard to appreciate the reputation he once enjoyed. Although he modestly described himself as being beaten out of the field of poetry by Byron (q.v.) and generously praised Jane Austen (q.v.) for her delineation of ordinary life, he effortlessly outdistanced both these writers in his appeal to the reading public of his day. Scott's day, in fact, was a long one: to Dickens and George Eliot (qq.v.) he was still the acknowledged master of the genre in which they worked. If his popularity has faded, it has left its lasting influence. Scott wrote at a time when the fashion for wild landscape and for picturesque evidence of the medieval past was in the ascendant, and he gave this taste a local form and shape. His poems and novels sent people out to look at abbeys and views, castles and waterfalls, adding items to a tourist's map we still in large part observe even when we forget the name of Scott. Perhaps the most striking aspect of his achievement was that it changed the English attitude to Scotland. Scottish landscape had long been regarded as merely savage and its culture as suspect, attitudes which Bonnie Prince Charlie's rebellion not only intensified but turned into official doctrine. Living when time had lent the events of 1745 a romantic charm, Scott could make his country's history fashionable—a triumph neatly epitomised by his success in persuading George IV to wear the once forbidden tartan during his visit.

Edinburgh was the city not only of Scott's birth but of his working life as advocate and author. The obvious place to start a walking tour is the Scott Monument, designed by George Kemp in 1840, on the south side of Princes Street. The novelist sits with his dog Maida beside him under a prominent Gothic spire and canopy; characters from the novels are represented in the niches. Our first excursion takes us north into the Georgian New Town, still being developed during Scott's lifetime. We begin by walking west along Princes Street, turn right into Hanover Street and then take a left on George Street, where Scott lived briefly after his marriage in 1797. On its south side is the 18C Music Hall where, at a banquet in 1827, Scott first emerged from his technical anonymity as 'The Great Unknown' and publicly acknowledged the 'Waverley' novels as his own. On that occasion he modestly echoed Macbeth's words:

> I am afraid to think what I have done
> Look on't again, I dare not . . .

George Street leads to Castle Street where he lived at No. 39 from 1802 until his financial crash in 1826. These were the years when the steady stream of poetry and novels issuing from his pen made him the most prominent figure in Edinburgh—indeed, in Scottish—literary life. Visitors to Castle Street included the peasant poet James Hogg (q.v.), who astonished the company by stretching full length on the sofa in imitation of Scott's wife, and the English poet George Crabbe (q.v.). Crabbe's stay in 1822 coincided awkwardly with the arrival of George IV in Edinburgh, an event that gave Scott particular pride. He returned hurriedly from greeting his sovereign, with the glass from which the King had drunk stowed safely in his formal clothes:

> The royal gift was forgotten—the ample skirt of the coat within which it had been packed, and which he had hitherto held cautiously in front of his person, slipped back to its more usual position—he sat down beside

Crabbe, and the glass was crushed to atoms. His scream and gesture made his wife conclude that he had sat down on a pair of scissors, or the like; but very little harm had been done except the breaking of the glass, of which alone he had been thinking.

From the north end of Castle Street we turn right on Queen Street and its continuation as York Place to the church of St Paul and St George. The early 19C church preserves Scott's customary pew. From St Paul and St George we can return directly to Princes Street on Leith Street, but a more interesting route goes south from York Place on St Andrew Street, cuts across St Andrew Square and completes the walk on St David Street.

The second part of our walking tour leads south from Princes Street into the Old Town. The Mound, almost opposite Hanover Street, quickly brings us to Lady Stair's House, a charming 17C building which is now a museum devoted to Robert Burns and Robert Louis Stevenson (qq.v.) as well as Scott. From the museum Lawnmarket and Castle Hill, part of Edinburgh's Royal Mile, lead to the Castle. Always patriotic and always fascinated by his country's history, Scott was instrumental in the search for the traditional Scottish Regalia—including the crown, sceptre and sword—which had been forgotten since the Act of Union in 1707. They were rediscovered in 1818 and are now on display in the Crown Room. Mons Meg, the historic cannon which stands on the Castle Esplanade, was returned from the Tower of London as a result of Scott's request to George IV on his 1822 visit. Its history is described in a note to Chapter 27 of *Rob Roy*.

We now return along Castle Hill and Lawnmarket, and take George IV Bridge to the right. Chambers Street, on the left, occupies the site of College Wynd, the street where Scott was born. The birthplace was demolished during his lifetime. The Old University at the end of Chambers Street replaces the College buildings he attended (1783–85). At the southern end of King George IV Bridge is the church of the 17C Covenanters, Greyfriars. Scott's father—also Walter—is buried in its churchyard. From this point Bristo Street and Charles Street lead to George Square, a handsome 18C addition to the city whose dignity has been lessened by the university buildings which now occupy two of its sides. At No. 25, which survives, Scott lived from infancy, when his family moved from College Wynd, until his marriage in 1797.

From George Square we return north to the junction with Lawnmarket and follow High Street eastwards. On the right we find Parliament Square, dominated by St Giles Cathedral. In the western part of the square an arrangement of stones marks the site of the old Tolbooth Prison, demolished in 1817, which gave its name to *The Heart of Midlothian*. The novel begins with an account of the Porteous Riots (1736) here. The south side of the square is occupied by Parliament House, a 17C building whose exterior was disguised by the addition of an early 19C façade. As headquarters of the Court of Session and High Court it was familiar to Scott during his years as an attorney.

On Canongate, continuation of the High Street, we find the 17C Huntly House, now home of the City Museum, whose collection includes Scott relics. The tour ends at Holyrood Palace, whose double connection with Scott neatly illustrates the two aspects of his temperament. The fact that the Young Pretender, Prince Charlie, held court here in 1745 stirred his imagination and he recreated the scene in Chapter 43 of *Waverley*. But for all his attraction to Jacobitism, he was both a political realist and a loyal Hanoverian, and he proudly attended the state occasions in the Palace during George IV's Edinburgh visit. The King, who had made Scott a baronet in 1818, regarded him as 'the man in Scotland I most wish to see.'

Although Edinburgh was the scene of Scott's professional life, his heart lay in the Border Country he came to love in childhood and chose for home in middle age. The chief interest and the obvious starting point of a tour is his country estate at ••Abbotsford, 26 miles SE of Edinburgh via A7. He bought the modest farm, set among fine countryside by his beloved Tweed, in 1811 and renamed it Abbotsford because the monks from Melrose Abbey used to cross the river here. In the years that followed he enlarged the estate and had, by 1822, demolished the original farmhouse to create the present splendid mansion. In a letter of 1824 he could, with justice, say of his achievement what Augustus had said of Rome: he had found it brick and left it marble. Abbotsford satisfied Scott's ambition of becoming a laird, the founder of a dynasty, and the life he led there smacked more of the country gentleman than the relentlessly busy novelist. Writing was reserved for the early morning and it is said that his sons took some time to realise their father was a successful author as well as landed proprietor. When Scott's finances crashed in 1826 he offered Abbotsford to his creditors but they refused it. He spent his last years struggling to fulfil the famous promise that his right hand would work off his debts. In 1831, suffering from gall stones and the effect of several strokes, he embarked on a Mediterranean cruise but returned to die at Abbotsford the following year.

Abbotsford and its contents have been remarkably well preserved, allowing the visitor to appreciate the expressive statement that the house embodied: a statement of taste as well as wealth and gentility. The 'Waverley' novels probably did more than any other single force to encourage nostalgia for the Middle Ages, and Scott chose to build in the medieval style later known as 'Scottish Baronial.' The interior is lavishly filled with armour and heraldic devices. Yet the fanciful pinnacles and Gothic corridors were discreetly combined with the modern conveniences that appealed to an Edinburgh lawyer who believed in rational progress. There is a steam central heating system, and the servants' bells work by air compression. The contents of Abbotsford remind us that Scott was also an indefatigable collector of souvenirs and mementoes: Napoleon's cloak clasp, Rob Roy's purse, Burns' tumbler and a lock of the Young Pretender's hair are on display. In the library is a fine portrait of Scott by Raeburn.

From Abbotsford we may explore the surrounding Border Country in two tours. The first (65 miles) begins by taking A6091 east to •Melrose Abbey, notable for its delicate stone carving. *The Lay of the Last Minstrel* praises its lovely east window:

> The Moon on the east oriel shone
> Through slender shafts of stately stone,
>   By foliaged tracery combined;
> Thou would'st have thought some fairy's hand
> 'Twixt poplars straight the osier wand
> In many a freakish knot, had twined;
> Then framed a spell, when the work was done,
> And changed the willow wreathes to stone.
>
> (Canto 1, stanza 11)

Scott was in the habit of showing it to his guests, like Wordsworth and his sister Dorothy, who came in 1803 (s.v. Lake Poets, Rte 14). We then continue SE, joining A68, to St Boswells, where we follow B6404 and then take a left on B6356 for *Dryburgh Abbey, beautifully sited in a loop of the Tweed. Scott is buried in the Abbey Church. 2 miles north on B6356 is *Scott's View, a lovely panorama of the Tweed and the Eildon Hills, where it is said that the horses pulling his hearse stopped out of habit.

From here we return south to B6404, which is followed to the junction with B6397, where a left turn brings us to Smailholm (8 miles). As an infant Scott was brought here to his grandfather's farm, Sandyknowe, and he later remembered the attempts made to cure the lameness that poliomyelitis had caused:

> some one had recommended that so often as a sheep was killed for the use of the family, I should be stripped, and swathed up in the skin warm as it was flayed from the carcass of the animal. In this Tartar-like habiliment I well remember lying upon the floor of the little parlour in the farmhouse, while my grandfather, a venerable old man with white hair, used every excitement to make me try to crawl.

Robert Scott's land included a 16C Border tower perched on a little hill by a small loch, and in the introduction to Canto 3 of *Marmion* Scott looked back on the days when he had

> thought that shatter'd tower
> The mightiest work of human power;
> And marvell'd as the aged hind
> With some strange tale bewitch'd my mind,
> Of forayers, who, with headlong force,
> Down from that strength had spurr'd their horse,
> Their southern rapine to renew,
> Far in the distant Cheviots blue,
> And home returning, fill'd the hall
> With revels, wassel-rout, and brawl

(lines 176–185)

From Smailholm we return SE, joining A6089 to Kelso (5 miles). Scott first came to this charming little town by the confluence of the Teviot and the Tweed in 1783, when he briefly attended the grammar school and met James Ballantyne, later to be printer of his first books and his partner in business. Scott returned to Kelso in 1785, when he was eighteen, to stay with his uncle, Captain Robert Scott.

10 miles SW of Kelso via A698 and A68 is Jedburgh, where he made his first appearance as an advocate in 1793, the year after he had been admitted to the Bar. In 1803 he visited Wordsworth and his sister Dorothy at their lodging, No. 5 Abbey Close, and read them his *Lay of the Last Minstrel* (s.v. Lake Poets, Rte 14).

Further SW (via A68 and B6357, briefly interrupted by A6088) lies Liddesdale, the lovely region that Scott toured in the 1790s, collecting ballads for his *Minstrelsy of the Scottish Border*, the work that first brought him to public attention. Among the sights he visited is the romantic Hermitage Castle, 13C–14C stronghold of the Soulis family. We reach it by turning north from B6357 on B6399, a journey of 28 miles from Jedburgh.

The second tour from Abbotsford, some 75 miles in all, begins by taking A7 south to Selkirk (4 miles). Scott knew the town well from his duties as Sheriff of Selkirkshire, a post he held from 1800 until his death. A statue stands in the Market Place outside the former

Court House, which is now the Town Hall and has Scott relics. Bowhill, 2 miles west via A708 near the confluence of the Ettrick and the Yarrow, was the home of the Scotts of Buccleuch, whom Scott regarded as the head of his clan. The present building was begun in 1795 by the third Duke, to whom *Minstrelsy of the Scottish Border* was dedicated. Scott knew it well—his horse would turn up the avenue by habit—and it has relics of him as well as a fine art collection. Nearby Newark Castle, seen across the valley, is the setting for *The Lay of the Last Minstrel*. Wordsworth (s.v. Lake Poets, Rte 14) walked among the ruins with Scott in 1831. 'Yarrow Revisited' records Wordsworth's last impression of his friend, then obviously exhausted and near death.

A708 continues SE into the lovely valley of the Yarrow, associated like its sister valley of the Ettrick, with Scott's *protégé*, James Hogg. Like Hogg, Scott was a patron of Tibbie Shiel's Inn at the southern end of St Mary's Loch (8 miles). A708 then descends to Moffat, where we take A701 north and branch right up the Tweed valley via B712 to A72 (42 miles). Four miles east we find Neidpath Castle, home of the notorious fourth Duke of Queensberry, whom Scott visited. South of A72 8 miles further east is Traquair, claimed as the oldest continuously inhabited house in Scotland and as the original of 'Tully-Veolan,' the seat of the Baron of Bradwardine in *Waverley* (Chs 8 and 9). The journey, which is now leading us back towards Abbotsford, is completed by a glimpse of Ashietiel, the house Scott rented from 1804 to 1812. It lies on the south bank of the Tweed about 7 miles east of Traquair.

Although Scott's name is most indelibly stamped on the Border Country near Abbotsford, his use of The Trossachs as setting for *The Lady of the Lake* and his romantic tale of the 18C outlaw Rob Roy MacGregor played a vital role in attracting tourists to the region. Its lochs and wooded countryside were already to the Romantic taste—Wordsworth and Coleridge had come on a walking tour in 1803 (s.v. Lake Poets, Rte 15)—but later visitors, like Ruskin (q.v.), saw them through Scott's eyes. A tour of the area may begin at Aberfoyle (off A81 27 miles north of Glasgow), where the name of the hotel recalls that in Scott's novel Bailie Nichol Jarvie met Rob Roy here (Chs 28–30). The waterfall at Ledard near the northern shore of Loch Ard (off B829 4 miles west of Aberfoyle) suggested the setting for Flora MacIvor's harp-playing in *Waverley* (Ch. 22). Scott later regretted the theatricality of the episode but defended the beauty of the waterfall: 'It is upon a small scale, but otherwise one of the most exquisite cascades it is possible to behold.' A821 leads north from Aberfoyle into The Trossachs (5 miles), the gorge whose name means 'bristly country' separating Loch Katrine and Loch Achray. In *Rob Roy* Francis Osbaldistone describes his first view of this area:

> Our route, though leading towards the lake, had hitherto been so much shaded by wood, that we only from time to time obtained a glimpse of that beautiful sheet of water. But the road now suddenly emerged from the forest ground, and, winding close by the margin of the loch, afforded us a full view of its spacious mirror, which now, the breeze having totally subsided, reflected in still magnificence the high dark heathy mountains, huge grey rocks, and shaggy banks by which it is encircled. The hills now sunk on its margin so closely, and were so broken and precipitous, as to afford no passage except just upon the narrow line of the track which we occupied, and which was overhung with rocks . . . Add to this,

Loch Katrine, engraved from a sketch by Thomas Allom. From
William Beattie, Scotland Illustrated *(1838). Courtesy of*
Cambridge University Library

that, as the road winded round every promontory and bay which indented
the lake, there was rarely a possibility of seeing a hundred yards before
us. (Ch. 30)

*Loch Katrine is best seen from a cruise on the suitably named *Sir
Walter Scott,* which in summer makes the journey several times each
day from the pier to Stronachlachar on the western shore. Ellen's
Isle, named after the heroine of *The Lady of the Lake,* can also be
seen by taking the road one mile north from the car park and pier to
the Silver Strand (cars by permit only). A821 east to Callander (8
miles) gives a fine journey along the northern shores of Loch Achray
and Loch Venachar.

Two other places in Scotland demand mention. Glasgow, beating
Edinburgh to the honour by several years, was in 1837 the first city
to erect a statue of Scott. In George Square the figure by John
Greenfield stands on top of a column originally intended for George
III. Perth, by the Firth of Tay on the east coast, is proud of Scott's
treatment of its history in *The Fair Maid of Perth.* North Inch, the
100-acre park by the Tay, was the scene of the Clan Combat of 1396
described in the novel (Ch. 34). The Fair Maid's House on Blackfriars
Wynd is a rebuilt version of the one occupied by Simon Glover and
his daughter Catharine.

Neither Scott's life nor the antiquarian interests so richly expressed
in his fiction was by any means confined to Scotland. The English
places associated with his name may briefly be listed region by
region, proceeding from north to south.

In Northern England there are two important landmarks near his beloved Border Country. Norham Castle, once the stronghold of the Bishop Princes of Durham, is the setting for the first Canto of *Marmion*. It lies off A698 7 miles south of Berwick-upon-Tweed. The second Canto of *Marmion* takes place in the ruined Benedictine Priory at Lindisfarne, or Holy Island: 'A solemn, huge, and dark-red pile,/ Placed on the margin of the isle' (stanza 9). The island lies 4 miles from Beal (near A1 8 miles south of Berwick-upon-Tweed) and can be reached by car except at high tide.

Scott's visits in 1809 and 1812 to Greta Bridge (on A66 9 miles NW of Scotch Corner and A1) led him to use Rokeby Park and the surrounding landscape in his poem of the Civil War, *Rokeby*. The subject of the lovely song 'Brignall Banks' lies 2 miles SW.

Scott's life connected him with the Lake District in several ways. Carlisle (off M6) was the scene of his courtship and marriage. His wife, Charlotte Charpentier, lodged at No. 81 Castle Street and the couple were married in Carlisle Cathedral on Christmas Eve 1797. In *Waverley* (Ch. 49) the hero visits the Jacobite rebel Fergus MacIvor when he is imprisoned in the Norman keep of the Castle. Further south, Scott was a guest of both Wordsworth and Southey (s.v. Lake Poets, Rtes 12A and 12C). In 1825 his friend John Wilson, better remembered as 'Christopher North' of *Blackwood's Edinburgh Magazine*, honoured his fifty-fourth birthday with a regatta on Windermere. Scott watched it from Storrs Point, on the eastern shore 2 miles south of Bowness-on-Windermere.

The Isle of Man, west of the Lake District but nowadays usually reached from Liverpool, appears in one of his late novels, *Peveril of the Peak*. Peel Castle on the west coast is introduced as 'one of those singular monuments of antiquity with which this singular and interesting island abounds' (Vol. 3, Ch. 3). Julian Peveril and Fenella escape by boat from Fenella's Tower in Volume 3, Chapter 7.

Yorkshire is the setting for much of *Ivanhoe*, Scott's first and probably his most successful English historical novel. 'Templestowe,' where Sir-Brian-de-Bois-Guilbert holds Rebecca captive, is based on the 17C Temple Newsam. It lies near the River Aire off an unclassified road 4 miles east of Leeds. *Conisbrough Castle, home of Rowena's intended husband Athelstane, survives and its superb keep is quite as magnificent as Scott suggests, even if he wrongly insisted on its being Saxon rather than Norman:

> There are few more beautiful or striking scenes in England than are presented by the vicinity of this ancient Saxon fortress. The soft and gentle river Don sweeps through an amphitheatre, in which cultivation is richly blended with woodland, and on a mount, ascending from the river, well defended by walls and ditches, rises this ancient edifice, which, as its Saxon name implies, was, previous to the Conquest, a royal residence of the kings of England. The outer walls have probably been added by the Normans, but the inner keep bears token of very great antiquity. It is situated on a mount at one angle of the inner court, and forms a complete circle of perhaps twenty-five feet in diameter. The wall is of immense thickness, and is propped or defended by six huge external buttresses which project from the circle, and rise up against the sides of the tower as if to strengthen or to support it. These massive buttresses are solid when they arise from the foundation, and a good way higher up; but are hollowed out towards the top, and terminate in a sort of turrets communicating with the interior of the keep itself. The distant appearance of this huge building, with these singular accompaniments, is as interesting to the lovers of the picturesque, as the interior of the castle is to the eager antiquary . . . (Ch. 41)

The Castle is on A630 5 miles SW of Doncaster and A1.

Yet the most memorable episode of *Ivanhoe* takes place in Central England. Prince John's tournament (Chs 7–13) is held on the field 1 mile north of Ashby-de-la-Zouch, on A50 between Leicester and Burton-upon-Trent. Scott, however, is careful to point out that Ashby Castle, where Prince John holds his festival after the tournament, is 'not the same building of which the stately ruins still interest the traveller' (Ch. 14).

The rest of Central England is the territory of *Kenilworth* and *Woodstock*, novels whose 19C popularity vied even with Shakespeare's reputation in attracting visitors to the area. In Kenilworth itself (on A452 and A46 between Coventry and Royal Leamington Spa) Scott stayed at the King's Arms Hotel, where his room is still pointed out. His novel recreated the splendour of the Castle in the time of Queen Elizabeth, most notably by its description of the revels in Chapter 35. The same novel made adroit use of the legend which associated Charlecote Park, outside Stratford-upon-Avon, with Shakespeare (q.v., Rte 6). *Woodstock* takes as its scene the vanished royal manor (built by Henry I) on A34 30 miles SE of Stratford and 8 miles NW of Oxford. Its deer park was assimilated into the grounds of Blenheim Palace. The legends connected with Wayland Smith's Cave, the striking dolmen in the Vale of the White Horse (off B4507 4 miles west of Wantage) are adapted to help the plot of *Kenilworth* (see especially Chs 9–11).

Scott first saw London at the age of four and, returning some twenty-five years later, was surprised to discover how accurate his memory of Westminster Abbey had been. Fittingly, he is now honoured by a prominent memorial in Poets' Corner (fee).

Lady Stair's House, Edinburgh. Open Mon to Sat 10–5 (June to Sept, 10–6).

Edinburgh Castle (DoE/SDD). Open May to Oct, Mon to Sat 9.30–6, Sun 11–6; Nov to Apr, Mon to Sat 9.30–5, Sun 12.30–4.30. Closed Christmas Day, Boxing Day & First 3 days of Jan. Fee.

Huntly House, Edinburgh. Open Mon to Sat 10–5 (June to Sept, 10–6).

Palace of Holyroodhouse, Edinburgh (DoE/SDD). State & historical apartments open 5 Jan to 31 March & 21 Oct to 31 Dec (except Christmas Day & Boxing Day), Mon to Sat 9.30–4.30; 1 Apr to 20 Oct, Mon to Sat 9.30–6, Sun 10.30–5.15. Historical apartments open 7 May to 13 May, 30 May to 20 June & 10 July to 14 July, Mon to Sat 9.30–6, Sun 10.30–5.15. Closed during Royal & State visits. Fee.

Abbotsford. Open 19 March to 31 Oct, Mon to Sat 10–5, Sun 2–5. Fee.

Melrose Abbey (DoE/SDD). Open Apr to Sept, Mon to Sat 9.30–7, Sun 2–7; Oct to March, Mon to Sat 9.30–4, Sun 2–4. Closed Tues & alternate Wed in winter, Christmas Day, Boxing Day, New Year's Day & 2 Jan. Fee.

Dryburgh Abbey (DoE/SDD). Open 15 March to 15 Oct, Mon to Sat 9.30–6.30, Sun 2–6.30; 16 Oct to 14 March, Mon to Sat 9.30–4, Sun 2–4. Closed Christmas Day, Boxing Day, New Year's Day & 2 Jan. Fee.

Smailholm Tower (DoE/SDD). Visitors should apply to key keeper at the farm.

Hermitage Castle (DoE/SDD). Open Apr to Sept, Mon to Sat 9.30–7, Sun 2–7; Oct to March, Mon to Sat 9.30–4, Sun 2–4. Closed Tues & alternate Wed in winter, Christmas Day, Boxing Day, New Year's Day & 2 Jan. Fee.

Bowhill. Open Easter, May, June, Sept, Mon, Wed, Thurs, Sat, 12.30–5, Sun 2–6; July, Aug, Mon to Thurs & Sat 12.30–5, Sun 2–6. Fee.

Newark Castle. Apply to Buccleuch Estates, Bowhill.

Neidpath Castle. Open 19 Apr to mid Oct, Mon to Sat 10–1, 2–6, Sun 1–6. Fee.

Traquair House. Open 15 Apr to 30 Sept, daily 1.30–5.30 (10.30–5.30 July, Aug and first 2 weeks of Sept). Fee.

Norham Castle (English Heritage). Open 15 March to 15 Oct, Mon to Sat 9.30–6.30, Sun 2–6.30 (Apr to Sept, Sun 9.30–6.30); 16 Oct to 14 March, Mon to Sat 9.30–4, Sun 2–4. Closed Christmas Eve, Christmas Day, Boxing Day & New Year's Day. Fee.

Lindisfarne Priory (English Heritage). Open 15 March to 15 Oct, Mon to Sat 9.30–6.30, Sun 2–6.30 (Apr to Sept, Sun 9.30–6.30); 16 Oct to 14 March, Mon to Sat 9.30–4, Sun 2–4. Closed Christmas Eve, Christmas Day, Boxing Day & New Year's Day. Fee.

Carlisle Castle (English Heritage). Open 15 March to 15 Oct, Mon to Sat 9.30–6.30, Sun 2–6.30; 16 Oct to 14 March, Mon to Sat 9.30–4, Sun 2–4. Closed Christmas Eve, Christmas Day, Boxing Day & New Year's Day. Fee.

Peel Castle. Open Good Fri & Easter Mon 10–5; 1 May to 30 Sept, Mon to Sat 10–6, Sun 2–5. Fee.

Temple Newsam. Open Tues to Sun & BH Mon 10.30–6.15 or dusk; also May to Sept, Wed 10.30–8.30. Fee.

Conisbrough Castle (English Heritage). Open 15 March to 15 Oct, Mon to Sat 9.30–6.30, Sun 2–6.30 (Apr to Sept, Sun 9.30–6.30); 16 Oct to 14 March, Mon to Sat 9.30–4, Sun 2–4. Closed Christmas Eve, Christmas Day, Boxing Day & New Year's Day. Fee.

Kenilworth Castle. (English Heritage). Open 15 March to 15 Oct, Mon to Sat 9.30–6.30, Sun 2–6.30 (Apr to Sept, Sun 9.30–6.30); 16 Oct to 14 March, Mon to Sat 9.30–4, Sun 2–4. Closed Christmas Eve, Christmas Day, Boxing Day & New Year's Day. Fee.

Charlecote Park (NT). Open Apr & Oct, Sat, Sun, BH Mon & Tues after Easter 11–5; May to end Sept, Tues, Wed, Fri to Sun, & BH Mon 11–6. Fee.

Blenheim Palace. Park open all year 9–5. Fee. House open 15 March to 31 Oct, daily 11–6. Fee.

Wayland Smith's Cave (English Heritage). Open at all reasonable times.

George Bernard Shaw

b. Dublin, 1856; d. Ayot St Lawrence, Hertfordshire, 1950. *Cashel Byron's Profession: A Novel* (1886); *An Unsocial Socialist* (1887); *The Quintessence of Ibsenism* (1891); *Widowers' Houses* (1893); *Arms and the Man* (1898); *Candida* (1898); *The Devil's Disciple* (1901); *The Man of Destiny* (1898); *The Perfect Wagnerite* (1898); *Mrs Warren's Profession* (1898); *The Philanderer* (1898); *Caesar and Cleopatra* (1901); *Love Among the Artists* (1900); *Man and Superman: A Comedy and a Philosophy* (1903); *John Bull's Other Island* (1907); *Major Barbara* (1907); *The Sanity of Art* (1908); *The Doctor's Dilemma* (1911); *The Shewing-up of Blanco Posnet* (1909); *Misalliance* (1914); *Androcles and the Lion* (1916); *Heartbreak House* (1919); *Back to Methusaleh: A Metabiological Pentateuch* (1921); *Saint Joan* (1924); *The Intelligent Woman's Guide to Socialism and Capitalism* (1928); *The Apple Cart: A Political Extravaganza* (1930); *The Adventures of the Black Girl in Her Search for God* (1932); *Too True To Be Good* (1934); *The Millionairess* (1936); *In Good King Charles's Golden Days* (1939).

Shaw's birthplace in Dublin at No. 33 (then No. 3) Synge Street, SW of St Stephen's Green, is marked with a plaque. His childhood in this modest house was quietly unhappy, overshadowed by his father's habitual drunkenness and his mother's cold, unloving manner. The dreariness of his circumstances was partly relieved after 1866, when the family was able to take a summer cottage on the coast at Dalkey, SE of the city, with its fine views of Dublin Bay.

In 1872 his mother took her two daughters to London, leaving her husband and son behind. After working for an estate agent, Shaw followed her in 1876. From 1887 until his marriage in 1898 they lived together at No. 29 Fitzroy Square, south of Euston Road west of its junction with Tottenham Court Road, and now marked with a GLC blue plaque. His own description of himself (in *Sixteen Self-Sketches*) as sponging ruthlessly off his mother during these years is a characteristic exaggeration, but the account of his long disheartening struggle to make his way as a writer is not. After his failure as a novelist he turned to reviewing art, music and, eventually, drama; it was not until the 1890s, when he was in his forties, that he began to be recognised as a playwright. The most important scene of his success is the Royal Court Theatre in Sloane Square, Chelsea (between Knightsbridge and the King's Road). His connection with the Royal Court and its adventurous manager, Harley Granville-Barker, began with the production of *Candida* in 1904. In the years that followed Shaw was a close friend of the actress Mrs Patrick Campbell, the first Eliza Doolittle, whose home was at No. 33 Kensington Square (south of Kensington High Street via Young Street).

By this time he had cured the shyness from which he suffered in youth, to become an effective speaker and campaigner on behalf of Socialism. His friends in the Fabian Society included H.G. Wells (q.v.) as well as Beatrice and Sidney Webb. The interest in politics can be traced back to visits to William Morris (q.v.) at his house in Hammersmith.

After his marriage to Charlotte Payne-Townshend Shaw lived at Adelphi Terrace (between the Strand and Victoria Embankment Gardens), an address favoured by several literary men of his generation. James Barrie (q.v.) was a neighbour but never an intimate friend.

The Shaws kept their London flat but after 1906 made their main home in Hertfordshire at Ayot St Lawrence (near A1 3 miles NW of Welwyn Garden City). Shaw's Corner is hardly an attractive house but it is impeccably respectable. It reminds the visitor of that streak of conventionality, even Puritanism, which underlay his flamboyantly eccentric views about diet, dress and medicine—about, indeed, any subject on which the Press cared to ask his opinion. On his death in 1950 his ashes were scattered in the garden and the house itself bequeathed to the National Trust. It remains virtually unaltered since his day, its atmosphere still bespeaking the organised regime which Charlotte imposed on her husband's rather disorderly habits. In the garden is the summerhouse where Shaw did much of his writing, safe from the possibility of interruption by visitors.

Shaw's Corner, Ayot St Lawrence (NT). Open Apr to end Oct, Mon to Thurs 2–6, Sun & BH Mon 12–6. Closed Good Fri. Fee.

Percy Bysshe Shelley

b. Field Place, West Sussex, 1792; d. at sea between Leghorn and Lerici, Italy, 1822. *Original Poetry by Victor and Cazire* (1810); *The Necessity of Atheism* (with Thomas Jefferson Hogg; 1811); *A Poetical Essay on the Existing State of Things* (1812); *An Addrress to the Irish People* (1812); *Declaration of Rights* (1812); *The Devil's Walk: A Ballad* (1812); *Queen Mab: A Philosophical Poem, with Notes* (1813); *A Refutation of Deism, In a Dialogue* (1814); *Alastor: Or the Spirit of Solitude, and Other Poems* (1816); *A Proposal for Putting Reform to the Vote Throughout the Kingdom, by the Hermit of Marlow* (1817); *An Address to The People on the Death of Princess Charlotte, by the Hermit of Marlow* (1817); *History of a Six Weeks' Tour Through a Part of France, Switzerland, Germany and Holland* (with Mary Wollstonecraft Shelley; 1817); *The Revolt of Islam; A Poem in Twelve Cantos* (originally called *Laon and Cythna*; 1818); *Rosalind and Helen: A Modern Eclogue; with Other Poems* (1819); *The Cenci: A Tragedy in Five Acts* (1819); *Prometheus Unbound: A Lyrical Drama in Four Acts, with Other Poems* (1820); *Oedipus Tyrannus or Swellfoot the Tyrant: A Tragedy in Two Acts* (1820); *Defence of Poetry* (1821); *Epipsychidion* (1821); *Adonais: An Elegy on the Death of John Keats* (1821); *Hellas: A Lyrical Drama* (1822).

Field Place, where Shelley was born, is a modest country house NW of Horsham; it is reached by following A264 toward Guildford for 1½ miles, turning right on B2199 at Broadbridge Heath and taking a left after 400 yards. Here the poet and his sister Elizabeth wrote the youthful verses for which they adopted the pseudonyms 'Victor' and 'Cazire.' His youthful radicalism and marriage to Harriet Westbrook alienated Shelley from his father, Sir Timothy, and he was refused admission to the house in 1815 when he arrived for the reading of his grandfather's will. He spent the afternoon in the grounds reading Milton's *Comus.*

During his years at Eton College (1804–10) Shelley's opinions and his love of chemical experiments earned him the nicknames of 'Mad Shelley' and 'Shelley the Atheist' from his fellow pupils. The school is west of London and most easily reached from Junction 6 of M4.

Shelley's undergraduate career at University College, Oxford continued the pattern he had established at Eton and so was brief but spectacular. Shortly after his entrance in October 1810 he sent copies of his anonymous pamphlet, *The Necessity of Atheism*, to the heads of the Colleges. Questioned about its authorship, he refused to answer and was expelled in March 1811. Thomas Jefferson Hogg, fellow student, fellow radical and co-author, suffered the same fate. The modern visitor to the College can find a memorial of 1893, originally intended for the Protestant Cemetery in Rome, by following a passage from the NW corner of Front Quad. The dome is by Basil Champneys and the effigy of the drowned poet by Onslow Ford.

After Oxford Shelley's life was restless and mobile; many of the places he visited preserve no trace of his brief residence. In the winter of 1811–12 he took Harriet Westbrook to Keswick in the Lake District, renting what is now known as Shelley's Cottage on Chestnut Hill. He wrote enthusiastically of his surroundings:

> Oh! how you will delight in this scenery. The mountains are now capped with snow. The lake [Derwentwater] as I see it here is glassy and calm. Snow vapours tinted by the loveliest refractions pass far below the summit of these gigantic rocks. The scene even in winter is inexpressibly lovely. The clouds assume shapes which seem peculiar to these regions. . . Oh!

give me a little cottage in *that* scene, let all live in peaceful little houses, let temples and palaces rot with their perishing masters.

He had been drawn to the area by the presence of the Lake Poets (q.v., Rte 12A) but Coleridge was absent and Wordsworth was oblivious of his existence, so he met only Southey, then living at nearby Greta Hall. The older writer's radicalism had waned with the years and he was made uncomfortable by the presence of a youth who 'acts upon me as my own ghost would do.' Shelley recovered from his mild disappointment by starting a correspondence with William Godwin, radical philosopher and his future father-in-law.

He first met Harriet Westbrook in London in 1811, when he was lodging at No. 15 Poland Street, south of Oxford Street. He returned to the area in 1814 to resolemnise their Scottish marriage at St George's Church, Hanover Square, SW of Oxford Circus. The ceremony made their marriage legally binding but no more success-ful, for she left him less than a month later. The curious and unhappy story ended in Hyde Park to the SW, where Harriet drowned herself in the Serpentine some two years later. In Hampstead Shelley visited Leigh Hunt (q.v.) at his cottage in the Vale of Health, reached from East Heath Road. His host introduced him to Keats (q.v.), but the two poets never became close friends and Keats later declined an invitation to stay with Shelley.

Shelley several times stayed in the Berkshire and Buckinghamshire countryside west of his old school. In 1816 he visited Thomas Love Peacock (q.v.) at Marlow, on A4155 between Slough and Reading. In 1817–18 he bought Albion House (now divided but marked with a plaque) on West Street; it was here that his second wife, Mary, daughter of Godwin and Mary Wollstonecraft, wrote *Frankenstein* while he wrote *The Revolt of Islam* and pamphlets as 'the Hermit of Marlow.' His favourite walk was to Bisham Woods, over Marlow Bridge and south of A404. He also went with Peacock on a boating expedition up the Thames to Lechlade, at the junction of A417 and A361 10 miles NE of Swindon. The occasion is remembered in the fine poem, 'A Summer Evening Churchyard,' quoted on a plaque on the churchyard wall.

When Shelley left Marlow he went abroad to an equally itinerant life and an early death by drowning. His body was cremated on the beach at Viareggio by a party that included Byron, Leigh Hunt (qq.v.) and Captain Edward Trelawny, who later wrote unreliable memoirs of both poets. The ashes were buried in the Protestant Cemetery at Rome with an epitaph by Hunt, but before the funeral pyre had burnt down Trelawney snatched what he declared to be Shelley's heart from the flames, though it is more likely to have been his liver. The heart—or liver—was returned to Mary Shelley and finally buried with her at St Peter's Church, Bournemouth, on the south coast. The fine Priory Church at Christchurch, 8 miles east of Bournemouth on A337, has a monument of 1854 originally intended for St Peter's.

Westminster Abbey has been slow and grudging in its recognition of the Romantic poets. The present memorial to Shelley and Keats in Poets' Corner (fee) was not erected until 1954.

Eton College. Open Daily 2–5 during term, 10.30–5 during spring holiday, 9–5 during summer holiday. Fee.

William Shenstone

b. Halesowen, West Midlands, 1714; d. Halesowen, 1763. *The Schoolmistress* (1742); *A Pastoral Ballad* (1755).

Though he left Oxford without taking a degree, Shenstone's residence at Pembroke College helped that institution's claim to be a 'nest of singing birds' of which his near-contemporary, Dr Johnson (q.v.), liked to boast.

In his youth Shenstone spent time in London and the fashionable spas but in 1745 he retired more or less permanently to The Leasowes, the small estate where he had been born, at Halesowen, SW of Birmingham. Here he devoted himself to writing poetic trifles and, mainly, to laying out his land in the Picturesque manner. His achievement managed to provoke chilly admiration from a man as indifferent to natural beauties as Dr Johnson:

> Now was excited his delight in rural pleasures, and his ambition of rural elegance: he began from this time to point his prospects, to diversify his surfaces, to entangle his walks, and to wind his waters; which he did with such judgment and such fancy, as made his little domain the envy of the great and the admiration of the skilful; a place to be visited by travellers and copied by designers.

Shenstone's estate has since vanished beneath a park and golf course to the east of the town centre, though a fragment of the ruined Priory he incorporated into his effects remains. He was buried in the parish church and is commemorated by a large urn of 1771 with an inscription by his friend Richard Graves, author of *The Spiritual Quixote*.

At Hagley Hall (5 miles SW on A456), where Shenstone was frequently a guest of Lord Lyttleton, we can find surviving examples of the poet's taste. The rather plain house itself is by Sanderson Miller but the delightfully contrived *park, cunningly dotted with garden buildings, was laid out with Shenstone's help. He met James Thomson (q.v.) here in 1743.

The legend connected with Shenstone's poem 'Written at an Inn At Henley,' probably dating from 1750, illustrates the pitfalls awaiting the literary topographer. Boswell's *Life* for 1776 tells how Johnson, relaxing in an unnamed inn after a visit to Blenheim Palace, quoted the last stanza with approval:

> Whoe'er has travell'd life's dull round,
>   Where'er his stages may have been,
> May sigh to think he still has found
>   The warmest welcome at an Inn.

Boswell adds: 'We happened to lie this night at the inn at Henley, where Shenstone wrote these lines.' Tradition and the guidebooks following in its wake have presumed this to be the 15C Red Lion at Henley-on-Thames, on A423 24 miles SE of Oxford. The Red Lion now has rooms named after all three writers and a replica of the stanza scratched on one of its windows. Yet Boswell's account makes it clear that their overnight stop was between Stratford-upon-Avon and Birmingham, which they were able to reach by nine the next morning, and hence that the town must be Henley-in-Arden, Warwickshire, 6 miles NW of Stratford on A34, where the picturesque

White Swan would seem a likely candidate. The objection is that Shenstone, a frequent guest of Lady Luxborough at The Barrels nearby, would have had little need to celebrate the hospitality of local inns. In fact, Richard Graves' *Recollections* (1788), based on personal knowledge of Shenstone and partly intended to correct the portrait Johnson gave in *Lives of the Poets*, states unequivocally that the poem was written in a 'summer house'—unnamed and unidentifiable—at Edge Hill, 6 miles north of Banbury, Oxfordshire. The misleading title may well have been supplied not by the poet but by his publisher, Dodsley.

Hagley Hall. Open from Easter Sun, BH Sun & Mon 12.30–5; 1 July to 2 Sept, daily except Sat 12.30–5. Fee.

Richard Brinsley Sheridan

b. Dublin, 1751; d. London, 1816. *The Rivals* (1775); *The School for Scandal* (1799); *The Critic* (1781).

Sheridan was born at No. 12 Upper Dorset Street, now marked by a plaque, in an undistinguished part of north Dublin and baptised at St Mary's, Mary Street, off Capel Street to the south.

His father's declining fortunes as actor and manager brought him to Bath in 1770, where he organised 'Attic Entertainments.' The family lodged at No. 9 New King Street (with a tablet), south of the fashionable Royal Crescent and in a distinctly less fashionable quarter. In 1772 Sheridan became involved in a romance with the beautiful singer Eliza Linley and a train of melodramatic events that were transmuted into the comedy of his first success, *The Rivals*. In order to protect Eliza from the attentions of another suitor, a Major Mathews, he eloped with her to France from her lodgings at No. 11 Royal Crescent; on his return he found himself embroiled in local scandal, family disagreements and two abortive duels with the quarrelsome Major.

The couple were eventually married in 1773 at Marylebone Parish Church in London. Its site near the north end of Marylebone High Street is now a Garden of Rest. The couple lived nearby at No. 22 Orchard Street, the southern continuation of Baker Street to its junction with Oxford Street. Two of Sheridan's later London addresses are worth noting: No. 10 Hertford Street (tablet), which leads from near the south end of Park Lane by the Hilton Hotel, acquired in 1795 on the death of General Burgoyne; and the home of his last years, No. 14 Savile Row (tablet), running parallel with Regent Street. Two other sites recall the twin directions of Sheridan's career after his playwriting days were over. As theatrical manager he built a new Theatre Royal, Drury Lane at the corner of Russell Street in Covent Garden. Its destruction by fire in 1809 robbed London of a major landmark but provoked a typical witticism from Sheridan. Watching the blaze from a nearby coffee house he remarked: 'A man may surely take a glass of wine by his own fireside.' As Whig politician, notably active in the impeachment of Warren Hastings, he frequented Brooks's Club on St James's Street.

Sheridan was MP for Stafford. His residence, Chetwynd House in Greengate Street, is now the Post Office.

Despite the reduced and unhappy circumstances of his last years —caused by the loss of his theatre, the difficulties of the Whig faction to which he had adhered and by his excessive drinking—Sheridan received a public funeral at Westminster Abbey. He was buried in Poets' Corner (fee) and not, as he would have preferred, near the grave of his old political ally, Charles James Fox, at the west end of the north aisle.

Sir Philip Sidney

b. Penshurst, Kent, 1554; d. Zutphen, Holland, 1586. *Arcadia* (1590); *Astrophel and Stella* (1591); *An Apologie for Poetrie* (1598).

Sir Philip Sidney, whom contemporaries and later generations praised as the pattern of the Renaissance courtier, was born at **Penshurst Place, SW of Tonbridge in Kent. Later celebrated in a famous poem by Ben Jonson (q.v.), the house remains a magnificent example of a medieval mansion lightly refurbished in the Elizabethan manner. The 14C hall is particularly notable. Penshurst's collection includes portraits of the poet and parts of his armour.

Sidney was educated at Shrewsbury, county town of Shropshire, in the old buildings of the School (now a Library) on Castle Gates opposite the Castle. A statue, erected in 1923 as a First World War Memorial, stands outside the School's present buildings (1882) near the south bank of the River Severn. Because of his father's position as President of the Court of the Marches he also stayed at Ludlow Castle to the south.

In 1568 he entered Christ Church, Oxford. Family connections with the Earl of Leicester made him a visitor to Kenilworth Castle, now ruined but then a centre of aristocratic life, on A452 north of Oxford and Royal Leamington Spa.

His charm, learning and favourable position at court assured Sidney's familiarity with other great houses. In 1578 he received a deputation of university dons at Audley End, Essex to the south of Cambridge; it included Gabriel Harvey, fellow member of the Areopagus, a group committed to introducing classical principles into English literature. More important were Sidney's visits to his sister Mary Herbert, Countess of Pembroke, at the splendid Renaissance mansion of **Wilton House, west of Salisbury in Wiltshire. He began the *Arcadia* at Wilton during a brief period of disgrace from the court in 1580. Its Single Cube Room has wall paintings by Thomas de Critz illustrating scenes from the prose romance.

After his death at the battle of Zutphen, Sidney's body was returned to London and buried in old St Paul's Cathedral.

Penshurst Place. Open Apr to end Oct, Tues (except after BH), Wed, Thurs, Sat, Sun, BH Mon 2–6. Fee.

Shrewsbury Library. Open Mon & Wed 9.30–6, Tues & Fri 9.20–2, Sat 9.30–5.

Ludlow Castle. Open May to Sept, daily 10.30–6; Oct to Apr, Mon to Sat 10.30–4. Fee.

Kenilworth Castle (English Heritage). Open 15 March to 15 Oct, Mon to Sat 9.30–6.30, Sun 2–6.30 (Apr to Sept, Sun 9.30–6.30); 16 Oct to 14 March, Mon to Sat 9.30–4, Sun 2–4. Closed Christmas Eve, Christmas Day, Boxing Day &

New Year's Day. Fee.

Audley End (English Heritage). Open Apr to Sept, Tues to Sun 1–6.30. Closed Good Fri but open BH Mon except May Day. Fee.

Wilton House. Open mid Apr to mid Oct, Tues to Sat & BH Mon 11–6, Sun 1–6. Fee.

John Skelton

b. place unknown, 1460; d. London, 1529. Poet.

From 1498 until his death Skelton was rector of St Mary at Diss (on A1066 20 miles south of Norwich). Although there is good reason to believe that he merely held the living rather than being permanently resident there, he spent enough time in his parish to write a poem ('Ware the Hauke') excoriating a curate for unleashing his bird in the church, to direct satirical jibes against some of his parishioners, and to acquire a reputation for irregular behaviour that accords well with the often boisterous nature of his verse.

He was buried in London at St Margaret's near Westminster Abbey.

Christopher Smart

b. Shipbourne, Kent, 1722; d. London, 1771. *Poems on Several Occasions* (1752); *A Song to David* (1763); *Jubilate Agno* (edited as *Rejoice in the Lamb* by William Force Stead; 1939).

The Kentish scenes of Smart's childhood in the villages of Shipbourne (on A227 4 miles north of Tonbridge) and East Barming (on A26 2 miles SW of Maidstone) are evoked in his poem 'The Hop-Garden.'

After his father's death in 1733 the family moved to Durham. Smart became a frequent guest of the Vane family, whom his father had served as steward, at Raby Castle (on A688 20 miles SW of the city and near Staindrop). At this fine 14C building, not yet reconstructed and modernised, he mixed on terms of apparent equality with the Vane children and fell in love with Anne, later remembered in *Jubilate Agno*.

In 1739 he entered Pembroke College (then Pembroke Hall), Cambridge, thanks to the generosity of Henrietta, Duchess of Cleveland and wife to Lord Barnard of Raby. Smart's academic career was distinguished: he rose from the humble position of sizar (or poor student) to Scholar of the University in 1742 and to Fellow of Pembroke in 1745, writing prize-winning poems as he went. Yet it was also marred by extravagance, as a 1747 letter by his colleague at Pembroke, the poet Gray (q.v.), vividly testifies:

> your mention of Mr Vane, reminds me of poor Smart (not that I, or any other Mortal, pity him) about three weeks ago he was arrested here at the Suit of a Taylor in London for a Debt of about 50£ of three Years standing. the College had about 28£ due to him in their Hands, the rest (to hinder him from going to the Castle, for he could not raise a Shilling) Brown, May & Peele, lent him upon his Note. upon this he remain'd confined to his Room, lest his Creditors here should snap him; & the

Fellows went round to make out a List of his Debts, wch amount in Cambridge to above 350£. that they might come the readier to some Composition, he was advised to go off in the Night, & lie hid somewhere or other.

His friend Charles Burney, father of the novelist (q.v.), offered a clue to at least one cause of Smart's difficulties: 'he ruined himself by returning the tavern treats of strangers who had invited him as a wit and an extraordinary personage.'

Although he maintained a formal connection with Pembroke until 1755, Smart went to London in 1749 to make his way as a professional author. The circumstances of his wedding in 1752 to Anna Maria (Nancy) Carnan are obscure, perhaps because it violated the conditions of his Fellowship, but it may have taken place at St Bride's off Fleet Street. It is certain, however, that he and his wife went to live at Canonbury Tower, facing Canonbury Place SE of Highbury and Islington Station (British Rail and Victoria Line). The fine 16C building, now headquarters of the Tower Theatre, was rented out as apartments; its tenants included Smart's father-in-law, the publisher John Newbery, who was also responsible for bringing Oliver Goldsmith (q.v.) to live at Canonbury.

In 1756 Smart suffered his first attack of religious mania, which took the form of literal obedience to the Biblical injunction that he should pray without ceasing. His friend Dr Johnson (q.v.) regarded these symptoms with gruff compassion ('I'd as lief pray with Kit Smart as anyone else. Another charge was that he did not love clean linen; and I have no passion for it') but their recurrence consigned the poet to asylums and, finally, debtors' prison. Such places have long since vanished from the map of London and the best memorial to Smart's later years of suffering is his religious poetry, especially *A Song to David*.

Raby Castle, near Staindrop. Open Apr to June & Sept, Wed & Sun 2–5; July & Aug, daily except Sat 2–5. Fee.

Canonbury Tower (Tower Theatre). Tours by arrangement, and for parties after Sat evening performance.

Tobias Smollett

b. Dalquharn, Strathclyde, 1721; d. Leghorn, Italy, 1771. *The Adventures of Roderick Random* (1748); *The Adventures of Peregrine Pickle* (1751); *The Adventures of Ferdinand Count Fathom* (1753); *The Adventures of Sir Launcelot Greaves* (1760–62); *Travels in France and Italy* (1766); *The Expedition of Humphry Clinker* (1771).

Smollett's birthplace, Dalquharn House, no longer stands but his family has left traces of its presence in the area where they had long been rooted and were of some importance. In 1763 his cousin James bought Cameron House, 4 miles NW of Dumbarton, 'ready-built rather than be at the trouble of repairing his own family-house of Bonhill, which stands two miles from hence on the Leven.' The writer came here on a visit in 1766 and described it in his epistolary novel, *Humphry Clinker*, a book that never misses an opportunity to praise his native land:

> We have fixed our head-quarters at Cameron, a very neat country-house belonging to commissary Smollett, where we found every sort of accommodation we could desire—It is situated like a Druid's temple, in a grove of oak, close by the side of Lough Lomond, which is a surprising body of pure transparent water, unfathomably deep in many places, six or seven miles broad, four and twenty miles in length, displaying above twenty green islands, covered with wood; some of them cultivated for corn, and many of them stocked with red deer. (Letter by Jeremy Melford, 3 September)

Cameron House was largely rebuilt in the 19C.

It was James Smollett who erected the monument to his famous relative at Renton (2 miles south). Consulted on the matter, Dr Johnson (q.v.) voiced his customary preference for a Latin tribute ('An English inscription would be a disgrace to Dr Smollett') and revised the proposed text. Not all his suggestions were adopted, and when Dorothy Wordsworth visited the spot in 1803 with her brother and Coleridge (s.v. Lake Poets, Rte 15) she noted: 'The Latin is miserably bad—as Coleridge said, such as poor Smollett, who was an excellent scholar, would have been ashamed of.'

The same Scottish trip of 1766, Smollett's last, took him to Edinburgh and so helped the eulogies of that city which appear in the August letters of *Humphry Clinker*. No. 22 John Street, off Canongate, where he stayed with his mother and sister, is marked with a plaque.

Most of his working life was spent in London. On his return from several years aboard ship as a surgeon's mate in the mid 1740s he set up medical practice in Downing Street off Whitehall. From 1750 to 1762 he lived at No. 16 Lawrence Street (plaque) off Cheyne Walk in Chelsea, making his combative, sometimes ill-tempered way as a journalist and writing the novels that established his reputation.

Yet it was *Humphry Clinker*, written during his retirement in Italy (1769–71), which most vividly and completely reflected Smollett's familiarity with Britain. Its Scottish references have already been noted but the English section of the itinerary followed by Matthew Bramble and his party deserves some summary.

Their first major stop is at Bristol, where the Georgian architecture of Clifton and Hotwells, to the west of the city, still reminds visitors of the fashionable status enjoyed by the area. At Bath nearby, which Smollett himself visited many times during the season, Mr Bramble first lodges in South Parade but is driven to Milsom Street by the noise of a fellow guest's French horns. He is sceptical of Bath's waters, contemptuous of the local society and grudging at best in his praise for John Wood the elder's famous Circus, then only recently completed:

> The Circus is a pretty bauble; contrived for shew, and looks like Vespasian's amphitheatre turned outside in. If we consider it in point of magnificence, the great number of small doors belonging to the separate houses, the inconsiderable height of the different orders, the affected ornaments of the architrave, which are both childish and misplaced, and the areas projecting into the street, surrounded with iron rails, destroy a good part of its effect upon the eye; and perhaps, we shall find it still more defective, if we view it in the light of convenience. The figure of each separate dwelling house, being the segment of a circle, must spoil the symmetry of the rooms, by contracting them towards the street windows, and leaving a larger sweep in the space behind. (Letter of 23 April)

'The same artist,' he gloomily adds, 'who planned the Circus, has likewise projected a Crescent; when that is finished, we shall probably have a Star; and those who are living thirty years hence, may, perhaps, see all the signs of the Zodiac exhibited in the architecture at Bath.' The Royal Crescent (1769)—by the younger and not the elder Wood—stands in magnificent rebuttal of this cynicism.

In their progress north the party visits the then fashionable spa of Harrogate, 8 miles west of A1 in North Yorkshire, now more redolent of the 19C than the 18C. At York Mr Bramble indulges the prejudices of his age and generation in an exaggerated form. He is unimpressed by the Minster:

> The external appearance of an old cathedral cannot be but displeasing to the eye of every man, who has any idea of propriety of proportion, even though he may be ignorant of architecture as a science; and the long slender spire puts one in mind of a criminal impaled, with a sharp stake rising up through his shoulder.

Praise is reserved for the 18C Assembly Rooms on Blake Street: 'There is nothing of this Arabic architecture in the Assembly Room, which seems to me to have been built upon a design of Palladio, and might be converted into an elegant place of worship' (Letter of 4 July).

At Scarborough on the North Yorkshire coast they join in the recent fashion for sea-bathing until Mr Bramble's embarrassing experience on the beach cuts the stay short. Though the town is, of course, greatly changed the visitor can still recognise its main features from Jeremy Melford's description:

> Scarborough, though a paltry town, is romantic from its situation along a cliff that overhangs the sea. The harbour is formed by a small elbow of land that runs out as a natural mole, directly opposite to the town; and on that side is the castle, which stands very high, of considerable extent, and before the invention of gun-powder, was counted impregnable. (Letter of 1 July)

In Durham, further north and much less damaged by time than Scarborough, the party is joined by the eccentric Lismahago and Mr Bramble is given a final opportunity to express his distaste for medieval things:

> The city of Durham appears like a confused heap of stones and brick, accumulated so as to cover a mountain, round which a river winds its brawling course. The streets are generally narrow, dark, and unpleasant, and many of them almost impassible in consequence of their declivity. The cathedral is a huge gloomy pile; but the clergy are well lodged. (Letter of 15 July)

Assembly Rooms, York. Open all year Mon to Fri 10–4 except when in use for meetings.

Edmund Spenser

b. London, 1552?; d. London, 1599. *The Shepheards Calender* (1579); *The Faerie Queene* (unfinished; 1590–96); *Amoretti* (1595); *Epithalamion* (1595); *Colin Clouts Come Home Againe* (1595); *Prothalamion* (1596).

Disappointingly little remains by which the traveller can remember

Spenser. The only record of the London scenes of his birth and childhood is his own tribute in the *Prothalamion* to 'mery London, my most kyndly Nurse,/ That to me gaue this Lifes first natiue sourse' (stanza 8). His education at Pembroke College (then Hall), Cambridge between 1569 and 1576 was marked by a similar tribute in *The Faerie Queene*: 'My mother Cambridge. . ./ With many a gentle Muse, and many a learned wit' (Bk 4, Canto 11, stanza 34).

Spenser's appointment in 1580 as secretary to Arthur Grey, Lord Grey de Wilton, Lord President of Ireland, and his subsequent posts in Irish public life made that country his home until just before his death. In 1580 he apparently witnessed the English massacre of the Spanish garrison at Forte del Oro near the harbour town of Smerwick, County Kerry on the Dingle Peninsula. He profited several times from the 'plantation' scheme that deprived disaffected Irish land-owners of their property, most importantly in 1586 when he acquired an estate including Kilcolman Castle, 3 miles north of Doneraile, which lies to the east of N20 halfway between Limerick and Cork. He settled there in 1588 and wrote substantial parts of his epic allegory, *The Faerie Queene* during his residence. Sir Walter Ralegh (q.v.) came as a visitor in 1589 from his nearby estate at Youghal, County Cork, a fishing town on the south coast to the east of Cork. Both this occasion and Spenser's trip to England the following year are described in *Colin Clouts Come Home Againe*. Kilcolman Castle and the house Spenser had added to it were destroyed in Tyrone's rebellion of 1598. Today the area is a wildfowl refuge and only the ruined tower and bailey survive, difficult of access. The surrounding countryside, however, is notable for both its intrinsic beauty and the contributions it may have made to the pastoral aspects of *The Faerie Queene*, especially in Book 4 (where, in Canto 11, stanza 41, the local river Awbeg is referred to as 'Mulla mine') and Book 6.

After the loss of his Irish home Spenser returned to London, though perhaps not in the condition of miserable poverty that earlier commentators believed. He was buried at the expense of the Earl of Essex in what is now Poets' Corner (fee) of Westminster Abbey, near the tomb of Chaucer (q.v.). In 1620 Lady Anne Clifford commissioned a *monument by Nicholas Stone—who also made the statue of Donne (q.v.) in St Paul's Cathedral—notable for its description of Spenser as 'the prince of poets in his tyme' and for its inaccuracy about the dates of his life. The monument was corrected and repaired in 1778.

Sir Richard Steele

b. Dublin, 1672; d. Carmarthen, Dyfed, 1729. *The Christian Hero* (1701); contributions to *The Tatler* (1709–11); contributions to *The Spectator* (1711–12); *The Conscious Lovers* (1722).

Like so many 18C writers of Irish birth, Steele was quick to declare himself an Englishman. He was educated at Charterhouse in the City of London, where he struck up the friendship with Joseph Addison (q.v.) that led to their collaboration on *The Tatler* and *The Spectator*. Though the school moved to Godalming, Surrey in 1872 its fine 16C–18C buildings on Charterhouse Square near the Central Meat Market survive and have been well restored.

From Charterhouse Steele proceeded to Oxford, studying at Christ Church (1690) before transferring to Merton College, which he left in 1694 without taking a degree in order to join the army. Despite this premature departure he paid the University and Merton frequent tributes in later life, including this account of the characteristic sensations of a former undergraduate revisiting his old college:

> The sight. . . filled my heart with unspeakable joy. Methought I grew younger the moment I stepped within the gate, and upon my entering the hall in which I had so often disputed, I found my logic come afresh into my head, and that I could have formed syllogisms in figures whose very names I had not once thought of for several years before. The libraries, quadrangles, and grove, all renewed in my mind, an hundred little pleasant stories and innocent amusements, though in the last place I could not help observing with some regret the loss of a tree, under whose shade I had often improved my acquaintance with Horace. (*The Englishman*, No. 34 [1713])

The only surviving reminder of Steele's adult life in London, where he was soldier, dramatist, pamphleteer and politician as well as essayist, has its own special interest. It is the simple gravestone of his second wife, Mary (d. 1718), the 'dear Prue' of his letters and imperious governor of his own somewhat unregulated habits, in the middle of the south transept of Westminster Abbey. The restrained, factual inscription that Steele composed in her memory is in marked contrast to the romantic enthusiasm with which he elsewhere spoke of Lady Steele.

He retired in 1724 to his wife's estate at Llangumnor, east of Carmarthen on the south coast of Wales, where he is remembered in the parish church on the hilltop. Shortly before his death he moved into Carmarthen itself and was buried in St Peter's Church, which has a stone tablet in his memory.

Charterhouse, City of London. Visitors by written appointment only.

Laurence Sterne

b. Clonmel, Tipperary, 1713; d. London, 1768. *The Life and Opinions of Tristram Shandy, Gentleman* (1760–67); *The Sermons of Mr Yorick* (1760–66); *A Sentimental Journey through France and Italy* (1768); *Letters from Yorick to Eliza* (1773).

Sterne entered Jesus College, Cambridge, where his great-grandfather Archbishop Sterne of York had been Master, as a sizar (or poor student) in 1733. Tradition remembers him reading Rabelais with John Hall, afterwards John Hall-Stevenson, under a walnut tree that grew in the First Court; he himself remembered the College by sending his most famous creation, Tristram Shandy, to it in Volume 1, Chapter 19 of the novel. A portrait by Allan Ramsay believed to represent the novelist hangs in the Hall.

After receiving his B.A. in 1737 Sterne embarked on a clerical career, more through necessity than vocation. He held his first curacy at the 15C church of All Saints in St Ives, 17 miles NW of Cambridge.

In 1738 he began an association with York and its surrounding area that lasted for the rest of his life, though after the fame of *Tristram Shandy* he frequently travelled to more fashionable parts of

England and the Continent. The city's social life appealed to his taste for coffee houses and female company, while his family connections with the Minster (where his uncle, Dr Jaques Sterne, was Canon Residentiary and Precentor) ensured a steady flow of minor ecclesiastical appointments. He delivered sermons at St Michael-le-Belfrey, immediately south of the Minster, and in the Minster itself, which was also the scene of his wedding to Elizabeth Lumley in 1741. Before her marriage Miss Lumley lodged on College Street (then Little Alice Lane), which runs east from Minster Yard, perhaps at the building known as St William's College.

From 1738 to 1759 Sterne lived at Sutton-on-the-Forest, 8 miles north of York on B1363, where he was rector of All Hallows. Except for its tower the church was heavily restored by the Victorians but its 18C pulpit, the one from which Sterne must surely have preached, still survives. A dedicated pluralist in an age of pluralists, he further acquired the living of Stillington, 3 miles further north, in 1741; his little church of St Nicholas is another victim of 19C restoration. If an anecdote told by the local squire is to be believed, he bore his pastoral responsibilities lightly: 'going over the fields on a Sunday to preach at Stillington, it happened that his pointer dog sprung a covey of partridge, when he went directly home for his gun and left his flock that was waiting for him in the church in the lurch.' His occupations were painting, music, unsuccessful attempts at farming and, according to contemporary rumour, infidelities that led to his wife's temporary insanity as well as, in 1759, the first of a series of separations that eventually became permanent. In his wife's absence he turned to literary composition, writing the first two volumes of *Tristram Shandy* in his Sutton parsonage. The parsonage burned down in 1757, apparently through the carelessness of the unlicensed curate in whose care Sterne had by that time left his living. It was rebuilt only after Sterne's death.

In 1760 he was granted the living of Coxwold (22 miles north of York, east of A19), a picturesque village whose hilly situation suited his delicate health better than the low-lying Sutton. 'O 'tis a delicious retreat!' he exclaimed in a letter, 'both from its beauty, & air of Solitude; & so sweetly does every thing abt it invite yr mind to rest its Labours—and be at peace with itself & the world.' The *house he rented at £12 per year and inevitably named Shandy Hall is a charming building of c. 1450 at the west end of the village. Sterne's income from his writing allowed him to make substantial improvements to it, including the installation of fireplaces in the Adam style. To the right of the main hallway is his study, the 'Philosophical Hut' where he wrote the later volumes of *Tristram Shandy* and the *Letters from Yorick to Eliza*, sentimental record of his attachment to Mrs Elizabeth Draper. Shandy Hall is now owned by the Laurence Sterne Trust. The church of St Michael, with a striking octagonal tower, preserves the pulpit from which he preached. Although he died and was buried in London, Sterne's body was removed to Coxwold in 1969 and reinterred near the south wall.

Sterne visited the patron of his living, Lord Fauconberg, at Newburgh Priory, SE of the village. Towards the end of his life he sometimes took 'a delicious Walk of Romance' to the ruins of Byland Abbey to the NE where he liked to indulge in the prospect of reunion with Mrs Draper.

Shandy Hall, Coxwold. Open June to Sept, Wed 2–5 & at other times by appointment with the Curator. Fee.

Newburgh Priory. Open 18 May to 31 Aug, Wed 2–6. Fee.

Byland Abbey (English Heritage). Open 15 March to 15 Oct, Mon to Sat 9.30–6.30, Sun 2–6.30; 16 Oct to 14 March, Mon to Sat 9.30–4, Sun 2–4. Closed Christmas Eve, Christmas Day, Boxing Day & New Year's Day. Fee.

Robert Louis Stevenson

b. Edinburgh, 1850; d. Vailima, Samoa, 1894. *An Inland Voyage* (1878); *Edinburgh: Picturesque Notes* (1879); *Travels With a Donkey in the Cévennes* (1879); *Deacon Brodie, or The Double Life* (with W.E. Henley; 1880); *Virginibus Puerisque and Other Papers* (1881); *New Arabian Nights* (1882); *Treasure Island* (1883); *A Child's Garden of Verses* (1885); *More New Arabian Nights: The Dynamiter* (1885); *Prince Otto: A Romance* (1885); *The Strange Case of Dr Jekyll and Mr Hyde* (1886); *Kidnapped: Being Memoirs of the Adventures of David Balfour in the Year 1751* (1886); *The Black Arrow: A Tale of Two Roses* (1888); *The Master of Ballantrae: A Winter's Tale* (1889); *The Wrong Box* (with Lloyd Osbourne; 1889); *The Wrecker* (with Lloyd Osbourne; 1892); *Island Nights Entertainments* (1893); *Catriona: A Sequel to Kidnapped* (1893); *The Body-Snatcher* (1895); *Weir of Hermiston: A Unfinished Romance* (1896); *St Ives: Being the Adventures of a French Prisoner in England* (finished by Sir Arthur Quiller-Couch; 1897).

Although posterity chose to construct a romanticised image of Robert Louis Stevenson from his final years in the South Seas, he was in fact a native of Edinburgh and never managed—nor, indeed, wished—to escape entirely from the city's shaping influence. As his friend W.E. Henley concluded in a sonnet, Stevenson's temperament embraced not only 'a deal of Ariel, just a streak of Puck,/ Much Antony, of Hamlet most of all' but also 'something of the Shorter Catechist.' Edinburgh today is still the best place to remember him. He was born into a prosperous and famous family of engineers who lived in the New Town, the Georgian development whose beauty he rightly defended against contemporary criticism in his second book. His home for the first three years of his life was at No. 8 Howard Place, by Inverleith Row just north of the Leith. From 1857 until he left the city in 1879 he lived at No. 17 Heriot Row, the wide and elegant street which forms the north side of Queen Street Gardens. The main landmark in the Old Town is Lady Stair's House, just off Lawnmarket, a 17C building which now houses a collection devoted to Stevenson, Burns and Sir Walter Scott (qq.v.). Brodie's Close opposite is named after the notorious 18C resident who was both town councillor and thief. His exploits suggested the play Stevenson wrote in collaboration with Henley and lie behind his far more serious study of the double life, *The Strange Case of Dr Jekyll and Mr Hyde*. The Castle nearby is the setting for the opening chapters of *St Ives*, a late work left incomplete at Stevenson's death. He is remembered by a plaque in St Giles Cathedral.

In *St Ives* Flora Gilchrist lives at Swanston Cottage, the Stevenson family's second home from 1867. Swanston, a neat little village now technically incorporated into the city, lies about 4 miles south and is reached by following A702, turning right on A720 (Oxgangs Road) and then taking a left on Swanston Road. The cottage is to the right, near the golf course. The Pentland Hills which rise SW of the village were well known to Stevenson and are praised in the last chapter of *Edinburgh: Picturesque Notes.*

In his youth Stevenson's delicate health forced him to study the law rather than follow the family tradition of engineering. In adult life it forced him to travel ever further from his country's uncongenial climate. In 1881, however, he did make a significant Scottish tour with his mother, his American wife and his stepson, Lloyd Osbourne. In June and July they stayed among the mountainous scenery of central Scotland at Moulin, a village on A924 north of Pitlochry. Stevenson wrote his fine short story 'Thrawn Janet' at Kinnaird Cottage. In August and September the party was at Braemar (on A93 NE of Pitlochry), staying in the cottage opposite what was then the church but is now the Invercauld Festival Theatre. During this visit Stevenson began *Treasure Island,* a story that neither he nor his wife regarded very seriously but which quickly became and has remained his most popular work.

South of the border Stevenson twice stayed in Surrey at the Burford Bridge Hotel, $1\frac{1}{2}$ miles north of Dorking on A24. During both visits (1878 and 1879) he met George Meredith (q.v.), who lived at Flint Cottage on Box Hill nearby. On the second occasion Meredith read him parts of *The Egoist* and, when Stevenson exclaimed that the character of Sir Willoughby Patterne must have been modelled on himself, made his famous reply: 'I've taken him from all of us, but principally from myself.' However, 'Owen Woodseer' in Meredith's *The Amazing Marriage* (1895) is certainly a portrait of Stevenson, intended as a tribute to the younger writer's slightly fey, Bohemian charm.

Stevenson's last years in Britain (1884–87), when he was virtually a housebound invalid, were spent on the south coast at Bournemouth. From 1885 his home here was Skerryvore, a house bought for him by his father and named 'in commemoration of the most beautiful and difficult of all the lighthouses erected by the family.' It no longer stands but its site on Alum Chine Road, south of Poole Road in Westbourne, is now a memorial garden.

Lady Stair's House, Edinburgh. Open Mon to Sat 10–5 (June to Sept, 10–6).

Edinburgh Castle (DoE/SDD). Open May to Oct, Mon to Sat 9.30–6, Sun 11–6; Nov to Apr, Mon to Sat 9.30–5, Sun 12.30–4.30. Closed Christmas Day, Boxing Day & first 3 days of Jan. Fee.

Bram Stoker

b. Dublin, 1847; d. London, 1912. *The Duties of Clerks of Petty Sessions of Ireland* (1878); *Under the Sunset* (1881); *The Gombeen Man* (1890); *The Watter's Mou'* (1895); *Dracula* (1897); *The Mystery of the Sea* (1902); *The Jewel of Seven Stars* (1904); *Personal Reminiscences of Henry Irving* (1906); *The Gates of Life* (1908); *Lady Athlyne* (1908); *The Lady of the Shroud* (1909); *Famous Impostors* (1909); *The Lair of the White Worm* (1911).

Stoker was educated at Trinity College, Dublin before coming to England in 1878 as acting manager to Sir Henry Irving. During the years of his prosperity he lived in Chelsea, first on Cheyne Walk by the river and later at No. 4 Durham Place, off Ormond Gate behind the Royal Hospital. Just round the corner is Tite Street and the home of Oscar Wilde (q.v.), whose parents Stoker knew during his youth in Dublin.

The popularity of *Dracula* now attracts tourists to Transylvania, a region Stoker never visited, but most of his novel is set closer to home. The Westenra family live in Hampstead and the undead Lucy Westenra makes her nocturnal appearances on Hampstead Heath. She had been buried nearby in 'the tomb of her kin, a lordly death-house in a lonely churchyard, away from teeming London; where the air is fresh, and the sun rises over Hampstead Hill, and where wild flowers grow of their own accord' (Ch. 13, 'Dr Seward's Diary'). We may be tempted to identify the spot with Highgate Cemetery, whose western part has catacombs and mausoleums entirely appropriate to Stoker's Gothic effects, especially the scene (Ch. 16) when Van Helsing and his helpers confront the vampire Lucy as she returns to her grave.

Count Dracula makes his landfall in England on the North Yorkshire coast at the old whaling port of *Whitby. The dramatic storm heralding his arrival is described in Chapter 7. He claims Lucy as his victim in the churchyard of St Mary, which lies between the Abbey and the town and enjoys a fine view of the harbour. The Westenra family, and perhaps Stoker himself on his holiday visits to Whitby, lodged on East Crescent nearby.

Stoker began the novel in 1895 at another of his favourite holiday retreats, Cruden Bay on the east coast of Scotland 24 miles north of Aberdeen. New Slains Castle, which overlooks this dramatic stretch of coastline from the north, may well have shaped his conception of Castle Dracula. The area is also the setting for several other works: *The Watter's Mou'*, *The Mystery of the Sea* and the short story 'Crooken Sands'.

Highgate Cemetery. Tours leave from Swains Lane daily on the hour, Apr to Sept 10–4, Oct to March 10–3.

Henry Howard, Earl of Surrey

b. Kenninghall, Norfolk?, 1517?; d. London, 1547. Poet.

The only surviving places to remind us of Surrey, sonneteer and near-contemporary of Sir Thomas Wyatt (q.v.) to whom he wrote an elegy, are connected with the unhappy close of his life. In 1547 he was indicted for treason in the Great Hall of London's Guildhall. The charge apparently owed more to his enemies' political power and to his own quarrelsome disposition than to evidence of any substance. After being committed to the Tower of London and executed on Tower Hill, he was buried at the nearby church of All Hallows (substantially rebuilt after bomb damage in the Second World War).

His body was later reinterred at St Michael in Framlingham, off A1120 between Stowmarket and the coast in Suffolk. His monument of 1614 stands among several fine Renaissance memorials to other members of the family of the Dukes of Norfolk.

Guildhall, City of London. Open Mon to Sat 10–5; also May to Sept, Sun (including BH) 10–5. Closed Christmas, Boxing Day, New Year's Day, Good Fri & Easter Mon.

Tower of London (DoE). Open March to Oct, Mon to Sat 9.30–5, Sun 2–5; Nov to Feb, Mon to Sat 9.30–4. Closed Christmas Eve, Christmas Day, Boxing Day, New Year's Day, Maundy Thurs, Good Fri. Fee.

R.S. Surtees

b. Milkwell Burn?, County Durham, 1803 or 1805; d. Brighton, East Sussex, 1864. *Jorrocks' Jaunts and Jollities* (1838); *Handley Cross, or the Spa Hunt: A Sporting Tale* (1843); *Hillingdon Hall, or the Cockney Squire: A Tale of Country Life* (1845); *Hawbuck Grange: or the Sporting Adventures of Thomas Scott, Esq.* (1847); *Mr Sponge's Sporting Tour* (1853).

The sporting novelist and creator of Jorrocks spent most of his life at Hamsterley Hall, County Durham, a late 18C Gothic house his family acquired in 1810 and he inherited in 1838. It stands about a mile SE of Hamsterley Mill, on A694 12½ miles SW of Newcastle upon Tyne. Surtees is buried in the churchyard at Ebchester 3½ miles beyond Hamsterley Mill on A694.

Jonathan Swift

b. Dublin, 1667; d. Dublin, 1745. *A Tale of a Tub* (1704); *The Battle of the Books* (1704); *A Meditation upon a Broom-Stick* (1710); *An Argument against Abolishing Christianity* (1711); *The Conduct of the Allies* (1711); *The Drapier's Letters* (1724); *Cadenus and Vanessa* (1726); *Travels in Several Remote Nations of the World. In Four Parts. By Lemuel Gulliver* (ie. *Gulliver's Travels*; 1726); *A Modest Proposal for Preventing the Children of the Poor from being a Burden to their Parents or Country* (1729); *A Beautiful Young Nymph Going to Bed* (1734); *Strephon and Chloe* (1734); *Verses on the Death of Dr Swift, Written by Himself* (1739); *Directions to Servants* (1745).

Swift's life was divided between two countries: Ireland, 'where there is nothing I shall be sorry to lose' (or so he claimed in a letter written when he was sixty-two), whose ecclesiastical and political affairs absorbed much of his energies; and England, where the disappointment of his youthful hopes for advancement was counterbalanced by his later acceptance in literary society. He himself encouraged doubts as to his country of origin, to the annoyance of Johnson (q.v.) in his *Lives of the Poets*:

> During his life the place of his birth was undetermined. He was contented to be called an Irishman by the Irish; but would occasionally call himself an Englishman. The question may, without much regret, be left in the obscurity in which he delighted to involve it.

In fact, Swift was an Irishman, and it is most convenient to begin by considering his connections with that country.

From the age of six he attended Kilkenny College in the county town of Kilkenny, beginning there a life-long friendship with his near-contemporary, Congreve (q.v.). The present buildings of the College stand on the north bank of the Nore near St John's Bridge; its former buildings were in the Close of St Mary's Cathedral.

Swift entered Trinity College, Dublin when he was fourteen—an early age though not so unusual as one might think. His connection

Bust of Swift by Louis François Roubiliac. Courtesy of Trinity College, Dublin

with the College is best remembered by Roubiliac's fine *bust in the Long Room of the Old Library. The various legends of his poor academic performance and bad behaviour, encouraged by his own references in old age to his 'dullness and insufficiency' as an undergraduate, are not fully supported by the College records.

After several years of frustrated clerical ambition he was appointed Dean of St Patrick's Cathedral in 1714. The position earned him the universal title, 'Dean Swift,' and he held it until his death. His house in Deanery Garden does not survive but the Cathedral itself is rich in reminders. On entering we find, near the foot of the second column from the west end of the nave, brass tablets commemorating him and Esther Johnson, recipient of the letters later collected as *Journal to Stella*, constant companion and possibly wife by a secret marriage. Swift's diary for 30 January 1728 contained this entry:

> This is the night of her funeral which my sickness will not suffer me to attend. It is now nine at night, and I am removed into another apartment that I may not see the light in the church, which is just over against the window of my bed-chamber.

The tablets do not necessarily mark the exact places where Swift and Stella were buried, for they have been moved over the years in obedience to the differing opinions of successive Deans about the real relationship between the couple. A bust by Patrick Cunningham (1775) stands by the door leading to the Vestiaries nearby. Above is the tablet with Swift's Latin epitaph on himself, famous for its inscription of his eventual destination as 'Ubi saeva Indignatio/ Ulterius/ Cor lacerare nequit.' Another poet, Yeats (q.v.), has offered a fine free translation of the text:

> Swift has sailed into his rest;
> Savage indignation there
> Cannot lacerate his breast.
> Imitate him, if you dare,
> World-besotted traveller; he
> Served human liberty.

Swift's epitaph on Stella is at the other side of the doorway.

The north transept contains the pulpit from which he preached, while in a corner of the south transept we find, above the monument to Lady Doneraile, a memorial to his servent, McGee. The north choir aisle has a tablet to Frederick Herman, Duke of Schomberg, who died at the Battle of the Boyne (1690). In 1729 Swift wrote to the Duke's grand-daughter urging the propriety of a memorial but received no reply. The project went ahead at the expense of the Dean and Chapter, and Swift himself wrote the inscription with its reference to the ingratitude of Schomberg's descendants.

Swift was thoroughly familiar with Dublin Castle, having been born at No. 7 Hooey Court (gone) within its shadow. In 1724, after having spent several futile hours waiting for an interview with Lord Carteret there, he is reputed to have left two lines on a card:

> My very good Lord, it's a very hard task
> To wait so long and have nothing to ask.

By following James Street to the west of Dublin we reach the 18C buildings of St Patrick's Hospital, opened in 1757 and founded by a bequest in Swift's will.

After the death of Esther Vanromigh ('Vanessa') in 1723 Swift made an extended tour through the south of Ireland. While staying at or near Skull, County Cork on L57 14 miles SW of Bantry, he wrote 'Carberiae Rupes,' a Latin poem about the wild scenery of the area; it was translated into English by William Dunkin.

Swift's connection with England began with childhood visits to his widowed mother, from whom he was separated for several years at a time. It was strengthened by his stay at Moor Park, near Farnham off A31 in Surrey. He served as secretary to Sir William Temple from 1689 or 1690 until that gentleman's death in 1699, with an interlude in Ireland (1694–96) after his ordination, editing Sir William's papers and becoming increasingly frustrated that the position did not lead to the advancement he had anticipated. It was here he first met Esther Johnson, daughter of the housekeeper. Moor Park, greatly changed and now a College of Adult Christian Education, lies 2 miles SE of the town near the ruins of Waverley Abbey.

In June–August 1714 he stayed with a friend from his Moor Park days, Rev. John Geree, at the village of Letcombe Bassett 2½ miles SW of Wantage in the Berkshire Downs. As he explains in his poem, 'The Author Upon Himself,' he was seeking refuge from the political fighting between Oxford and Bolingbroke which accompanied the closing months of Queen Anne's reign:

> By Faction tir'd, with Grief he waits a while,
> His great contending Friends to reconcile,
> Performs what Friendship, Justice, Truth require:
> What could he more, but decently retire?
>
> (lines 71–74)

His rural peace was disturbed by an unexpected and injudiciously public visit from Esther Vanromigh; Swift included 'the Berkshire Surprise' among the subtitles he originally planned for *Cadenus and Vanessa*, the poem that tells the story of their attachment. The house where Swift stayed no longer stands but Geree's church of St Michael survives.

Swift's closest friendships in England were with Pope and Gay (qq.v.), though *Verses on the Death of Dr Swift* prophesied cynically: 'Poor POPE will grieve a Month; and GAY/ A week' (lines 207–208). His most important visits to them took place in 1726, when he arrived with the manuscript of *Gulliver's Travels*, and in 1727, when he stayed at Pope's Villa in Twickenham and travelled with him to Lord Bathurst's estate at Cirencester, both described under the entry for his friend.

Old Library, **Trinity College**, Dublin. Open Mon to Fri 9.30–5, Sat 9.30– 1.

Dublin Castle. State Apartments open Mon to Fri 10–12.15, 2–5, Sat & Sun 2–5. Closed occasionally for State functions. Fee.

Algernon Charles Swinburne

b. London, 1837; d. London, 1909. *Atalanta in Calydon* (1865); *Poems and Ballads* (1866); *A Song of Italy* (1867); *An Appeal to England* (1867); *Songs Before Sunrise* (1871); *Bothwell* (1874); *Poems and Ballads: Second Series* (1878); *Mary Stuart* (1881); *Tristram of Lyonesse and Other Poems* (1882); *A Century of Roundels* (1883); *Poems and Ballads: Third Series* (1889); *Love's Cross Currents: A Year's Letters* (1901); *Lesbia Brandon* (edited by R. Hughes; 1952).

Though born in London, Swinburne divided his childhood between the countryside of South-Eastern and Northern England. His parents lived on the Isle of Wight at Bonchurch, a village beneath the downs on the south coast 1 mile east of Ventnor. Their home, East Dene, is now a hostel. When Dickens (q.v., Rte 12) came for a holiday in 1849 his attention was caught by 'the golden-haired lad of the Swinburnes.' His parents' connection with Bonchurch ended in the 1860s but the poet, like his father and sisters, is buried in its newer churchyard.

Always eager to prove a physical courage that his small stature might have seemed to belie, Swinburne undertook in 1851 the remarkable feat of climbing Culver Cliff, which rises some 254ft from the sea 8 miles NE of Bonchurch near the island's eastern tip. In 1857, and presumably in tamer mood, he called on Tennyson (q.v.) at Farringford near Freshwater on the western end of the Isle. The

Poet Laureate invited him to dinner, treated him to the inevitable reading of *Maud* and reported favourably in a letter to a friend: 'what I particularly admired in him was that he did not press upon me any verses of his own.'

Throughout his early years Swinburne paid frequent visits to his grandfather at Capheaton, the family home in Northumberland, a fine 17C building off A696 18 miles NW of Newcastle upon Tyne. He was greatly impressed and influenced by the eccentric Sir John: 'It was said that the two maddest things in the North country were his horse and himself; I don't think his horse can have been the madder.' The bleak moors and coasts of Northumberland, too, left a lasting mark on his sensibility:

> Between our eastward and our westward sea
> > The narrowing strand
> Clasps the noblest shore fame holds in fee
> Even here where English birth seals all men free—
> > Northumberland:

> ('Northumberland,' lines 1–5)

He was also a guest of Lady Pauline Trevelyan at Wallington, 3 miles north of Capheaton via B6342. It was here that he first met Ruskin (q.v.), apparently in 1857 when the critic came to assist the artist William Bell Scott in redecorating the house. In fact, the young Swinburne made a habit of meeting the great, for in 1849 his parents had taken him to visit Wordsworth at Rydal Mount in the Lake District (s.v. Lake Poets, Rte 12C). It is reported that the elderly Wordsworth, who died only six months later, recommended his poetry on the grounds that 'there was nothing in his writings that would do the boy harm, and there were some things which might do him good.'

In 1849 Swinburne entered Eton College, south of M4 near Windsor. Lord Redesdale's famous description of his new schoolfellow shows that the future poet's highly distinctive appearance was by then already established: 'He was strangely tiny. His limbs were small and delicate; and his sloping shoulders looked far too weak to carry his great head, the size of which was exaggerated by the touzled mass of red hair standing almost at right angles to it.' He was soon called 'Mad Swinburne,' a nickname that echoed the one bestowed by the same school on an earlier poet he much admired and emulated, Shelley (q.v.). A late work, 'Eton: An Ode,' praised his old school in the stately language appropriate to public verse, but the writings he did not choose to make public show that its most permanent legacy seems to have been a lifelong obsession with flagellation.

Swinburne's career at Balliol College, Oxford, which began in 1856, was both distinguished and controversial. Its most important result, perhaps, was the friendship with William Morris, Rossetti (qq.v.) and the painter Edward Burne-Jones formed during their visit to the university for 'The Jovial Campaign' to decorate the Oxford Union building in 1857; this is briefly noted under the entry for Morris. Otherwise, Swinburne devoted more time to writing poetry than the authorities judged prudent. This—together with his republicanism, agnosticism, and complaints from the landlady of his lodgings in Broad Street about irregular behaviour—made Benjamin Jowett fear that his college would send him down and so 'make Balliol as ridiculous as University had made itself about Shelley.' In the event, Swinburne was apparently advised to leave without taking a degree, which he did in 1860.

A selection of the places Swinburne visited during the next decade indicates the range of his friendships, interests and activities. In 1864 he toured Cornwall with the landscape painter Inchbold. The ruined Tintagel Castle on the north coast 4 miles SW of Boscastle is described in a letter to his cousin Mary Gordon: 'The outer half of the castle, on the headland beyond the isthmus is on the very edge (and partly over the edge and on the slant) of the cliff; and has indescribable views of the double bay, broken cliffs, and outer sea.' The trip influenced *Tristram of Lyonesse* and is remembered in a poem of 1888, 'In Memory of John William Inchbold.'

Swinburne became a *protégé* and close friend of Richard Monckton Milnes (Lord Houghton), politician, biographer of Keats and book collector whose library contained many volumes of erotica. He was several times a guest at Milnes' country house, Monk Fryston Hall in North Yorkshire, 2 miles east of A1 on A63 towards Selby. The Hall is now a hotel that preserves much of its former character. In 1861 the poet met Richard Burton, explorer and translator of *The Arabian Nights* here. The following year he struck a fellow guest as 'a cross between the devil and the Duke of Argyll.' Henry Adams, the American writer who was then acting as Milnes' private secretary, remembered Swinburne in his *Education* as

> a tropical bird, high-crested, long-beaked, quick-moving, with a rapid
> utterance and screams of humour quite unlike any English lark or
> nightingale. One could hardly call him a crimson macaw among owls,
> and yet no ordinary contrast availed.

Another powerful literary friend was the novelist Edward Bulwer-Lytton (s.v. Lytton), who wrote to Swinburne expressing admiration for *Atalanta in Calydon*. In the summer of 1866, when the controversy stirred up by the publication of *Poems and Ballads* was at its height, Swinburne stayed at Knebworth House, the 16C mansion Lytton had extravagantly enlarged. Knebworth lies ½ a mile west of A1(M) and is reached from the junction north of Welwyn Garden City via B656.

During these years, when his fame and notoriety grew in equal proportions, Swinburne was living in London. In 1862 he went to lodge with Rossetti at Tudor House, No. 16 Cheyne Walk, by the Chelsea Embankment. The ensuing domestic chaos quickly drove away George Meredith (q.v.), a fellow tenant, and Swinburne's outrageous, frequently drunken behaviour appears to have been too much even for a man of Rossetti's easygoing habits. In 1865–70 Swinburne was at No. 22 Dorset Street, west of Baker Street just south of its junction with Marylebone Road. By 1872 he was at No. 3 Great James Street, which runs north from Theobald's Road near Gray's Inn Gardens and Gray's Inn Road. At a later date he moved a few streets north to Guilford Street.

This mobility may in part have been designed to escape the watchful eye of his family, who had joined his friends in concern about his heavy drinking. By 1879 the problem had reached a point where it justified fears for his health, if not his life, and demanded a drastic remedy. This appeared in the surprising form of Theodore Watts (later Watts-Dunton), a solicitor of literary tastes. With the approval of Swinburne's family he took the poet firmly in hand and removed him to Putney in south-west London. No. 2 The Pines, the house he rented on Putney Hill, still stands (though its number has been altered to 11) and is only a few minutes' walk from Putney

Station (British Rail).

To contemporaries the suburb, then newly developed and still remote from London, seemed a strange, even comic destination for a fiery poet and No. 2 The Pines an inappropriately bourgeois address

'At the Pines,' by Max Beerbohm (q.v.). Courtesy of Ashmolean Museum

The elderly Swinburne (left) with the companion of his Putney years, Theodore Watts-Dunton, who also appears in the picture of Rossetti (q.v.)

for an admirer of Mazzini and De Sade. Yet Swinburne remained there for the rest of his life, settling into a quiet and apparently contented routine: admiring the children in their baby carriages during his morning walk on nearby Putney Heath, confining himself to a single bottle of beer over lunch, and devoting afternoons to energetic but uninspired composition. He rarely went into central London or, indeed, left Putney at all. Visitors regarded his transformation with surprise tinged by disappointment. G.K. Chesterton (q.v.) came and found not the 'Anti-Christ in purple' he had expected but 'a very well-read Victorian old maid.' The atmosphere of the house and of Swinburne's later years was deftly caught by the young Max Beerbohm (q.v.) in his essay, 'No. 2 The Pines.'

Wallington Hall (NT). Open Apr to end Sept, daily except Tues 1–6; Oct, Wed, Sat & Sun 2–5. Fee

Rydal Mount. Open March to Oct, daily 10–5.30; Nov to mid Jan 10–12.30, 2–4. Fee.

Eton College. Open daily 2–5 during term, 10.30–5 during spring holiday, 9–5 during summer holiday. Fee.

Tintagel Castle (English Heritage). Open 15 March to 15 Oct, Mon to Sat 9.30–6.30, Sun 2–6.30 (from 9.30 Apr to Sept); 16 Oct to 14 March, Mon to Sat 9.30–4, Sun 2–4. Closed Christmas Eve, Christmas Day, Boxing Day & New Year's Day. Fee.

Knebworth House. Open 1 Apr to 21 May, Sun & BH Mon 11.30–4.30; 1 June to 15 Sept, Tues to Sun & BH Mon 11.30–4.30; 15 Sept to 30 Sept, Sun 11.30–4.30. Fee.

John Millington Synge

b. Dublin, 1871; d. Dublin, 1909. *In the Shadow of the Glen* (1905); *Riders to the Sea* (1905); *The Well of the Saints* (1905); *The Playboy of the Western World* (1907); *The Aran Islands* (1907); *The Tinker's Wedding* (1907); *Deirdre of the Sorrows* (1910).

Synge was born at No. 2 Newtown Villas, a substantial semi-detached house in the southern Dublin suburb of Rathfarnham. After his father died the following year his mother moved the family north to the suburb of Rathgar and a house at No. 4 Orwell Park, immediately north of the River Dodder.

The Synges were affluent and pious members of the Protestant Ascendancy and as a child, at a time when protests against landlordism were at their height, he was frequently taken to the family estates in County Wicklow, south of Dublin. He several times stayed with his mother in the little coastal resort of Greystones (on L29 4½ miles south of Bray) and visited his grandfather, Francis Synge, at Glanmore Castle in the romantic Devil's Glen west of Ashford (9 miles south of Greystones on N11). The building later fell into ruins but has been partly rebuilt.

In 1888, already starting to reject the family's politics and religion, Synge entered Trinity College, Dublin. He was later to insist that his education here made little impression on him. The Manuscript Room in the Old Library has mss. of his works.

After graduating in 1892 Synge spent several years on the Continent studying music and writing in a desultory fashion. In 1896 came a

'Thatching,' by Jack B. Yeats. From The Aran Islands *(1907).*
Courtesy of Cambridge University Library

momentous meeting with Yeats (q.v.) in Paris. Afire with enthusiasm
for the Irish literary revival and with the belief that artists should
deal with Irish subjects, the older writer advised him to study folk
life on the Aran Islands, and Synge's obedience to this suggestion
helped him at last to find his literary voice. His visits each summer
from 1898 to 1902 led not only to a fine prose account of the islands
but also to the mastery of folk idiom that distinguishes his plays.

The little group of three islands lies in the Galway Bay some 30
miles SW of Galway, from which it can be reached by steamer or by
air. The modern visitor can still find much to recognise from Synge's
descriptions. Fishing remains the chief means of livelihood, and the
islanders still sometimes wear 'pampooties,' the locally made cowhide
shoes which Synge, always a stickler for authentic detail, made the
original cast of *Riders to the Sea* wear. That play comes directly from

his experience of Inishmaan, the central island in the group, where he spent much time strolling round the impressive ruins of Dún Conor, one of the many ancient fortifications which dot the landscape.

By the time Synge's plays were achieving success and causing controversy in Dublin's Abbey Theatre (see entry for Yeats), Synge was already suffering from Hodgkin's disease. He died in Dublin at No. 130 Northumberland Road (reached by following Lower Mount Street SE from Merrion Square) and was buried at Mount Jerome Cemetery in the suburb of Harold's Cross.

Manuscript Room, Old Library, Trinity College, Dublin. Open Mon to Fri 10–5, Sat 10–1.

Alfred Lord Tennyson

b. Somersby, Lincolnshire, 1809; d. Haslemere, Surrey, 1892. *Poems by Two Brothers* (with contributions by Charles and Frederick Tennyson; 1827); *Poems, Chiefly Lyrical* (includes 'The Kraken,' 'Mariana'; 1830); *Poems* (Includes 'The Lady of Shalott,' 'The Palace of Art,' 'The Lotos-Eaters'; 1833); *Poems* (includes 'Ulysses,' 'Break, Break, Break,' 'Morte d'Arthur,' 'Locksley Hall'; 1842; *The Princess* (1847); *In Memoriam A.H.H.* (1850); *Maud, and Other Poems* (1855); *Idylls of the King* (1859); *Enoch Arden* (1864); *Ballads and Other Poems* (1880); *Tiresias and Other Poems* (1885); *Demeter and Other Poems* (1889).

Of the poet's various connections with Eastern England by far the deepest are in Lincolnshire, where the Tennyson family originated and where he himself spent his childhood, youth and much of his early adulthood. The county town of Lincoln makes a convenient starting point for a tour. Outside the east end of the Cathedral, between the chapter house and Priory Gate, stands a statue of 1905 by G.F. Watts that shows him, dog by his side, wearing the characteristic broad-brimmed hat and flowing cloak. The Usher Art Gallery on Deansgate south of the Cathedral contains a collection of personal memorabilia.

By heading east via Horncastle and branching north on country roads we enter the Wolds, an area still virtually as remote and rural as it was in Tennyson's day. He was born in the small village of Somersby, at Somersby House (formerly the Rectory) opposite the church, and passed a childhood, youth and early poetic career there overshadowed by family difficulties in the form of his father's poverty, epilepsy, alcoholism and opium-addiction. Rev. George Clayton Tennyson (d. 1831) was rector of the small church and is buried outside its door; a bust of the poet is inside. Holywell Wood behind the Rectory was a favourite walk of Tennyson and his brothers. Nearby to the SE Bag Enderby, of which Tennyson's father also held the living, has a Perpendicular church of extreme and touching simplicity.

In the small town of Tetford to the north, a useful centre for tours of the Wolds, is the White Hart Inn where Tennyson was a customer; the oak settle he reputedly used is displayed in the bar. At Louth, a market town further north distinguished by the magnificent spire of its church, Tennyson attended the Old Grammar School (rebuilt) on Westgate from 1816 to 1820, upholding the time-honoured tradition by which poets dislike their schooldays and find their masters brutally insensitive. A day scholar, he lodged with his grandmother in the same street. His first volume of poetry was issued by a bookseller in the Market Place.

Near the village of Tealby, to the west of Louth and outside Market Rasen, stood the now-demolished Bayons Manor, home of the poet's grandfather, always on bad terms with the Somersby family. His heir Charles Tennyson d'Eyncourt added to the house, originally just a small Regency building, in the same spirit that led him to extend the family name. His achievement provoked a contemptuous passage in *Maud*:

> Seeing his gewgaw castle shine,
> New as his title, built last year,
> There amid perky larches and pine,
> And over the sullen-purple moor
> (Look at it) pricking a cockney ear.

(lines 347–351)

Suitably elaborate monuments to his branch of the Tennysons may be found in the chancel of Tealby church. The florid inscription honouring his grandfather, George, provoked another outburst from the poet, this time in 'Locksley Hall Sixty Years After' (1886):

> Gone the tyrant of my youth, and mute below the chancel stones,
> All his virtues—I forgive them—black in white above his bones.

(lines 43–44)

Tennyson's connections with Eastern England were extended by his studies (1827–31) at Trinity College, Cambridge. During his undergraduate years he was elected to the exclusive society of the Apostles and won the Lord Chancellor's medal for his poem 'Timbuctoo' (1829). Of special importance was his close friendship with Arthur Henry Hallam, whose early death led to the great elegiac sequence 'In Memoriam'. No. 87 deals with a later visit to Cambridge that evoked memories of his dead friend. Tennyson is commemorated in Trinity by Thomas Woolner's good bust in the Library and Sir Hamo Thornycroft's less successful statue of 1909 in the ante-chapel, which, according to one observer, makes him look like 'the prima donna's noble father in Victorian opera.'

Hallam had rooms in New Court while Tennyson himself lodged first in Rose Crescent, off Trinity Street, and then at the King's Parade end of Trumpington Street, in No. 57, whose bricked-over doorway is still clearly distinguishable between the neighbouring houses. The neo-classical building immediately opposite, now part of St Catharine's College, was once the Bull Hotel, from which Tennyson departed Cambridge in 1831.

He was a frequent guest at the Hallams' London home, No. 67 Wimpole Street, which runs south from Marylebone Road as an extension of Devonshire Place. This is the scene of the finely tuned seventh lyric of *In Memoriam*:

> Dark house, by which once more I stand
> Here in the long unlovely street. . .

Hallam's death in 1833 and the Tennyson family's move from Somersby in 1837 made the years that followed disturbed and restless: Tennyson became a traveller and a visitor to other men's houses. London connections are represented by: No. 14 Percy Street, off Tottenham Court Road, home of the poet Coventry Patmore (q.v.)

and now marked by a plaque; Carlyle's House in Cheyne Row, Chelsea, described under that author; and the Star and Garter Inn, Richmond (for which see Dickens, Rte 6). His friendship with three other famous contemporaries is best remembered by a later occasion, in 1855, when he read *Maud* to an assembled company at the Brownings' lodging in Dorset Street, near Wimpole Street, and was covertly sketched by Dante Gabriel Rossetti (q.v.): see the entry for Robert and Elizabeth Barrett Browning. A London inn, the Cock Tavern, is celebrated in 'Will Waterproof's Lyrical Monologue' (1842), one of his rare ventures into light verse; relics of the building are preserved in the present inn of that name on the south side of Fleet Street near Temple Bar Memorial.

A more serious example of the relation between literature and topography was his visit in 1848 to the ruins of Tintagel Castle on the north coast of Cornwall, south of Boscastle, made during the long gestatory years of his Arthurian cycle. The same trip also took him to the village of Morwenstow, north of Bude, where he met the eccentric poet-clergyman R.S. Hawker (q.v.).

Tennyson's appointment as Poet Laureate on the death of Wordsworth in 1850 and his marriage the same year to Emily Sellwood, whom he had met in Somersby, marked the beginning of a more settled life. From 1851 to 1853 they lived at Chapel House on Montpelier Row, a superb terrace of early 18C houses on the edge of Marble Hill Park in Twickenham.

From 1853 onwards his life centred on South Eastern England. In that year he moved, first as tenant and later as owner, to Farringford near Freshwater on the western end of the Isle of Wight. The location answered his need for seclusion, while the house, originally built in 1806 but later enlarged, appealed to his love of the Gothic style: 'It is like blank verse. It will suit the humblest cottage and the grandest cathedral.' Literary friends who came to stay included William Allingham, Francis Turner Palgrave (editor of *The Golden Treasury*), Edward Lear (q.v.) and Edward FitzGerald (q.v.), whom Tennyson visited at Woodbridge in Suffolk. The young Swinburne (q.v.), who called uninvited in 1857, recommended himself by not attempting to press any of his own poetry on the Laureate. Among the public men who paid visits were Prince Albert and, in 1864, Garibaldi, who planted a tree which still stands outside the house. Farringford is now a hotel.

Emily Tennyson, who outlived her husband until 1896, is buried in the churchyard at Freshwater and there is, inevitably, a memorial to him in the church. Tennyson Down (NT) on the southern shore between Easton and The Needles is named to commemorate a favourite walk and has a striking monument. 'Crossing the Bar' was written on a voyage across the Solent between the Isle of Wight and the mainland.

Tennyson acquired a second and larger establishment with the building (1868–69) of Aldworth on Blackdown Hill (NT; 919ft) south of Haslemere, Surrey and reached from the town via Tennyson's Lane (NT). It was designed by his friend, the architect James Knowles, who refused a fee on the grounds that his pleasure in Tennyson's poetry was sufficient reward. Of the result—eclectically Gothic with the French style predominating, deliberately grand and at odds with its natural setting—Tennyson's modern biographer has remarked: 'It may not look like a poet's home, but it could not be a more suitable seat for a Poet Laureate.' To Aldworth came visitors like Carlyle (q.v.), who could not be lured as far as the Isle of Wight, and Gladstone, who like Tennyson had been a close friend of Hallam.

Tennyson's funeral was held in Westminster Abbey (though several friends found the occasion hollow and disappointing) and he is honoured by a memorial in Poets' Corner (fee). In 1875 he had written the inscription for the monument to the Arctic explorer Sir John Franklin (d. 1847) in the Chapel of St John the Evangelist. He considered it his best epitaph.

Usher Gallery, Lincoln. Open Mon to Sat 10–5.30, Sun 2–5. Fee.

Trinity College Library, Cambridge. Open Mon to Fri 12–2, and also Sat 10.30–12.30 during Full Term.

Carlyle's House, Chelsea (NT). Open Apr to end Oct, Wed to Sun & BH Mon 11–5. Closed Good Fri. Fee.

Tintagel Castle (English Heritage). Open 15 March to 15 Oct, Mon to Sat 9.30–6.30, Sun 2–6.30 (from 9.30 Apr to Sept); 16 Oct to 14 March, Mon to Sat 9.30–4, Sun 2–4. Closed Christmas Eve, Christmas Day, Boxing Day & New Year's Day. Fee.

William Makepeace Thackeray

b. Calcutta, India, 1811; d. London, 1863. *The Paris Sketch Book, by Mr Titmarsh* (1840); *The Irish Sketch Book, by Mr M.A. Titmarsh* (1843); *The Luck of Barry Lyndon: A Romance of the Last Century. By Fitz-Boodle* (1844; revised 1856); *Notes of a Journey from Cornhill to Grand Cairo* (1846); *The Book of Snobs* (1848); *Vanity Fair: A Novel Without a Hero* (1848); *The History of Pendennis: His Fortunes and Misfortunes, His Friends and His Greatest Enemy* (1849–50); *The History of Henry Esmond, Esq. a Colonel in the Service of Her Majesty Q. Anne, Written by Himself* (1852); *The English Humourists of the Eighteenth Century* (1853); *The Newcomes: Memoirs of a Most Respectable Family, Edited by Arthur Pendennis Esqre* (1854–55); *The Virginians: A Tale of the Last Century* (1858–59); *The Four Georges: Sketches of Manners, Morals, Court and Town Life* (1861); *Lovel the Widower* (1861); *The Adventures of Philip on His Way Through the World* (1862); *Roundabout Papers* (1863); *Denis Duval* (unfinished; 1867).

When he first arrived from India in 1817 Thackeray was sent to Dr Turner's Academy at Chiswick in SW London, a borough whose connections with genteel education he later immortalised in the opening chapter of *Vanity Fair*. Miss Pinkerton's establishment in the novel has been identified as Walpole House on the delightful 18C Chiswick Mall.

We do not know if Thackeray shared Becky Sharp's sentiments —'thank God, I'm out of Chiswick' (Ch. 2)—but he did leave Dr Turner's Academy slightly earlier than expected and was certainly ill-prepared for the rigours of •Charterhouse. The school was then still in its fine old buildings on Charterhouse Square near the Central Meat Market in the City. The novelist quickly showed himself indifferent to sport and given to reading novels, especially the 'Waverley' novels of Sir Walter Scott (q.v.). These do not appear to have been happy years, for his later memories centred on the brutality of public school life: his schoolmasters bear names like 'Birch' and 'Swishtail' while Charterhouse itself is nicknamed 'Slaughterhouse.' A certain mellowing is apparent in *The Newcomes*, where the school

Pensioner's Hall, Charterhouse, by Thomas Shepherd. From James Elmes, London and its Environs in the Nineteenth Century (1829). Courtesy of Cambridge University Library

appears under the transparent disguise of 'Grey Friars.' The aged and broken Colonel Newcome is received as a Poor Brother in Chapter 76, which includes a description of Founder's Day at the school, and dies here in the final chapter:

> At the usual evening hour the chapel bell began to toll, and Thomas Newcome's hands outside the bed feebly beat time. And just as the last bell struck, a peculiar sweet smile shone over his face, and he lifted up his head a little, and quickly said 'Adsum!' and fell back. It was the word we used at school, when names were called; and lo, he whose heart was as that of a little child, had answered to his name, and stood in the presence of the Master.

Thackeray spent holidays with his mother and stepfather, Major Carmichael-Smyth, at their Devon home, Larkbeare, near Ottery St Mary, a mile south of A30 between Honiton and Exeter. His description of 'Clavering St Mary' in *Pendennis*, his most autobiographical novel, shows that mixture of sentiment and irony which is Thackeray's most distinctive trait:

> Looking at the little old town of Clavering St Mary from the old London road as it runs by the lodge at Fairoaks [Larkbeare], and seeing the rapid and shining Brawl [the Otter] winding down and skirting the woods of Clavering Park [Escot Lodge], and the ancient church tower and peaked roofs of the houses rising up amongst trees and old walls, behind which swells a fair background of sunshiny hills that stretch from Clavering westwards towards the sea—the place appears to be so cheery and comfortable that many a traveller's heart must have yearned towards it from the coach-top, and he must have thought that it was in such a calm and friendly nook he would like to shelter at the end of life's struggle . . . Like Constantinople seen from the Bosphorus; like Mrs Rougemont viewed in her box from the opposite side of the house; like many an object which we pursue in life, and admire before we have attained it; Clavering is rather prettier at a distance than it is on closer acquaintance. The town so cheerful of aspect a few furlongs off, looks very blank and dreary. (Ch. 15)

The lovely collegiate Church of St Mary, rebuilt 1337–42 by Bishop Grandison, is remembered less cynically for 'its grey towers, of which the sun illuminates the delicate carving; deepening the shadows of the huge buttresses, and gilding the glittering windows and flaming vanes' (Ch. 15). In the same book the quiet coastal resort of Sidmouth, 5 miles south, appears as 'Baymouth' and Exeter as 'Chatteris,' the city treated to an exhibition of Miss Fotheringay's dramatic talents; she lodges with Captain Costigan near the Cathedral Close.

Though the Carmichael-Smyths did not long remain in Devon Thackeray kept his connections with South-Western England in later years. In 1848 he stayed with the Elton family at Clevedon Court on B3130 12 miles west of Bristol. The visit confirmed his unfulfilled romantic attachment to their daughter, Mrs Brookfield. The building itself, 14C with Elizabethan alterations, is generally identified with the 'Castlewood' of *Henry Esmond*, though the novel places it in Hampshire.

When he entered Trinity College, Cambridge in February 1829 he was given ground-floor rooms between the main gatehouse and Chapel in Great Court, and wrote to his mother: 'Men will say some day, that Newton and Thackeray kept near one another!' He gave the same rooms to his hero Henry Esmond (Bk 1, Ch. 10), but his own Trinity career more closely resembled the misadventures of Pendennis, whom he made a student of 'St Boniface, Oxbridge' (Ch. 18ff). The love of novel-reading continued but to this blameless pastime he added a fondness for wine parties and gambling. Discouraged by poor exam results and with part of his patrimony wasted, he left in the spring of 1830. His fellow undergraduate Edward FitzGerald (q.v.) remained a lifelong friend.

From Cambridge Thackeray went to London and settled thoroughly into the life of a 'cockney,' to use his own term for the urban spirit that pervades his fiction, whether it deals with elegant West End houses and clubs or with dubiously Bohemian quarters. In 1831 he entered the Middle Temple, south of Fleet Street near its junction with the Strand; his lodgings were at No. 1 Hare Court, off Inner Temple Lane. Though he never seriously applied himself to the study of law, he developed a lasting taste for the 18C literary associations of the Temple:

> I don't know whether the student of law permits himself the refreshment of enthusiasm, or indulges in poetical reminiscences as he passes by historical chambers. . . but the man of letters can't but love the place which has been inhabited by so many of his brethren, or peopled by their creations as real to us at this day as the authors whose children they were—and Sir Roger de Coverley walking in the Temple Garden, and discoursing with Mr Spectator about the beauties in hoops and patches who are sauntering over the grass, is just as lively a figure to me as old Samuel Johnson rolling through the fog with the Scotch gentleman at his heels on their way to Dr Goldsmith's chambers in Brick Court; or Harry Fielding, with inked ruffles and a wet towel round his head, dashing off articles at Midnight for the *Covent Garden Journal*, while the printer's boy is asleep in the passage. (*Pendennis*, Ch. 29)

In 1838, after his marriage to Isabella Shawe, Thackeray settled in Bloomsbury at No. 13 Coram Street (then Great Coram Street), off Woburn Place. But his domestic happiness was destroyed by his wife's mental breakdown in 1840. He left his two daughters in the care of his mother and travelled with Isabella on the Continent, before surrendering her permanently into professional hands. He returned only briefly to Coram Street before the lease expired in 1843 and lived a bachelor life for the next few years.

It was not until 1846 that he was again able to provide a home for his children. In that year he began his long association with Kensington by moving into No. 13 Young Street (now marked with a GLC plaque), south of Kensington High Street near the SW corner of Kensington Gardens. *Vanity Fair* was written here, and in 1850 Charlotte Brontë (q.v.), a great admirer of the novel, was entertained to a memorably unsuccessful dinner. In 1854 he moved SE to the more fashionable Brompton. Although pleased by his 'neat new house' at No. 36 Onslow Square (marked with a GLC plaque) Thackeray was never entirely at home in the neighbourhood.

It comes as no surprise, then, that he should have moved back to Kensington in 1861; yet the importance, elegance and expressiveness of the home he built for himself are a pleasant shock to the literary pilgrim. *No. 2 Palace Green, facing Kensington Gardens off Kensington High Street, is convincing evidence of the affluence his writing had at last won him—a gesture to show the world that his years of labour in Fleet Street had been rewarded. He acknowledged that the house was paid for by his salary as editor of the *Cornhill Magazine* and joked that it should have the emblem of the wheatsheaf at its door. As the cost rose to £8000 he ruefully agreed with the suggestion it should be called 'Vanity Fair House.' Yet the Palace Green home was more than just an announcement of the social position he had achieved. Thackeray chose to build in the Queen Anne style—and did so with immaculate taste—long before it was being generally revived by the Victorians. The house embodies the mild unease with mid-nineteenth century culture and the preference for the early 18C we find in his writings, particularly *Henry Esmond* and the *Lectures on the English Humourists*. It now belongs to the Israeli Embassy.

Thackeray's interest in another period, the Regency, is shown by his deft use of Brighton in *Vanity Fair*, where the fashionable resort is hailed as 'a clean Naples with genteel lazzaroni—. . . Brighton, that always looks so brisk, gay, and gaudy, like a harlequin's jacket—. . . Brighton, which used to be seven hours distant from London at the time of our story; which is now only a hundred minutes off; and which may approach who knows how much nearer' (Ch. 22). His last novel, *Denis Duval*, retreats again into his beloved eighteenth century and is set east of Brighton in the picturesque little towns of Winchelsea and Rye. Its hero attends the 17C Peacocke's School in Rye's High Street. Henry James (q.v.), who lived in Rye, included a finely appreciative essay, 'Winchelsea, Rye and *Denis Duval*,' in his *English Hours*.

Thackeray died in 1863 at Palace Green, with *Denis Duval* unfinished and his projected history of Queen Anne's reign unattempted. The offer of a grave near Oliver Goldsmith (q.v.) in the Temple Church was declined and he was buried in Kensal Green Cemetery, opposite Kensal Green Station (British Rail and Bakerloo Underground Line). His grave is No. 18177 in square 36 between South Avenue and the canal. Its simplicity and modest position prompted Richard Monckton Milnes, Lord Houghton, a friend since their days at Trinity College, to write:

> But, may be, he—who could so draw
>   The hidden great—the humble wise,

Yielding with them to God's good law
Makes the Pantheon where he lies.

Some were surprised that the question of a funeral in Westminster Abbey had not been raised, and Shirley Brooks, a friend from *Punch*, started a subscription for a bust to be placed in Poets' Corner (fee). It was designed by Baron Carlo Marochetti, Thackeray's old neighbour in Young Street.

Charterhouse, City of London. Visitors by written appointment only.

Clevedon Court, near Clevedon (NT). Open Apr to end Sept, Wed, Thurs, Sun & BH Mon 2.30–5.30. Fee.

Kensal Green Cemetery. Open Mon to Sat 9–5.30 (or dusk, if earlier), Sun 2–5.30 (or dusk); Good Fri 2–5.30, Christmas Day 10–2. Closes at 1 on BH.

Dylan Thomas

b. Swansea, West Glamorgan, 1914; d. New York, USA, 1953. *18 Poems* (1934); *Twenty-Five Poems* (1936); *The Map of Love: Verse and Prose* (1939); *Portrait of the Artist as a Young Dog* (1940); *New Poems* (1943); *Deaths and Entrances: Poems* (1946); *Twenty-Six Poems* (1950); *In Country Sleep and Other Poems* (1952); *Collected Poems 1934–1952* (1952); *The Doctor and the Devils* (1953); *Under Milk Wood: A Play for Voices* (1954); *Quite Early One Morning: Broadcasts* (1954); *Adventures in the Skin Trade and Other Stories* (1955); *A Prospect of the Sea and Other Stories and Prose Writings* (edited by Daniel Jones; 1955); *The Beach of Falesá: Based on a Story by R.L. Stevenson* (1963).

For Dylan Thomas Wales was the magic territory of childhood, the culture that shaped his gifts, the narrow province from which he needed to escape and, always, the place where he could do his best writing. His family home is in the western part of Swansea, the Uplands, at No. 5 Cwmdonkin Drive, a street that proclaims its Edwardian respectability. Here, after leaving school and abandoning his job as a local reporter, Thomas first dedicated himself to poetry. Cwmdonkin Park, to the west, where he used to play as a child, now has a memorial.

In adult life his connection with Wales centred on the pleasant little town of Laugharne, on the coast and A4066 NW of Swansea. He first came in 1938 as a guest of the novelist Richard Hughes, returning later to rent Sea View near the town centre and finally, for the last years of his life, to live by the sea in The Boat House (beyond Cliff Road). He is buried in the churchyard. Several Welsh Towns have claimed themselves as the original of 'Llaregyb,' setting for *Under Milk Wood*, but it is certain that the radio play could not have been conceived without the influence and example of Laugharne.

Thomas' life in London—and, at the end, in America—made the need for such a retreat the more urgent. He first went to London in 1934, frequenting 'Fitzrovia' (north of Oxford Street and west of Tottenham Court Road) and later, when he was connected with the BBC, the area round Broadcasting House in Langham Place (north of Oxford Circus). In 1982 a memorial to Thomas was added to Poets' Corner (fee) of Westminster Abbey.

Edward Thomas

b. London, 1878; d. Arras, France, 1917. *The Woodland Life* (1897); *Horae Solitariae* (1902); *Oxford* (1903); *Rose Acre Papers* (1904); *Beautiful Wales* (1905); *The Heart of England* (1906); *Richard Jefferies* (1909); *The South Country* (1909); *Windsor Castle* (1910); *The Isle of Wight* (1911); *Light and Twilight* (1911); *Algernon Charles Swinburne* (1912); *George Borrow* (1912); *The Icknield Way* (1913); *The Country* (1913); *The Happy-Go-Lucky Morgans* (1913); *Walter Pater* (1913); *In Pursuit of Spring* (1914); *Four-and-Twenty Blackbirds* (1915); *Keats* (1916); *A Literary Pilgrim in England* (1917); *Poems* (1917); *Last Poems* (1918).

Son of a railway clerk, Thomas went to Oxford as a non-collegiate student in 1897 and entered Lincoln College the next year. His rooms were in the Front Quad above those once occupied by John Wesley.

Thomas' first book had appeared the year he began his studies. After university he supported himself, with determination but often with great difficulty, by a stream of books ranging from the merest hackwork to writings on nature and topography that place him in the tradition of Richard Jefferies and George Borrow (qq.v.). The headnote above gives only a sample for, as Thomas himself remarked to a friend, if 'they put a list of books on my tombstone I shall want one as big as one of the stones at Stonehenge.'

The same love of nature that characterises his best work governed his choice of homes. In 1901–04 he lived in Kent at Bearsted, now virtually assimilated into its western neighbour, Maidstone. Above the village rise the North Downs where he delighted to walk. He then moved west to Else's Farm in Sevenoaks Weald, 4 miles south of Sevenoaks. Thomas brought W.H. Davies to the village and, despite his own poverty, helped support him while he began the *Autobiography of a Super-Tramp* (1908). From 1906 onwards he lived in the area round Petersfield (on A3 in Hampshire) to be near Bedales school, where he sent his son. Of his homes here the most interesting is the last: Yewtree Cottage, a cheap semi-detached workman's dwelling near the church in Steep (2 miles north of Petersfield). There is a memorial stone on the hill opposite.

In 1914 he visited the American poet Robert Frost, then staying in the village of Dymock (4 miles south of Ledbury in Hereford and Worcester). In his walks on the nearby Malvern Hills with Frost that summer, Thomas first saw how his precise, unsentimental vision of nature could be recorded in deceptively simple verse. It is, of course, for his career as a poet—cut short by his death in the First World War—that he is now chiefly remembered.

Francis Thompson

b. Preston, Lancashire, 1859; d. London, 1907. *Poems* (includes 'The Hound of Heaven'; 1893); *Sister Songs* (1895); *New Poems* (1897); *Health and Holiness* (1905).

The poet's strange and haunted life began among distinctly mundane surroundings in Northern England. In Preston (28 miles NW of Manchester) his birthplace at No. 7 Winckley Street, south of

Fishergate near St George's Shopping Centre, is marked with a plaque. When he was still a child his family moved to Ashton-under-Lyne, 6 miles east of Manchester via A635. Their home, which his father also used as surgery for his practice in homeopathic medicine and made a gathering place for the local Catholic clergy, was at No. 226 Stamford Street, the main thoroughfare which runs NE from Chester Square. In 1870 Thompson was sent to Ushaw College, 4 miles west of Durham. The College's most interesting feature, the chapel designed by Pugin in 1840, was rebuilt on a larger scale in 1885 after Thompson had left. At the age of seventeen he returned to Manchester and entered Owens College, now the University of Manchester, in Oxford Road a mile SE of St Peter's Square. He spent six unsuccessful years here as a medical student, failing his exams three times.

In 1885 he abandoned medicine, broke permanently with his father and came to London. He quickly sank into destitution and opium addiction. From this state he was rescued in 1888 by Wilfrid Meynell, editor of *Merry England*, to whom he had submitted several poems written on ragged scraps of paper. Meynell and his wife Alice, poet, essayist and critic, became Thompson's unofficial guardians, not merely establishing his reputation as a poet but making possible the circumstances under which most of his verse was written. He was a regular visitor to their home at No. 47 Palace Court, which runs north from Bayswater Road near its continuation as Notting Hill Gate. Here he met Coventry Patmore (q.v.), a poet of an older generation and by then almost a forgotten figure.

Thompson's life in London was relieved by retreats into the country, though neither they nor the Meynells' good offices permanently saved him from opium. In 1889 he stayed at a monastery in Storrington, a large West Sussex village 8 miles NW of Worthing. His 'Ode to the Setting Sun' and much of his most famous poem, 'The Hound of Heaven,' were written while walking on Kithurst Hill south of Storrington and A283. In 1907, prematurely aged by drugs and obviously near death, he returned to West Sussex on a visit to the writer Wilfrid Scawen Blunt at Newbuildings Place, south of Horsham. To reach it from A24 we take A272 west to Green Street (1½ miles), where we follow an unclassified road to the right for 1 mile, forking right in the hamlet of Dragons Green. In the intervening years Thompson had also lived (1892–96) with the Roman Catholic community at Pantasaph near the Dee estuary and the North Wales coast. It lies 2 miles west of Holywell and is reached via A55 and an unclassified road leading south.

Thompson was buried in London at St Mary's, the Roman Catholic annexe to Kensal Green Cemetery, opposite Kensal Green Station (British Rail and Bakerloo Underground Line). His gravestone bears the epitaph 'Look for me in the nurseries of Heaven.'

Newbuildings Place, near Southwater. Visitors by written appointment with the Viscount Knebworth.

Kensal Green Cemetery. Open Mon to Sat 9–5.30 (or dusk, if earlier), Sun 2–5.30 (or dusk); Good Fri 2–5.30, Christmas Day 10–2. Closes at 1 on BH.

James Thomson

b. Ednam, Borders, 1700; d. London, 1748. *The Seasons* (1726–30; revised edition 1744); *Liberty* (1734–36); *The Castle of Indolence* (1748).

Thomson was born in the former manse at the village of Ednam, 2 miles north of Kelso on B6461. On nearby Ednam Hill there is an obelisk commemorating him, erected by David Stewart, Earl of Buchan in 1819. The enthusiastic peer had opened his campaign on behalf of the poet's memory by holding an anniversary ceremony on the spot in 1791, an occasion to which Robert Burns (q.v.) contributed a poem. Thomson went to school at Jedburgh, on A68 11 miles south of Kelso, attending classes in the aisle of the splendid Abbey. The rugged and impressive landscape of surrounding ˙Teviotdale contributed greatly to that new feeling for nature which he introduced into 18C poetry; its influence is particularly apparent in the 'Winter' section of *The Seasons*.

After studying at Edinburgh University, Thomson came permanently to England in 1725. The popularity of his verse and his own fluency in finding aristocratic patrons and friends made him a frequent visitor to country houses. In 1727 he stayed for the first time with the literary-minded Countess of Hertford at Castle House in Marlborough, Wiltshire. The house is now part of Marlborough College. It is hard to credit Dr Johnson (q.v.) when he reports that Thomson 'took more delight in carousing with Lord Hertford and his friends than assisting her Ladyship's poetical operations,' for the poet was writing 'Spring' during his visit. As a guest of the Talbot family he found the 17C Ashdown House (off B4000 10 miles east of Swindon) a 'little solitary island, in the midst of a vast verdant ocean.' At Cliveden (by the Thames NE of Maidenhead) a 19C mansion has replaced the 17C building where Thomson's *Masque of Alfred*, with music by Dr Thomas Arne, was first performed in 1740. The occasion would hardly deserve remembering were it not for the inclusion of 'Rule Britannia' among the songs.

Two country houses are of special importance, for they remind the visitor of the close connection between Thomson's poetry and 18C landscape gardening, and of the appropriateness that made William Kent an illustrator of *The Seasons*. The magnificent grounds of Stowe, in Buckinghamshire, to which Kent contributed, are praised in the revised version of 'Autumn':

> Oh! lead me to the wide extended walks,
> The fair majestic paradise of Stowe!
> Not Persian Cyrus on Ionia's shore
> E'er saw such sylvan scenes, such various art
> By genius fired, such ardent genius tamed
> By cool judicious art, that in the strife
> All-beauteous Nature fears to be outdone.
>
> (lines 1041–1047)

Now a public school, Stowe is 2 miles NW of Buckingham. Hagley Hall (on A456 between Birmingham and Kidderminster) receives a tribute in 'Spring':

> There among the dale
> With woods o'erhung, and shagged with mossy rocks
> Whence on each hand the gushing waters play,

And down the rough cascade white-dashing fall
Or gleam in lengthened vista through the trees,
You silent steal; or sit beneath the shade
Of solemn oaks, that tuft the swelling mounts
Thrown graceful round by Nature's careless hand,
And pensive listen to the various voice
Of rural peace. . .

(lines 909–918)

At Hagley Thomson met the poet Shenstone (q.v.) and revised *The Seasons*, accepting suggestions from his host, Lord Lyttleton.

The same appreciation of landscape led Thomson from central to south-west London, then a series of outlying but fashionable villages. In Hammersmith he frequented the Doves Inn (now a restaurant) at No. 19 Upper Mall by the river. From 1736 he lived in Richmond, celebrating the view from its Hill in 'Summer' (lines 1408–1445). The Royal Hospital on Kew Foot Road, near the Old Deer Park at the southern end of Kew Road, now incorporates the house where he lived from 1739 until his death. It was here that he received visits from Pope (q.v.) and William Collins (q.v.), and cultivated the habit he made the subject of his last poem, *The Castle of Indolence*. Charles Burney, father of the novelist (q.v.), 'one day at two o'clock in the afternoon, found him in bed, with the curtains closed and the windows shut' and was told: 'Why, Mon, I had not motive to rise.' Thomson found his final rest at the church of St Mary Magdalene between Paradise Road and George Street, where he is commemorated by a tablet of 1792, another fruit of Lord Buchan's admiration for his work.

Poets' Corner (fee) in Westminster Abbey has a memorial of 1762.

Jedburgh Abbey (DoE/SDD). Open 15 March to 15 Oct, Mon to Sat 9.30–6.30, Sun 2–6.30; 16 Oct to 14 March, Mon to Sat 9.30–4, Sun 2–4. Closed Christmas Day, Boxing Day, New Year's Day & 2 Jan. Fee.

Ashdown House (NT). Open Apr, Wed only 2–6; May to end Sept, Wed & 1st & 3rd Sat of each month 2–6. Fee.

Cliveden (NT). Grounds open March to end Dec, daily (including Good Fri) 11–6 or sunset if earlier. Fee. House (only 2 rooms shown) open Apr to end Oct, Sat & Sun 2–6. Fee.

Stowe, near Buckingham. Grounds and garden buildings open Easter & summer school holidays, Fri, Sat, Sun & Aug BH Mon 1–6. Fee.

Hagley Hall. Open from East Sun, BH Sun & Mon 12.30–5; 1 July to 2 Sept, daily except Sat 12.30–5. Fee.

Thomas Traherne

b. Hereford, 1638?; d. London, 1674. Metaphysical poet.

Traherne was educated at Brasenose College, Oxford and apparently continued to live in the city for most of his life, despite holding a living at the village of Credenhill near his hometown in Hereford and Worcester. His appointment as chaplain to the Lord Keeper, Sir Orlando Bridgeman, brought him to Teddington in south-west London in 1672. From that year until his death he served as rector of St Mary, on Ferry Road near Teddington Lock, and is buried in the small brick church; it also contains a monument of 1674 to Bridgeman.

Traherne's *Centuries of Meditation*, upon which his reputation as a devotional poet depends, was not discovered and published until the closing years of the 19C.

Anthony Trollope

b. London, 1815; d. London, 1882. *The Macdermotts of Ballycloran* (1847); *The Kellys and the O'Kellys, or Landlords and Tenants: A Tale of Irish Life* (1848); *The Warden* (1855); *Barchester Towers* (1857); *Doctor Thorne* (1858); *Framley Parsonage* (1861); *Orley Farm* (1862); *North America* (1862); *The Small House at Allington* (1864); *Can You Forgive Her?* (1864); *The Claverings* (1867); *The Last Chronicle of Barset* (1867); *Phineas Finn: The Irish Member* (1869); *He Knew He Was Right* (1869); *The Vicar of Bullhampton* (1870); *Sir Harry Hotspur of Humblethwaite* (1871); *The Eustace Diamonds* (1873); *Australia and New Zealand* (1873); *Phineas Redux* (1874); *The Way We Live Now* (1875); *The Prime Minister* (1876); *The American Senator* (1877); *Is He Popenjoy?* (1878); *The Duke's Children* (1880); *Dr Wortle's School* (1881); *Mr Scarborough's Family* (1883); *An Autobiography* (1883).

The novelist spent most of his childhood in a succession of homes at Harrow in north-west London, where his father made a characteristically ill-planned and unsuccessful attempt to establish himself as a farmer. He was sent as a dayboy to the famous public school at Harrow on the Hill. Poor and shabbily dressed, Trollope was uncomfortable among his affluent fellow pupils and his *Autobiography* remembered the walk between home and school as 'a daily purgatory' (Ch. 1).

He was no happier when his education at Harrow was interrupted by a brief spell (1825–27) at another famous school, Winchester College. The experience was, if anything, more miserable since Trollope's father—then embarked on an equally unsuccessful attempt to run a general store in America—was unable to pay his son's bills and the local tradesmen withdrew their credit:

> My schoolfellows of course knew that it was so, and I became a Pariah. It is the nature of boys to be cruel. I have sometimes doubted whether among each other they do usually suffer much, one from the other's cruelty; but I suffered horribly! I could make no stand against it. I had no friend to whom I could pour out my sorrows. I was big, and awkward, and ugly, and, I have no doubt, skulked about in a most unattractive manner. Of course I was ill-dressed and dirty. But, ah! how well I remember all the agonies of my young heart; how I considered whether I should always be alone; whether I could not find my way up to the top of that college tower, and from thence put an end to everything? (*Autobiography*, Ch. 1)

Despite these unhappy memories, obviously still fresh in old age, Trollope made use of Winchester at least once in his fiction. The conflict over 'Hiram's Hospital' in *The Warden* clearly derives from a legal dispute, eventually settled in 1857, involving the city's medieval *Hospital of St Cross. The Hospital stands on St Cross Road south of the centre. Its church is particularly notable.

This link between Winchester and *The Warden* has prompted speculation that the city might be the original of 'Barchester,' centre of the 'Barsetshire' novels. Indeed, identifying 'Barchester' used to be a favourite pastime, and a source of much friendly rivalry, among clerics attached to various English cathedrals. Trollope may have seemed to encourage this by speaking of 'Barsetshire' in language that Hardy (q.v.) might have used about 'Wessex':

> I had it all in my mind,—its roads and railroads, its towns and parishes, its members of Parliament, and the different hunts which rode over it. I knew all the great lords and their castles, the squires and their parks, the rectors and their churches. . . Throughout these stories there has been no name given to a fictitious site which does not represent to me a spot of which I know all the accessories, as though I had lived and wandered there. (*Autobiography*, Ch. 8)

Yet Trollope's familiarity with 'Barsetshire' was limited to his mind. Unlike Hardy, he never suggested that it had any existence outside the pages of his novels. The furthest he would go was this reference to a visit to Salisbury, apparently made in 1851: 'whilst wandering there on a mid-summer evening round the purlieus of the cathedral I conceived the story of *The Warden*.' He added: 'I stood for an hour on the little bridge in Salisbury, and had made out to my own satisfaction the spot on which Hiram's Hospital should stand' (*Autobiography*, Ch. 5). The bridge is presumably Harnham Bridge, south of the Cathedral Close. St Nicholas' Hospital stands nearby but the visitor will look in vain for any further warrant to give a local habitation and a name to Trollope's invention.

Trollope went to Salisbury in the course of his work for the Post Office, a job that took him to Ireland for most of the 1840s and 1850s. He was a guest of Sir William Henry Gregory at Coole Park by N18 north of Gort in Galway. The house itself, closely associated with Yeats (q.v.) and his circle, has been demolished but the grounds where Trollope indulged his passion for fox-hunting remain. In 1854–59 he lived SE of Dublin in the suburb of Donnybrook. His home, No. 5 Seaview Terrace, is reached by turning left from the main road between Dublin and Bray on to Ailesbury Road.

From 1872 to 1880, when he had abandoned 'Barsetshire' for his novels of political life, Trollope lived in London at No. 39 Montagu Square (GLC plaque), north of Marble Arch. He then moved to the village of South Harting, on B2141 11 miles NW of Chichester in West Sussex, where his home survives as Northend House. He died in London and, like so many eminent Victorian writers, was buried in Kensal Green Cemetery, opposite Kensal Green Station (British Rail and Bakerloo Underground Line). His grave is No. 28529 in square 138, SW of the church.

Harrow School. Visits by prior appointment with the Custos of the Old Schools.

Winchester College. Open Apr to Sept, Mon to Sat 10–6, Sun 2–6 (guided tours start Mon to Sat 11, 2 & 3.15, Sun 2 & 3.15); Oct to March, Mon to Sat 10–4, Sun 2–4. Fee.

Hospital of St Cross, Winchester. Open daily except Sun and Christmas Day, summer 9–12.30 & 2–5, winter 10.30–12.30 & 2–4.30. Fee.

Kensal Green Cemetery. Open Mon to Sat 9–5.30 (or dusk, if earlier), Sun 2–5.30 (or dusk); Good Fri 2–5.30, Christmas Day 10–2. Closes at 1 on BH.

Nicholas Udall (or Uvedale)

b. place unknown, 1505; d. London, 1556. *Ralph Roister Doister* (n.d.)

Udall, author of the first known English stage comedy, spent his life in some of the country's best known educational institutions. He received his boyhood schooling at Winchester College. From 1520 to 1524 he studied at Corpus Christi, Oxford, distinguishing himself by a zealous Protestantism later prudently abandoned during the reign of Queen Mary. In c. 1534 he became headmaster of Eton College, south of M4 near Windsor, perhaps writing *Ralph Roister Doister* for performance by his pupils. He gained a reputation for physical brutality and was dismissed on charges of misconduct in 1541. He had acquired the living of Braintree, 12 miles north of Chelmsford, Essex in 1537, retaining it until 1544. The church of St Michael the Archangel underwent heavy 19C restoration; only its 13C tower remains untouched. For the last two years of his life he was headmaster of Westminster School, in Little Dean's Yard to the south of Westminster Abbey in London. Udall was buried at nearby St Margaret's, Westminster.

Winchester College. Open Apr to Sept, Mon to Sat 10–6, Sun 2–6 (guided tours start Mon to Sat 11, 2, & 3.15, Sun 2 & 3.15); Oct to March, Mon to Sat 10–4, Sun 2–4. Fee.

Eton College. Open daily 2–5 during term, 10.30-5 during spring holiday, 9–5 during summer holiday. Fee.

Sir John Vanbrugh

b. London, 1664; d. London, 1726. *The Relapse* (1697); *The Provok'd Wife* (1697).

After his early success as auther of elegant comedy Vanbrugh, in Swift's ironic phrase, 'without thought or lecture/... hugely turn'd to architecture.' Apparently without formal training but with the technical assistance of Nicholas Hawksmoor he raised the English Baroque style to a new scale and a new pitch of grandeur. Walpole's reaction to Castle Howard sums up admiration for his achievement:

> Nobody had informed me that I should see at once a palace, a town, a fortified city, temples on high places, woods worthy of being each a metropolis of the Druids, the noblest lawn in the world fenced by half the horizon, and a mausoleum that would tempt one to be buried alive; in short I have seen gigantic palaces before, but never a sublime one.

His chief works, mostly too well known to require special commentary, may be listed briefly, with their arrangements for opening to the public:

Castle Howard, 17 miles NE of York. Begun in 1701 for the Earl of Carlisle. Open 25 March to end Oct, daily 11.30–5. Fee.

Blenheim Palace, 8 miles NW of Oxford. Begun in 1705 for the Duke of Marlborough. Park open all year 9–5. Fee. House open 15 March to end Oct, daily 11–6. Fee.

Seaton Delaval Hall, 11 miles NE of Newcastle upon Tyne. 1720–28, for Admiral George Delaval. Badly damaged by fire in 1822. Open 1 May to 30 Sept, Wed,

Sun & BH Mon 2–6. Fee.

Audley End (English Heritage), 11 miles south of Cambridge. In 1721–22 Vanbrugh performed what one of his biographers has called 'the least creditable of all his undertakings,' the reduction of the Jacobean mansion to its present sadly diminished proportions. Open Apr to Sept, Tues to Sun 1–6.30. Closed Good Fri but open BH Mon except May Day. Fee.

Stowe House, 2 miles NW of Buckingham. In 1710 Sir Richard Temple (later Viscount Cobham) began to enlarge his house and landscape its grounds, eventually creating a magnificent essay in 18C taste that includes work by Kent and Gibbs as well as Vanbrugh. Vanbrugh may have had a hand in alterations to the house but his main surviving contributions are to the garden buildings: the Lake Pavilions on the SE side of the Octagon Lake, unfortunately altered in 1770; the Rotondo on the main lawn south of the house, with unhappy alterations to its dome made later in the 18C; and the Bourbon Tower, outside the grounds to the NE, an early example of medievalism. Stowe House is now a public school. The grounds and garden buildings are open during the Easter and summer holidays, Fri, Sat, Sun & August BH Mon 1–6. Fee.

Of the several houses he built and occupied in London only one survives. It stands in Greenwich at the corner of Maze Hill and Westcombe Park Road and is now an RAF Memorial School. The present name, Vanbrugh Castle, replaces his own more whimsical choice, the Bastille, recalling the prison where he had the misfortune to spend some eighteen months during a youthful visit to the Continent.

Vanbrugh is buried in the City of London at St Stephen's, Walbrook, immediately south of the Mansion House and Bank Underground Station (Central and Northern Lines), a church by his most famous contemporary in architecture, Wren.

Edmund Waller

b. Coleshill, Buckinghamshire, 1606; d. Beaconsfield, Buckinghamshire, 1687. Lyric poet.

The manor house at Coleshill, off A404 6 miles NE of High Wycombe, where Waller was born does not survive but the parish church of Amersham, 2 miles further north, where he was baptised can still be visited. The Waller family later moved to Beaconsfield, 4 miles south, the poet's home for the rest of his life except his years of exile on the Continent. His house, Hall Barn, has since been rebuilt but his grave survives in the parish churchyard.

In 1620 Waller entered King's College, Cambridge where he left no mark and apparently took no degree.

In London he married Anne Bankes at St Margaret's, Westminster, near the Abbey, in 1631. A less happy period of his life is recalled by the Tower of London, where he was imprisoned in 1643–44 for his part in a plot to secure the City of London for the King. He was banished from England, only escaping a heavier penalty by abject displays of remorse and perhaps by betrayal of his confederates. After his return (c. 1652) he behaved more prudently and wrote a panegyric to Oliver Cromwell.

Waller is also one of the impressive list of writers connected with Penshurst Place, SW of Tonbridge in Kent. In the 1630s he addressed a series of poems to Lady Dorothy Sidney ('Sacharissa') which compliment her in extravagant conceits and invoke the memory of Sir Philip Sidney (q.v.).

Tower of London (DoE). Open March to Oct, Mon to Sat 9.30–5, Sun 2–5; Nov to Feb, Mon to Sat 9.30–4. Closed Christmas Eve, Christmas Day, Boxing Day, New Year's Day, Maundy Thurs, Good Fri. Fee.

Penshurst Place. Open Apr to end Oct, Tues (except after BH), Wed, Thurs, Sat, Sun, BH Mon 2–6. Fee.

Horace Walpole, Earl of Orford

b. London, 1717; d. London, 1797. *The Castle of Otranto* (1764); *The Mysterious Mother* (1768).

Walpole was born at No. 22 Arlington Street, south of Piccadilly, the London residence of his father, Sir Robert, Prime Minister to George I and George II. It is now marked by a GLC plaque. No. 5 opposite, bought by the father in 1742 and inherited by the son in 1745, has been demolished—a fate also suffered by Horace's later town house on the east side of Mayfair's much vandalised Berkeley Square.

From 1735 to 1739 Walpole studied at King's College, Cambridge but was in residence only intermittently. Unlike his father, who had contributed largely to the Fellows' Building of 1724 by James Gibbs, he left no interesting trace of his presence there. The Great Court of Trinity College, however, enjoys an intriguing connection with his only novel. Revisiting Cambridge more than a decade after writing *The Castle of Otranto* Walpole realised that for its Gothic setting he had unconsciously drawn on memories of one of the colleges. The letter to Madame du Deffand (27 January 1775) explaining this curious fact does not name the spot but, with its gatehouses, towers, chapel and hall with oriel window, only Great Court fully matches the scattered hints offered by the novel.

During his undergraduate years and again in 1743–45 Walpole passed summers at *Houghton Hall, 16 Miles NE of King's Lynn in Norfolk, the Palladian mansion built by his father in 1722–31. He did not find county society congenial:

> Only imagine that I here every day see men, who are mountains of roast beef, and only seem just roughly hewn out into the outlines of human form, like the giant-rock at Pratolino! I shudder when I see them brandish their knives in act to carve, and look at them as savages that devour one another. I should not stare at all more than I do, if yonder Alderman at the lower end of the table was to stick his fork into his neighbour's jolly cheek, and cut a brave slice of brown and fat.

Characteristically, he took refuge in writing *Aedes Walpolianae* (1747), a descriptive catalogue of the many fine paintings his father had gathered. Their sale and dispersal in 1779, made necessary by the dissolute ways of Lord Orford, was a lasting source of grief to him. Like his father, Walpole is buried in the little church that stands in the park.

During his Norfolk summers he also visited his uncle Horatio at another 18C mansion: Wolterton Hall, 3½ miles west of Erpingham, a village on A140 between Aylsham and Cromer.

At **Strawberry Hill Walpole found a house more suited to his

The Cabinet at Strawberry Hill. From A Description of the Villa of Mr Horace Walpole ... at Strawberry-Hill near Twickenham, Middlesex *(1784). Courtesy of Cambridge University Library*

taste than the provincial grandeurs of Houghton and devoted much of his life to making it perhaps the most self-expressive environment any English writer has ever created. Well-preserved despite Walpole's own fears for its fragility and its fate after his death, Strawberry Hill still stands as his best monument. It is situated in Twickenham, today thoroughly assimilated into SW London, between Strawberry Hill Station (British Rail) and the Thames; it now houses St Mary's Training College.

When Walpole first rented Chopped-Straw Hall (as it was then known) it was a coachman's cottage whose chief attraction lay in its modesty and its rural but not remote location:

> It is a little plaything-house . . . and is the prettiest bauble you ever saw. It is set in enamelled meadows, with filigree hedges:

A small Euphrates through the piece is roll'd,
And little finches wave their wings in gold.

Two delightful roads, that you would call dusty, supply me continually with coaches and chaises: barges as solemn as Barons of the Exchequer move under my window; Richmond Hill and Ham Walks bound my prospect; but, thank God! the Thames is between me and the Duchess of Queensbury. Dowagers as plenty as flounders inhabit all around, and Pope's ghost is just now skimming under the window by a most poetical moonlight. I have about land enough to keep such a farm as Noah's, when he set up in the ark with a pair of each kind; but my cottage is rather cleaner than I believe his was after they had been cooped up together forty days.

After buying the property in 1749 he began, with the aid of various architectural 'Committees of Taste,' to transform it into 'a little Gothic castle.' The full story, told by running commentary in his letters and more formally in his *Description of Strawberry Hill* (1774), can here only be summarised. By 1753 the original exterior had been decorated with battlements and the interior remodelled, most successfully in the charming Staircase Hall. In the course of the next twenty years there followed Library, Great Parlour, Holbein Chamber, Cloister, Gallery, and Chapel, until the building's original size had been more than doubled and its outlines rendered pleasingly asymmetrical.

In Walpole's lifetime Strawberry Hill became an object of curiosity to a steady flow of visitors. He even needed to print a list of regulations: advance notice was required, parties were limited to four people, and children were not admitted. Contemporaries sometimes reacted with amusement, derision or bewilderment, as in the case of the Frenchman who first removed and then replaced his hat in the unconsecrated chapel where the owner housed his cabinet of secular curiosities. And so began the long history of misunderstanding from which Strawberry Hill can still suffer today. Walpole has been credited with beginning a Gothic revival that was already underway before he ever added a battlement. He has been accused of gimcrack inaccuracy in his use of Gothic motifs, whereas in fact the details of Strawberry Hill constitute a jackdaw history of English ecclesiastical architecture. And he is sometimes supposed to have created an effect of Gothic gloom suitable to the author of *The Castle of Otranto*. Though he may at times have strived to achieve this note, it was always relieved by the Rococo aspect of his sensibility, the use of very un-Gothic materials and by an eclectic assembly of *objets d'art* (unfortunately later dispersed). However much Strawberry Hill may have grown in size and elaborateness it never entirely ceased to be the 'little plaything-house' its creator had first rented.

Like Pope (q.v.) before him, Walpole was both a frequent visitor to Marble Hill House nearby and an unofficial adviser to Mrs Howard (later Lady Suffolk), mistress to George II, in the laying out of her garden.

Houghton Hall. Open Easter Sun to last Sun in Sept, Thurs and BH 12–5.30, Sun 1.30–5.30. Fee.

Strawberry Hill (St Mary's College), Twickenham. Visitors by appointment with the Principal for Wed or Sat afternoons.

Marble Hill House, Twickenham (GLC). Open daily except Fri 10–5 (Nov to Jan, closes at 4).

Evelyn Waugh

b. London, 1903; d. Combe Florey, Somerset, 1966. *PRB: An Essay on the Pre-Raphaelite Brotherhood 1847–1854* (privately printed; 1926); *Decline and Fall* (1928); *Rossetti: His Life and Works* (1928); *Vile Bodies* (1930); *Black Mischief* (1932); *A Handful of Dust* (1934); *Edmund Campion* (1935); *Waugh in Abyssinia* (1936); *Scoop* (1938); *Put Out More Flags* (1942); *Work Suspended* (1942); *Brideshead Revisited: The Sacred and Profane Memories of Captain Charles Ryder* (1945); *When the Going Was Good* (1946); *Scott-King's Modern Europe* (1947); *The Loved One* (1948); *Helena* (1950); *Men At Arms* (1952); *Love Among the Ruins* (1953); *Officers and Gentlemen* (1955); *The Ordeal of Gilbert Pinfold* (1957); *The Life of Ronald Knox* (1959); *Unconditional Surrender* (1961); *A Little Learning* (1964).

Waugh was born in Hampstead at No. 11 Hillfield Road (west of Finchley Road near Westfield College). In the normal course of events he would have followed his older brother's footsteps and gone to Sherborne School in Dorset but the appearance of Alec Waugh's novel *Loom of Youth*, highly critical of public school life, made a different choice expedient. So Waugh was educated at Lancing College (7½ miles west of Brighton via A27). *A Little Learning*, his own account of his early life, shows little fondness for the school except for the fine, massive Victorian chapel which dominates its architecture.

He himself was acutely conscious that Hertford College was not then among the more prestigious institutions in Oxford and that he accepted a scholarship there mainly because of his father's strained finances. 'I have to make a noise,' he told his contemporary Cyril Connolly, 'because I'm poor.' The legend of his flamboyantly drunken behaviour during his undergraduate years (1922–24) has no doubt grown in the telling, including his own telling, but his bad relations with his History tutor and equally bad Third are a matter of record. Waugh the novelist, however, possessed Oxford with a confidence that Waugh the undergraduate could not. His fictional portraits of the University range from the farcical 'Scone College,' whose quad echoes to 'the sound of the English county families baying for broken glass,' at the beginning of *Decline and Fall*, to the richly nostalgic account in *Brideshead Revisited*. This novel mourned an Oxford 'submerged now and obliterated, irrecoverable as Lyonesse, so quickly have the waters come flooding in' (Part 1, Ch. 1).

Television has recently identified Brideshead Castle, which the novel locates in Wiltshire, with Castle Howard (off A64 17 miles NE of York). Waugh, in fact, did pay a visit in 1937 and Vanbrugh's Baroque splendours may well have contributed to the fictional country house, but Castle Howard's current popularity with visitors is in striking contrast to the picture of aristocratic decline offered by the novel. In a 1959 preface Waugh himself noted 'the present cult of country houses' and remarked with prophetic irony: 'Brideshead today would be open to trippers, its treasures rearranged by expert hands and the fabric better maintained than it was by Lord Marchmain.'

His passionate attachment to the old order of society made it fitting that he should acquire a country house for himself as soon as the success of his writing permitted such an elevation. In 1937 he bought Piers Court in Stinchcombe, on B4060 12 miles NW of Stroud and

near the western edge of the Cotswolds. In 1957, defying the era of
austerity, he moved to the larger and grander manor at Combe Florey
in Somerset (on the edge of the Quantock Hills, off A358 8 miles NW
of Taunton). These surroundings allowed him to indulge his taste for
Victorian interior decoration, and he celebrated his arrival at Combe
Florey by commissioning the famous factory in Wilton to reproduce
a prize-winning carpet from the Great Exhibition of 1851.

Castle Howard. Open 25 March to end Oct, daily 11.30–5. Fee.

H.G. Wells

b. London, 1866; d. London, 1946. *The Time Machine* (1895); *The Island of Dr
Moreau* (1896); *The Invisible Man, A Grotesque Romance* (1897); *The War of
the Worlds* (1898); *When the Sleeper Wakes: A Story of Years to Come* (1899);
Love and Mr Lewisham (1900); *The First Men in the Moon* (1901); *The Discovery
of the Future* (1902); *Mankind in the Making* (1903); *A Modern Utopia* (1905);
Kipps: The Story of a Simple Soul (1905); *The War in the Air, and Particularly
How Mr Bert Smallways Fared While It Lasted* (1908); *Tono-Bungay* (1909);
Ann Veronica (1909); *The History of Mr Polly* (1910); *The New Machiavelli*
(1911); *Marriage* (1912); *Bealby: A Holiday* (1915); *Boon* (1915); *Mr Britling
Sees It Through* (1916); *The Outline of History* (1920); *Russia in the Shadows*
(1920); *The Salvaging of Civilization* (1921); *A Short History of the World* (1922);
Men Like Gods (1923); *A Year of Prophesying* (1924); *The World of William
Clissold* (1926); *The Way to World Peace* (1930); *The Autocracy of Mr Parham*
(1930); *The Science of Life: A Summary of Contemporary Knowledge About
Life and Its Possibilities* (1930); *The Work, Wealth and Happiness of Mankind*
(1932); *The Bulpington of Blup* (1933); *The Shape of Things to Come* (1933);
*Experiment in Autobiography: Discoveries and Conclusions of a Very Ordinary
Brain—Since 1866* (1934); *The Fate of Homo Sapiens* (1939); *The Outlook for
Homo Sapiens* (1942); *Mind at the End of Its Tether* (1945).

Not all the scenes of Wells' insecure and unhappy childhood, a rich
trove of experience mined by his best novels, survive. At Bromley,
then a separate town but now absorbed into SE London, a plaque in
the High Street (A21) marks the site of Atlas House, a grand name
for the modest building where he was born and his father ran a china
shop. The draper's premises in Windsor and Portsmouth where he
was sent to work after the failure of the family business have gone.

The most interesting reminder of his early years is *Uppark in West
Sussex (on B2146 6 miles SE of Petersfield), a charming country
house built in the reign of William and Mary. Wells' mother had been
in service with the Featherstonhaugh family here before her marriage
and she returned as housekeeper in 1880 when the Bromley shop
failed. So Uppark became Wells' intermittent home, and he was
allowed the run of its library. It appears in *Tono-Bungay* as 'Bladesover
House,' which seems to the young hero 'a closed and complete social
system' (Ch. 1). Chapter 2 of the novel gives a lightly fictionalised
account of the famous episode in 1883 when Wells ran away from
Portsmouth and returned unexpectedly home. The result of this
rebellion against his fate as a draper's assistant was that he was sent
to school in Midhurst (12 miles NE of Uppark via unclassified roads),
the 'Wimblehurst' of *Tono-Bungay*.

In 1884 Wells' success at Midhurst won him a place in London at
the Normal School of Science (now Imperial College) on Exhibition
Road in Kensington. His teacher, T.H. Huxley, had considerable

influence over his later scientific writings. Another aspect of Wells' intellectual development, his Socialism, was represented by visits to William Morris (q.v.) at his Hammersmith home.

Despite his early promise Wells left the Normal School without distinguishing himself and, like so many young writers, was condemned to spend the next few years following a desultory career as a schoolmaster. In 1898, already on the way to success in the literary world, he went to live at Sandgate, 2½ miles west of Folkestone on the Kent coast. In 1900 he was able to exchange his rented home for Spade House, designed for him by C.F. Voysey, on Radnor Cliff Crescent. Here he wrote several of his most famous novels, including *Kipps*, whose final chapters reflect the problems Wells had encountered in building a house of his own. During these years he was frequently in contact with Conrad and Henry James (qq.v.), who both lived nearby.

Wells' life at Spade House epitomised the affluent, domesticated comfort to which writers of his generation aspired, but he was destined never to be content as either successful novelist or family man. In 1909 he abandoned Sandgate for London and bought No. 17 Church Row, one of the pleasant Georgian houses near St John's church in Hampstead. Finding it too cramped he moved back to the country in 1912, buying The Glebe, a Georgian house near the church in the village of Little Easton (off B184 6 miles south of Thaxted in Essex).

Little Easton was his main home until 1930, when he returned to London and a flat in Chiltern Court Mansions, south of Regent's Park at the junction of Marylebone Road and Baker Street. Arnold Bennett (q.v.), long a close friend and now a neighbour at Chiltern Court, died only a few months after Wells' arrival. In 1937 he moved a short distance north to his last home at No. 13 Hanover Terrace (now marked with a GLC blue plaque), a fine street by Nash between Regent's Park and Baker Street's northern continuation as Park Road.

Uppark (NT). Open Apr to end Sept, Wed, Thurs, Sun & BH Mon 2–6. Fee.

Gilbert White

b. Selborne, Hampshire, 1720; d. Selborne, 1793. *The Natural History and Antiquities of Selborne, in the County of Southampton* (1789); *A Naturalist's Calendar With Observations in Various Branches of Natural History; Extracted from the Papers of the Late Rev. Gilbert White, M.A.* (1795).

'The parish of Selborne lies in the extreme eastern corner of the county of Hampshire, bordering on the county of Sussex, and not far from the county of Surrey; is about fifty miles south-west of London, in latitude 51, and near midway between the towns of Alton and Petersfield.' In these precise terms White's classic work introduced the village where he was born, spent most of his life and died. The very nature of his achievement, rooted in the gentle, vivid observation that comes from long familiarity, has attracted visitors to *Selborne ever since the book enjoyed its first success. They have rarely been disappointed. William Cobbett (q.v.) came in the course of his *Rural Rides* and found the village 'precisely what it is described by Mr White. . . Nothing can surpass in beauty these dells and hillocks and hangers, which last are so steep that it is impossible to ascend them, except by means of a serpentine path' (entry for 7 August 1823).

In Selborne today White's home, The Wakes, is a museum dedicated jointly to his memory and that of Captain Oates, the Antarctic explorer. It contains a reconstruction of White's study as well as personal relics and editions of his work. The garden still has the ha-ha (or sunken wall) he built and his sundial. They face west towards The Hanger, a wooded hill offering fine views. White's very simple grave can be found in the churchyard north of the chancel; nearby is the ancient yew whose annual growth he measured. Inside the church, where White served as curate in 1757–59 and again from 1784 until his death, is a memorial window contributed by the Gilbert White Fellowship in 1920 and monuments to other members of his family.

Although Selborne is rich enough to satisfy the interest of most lovers of White's work, his connection with Oriel College, Oxford should not be forgotten. He studied here as an undergraduate (1740–43) and remained as a Fellow for an additional probationary year. The poet William Collins (q.v.) was among his contemporaries.

The Wakes, Selborne. Open March to Oct, Tues to Sun 12–5.30: Fee.

Oscar Wilde

b. Dublin, 1854; d. Paris, France, 1900. *Poems* (1881); *The Happy Prince and Other Tales* (1888); *The Picture of Dorian Gray* (1891); *Intentions* (1891); *Lord Arthur Savile's Crime, and Other Stories* (1891); *Lady Windermere's Fan: A Play About a Good Woman* (1893); *A Woman of No Importance* (1894); *An Ideal Husband* (1899); *The Importance of Being Earnest: A Trivial Comedy for Serious People* (1899); *The Soul of Man* (1895); *Salomé: Drame en un Acte* (1893); *The Ballad of Reading Gaol, By C.3.3.* (1898); *De Profundis* (1905);

Wilde was educated in Enniskillen, the county town of Fermanagh, at the Portora Royal School. His childhood and youth otherwise belonged to Dublin, where his father was a distinguished eye and ear surgeon and his mother, Lady 'Speranza' Wilde, a well-known advocate of Irish nationalism. He was born just east of Trinity College at No. 21 Westland Row, now marked with a plaque; the family later moved a few streets south to No. 1 Merrion Square. Wilde continued to live here during the first year of his studies at Trinity College but later moved into the college quadrangle known as Botany Bay. Edward Carson, whose savage cross-examination helped bring about Wilde's downfall in court, was a contemporary at Trinity but never a close friend.

In 1874 Wilde's academic success won him a Classical Demyship (or scholarship) at Magdalen College, Oxford. His lodgings were first in Chaplain's Quad, then in Cloister Quadrangle and, for his last two years, on Kitchen staircase overlooking the river and Magdalen Bridge. He was 'the happiest man in the world,' attending lectures by Walter Pater (q.v.), helping Ruskin (q.v.) in the famous road-building experiment at North Hinksey, and winning the Newdigate Prize for Poetry. By the time he left he had become the most conspicuous member of a cult which rejected Victorian moral earnest-ness and cultivated exquisite style. His rooms at Magdalen were famous for their blue china and sumptuous furnishings.

In London his fame quickly grew, aided by the fun Gilbert (q.v.) and Sullivan poked at the Aesthetes in *Patience*. Despite the legend, he never walked down Piccadilly with a poppy or a lily in his medieval hand as Bunthorne sings of doing in the opera. Anyone could do that, he liked to point out: 'The difficult thing to achieve was to make people think that I had done it.' A favourite gathering place for Wilde and his circle was the Café Royal on Regent Street north of Piccadilly Circus. Here he dined with Frank Harris, Aubrey Beardsley, Richard Le Gallienne, Lionel Johnson, Lord Alfred Douglas and Max Beerbohm (q.v.) among others.

After his marriage to Constance Lloyd in 1884 he moved to No. 34 Tite Street, west of the Royal Hospital in Chelsea. Edward William Godwin, the architect responsible for Whistler's White House (now demolished) on the same street, was hired to make expensive alterations. Both the decor and the host greatly impressed Yeats (q.v.) when he came for Christmas dinner in 1888:

> He had a white dining room, the first I had seen, chairs, walls, cushions all white, but in the middle of the table a red cloth table-centre with a red terracotta statue and above it a red hanging lamp. I have never and shall never meet conversation that could match his. Perplexed by my own shapelessness, my lack of self-possession and of easy courtesy, I was astonished by this scholar who as a man of the world was so perfect.

The house is now marked by a GLC plaque that remembers Wilde rather inadequately as 'wit and dramatist'.

No. 34 Tite Street saw both the height of Wilde's success and the disaster that followed, for it was sold up by bailiffs during his trials in 1895. The two main scenes of Wilde's humiliation and suffering do not survive: the Old Bailey, where he was sentenced to two years' hard labour for committing 'indecent acts,' and Reading Jail, where he served most of the sentence, have both been rebuilt. However, the visitor to London can still see the Cadogan Hotel (on Sloane Street by Cadogan Place in Chelsea), where Wilde was arrested, and Pentonville Prison on the Caledonian Road north of King's Cross. It was here that Wilde started and ended his imprisonment. After his release in 1897 he lived on the Continent, adopting the name 'Sebastian Melmoth' in oblique allusion to his ancestor, Charles Maturin (q.v.).

Virginia Woolf (née Stephen)

b. London, 1882; d. Rodmell, East Sussex, 1941. *The Voyage Out* (1915); *Kew Gardens* (1919); *Night and Day* (1919); *Monday or Tuesday* (1921); *Jacob's Room* (1922); *Mrs Dalloway* (1925); *The Common Reader* (1925); *To the Lighthouse* (1927); *Orlando: A Biography* (1928); *A Room of One's Own* (1929); *On Being Ill* (1930); *The Waves* (1931); *The Common Reader: Second Series* (1932); *Flush: A Biography* (1933); *The Years* (1937); *Three Guineas* (1938); *Roger Fry: A Biography* (1940); *Between the Acts* (1941); *The Death of the Moth, and Other Essays* (1942); *A Haunted House, and Other Short Stories* (1943); *The Moment, and Other Essays* (1947); *The Captain's Death Bed, and Other Essays* (1950); *Granite and Rainbow: Essays* (1958).

A plaque now marks No. 22 Hyde Park Gate (off Kensington High

Street west of the Royal Albert Hall), the London home of Sir Leslie Stephen after his second marriage, to Julia Duckworth, in 1878. Vanessa, Thoby, Virginia and Adrian Stephen were all born here and brought up in the top-floor nursery. Julia died in 1895 and, after several years of gloomy, distracted bereavement like Mr Ramsay's in *To the Lighthouse*, Sir Leslie followed in 1904.

It was then that the Stephen children decided to leave Kensington for Bloomsbury, the then unfashionable and not quite respectable area round the British Museum. Their first home (from 1905) was at No. 46 Gordon Square, east of Gower Street and University College. In the various Cambridge friends of Thoby and Adrian who came to visit was the nucleus of the famous 'Bloomsbury circle': the artist Clive Bell (who married Vanessa), Leonard Woolf (later, of course, Virginia's husband), Lytton Strachey, and two young men of whom great things were expected, Saxon Sydney-Turner and Desmond MacCarthy. After Clive's marriage to Vanessa and the death of Thoby, Virginia and Adrian went to live at No. 29 Fitzroy Square, west of Tottenham Court Road, a house once occupied by Bernard Shaw (q.v.). It is some indication of the neighbourhood's reputation in those days that Virginia thought it necessary to consult the police about safety before making the move. In later years—when the Bloomsbury group had expanded to include the economist Maynard Keynes, the artists Roger Fry and Duncan Grant, and had made friendly contact with E.M. Forster (q.v.)—Virginia lived at several other Bloomsbury addresses, now gone or drastically altered: in Brunswick Square (1911–12), Tavistock Square (1924–39) and Mecklenburgh Square (1939–40).

These last two places also served as headquarters of the Hogarth Press, a venture begun in the early days of her marriage to Leonard and begun not in Bloomsbury but in the west of London at Richmond. The name was taken from its first home, Hogarth House in Paradise Road, between the Park and Richmond Station (British Rail and District Underground Line). Here she and Leonard published her own early work, as well as *The Waste Land* by their friend T.S. Eliot (q.v.).

A large part, then, of Virginia Woolf's life and sensibility was urban: *Mrs Dalloway* is obvious testimony to her rich absorption in the moods of city life. Yet 'Bloomsbury' also had its intermittently rural aspect: a summer and weekend life of picnics and dog-walking and adultery. Her own taste for the country had begun with childhood visits to Talland House (now flats) overlooking the bay at St Ives on the north Cornish coast. Sir Leslie Stephen abandoned the house after his wife's death but Virginia returned to Cornwall throughout her life. *To the Lighthouse*, nominally set in the Hebrides but clearly Cornish in atmosphere, is the fruit of this association and of the adult contemplation of her parents it provoked. Her connection with Sussex dated from youth but was confirmed after her marriage when she and Leonard bought *Monk's House in the village of Rodmell, on A275 between Lewes and Newhaven. It was their home from 1914 until 1941, when she drowned herself in the nearby Ouse. Her ashes were buried in the garden.

For much of her life Virginia Woolf felt herself at a disadvantage because, unlike her brothers, she had not been sent to university. In 1928 she went some way toward making the score even by lecturing the students of Newnham and Girton Colleges in Cambridge on the need to have a room of their own. Earlier she had visited Rupert Brooke (q.v.) in nearby Grantchester. In larger terms, she never lacked the *entrée* to the literary society of her day, calling on her father's old friend Thomas Hardy (q.v., Rte 5) in Dorchester and, like virtually all the writers of her generation, visiting Lady Ottoline and Philip Morrell at Garsington Manor (off B480 4 miles SE of Oxford). Her friendship with Victoria Sackville-West took her to *Knole, the splendid Elizabethan mansion outside Sevenoaks in Kent (east of A225). *Orlando* is an affectionate tribute to both Vita and the house. The lovely *Sissinghurst Castle, where Vita lived with her husband Sir Harold Nicolson, lies off A262 in Kent, 2 miles NE of Cranbrook and 1 mile east of Sissinghurst village.

Monk's House, Rodmell (NT). Open Apr to end Oct, Wed & Sat 2–6. Fee.

Garsington Manor. Gardens open under NGS. Fee.

Knole, Sevenoaks (NT). Park open all year to walkers. House open Apr to end Nov, Wed to Sat 11–5, Sun 2–5; Good Fri & BH Mon 11–5. Fee.

Sissinghurst Castle & Garden (NT). Open Apr to 15 Oct, Tues to Fri 1–6.30, Sat, Sun & Good Fri 10–6.30. Fee.

Sir Thomas Wyatt

b. Allington, Kent, 1503; d. Sherborne, Dorset, 1542. Poet.

Quite as much as the very real distinction of his poetry, Wyatt's position as court favourite, his appointment to various diplomatic missions and his sometimes unhappy involvement in the political turmoil of the early Tudor period ensured that his life was well documented and spent in public places that have survived.

He was born at *Allington Castle, on the northern outskirts of Maidstone in Kent, returning there periodically in adult life—most notably the time somewhere between 1536 and 1540 when his unjustly neglected satires and *Penitential Psalms* were written. His father, Sir Henry Wyatt, had acquired the late 13C building in 1492 and many of the alterations to it date from his ownership. The visitor today, however, is less aware of their presence than of the restrained and scholarly repairs carried out by a later owner, Sir Maurice Conway, who rescued the castle from near-ruin between 1905 and 1929. It is now owned by the Carmelites.

In 1536 charges of complicity in Ann Boleyn's adultery made Wyatt a prisoner in the Tower of London. His relationship with Henry's wife, whose exact nature still remains unclear, had prompted the fine sonnet, 'Who so list to hount, I know where is an hynde.' His sojourn in the Tower provoked a poem complaining of his unjust imprisonment. ('Who list his welthe and eas Retayne/ Hym selffe let hym vnknowne contayne') and an elegy for Ann Boleyn's lovers, whose execution he witnessed, 'In mornyng wyse syns daylye I increase.' Another execution on Tower Hill, this time of his friend and patron Thomas Cromwell in 1540, led to another poem ('The piller pearisht is whearto I lent,/ The strongest staye of myne vnquiet mynde') and a second term of imprisonment in the Tower (1540–41).

Wyatt died the following year at Sherborne in Dorset, in the course of a diplomatic mission that was taking him to Falmouth. His grave in the fine Abbey Church is without proper memorial. A small tablet in the north transept marks its possible site, but it is equally reasonable to suppose that he may rest in the nearby Wykeham Chapel where his friend Sir John Horsey (d. 1546) and other members of the Horsey family are buried.

Allington Castle, near Maidstone. Open all year daily 2–4. Fee.

Tower of London (DoE). Open March to Oct, Mon to Sat 9.30–5, Sun 2–5; Nov to Feb, Mon to Sat 9.30–4. Closed Christmas Eve, Christmas Day, Boxing Day, New Year's Day, Maundy Thurs, Good Fri. Fee.

William Wycherley

b. Preston Brockhurst, Shropshire, 1640; d. London, 1716. *The Country Wife* (1675); *The Plain Dealer* (1677).

Wycherley was born on the family estate of Clive Hall, 1½ miles west of Preston Brockhurst, itself 9 miles north of Shrewsbury. He was educated first in France and then at The Queen's College, Oxford. He died in London, eleven days after a second marriage undertaken in curious and possibly disreputable circumstances, and was buried at St Paul's, Covent Garden, west of the old market. The church burnt down in 1795 but was rebuilt after Inigo Jones' original design.

William Butler Yeats

b. Dublin, 1865; d. Roquebrune, France, 1939. *The Wanderings of Oisin and Other Poems* (1889); *The Countess Cathleen and Various Legends and Lyrics* (1892); *The Celtic Twilight: Men and Women, Dhouls and Fairies* (1893); *The Land of Heart's Desire* (1894); *The Secret Rose* (1897); *The Wind Among the Reeds* (1899); *The Shadowy Waters* (1900); *Cathleen ni Houlihan* (1902); *In the Seven Woods: Being Poems Chiefly of the Irish Heroic Age* (1903); *Deirdre* (1907); *The Green Helmet and Other Poems* (1910); *Responsibilities* (1916); *Easter 1916* (1916); *The Wild Swans at Coole, Other Verses and a Play* (1917); *Two Plays For Dancers* (1919); *Michael Robartes and the Dancer* (1920); *The Player Queen* (1922); *The Cat and the Moon and Certain Poems* (1924); *A Vision* (1925); *The Tower* (1928); *Sophocles' King Oedipus: A Version For the Modern Stage* (1928); *A Packet For Ezra Pound* (1929); *Words For Music Perhaps and Other Poems* (1932); *The Winding Stair and Other Poems* (1933); *The Autobiography of Yeats* (1938); *Last Poems and Two Plays* (1939).

Like Swift (q.v.), whom he admired, Yeats divided his life between Ireland and England. In childhood he moved from Dublin to London and back as his father, Jack Butler Yeats, built a minor reputation in both cities as a portrait painter and artist in the Pre-Raphaelite tradition. Once his own poetic reputation was established, Yeats played a leading role in both the Irish literary revival and the various English movements which bridged the gap between Pre-Raphaelitism and Modernism.

His connection with England is best described first, for it is limited almost entirely to London. His earliest homes in the city were at No. 23 Fitzroy Road (off Regent's Park Road north of the Park and east of Primrose Hill) where he lived from 1867 to 1874, and at No. 14 Edith Villas (by the junction of West Cromwell Road and North End in Earl's Court) where the family stayed until 1876. Yeats was sent to school in Hammersmith at the Godolphin School in Iffley Road, reached from Hammersmith Underground Station (Metropolitan, Piccadilly and District Lines) by taking Beadon and Glenthorne Roads from Hammersmith Broadway and then turning right. 'Reveries Over Childhood and Youth' (later included in his *Autobiography*) remembers his painful shyness and sense of estrangement from his English fellow pupils.

From 1876 until 1880 the Yeats family lived at the most interesting of their London homes: No. 8 Woodstock Road in Bedford Park, above Chiswick High Road in north Chiswick. Begun by Norman Shaw in 1875, Bedford Park was England's earliest experiment in creating a planned garden suburb, noted for its tree-lined avenues, the quaint variety of its architecture and the artiness of its inhabitants. 'Reveries Over Childhood and Youth' vividly describes the 'romantic excitement' of moving there:

> We were to see De Morgan tiles, peacock-blue doors and the pomegranate pattern and the tulip pattern of Morris, and to discover that we had always hated doors painted with imitation grain, the roses of mid-Victoria, and tiles covered with geometrical patterns that seemed to have been shaken out of a muddy kaleidoscope. We went to live in a house like those we had seen in pictures and even met people dressed like people in the story-books. The streets were not straight and dull . . . but wound about where there was a big tree or for the mere pleasure of winding, and there were wood palings instead of iron railings. The newness of everything, the empty houses where we played at hide-and-seek, and the strangeness of it all, made us feel that we were living among toys. We could imagine people living happy lives as we thought people did long ago when the poor were picturesque and the master of a house could tell of strange adventures over the sea. (Part 8)

On his return to London from Dublin in 1887 Yeats quickly began to move in the literary circles for which such a childhood had prepared him. He visited William Morris (q.v.) at his home in Hammersmith and Oscar Wilde (q.v.) in Tite Street. In 1891 he formed the Rhymers' Club, whose meeting place was the Cheshire Cheese, on the north side of Fleet Street by Wine Office Court. Regular attendants included Lionel Johnson, Edward Dowson, Arthur Symons, Richard Le Gallienne, and John Davidson. They would dine in the restaurant downstairs before adjourning upstairs to read their poetry to each other. One evening Yeats surveyed the company and remarked: 'None of us can say who will succeed or even who has or has not talent. The only thing certain about us is that we are too many.' From 1895 until 1919 he lived at *No. 5 Woburn Walk (then Woburn Buildings, now marked with a plaque), a charming little street of 18C shopfronts running east of Upper Woburn Place just before it joins the Euston Road. Here, in a living room which his friend Lady Gregory (see below) had helped to decorate, Yeats continued to hold literary gatherings, bringing Ezra Pound and John Masefield (q.v.) among others to Monday evening meetings where he distributed 'cigarettes and Chianti, and laid down the law about poetry.'

When he left Woburn Walk in 1919 Yeats lived for two years in Oxford. Like so many literary men of the age, he was a guest of Lady Ottoline and Philip Morrell at Garsington Manor, off B480 4 miles SE of the city.

Caricature of Yeats by Edmund Dulac (1915). Courtesy of National Gallery of Ireland

Yeats' life in Ireland began and ended in Dublin and its environs. He was born in Sandymount, a south-eastern suburb of the city, at Georgeville, a large semi-detached house on Sandymount Avenue (which runs NE from Merrion Road near the buildings of the Royal Dublin Society). On their return from England in 1880 the Yeats family lived first at Howth, on the coast NE of the city, and then in the southern suburb of Harold's Cross.

His passionate involvement in the Irish literary revival was epitomised by his work for the Abbey Theatre (founded in 1904) where, as producer and manager, he showed selfless determination in bringing the controversial plays of Synge (q.v.) before the public. The original theatre, near the Custom House on Lower Abbey Street in north Dublin, burnt down in the 1950s and the present building dates from 1966. From 1922, when he left the Oxford area and severed his long connection with England, until 1928 Yeats lived at No. 82 Merrion Square (NE of St Stephen's Green), a fine Georgian house which he made a meeting place for writers as he had earlier made

Woburn Walk in London. It is now marked with a plaque. He left Merrion Square for a smaller house at No. 42 Fitzwilliam Square to the south, where he remained until 1932.

On the whole, Yeats' connection with rural Ireland is better commemorated than his life in Dublin. Particularly rich is the area round Gort, on the west coast SE of Galway. Off N18 2½ miles NW lay Coole Park, home of Lady Augusta Gregory (1859–1932) from 1880 until her death. Yeats first met her in 1896 and their friendship was strengthened by common involvement in the Irish theatre during the years that followed. When she died he wrote: 'I cannot realise the world without her. She has been to me mother, friend, sister and brother.' His first visit to Coole Park in 1897 is finely remembered in 'The Wild Swans at Coole,' and the house recurs throughout his poetry of the 1920s, embodying the traditional, aristocratic order to which he turned as a value in an age of civil discontent and anarchy:

> Great works constructed there in nature's spite
> For scholars and for poets after us,
> Thoughts long knitted into a single thought,
> A dance-like glory that those walls begot.
>
> ('Coole Park 1929,' lines 5–8)

As Yeats himself prophesied, the house itself has gone: it was bought by the Eire Government in 1934 and demolished in 1941. All that remains is the grounds, the lake where Yeats counted the swans and the famous Autograph Tree, a copper beech carved with the initials of Yeats and other writers and artists connected with the Irish literary revival.

Nearby is **Thoor Ballylee, 3 miles NE of Gort off N66 to Loughrea. The Norman tower and the cottages that huddle at its base had originally been part of the Gregory estate before they were acquired by the Congested Districts Board. Yeats bought the buildings for £35 in 1916 and lived there intermittently until 1929, when the damp location and the cost of repairs no longer made it a practicable home. His lines, 'To Be Carved On A Stone at Thoor Ballylee,' record the work he put into restoration:

> I, the poet William Yeats,
> With old mill boards and sea-green slates,
> And smithy work from the Gort forge,
> Restored this tower for my wife George;
> And may these characteristics remain
> When all is ruin once again.

The poem has now been carved on the tower, which has been rescued from the fate he foresaw. Inside the collection includes editions of his work and the oak furniture he installed, so large that it was built on the spot and could not be removed. Yet Thoor Ballylee is of interest as more than an unusually picturesque and well-preserved writer's house. Yeats' choice of it as home, like his admiration for Coole Park, expressed respect for the past and its traditional order in which art could flourish:

> I declare this tower is my symbol; I declare
> This winding, gyring, spiring treadmill of a stair is my ancestral stair.
>
> ('Blood and the Moon,' Section 2, lines 5–6)

The symbol is explored in some of his finest poems.

If Coole Park and Thoor Ballylee stand for the values that Yeats espoused in middle age, Sligo and its surrounding countryside embody the Irish traditions he inherited in childhood and which, as folklore, legend and superstition, nourished his imagination throughout his life. In Sligo itself (on the coast west of Enniskillen via N16) he paid childhood visits to his maternal grandparents, the Pollexfens. The County Library on Stephen Street north of the river has a *collection of Yeats family portraits by his father and his brother Jack. The adjacent Museum has a collection of Yeatsiana.

The splendid countryside nearby, full of intrinsic interest, is also rich in reminders of the poet. 3 miles SW of Sligo and visible from the town is Knocknarea (1083ft), surmounted by a cairn, Misgaun Meaghbh or Miosgán Meva, monument to Maeva, Queen of Connacht. Yeats' early hero, Oisin, included in his wanderings this 'cairn-heaped grassy hill/ Where passionate Maeve is stony-still' (Bk 1, Lines 17–18). Yeats returned to the subject in 'The Old Age of Queen Maeve' (1903). Immediately SE of Sligo via L16 is the beautiful *Lough Gill. Among the many islands that dot the surface of the lake is Innisfree (near the SE bank), made famous as a picturesque refuge from the world in an early poem. Near Aghamore Bay at the SE corner of the lake is the Dooney Rock, where Yeats' fiddler made 'Folk dance like a wave of the sea' (line 2). Four miles north of Sligo on N 15 we find Drumcliff and the Protestant church of which Yeats' grandfather was rector. Though he died and was buried on the French Riviera, the poet was reburied here in 1948 in a grave just north of the porch. The location and the epitaph now inscribed on his tomb obey the instructions in the final stanza of 'Under Ben Bulben':

> Under bare Ben Bulben's head
> In Drumcliff churchyard Yeats is laid.
> An ancestor was rector there
> Long years ago, a church stands near,
> By the road an ancient cross.
> No marble, no conventional phrase;
> On limestone quarried near the spot
> By his command these words are cut:
> > *Cast a cold eye*
> > *On life, on death.*
> > *Horseman, pass by!*

Ben Bulben (1730ft), which offers a magnificent view from the top, is 2 miles NE of the village.

Garsington Manor. Gardens open under NGS. Fee.

Thoor Ballylee. Open Apr to Oct, daily 10–6. Fee.

Sligo County Library & Museum. Library open Tues to Sat 10–1, 2–5, also Tues & Thurs 7–9. Museum & Art Gallery open 1 June to 30 Sept, Tues to Sat 10.30–12.30, 2.30–4.30.

Charlotte M. Yonge

b. Otterbourne, Hampshire, 1823; d. Otterbourne, 1901. *The Heir of Redclyffe* (1853); *Heartsease: or The Brother's Wife* (1854); *The Daisy Chain* (1856); *The Book of Golden Deeds of All Times and All Lands* (1864); *The Chaplet of Pearls* (1867); *A Book of Worthies, Gathered From the Old Histories and Now Written Out Anew* (1869).

Charlotte Yonge spent all her long, quiet and industrious life in Otterbourne, by A33 5 miles south of Winchester. Elderfield, the house to which she moved in 1862, stands opposite the school and the church of St Matthew. These were built in 1837–39 and, though a local architect was employed, Charlotte Yonge confirms in *John Keble's Parishes* (1898) that the blue-brick church was designed mainly by her father, squire of the village and patron of the living, 'who started with merely the power of military drawing (acquired before he was sixteen years old) and a great admiration for York Cathedral' (Ch. 9). The apse was added in 1875 by T.S. Wyatt and paid for by Miss Yonge. She is buried in the churchyard at the foot of the memorial cross to Keble, who held the living.

The location of her grave acknowledges the influence that Keble's High Church views exercised over her voluminous writings. He was appointed vicar of Hursley in 1835, when he was already leader of the Oxford Movement, and remained there until his death in 1866. The village, 2 miles NW on A3090 beyond its junction with A31, still has the church he built in 1846–48, paid for by the royalties from his popular sequence of religious poems, *The Christian Year* (1827). The stained glass windows, whose design was supervised by William Butterfield, are noteworthy. Keble himself is buried in the churchyard.

INDEX TO LONDON

The region covered by this index extends slightly beyond the formal boundaries of Greater London to include a few sights often visited from the city – Eton College and Windsor Castle, for example. They also appear in the general index to places outside London.

INDEX TO PLACES OUTSIDE LONDON

The Index includes a handful of places formerly in the Home Counties but now in Greater London, whose boundaries are wide and sometimes mysterious to the casual tourist. These places are also listed in the index to London.

The following abbreviations are used to distinguish between places of the same name or confusingly similar names:

Beds = Bedfordshire
Bucks = Buckinghamshire
Camb = Cambridgeshire
Corn = Cornwall
Derb = Derbyshire
Dor = Dorset
Herts = Hertfordshire

Lancs = Lancashire
Norf = Norfolk
Nthb = Northumberland
Oxon = Oxfordshire
Som = Somerset
Susx = Sussex
York = Yorkshire

Typeset by MCL Dataset Ltd, Ruislip, England, using a Prefis Book Machine.
Printed in Great Britain by Butler & Tanner Ltd, Frome and London.

Maps

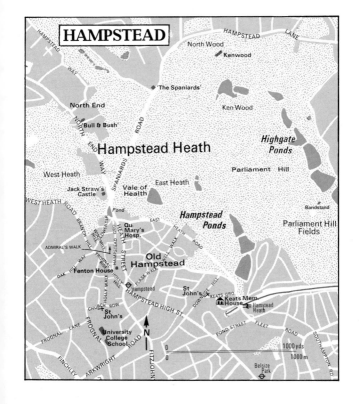

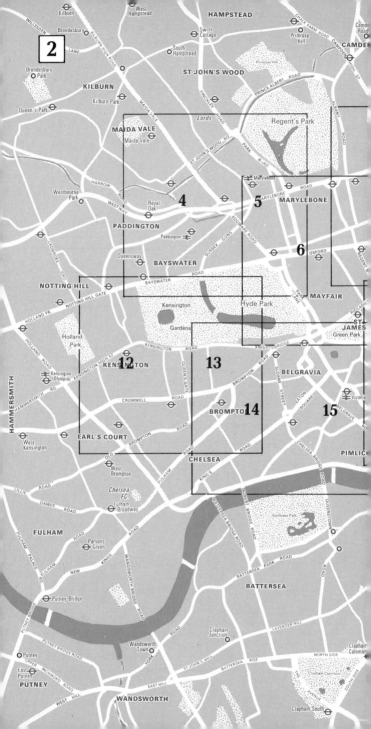

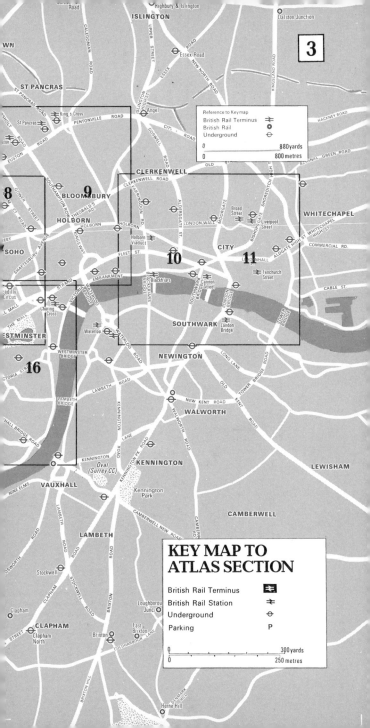

3

ISLINGTON

Highbury & Islington

Dalston Junction

WN

ST PANCRAS

St Pancras Road

King's Cross

PENTONVILLE ROAD

St Pancras

EUSTON ROAD

Angel

Essex Road

NEW NORTH ROAD

HACKNEY ROAD

8

GOWER STREET

BLOOMSBURY

9

THEOBALD'S RD

HOLBORN

HOLBORN

CLERKENWELL

CLERKENWELL ROAD

FARRINGDON RD

GOSWELL ROAD

OLD ST

BETHNAL GREEN ROAD

WHITECHAPEL

ALDERSGATE ST

LONDON WALL

MOORGATE

Broad Street

BISHOPSGATE

SHOREDITCH HIGH ST

Liverpool Street

ALDGATE HIGH ST

WHITECHAPEL RD

WHITECHAPEL

SOHO

SHAFTESBURY AVENUE

KINGSWAY

Holborn Viaduct

FLEET ST

CITY

Fenchurch Street

COMMERCIAL RD.

10

LEADENHALL

11

CABLE ST

FLEET

Piccadilly Circus

Charing Cross

STRAND

EMBANKMENT

VICTORIA EMBANKMENT

WATERLOO BRIDGE

Blackfriars

BLACKFRIARS BRIDGE

SOUTHWARK BRIDGE

Cannon Street

LONDON BRIDGE

Waterloo

SOUTHWARK

London Bridge

TOWER BRIDGE

ESTMINSTER

WATERLOO ROAD

NEWINGTON

LONG LANE

LEWISHAM

WESTMINSTER BRIDGE

16

OLD KENT ROAD

LAMBETH BRIDGE

LAMBETH

KENNINGTON

WALWORTH ROAD

New Kent Road

TOWER BRIDGE ROAD

WALWORTH

CTORIA STREET

HALL BRIDGE ROAD

KENNINGTON

KENNINGTON ROAD

KENNINGTON LANE

KENNINGTON PK ROAD

Oval (Surrey CC)

KENNINGTON

Kennington Park

CAMBERWELL

VAUXHALL

NINE ELMS

Kennington Park

CAMBERWELL NEW ROAD

CAMBERWELL

CAMBERWELL RD

LAMBETH

LAMBETH ROAD

Stockwell

DSWORTH

STOCKWELL ROAD

BRIXTON ROAD

Loughborough Junc.

East Brixton

COLDHARBOUR LANE

Clapham

CLAPHAM ROAD

CLAPHAM

Clapham North

Brixton

BRIXTON HILL

DENMARK HILL

Herne Hill

KEY MAP TO
ATLAS SECTION

British Rail Terminus	🚆
British Rail Station	🚉
Underground	⊖
Parking	P

0 _____ 300 yards
0 _____ 250 metres

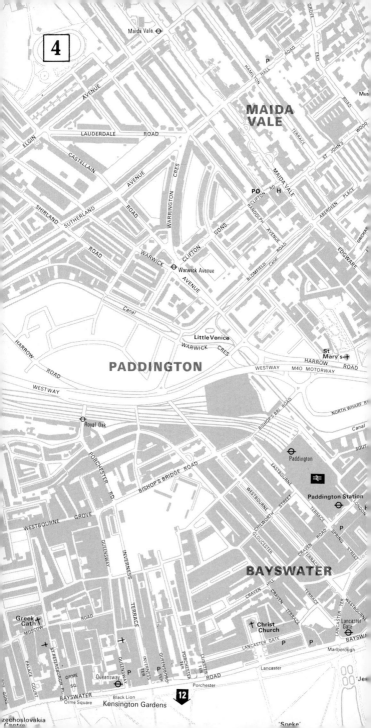

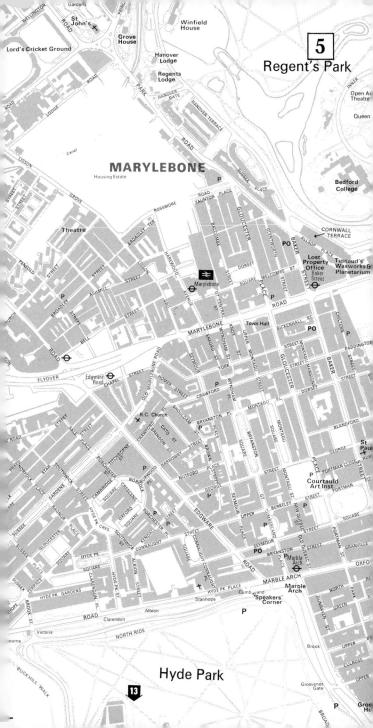

St John's

Wellington Road

Grove House

Winfield House

Lord's Cricket Ground

Hanover Lodge

Regents Lodge

Gardens

INNER

Open Air Theatre

Queen

PARK

HANOVER GATE

HANOVER TERRACE

ROAD

Canal

MARYLEBONE
Housing Estate

LISSON

STREET

STREET

GROVE

Theatre

PENFOLD

STREET

ROSSMORE

BROADLEY TER

HARDWOOD

LISSON

STREET

BROADLEY

P

ASHMILL

STREET

BELL

STREET

ROAD

FLYOVER

Edgware Road

CHAPEL

OLD MARYLEBONE ROAD

STREET

HOMER STREET

SHOULDHAM

ROAD

TAUNTON

PLACE

BALCOMBE

GLOUCESTER

PLACE

SUSSEX

PLACE

P

CORNWALL
TERRACE

Bedford College

ALLSOP PL

PO

BAKER

Lost Property Office
Baker Street

Tussaud's Waxworks & Planetarium

DORSET

SQUARE

MELCOMBE

PLACE

ROAD

GLENWORTH

AVENUE

Marylebone

CENTRAL

STREET

MARYLEBONE

HARCOURT

SEYMOUR

CRAWFORD

YORK

WYNDHAM

Town Hall

UPPER MONTAGU

GLOUCESTER

KNOX

STREET

BICKENHALL ST

MONTAGU MANSIONS

PO

BAKER

DORSET

CHILTERN

PADDINGTON

BLANDFORD

ST PAUL

R.C. Church

CRAWFORD

BRENDON ST

CATO ST

BRYANSTON PL

MONTAGU PLACE

MONTAGU SQUARE

GEORGE

PORTMAN CLOSE

SALE STREET

NORFOLK

STAR STREET

SOUTHWICK

GARDENS

CAMBRIDGE

TITCHBORNE ST

NORTH WHARF

CRESCENT

HARROWBY

BROWN

NUTFORD

PLACE

GEORGE

STREET

BRYANSTON

STREET

SEYMOUR

MONTAGU

STREET

UPPER BERKELEY

PORTMAN

GEORGE

PLACE

NEW QUEBEC

PORTMAN SQUARE

GRANVILLE

PL

OXFO

PRAED

NORFOLK

PLACE

RADNOR

PLACE

SUSSEX

HYDE PK CRES

OXFORD

PORCHESTER PLACE

KENDALL

P

CONNAUGHT

SQUARE

SEYMOUR

PO

UPPER

BERKELEY

P

SEYMOUR

BRYANSTON

P

Courtauld Art Inst

P

SQUARE

NORTH

OLD QUEBEC ST

PORTMAN

STREET

Marble Arch

DURWESTERN

SUSSEX

SQUARE

GLOUCESTER

SQUARE

HYDE PK

SQUARE

HYDE PK GARDENS

SOUTHWICK

ALBION STREET

CLARENDON

CONNAUGHT STREET

CONNAUGHT SQUARE

EDGWARE

ROAD

STREET

HYDE PK PLACE

Stanhope

Cumberland

MARBLE ARCH

Marble Arch

'Speakers' Corner'

NORTH

GREEN

DUNRAVEN

ST

OXFO

HOPE

BROOK ST

SUSSEX TERRACE

CLARENDON

ROAD

Albion

Victoria

NORTH RIDE

Clarendon

P

Brook

UPPER

CULROSS

bourne

BUCKHILL WALK

13

Hyde Park

Grosvenor Gate

Grosvenor House

GROS